New Products Management

New Products Management

Twelfth Edition

Merle Crawford
University of Michigan—Emeritus

Anthony Di Benedetto
Temple University

NEW PRODUCTS MANAGEMENT, TWELFTH EDITION

Published by McGraw-Hill Education, 2 Penn Plaza, New York, NY 10121. Copyright ©2021 by McGraw-Hill Education. All rights reserved. Printed in the United States of America. Previous editions ©2015, 2011, and 2008. No part of this publication may be reproduced or distributed in any form or by any means, or stored in a database or retrieval system, without the prior written consent of McGraw-Hill Education, including, but not limited to, in any network or other electronic storage or transmission, or broadcast for distance learning.

Some ancillaries, including electronic and print components, may not be available to customers outside the United States.

This book is printed on acid-free paper.

1 2 3 4 5 6 7 8 9 LCR 24 23 22 21 20

ISBN 978-1-259-91182-8 (bound edition)
MHID 1-259-91182-9 (bound edition)
ISBN 978-1-260-51202-1 (loose-leaf edition)
MHID 1-260-51202-9 (loose-leaf edition)

Portfolio Manager: *Laura Hurst Spell*
Product Developer: *Sarah Blasco*
Marketing Manager: *Lisa Granger*
Content Project Manager: *Lisa Bruflodt*
Buyer: *Laura Fuller*
Designer: *Beth Blech*
Content Licensing Specialist: *Jacob Sullivan*
Cover Image: *Background: McGraw-Hill Education; Inset (left to right): grinvalds/123RF; conejota/Shutterstock; Syda Productions/Shutterstock; nonwarit/123RF; GaudiLab/Shutterstock; fizkes/Shutterstock*
Compositor: *Aptara®, Inc.*

All credits appearing on page or at the end of the book are considered to be an extension of the copyright page.

Library of Congress Cataloging-in-Publication Data

Names: Crawford, C. Merle (Charles Merle), 1924-2012, author. | Di
  Benedetto, C. Anthony, author.
Title: New products management / Merle Crawford, University of Michigan,
  Emeritus, Anthony Di Benedetto, Temple University.
Description: Twelfth edition. | New York, NY : McGraw-Hill Education,
  [2021] | Includes bibliographical references and index.
Identifiers: LCCN 2019030305 (print) | LCCN 2019030306 (ebook) | ISBN
  9781259911828 (hardcover ; alk. paper) | ISBN 9781260512021 (loose-leaf ;
  alk. paper) | ISBN 9781260512014 (pdf)
Subjects: LCSH: New products—Management.
Classification: LCC HF5415.153 .C72 2021 (print) | LCC HF5415.153 (ebook)
  | DDC 658.5/75—dc23
LC record available at https://lccn.loc.gov/2019030305
LC ebook record available at https://lccn.loc.gov/2019030306

The Internet addresses listed in the text were accurate at the time of publication. The inclusion of a website does not indicate an endorsement by the authors or McGraw-Hill Education, and McGraw-Hill Education does not guarantee the accuracy of the information presented at these sites.

mheducation.com/highered

About the Authors

Merle Crawford was Professor of Marketing (Emeritus) at the University of Michigan, where he taught from 1965 until his retirement in 1992. Prior to his appointment at Michigan, he was marketing director at Mead Johnson & Co. Professor Crawford was an original member of the Product Development & Management Association from its founding in 1976, and he served as the charter president from 1977 to 1978 and on the Board of Directors until 1994. He authored the first edition of the groundbreaking textbook *New Products Management*, published in 1983 and still widely used by managers, executives, and business students.

Anthony Di Benedetto is Professor of Marketing and Supply Chain Management and Senior Washburn Research Fellow at Temple University, Philadelphia. He held the Fulbright-Hall Chair in Entrepreneurship, Wirtschaftsuniversität Wien, Vienna, Austria, during 2010–2011. He has lectured worldwide on product development and marketing management. He was named one of the 50 leading research scholars worldwide in Innovation and Technology Management by the International Association of Management of Technology. Professor Di Benedetto served as editor-in-chief of the *Journal of Product Innovation Management* for nine years and is currently co-editor-in-chief of *Industrial Marketing Management*.

Preface

New products have always been of interest to both academics and practitioners, and organized, college-level instruction on the subject of new products management traces to the 1950s. By the 1990s, a new products management discipline had evolved. The Product Development & Management Association (PDMA) has flowered to close to 3,000 members in some 50 countries around the world, and there are over 20 local chapters in the United States alone, plus international affiliates in a dozen countries. Over 300 colleges have courses on the subject of new products, and the field's journal, the *Journal of Product Innovation Management,* has a track record of publication of over three decades. The job title of new products manager or director is becoming much more common and is offering much earlier entry than 20 or 25 years ago; we also see the emergence of higher level positions for careers to build to. The PDMA now offers a practitioner certification (New Product Development Professional, or NPDP), recognizes the best product developing firms (with its Outstanding Corporate Innovator award), and has been able to do what those in many fields have not, that is, merge the thinking and activity of professors and practitioners. Information on the PDMA can be found at www.pdma.org.

How This Book Views the Field of New Products Management

Such exploding growth means that we still take a variety of approaches to the teaching of the new products subject—marketing, technical, creative, design, and so on. This book provides the management approach with the perspective of marketing. In every organization (industry, retailing, government, non-profits, and any other kind of institution) there is a person or group of persons who, knowingly or unknowingly, are charged with getting new goods and services onto the market. More and more today, those people are new products managers, or project managers, or team leaders. They lead a multifunctional group of people, with the perspective of a general manager, operating as a company within a company. They must deal with the total task—strategy, organization, concept generation, evaluation, technical development, marketing, and so on. They are not finished with their work until the new product has achieved the goals assigned to the team—this usually means some form of sales or profit, and certainly means the task is not finished when the new product is put onto the shipping dock.

We try to avoid a functional myopia, and it is rare today to hear that "Marketing tells everyone what to do" or "R&D runs our new products activity." When a functional specialist is assigned leadership of a new products team, that person must learn the general manager viewpoint, but one usually has to succeed as a functional member of new products teams before getting a shot at being a team leader. Marketing people, working as team members or as team leaders, need the types of information in this book.

Some Basic Beliefs That Guided the Writing

People who have used the first 11 editions of this book know its unique viewpoints on the subject. But for newcomers, and of course all students are newcomers, here are some of them.

1. Product innovation is one single operation in an organization. It has parts (strategy, teams, plans, etc.), but they are all just parts. Any operation that runs as separate pieces misses the strength of the whole.

2. The field is still new enough that it lacks a systematic language. This makes it very difficult for students, who are accustomed to studying subjects where a term means one thing, and only that one thing. We use all product terms consistently throughout the book, and we urge students to use them. Naturally, new terms come and go; some survive and some don't.

   Because of the terminology problem in a rapidly growing field, every term that might require definition has been made bold the first time it is used, and the index directs the reader to that section. We don't include a glossary, but a useful one is available at the Product Development & Management Association Web site.

3. Ideas learned without application are only temporary residents in your mind. To become yours, a concept must be applied, in little ways or in big ones. Thus, we provide numerous short illustrative cases, which are opportunities for using the concepts studied. There are many examples from the business world, and up-to-date references on all important topics.

4. As much as we would like them and have diligently tried to find them, we believe there is no standard set of procedures for product innovators, nor particular sets for makers of consumer packaged goods, or of consumer durables, industrial goods, services, and so on. Like a marketing plan, there is a best plan for any particular situation. A manager must look at a situation and then compile a set of tools and other operations appropriate to that situation. All large firms use scores of different approaches, not one.

5. Next, there is the halo effect, which is a problem in the field of new products. The halo effect shows in the statement, "It must be a good thing for us to do—Apple does it, or Google does it, or Honda does it." Those are excellent companies, but one reason they're good is they spend lots of time and money studying, learning from others. They have huge training programs in product innovation and bring in every expert who appears on the scene with what looks like a good new products management idea. They assume everything they do is wrong and can be improved. You should too. This book does. Citations of their actions are given as examples, not recommendations. These well-known firms have many divisions and hundreds of new products under development at any one time. Managers there can't know what other managers are doing, nor do they care, in the prescriptive sense. Each group aims to optimize its situation, so they look around, see what others in comparable situations are doing (inside and outside their firm), and pick and choose to fit the situation. To the extent there are

generalizations (e.g., there should be some form of strategy), these will stand out as you work your way through the course. But what strategy, and exactly how should one determine it—that is situational.

6. An example of this lies in rejection of the belief that new products strategy should rest on the base of either technology or market. This choice has been argued for many years. But most firms seek to optimize on both, a dual-drive strategy. Of course, true to the previous point, firms will build on one or the other if the situation seems to fit.

7. We believe that students should be challenged to think about concepts they have been introduced to. This book contains lists of things from time to time, but such lists are just a resource for thinking. The above belief about the best approach being situational is based on the need to analyze, consider, discuss, apply. The great variety in approaches used by businesspeople is not a testimony to ignorance, but to thinking. On a majority of the issues facing us today, intelligent people can come down with different views. Decisions are the same—they are not necessarily right or wrong at the time they are made. Instead, the manager who makes a decision then has to work hard to make that decision turn out right. The quality of the work is more important than the quality of the decision.

8. Last, we have tried to implement more clearly the view that two things are being developed—the product and the marketing plan. There are two development processes going on in tandem. Marketing strategy begins at the very start and runs alongside the technical work and beyond it.

Changes in the Twelfth Edition

Past adopters of *New Products Management* will notice major changes in this edition. While there are some changes in virtually every chapter, some of the most substantial changes are as follows:

1. We have made major additions and updates to the cases to provide more plentiful and more current examples. We retired several cases from the previous edition, wrote many new cases, and thoroughly updated many others. New cases for this edition include: Oculus Rift, Adidas Parley sustainable running shoes, Google Glass, Indiegogo, Tesla, Chipotle, Chick-fil-A, Corporate Social Responsibility at Starbucks, and many others. As always, we aim to offer a mix of high-tech products and consumer products and services in the set of cases.

2. In addition, we have substantially updated examples throughout the text wherever possible. We try to make use of illustrative examples that will resonate with today's students wherever possible. Of course, we welcome the reader's comments and suggestions for improvement.

3. There continues to be much new research in new products, and we have tried to stay current on all of these topics. Readers will notice new or expanded coverage of portfolio management, value curve creation, the TRIZ method, crowdsourcing, crowdfunding, observational research, open innovation, organizational

structure, 3D modeling, beta testing, sustainable product development, and frugal innovation, among other topics.

4. We continue the practice of referencing Web sites of interest throughout the text, and we have added the web addresses for several useful Youtube videos and other resources.

Adopters of previous editions will notice that the format is slimmed down to 18 chapters. We have tried to streamline presentation and focus on the topics that will be of most importance and interest to new product managers. We still use analytical models to integrate the stages of the new products process. As in previous editions, perceptual mapping is introduced early in the new products process, during concept generation, but its output may guide selection of attributes in a conjoint analysis task, and may later be used in benefit segmentation and product positioning. Conjoint analysis results may be used in concept generation or evaluation and may provide a set of desired customer attributes for house-of-quality development. The sequence of three smartphone end-of-chapter cases illustrates how the analytical models bind the new products process together. As in previous editions, many other concepts—Product Innovation Charter, A-T-A-R models, evaluation techniques, the multifunctional nature of new products management—are also used to integrate topics horizontally throughout the text.

Because this book takes a managerial focus and is updated extensively, it is useful to the practicing new products manager. It has been used in many executive education programs. Great pains have been taken to present the "best practices" of industry and offer footnote references to business literature.

As always, effort has been aimed at making the book increasingly relevant to its users. We consider a text revision to be a "new product," and thus an opportunity for us to become even more customer-oriented. Academic colleagues have made many thoughtful suggestions based on their experiences with previous editions and have provided much of the driving force behind the changes you see in this edition. We gratefully acknowledge all the reviewers who provided extensive comments and suggestions that were extremely helpful in this revision, as well as all the instructors and students who contacted us to make suggestions and correct errors. In particular, Matt Bokovitz and Jacob Cheesebrough, both Temple University students, did a phenomenal job providing research support and case studies that allowed us to make the substantial improvements and updates you will see in this book. Sincere thanks to both of you!

We are thrilled about this new edition. It has been greatly updated and streamlined, and over half the cases are brand-new. We are really proud of all the changes in this edition, and sincerely hope this new version meets your instructional needs!

Online Resources

The instructor will find plenty of online support for this text at the companion Web site, **www.mhhe.com/crawford12e**. Available on the Web site are an online Instructor's Manual, a set of PowerPoint slides, a test bank, and exercises and cases that can be used to accompany the text materials. Some of these materials are also available to the students where appropriate.

Dedication

This edition is dedicated to Merle Crawford (1924–2012), Professor Emeritus (University of Michigan), sole author of the first five editions of this textbook, and co-founder of the Product Development & Management Association. I have tried to remain true to Professor Crawford's vision when he wrote the first edition of this book years ago. He continues to be an inspiration to all of us who teach and practice new products management.

A.D.B.

Contents in Brief

PART ONE
Opportunity Identification and Selection 3

1. The Strategic Elements of Product Development 5
2. The New Products Process 25
3. Opportunity Identification and Selection: Strategic Planning for New Products 58

PART TWO
Concept Generation 89

4. The Product Concept and Ready-Made New Product Ideas 90
5. New Product Ideas: The Problem Find-Solve Approach 119
6. New Product Ideas: Analytical Attribute Approaches 141

PART THREE
Concept/Project Evaluation 165

7. Concept Evaluation and Testing 166
8. The Full Screen 198
9. Sales Forecasting and Financial Analysis 214
10. Product Protocol 244

PART FOUR
Development 271

11. Design 275
12. Development Team Management 296
13. Product Use Testing 322

PART FIVE
Launch 343

14. Strategic Launch Planning 346
15. Implementation of the Strategic Plan 375
16. Market Testing 395
17. Launch Management 419
18. Public Policy Issues 440

APPENDIXES

A Sources of Ideas Already Generated 463
B Other Techniques of Concept Generation 468

INDEX 476

Contents

PART ONE
**OPPORTUNITY IDENTIFICATION
AND SELECTION   3**

Chapter 1
**The Strategic Elements of Product
Development   5**

Setting   5
The Importance of New Products   6
Globalization and New Product Development   9
How Product Development Is Different   11
What Is a New Product, and What Leads to
    Success?   14
Does This Field of Activity Have a Unique
    Vocabulary?   16
Does the Field of New Products Offer
    Careers?   17
The Strategic Elements of Product
    Development   18
The Basic New Products Process   18
The Other Strategic Elements   22
Product Development in Action   23
Summary   24

Chapter 2
The New Products Process   25

Setting   25
The LEGO New Products Saga   25
    The Product Innovation Charter (PIC)   27
    The New Products Process   28
    The New Product Portfolio   28
    What Happened in That Saga?   29
The Phases in the New Products Process   29
    Phase 1: Opportunity Identification and Selection   29
    Phase 2: Concept Generation   31
    Phase 3: Concept/Project Evaluation   32
    Phase 4: Development   33
    Phase 5: Launch   34

Evaluation Tasks Throughout the New Products
    Process   34
Agile Product Development   37
Speeding the Product to Market   38
    Risks and Guidelines in Speeding to Market   41
What about New Services?   43
New-to-the-World Products   46
Disruptive Innovation   48
The Role of the Serial Innovator   50
Spiral Development and the Role of
    Prototypes   51
Closing Thoughts about the New Products
    Process   52
Summary   53
Case: Oculus Rift   54
Case: The Levacor Heart Pump   55

Chapter 3
**Opportunity Identification and
Selection: Strategic Planning for
New Products   58**

Setting   58
A Product Strategy for a "Company within
    a Company"   59
New Product Strategy Inputs and Identifying
    Opportunities   59
    Product Platform Planning   59
    Opportunity Identification   63
    Noncorporate Strategic Planning   64
    Miscellaneous Sources   65
The Product Innovation Charter   66
    Why Have a PIC?   68
The Sections of the PIC   70
    Background Section of the PIC   70
    The Arena (Area of Focus) Section of the PIC   70
    Goals and Objectives Section of the PIC   73
    Special Guidelines Section of the PIC   74
How to Prepare a Product Innovation
    Charter   75

Product Portfolio Analysis: The New Product's
   Strategic Fit   76
Summary   82
Case: Adidas Ultraboost X Parley Shoes   82
Case: The Honda Element   83

PART TWO
CONCEPT GENERATION   89

Chapter 4
The Product Concept and Ready-Made
New Product Ideas   90

Setting   90
Preparation   90
   The Product Innovation Charter   90
   Creativity and Innovation   91
   Management's Role in Creativity   92
   Activities to Encourage Creativity   93
   Special Rewards   95
   The Removal of Roadblocks   95
The Product Concept   96
   The Designer Decaf Example   99
   The Product Concept Statement   100
Approaches to Concept Generation   102
Important Sources of Ready-Made
   New Product Ideas   102
   User Toolkits and Customization   103
   Crowdsourcing   106
   Lead Users   108
   Open Innovation   109
Summary   114
Case: Google Glass   115
Case: Indiegogo   116
Case: Aquafresh White Trays   117

Chapter 5
New Product Ideas: The Problem
Find-Solve Approach   119

Setting   119
The Overall System of Internal Concept
   Generation   119
Gathering the Problems   120
   Internal Records   121

Direct Inputs from Technical and Marketing
   Departments   121
   Problem Analysis   122
   Scenario Analysis   130
Solving the Problems   133
   Group Creativity   134
   Brainstorming   134
   Electronic Brainstorming and Computer-Assisted
   Creativity Techniques   135
   Online Communities   136
   Disciplines Panel   137
Concept Generation Techniques
   in Action   138
Summary   138
Case: Creative Customer Problem Solving   139

Chapter 6
New Product Ideas: Analytical Attribute
Approaches   141

Setting   141
Understanding Why Customers Buy
   a Product   141
   Products Are Groups of Attributes   141
   Analyzing Product Attributes for Concept Generation
   and Evaluation   143
Gap Analysis   143
   Determinant Gap Maps   143
   Perceptual Gap Maps   145
   Comments on Gap Analysis   146
Trade-Off Analysis   147
   Using Trade-Off Analysis to Generate Concepts   147
   Is Conjoint the Right Method?   150
   Alternatives to Full-Profile Conjoint Analysis   151
   Prototypes in Concept Testing   151
Qualitative Techniques   152
   Dimensional Analysis   152
   Checklists   152
   Analogy   154
   Value Curve Creation   155
   Product Enhancements   156
   TRIZ   157
Summary   158
Case: Comparing Smartphones (A)   158
Case: Ray-Ban   160
Case: Rubbermaid   161

PART THREE
CONCEPT/PROJECT EVALUATION   165

Chapter 7
Concept Evaluation and Testing   166

Setting   166
What's Going On in the New Products
Process?   166
The Evaluation System for the Basic New Products Process   167
Product Line Considerations in Concept Evaluation   169
The Cumulative Expenditures Curve   170
The Risk/Payoff Matrix   170
The Decay Curve and the New Products Process   172
Planning the Evaluation System   172
Everything Is Tentative   173
Potholes   173
The People Dimension   174
Surrogates   175
The A-T-A-R Model   176
Where Do We Get the Figures for the A-T-A-R Model?   179
Further Uses of the A-T-A-R Model   179
Concept Evaluation: Fit with Product
Innovation Charter   180
Concept Testing and Development   180
What Is a New Product Concept?   181
The Purposes of Concept Testing   182
Considerations in Concept Testing Research   183
Prepare the Concept Statement   183
Define the Respondent Group   187
Select the Response Situation   188
Prepare the Interviewing Sequence   188
Analyzing Research Results   189
Identifying Benefit Segments   189
Conjoint Analysis in Concept Testing   192
Conclusions   193
Summary   193
Case: Concept Evaluation at Amazon   194
Case: Domino's   195
Case: Comparing Smartphones (B)   197

Chapter 8
The Full Screen   198

Setting   198
Purposes of the Full Screen   199
The Scoring Model   201
Introduction to Scoring Models   201
The Screening Procedure   202
Profile Sheet   207
The Analytic Hierarchy Process   208
Special Aspects   211
Summary   212
Tesla (A)   212

Chapter 9
Sales Forecasting and Financial Analysis   214

Setting   214
Sales Forecasting for New Products   215
Forecasting Sales Using Traditional
Methods   216
Forecasting Sales Using Purchase Intentions   218
Forecasting Sales Using the A-T-A-R Model   219
Techniques for Forecasting Product
Diffusion   221
Observations on Forecasting Models   223
Problems with Sales Forecasting   224
Summary of the Problems   225
Actions by Managers to Handle These
Problems   225
Improve the New Product Process Currently in Use   225
Use the Life Cycle Concept of Financial Analysis   226
Reduce Dependence on Poor Forecasts   227
Return to the PIC   232
Summary   234
Case: Bay City Electronics   235
Case: Mercedes Benz   241

Chapter 10
Product Protocol   244

Setting   244
The Product Protocol   245
Purposes of the Protocol   247

Protocol's Specific Contents 249
   Target Market 249
   Positioning 251
   Product Attributes 251
   Competitive Comparisons and Augmentation
   Dimensions 253
   Other Components of the Product Protocol 253
Protocol and the Voice of the Customer 254
   Hearing the Voice of the Customer 254
Protocol and Quality Function
   Deployment (QFD) 257
   QFD and the House of Quality 257
   Outcomes of QFD 262
Some Warnings about the Difficulty of the
   Protocol Process 264
Summary 265
Case: Product Protocol for Entrepreneurs 265
Case: DuPont 267

PART FOUR
DEVELOPMENT 271

Chapter 11
Design 275

Setting 275
What Is Design? 276
Design-Driven Innovation 277
The Role of Design in the New Products
   Process 278
   Contributions of Design to New Product Goals 278
Product Architecture 283
   A Process for Product Architecture 283
   Product Architecture and Product Platforms 285
Assessment Factors for Industrial Design 285
Prototype Development 286
Managing the Interfaces in the Design
   Process 287
Improving the Interfaces in the Design
   Process 289
Computer-Aided Design and Design
   for Manufacturability 291
Continuous Improvement in Design 293
Summary 294
Case: The IDEA Awards 294

Chapter 12
Development Team Management 296

Setting 296
What Is a Team? 296
Structuring the Team 297
   Another Look at Projectization 301
Building a Team 302
   Establishing a Culture of Collaboration 302
   Selecting the Team Leader 303
   Selecting the Team Members 304
   The Role of the Project Champion 305
   Network Building 306
   Training the Teams 306
Managing the Team 306
   Cross-Functional Interface Management 308
   Overcoming Barriers to Market Orientation 310
   Ongoing Management of the Team 310
   Team Compensation and Motivation 311
   Closing the Team Down 312
Virtual Teams 313
Managing Globally Dispersed Teams 314
Summary 317
Case: Provo Craft 318
Case: Ford Fusion 319

Chapter 13
Product Use Testing 322

Setting 322
The Role of Marketing During
   Development 323
   Marketing Is Involved from the Beginning
   of the Process 323
   Marketing Ramp-Up, or the "I Think We've
   Got It" Phase 324
Why Do Product Use Testing? 324
Is Product Use Testing Really Necessary? 325
   Are These Arguments Correct? 325
Knowledge Gained from Product Use
   Testing 328
   Pre-Use Sense Reactions 328
   Early Use Experiences 328
   Alpha and Beta Tests 329
   Gamma Testing 330
   Diagnostic Information 331

Decisions in Product Use Testing   331
  Who Should Be in the User Group?   331
  How Should We Reach the User Group?   332
  Should We Disclose Our Identity?   333
  How Much Explanation Should We Provide?   333
  *How Much Control over Product Use
  Should There Be?*   333
  How Should the Test Be Conducted?   334
  *Over What Time Period Should the Test
  Be Conducted?*   335
  *What Should Be the Source of the Product
  Being Tested?*   336
  *What Should Be the Form of the Product
  Being Tested?*   336
  How Should We Record Respondents' Reactions?   336
  How Should We Interpret the Figures We Get?   338
  Should We Compensate the Testers?   339
Summary   339
Case: Chipotle   339
Case: Product Use Testing for New Consumer
Nondurables   341

PART FIVE
LAUNCH   343

Chapter 14
Strategic Launch Planning   346

Setting   346
The Strategic Givens   347
Revisiting the Strategic Goals   348
Strategic Platform Decisions   349
  Type of Demand Sought   349
  Permanence   350
  Aggressiveness   350
  Product Line Replacement   351
  Image   352
The Target Market Decision   352
  Alternative Ways to Segment a Market   352
  Micromarketing and Mass Customization   354
  Targeting May Also Use Diffusion of Innovation   356
Product Positioning   358
Branding and Brand Management   360
  Trademarks and Registration   360
  What Is a Good Brand Name?   363

  Managing Brand Equity   363
  Brand Equity and Branding Strategies   368
  *Global Branding and Positioning: Standardize
  or Adapt?*   369
  Global Brand Leadership   370
Packaging   371
  The Role of Packaging   371
  The Packaging Decision   371
Summary   372
Case: Tesla (B)   373
Case: Comparing Smartphones (C)   **373**

Chapter 15
Implementation of the Strategic Plan   375

Setting   375
The Launch Cycle   375
  Prelaunch and Preannouncement   375
  Announcement, Beachhead, and Early Growth   378
Lean Launch and Launch Timing   379
Launch Tactics   381
  The Communications Plan   381
  The Copy Strategy Statement   383
  Personal Selling   383
Alliances   384
A-T-A-R Requirements   385
  Awareness   385
  Stocking and Availability   386
  Trial   388
  Repeat Purchase   391
Summary   391
Case: Coca-Cola Life   392

Chapter 16
Market Testing   395

Setting   395
The Market Testing Decision   395
  When Is the Decision Made?   395
  Is This an Easy Decision to Make?   396
  Market Tests Must Have Teeth   397
  The Factors for Deciding Whether to Market Test   398
Methods of Market Testing   400
  Pseudo Sale   400
  Controlled Sale   400
  Full Sale   401

Pseudo Sale Methods   401
   Speculative Sale   402
   Simulated Test Market   403
Controlled Sale Methods   406
   Informal Selling   406
   Direct Marketing   407
   Minimarkets   407
   Scanner Market Testing   409
Full Sale Methods   410
   Test Marketing   410
   The Rollout   413
Wrap-Up on Market Testing
   Methodologies   417
Summary   417
Case: Chick-fil-A   418

Chapter 17
Launch Management   419

Setting   419
What We Mean by Launch
   Management   419
The Launch Management System   420
   Step One: Spot Potential Problems   421
   Step Two: Select the Control Events   425
   Step Three: Develop Contingency Plans   426
   Step Four: Design the Tracking System   427
Effective Innovation Metrics   430
A Sample Launch Management Plan   432
Launch Management and Knowledge
   Creation   432
Product Failure   435
Summary   437
Case: Gillette   438

Chapter 18
Public Policy Issues   440

Setting   440
Bigger Picture: A Cycle of Concerns   440
   Phase I: Stirring   441
   Phase II: Trial Support   441
   Phase III: The Political Arena   442
   Phase IV: Regulatory Adjustment   442
Business Attitudes toward Product Issues   442
Current Problem Areas   443
Product Liability   443
   Typology of Injury Sources   443
   The Four Legal Bases for Product Liability   445
   Other Legislation   447
Planning for the Product Recall   447
Sustainability and the Environment   448
Product Piracy   452
Designing Products for Emerging Markets   453
The Underlying Issues   456
Summary   456
Case: Clorox Green Works   457
Case: Sustainability and the Fashion
Industry   459
Case: CSR at Starbucks   461

Appendix A   Sources of Ideas Already
                Generated   463

Appendix B   Other Techniques of Concept
                Generation   468

Index   476

New Products Management

FIGURE I.1

Opportunity Identification and Selection

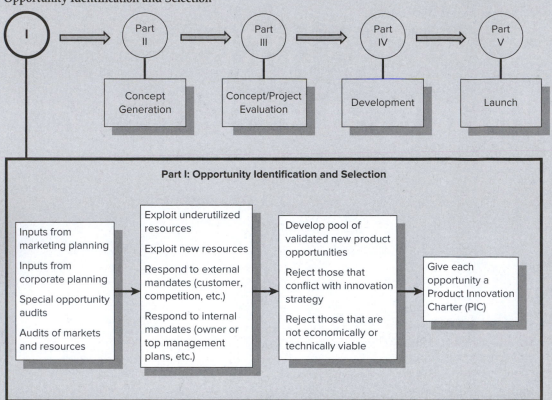

PART ONE

Opportunity Identification and Selection

This book is divided into parts. They are (1) Opportunity Identification and Selection, (2) Concept Generation, (3) Concept/Project Evaluation, (4) Development, and (5) Launch. They follow the general flow of the new products process, which we will present in Chapter 1, Figure 1.5. We will see later, however, that the phases are not sequential, compartmentalized steps. They are quite fluid and overlap each other.

At the beginning of each part is a short Part Introduction (noted with a Roman numeral) and a figure (see Figure I.1). The introduction describes briefly what aspects of the new products process will be covered in the upcoming chapters. The figure provides detailed information about what goes on at that phase in the new products process and shows what phases come immediately before and after. Figure I.1, for example, details the opportunity identification and selection process, ending with the product innovation charter, a key topic of Chapter 3. Hence, the five part figures (Figures I.1, II.1, III.1, IV.1, and V.1) actually make up one long, detailed new products process, the essence of which is presented briefly in Figure 1.5.

Before getting to opportunity identification and selection, we begin Part I with two introductory chapters. The first introduces the three *strategic elements of product development:* the new products process, the product innovation charter, and the product portfolio. It presents the first of these, the new products process, in relatively simplified form, as a kind of introduction to the rest of the book. Chapter 1 also attempts to answer the questions most often asked about such a course and helps to define some of the concepts we will be returning to throughout the text (such as, what exactly is a new product, how many new products really do succeed, and how do firms achieve globalization in product development). Chapter 2 goes much deeper into the new products process. Chapter 2 also introduces the key concepts of radical innovation, new service development, and speed to market and how each of these may have an impact on the new products process as presented in the chapter.

Chapter 3 completes the introductory part of the book, as it presents the second and third strategic elements. First, opportunity identification and selection are presented, which deal with the strategic planning lying at the very base of new products work that guides a new products team, just as corporate or strategic business unit strategy guides the unit as a whole. Figure I.1 provides a flow model that describes the process of opportunity identification. Chapter 3 then discusses the product innovation charter (PIC). This can be thought of as a statement of strategy that will guide the new product development team: the arena in which they will operate, their goals and objectives, and other considerations. The last part of Chapter 3 discusses the product portfolio. Innovative ideas that can be converted into high-potential new product opportunities can come from many sources; but however the new product idea is arrived at, its fit with the firm's product innovation strategies needs to be assessed. This is a portfolio issue: When assessing any potential new product, the firm needs to consider its technical viability (can we make it?) and its market viability (will customers buy it?). Most firms will have many other criteria, both financial and strategic, that they consider at this important step.

As seen in Figure I.1, once the PIC has been determined, the next step is to generate product concepts. This will be taken up in Part II of this book.

The Strategic Elements of Product Development

Setting

Mention new products and people think about technology—iPhones, online shopping, smart watches, self-driving cars, virtual realities, and the like. But most new products are far simpler—low-carb colas, new movies, new singing stars, fast foods, and new flavors of frozen yogurt. New products run the gamut from the cutting edge of technology to the latest version of the ballpoint pen. New products can be tangible goods or services. New products can be destined for the consumer market, the business-to-business market, or both.

You have chosen to study how new products are developed and managed, so it would be nice to say they come from an orderly process, managed by experienced persons well versed in product innovation. Some do, but some don't. Years ago, Art Fry became famous for an idea that became Post-it notes, when his hymnal page-marking slips kept falling out. He had a rough time persuading others at 3M that the idea was worth marketing, even though it soon became one of the highest volume supply items in the office supply industry! Or consider James Dyson, an industrial designer by training who was dissatisfied with the performance of commercially available vacuum cleaners and set out to create a better one. After five years and about 5,000 prototypes, he created the Dual Cyclone bagless vacuum cleaner. Over the next eight years, he was unable to interest vacuum cleaner manufacturers or venture capitalists in the new product, frequently hearing that since he was a designer, he couldn't possibly know anything about manufacturing or marketing! In 1985 and on the verge of bankruptcy, Dyson found an interested Japanese investor, and by 1993 he had set up Dyson Appliances in the United Kingdom (his home country). Since that time, Dyson Appliances has sold over $2 billion worth of vacuums worldwide.[1]

So you may be confused by the uncertainty you meet in this book. If so, welcome to the land of creative exploration. The activity we study in this book is sometimes called

---

[1]Anonymous, "Dyson Fills a Vacuum," @ *Issue*, 8(1), 2003.

product innovation management; some call it product planning, and some (from a very biased perspective) call it *research and development* (R&D) or *marketing*. In this book, we use the most descriptive term we have—new products management—and we adopt the viewpoint of the marketing manager; that is, we are primarily concerned about the specific role for marketing in the overall task.

The Importance of New Products

New products are *big business.* Over a $100 billion are spent yearly on the technical development phase alone. Untold thousands of new products are marketed every year, perhaps millions if we call each new Web site a new product. Hundreds of thousands of people make their living producing and marketing new products. Many managers realize that *radical innovation* is critical to future growth and even the survival of the firm. Here, we are defining radical innovation as innovation that displaces or makes obsolete current products and/or creates totally new product categories.[2] The Industrial Research Institute identified "accelerating innovation" and "business growth through innovation" as the top challenges faced by technology leaders, and business writer Gary Hamel has described the creation of radical innovation as "the most important business issue of our time."[3]

The reason firms invest this much in new products is that they *hold the answer to most firms' biggest problems.* Competitors do the most damage when (1) there is so little product differentiation that price-cutting takes everyone's margins away or (2) when they have a desirable new item that we don't. The fact is: *A successful new product does more good for a firm than anything else.* The very reason for a firm's existence is the value its operations provide to others, and for which they pay. And in a competitive world this means that what we offer—be it a physical good or a service—must be better than what someone else offers, at least part of the time. This is true in all organizations, including hospitals, churches, colleges, and political parties. Look at the winners in those arenas and ask yourself which ones are popular and growing.

Another reason for studying about new products is that *the new products process is exceedingly difficult.* Hundreds of individuals are involved in the creation of a single product, but all are from separate departments (sales, engineering, manufacturing, and so on) where they may have their own agendas. When a product flops miserably, it often generates huge publicity, much to the chagrin of the producers: think of New Coke, Google Glass, the Amazon Fire Phone, recent movie duds, or countless others. Perhaps, as a result, we think failure rates are higher than they really are. New products do fail, of course, but at around a 40 percent rate, not the

[2]M. Rice, R. Liefer, and G. O'Connor, "Assessing Transition Readiness for Radical Innovations," *Research-Technology Management,* 45(6), 2002, pp. 50–56; and Gina O'Connor, Joanne Hyland, and Mark P. Rice, "Bringing Radical and Other Innovations Successfully to Market: Bridging the Transition from R&D to Operations," in *The PDMA Toolbook 2 for New Product Development,* ed. P. Belliveau, A. Griffin, and S. M. Somermeyer (Hoboken, NJ: Wiley, 2004), pp. 33–70.

[3]Industrial Research Institute 2001/2002 Annual Reports, Washington, DC, Industrial Research Institute; and Gary Hamel, "Innovation Now! (It's the Only Way to Win Today)," *Fast Company,* December 2002, pp. 114–124.

90 percent rate you often hear, and this percentage holds for both goods and services. The best product-developing firms can improve their odds further: They require only about four ideas to generate one winning product, as compared to over nine ideas for other firms. This is probably because the best firms are better at screening out bad ideas earlier.[4] And after many years of research, we know many of the most important reasons why products fail. The firm doesn't understand the customer, or underfunds the required R&D, or doesn't do the required homework before beginning development (sometimes called the *ready–fire–aim approach*), or doesn't pay enough attention to quality, or lacks senior management support, or chases a moving target (we will see moving-target issues such as unstable specifications and scope creep in Chapter 3).[5]

The goal at most firms is not necessarily to reduce failure rates to zero. Having too low a failure rate might mean that the firm is playing it too safe with close-to-home innovations, while missing out on the (risky) breakthroughs. The definition of "too low" probably depends on the industry and on how inherently risky product development is. The goal here is to minimize the dollar losses on the failures (don't bankrupt the company!) and to learn from them. Regardless of the actual failure rate you encounter, the amount at stake and the risk of failure are high in new product development.

Success rates have remained remarkably consistent over the years. The Comparative Performance Assessment Study (CPAS) is periodically conducted by the Product Development & Management Association (PDMA), most recently in 2012.[6] In these studies, for every 100 ideas, a little under 70 make it through the initial screen; fewer than 50 pass concept evaluation and testing and are moved to the development phase; a little more than 30 make it through development; about 30 make it through testing; about 25 of them are commercialized; and about 15 are considered to be successes (about 60 percent of those that were commercialized). Interestingly, the percent success rate does not vary too much from one category to the next. The percent success rate ranges from 51 percent (frequently purchased consumer goods) to 65 percent (health care). If one splits the CPAS sample into two groups, the "Best" (the top-performing 25 percent of firms) and the "Rest," a slightly different pattern emerges: In 2012, the Best firms attained a success rate of over 80 percent, while the Rest's success

---

[4]Marjorie Adams, *Competitive Performance Assessment Study (CPAS) Results,* PDMA Foundation, 2004; and Stephen K. Markham and Hyunjung Lee, "Product Development and Management Association's 2012 Comparative Performance Assessment Study," *Journal of Product Innovation Management,* 30(3), 2013, pp. 408–429. Success rate has held steady at around 60 percent of products marketed since the 1995 CPAS study; the 2012 study suggests the success rates are slightly lower in Europe and Asia.

[5]Robert Cooper, *Winning at New Products: Accelerating the Process from Idea to Launch,* 3rd ed. (New York: Perseus Books, 2001).

[6]2003 CPAS results are found in Doug Boike and Marjorie Adams, "PDMA Foundation CPAS Study Reveals New Trends—While the 'Best-Rest' Gap in NPD Widens," *Visions,* 28(3), July 2004, pp. 26–29; and Gloria Barczak, Abbie Griffin, and Kenneth B. Kahn, "Perspective: Trends and Drivers of Success in NPD Practices: Results of the 2003 PDMA Best Practices Study," *Journal of Product Innovation Management,* 26(1), January 2009, pp. 3–23. The 2012 results are summarized in Markham and Lee (2012), op. cit.

FIGURE 1.1
The Best Firms Achieve Superior NPD Results

	The Best (top 25% of firms)	The Rest (bottom 75% of firms)
Percent Successes	82.2	52.9
Percent of Sales from New Products	47.9	25.4
Percent of Profits from New Products	48.5	25.0
Number of Ideas Per Successful New Product	4.5	11.4

Source: Adapted from Stephen K. Markham and Hyunjung Lee, "Product Development and Management Association's 2012 Comparative Performance Assessment Study," *Journal of Product Innovation Management*, 30(3), 2013, pp. 408–429.

rate was much lower at about 50 percent. The Best, therefore, have greater success with new product development![7]

Figure 1.1 shows that the Best firms not only have a higher percentage rate of successes but also derive almost twice as many sales and profits from new products (defined as five years old or younger) than do the Rest. Best firms are also more efficient in developing successful products: they require about 4.5 ideas to generate one success, while the Rest firms require almost three times as many ideas per success. In addition, the development cost per successful project for Best firms is roughly half the cost per successful project for the Rest.[8]

The 2012 CPAS study also reveals that the Best companies at product development manage their new products process differently than do the Rest. In sum, the Best companies are better at implementing many of the new products process concepts and principles that we discuss in upcoming chapters of this book. Relative to the Rest, the Best:

- Have an effective new products process, which allows them to spend more time per project but on fewer projects (which we explore in Chapter 2).
- Are more likely to use market research tools such as creativity sessions (Chapter 5), trade-off analyses (Chapter 6), concept tests (Chapter 7), voice of the customer (Chapter 10), alpha and beta testing (Chapter 13), and test markets (Chapter 16).
- Rely more on portfolio analysis for product selection (Chapter 3).
- Are more likely to have global market and operations strategies (Chapters 3 and 12).
- Tend to use social media and online communities more for information gathering (Chapter 5).
- Employ formal processes for idea generation (Chapter 5) and concept development (Chapter 8).
- Adopt an open-innovation approach (Chapter 5).
- Involve senior management in decision making (Chapters 10 and 12).
- Use design and engineering tools (Chapter 11).

[7]The "Best" are defined in the CPAS study as those firms that are in the top 25 percent in their industry and above the mean in both program success and sales and profit success from new product development.

[8]Stephen K. Markham and Hyunjung Lee, op. cit.

- Use cross-functional teams effectively (Chapter 12).
- Are better at using team support tools and team incentives (Chapter 12).[9]

In sum, the concepts of new products management as presented throughout this book are used extensively, and well, by the top innovating companies, who achieve superior results from their new products!

Globalization and New Product Development

Like all aspects of modern business, product development has become more challenging due to increased **globalization**. To a greater extent than ever before, firms are seeing new product development as a global process in order to take advantage of worldwide opportunities and increase their efficiency and effectiveness of innovation. According to a 2007 study by consultants Booz & Company, the top global firms in terms of R&D spending deployed about 55 percent of their R&D spending in foreign countries. Among the 80 top U.S. R&D firms, $80.1 billion out of $146 billion was spent overseas, and similar percentages were found for top European and Japanese R&D firms.[10] The Booz & Company study also showed that the firms with higher percentages of R&D spending deployed elsewhere did better than average on many important performance measures, such as return on investment and total shareholder return.

This study found that firms have multiple reasons for increasing their global R&D efforts. In many foreign countries, R&D engineers are lower paid than in the United States, Western Europe, or Japan—but the salary gap is narrowing, especially for the most skilled engineers and scientists. Now, many firms look overseas not just to access a cheaper labor force but to access the talent residing in these markets and the ideas generated by these skilled personnel. Huge markets such as India and China are obvious sources of talented engineers, and there is some evidence of specialization: India boasts strengths in automotive engineering, China in electronics.

Another reason for increased global R&D is the increasing globalization of the innovating firms themselves. For example, as automakers seek to penetrate new markets such as China or India, it makes sense to conduct more of their design work in or near these markets than back in the home office located in Michigan or Bavaria. In addition, firms are under increased pressure to reduce product development times, or may be competing in increasingly turbulent market environments. These factors lead firms to leverage all the global resources they have at their disposal for product development.[11]

---

[9]Stephen K. Markham and Hyunjung Lee, op. cit.

[10]For a summary of the Booz & Company findings, see Barry Jaruzelski and Kevin Dehoff, "'Beyond Borders: The Global Innovation 1000' Study Reveals a Global Shift in R&D Spending," *Visions*, 33(3), October 2009, pp. 27–30.

[11]Elko J. Kleinschmidt, Ulrike de Brentani, and Sören Salomo, "Performance of Global New Product Development Programs: A Resource-Based View," *Journal of Product Innovation Management*, 24(5), September 2007, pp. 419–441; see summary in K. Sivakumar, "Global Product Development," in Jagdish N. Sheth and Naresh K. Malhotra, *Wiley International Encyclopedia of Marketing*, Volume 5, Product Innovation and Management (West Sussex, UK: John Wiley, 2011), pp. 68–74.

Many multinational firms seek to leverage their product development skills across their subsidiaries and gain competitive advantage by setting up *global new product teams*.[12] A large firm may have R&D skills in its German subsidiary, its manufacturing in Asia, and its suppliers somewhere else again. A firm's global presence, however, is no guarantee that it will automatically know how to efficiently manage its global operations. Effectively coordinating and marshaling the efforts across multiple countries to develop and to launch successful new products is a major challenge. There are many decisions to make that impact global product development effectiveness: how much autonomy should the subsidiaries have, how should they be rewarded, what work conditions should be imposed such that teamwork within and between subsidiaries is encouraged, and so forth. There is also the possibility of outsourcing some of the required new product capabilities, for example, through strategic alliances with global partners. Similarly, the global network of suppliers and distributors needs to be managed and coordinated so as to improve global product development as well as global launch. Selecting the best organizational structure for the global product team is more difficult than if only one culture is involved, as differences among team individuals as well as linguistic barriers and national culture differences must be taken into account. At the time of launch, even more decisions arise: Should a product be positioned the same way throughout the world, or should positioning, branding, or packaging decisions be localized? Many firms react to these challenges with well-defined, formal processes, while others leave the new products process relatively unstructured and adaptable to product or environmental considerations.

The best research available on this topic finds that firms with a *global innovation culture* have the most effective global new product programs.[13] Having a global innovation culture means that a firm is open to global markets, mindful of differences in customer needs and preferences, and respectful of different national cultural and business environments. Firms with such a corporate culture are able to recognize the specialized skills, resources, and ideas they possess in different subsidiaries around the world. In fact, at these firms, all operations and strategies (not just new product development) are defined in terms of the realities of the international market. A firm with a global innovation culture is better at integrating its global knowledge, can better manage the R&D tasks associated with the new products process, and has an advantage in implementing global launches.[14] All of these factors contribute to improved global new product performance. Throughout this book, you will see examples of firms that practice innovation on a global basis, which includes managing virtual and highly diverse global product development teams—no easy task! Figure 1.2 provides several samples of firms that take the global aspect of product development very seriously.

[12]Good references are Roger J. Calantone and David A. Griffith, "From the Special Issue Editors: Challenges and Opportunities in the Field of Global Product Launch," *Journal of Product Innovation Management,* 24(5), September 2007, pp. 414–418; and Ram Mudambi, Susan Mudambi, and Pietro Navarra, "Global Innovation in MNCs: The Effects of Subsidiary Self-Determination and Teamwork," *Journal of Product Innovation Management,* 24(5), September 2007, pp. 442–455.

[13]Elko J. Kleinschmidt, Ulrike de Brentani, and Sören Salomo, op. cit.

[14]Roger J. Calantone, S. T. Cavusgil, J. B. Schmidt, and G.-C. Shin, "Internationalization and the Dynamics of Product Adaptation: An Empirical Investigation," *Journal of Product Innovation Management,* 22(2), March 2004, pp. 185–198.

FIGURE 1.2   **Product Development as a Global Process**

Procter & Gamble: According to the P&G Web site, P&G products are developed as global R&D projects. P&G has 22 research centers in 13 countries from which they can draw expertise. As a good example of a global product, consider the Swiffer mop. P&G made use of its research centers in the United States and France to conduct market research and testing in support of this new product.

Apple: In the development of the iPod, Apple worked with about ten different firms and independent contractors throughout the world, and did product design and customer requirement definition in both the United States and Japan.

Ikea: The Swedish furniture retailer knows that its target market (middle-class strivers) crosses international and intercontinental lines, so it operates globally in a streamlined fashion. It identifies an unmet customer need (say a certain style of table at a given price point), commissions in-house and outsourced designers to compete for the best design, then its manufacturing partners worldwide compete for the rights to manufacture it. Excellent global logistics complete the value delivery to customers.

Ford: The carmaker has moved to a Global Product Development System, in which different groups are assigned the engineering task for one car system, and this is shared globally. One group does the exhaust system for all cars sold globally, one does the steering system, and so on. This efficient method has slashed time to market by 25 to 40 percent and cut engineering costs by 60 percent in the first few years of operation. The fact that car customers have similar wants around the world (fuel economy, safety, sustainability, attractive design, and a good entertainment system) makes the Global Product Development System feasible.

Source: Some examples are from Loida Rosario, "Borderless Innovation: The Impact of Globalization on NPD Planning in Three Industries," Visions, June 2006.

Global new product teams are a way of life now for many firms, and we will see more about the challenges facing such teams in Chapter 12. There, we will focus on the issues facing the global new product development team, and how firms overcome these hurdles to take advantage of product knowledge residing in many corners of the world. We touch on some of the issues regarding global positioning and branding decisions in Chapter 14.

How Product Development Is Different

It is likely that this course is located in your university's business school, within the marketing department. Or it might be part of your engineering training, or part of a specialized program in technology innovation management. In any case, this is a good time to note an underlying principle of product development: It's all about teamwork. The *new products team* ideally is cross-functional, comprising personnel from marketing, R&D, engineering, manufacturing, production, design, and other functional areas as well. Unlike other courses you may be taking, we spend much time in this text on *how you interact with people from other fields of study*: discussing how team members work together, how they can improve communication, what they need to achieve when working together, and so on. So, whatever your background, and whatever course of study you are pursuing, remember that in product development you will spend a lot of your time coordinating and working closely with people from other functional areas. Above all else, product development is a joint effort.

All members of a new products team make an important contribution to product development, so we must be aware of, and try to avoid, narrow functional viewpoints. Marketers have to learn to work with scientists, engineers, lawyers, production managers, and so on. We may come from marketing, and we will often return there when the project is finished, but, for now, we are all *new products people,* working with all functions, being biased to no one. A marketing type may not appreciate the thoroughness of a research scientist. And that scientist may not appreciate the marketer's enthusiasm, which sometimes leads to what the scientist thinks are rash and unwarranted conclusions. Now is a good time to begin thinking like a general manager.

This course of study calls for a *strong creative contribution*. Not only do we create new product concepts; in many firms, that's easy. The tough part is *how best to develop and market them*—devising a concept-testing method that works, screening a totally new idea the firm has never faced, and figuring out how to integrate engineers into a trade show booth effectively, how to position a product that creates its own new category, how to produce it on present equipment, how to name it in a way that communicates and is not confusing, and so on. No answers are found in the back of this book. We never will know whether any one decision was right, just whether the total package of decisions worked out.

Being creative means we *travel on unmarked roads*. Most of our decisions are made on grossly inadequate facts. Not that we don't know what facts we need or how to get good estimates of them—we usually do. But there's never enough time or money. Worst of all, *what seems to be a fact in January may not be a fact come June, when we actually introduce the new item.* As a result, we often do things that make others nervous. For example, we use **heuristics**—rules of thumb that firms have found work for them: "On items such as this, about 30 percent of the people who hear of a new brand, try it," or "When the product engineer from R&D disagrees with the process engineer from manufacturing, it's better to go with manufacturing." Heuristics sometimes leave us holding an empty bag; but without them, projects just won't move forward fast enough. Another technique is to use *simple intuition:* hunch, or gut feel. This explains why most managers want new products people to have spent time in ongoing operations before moving on to new products work.

This suggests another key difference between this course and many of your others. This course is about the activities of *people working under intense pressure*, making tough decisions under impossible conditions. Consider the development and launch of the Amazon Fire Phone. Strategically, the phone was supposed to grab a share of the smartphone market and also drive shoppers to Amazon's online store. From a technology viewpoint, the phone was actually quite adequate compared to competitors, in terms of important attributes such as screen size and memory. But it needed to be better than adequate in order to gain traction in a market dominated by Apple and Android phones. Despite the best efforts of the company and the huge investment in human and financial resources, the phone was declared a failure soon after launch.[15] When studying how strategy guides teams throughout a project, or how firms telescope their market testing into simultaneous regional rollouts, remember that pressure.

---

[15]J. P. Mangalindan, "Why Amazon's Fire Phone Failed," *Fortune*, September 29, 2014.

FIGURE 1.3   **Not All New Products Are Planned**

A Raytheon engineer working on experimental radar noticed that a chocolate bar in his shirt pocket melted. He then "cooked" some popcorn. The firm developed the first commercial microwave oven.

A chemist at G. D. Searle licked his finger to turn a page of a book and got a sweet taste. Remembering that he had spilled some experimental fluid, he checked it out and produced aspartame (NutraSweet).

A 3M researcher dropped a beaker of industrial compound and later noticed that where her sneakers had been splashed, they stayed clean. ScotchGard fabric protector resulted.

A DuPont chemist was bothered by an experimental refrigerant that didn't dissolve in conventional solvents or react to extreme temperatures. So the firm took the time to identify what later became Teflon.

Another scientist couldn't get plastic to mix evenly when cast into automobile parts. Disgusted, he threw a steel wool scouring pad into one batch as he quit for the night. Later, he noticed that the steel fibers conducted the heat out of the liquid quickly, letting it cool more evenly and stay mixed better. Bendix made many things from the new material, including brake linings.

Others? Gore-Tex, dynamite, puffed wheat, Dextro-Maltose, LSD, penicillin, Dramamine, X rays, pulsars, and many more. In each case, a prepared mind.

Sources: DuPont and Bendix cases, *The Innovators* (New York: Dow Jones, 1968); Raytheon, Searle, and 3M cases, Kenneth Labrich, "The Innovators," *Fortune,* June 6, 1988, p. 56.

You may also be taking a course that deals with innovation in manufacturing or operations, and you may wonder how *process* innovation differs from *product* innovation. The term *process innovation* usually applies to functions, especially the manufacturing or distribution process, and every new product benefits from this type of innovation. The term *product innovation* applies to the total operation by which a new product is created and marketed, and it includes innovation in all of the functional processes.

The last difference worth noting here is in *application*. Sometimes the new product process is accidental, or **serendipitous** (see Figure 1.3). But remember the old adage that chance favors the prepared mind. At least two dozen scientists had observed mold killing their bacteria colonies before Alexander Fleming pursued the phenomenon into the discovery of penicillin. More recently, Pfizer researchers noticed that several of the men in a test study of a new angina medication reported that it was ineffective at treating their angina, but it did have an unexpected alternative effect on the body. Soon, Pfizer was marketing Viagra, a leading product of theirs for several years.[16] So, we must practice. You cannot learn how to develop a new product concept by reading about attribute analysis or gap analysis. You must *do* them. The same goes for product use testing, positioning, contingency planning, and many more. There are opportunities at the end of every chapter to apply the chapter's material in one or more real-life short cases.

[16]Jenny Darroch and Morgan P. Miles, "Sources of Innovation," in V. K. Narayanan and Gina C. O'Connor (eds.), *Encyclopedia of Technology & Innovation Management* (Chichester, UK: John Wiley, 2010), Chapter 14.

What Is a New Product, and What Leads to Success?

The term **new product** can mean different things to different people. Figure 1.4 shows that new products can include **new-to-the-world** (sometimes called **really new**) products, as well as minor repositionings and cost reductions. The list in Figure 1.4 may include things you would exclude. For example, can we have a new item just by repositioning an old one (telling customers it is something else)? Arm & Hammer did, several times, by coming up with a new refrigerator deodorant, a new carpet freshener, a new drain deodorant, and more, all in the same package of baking soda, even with the same brand name. These may be considered just new uses, but the firm still went through a process of discovery and development. And a new use (particularly in industrial firms) may occur in a completely separate division. DuPont, for example, uses basic fibers in many different ways, from technical to consumer. Financial firms use their common databases for different markets. Similarly, brand names have long been used as platforms for launching line extensions. The Dove soap name, for example, has been extended to almost two dozen box soaps and almost as many liquid body washes, and more recently, to a very successful Dove Men+Care line.[17]

FIGURE 1.4   **What Is a New Product?**

New products can be categorized in terms of how new they really are to the world or to the firm. One common set of categories is as follows:

1. **New-to-the-world products, or really new products.** These products are inventions that create a whole new market. Examples: Polaroid camera, the smartphone and iPad, Hewlett-Packard's laser printer, Rollerblade brand inline skates, P&G's Tide Pods.

2. **New-to-the-firm products, or new product lines.** Products that take a firm into a category new to it. The products are not new to the world but are new to the firm. Examples: P&G's first shampoo or coffee, Hallmark gift items, Virgin Atlantic Airlines or Virgin Mobile phone service, Canon's laser printer.

3. **Additions to existing product lines.** These are "flanker" brands, or line extensions, designed to flesh out the product line as offered to the firm's current markets. Examples: Dove Men+Care, Tide Pods with Downy, Special K line extensions (drinks, snack bars, and crystals).

4. **Improvements and revisions to existing products.** Current products made better. Examples: P&G's Ivory Soap and Tide powder laundry detergent have been revised numerous times throughout their history; countless other examples.

5. **Repositionings.** Products that are retargeted for a new use or application. Example: Arm & Hammer baking soda repositioned as a drain or refrigerator deodorant; aspirin repositioned as a safeguard against heart attacks. Also includes products retargeted to new users or new target markets; Marlboro cigarettes were repositioned from a woman's cigarette to a man's cigarette years ago.

6. **Cost reductions.** New products that simply replace existing products in the line, providing the customer similar performance but at a lower cost. May be more of a "new product" in terms of design or production than marketing.

Sources: The categorization scheme was originally presented in Booz, Allen & Hamilton Inc., *New Product Management for the 1980s* (New York: Booz, Allen & Hamilton Inc., 1982) and is now standard in new product development. Some of the examples are from Robert G. Cooper, *Winning at New Products: Accelerating the Process from Idea to Launch,* 3rd ed. (Cambridge, MA: Perseus Publications, 2001).

[17]Deborah L. Vence, "Just a Variation on a Theme," *Marketing News,* February 2007, pp. 18–20.

All the categories in Figure 1.4 are considered new products, but it is plain to see that the risks and uncertainties differ, and the categories need to be managed differently. Generally, if a product is new to the world or new to the firm (the first two categories), the risks and uncertainties faced by the firm are higher, as are the associated costs of development and launch. It cost Gillette far more, for example, to launch its newest shaving system (the Fusion) than to do upgrades to the earlier Mach 3 system (such as developing the women's version, named Venus, which used the same blade technology). A greater commitment of human and financial resources is often required to bring the most innovative new products to market successfully.

Note also that not all the new product categories in Figure 1.4 are necessarily innovations. Line extensions, like the Dove soap bars and men's products mentioned earlier, or new flavors of Oreo cookies, may have resulted from the company's desire to increase display space and shelf space, or boost sales of the product category. Line extension shouldn't be confused with "true" innovation—and management must recognize that true innovation that provides enhanced value to customers is where their long-term competitive advantage may lie.[18]

New-to-the-world products revolutionize existing product categories or define wholly new ones. They are the most likely to require consumer learning and/or incorporate a very new technology. Desktop computers with word processing software defined a new product category that made electric and manual typewriters virtually obsolete, and consumer learning was required by those who type for a living. Hewlett-Packard LaserJet printers did much the same thing in the printer category. The launch of CDs required major differences at the retail level in terms of store layout and distribution of related components (such as CD players). Other familiar examples, such as Tesla and other electric cars, smart TVs, and wearable technology such as smart watches, illustrate the use of new technologies in new-to-the-world products. Manufacturers had to overcome perceived risks, perceived incompatibility with prior experience, or other barriers to customer adoption (more on this subject in Chapter 14).

Of course, launching new-to-the-world products means risk—and the encouragement to take on the risk must permeate the whole firm and must start at the highest levels of management. At highly innovative firms like Intel and Gillette (a division of Procter & Gamble), top management may even abandon the use of quarterly earnings estimates in order to keep the business units focused on innovation and other long-term strategic goals.[19]

The **new product line** category in Figure 1.4 raises the issue of the imitation product, a strictly "me-too." If a firm introduces a brand of light beer that is new to them but is identical to those already on the market, is it a new product? Yes, it is new to the firm, and it requires the new products process. Canon was not the first laser printer manufacturer, Coca-Cola was not the first orange-juice bottler, and P&G was not the first competitor in the coffee business. These were new products to these firms, however, managerially speaking, and they are managed as such by the companies.

---

[18]Deborah L. Vence, op. cit.

[19]Thomas D. Kuczmarski, "What Is Innovation? And Why Aren't Companies Doing More of It?" *Journal of Consumer Marketing*, 20(6), 2003, pp. 536–541.

Figure 1.4 shows that many new products can be considered additions to existing product lines or improvements and revisions to existing products. Many of these line extensions round out or add to existing product lines extremely well: Dove Men+Care, Bud Light, Special K snack bars or shakes. Nevertheless, studies suggest that the most innovative new product categories account for many more product successes. In one study, the two most innovative categories accounted for about 30 percent of new product launches, but about 60 percent of the most successful products. (Percentages, of course, will vary by industry: High-tech industries will produce proportionately more highly innovative new products.) In fact, a U shape between innovativeness and success was found: The most innovative new product categories and the least innovative categories (the repositionings and cost reductions) outperformed the middle categories in terms of meeting financial criteria, returns on investment, and resulting market shares![20] This is because new products in the "middle ground" are not new enough to really excite new customers, yet different enough from existing products that there are fewer synergies. The results suggest that many firms need to reconsider the importance and potential contribution of innovative new products when making project selection decisions. In Chapter 3, we shall look at building a strategic portfolio of products that strives for balance among the innovation categories.

We have already seen that, even among the best firms, there are some product failures, and this entire book is devoted to developing new successful products, so there can be no easy answer to the question "What leads to new product success?" Nevertheless, several studies over the years on this question have yielded a consistent answer: The number one reason for success is a *unique superior product*. Additionally, common causes of failure include "no need for the product" and "there was a need but the new product did not meet that need." In other words, it was not unique and superior.[21] It did not offer the user sufficient **value added** relative to the costs of purchasing and use. Value added is a key concept to keep in mind as you travel the new product highway.

Does This Field of Activity Have a Unique Vocabulary?

Yes, it does, for two reasons. One, it is an *expanding field*, taking on new tasks and performing them in new ways. Second, it is a *melting pot field*, bringing in the language of scientists, lawyers, marketing people, accountants, production people, corporate strategists, and many more. Because many of these people talk about the same event but using different terms, communication problems abound.

[20]Elko J. Kleinschmidt and Robert G. Cooper, "The Impact of Product Innovativeness on Performance," *Journal of Product Innovation Management*, 8(4), December 1991, pp. 240–251; see also Abbie Griffin, *Drivers of NPD Success: The 1997 PDMA Report* (Chicago: Product Development & Management Association, 1997).

[21]Discussions of product success and failure can be found in R. G. Cooper, "New Products: What Separates the Winners from the Losers?" in M. D. Rosenau, A. Griffin, G. Castellion, and N. Anscheutz (eds.), *The PDMA Handbook of New Product Development* (New York: John Wiley, 1996), pp. 3–18; and R.G. Cooper, "The Impact of Product Innovativeness on Performance," *Journal of Product Innovation Management*, 16(2), April 1999, pp. 115–133.

For example, there is sometimes confusion over the terms **invention** and **innovation**. To managers invention refers to the dimension of uniqueness—the form, formulation, function of something. It is usually patentable. Innovation refers to the overall process whereby an invention is transformed into a commercial product that can be sold profitably. The invention may take but a few moments. We have far more inventions than we do innovations. Similarly, the average person might think that a product idea, a product concept, a product prototype, and maybe even a product are all about the same thing. As you will see in the pages of this book, we have specific, distinct definitions for each of these terms, and they are not interchangeable.

The term **design** can be confusing as well. It can refer to industrial design or engineering (premanufacturing) design; creative design focused on appearance and aesthetics; or the entire technical creation function from initial specs to the shipping dock. Some might even use the term to refer to the entire product innovation function. In this text, we will adopt an *industrial design* perspective, considering the functionality and ergonomics of the product as well as its appearance, and we will explore how design can itself be a driver of innovation.

When in doubt, a complete glossary of new product terms is published online by the Product Development & Management Association (**www.pdma.org**; follow the link to the glossary).

Does the Field of New Products Offer Careers?

It does, though not many are entry positions for people right out of college. Generally, top managers want new products people to know the industry involved (for the customer understanding mentioned earlier) and the firm's various operations (that multidimensional, orchestration task also mentioned). So, most new products managers get assigned to new products work from a position in a functional department. For example, a scientist finds working with marketing and manufacturing people interesting, a market researcher specializes in benefit segmentation, or a salesperson earns a reputation for good new product concepts. Each of these people is a candidate for full-time work on new products.

The specific jobs in this field are three. First is **functional representative** on a team, sometimes full time, more often part time. An example is a marketing researcher or a production planner. These people may be representatives on several teams or just one. The second job is **project manager** or **team leader**. This role is leader of a team of people representing the functions that will be required. The third position is **new products process manager**, responsible for helping project managers develop and use good new product processes.

Some of the career tips we hear are:

1. Be multifunctional, not functionally parochial. Have experience in more than one function (marketing, manufacturing, and so on).
2. Be a risk taker, willing to do whatever is necessary to bring a product to market, including facing the wrath of coworkers.
3. Think like a general manager. Scientists and sales managers can lead new products teams, but they must cease being scientists and sales managers.

4. Be a combination of optimist and realist, aggressor and team player, leader and follower.

5. Develop your creative skills, both for new product concepts and for new ways of doing things.

6. Be comfortable in chaos and confusion. Learn to work with depressives, euphorics, and those with no emotion at all.

Fortunately, such managers do exist—and in increasing numbers. We hope you become one of them.

The Strategic Elements of Product Development

We cover a lot of product development material in this book, from opportunity identification right through to launch and postlaunch. Underlying all of this are three **strategic elements**, which will be a major focus in this book. These strategic elements provide a framework to guide management through product development and help them focus on what is most important. Top product development consultants, like Robert Cooper of the Product Development Institute, recommend a framework of this type to firms of all sizes to help guide product development.[22] A key point here is that *all three of the strategic elements must be in place*, and each is coordinated with, and supports, all the others. The three elements are a **new products process**, a **product innovation charter**, and a well-managed **product portfolio**.

The *new products process* is the procedure that takes the new product idea through concept evaluation, product development, launch, and postlaunch. This procedure is usually depicted as a phased process with evaluative steps between the phases, but as you will see in upcoming chapters, it is rarely so straightforward. The *product innovation charter* is essentially a strategy for new products. It ensures that the new product team develops products that are in line with firm objectives and strategies and that address marketplace opportunities. *Product portfolio management* helps the firm assess which new products would be the best additions to the existing product line, given both financial and strategic objectives. In this chapter, we introduce the first strategic element, the new products process, as it serves as a framework for everything that follows in this book, and explore it more deeply in Chapter 2. In Chapter 3, we discuss the last two strategic elements, the product innovation charter and product portfolio management.

The Basic New Products Process

Figure 1.5 shows a simple new products process. Research has shown that about 70 percent of firms use some kind of formal, cross-functional, phased new products process, and about 47 percent use clearly defined evaluation criteria after each phase.

---

[22]Roger J. Calantone, S. T. Cavusgil, J. B. Schmidt, and G.-C. Shin, "Internationalization and the Dynamics of Product Adaptation: An Empirical Investigation," *Journal of Product Innovation Management,* 22(2), March 2004, pp. 185–198.

FIGURE 1.5

The Basic New Products Process

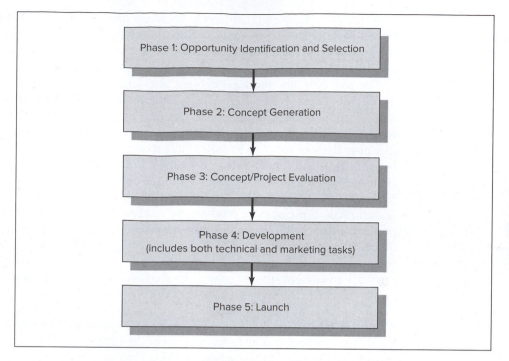

At least 40 percent of firms assign a process manager whose job is to manage the phased new products process.[23] The phased new products process is well established among firms involved in new product development.

The actual form of the phased new products process is by no means standardized. The number of phases can vary across companies. But the first component of the process is the pre-development period, sometimes called the front end of innovation, which encompasses identifying opportunities, generating and screening ideas, developing and refining concepts, evaluating the concepts for their financial and strategic potential, and then making a decision on which concepts to put into development. Predevelopment corresponds to the first three phases in Figure 1.5. Next comes the development phase, which includes both technical development and developing the marketing plans for the upcoming launch. The final phase, launch, starts at the time the product is launched but also includes management of the product post-launch to guide it toward successfully reaching its objective. In short, no matter how many phases, there is an underlying process of predevelopment, development, and launch.

The phases of the new products process represent *activities* that are conducted by the new product team; between the phases are *evaluation tasks*, or decision points.[24] It is at

[23]Markham and Lee (2012), op. cit.; Robert G. Cooper, Scott J. Edgett, and Elko J. Kleinschmidt, *Improving New Product Development Performance and Practices: Benchmarking Study* (Houston, TX: American Productivity and Quality Center, 2002); Marjorie Adams (2004), op. cit., and Kenneth B. Kahn, Gloria Barczak, and Roberta Moss (2002), op. cit.

[24]Robert G. Cooper, *Winning at New Products: Accelerating the Process from Idea to Launch,* 3rd ed. (Cambridge, MA: Perseus Publishing, 2001).

these points that the hard Go/No Go decisions need to be made (that is, whether the project looks promising enough to go on to the next phase). Throughout this book, we will be looking at the kinds of tests (from concept tests, to product use tests, to market tests) that are used to gather information for project evaluation.

The goal of a new products process is to manage down the amount of risk and uncertainty as one passes from idea generation to launch. There are periodic evaluations all the way through the process. A firm may have access to hundreds of ideas; weaker ones are immediately eliminated, and the better ones are refined into concepts. (For now, think of concepts as "more fully formed ideas." We will make the distinction between ideas and concepts clear in Chapter 4.) Later in the process, only the best concepts are approved and moved forward to the development phase. The product is continuously refined during the development phase and could still be halted before the launch phase if preliminary product use test results are not positive. By the time the product is launched, it has a much higher likelihood of succeeding (recall the roughly 60 percent success rate across many product categories cited earlier). Managing down the amount of uncertainty is important, because each additional phase means greater financial investment (possibly much greater), not to mention greater commitment of human resources. Firms using a new products process have reported improvements in product teamwork, less rework, greater success rates with new products, earlier identification of failures, improved launch, and up to 30 percent shorter cycle times.[25] This is not to say, however, that all firms implement the process well. Other studies show that many firms that claim to have a new products process either designed it or implemented it poorly; thus, there is much room for improvement.[26]

Note, however, that the neat, linear new products process shown in Figure 1.5 is not typical of product development in the real world. The reality is that the activities are not sequential, but overlapping. It is not implied that one phase must be completed before work can begin on the next one, like a pass-the-baton relay race. In fact, overlapping is encouraged. There is much pressure for firms to **accelerate time to market** for new products, and a certain amount of phase overlapping is an important tool in speeding new products to market. To do this right, of course, requires that the product team members from different functional areas (marketing, R&D, manufacturing, design, engineering) communicate very effectively.[27] Product development is truly **multifunctional**, where all functions (and, increasingly, the customer as well) work together on a **cross-functional team** to accomplish the required tasks. The whole of Chapter 12 investigates the organization and management of these cross-functional teams in depth. But even though we discuss teams later in the text, keep in mind that

[25]Robert G. Cooper, "New Products: What Separates the Winners From the Losers and What Drives Success," in K. B. Kahn, S. E. Kay, R. J. Slotegraaf, and S. Uban (eds.), *The PDMA Handbook of New Product Development* (Hoboken, NJ: Wiley, 2013), Ch. 1, pp. 3–34.

[26]Robert G. Cooper, Scott J. Edgett, and Elko J. Kleinschmidt, *Best Practices in Product Innovation: What Distinguishes the Top Performers,* Product Development Institute, 2003; Robert G. Cooper, "Perspective: The Stage-Gate® Idea-to-Launch Process—Update, What's New, and NexGen Systems," *Journal of Product Innovation Management,* 25(3), May 2008, pp. 213–232.

[27]Preston G. Smith and D. G. Reinertsen, *Developing Products in Half the Time* (New York: Van Nostrand Reinhold, 1991).

the team must become involved as early as possible in the new products process. It is the responsibility of the team leader to bring together the right individuals with the right skill sets, and to encourage communication within the team, between the team and top management, and between the team and communities of customers. The effective team leader knows how to deal with power conflicts as well as technical complexity.[28]

Another way that firms have been able to avoid delays and speed up time to market is to streamline the evaluation tasks. At Johnson & Johnson, the preparation for an evaluation task might have included preparing a 30- to 90-page review document. This was cut to a standardized presentation, with a one-page summary and a handful of slides—enough to inform senior management about the risks and commitments being decided upon. It was reported that weeks of preparation time were saved with the new format.[29]

Furthermore, Figure 1.5 implies that each phase is always followed by a Go/No Go decision. While this is often the case, it might be an oversimplification. If some key information is still missing or unavailable, a third option is possible, which we can call an "On decision." This means that the project will move forward (a conditional "Go," if you will), but the missing information must be gathered and the project could still be halted at a later phase. An evaluation task that includes conditional Go decisions is sometimes called a **fuzzy gate**. For example, a new packaged food product might do reasonably well at a concept test, but management might feel they don't really have a read on the market until some product use testing (letting the customer actually taste the product) is conducted. An On decision would mean that the product is approved to move to development, but the product use test must yield positive results, otherwise the project would be halted at that point. Fuzzy gates, therefore, speed up the process because time is not wasted in obtaining complete information before the decision is made. They are relatively common; in the CPAS study, about 50 percent of projects move forward with some conditional decisions along the way. Nevertheless, the team must indeed make a firm decision once the necessary information is obtained; in other words, fuzzy gates still have teeth. A related problem occurs when teams actually make a full "Go" decision, but fail to commit any resources to the project. This is known as a *hollow-gate* problem and results in too many projects underway and, inevitably, cost overruns and launch delays. Similarly, a poor project may never be critically evaluated because it is the CEO's pet project, or because a hidden personal or political agenda is influencing decision making. Gates without teeth, hollow gates, special treatment for executives, or hidden agendas can all hinder effectiveness of the new products process, but all are identifiable and avoidable.[30]

Another consideration is that the new products process might look very different for new-to-the-world, **breakthrough products** (more on these in Chapter 2) as

---

[28]Hans J. Thamhain, "Managing Product Development Project Teams," in Kenneth B. Kahn, George Castellion, and Abbie Griffin (eds.), *The PDMA Handbook of New Product Development* (New York: John Wiley & Sons, 2005), pp. 127–143.

[29]Robert G. Cooper, "What Leading Companies Are Doing to Reinvent Their NPD Processes," *Visions*, 32(3), September 2008, pp. 6–10.

[30]For more on all of these problem areas, see Cooper (2008), op. cit.

compared to more **incremental new products**. A firm like P&G might use a simplified process for a low-risk project (such as a new detergent) in which some phases and evaluation tasks are combined or may even be omitted. The CPAS study showed that only about 40 percent of radical projects have phases that overlap or are skipped, while for incremental new products, about 59 percent have overlapping phases or skip some phases entirely. For a new-to-the-world product, such as Febreze or Dryel, P&G faces greater risks and higher expenses, and the complete new products process in all its detail will probably be followed. Thus, it is helpful to think of the process in Figure 1.5 as a guideline or framework, but to recognize that the new products process is really quite flexible. In fact, these characteristics (overlapping phases, fuzzy gates, and flexibility) are features of what is called the **third-generation new products process**, which is the way most firms interpret the process depicted in Figure 1.5.[31]

There is something else significant in Figure 1.5. The phases do not refer to functions or departments. Technical people may *lead* the technical portion of the development, but others participate, some very actively, including market research, sales, design, and others. Launch sounds like a marketing activity, but much of the marketing is done back during earlier phases. We discuss what we call the "marketing ramp-up" in detail in Chapter 13. Also, during launch, the manufacturing people are busy setting up production capability. Legal people are clearing brand names, and lab people are running tests on early product output. It is clear that the new products process is a job for a well-organized, efficient cross-functional team.

Additionally, different firms group the new product activities differently. There is certainly no agreement on the exact number of steps. That is not a cause for concern. Rather than thinking of the process as some number of discrete phases, look for the bigger picture of a large, evolving, general-purpose process, which we break up into five phases partly for our benefit in presenting the story about new product activities. Different firms simply break up the same underlying process differently.

We will go much deeper into the new products process in Chapter 2.

The Other Strategic Elements

The process depicted in Figure 1.5 is part of a firm's new product strategy, but it leaves some questions unanswered. First, what is the firm's underlying strategy for new products? What market and/or technology opportunities is it seeking to exploit? What is the strategic arena within which the firm will compete? How innovative does management want to be? Lacking a new product strategy, the firm will approach new product development in an unfocused manner. Without a clear boundary defining what new market or technology opportunities to pursue, *any* idea would seem to be all right, which leads to too many underfunded products. We call this new product strategy a **product innovation charter**, or PIC. The PIC is developed by senior management and provides guidance to all functional areas involved in innovation. It

---

[31]See Robert G. Cooper, "Perspective: Third-Generation New Product Processes," *Journal of Product Innovation Management,* 11(1), 1994, pp. 3–14; also Cooper (2008), op. cit.; also Robert G. Cooper, "Effective Gating," *Marketing Management,* 18(2), 2009, pp. 12–17.

defines a scope of activity for new product development, helping the product team identify what opportunities lie within the boundaries and where they should focus their efforts. That way, perhaps fewer projects may be pursued, but they will generally be of higher value to the firm. And the advantages of establishing a PIC are obvious. In Robert Cooper's research, a clear new product strategy (well-stated goals, match between product innovation and overall business goals, identifiable strategic focus, product roadmap in place) is closely related to new product performance.[32]

Additionally, many new product concepts may seem to be technically feasible and marketable. Before committing scarce financial and human resources, top management must also consider whether the new product, if developed, would fit the firm's overall business strategy: whether it adds strategically to the products already being offered, or whether it throws the firm's product line off balance. This is an issue of product portfolio management. While almost every firm will consider financial criteria such as expected sales revenues or profits when approving a new product development project, the best performing firms balance financial criteria with strategic considerations, such that the firm's long-term objectives will be met and there will be a dependable flow of new products into the future.[33]

The product innovation charter, product portfolio management, and related issues are covered more deeply in Chapter 3.

Product Development in Action

To see the ongoing efforts of the best product developers in the business, check the Web site for the Product Development & Management Association (**www.pdma .org**). Among other things, the PDMA sponsors an Outstanding Corporate Innovator award. This award is not for a single great new product, but rather for a sustained program of new product success over at least five years. And award winners must tell attendees at the association's annual conference how they did it. As we noted before, innovation can be taught—and managers from the best innovating firms serve as the teachers in these conference sessions. In most of these cases, one could take their systems right from this book. Winners have included Corning, Royal DSM, Merck, Hewlett-Packard, Sherwin-Williams, Maytag, Becton-Dickinson, Novozymes, Harley-Davidson, and many others (the full list is on the PDMA Web site).

The PDMA Web site also provides links to their academic journal, the *Journal of Product Innovation Management*, and their practitioner-oriented newsletter, *Visions,* as well as to the glossary mentioned earlier. As you take this course, you may want to check these publications for the most recent and timely articles on many aspects of new product development and innovation, and for the current hot topics among new product development professionals.

---

[32]Robert Cooper, "Best Practices and Success Drivers in New Product Development," in Peter N. Golder and Debanjan Mitra (eds.), *Handbook of Research on New Product Development,* Cheltenham, UK: Edward Elgar, 2018, pp. 410–434.

[33]Gary E. Blau, Joseph F. Pekny, Vishal A. Varma, and Paul R. Bunch, "Managing a Portfolio of Interdependent New Product Candidates in the Pharmaceutical Industry," *Journal of Product Innovation Management,* 21(4), July 2004, pp. 227–245.

Summary

This chapter has introduced you to the general field of new products management. You read how the activity is (or should be) found in all organizations, not just business. You read how this course of study relates to others, what a new product actually is, and that services and business products are covered, not just cake mixes, cell phones, and cars. You learned about where the field stands today, the hallmarks of our activity, our problems with vocabulary, and possible careers. Chapter 2 will take us directly into the new product process.

CHAPTER TWO

The New Products Process

Setting

Chapter 1 provided a view of the *overall new products process*—the phases and evaluative tasks that, if performed well, will churn out the new products the organization needs. This process appeared in Figure 1.5, which serves as a framework for the rest of this book. As noted in the introduction to Part I, the five figures that introduce each part of this book (Figures I.1, II.1, and so on) are indeed the five boxes of Figure 1.5, but expanded to show more detail on what happens at each phase in the process. In this chapter, we go more deeply into the phases of the new products process model of Figure 1.5, illustrating what tasks are required at each phase and who is responsible for what. We then explore several issues important to product managers: how the new products process can be sped up (without sacrificing product quality or running up the budget), how the process would have to be adapted for the development of new services, how to develop breakthrough innovations, and how the skills and resources of external partners can be leveraged to improve the process.

We begin by relating a short new product story to illustrate some of the key activities in the new products process in action. This will lead into a deeper discussion of the new products process and its managerial aspects. In particular, the story clearly shows how the new products process is interwoven with the other strategic elements introduced in Chapter 1, that is, the product innovation charter and the new product portfolio. It also introduces the idea of the cross-functional team and the importance of effective team management in implementing the new products process.

The LEGO New Products Saga[1]

The LEGO Group, manufacturer of those plastic bricks popular with children worldwide, was founded in 1932 in Denmark by Ole Kirk Christiansen. The name LEGO was picked as a short form of "leg goet," or "play well" in Danish, but by coincidence,

[1]This saga is adapted from several sources, including David Robertson, "Innovation at Lego," *Visions*, 35(3), 2011, pp. 10–17; Anonymous, "So What Did Lego Do Anyway," *Visions*, 36(1), 2012, pp. 24–25; Bradford Wieners, "Lego Is for Girls," *Bloomberg BusinessWeek*, December 15, 2011; and *Innovation at the LEGO Group*, International Institute for Management Development, Case IMD-380, 2008.

it also means "I connect" in Latin, and one cannot imagine a more appropriate name for the little connecting bricks. LEGO manufactured wooden toys for the first few years of its existence, but in 1947, Christiansen bought a plastic injection molding machine, and by 1958, the company was manufacturing the familiar plastic bricks. From 1958 to 1978, sales grew at a steady pace to about $180 million worldwide. By 1978, LEGO had introduced the Castle, Space, and Fabuland play themes and the Technic building system. Buoyed by these and other product innovations, sales really took off, doubling once every five years up to about 1993.

Faced with slowing sales in the early 1990s, LEGO began product line extensions, tripling the number of stock-keeping units (SKUs), but these only cannibalized existing products. Overall company sales were unaffected, and the product development efforts ate into LEGO profits. In 1998, LEGO lost money (a company first) and laid off 1,000 workers.

Customer and industry research suggested several reasons for the declines in sales and profits. A generation earlier, kids would have played with LEGO until they reached about 10 or 11 years old; by the late 1990s, they were losing interest earlier. In addition, many children, including the very young, were getting into video and electronic games and preferred these to building blocks. These consumer trends were unlikely to change soon. Industry changes were also taking place. Most competitors were manufacturing in China, while LEGO still produced bricks at more expensive European locations. The channel power in the toy and game industry had shifted away from manufacturers and now belonged to huge discount retailers. LEGO's patent on the plastic brick was also about to expire, truly leaving LEGO in a "change or die" situation.

In 2000, LEGO developed a new mission statement: "To become the world's strongest brand among families with children by 2005." This mission statement was designed to boost innovation throughout the company. To pursue the mission and spur the innovative process, LEGO followed the wisdom of the best business consultants and academics. Some of the most notable activities were as follow:

- LEGO hired creative people internationally, from Italy to Japan to the United States, for their Concept Lab, a new products center to increase diversity and stimulate creativity.

- LEGO created a wide spectrum of innovations, including LEGOLAND amusement parks and education centers, and also opened LEGO retail stores.

- For the first time, LEGO partnered with movie producers to develop Star Wars and Harry Potter LEGO sets in addition to Steven Spielberg Movie-Maker toys.

- New electronic toys such as Galidor, Bionicle, and Mindstorms were added. Galidor interacted with a TV program of the same name, and Bionicle was paired with a movie. A line of Explore electronic toys was also designed for very young children.

- LEGO launched the Digital Designer, with which children could use virtual LEGO bricks to design creations on the computer.

Unfortunately, nothing worked. By 2003, LEGO had lost about $300 million and was almost bankrupt. It was very likely that the company would be sold within a year.

LEGO seemed to have implemented effective strategies: boosting creativity, finding innovation partners, looking for disruptive opportunities, and building an innovation culture. All of these activities were investments in the innovation "engine." With the power of this engine, LEGO was capable of rapid new product development. This did not guarantee successful new products, however. The Concept Lab was charged with developing new products but was not held responsible if its products were not very innovative or good (hence, adding a seventh line of LEGO people to an already wide-enough product line). Movie licensing was only profitable in the years when Harry Potter or Star Wars movies were released, and that was out of LEGO's control. Something still needed to be done.

The big turnaround to save the company began in earnest in 2003. LEGO sold most of the LEGOLAND parks and its headquarters building. Brick production was outsourced to cheaper locations (Mexico and Czech Republic). The number of SKUs was cut in half, as many of these were redundant (for example, at one time, there were seven different lines of LEGO people, all with slightly different faces). Within a year, LEGO had raised enough cash to stave off bankruptcy, but now a long-term plan was required.

The Product Innovation Charter (PIC)

The starting point for the turnaround was a clear product innovation charter (PIC), which begins with an honest situation assessment and opportunity identification. According to Professor David Robertson of the Wharton School, what was missing at LEGO was an innovation guidance system: "Like a rocket car without a steering wheel, LEGO's innovation engine had launched them down a path at high speed, without the ability to navigate the curves in the road ahead. And like such a car, the end of such a ride is destined to be disastrous." To be sure, there were successes, such as the very popular Mindstorms, which LEGO could build upon. But to improve the success rate substantially, LEGO needed to institute an effective guidance system, which, according to Robertson, would have to provide answers to three questions: Where are you now, where do you want to go, and how will you get there?

LEGO's new strategy for innovation centered not on making toys but rather on "developing new experiences that were obviously LEGO but never seen before." Organizational changes were also made to facilitate this new strategy: The Concept Lab was separated from the product development department and set up as an independent profit center. Concept Lab designers were now working with a smaller number of SKUs and were encouraged to use the principle "less is more" by combining familiar elements in different ways. This appealed to the designers, as it was not too different from the LEGO experience itself: making an unlimited number of creative models using a simple system of bricks.

While you will learn more about the PIC in Chapter 3, the important thing to know is that it is a systematic way for managers to develop a new product strategy that considers the goals for their product innovation efforts and how these efforts fit overall business strategy. It involves identifying a strategic focus (i.e., which markets and technologies will be targeted). Any new product opportunities that did not clearly help LEGO achieve its objectives would no longer be pursued.

The New Products Process

A second strategic element is the new products process, which is the path the new product takes from idea to the time of launch and beyond. While LEGO had a new products process in place, it was formalized at this time to a phased process with specific evaluation points and deadlines. LEGO begins by collecting input from customers, suppliers, and other outside sources. A two-day workshop is held in February to examine market trends and identify ideas sourced from inside the company and from the outside sources, and a two-year roadmap is planned for product innovation. In June, product team members present their findings on trends and themes and suggest concepts; the concepts are screened, and the best ones are selected for further consideration. By September, the concepts are more fully developed, business plans and sales projections are prepared, and early prototypes (such as sketches) are prepared and presented. The concepts with the most potential are approved for further work. Then, in December, a full screen is done: the product teams select the concepts that will go into product development, more fully designed prototypes (realistic models, package design ideas) are created and evaluated, business plans are finalized, and required resources are planned. In January, these concepts go into development, with a planned launch later in the year (in time for the November–December peak buying season), and the cycle begins again. This formalized process aided in screening out the weaker ideas, allowing LEGO to concentrate on the highest-potential concepts while keeping to the two-year innovation cycle.

The New Product Portfolio

In addition to a well-functioning new products process, there also needs to be an assurance that the firm is developing the right products with respect to its product portfolio. LEGO management established a plan for thinking about the categories of innovation they were involved in and which ones needed to be focused on. Management defined three broad innovation categories. *Adjusted innovation* is continuous improvement of existing product categories, based on experience and insight. *Reconfigured innovation* involves creating new and better value-providing solutions, supported by studies of customer needs and marketplace changes. And *redefined innovation* means never-before-seen solutions that provide new strategic directions for the future, based on an understanding of social and cultural trends as well as industry trends.

LEGO's product launches during this time reveal the new product portfolio in action. A key component of LEGO's turnaround was the development of Mindstorms NXT, an extension of the original Mindstorms robotic set. LEGO worked with dedicated Mindstorms hobbyists, who enthusiastically made many useful suggestions on potential applications and new components to add to the set. In the words of LEGO management, the hobbyists "came up with ideas we had not even dreamed of." Mindstorms NXT was launched at the Consumer Electronics Show in January 2006 and featured powerful programming capabilities with a visual interface. Mindstorms NXT was targeted to consumers and also to educators through its LEGO Education Group. It became one of the most profitable products in the company's history.

LEGO did not ignore its traditional brick playset line either. When consumer research found that LEGO sets were much more popular with boys, it began to work on a playset specifically targeted to girls. Launched in late 2011, the LEGO Friends line featured realistic-looking play figures, settings, and storylines designed to appeal to girls. And, noting how movie licensing had been profitable in the past, the company got into that business as well, with the 2014 release of *The Lego Movie*, followed by other successful titles.

What Happened in That Saga?

We just read several years' worth of product development activity in a few minutes. The story began with an ongoing operation that was facing a difficult situation. The saga illustrates how the managers involved applied the strategic elements effectively. We also saw how important it was to get support for the process from top management.

This situation is typical in that the new products process *does not usually begin with a new product idea*. It is folklore that someone, somewhere, wakes up in the middle of the night with a great insight. It can happen, but successful new product programs are not built on such slender hopes. As the saga shows, the process usually begins with what amounts to strategy. With top management's support and good execution of all the strategic elements, LEGO was able to revitalize its innovation process and get back on course.

Note too that development does not take place behind the closed doors of a research lab. Along the way, LEGO's creative people worked with enthusiastic hobbyists, as well as educators and other partners. Also, marketing doesn't start when the product is finished. It becomes involved very early in the process—in this saga, marketing provided key information for the development of the PIC.

Last, the process is not over when the new product is launched. It ends when the new product is *successful,* usually after some in-flight corrections. LEGO monitors the sales, profits, and market shares of its new products and takes corrective actions if interim goals are not reached.

The next section looks more deeply at the phases of the new products process, first introduced in Chapter 1.

The Phases in the New Products Process

Figure 2.1 shows a more detailed version of the **new products process**. Let's examine each of the phases individually to understand the basics.

Phase 1: Opportunity Identification and Selection

The first phase is strategic in nature; successful completion of this phase yields strategic guidance to the new products team, which guides idea generation and all remaining phases in the new products process.

At least three main streams of activity feed strategic planning for new products. They are as follows.

- **Ongoing marketing planning.** Example: The annual marketing plan for a CD-ROM line calls for a line extension to meet encroachment of a new competitor selling primarily on price.
- **Ongoing corporate planning.** Example: Top management adopts a strategy that says either own a market (meaning get either a first- or second-place share) or get

FIGURE 2.1
The Phases of the New Products Process

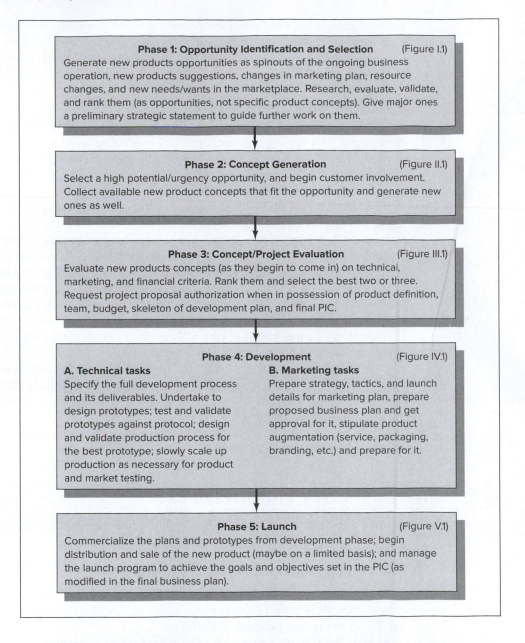

Phase 1: Opportunity Identification and Selection   (Figure I.1)

Generate new products opportunities as spinouts of the ongoing business operation, new products suggestions, changes in marketing plan, resource changes, and new needs/wants in the marketplace. Research, evaluate, validate, and rank them (as opportunities, not specific product concepts). Give major ones a preliminary strategic statement to guide further work on them.

Phase 2: Concept Generation   (Figure II.1)

Select a high potential/urgency opportunity, and begin customer involvement. Collect available new product concepts that fit the opportunity and generate new ones as well.

Phase 3: Concept/Project Evaluation   (Figure III.1)

Evaluate new products concepts (as they begin to come in) on technical, marketing, and financial criteria. Rank them and select the best two or three. Request project proposal authorization when in possession of product definition, team, budget, skeleton of development plan, and final PIC.

Phase 4: Development   (Figure IV.1)

A. Technical tasks

Specify the full development process and its deliverables. Undertake to design prototypes; test and validate prototypes against protocol; design and validate production process for the best prototype; slowly scale up production as necessary for product and market testing.

B. Marketing tasks

Prepare strategy, tactics, and launch details for marketing plan, prepare proposed business plan and get approval for it, stipulate product augmentation (service, packaging, branding, etc.) and prepare for it.

Phase 5: Launch   (Figure V.1)

Commercialize the plans and prototypes from development phase; begin distribution and sale of the new product (maybe on a limited basis); and manage the launch program to achieve the goals and objectives set in the PIC (as modified in the final business plan).

out of it. This will require new product activity in all desirable markets where the firm holds a minor position.

- **Special opportunity analysis.** One or more persons (in the firm or a consulting firm) are assigned to take an inventory of the firm's resources (people, facilities, reputations, to name a few). Example: A firm in the auto parts business called for an audit of its manufacturing operation. It turned out that manufacturing process engineering had been overlooked or just not appreciated; that skill could serve as the base for a new products program.

From these activities, the opportunities identified can be sorted into four categories. Here are illustrations:

- **An underutilized resource:** A bottling operation, a strong franchise with dealers, or that manufacturing process engineering department.
- **A new resource:** A chemical company discovers a new compound with hundreds of potentially commercial uses and applications.
- **An external mandate:** The market may be stagnant, the competition may be threatening, or customer needs may be evolving. Challenges like this will cause the firm to search for new opportunities, as we saw in the LEGO saga earlier.
- **An internal mandate:** Long-range planning often establishes a five-year-out dollar sales target, and new products people often must fill part of the gap between current sales and that target. That assignment is called the **product innovation** (and/or *acquisition*) **gap**. Other common internal mandates are simply upper management desires, such as Steve Jobs's stated goal to "reinvent the phone" with the iPhone project.[2]

The process of creatively recognizing such opportunities is called **opportunity identification**. The opportunities are carefully and thoroughly described, then analyzed to confirm that a sales potential does, indeed, exist. Recall that LEGO recognized that robotic-based building toys could be a viable business direction and also realized that the new products process needed to be fixed in order to support new products of this type. Opportunities can be anywhere, and firms like Corning have "opportunity scouts" and "tech scouts" who work with networks of external technologists and business leaders to find promising opportunities.[3]

Of course, no firm wants to exploit *all* opportunities; some are better than others. Some may not fit with company skills, some are too risky, some require more money than the firm has. So, most firms have **ongoing strategies** covering product innovation. For example, Waterford had a strategy that no new product would jeopardize the firm's great image. Gillette and Sony usually choose leading-edge innovation strategies.

Once an opportunity is approved, managers turn to various techniques to guide new product people in exploiting it. This we will call the **product innovation charter (PIC),** and it will be explained in Chapter 3.

Phase 2: Concept Generation

In some cases, merely identifying an opportunity spells out what is wanted (for example, an opportunity to add a small size of deodorant for travelers). Most times, however, it is not so clear, so an immense set of ideation tools has evolved. Creating viable **product concepts** sounds fun and interesting, but it is hard and sometimes frustrating work.

The most fruitful ideation involves identifying problems people or businesses have and suggesting solutions to them. For example, if the opportunity focused on "people

[2]Henry Robben, "Opportunity Identification," in Jagdish N. Sheth and Naresh K. Malhotra, *Wiley International Encyclopedia of Marketing*, Volume 5, Product Innovation and Management (West Sussex, UK: John Wiley, 2011), p. 153.

[3]Jacquelin Cooper, "How Industry Leaders Find, Evaluate and Choose the Most Promising Open Innovation Opportunities," *Visions*, 36(1), 2012, pp. 20–23.

moving their families over long distances," the first ideation step is to study those people and find what problems they have. This is the **problem find-solve** approach.

While this problem-based ideation is going on, unsolicited ideas are pouring in via phone, mail, and e-mail from customers, potential or former customers, employees (especially sales, technical, and operations), and every other source imaginable. These ideas are reviewed briefly by whomever receives them to see if they are even relevant to the firm and its strategies. They are then put into the pool with the ideas that came from problem-solving activities.

Concept generation is covered in Part II, Chapters 4 through 6.

Phase 3: Concept/Project Evaluation

Before development work can begin on new ideas, they need to be evaluated, screened, sorted out. This activity, sometimes called **screening** or **pretechnical evaluation**, varies tremendously. But most firms generally follow a sequence from quick looks to complete discounted cash flows and a net present value. The quick look is necessary because the flow of new product concepts is huge and can easily reach the thousands in many firms.

But what happens next is the first formal type of evaluation. Depending on the idea, this may be end-user screening or technical screening, or both. The work may be extensive and difficult, or it may take no more than a few phone calls or e-mails. In the LEGO example, many of the proposed new products may have originated among the Concept Lab people; this would have to be followed by a **concept test** to see what potential consumers thought about it. Ultimately, these views all come together in what is often called the **full screen**. It uses a scoring model of some type and results in a decision to either undertake development or quit.

If the decision is to go ahead, the evaluation turns into **project evaluation**, where we no longer evaluate the idea but rather the plan we propose for capitalizing on that idea. This involves preparing a statement of what is wanted from the new product. Firms using **Quality Function Deployment** (a method of project management and control, which we explore in Chapter 10) see this as the first list of customer needs. A more common generic term is **product description** or **product definition**. In this book it will be called **product protocol**. Protocol here means a kind of agreement, and it is important that there be agreement between the various groups *before* extensive technical work gets under way. The protocol should, to the extent possible, be *benefits* the new item is to yield, not the features the new item is to have.

The lack of good hard information complicates all pretechnical evaluation. In fact, the first three phases (strategic planning, concept generation, and, especially, concept/project evaluation) comprise what is popularly called the **fuzzy front end** or simply **front end** (of the new product process). By the end of the project, most fuzz will have been removed, but for now, we move with more daring than the data allow.[4] The various pretechnical evaluation actions are covered in Part III, Chapters 7 through 10.

---

[4]The fuzzy front end has been the subject of much research the past few years. A good resource is Peter A. Koen, Greg A. Ajamian, Scott Boyce, Allen Clamen, Eden Fisher, Stavros Fountoulakis, Albert Johnson, Pushpinder Puri, and Rebecca Seibert, "Fuzzy Front End: Effective Methods, Tools, and Techniques," in P. Belliveau, A. Griffin, and S. M. Somermeyer, *The PDMA Toolbook for New Product Development* (New York: John Wiley, 2002), Ch. 1.

Phase 4: Development

This is the phase during which the item acquires finite form—a tangible good or a specific sequence of resources and activities that will perform an intangible service. It is also the phase during which the **marketing plan** is sketched and gradually fleshed out. Business practice varies immensely, but we often find the following components.

Resource Preparation

Often overlooked by new products managers is a step called **resource preparation**. For product improvements and some line extensions, this is fine, because a firm is already up and running in a mode that fits products that are close to home. The culture is right, market data are more reliable, and ongoing managers are ready to do the work. But a particular innovation charter may leave familiar territory, forcing problems of fit. If a firm wants new-to-the-world products (more about them later in this chapter), then the team will need to be adequately prepared: it may need special training, new reward systems, revisions in the firm's usual project review system, and special permissions.

The Major Body of Effort

Next comes what all of the previous steps have been leading up to—the actual development of not one thing, but three—the item or service itself, the marketing plan for it, and a business (or financial) plan that final approval will require. The product (or concept) stream involves industrial design and bench work (goods) or systems design (services), **prototypes**, product specifications, and so on. It culminates in a product that the developers hope is finished: produced, tested, and costed out.

While the technical developers are at work, marketing planners are busy making periodic market scans (to keep up with changes out there) and making marketing decisions as early as they can be made—first strategic and then tactical. Marketing decisions are completely interlaced with technical ones and involve package design, brand name selection, and tentative marketing budgets. A technical disappointment down the line may junk the early package design, name, or whatever. But we have to pay that price; we can't wait for each step to be conclusive before going to the next one.

Along the way, concept evaluation continues; we evaluated the concept well enough to permit development work (discussed earlier), but we have to keep evaluating technical and marketing planning *results*. We evaluate prototypes primarily, checking to be sure that the technology being developed meets the needs and desires of the customers in a way that creates value for them, while at the same time being profitable commercially.[5] By the time this phase winds down, we want to be assured that the new product actually does solve those problems we began with.

Comprehensive Business Analysis

If the product is real and customers like it, some firms make a comprehensive **business analysis** before moving into launch. The financial analysis is still not firm, but it is good enough to assure management that this project will be worthwhile. The financials will gradually be tightened during the launch phase, and where the actual Go/No Go point

[5]Edward U. Bond, III and Mark B. Houston, "Barriers to Matching New Technologies and Market Opportunities in Established Firms," *Journal of Product Innovation Management,* 20(2), March 2003, pp. 120–135.

is reached varies with the nature of the industry. Approval for a new food product can be held until just before signing advertising contracts, but a new chemical that requires a new manufacturing facility has to Go much earlier, and the pharmaceutical industry really makes the Go decision when it undertakes the 10-year, $50 million R&D research effort. The development phase is covered in Part IV, Chapters 11 through 13.

Phase 5: Launch

Traditionally, the term **launch**, or *commercialization*, has described that time or that decision when the firm decides to market a product (the Go in Go/No Go). We associate this decision with building factories or authorizing agencies to proceed with multi-million-dollar advertising campaigns.

But launch is more complex than that. The launch is not a single point in time, the "opening night," so to speak. Rather, product teams think of launch as a *phase*, including the last few weeks or months before and after the product is launched. During the launch phase, the product team is living life in the fast lane (or in the pressure cooker). Manufacturing is doing a gradual scale-up of output. The marketing planners, who got a good look at their ultimate target market as early as the opportunity, are now deep into the hundreds of tactical details required for launch. The critical step (if a company takes it) is the **market test**, a dress rehearsal for the launch, and managers hope any problems discovered are fixable between dress rehearsal and opening night. If not, the opening has to be delayed. We will review many market test techniques in Chapter 16.

Sooner or later, the preparation activities lead to a public announcement of the new product through advertising, sales calls, and other promotional tactics. The announcement is often called *launch*. Most firms today execute the launch gradually, over a period of at least several weeks, since there are suppliers to bring on line, sales forces to be trained, distributors to be stocked and trained, and a large set of market support people to be educated (columnists, scientists, government people, and others).

One thing that is often overlooked at this point is the activity of planning for **launch management**. When spacecraft are launched, a plan of tracking has been carefully prepared. The space control center implements the tracking plan, seeking to spot every glitch that comes up during launch and hoping it was anticipated so that a solution is on board, ready to use. New products managers often do the same thing, sometimes formally but often *very* informally.

The launch phase is covered in Part V, Chapters 14 through 18.

Evaluation Tasks Throughout the New Products Process

Figure 2.2 illustrates the evaluation tasks encountered in the new products process. As shown, different kinds of questions need to be asked after different phases. For example, once concepts are generated, each is subject to an initial review: Is it any good, and is it worth refining? At the concept evaluation phase, careful screening is required, as concepts that pass this phase move on to development and begin incurring significant costs. In development, relevant questions are "Are we done yet?" and "If not, should we continue to try?" These questions are best answered through progress reports. Finally, at launch, the main questions concern whether the product should be launched, and later, how well it has done relative to expectation. We pick up discussion of

FIGURE 2.2

The Evaluation
Tasks in the
New Products
Process

New Products Process Phase	Evaluation Task at End of Phase
Opportunity Identification and Selection	*Direction:* Where should we look?
Concept Generation	*Initial Review:* Does the idea pass initial screen and go on to concept development?
Concept/Project Evaluation	*Full Screen:* Should we put the concept into development?
Development	*Technical Questions:* Have we developed the product? And if not, should we continue to try? *Marketing Questions:* Should we market it? And if so, how?
Launch	*Post-Launch Evaluation:* How are we doing relative to objectives?

Figure 2.2 later, in Chapter 7, when we go much more in depth into which evaluation techniques are the most useful at each point in the new products process.

You may have noticed by now that the new products process essentially turns an opportunity (the real start) into a profit flow (the real finish). It begins with something that is not a product (the opportunity) and ends up with another thing that is not a product (the profit). The product comes from a situation and turns into an end.

What we have, then, is an **evolving product**, or better, an evolving concept that, at the end, if it is successful, becomes a new product. Even a new product announcement just tells the world about a concept, hopefully a winner, but actually just in temporary form. Forces are standing by to see what revisions need to be made, even now, if it is off track.

This evolution is linked to the phases of the new products process (see Figure 2.3). Here are the phases in that process, using a new skim milk product as an example:

Phase 1: Opportunity Identification

- *Opportunity concept*—a company skill or resource, or a customer problem. (Assume that skim milk drinkers tell us they don't like the watered look of their favorite beverage.)

Phase 2: Concept Generation

- *Idea concept*—the first appearance of an idea. ("Maybe we could change the color... .")
- *Stated concept*—a form or a technology, plus a clear statement of benefit. (See Chapter 4.) (Our firm's patented method of breaking down protein globules might make the liquid more cloudy; emphasis on the *might*, at this time.)

Phase 3: Concept/Project Evaluation

- *Tested concept*—it has passed an end-user concept test; need is confirmed. (Consumers say they would very much like to have such a milk product, and the method of getting it sounds fine.)

FIGURE 2.3
The Evolution from Concept to New Product

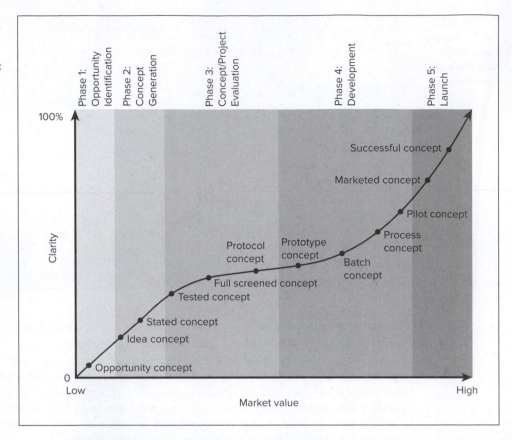

- *Fully screened concept*—it passes the test of fit with the company's situation.
- *Protocol concept*—a product definition that includes the intended market user, the problem perceived, the benefits that a less watery skim milk would have to have, plus any mandatory features. (Our new product must taste as good or better than current skim milk, and it must yield exactly the same nutritional values.)

Phase 4: Development

- *Prototype concept*—a tentative physical product or system procedure, including features and benefits. (A small supply of a full-bodied skim milk, ready to consume, though not yet produced in quantity.)
- *Batch concept*—first full test-of-fit with manufacturing; it can be made. Specifications are written stating exactly what the product is to be, including features, characteristics, and standards. (Skim milk ingredients: Vitamin A source, fat, fiber, and so on.)
- *Process concept*—the full manufacturing process is complete.
- *Pilot concept*—a supply of the new product, produced in quantity from a pilot production line, enough for field testing with end users.

Phase 5: Launch

- *Marketed concept*—output of the scale-up process from the pilot—a milk product that is actually marketed, either for a market test or for full-scale launch.

- *Successful concept (i.e., new product)*—it meets the goals set for it at the start of the project. (New, Full Body Skim has achieved 24 percent of the market, is very profitable, and already competitors are negotiating licenses on our technology.)

The idea that a new product suddenly emerges from R&D—like a chicken from an egg—is simply incorrect. In fact, throughout this book we will be examining how analytical techniques are applied throughout the new product process, from early idea generation and concept evaluation, through screening, and on to positioning, market testing, and launch management.

Agile Product Development[6]

A complementary process to the phased new product process is **agile product development**. This has gained popularity in the software industry due to the continuous and incremental nature of the development process. The objective of agile product development is to provide customer satisfaction by continuous software improvement and delivery. To achieve this objective, software developers often adhere to the Agile Manifesto, favoring individuals, customer collaboration, and responding to changing requirements throughout the process (see www.agilemanifesto.org for more detail).

Agile product development requires some changes in product team organization to build in the required amount of flexibility. The process is described as a "scrum" (think of an American football huddle, or rugby scrum) where the team engages in a series of sprints to continuously develop and deliver software. There is a product owner (a single individual who ensures that customer requirements are addressed in every iteration, participates in sprint planning, and keeps the product moving forward). Sprints are managed by scrum masters working with the required team members (software engineers, programmers, and architects), and the team has much autonomy on how to meet the goals for each sprint.

Although agile product development originated in the software industry, there is some evidence that its principles can be adapted to manufactured products as well, especially in cases of high uncertainty and significant customer involvement. **Agile-Stage-Gate**, a blending of agile product development with the traditional new products process, has been successfully employed with computer hardware and other manufactured goods. The scrum, having the dedicated and autonomous product team, seems to be a feature of agile product development that has caught on for manufactured goods. Corning, for example, uses Agile-Stage-Gate and dedicated teams for its most critical projects—constituting about 20 percent of all projects.[7]

LEGO Education uses Agile-Stage-Gate for almost all of its new products. In 2011, LEGO Education started development of its Story Starter product, aimed at the elementary school market. Story Starter was viewed internally as a radical and uncertain project, and the intense customer interaction that was required initially slowed

---

[6]Details on agile software development can be found on the Agile Manifesto Web page, agilemanifesto.org.

[7]R. G. Cooper, "New Products: What Separates the Winners from the Losers?," in K. B. Kahn (ed.), *PDMA Handbook of New Product Development*, 3d ed., Hoboken, NJ: Wiley, 2013, pp. 25–33.

down the process. Thanks to input from LEGO Digital Solutions, another LEGO division that was already familiar with agile product development, LEGO Education decided to try managing the Story Starter as an Agile-Stage-Gate hybrid (sprints, daily scrums, planning meetings, and pilot tests with over 50 schools to understand customer requirements). Story Starter was successfully brought to market in only 12 months; it was soon followed by another successful new educational product, More to Math, soon after.[8]

Speeding the Product to Market

One of today's most discussed management goals in product development is **accelerated product development (APD)**, or speeding the product to market. Accelerating time to market offers many benefits to the firm. The product will be on the market for a longer period of time before becoming obsolete, it can attract customers early and possibly block competitors with similar products that hit the market at a later time, or it can help to build or support a firm's reputation. A firm that implements the strategic elements outlined in Chapter 1—the product innovation charter, the new products process, and portfolio management—has advantages in reducing cycle time. New product consultant Robert Cooper identifies five sure methods to accelerate time to market, some of which have been mentioned previously:

- A clear product innovation charter—doing the opportunity identification homework and having a clean product definition—leads to better product design specifications and less time lost due to "recycling" (returning to earlier phases in the process to fix errors).

- A third-generation new products process that permits overlapping phases or *parallel processing* results in more getting accomplished in a shorter span of time; streamlined evaluation tasks means that less time is wasted in evaluation.

- A portfolio management approach minimizes the chance that the firm's human and financial resources are spread too thinly over too many projects; better project selection focuses the firm's scarce resources and uses them more efficiently.

- A focus on quality at every phase complements the PIC; by following the adage "do it right the first time," the firm will avoid unnecessary recycling.

- An empowered *cross-functional team*, including individuals from marketing, R&D, manufacturing, and other functional areas, that works on the project from the earliest phases, supports parallel processing and eliminates "over-the-wall" product development (for example, marketing or production do not even begin their participation until the product is out of technical product development).[9]

[8]For more information on Agile-Stage-Gate and other examples, see Robert G. Cooper and Anita F. Sommer, "From Experience: The Agile-Stage-Gate Hybrid Model: A Promising New Approach and a New Research Opportunity," *Journal of Product Innovation Management*, 33(5), 2016, pp. 513–526.

[9]Robert G. Cooper, *Winning at New Products: Accelerating the Process from Idea to Launch*, 2nd ed. (Reading, MA: Addison-Wesley, 1993), p. 210.

Notice that the first three methods are the three strategic elements, while the last two (focus on quality and multifunctional product teams) are methods that help the firm to implement the strategic elements.

There is plenty of evidence that these techniques contribute greatly to increasing speed to market. Software development is often marked by intensive "crunch time" periods due to approaching deadlines, and many firms in this industry rely on small, cohesive cross-functional teams to meet time goals while at the same time not sacrificing quality.[10] Parallel processing is typical in the car industry: A car's drive train may be 70 or 80 percent designed (but not 100 percent) before body design work is initiated. Then, an early prototype (but not the final car) may be built and ready for controlled test-driving. The use of parallel processing by Japanese automakers was a big factor in their emergence on the world market.[11] Figure 2.4 shows many techniques that have been advocated for shortening cycle times.

Note that the *cycle time metric,* that is, the way management measures speed to market (or, frequently, *time to market*), is often "getting the idea to the shipping dock faster." This assumes that there has already been technical accomplishment—the R of R&D has been concluded successfully. But from the point of view of technical development, speed to market success means not just time to the shipping dock, but also *postshipping technical speed.* For example, are corporate services (such as legal and environmental) in place? Also, if one uses the metric of "time to success" rather than "time to the shipping dock," marketing has a much bigger role to play in accelerating cycle time. Marketing can strive to accelerate *premarket speed* (i.e., pretesting the marketing plan more quickly, or getting up to speed on field coverage through alliance formation), and also *postannouncement* speed (i.e., speeding up coupon redemption, or getting the sales reps into the field more quickly).

We are now also hearing about the value of being **first to mindshare** rather than being first to market. The firm with mindshare in a given product category is the one that the target market associates with the product category and that is seen as the standard for competitors to match (such as Intel microprocessors, Tesla electric cars, or Apple or Samsung smartphones). Firms that strive for mindshare think not about the speed of an individual product's development and launch, but rather about creating a dominant position in the mind of the customer.[12]

Finally, the role of *top management* in speeding products to market cannot be ignored. It is not enough for top management simply to say "Cycle times are to be cut by 50 percent, effective now!" Employees will no doubt interpret such blanket statements as a thinly disguised command to work twice as hard. Real resources need to be

[10]B. J. Zirger and Janet L. Hartley, "The Effect of Acceleration Techniques on Product Development Time," *IEEE Transactions on Engineering Management,* May 1996, pp. 143–152, look at cross-functional teams in electronics firms; and Alfredo M. Choperena, "Fast Cycle Time: Driver of Innovation and Quality," *Research-Technology Management,* May–June 1996, pp. 36–40, examines the development of an immunoassay diagnostic system. Both found evidence that teams drive speed to market without sacrificing quality.

[11]K. B. Clark and T. Fujimoto, *Product Development Performance: Strategy, Organization, and Management in the World Auto Industry* (Boston, MA: Harvard Business School Press, 1991).

[12]Denis Lambert and Stanley F. Slater, "First, Fast, and On-Time: The Path to Success. Or Is It?" *Journal of Product Innovation Management,* 16(5), September 1999, pp. 427–438.

FIGURE 2.4 **Techniques for Attaining Speed in a New Product Project**

Organization Phase

1. Use dedicated cross-functional teams.
2. Use small groups and other techniques to minimize bureaucracy.
3. Empower a team, motivate it through incentives and rewards, and protect it.
4. Destroy turf and territory.
5. Make sure the supporting departments are ready when called on.
6. Develop effective team leadership.
7. Encourage organizational learning; transfer knowledge from one project to the next.

Intensify Resource Commitments

1. Integrate vendors; reduce numbers as necessary.
2. Integrate other technology resources.
3. Integrate resellers; reduce numbers as necessary.
4. Get users involved early; capture the voice of the customer.
5. Use simultaneous or concurrent engineering.
6. Get suppliers involved through alliances, ventures, etc.; develop long-term relations with them.

Design for Speed

1. Computer-aided design and other forms of rapid prototyping.
2. Design-aided manufacturing, reduce number of parts, consider the manufacturing process.
3. Use common components across families.
4. Make the product easy to test.
5. Design in the qualities that lead to fast trial, including relative advantage.
6. Use effective design practices; minimize costly design changes late in the new products process.

Prepare for Rapid Manufacturing

1. Simplify documentation.
2. Use standardized process plans.
3. Use computer-aided manufacturing.
4. Go to just-in-time delivery of materials and components (flexible manufacturing).
5. Integrate product use testing, and start it early.

Prepare for Rapid Marketing

1. Use rollouts in place of test markets.
2. Seed the firm's reputation ahead of marketing.
3. Spend what it takes to get immediate market awareness.
4. Make trial purchasing as easy as possible.
5. Get customer service capability in place ahead of need, and test it.

Sources: Compiled from many sources, but a good overview of the topic is found in Pinar Cankurtaran, Fred Langerak, and Abbie Griffin, "Consequences of New Product Development Speed: A Meta-Analysis," *Journal of Product Innovation Management*, 30(3), 2013, pp. 465–486.

committed to a cycle time reduction program. An expert in cycle time reduction, Preston Smith, reports that many firms expect the process to be quick and easy. Executives sometimes ask for a one- or two-day training program in cycle-time reduction, believing that to be adequate training. The idea is not to skip critical steps in the new products process, but to get through the process faster without sacrificing quality.

Senior management will also know the value of strategic alliances to obtain technical and marketing resources and assistance. Alliances can be upstream to vendors, downstream to resellers and customers, and even sideways to competitors. Apple, for example, turned to Sony for assistance in speeding up the development of the PowerBook notebook.[13]

Risks and Guidelines in Speeding to Market

There are plenty of advantages to speeding to market, not the least of which is that the product that is launched early is on the market for a longer period of time before becoming obsolete. A launch delay of, say, six months means six months less to earn profits and may give a competitor a chance to be first to market and establish a positive reputation.

Nevertheless, there are lots of costs involved in speed, costs that are not evident and which can sometimes be disastrous. A firm facing increased competitive intensity, rapid technological change, and fast-changing market demographics may be tempted to concentrate on only easy, incremental product projects, or to cut critical steps in the new products process in order to get cycle time down. Cutting corners in technical product development may result in quality sacrifices, resulting in annoyed customers and distributors. By rushing the early steps, the firm may decide late in the process that the product quality is inadequate, which delays the launch, further infuriates dealers, and encourages customers to drift to the competition. Alternatively, rushing through the marketing ramp-up may result in inadequate attention to key marketing tasks in readying the product for launch. In these cases, the firm wins the speed-to-market battle but may lose the war.

The temptation to go too fast must be resisted, so that the firm does not mishandle a new-to-the-world opportunity, miss out on key customer information, or develop a technologically inferior product.[14] A better way to cope when facing a high-turbulence environment is to keep product development as flexible as possible: Do not freeze the product concept until the last possible moment, but allow later phases in the new products process to run concurrently with concept development.[15] This is the principle of *postponement*, which we revisit in our discussion of the launch phase in Chapter 15.

[13]For the Apple example, see Douglas W. LaBahn, Abdul Ali, and Robert Krapfel, "New Product Development Cycle Time: The Influence of Project and Process Functions in Small Manufacturing Companies," *Journal of Business Research,* June 1996, pp. 179–188.

[14]Christer Karlsson and Pär Åhlström, "Technological Level and Product Development Cycle Time," *Journal of Product Innovation Management,* 16(4), July 1999, pp. 352–362; R. G. Cooper and S. J. Edgett, "The Dark Side of Time and Time Metrics in Product Innovation," *Visions,* April–May 2002, pp. 14–16; see also C. Merle Crawford, "The Hidden Cost of Accelerated Product Development," *Journal of Product Innovation Management,* 9(3), September 1992, pp. 188–199; and Abdul Ali, Robert Krapfel, Jr., and Douglas LaBahn, "Product Innovativeness and Entry Strategy: Impact on Cycle Time and Break-Even Time," *Journal of Product Innovation Management,* 12(1), January 1995, pp. 54–69.

[15]Marco Iansiti, "Shooting the Rapids: Managing Product Development in Turbulent Environments," *California Management Review,* Fall 1995, pp. 37–58. Roger J. Calantone, Jeffrey B. Schmidt, and C. Anthony Di Benedetto, "New Product Activities and Performance: The Moderating Role of Environmental Hostility," *Journal of Product Innovation Management,* 14(3), May 1997, pp. 179–189, looked specifically at high-hostility environments.

FIGURE 2.5 **Other Considerations in Cycle Time Acceleration**

Do the job right the first time. A small amount of time in the early phases can save many times that later, in rework alone.

Seek lots of platinum BBs rather than one silver bullet. This means look at every step, every action, every meeting; small savings add up.

Train everyone involved. People who don't know their jobs, who are assigned work without proper skill-building, won't know how to speed things up.

Communicate. Huge amounts of delay can be traced to someone, somewhere, waiting for a piece of information. E-mail and the Internet have made collaboration much easier and quicker, speeding up communication.

Be flexible. Look for machines that can do many jobs, people who can switch from one job to another, stand-by vendors, and more. Attitudes too: a new product may require finding a more open-minded designer.

Make fast decisions. Managers know that people sometimes get blamed more for things they *do* than for things they *don't do*. Retraining them to make decisions as soon as they reasonably can, *and* managing them in such a way that we don't destroy that willingness, is a key step to a fast program.

Cut things wisely. There is a common bureaucratic practice of meeting a budget cut of 10% by cutting all of its components 10%. A better method is to take perhaps a 50% cut in noncritical steps, and 0% in the key ones. It's all risky, but why not take the risk on things that are more forgiving?

Another related concern is that accelerating time to market might result in bringing the product out too soon, while it still has bugs. In some situations, where there are high opportunity costs and relatively low development risks (such as with a new personal computer), it would be better to speed up cycle time. When Boeing develops and launches a new aircraft, however, there are relatively low opportunity costs (fewer direct competitors) but much higher development risks. In this case, getting the product "100 percent right" is the more appropriate goal.[16] Another risk of focusing exclusively on speed to market is that management might be tempted to concentrate on quick, close-to-home innovations at the expense of really new products, thus putting new product development efforts out of strategic balance.[17]

Some other considerations in cycle time acceleration are summarized in Figure 2.5.

P&G successfully cut development time on a pharmaceutical product by over 80 percent, while improving quality by over 60 percent, using many of the techniques described above. New product personnel carefully documented all work activities involved in product development and set aggressive goals for time reduction—"This activity should take 50 percent of the time it currently takes" (more modest goals could be easily achieved through only minor improvements). Stretch goals were set: To achieve a 75 percent reduction, one could set a goal of 50 percent reduction in the first year and a further 50 percent reduction in the second year. They also practiced several of the techniques described in this chapter and the previous one: team motivation

[16]E. G. Krubasik, "Customize Your Product Development," *Harvard Business Review,* 66, November–December 1988, pp. 46–52.

[17]C. Merle Crawford, op. cit.

through clear goal setting, empowerment, and reward mechanisms; and senior management commitment.[18]

In Chapter 14 we will see other metrics that can be used to complement speed-to-market, such as the *cash-to-cash metric*. Using this tool, the firm will measure not just how quickly the product is launched, but also how long it takes to break even. Using metrics such as this helps the firm manage the *whole* launch phase, not just the moment of launch.

What about New Services?

Before we leave the new products process, let's consider products that seem not to have a technical component to their development—**services**. Services and goods are often arrayed on a scale of (1) pure service, (2) primarily service and partly a good, (3) primarily a good and partly service, and (4) pure good. Examples, in order, are counseling, insurance policy, automobile, and candy bar. Only in the first category does the product provider have nothing tangible on which to do R&D, and there are very few of them. Even on pure or primarily service products, there are tangible support items such as ads, warranties, policies, and instructions, which need design and production. For an example of a good/service blend, consider a smartphone. The phone itself is tangible, yet it provides services: communication, as well as entertainment (music, games), information (maps), and other applications.

The creation of service products tends to mirror the systems used for goods. The strategic elements all fit (the product innovation charter, the new products process, and the balanced portfolio). Perhaps the concepts must be applied creatively, but still the parallels are there. Indeed, a study of successful new services found that these tended to come from companies that used a systematic, comprehensive new service development process with clearly defined phases and regular evaluations and reviews. In fact, according to the most recent CPAS study, the new services process is very similar to the new products process we have presented in this chapter, with only a few key differences. While the basic phases of Figure 2.1 apply, on average, new services take substantially less time in development, and this is true for radical as well as incremental service innovations. For example, a radical new tangible product may require on average over 122 weeks in development, while a radical new service could be completed in about 55 weeks. On other measures, though, services show little difference from tangible products.[19]

The new products process needs a little refinement to be most useful in service development, mostly due to fundamental differences between services and manufactured goods.[20] Services are individualized to the individual customer. Whereas goods are mass-produced, services are provided through interaction between service provider

[18]R. W. Boggs, Linda M. Bayuk, and David A. McCamey, "Speeding Development Cycles," *Research-Technology Management*, September–October 1999, pp. 33–38.

[19]Stephen K. Markham and Thomas Hollmann, "The Difference Between Goods and Services Development: A PDMA CPAS Research Study," in K. B. Kahn, S. E. Kay, R. J. Slotegraaf, and S. Uban (eds.), *The PDMA Handbook of New Product Development* (Hoboken, NJ: John Wiley, 2013), Ch. 25, p. 408.

[20]The next paragraphs, and the JetBlue example, are drawn from Thomas D. Kuczmarski and Zachary T. Johnston, "New Service Development," in Kenneth B. Kahn, George Castellion, and Abbie Griffin (eds.), *The PDMA Handbook of New Product Development* (New York: John Wiley, 2005), pp. 92–107.

and customer, and the most successful service providers are those that can deliver a "customized" experience to each customer. Services, unlike goods, are also intangible, which means that a key component of the service is indeed the experience of receiving the service. For this reason, the human interaction between service provider and customer is of utmost importance; service providers must strive to meet customer expectation and leave a positive impression. Services are also instantly and continuously being evaluated by customers at every interaction with the service provider. The service provider therefore needs to obtain feedback from the customer and act on it quickly so as to continuously improve performance. Finally, services are often evaluated by customers as the sum of their parts. A family looking back on a trip to a theme park considers the ease of transfer from the airport, the convenience of parking, the number and entertainment value of rides and other activities, the cleanliness of the park, and the friendliness of park personnel when forming an overall opinion of the experience. Poor performance on any of these leads to a lower evaluation of the whole trip. These fundamental differences between services and products pose challenges to the service provider, but the same basic new products process can still be used.

Consider how JetBlue has been successful in an extremely competitive air travel market through excellent service development. Rather than focusing on cost-cutting, as many of its competitors have done, JetBlue strove to provide a customized experience, offering travelers free television, friendlier flight crews, comfortable seats, and a simple but useful Web site. JetBlue also is a leader in adding safety measures, such as "paperless cockpit" flight technology and security cameras in the passenger cabin. These safety measures, important to today's air travelers, help to differentiate JetBlue from competitors. Also, JetBlue obtains opinions (good and bad) from customers throughout the service experience: when the customer is on the company Web page, at the ticket counter, or on the actual flight, JetBlue strives to obtain customer satisfaction information so they can target any areas for improvement and increase the customer's overall level of satisfaction with the firm. The guiding objective at JetBlue, according to its founding CEO, David Neeleman, was to bring "humanity back to air travel." This is clearly a service provider that understands the importance of customer interaction!

Given the importance of customer interaction in service success, it is no surprise that getting customer participation early is critical to successful new service development. Service delivery personnel—the staff that actually deals with customers, obtains their feedback, and handles their complaints—are in the best position to identify unmet customer needs and are therefore critical players at the concept generation phase. Involving them this early in the new products process increases their motivation and excitement about the new service, which results in more enthusiastic service delivery and more satisfied customers. As the service progresses through development, the best prototype concepts can be taken to customers and tested in product use tests much like those outlined above. Unfortunately, prototype testing is not always well done by service providers. Since services are by definition unpatentable and often easy for competitors to replicate, it is important to ensure that the service has been "tweaked" as much as possible before launch to make sure customers are very satisfied with the offering. A prototype test would be an ideal opportunity to do this kind of tweaking.

Finally, the launch phase for services can be particularly challenging. For one thing, services need constant monitoring to ensure they are efficiently meeting customer needs and expectations; this is why the best service providers (think restaurants, hotels, and hospitals) are constantly getting customer feedback. Also, the successful launch of a new service depends greatly on the service delivery personnel training. Coca-Cola employees, for example, rarely interact with the final consumer; by contrast, services of all types are delivered by company personnel (the bank teller, the hotel clerk, the hairdresser, the financial advisor). Excellent training of the service delivery personnel is a key component of any service firm's customer retention program. A training program will include instruction on the strategic importance to the firm of excellent service delivery as well as lessons on crisis management and troubleshooting, in addition to basic service delivery training.

FedEx is a prime example of a service provider that excels in new service development.[21] FedEx places the customer experience at the center of its new products process. Customers are involved early in the new products process as co-innovators; this helps FedEx identify their needs early. FedEx has set up market councils comprising executives, sales and marketing personnel, and even corporate lawyers to call on key customers and learn from them. They complement these activities with ethnographic studies (such as the observational techniques to be discussed in Chapter 5) to get at the heart of emerging customer needs. A classic example of this was FedEx's realization that the customer's experience would be enhanced if they provided greater access and more digital services. The solution was the 2004 acquisition of Kinko's (now FedEx Office), which immediately increased the number of shipping points, and at the same time widened service offerings to include photocopying, faxing, binding, and printing. As customer needs evolved (in particular those of small business customers), FedEx was able to grow with them and keep pace.

A key factor in FedEx's new products success was the establishment of the Portfolio Management Team (PMT), a group of senior executives that lead business units and functional areas. The PMT is charged with developing strategic direction, conducting the evaluation tasks in the new products process, and maintaining a balanced portfolio of projects. FedEx has found that the principles stated in Chapter 1 are effective: Following a phased new products process, risk is managed down through time, such that it is effectively reduced by the time costly development and launch phases are reached, and there is a high degree of confidence that a newly launched service will be successful and provide expected returns on investment. For its excellent service development program, FedEx won the 2007 PDMA Outstanding Corporate Innovator award.

Service providers can be very successful with creative new service offerings that offer competitive advantages. Noticing the wide variety of languages spoken by its customers, Walgreen's instituted a Dial-A-Pharmacist service that permitted non-English speakers access to pharmacists that spoke their language using in-store phones. The service, which gets about 1,000 calls per month, reduced patient error and boosted customer satisfaction. Since the core benefit of a service is nontangible,

---

[21]The FedEx example is drawn from Donald Comer, "How FedEx Uses Insight and Invention to Innovate," *Visions*, 31(4), December 2007, pp. 12–14.

the goal often is to improve the overall customer experience, which Netflix did when it initiated its DVD service. Customers appreciated the easy-to-use Web site and convenient mailing. Finally, Amazon's Kindle has succeeded where other reader devices have not, because users don't buy just the reader—they buy the whole service, and this is where Kindle excels. It offers the largest selection of books, an easy-to-use Web site, and wireless syncing to the user's computer or other devices.[22]

New-to-the-World Products

As seen in Chapter 1, the term *new products* can refer to new-to-the world products, close-to-home extensions of existing products, or just about anything in between. But the phased process seen in Figure 2.1 may not work as well with new-to-the-world products. Research confirms that firms that launch new-to-the-world products incur a significantly lower long-term survival rate than those that enter the market later. But the lower survival rate for a new-to-the-world product is offset by higher profits, since the market for such a product is often larger and can offer bigger profit margins.[23] Managers are enticed to take educated risks on new-to-the-world products, buoyed by the phenomenal success of products such as Corning's optical fiber, General Electric's computed tomographic scanner, Apple's iPhone, and many others.[24]

Part of the reason for the higher failure rate for new-to-the-world products is that they are difficult to manage. Almost by definition, new-to-the-world products, like the first cell phones or the first personal computers, require discontinuities (sometimes several of them) in order to succeed. Consider the introduction of the personal computer. Contributing to its rapid adoption were discontinuities in technology (computer companies, including some new startups, had to design essentially a totally new computer), in the market (individual homeowners and small businesses now were buying computers, and not just big firms), organizational (personal computers were sold in electronics shops and department stores, not through a professional sales force), and social (millions of people realized how much they needed a computer).[25] Much new research is aimed at understanding the management processes that are most appropriate for high-uncertainty, high-ambiguity environments.[26]

While we still have a long way to go, a good starting point is the recognition that new-to-the-world products must be nurtured. Many business opportunities may present themselves, and some may look promising, but all have uncertain outcomes.

[22]The characteristics and examples are taken from Thomas D. Kuczmarski and Rishu Mandolia, "Service Development," in K. B. Kahn, S. E. Kay, R. J. Slotegraaf, and S. Uban (eds.), *The PDMA Handbook of New Product Development* (Hoboken, NJ: John Wiley, 2013), Ch. 3, pp. 52–54.

[23]Sungwook Min, Manohar U. Kalwani, and William T. Robinson, "Market Pioneer and Early Follower Survival Risks: A Contingency Analysis of Really New Versus Incrementally New Product-Markets," *Journal of Marketing*, 70(1), 2006, pp. 15–33.

[24]Much of this section derives from Gina C. O'Connor, Richard Liefer, Albert S. Paulson, and Lois S. Peters, *Grabbing Lightning: Building a Capability for Breakthrough Innovation* (San Francisco, CA: Jossey-Bass, 2008).

[25]Rosanna Garcia, "Types of Innovation," in V. K. Narayanan and Gina C. O'Connor (eds.), *Encyclopedia of Technology & Innovation Management* (Chichester, UK: John Wiley, 2010), Chapter 13.

[26]A good reference is O'Connor et al., op. cit.

Experimentation in the marketplace can assess the opportunities and may even identify new ones. The goal is to consider the innovation, together with the identified business opportunities, and to develop from this new business model that provides high customer value and, ultimately, is also profitable for the firm. This can be an expensive proposition, and certainly management must not plan on instant decision making, but the due diligence is required due to the uncertainties involved. This process sounds like a business laboratory, and it is sometimes called the *incubation* period.[27] As leading innovation researcher Gina O'Connor says, "Companies do not realize that breakthrough technologies do not yield breakthrough businesses without enormous investment far beyond the technology itself, requiring lots of experimentation on many fronts."

To do incubation correctly, failure must be tolerated, but at the same time learning from the failure so that the firm continues to move toward a successful launch. It should be noted that incubation is not the same as business development (finding new customers or managing acquisitions). Business development is often done over a one- to two-year time horizon and may be completely done by marketing or management personnel. Due to its focus on business model development for a radical innovation (in an uncertain environment), the time horizon for incubation can be three to five years, and typically technical development, as well as customer and market interaction, is involved.

Radical innovation requires a planning approach that acknowledges the unknowns and uncertainties involved. This approach, called *discovery-driven planning*,[28] requires that managers make assumptions about the future in order to build their forecasts and targets, recognizing that these assumptions may be quite wrong. As more information becomes available, the targets are rethought, the forecasts adjusted, and the plan evolves. This is different from the approach more typically seen in less uncertain markets, where past results can be used to build predictable forecasts of the future. A guiding principle in discovery-driven planning is the *reverse income statement*, which starts from the bottom (required profits) and works backward to required levels of revenues and costs. The firm should also be pursuing a real-options orientation to investment.[29] The firm can make low-cost test investments to gather information on the technology and its marketplace potential. The test investment can be thought of as buying an option to continue the development of the breakthrough innovation. If the small investment suggests there is great upside potential, the project is continued to the next phase; otherwise it is terminated.

There should be a clear connection between the radical innovation and the firm's strategic vision as articulated by senior management.[30] Without top management encouragement, business units involved in product development will often focus on

[27]O'Connor et al., Chapter 4; the quote is from p. 82.

[28]Rita Gunter McGrath, and Ian C. MacMillan, "Discovery-Driven Planning," *Harvard Business Review*, July–August 1995, pp. 44–54.

[29]Ian C. MacMillan, Alexander B. van Putten, Rita Gunther McGrath, and James D. Thompson, "Using Real Options Discipline for Highly Uncertain Technology Investments," *Research-Technology Management*, January–February 2006, pp. 29–37.

[30]A good general reference on radical new products is Gary S. Lynn and Richard R. Reilly, *Blockbusters: The Five Keys to Developing Great New Products* (New York: HarperCollins, 2002). An influential article on this topic is Erwin Danneels, "Disruptive Technology Reconsidered: A Critique and Research Agenda," *Journal of Product Innovation Management*, 21(4), July 2004, pp. 246–258.

improving operational efficiency and will therefore be reluctant to accept radically new product projects because of the new product personnel involvement in corporate strategic planning when the environment is very changeable and turbulent.[31] In order to move promising radical innovation projects forward, senior management at some firms establishes a *transition management* team charged with moving an R&D innovation project to business operating status. The transition team receives appropriate funding as well as support and oversight from senior management.[32]

Obviously, with a new-to-the-world product, it is especially important that the **voice of the customer (VOC)** be brought in as early as possible, preferably at the beginning of the process. A critical issue here is identifying the right customers to bring in: For example, a medical equipment manufacturer developing a next-generation diagnostic machine might want to partner with the leading research hospitals to determine what performance features need to be built in. Researchers at these hospitals, having found available products to be unsatisfactory, may already have internally developed simple working prototypes of their own. What better guidance could the equipment manufacturer obtain? Identifying and working with these customers is central to **lead user analysis**, which we will explore more fully in Chapter 5; we will more formally discuss the voice of the customer in Chapter 10.

Disruptive Innovation

Some innovations are described as **disruptive** innovations, a term first used by Harvard Professor Clayton Christensen.[33] These are innovations that create a new market or value network. Often, a disruptive innovation is launched by a smaller firm with few resources which targets segments that established firms have overlooked. The disruptor offers a product that suits the needs of the targeted segment at a good price, thus providing value to this segment, even if the product is inferior in some respects to existing products. Established firms may not immediately recognize or react to this threat. Over time, the disruptor improves functionality, moves "upmarket," and wins over mainstream customers.

A classic example of a disruptive innovation is the desktop copier. The first copier companies such as Xerox sold expensive, heavy-duty copiers to businesses. The needs

---

[31]Roger Calantone, Rosanna Garcia, and Cornelia Dröge, "The Effects of Environmental Turbulence on New Product Development Strategy Planning," *Journal of Product Innovation Management*, 20(2), March 2003, pp. 90–103.

[32]Gina O'Connor, Joanne Hyland, and Mark P. Rice, "Bringing Radical and Other Major Innovations Successfully to Market: Bridging the Transition from R&D to Operations," in P. Belliveau, A. Griffin, and S. M. Somermeyer (eds.), *The PDMA Toolbook 2 for New Product Development* (New York: John Wiley, 2004).

[33]For background on disruptive innovation, see Joseph L. Bower and Clayton M. Christensen, "Disruptive Technologies: Catching the Wave," *Harvard Business Review*, January–February 1995, pp. 43–53; Clayton Christensen, *The Innovator's Dilemma*, Harvard Business School Press, 1997; Anita M. McGahan, "How Industries Change," *Harvard Business Review*, October 2004, pp. 86–94; Maxwell Wessel and Clayton M. Christensen, "Surviving Disruption," *Harvard Business Review*, December 2012, pp. 56–65; Clayton M. Christensen, Michael Raynor, and Rory McDonald, "What Is Disruptive Innovation?," *Harvard Business Review*, December 2015, pp. 44–53.

of small business owners, people working in home offices, and students were not served by these machines. These customers wanted affordable copiers that could fit on their office desks, and they did not care as much if the pages were produced slowly or if the printing resolution was not perfect. They needed dozens of copies, not thousands, so cost per page was not so important. Ricoh, Canon, and others targeted these customers with the original desktop copiers, which, though slower and more expensive per page, were small and affordable. After gaining a foothold in this target market, the desktop copier manufacturers moved upmarket and became competitors in the giant office printer market as well. Some other recent examples include Amazon shaking up the retail industry (including both bricks-and-mortar and online competitors), Netflix revolutionizing how customers access movies and other entertainment (and putting movie rental companies like Blockbuster out of business), and digital photography severely disrupting the film photography business.

New product developers and planners should notice that a disruptive innovation is not necessarily the result of a radically new technology. Among these examples, digital photography certainly was a radical departure from film photography, but neither Amazon nor the desktop copier makers used radical technology to disrupt the market. Disruption can come from **business model innovation**, technology innovation, or both.[34]

Some argue that ride-share companies like Uber and Lyft are disruptive innovators in the taxi business, and most taxi fleet operators would probably agree with that statement. But, technically, they do not exactly fit Christensen's definition of disruptive innovation, since they did not gain traction by serving an ignored target segment. They focused on existing taxi riders, essentially providing a simple and reliable ride-share app that gave riders an alternative to traditional taxi service. Nevertheless, the outcome still was the same: new competitors with an innovative business model were able to gain a foothold in an existing industry and draw significant market share from the entrenched competition.

Finally, there are other innovations that do disrupt their respective industries even though they do not follow the classic disruptive innovation model. Instead, they exhibit *high-end* technology disruption, characterized as an innovation that is difficult for competitors to imitate initially. Instead of gradually improving performance through time (as a classic disruptor), high-end disruptors use technology to lower cost per unit of performance through time. Unlike classic disruptors, high-end disruptors initially sell at high prices, target price-insensitive customers, and outperform incumbents on important performance attributes; later, they lower prices and enter the mainstream market. Many examples come to mind: the iPod was a superior product to the Walkman; Starbucks has expanded globally with a high-price strategy; and Dyson vacuum cleaners and other appliances started at extremely high prices but now compete at more mainstream price levels.[35]

---

[34]See Gary P. Pisano, "You Need an Innovation Strategy," *Harvard Business Review*, June 2015, pp. 44-54.

[35]For a discussion of high-end disruptors, see Jeff Dyer and David Bryce, "Tesla's High End Disruption Gamble," *Forbes*, August 20, 2015.

The Role of the Serial Innovator

The most recent research on the new products process suggests that some rethinking of the traditional process is required for a firm to be consistently successful at commercializing new-to-the-world products. While many firms are capable of launching radical innovations successfully, few seem to be able to do it repeatedly over a long period of time. Those that can (Apple, Procter & Gamble, Caterpillar, and Intel come to mind) have something in common: **serial innovators**.[36] These are usually mid-level, technical employees who think and work differently and follow their own new products process. In fact, a challenge for senior management is to be able to identify serial innovators (there aren't many; they are estimated at one per 100 technical employees, or even one per 500), and once identified, to manage them and reward them properly.

The problem many firms have with radical innovation is that technology-driven innovation may be very exciting from a technical viewpoint, but doesn't really solve a customer problem, therefore there is no application that can be brought to market. (In Chapter 3 we will see how the Product Innovation Charter is designed to avert this problem by ensuring there is a market dimension that matches with the technology.) In other cases, a good technology may lack an internal product champion that ensures that the technology goes into the development process (see discussion of product champions in Chapter 12). The reason serial innovators are so good at breakthrough innovation is that they know how to bridge the gap between technology and market. They do this in iterative fashion. Generally, they begin by identifying and fully understanding a customer problem, and then discover possible technical solutions to those problems. They oscillate between customer need and technology solution. As time goes on and the serial innovators learn more about potential customer solutions, they will also bring in market information as well: is there a large enough market demand to justify bringing this technology to market?

The "process" followed by serial innovators is arguably not a process at all, since that implies a series of steps and a fixed order. There are several activities that need to be done, but there is no particular order and a lot of recycling and rethinking is necessary and expected. These steps include:

- Finding a problem that is important to customers, checking potential market size and revenue stream.
- Understanding the problem, including technology, currently available solutions, competition, and customer requirements.
- Determining if the problem is interesting to enough customers willing to pay for it, and also interesting to the firm in terms of fitting with product strategy.
- Inventing a solution to the problem and checking for customer acceptance with a prototype.
- Ensuring that the product goes into development, then gaining market acceptance for the product.[37]

[36]Abbie Griffin, Raymond L. Price, and Bruce A. Vojak, *Serial Innovators: How Individuals Create and Deliver Breakthrough Innovations in Mature Firms* (Stanford: Stanford Unversity Press, 2012).
[37]Griffin, Price, and Vojak, op. cit.

There is much room here for circling back: if customers don't accept the prototype, this may require further work to better understand the problem, or even rethinking if the right problem is being solved.

It is clear how serial innovators differ from other technology employees. They have a deeper understanding of customers, the firm's product strategy, and political processes, and can act themselves as the product champion. They focus not just on solving customer problems, but on understanding the situation so well, from so many different perspectives, that they find the optimal solution to the customer problem. They can handle discovery, invention, and launch themselves, and therefore are highly valuable to the firm, and allow the firm to be consistently successful with radical new products.

So how can a firm recruit serial innovators, or recognize serial innovators among its employees? New products researcher Abbie Griffin suggests that serial innovators have five innate characteristics one should look for:

- Systems thinking (can see ways to connect disjoint information).
- High creativity (though, interestingly, not exceedingly high!).
- Curiosity in several areas of interest.
- A knack for intuition based on expertise.
- A sincere desire to solve customer problems.[38]

Spiral Development and the Role of Prototypes

In the case of radical product innovation, a fluid, agile new products process might lead to more innovative results. If the final form of the product is truly unknown, it may make sense for the firm to try several prototypes in rapid succession, showing them to customers, getting feedback, trying another prototype, then continuing in this manner until an acceptable form is identified. The term **spiral development** is sometimes used to describe this process; the name refers to the many iterations between firm and customer. Spiral development can be described as a "build-test-feedback-revise" process:

- An early, nonworking version of the product, called a **focused prototype**, is built (this might be a new cell phone made of wood or foam, or perhaps it is a plastic nonfunctioning prototype that looks real but lacks wires).
- The prototype is tested with customers, who express likes, dislikes, purchase intentions, and so on.
- Customer feedback is obtained on what needs to be changed.
- Based on the feedback, the next prototype is prepared and the cycle continues.[39]

[38]Griffin, Price, and Vojak, op. cit.

[39]Robert G. Cooper, "New Products: What Separates the Winners from the Losers and What Drives Success," in K. B. Kahn, S. E. Kay, R. J. Slotegraaf, and S. Uban (eds.), *The PDMA Handbook of New Product Development* (Hoboken, NJ: Wiley, 2013), Ch. 1, p. 14.

Note that, essentially, the spiral development process allows phases in the new products process to be done out of order. Early prototypes are built even before customer specifications are determined! And there may be many prototypes built and tested in succession until one is finally selected.

The spiral development process is sometimes called **probe-and-learn**: Through interaction with customers, designers are inspired to probe, experiment, and improvise, and as a result, may come up with a successful new-to-the-world product. Another term sometimes used to describe this iterative process is **lickety-stick**: The developing team develops prototypes from dozens of different new product ideas ("lickety"), eventually settling on a prototype that customers like ("stick").[40] As Mike Santori of National Instruments said, the goal at this early stage is not to determine how to cut costs, but to see what functionality customers are looking for. Rolling out several prototypes quickly and efficiently "gives you flexibility to try out different ideas and audiences."[41]

The story of General Electric's (GE's) computed tomographic (CT) scanner illustrates the development of a new-to-the-world product with a large assist from the voice of the customer. The original instrument was developed as a head scanner; later versions included a breast scanner and a full-body scanner. In each case, the physicians said the product did not work appropriately. On the fourth try, GE developed the 8800 full-body scanner, which was a huge success when launched, eventually gaining a 68 percent market share. GE did not simply create a solution looking for a problem—that implies having no strategy. GE did have a strategy: Develop a breakthrough scanner technology for medical diagnostic applications, and learn from early trials specifically what applications would be the most valuable to their physician customers.[42]

Closing Thoughts about the New Products Process

As we discussed in Chapter 1, many firms use a new products process much like the one shown in this chapter (though of course the details will vary), and the CPAS studies have consistently shown that the majority of the Best firms implement new products processes and enjoy more success with new products as a result.[43]

Some exciting developments are being noted in the auto industry. Almost half of the automotive engineers in a recent survey said their companies used a traditional new products process, while about a third used a modified process, which allows them

[40]"Lickety-stick" was coined by Gary S. Lynn and Richard R. Reilly in *Blockbusters*, op. cit.

[41]Quoted in Heidi Bertels, "The 7th Annual Front End of Innovation Conference Adopts a New Format and Content," *Visions*, 33(3), October 2009, pp. 34–37.

[42]Gary S. Lynn, Mario Mazzuca, Joseph G. Morone, and Albert S. Paulson, "Learning Is the Critical Success Factor in Developing Truly New Products," *Research-Technology Management*, May–June 1998, pp. 45–51.

[43]Stephen K. Markham and Hyunjung Lee, "Product Development and Management Association's 2012 Comparative Performance Assessment Study," *Journal of Product Innovation Management*, 30(3), 2013, pp. 408–429.

to improve efficiency without sacrificing product novelty.[44] Using a modified process has allowed as much as a 50 percent reduction in time to market while maintaining new product quality and novelty.

The role of senior management cannot be overlooked, especially in the case of radical new products. Speaking at a PDMA meeting, Al Lopez, former vice president of R&D at ExxonMobil, mentioned his company's many radical new products, including high-strength steel for pipelines, low-sulfur fuel processes, improved catalysts, and so on. Senior management supports productive R&D in several key ways: by recognizing and building the firm's core technical competencies and capabilities, by encouraging knowledge flow (both internal and external) throughout the firm, by developing effective, streamlined work processes, by clearly linking basic and applied research, and by assuring an exciting work environment in which learning and achievement are rewarded.[45]

Finally one can ask whether firms can be ambidextrous—that is, be excellent in both new-to-the-world and incremental innovations. Barriers to ambidexterity no doubt exist: Fears of brand dilution, channel conflict, or even a "we've always done it this way" culture. There is also the issue of resource allocation: Investing in developing competencies that lead to radical new products may mean divesting those resources away from bettering one's existing competencies. These are serious concerns of managers at highly innovative firms; to avoid problems of this sort, often a highly projectized venture is spun out as a separate organizational unit to pursue the radical innovation;[46] more on this topic in Chapter 12.

Summary

In this chapter, we studied the system of phases and activities used in the process of developing and marketing new products. We looked at a simplistic version of this process as applied by the LEGO company and showed how it interacted with LEGO's product portfolio and PIC. We then went through the basic process phase by phase. Be careful: don't think that this, or any, new product process is etched in stone. It is a guide and an integrator, not a straitjacket.

We now turn to Chapter 3, in which we will discuss two more strategic elements: the product innovation charter and managing the portfolio of new products. Chapter 3 introduces the first of the five major phases in the process—Opportunity Identification and Selection. This will include the various forms of strategy to guide the evaluation of available opportunities. That will prepare us to begin the study of concept generation.

---

[44]John E. Ettlie and Jorg M. Eisenbach, "Modified Stage-Gate® Regimes in New Product Development," *Journal of Product Innovation Management*, 24(1), January 2007, pp. 20–33.

[45]For more information, see Peter Koen, "Tools and Techniques for Managing the Front End of Innovation: Highlights from the May 2003 Cambridge Conference," *Visions*, October 2003.

[46]Erwin Danneels, "From the Guest Editor: Dialogue on the Effects of Disruptive Technology on Firms and Industries," *Journal of Product Innovation Management*, 23(1), January 2006, pp. 2–4.

Case: Oculus Rift[47]

Palmer Luckey, a passionate virtual reality hobbyist and collector, formed the Oculus VR company with three partners in July 2012 with the intention of developing and selling virtual reality (VR) products. The company soon announced its first product, the Rift, a video-gaming VR headset. By August 2012, a Kickstarter campaign was initiated to make headsets and release them to developers. The target goal was $250,000; the campaign raised almost 10 times that amount ($2.4 million). The first preproduction model released to developers was the Oculus VR DK1, followed soon by the DK2. The Rift was finally launched in the consumer market in 2016. By that time, the Oculus VR company had been purchased by Facebook; the March 2014 acquisition cost Facebook $2.3 million in cash and stock.

VR was, at the time, a new technology whose potential was only beginning to be explored. There would be an immediate market for gamers in that it would provide a realistic and entertaining experience. There were many other applications outside the gaming industry as well, as it allowed users to interface with a realistic experience in many real-life settings, such as virtual education, tourism, or movies and other visual entertainment. In fact, the Oculus Rift was the first VR product successfully launched into the consumer market.

The DK1 kit was a very early preproduction kit, aimed primarily at developers and early adopters. Priced at $350, it had a low-resolution screen and lacked positional tracking. The improved DK2 offered much higher resolution and overcame a problem encountered in the DK1 (motion sickness experienced by some users) by using OLED technology. The DK2 also featured an external camera and positional tracking, and it sold for about the same price. These pre-production launches allowed developers to make content, which would be available to consumers at the time the Rift was released.

The first commercialized version featured several technologies improving the user's viewing experience, including the following:

- **Low-latency 360-degree head tracking:** The view reacts immediately to head movements due to accurate head tracking, allowing the user a very realistic view as he or she looks around the virtual world.
- **Stereoscopic 3D view:** Slightly different views for each eye permit realistic 3D viewing.
- **Wide field of view:** The Oculus Rift offers a 100-degree field of view, which means it mimics and even surpasses human peripheral vision. Rather than looking at a finite screen, this wide field of view (combined with the previous two points) truly immerses the viewer into the virtual world.

[47]This case was based on several sources, including www.oculus.com; Darrell Etherington, "How Oculus Plans to be Riding High When the Virtual Reality Wave Breaks," *Techcrunch*, December 13, 2013; Anonymous, "First Look at the Rift, Shipping Q1 2016," *Oculus Blog*, May 6, 2015; Peter Brown, "Oculus Rift Review: The Future Is Now," *Gamespot*, July 25, 2017; Nick Statt and Chaim Gartenberg, "Oculus Is Now Selling Its Rift Headset to Businesses with a New Bundle," *The Verge*, October 11, 2017; and others.

- **Wearability:** The Oculus Rift is designed to be lightweight and comfortable, allowing users the ability to wear it for extended periods.

The consumer launch was announced in May 2015, and pre-orders were taken up to January 2016 at an initial price of $600. Shipments to consumers began in March 2016; the consumer product was a technical improvement over the DK2, with better resolution and positional tracking, better audio, and improved ergonomics and appearance. By June 2017, a version of Oculus Rift for businesses was made available for $900. This version included the Rift, touch controllers and other peripherals, and improved warranty and customer service.

The Oculus Rift is a new-to-the-world product. What were the challenges and uncertainties facing the parent company, especially in its startup days before the Facebook purchase and when the company founders were raising Kickstarter funds? Based on what you see in the case and outside research on this product, how did they mitigate these uncertainties? Search online for the most recent Oculus Rift products. How would you describe the company's new products strategy?

Case: The Levacor Heart Pump[48]

Since 1982, when the first artificial heart (the Jarvik-7) was implanted in the chest of Barney Clark, a major quest of the medical device companies has been to improve the well-being of heart failure patients. The goal for the patient is independent existence. Dr. Clark needed to be attached to a large external machine that powered his mechanical heart, which managed to prolong his life for 112 days. Today, of course, the goal is to make the devices as thin as possible, such that they can be implanted in the body and allow the patient essentially to go about a normal existence. In view of the ultra-thin smartphones and other similar products already available to consumers, medical device engineers are eager to use similar technologies to develop slim devices to support the functioning of the heart.

According to the American Heart Association, about 80 million adults in the United States have cardiovascular disease of one type or another, and about 5 million suffer from heart failure. When looking at the demand for medical devices to aid the heart, the aging baby-boomer market cannot be ignored. This active age group "wants to live, and demands, a full, rich life. . . . now we have medical consumers, a market that didn't exist 20 years ago," notes designer Allan Cameron. This target audience would certainly be receptive to a device that would allow long-term freedom and independence, even if major heart disease strikes. In fact, the heart pump industry is profitable and growing. In 2005, the leading heart-pump maker, Thoratec, had annual sales of $201 million on its HeartMate XVE. Analysts see the market as going nowhere but up, especially after Medicare announced that it will be expanding the number of hospitals permitted to do heart-pump implants.

Recent efforts have been to develop implantable heart pumps that assist the patient's own heart, rather than mechanical devices that actually replace the heart.

---

[48]This case was based on information in Reena Jana, "A Smaller, Sleeker Heart Pump," businessweek.com, January 16, 2007.

One of the most promising of these is the Levacor, which by late 2006 was in development at WorldHeart, based in Oakland, California. By this time, the Levacor had been in feasibility trials in Europe only for a few months; clinical trials in the United States (and ultimate FDA approval) were still far into the future. The most distinctive feature of the Levacor is that it uses magnetically levitated rotary technology to power the pump.

The Levacor story begins in the early 1990s at a company called Medquest (since acquired by WorldHeart). Pratap Khanwilkar and his team at Medquest were studying the heart pumps of the time and identified several problems associated with their use. Their size limited their usefulness: A pump that fit into the body of a large man might not be supported by a small adult, teenager, or child. There was also the problem of longevity. The heart pumps needed to be replaced every so often, exposing the patient to the risks and stresses of repeat surgery; this would be a concern especially in the case of a very young patient who might be relying on the pump for decades. The term used in the medical community for an implant that will never need to be replaced is "destination therapy." Another concern is the actual functioning of the pump: It must be gentle enough not to rupture blood cells, cause as little vibration as possible, and not require much power to operate.

The Medquest team settled on magnetic levitation technology as a possible solution. Magnetic levitation involves suspending a rotor using a balance of magnetic fields so that it moves without touching other parts: It literally levitates. Since nothing contacts the rotor, there is no friction or heat buildup, and also no erosion due to wear and tear, leading to longer life. The technology had been used for some time in large-scale projects such as power turbines, but had never been tried on such a small commercial application and certainly never in a heart device. Together with an engineering firm, LaunchPoint Technologies, Medquest developed a small, proprietary magnetic levitation system that could serve to pump blood from the heart throughout the rest of the body. The "suspension in air" of the rotor had a distinct advantage in a heart pump application: since there was less to obstruct blood flow, life-threatening clots would be unlikely to form. The development team designed a three-dimensional version of the pump using computer-aided design software, which also was used to make a real-size, clear plastic prototype using rapid-prototyping technology. Using a blood substitute, the team was able to watch liquid flow through the prototype.

By early 2006, a working prototype made of a titanium alloy was available, about the size of a hockey puck and one-fourth the size of WorldHeart's previous model (which did not use the magnetic levitation technology). The device provides full mobility: The pump itself is implanted in the patient's abdomen, and the external device is a small battery pack and controller that the patient straps on. The first patient, a 67-year-old Greek man, was well enough 50 days after the implant to climb stairs on his own and was released from hospital to live a normal life at home not long thereafter. By this time, WorldHeart and LaunchPoint were also working on an even smaller device designed for babies.

As of early 2007, it was still unclear whether the magnetic levitation heart pumps would be the long-term industry standard; however, Mr. Khanwilkar (by now serving as WorldHeart's vice president for rotary systems and business development) was optimistic.

Based on the description in this case, discuss the new products process apparently under way at WorldHeart, in comparison to that outlined in this chapter. How is it similar or different? The launch phase is, of course, still well into the future at the time the case occurs. What are the problem areas the company might face at the time of launch? At the time of the case, what are the uncertainties that still exist? What could the company do now to manage these uncertainties?

CHAPTER THREE

Opportunity Identification and Selection: Strategic Planning for New Products

Setting

Chapter 1 introduced us to the strategic elements of new product development, and to the first of these elements, the new products process. Chapter 2 expanded on this process, showing us the phases, beginning with opportunity generation and ending with the launch of a new product. Chapter 3 details the first phase of the process, opportunity analysis and strategic planning. It is in this context that we present the two remaining strategic elements: the product innovation charter (PIC) and product portfolio management; these two strategic elements are essential parts of this first phase.

We will explore in detail the process shown in Figure I.1 in the Introduction to Part I. The first part of this chapter discusses the importance of product strategic planning, focusing on the role of product platforms and also on the process of opportunity identification. This leads up to the second part of the chapter, the development of the PIC. This is essentially the product team's new product strategy, and it can be thought of as a foundation for new products management that serves as a loose harness for the integration of all people and resources used in generating new products. We look at what a team needs in its strategy statement and then at where its inputs originate—that is, in corporate strategy, in platform strategy, and in influences from many other sources. We explore the components of the PIC—its drivers, its goals and objectives, and its rules of the road. The final part of the chapter presents new product portfolio strategy: the strategic importance of having a portfolio strategy, what the components of a good portfolio are, and how some of the top firms develop their portfolios.

A Product Strategy for a "Company within a Company"

The group of people who lead the development of a new product act as *a company within a company*. They may be loosely tied together in a committee, or they may be fully dedicated (full-time) managers sent off somewhere in a *skunkworks* to address a difficult assignment (see Chapter 12 for a discussion of skunkworks and other new product team structures). Regardless of the precise form, the group represents all of the necessary functions. They are led by a group leader, a team manager, or a project manager. As a group, they essentially do everything the company as a whole would do: develop and allocate a budget, do financial analysis and projections, assign and implement tasks and responsibilities, and so on.

For these people, a new products strategy does several things. It charts the group's direction—where it must go, and where it must *not* go. It also tells the group its goals and objectives and provides some rules of the road. As new product researcher Peter Koen said, the managers of the best firms at product innovation ask, "What sandbox should I be playing in?" before thinking of specific products—much as successful venture capitalists ask first what market areas they should be looking in for new businesses.[1] We first explore the inputs to this new products strategy—which we will later define as the **product innovation charter (PIC)**—then we detail the PIC's components and explore ways in which it can be built.

New Product Strategy Inputs and Identifying Opportunities

Corporate leaders make many strategy statements. Figure 3.1 shows a list of such statements, and you can see how important they would be to a new products team. Top-level statements like these guide a whole firm and are parts of what are sometimes called **mission statements**. Explicit consideration of the role of new products in the organization is strongly related to success. In Robert Cooper's research, 59 percent of managers from top-performing firms report that their new products are a key part of their stated business goals, while only 3 percent of the lowest-performing firms do so.[2]

Product Platform Planning

Many firms, especially those operating in a high-tech environment, think in terms of a **product platform strategy**. This is a basic or "core" technology and other common elements from which many new products can be developed efficiently over time.[3] A well-known example of product platforms exists in the car industry. Car platforms are notoriously expensive; a carmaker will use a single platform to support several models over several years in order to spread out the cost of the platform over many vehicles. At Chrysler, several Chryslers, Dodges, and Jeeps may share a platform for some of the

---

[1]Peter Koen, "Tools and Techniques for Managing the Front End of Innovation: Highlights from the May 2003 Cambridge Conference," *Visions*, October 2003.

[2]Robert G. Cooper, *Product Leadership: Pathways to Profitable Innovation*, 2nd ed. (New York: Basic Books, 2005).

[3]M. E. McGrath. *Product Strategy for High Technology Companies*. McGraw-Hill, 2001.

FIGURE 3.1 **Corporate Strengths**

These are examples of actual corporate strengths that managements have asked be used to differentiate the firm's new products. Many others are discussed in this chapter. These terms can be used to complete the following sentence: *New products in this firm will:*

Technologies

Herman Miller: Utilize our fine furniture designers.
Braun: Utilize innovative design in every product.
Otis Elevator: Build in new levels of service as a key benefit.
Coca-Cola: Gain value by being bottled in our bottling system.
White Consolidated: Be made on our assembly lines.

Markets

Gerber: Be for babies and only babies.
Nike: Be for all sports and not just shoes.
IBM: Be for all people in computers, not just techie types.
Budd: Be specially created to meet the needs of Ford engineers.

Guidelines

Lexus: Offer genuine value.
Cooper: Never be first to market.
Bausch & Lomb: Use only internal R&D.
Sealed Air: Offer more protection with less material.
Argo: Copy Deere, at a lower price.

mechanical components; the same thing happens with Volkswagen and Audi. Platform strategies are also seen in the software industry. Google has added YouTube, Gmail, Google Docs, and other features to its platform; Amazon and Apple have also similarly expanded from an early product to a full platform of products.[4]

These companies are making use of **modularization**, that is, decomposing complex systems into subsystems or modules. A car, for example, can be decomposed into its engine-transaxle combination, interior, body, dashboard, and so on.[5] For example, Chrysler and Volkswagen combine these subsystems into **modular products** built on the same platform. The procedure by which these subsystems are combined into modular products is tied to the product's architecture, which we shall revisit in Chapter 11.

Platforms can also be used to gain competitive advantage globally. Firms that take a multinational approach to new products on average do better than those that develop products just for their home market.[6] There are several strategies for selling one's products internationally. If the customer needs are not that different, one way is to sell a global product (in which one product is sold worldwide, such as Gillette blades or Canon cameras). If customers differ in their preferences, firms will often resort to a platform strategy. This provides the benefit of standardization and scale economies while still allowing for adaptation to particular market needs. A firm may offer a

[4]Simon, *The Age of the Platform: How Amazon, Apple, Facebook and Google Have Redefined Business.*
[5]Tucker J. Marion, op. cit., p. 194.
[6]U. De Brentani, E. Kleinschmidt, and S. Salomo, "Success in Global New Product Development: Impact of Strategy and the Behavioral Environment of the Firm," *Journal of Product Innovation Management*, 27(2), 2010, pp. 143–160; see Robert G. Cooper, op. cit., p. 15.

"glocal" product (one platform but several product variants adapted to local needs; a single Ford platform may be used to make cars with stick shifts in Europe but with automatic transmission and standard air conditioning in North America), or multiple glocal products (Volkswagen sells some kinds of cars in Europe and North America and different lines in Asian markets).[7] As examples, consider:

- From a common set of ingredients, Proctor & Gamble (P&G) developed Liquid Ariel, Liquid Tide, and Liquid Cheer for the European, U.S., and Japanese markets, respectively.

- Honda's World Car platform is used to make Accords for the North American, European, and Japanese markets, each slightly different in size according to market preferences. Honda also makes minivans, sport utility vehicles, and Acura luxury cars from the same platform.

The right choice depends on the situation, of course, but it should be guided by concept testing and product testing in each international market; it's not a safe bet to test the product only in the home market and then hope for the best internationally. It also makes sense to have global product teams with representatives of multiple countries.[8]

Many firms report promising results. Black & Decker redesigned its power tool groups into product families, allowing for more sharing of components. For example, where once 120 different motors were used in consumer power tools, a single universal motor is now used. The emphasis on platforms reduced product costs by 50 percent and helped Black & Decker achieve the highest market share in the category. IBM used a standard set of subcomponents for all ThinkPad products, cutting both the number of parts needed and base manufacturing costs in half.[9]

The examples illustrate a couple of different ways platforms evolve. In the Black & Decker example, the procedure was *bottom-up*: The firm found a way to consolidate components within an existing family of products to gain scale economies. But the Sony and Honda examples show a *top-down* platform procedure: The platform was designed at the outset to become the basis for a family of products, possibly for years into the future. Managers may need to be convinced to commit to top-down platform development rather than development of a single product, as it will certainly be more expensive and time-consuming. But the benefits are the cost and time efficiencies that will be obtained with future products built from the same platform and, ultimately, greater future competitive advantage. (Actually, once Black & Decker successfully converted to platform-based design, it then was able to generate even more products by "reusing" its platforms: It transformed its product design into a kind of top-down procedure.[10])

---

[7]Robert G. Cooper, op. cit., p. 15.

[8]U. De Brentani, E. Kleinschmidt, and S. Salomo, op. cit.

[9]Identified industries and examples are from Niklas Sundgren, "Introducing Interface Management in New Product Family Development," *Journal of Product Innovation Management*, 16(1), January 1999, pp. 40–51; Krichevsky, op. cit.; and Meyer and DeTore, op. cit.

[10]Marc Meyer and Alvin Lehnerd, *The Power of Product Platforms* (New York: Free Press, 1997).

Platforms are a possibility in service industries as well as for manufactured goods. From a single platform for managed health care services, one provider offered several derivative insurance products: self-insurance, group insurance, and extra coverage insurance.[11]

There is a trade-off involved here: Customers (or segments) want distinct products, while common products produce the greatest cost efficiencies.[12] To find the best balance, the manufacturer needs to decide on the level of commonality to be attained (that is, which designs or processes to standardize, and which to adapt). Suppose a product team is designing the dashboard for a new line of cars. The desired attributes in a dashboard no doubt depend on type of car being designed. A sports coupe buyer would probably like a roadster-like dashboard, while a family sedan buyer would prefer a more functional look. Once the key attributes have been identified, the team considers the components of the dashboard (heating, ventilation, and air conditioning [HVAC]; electrical; steering system; radio; insulation; and so on) and decides where commonalities could be found. Possibly the electrical and entertainment system designs could be shared, as could some HVAC parts (only the ends of the air conditioning ducts might need to be adapted). To achieve the desired differences between the two types of cars, the steering systems may need to be completely different, as would the insulation system: One might want to design the insulation for the sporty car such that it lets in more road noise![13]

Brand platforms can also be strategically important and are widely used. Brands may be billion-dollar assets, so many brand platforms are personally driven by chief executive officers (CEOs). Brands can serve as the launching pad for scores of products, all having in common the brand and any strategies applying to that brand. Kellogg's, for example, uses its company name as a brand platform, and it extended the Special K brand from simply a cereal to a whole range of diet-related products. Note, however, that any team using a platform brand must conform to the strategy of that brand; in the case of Waterford crystal, all products had to have top quality, no exceptions.[14]

The *value* of an established brand is called its **brand equity**. Market research can measure the value of any brand for any particular market (for example, the Duracell brand, if put onto a line of heavyweight industrial batteries). The measurements actually tell the amount of free promotion and integrity the brand equity brings to a new item that uses it. It is important to remember that a poor product concept won't succeed just because of a good brand name, and it may actually damage that brand's equity. We will return to the issue of managing brand equity in Chapter 14.

---

[11]James Walter, "Managing Services Platforms: The Managed Comp Experience," presentation at the 1999 Product Development & Management Association International Conference, Marco Island, FL.

[12]As the U.S. carmakers found out in the 1980s, it may have been more cost efficient for compacts and luxury sedans to share parts and design features, but customers complained that the cars looked too much alike.

[13]David Robertson and Karl Ulrich, "Planning for Product Platforms," *Sloan Management Review*, 39(4), Summer 1998, pp. 19–32.

[14]Guidance on using brand platforms for product innovation can be found in Dennis A. Pitts and Lea Prevel Katsanis, "Understanding Brand Equity for Successful Brand Extension," *Journal of Consumer Marketing*, 12(4), 1995, pp. 51–64. For a discussion of benefits and issues in platform planning, see David Robertson and Karl Ulrich, "Planning for Product Platforms," *Sloan Management Review*, Summer 1998, pp. 19–32.

FIGURE 3.2 Identifying the "Greenfield Markets"

1. Find another location or venue. Once McDonald's had taken up the best locations for traditional fast-food restaurants, it continued its U.S. expansion by placing stores inside Walmarts, in sports arenas, and elsewhere. Starbucks coffee complemented coffee-shop sales by selling its coffee beans and ice creams in supermarkets.

2. Leverage your firm's strengths in a new activity center. Nike has recently moved into golf and hockey, and Honeywell is looking into casino opportunities.

3. Identify a fast-growing need, and adapt your products to that need. Hewlett-Packard followed the need for "total information solutions" that led it to develop computing and communications products for the World Cup and other sporting events.

4. Find a "new to you" industry: P&G in pharmaceuticals, Disney in cruises, Rubbermaid in gardening products—either through alliance, acquisition, or internal development.

Recommendations for scouting for such opportunities:

1. Look for emerging trends: increased globalization of freight flow meant more global opportunities for FedEx.

2. Find fringe markets that are becoming mainstream: gourmet coffee, extreme sports, home carbon monoxide testing are recent examples that spelled opportunities for many firms.

3. Find bottlenecks in the flow of trade, and seek to eliminate them. Need for better hospital patient record retrieval led 3M to develop its Health Information Systems business.

4. Look for "ripple effects" on business opportunities. The trend toward "immediacy" has led to products such as electronic banking and 24-hour food stores. Health concerns have opened up opportunities in fitness products, vitamins, seminars, etc.

Source: Allen J. Magrath, "Envisioning Greenfield Markets," *Across the Board*, May 1998, pp. 26–30.

Another common platform is the **category platform**, either product type or customer. Most marketing effort today is conducted at category group levels—one overall plan for cake mixes, for do-it-yourself tools, or for finance courses in a college. For example, DuPont has special finishes platforms for doing business with the automobile industry, the marine industry, and the furniture industry, among others. Any strategic change in one of those areas influences all new products developed under that umbrella.

Opportunity Identification

Many firms have persons working full time looking for new opportunities. They essentially audit the firm and any environment relevant to it. Throughout the firm, people in the course of doing their jobs discover new opportunities—a salesperson learns that a customer is moving into a new market, a scientist finds unexpected activity in a compound, a finance vice president notes a fall in the prime rate, a director urges that we look more carefully at what the Environmental Protection Agency is doing. A new regulation, for example, may restrict the use of petroleum-based synthetics, and a CEO may want all divisions to seek new products that actively capitalize on the regulatory change.

As shown in Figure I.1, new opportunities can come from many different sources: underutilized or new resources, mandates originating external to the firm (e.g., new regulatory restrictions), or internal mandates (e.g., from new corporate leadership). Figure 3.2 suggests several ways in which firms can identify opportunities for growth in new markets by finding new ways to create value for customers.

Many futurists advocate studying the emerging trends in society and deriving product opportunities from them. A team of experts from the consulting firm Social Technologies identified six important and provocative modern trends:

Just-in-time life: People like making spur-of-the-moment decisions based on real-time information.

Sensing consumers: People can now sense their environment better than ever before; what might be "too much information" for some might be essential information for others.

The transparent self: More information about consumers is now available to product managers than ever before.

In search of "enoughness": Consumers are increasingly adopting simpler lifestyles marked by fewer material possessions and an increasing concern about quality of life.

Virtual made real: As more people become accustomed to virtual spaces, the boundary between these and the real world will become increasingly blurred.

Co-creation: Due to increases in e-commerce and online communities, it is easier for customers to communicate with each other, cooperate, and share information.[15]

Each one of these trends suggests possible opportunities for new product development, as shown in Figure 3.3. As an example, Tremont Electric developed the nPower PEG, a "personal energy generator" that allows the user to charge a phone or other electronic device just by plugging it in and putting it in his or her pocket—the device charges from the kinetic energy generated from walking or running. Product developers at Tremont may have been thinking about the "just-in-time life" trend. If one is traveling or camping, or just forgot to plug in the phone the night before, this product can help the person use the phone again quickly and without waiting to find a plug. It also adds a cost-saving benefit as well as an eco-friendly charging option.[16]

Truly, there is no end to these opportunities, every one of which may reveal additional opportunities for new products. Unfortunately, each opportunity takes time and money to investigate, so we don't exploit nearly as many as we would like.

Noncorporate Strategic Planning

Although the major thrust of strategic planning comes from the top down (i.e., corporate and platform strategy development), much of it also comes from the heads of the functions (**silos** or chimneys) in the firm—marketing, technical, manufacturing, and finance, and from the planning of suppliers, customers, and others. Such groups frequently have the power to affect new product work. For example, paper manufacturing is done on huge, expensive machines; such firms often have strategies with a statement: "All new items, if paper-related, must be manufacturable on our current lines." Financial conditions may warrant restrictions such as "no new products that require more than $3 million capital investments." Suppliers of materials (e.g., chemicals or metals) often require firms (usually smaller) to buy and use what

---

[15]Andy Hines, Josh Calder, and Don Abraham, "Six Catalysts Shaping the Future of Product Development," *Visions*, 33(3), October 2009, pp. 20–23.

[16]Tremont Electric's Web site for the charger is www.greennpower.com.

FIGURE 3.3 **Product Opportunities as Derived from Six Societal Trends**

Trend	Related Product Opportunities
Trend 1: Just-in-Time Life	PhillyCarShare or Zipcar: carsharing systems with hourly rentals. Twitter or related services that allow instantaneous updates about friends. Real-time people tracking services such as Loopt.
Trend 2: Sensing Consumers	Home-testing kits for cholesterol, allergens, and so on. Technology that allows parents to track their children around the clock. Consumers taking part in environmental sensing networks.
Trend 3: The Transparent Self	GyPSii displays friends' whereabouts. Services that generate personal data such as bank accounts. 23andme, a home DNA test (*Time* Invention of the Year in 2009).
Trend 4: In Search of "Enoughness"	Products servicing environmental concerns. "Slow food" and "slow life" related products. Products supporting leisure time activities.
Trend 5: Virtual Made Real	Products and services related to virtual economies. Websites offering avatars for socialization and play in virtual cities. Virtual nightclubs and similar activities.
Trend 6: Co-Creation	iPhone apps number in the tens of thousands and are still growing. LEGO has an online factory for visitors to make their own LEGO toys. NikeID for custom shoes, and other similar product "configurators."

Source: Andy Hines, Josh Calder, and Don Abraham, "Six Catalysts Shaping the Future of Product Development," *Visions*, 33(3), October 2009, pp. 20–23.

they make. But the greatest functional inputs may come from technical, especially in technology- or supply-push conditions, or from marketing, where ongoing planning uses a range of techniques designed to give sharper market focus and new positionings. For example, look at Figure 3.4. It shows a variation on the traditional **product-market matrix**. The cells show variations in *innovativeness risk* as a firm brings in new product types or technologies (operating mode change, across the top) or markets products that require changes in how people buy or use them (use mode down the left side). A simple flavor change (product improvement) would probably involve little or no risk, but substituting a computer line for face-to-face dealings in the field of medicine (**diversification** for a computer services firm) would involve dangerous risk to the producer of the service (great change in both technology and use mode).

Miscellaneous Sources

In contrast to the corporate-platform downward pressure approach and the horizontal functional pressure approach, some inputs can start at the lower level of activity and influence upward, as when a new product is so successful it drives corporate strategy to change. For example, an ethical pharmaceutical firm once unintentionally marketed a very successful new proprietary food product, with the result that a new division was created (to isolate the consumer advertising activity from the rest of the firm) and new strategies were created to optimize its opportunity. Sometimes, a slow and gradual

FIGURE 3.4
Degree of
Innovativeness
as a Matter of
Strategic Risk

Risk		Change in operations or marketing mode		
		None	*Some*	*Great*
Change in use/ user mode	*None*	Low	Low	Medium
	Some	Low	Medium	High
	Great	Medium	High	Dangerous

Application: This matrix has gone by several names: Product/Market, Technology/Application, and Market-Newness/Firm-Newness. In all cases, the issue is the risk of innovativeness. Risk on the user side is just as much a concern to us as risk within the firm. Every new product can be positioned on this chart somewhere, and that position is important if it is accepted as a project. Selecting one section to be preferred over the others is a matter of strategy.

restructuring of business practice can influence new product strategies almost without anyone realizing it. Managers of service products frequently add a tangible component (FedEx and UPS offer branded packaging materials and even require that their drivers look neat), and managers of tangible products may add or emphasize a service component (such as a car-warranty program).

The Product Innovation Charter

All of the preceding inputs (corporate mission, platform planning, strategic fit, and so on) are potentially used in the development of a company's new product strategy. Because of the importance of this step in driving all that comes later in product development, we advocate a special name for this strategy: the **product innovation charter**. Typically, the PIC is a document prepared by senior management that is designed to provide guidance to the business units on the role of innovation.[17] The term PIC reminds us that the strategy is for *products*, not processes and other activities, it is for *innovation*, and it is indeed a *charter* (a document that gives the conditions under which an organization will operate). The PIC can be thought of as a kind of mission statement, but applied at a more micro level within the firm and adapted to new product

[17]Erika B. Seamon, "Achieving Growth Through an Innovative Culture," in P. Belliveau, A. Griffin, and S. M. Somermeyer, *PDMA Toolbook 2 for New Product Development* (New York: John Wiley, 2004), Ch. 1.

activities.[18] It allows delegation, permits financing, and calls for personnel assignments, all within an agreed-upon scope of activity. For new product teams plowing off into unknown waters, such a charter is invaluable.[19]

Most firms have a PIC, though it may not go by that name. In fact, some firms claim they have no strategy and then go on to describe methods of project management that are clearly strategic![20] In an empirical study of Product Development & Management Association (PDMA) member managers, about three-fourths of the firms investigated had a formal new product policy of some type (that is, at least a partial PIC), while 29 percent reported having a formal, written PIC.[21] A more recent study of senior executives found that innovation rates are substantially higher in cases where the PIC has detailed and specific content and where there is general satisfaction with the new products process within the firm. The more specific the corporate mission is presented in the PIC, and the more clearly senior management's strategic directions are spelled out, the better the performance of new products developed by the firm.[22] The value of PICs is clearly shown in the Comparative Performance Assessment Study (CPAS) introduced in Chapter 1. In that study, 86 percent of the Best firms had a PIC, as opposed to only 69 percent for the Rest.[23]

The components of a PIC are provided in Figure 3.5. In the PDMA study, well over 80 percent of the firms had formalized at least some of these components. To ensure that the PIC is effective, it should be put in place early by senior management, and the latter should stay involved and not delegate its implementation.[24] An illustrative example of what the PIC might have looked like for Orosound, a small company that manufactures noise-filtering earphones, is shown in Figure 3.6.

We will expand the discussion of the PIC soon, but let's first examine the various inputs that help managers make strategic decisions.

Strategy statements take almost as many forms as there are firms preparing them, but they tend to build around the structure given in Figure 3.5. They can be for an *entire firm* (if very small or very narrowly conceived), or for a *standing platform* of activity within a larger firm (for example, Black & Decker brand of tools), or for a *specific project* (for example, Hewlett-Packard's newest laser printer). A PIC generally speaks to an opportunity (the focus), not to the specific product or products the group has yet to create. Of course, when products are very complex (a new car platform, an air express service for the Asian market, or a nation's new health plan), one product is all the team can handle.

---

[18]Christopher K. Bart, "Product Innovation Charters: Mission Statements for New Products," *R&D Management*, 32(1), 2002, pp. 23–34.

[19]See Robert G. Cooper and Elko J. Kleinschmidt, "Winning Businesses in Product Development: The Critical Success Factors," *Research-Technology Management*, July–August 1996, pp. 18–29. An example at Kodak is given in Diana Laitner, "Deep Needs and the Fuzzy Front End," *Visions*, July 1997, pp. 6–9.

[20]Albert L. Page, "Product Strategy for Product Development," *Visions*, July 1997, pp. 15–16.

[21]Bart, op. cit.

[22]Chris Bart and Ashish Pujari, "The Performance Impact of Content and Process in Product Innovation Charters," *Journal of Product Innovation Management*, 24(1), January 2007, pp. 3–19.

[23]Gloria Barczak, Abbie Griffin, and Kenneth B. Kahn, "Perspective: Trends and Drivers of Success in NPD Practices: Results of the 2003 PDMA Best Practices Study," *Journal of Product Innovation Management*, 26(1), January 2009, pp. 3–23.

[24]Seamon, op. cit.

FIGURE 3.5
The Product
Innovation
Charter

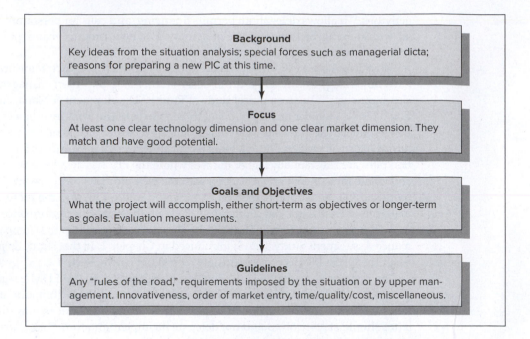

Background
Key ideas from the situation analysis; special forces such as managerial dicta; reasons for preparing a new PIC at this time.

Focus
At least one clear technology dimension and one clear market dimension. They match and have good potential.

Goals and Objectives
What the project will accomplish, either short-term as objectives or longer-term as goals. Evaluation measurements.

Guidelines
Any "rules of the road," requirements imposed by the situation or by upper management. Innovativeness, order of market entry, time/quality/cost, miscellaneous.

The PIC should be in writing and should be given to all participants, but for various reasons these things do not always happen. This is unfortunate, because a secret, mind-only strategy will not do much for a team of 30 people.

Why Have a PIC?

Think back to Peter Koen's "sandbox" comment mentioned earlier. We have already seen how many different places we can find opportunities for new product development. Without a strategy, it is easy to lose focus and to spend time and resources chasing the wrong opportunities. The PIC provides the direction, or directions, the team should concentrate on in new product development—in other words, it defines what sandbox the team is in, or wants to be in, and also where it does not want to be. Without placing the boards that define the size and shape of the sandbox (metaphorically speaking), then *any* opportunity would seem to be a good one!

Consider a team developing a small, portable computer printer. One member is thinking of using a new battery-based technology, while another team member is concentrating on potential customers who happen to work in environments where wall plugs are available. Marketing research people plan to pretest the product extensively, while manufacturing engineers assume time is critical and are designing finished production capability from the beginning. A vendor picked to supply the tractor mechanism has to check with the team leader almost every day because the team has not decided exactly what functions the printer will serve or the target user. In addition, the team is being guided by requests from the sales department, which is currently calling on smaller firms—although, in fact, the biggest potential is thought to be in large firms and governments. This team has not developed strategy.

FIGURE 3.6 **Product Innovation Charter for Orosound**

Orosound is a French company founded in 2015 with the goal of developing and manufacturing noise-filtering earphones. The founders, Pierre Guiu and Eric Benhaim, realized that workplace noise pollution was a concern and set out to develop a high-quality earphone to solve this problem. By mid-2016, a prototype was ready and the founders started a Kickstarter campaign that eventually raised almost 80,000 euro. Mass production of the product, carrying the Tilde brand name, began in 2017. Orosound focused on selling to companies in France and Japan and also to individuals who were Kickstarter donors.

The Tilde is a uniquely designed earphone that manages the surrounding noise in a way that is controllable by the user. The wearer can selectively hear a person speaking directly to them while filtering out ambient noise. This is preferable to head-phones, which may need to be removed completely to hear the speaker. The Tilde can also be used for high-quality music listening. Thus, Orosound saw potential for the Tilde in both workplace applications and for personal music enjoyment.

Background: There is an opportunity in the marketplace due to noise pollution that constantly surrounds us. Companies are especially concerned about the health and well-being of their employees, and reduction of ambient noise can lead to higher workplace satisfaction. While there are competitive headphones, there are none that offer all of the benefits that the Tilde provides.

Focus: Orosound has technology and R&D strength and owns several patents in acoustics that led to the development of the Tilde. On the marketing side, the Tilde satisfies an unmet need in the workplace—for effective, yet controllable and selective sound filtering that improves the well-being of workers. Given the growth of workplace collaboration, the ability to filter out ambient noise and still carry on a conversation is a definite plus.

Goals and objectives: Due to intense interest in France and Japan, Orosound targeted those two countries at first, allowing for an assessment of marketplace acceptance and some accurate sales forecasting for future global targets. The individual consumer market is a secondary target for the moment.

Guidelines: Orosound wants to take advantage of the growth in workplace collaboration, for which the Tilde is ideally suited. The product should make the workplace a more productive and happier place. The Tilde should be an indispensable part of any workplace environment.

Team guidance, just like corporate or strategic business units (SBUs) guidance, comes partly in the form of strategy. Its purpose is *to focus and integrate team effort and to permit delegation.* Bausch & Lomb almost lost its market position when its managers concentrated for too long on improving old products and thus almost missed new products like extended-wear contact lenses. Being forced to review their strategy, they found many more opportunities and went on to capitalize on them (e.g., disposable contact lenses).

Lacking a focused and integrated effort, new products teams are likely to face the related problems of *scope creep* and *unstable product specifications.*[25] Both of these problems occur if the "sandbox" is not defined, or only poorly or vaguely defined. Scope creep refers to the constant changing of a project's definition: Is the project meant to be a product designed for a specific customer, a large number of users, or a platform for a whole new line of products? *Unstable product specifications* refer to the product requirements or desired performance level changing as the product goes through the development phase. In either case, the product team is chasing an elusive target

[25]For more on scope creep and unstable specifications, see Robert G. Cooper, "What Separates the Winners from the Losers and What Drives Success," in Kenneth B. Kahn, George Castellion, and Abbie Griffin, *The PDMA Handbook of New Product Development*, 2nd ed. (Hoboken, NJ: John Wiley & Sons, 2005).

(Robert Cooper would call this the "moving goalpost"), with inevitable waste of both time and resources. A clear-cut PIC, designed to over-arch the entire new products process, helps to minimize these costly and time-consuming problems. There is even value to be gained in the very process of working together and formulating a PIC. A good process fosters high levels of commitment from the participants, consensus on goals and objectives, and agreement on the ways the goals will be achieved. Indeed, in a recent empirical study, the most innovative firms in the sample were those that had a clear PIC and also had a satisfactory process for PIC development.[26] This finding complements an earlier study, in which 70 percent of the highest-performing firms had a specific PIC, while only 51 percent of low-performing firms did.[27]

The Sections of the PIC

The PIC is a plan for the firm's initiatives in new product development. It provides clarification of goals and a common language for all personnel involved in new products. The roles of all participants throughout the new products process are clearly specified. An effective PIC communicates to the product team members exactly how their efforts fit into the big corporate picture.[28]

Background Section of the PIC

This section of the PIC answers the question: "Why did we develop this strategy, anyway?" To the extent necessary, it recaps the analysis behind it. As seen in Figure 3.5, this section will incorporate the situation analysis (strengths, weaknesses, opportunities, and threats [SWOT] analysis) and any other managerial input that may be relevant at this time.

The Arena (Area of Focus) Section of the PIC

In today's competitive marketplaces, it takes focus to unlock the necessary power of innovation. Just as a laser can take a harmless light and convert it into a deadly ray, so can a commitment to, say, the pizza delivery business or to the Web site construction process convert limited resources into a strong competitive thrust. As one developer said, "We like to play on fields that tilt in our direction."

In recent years we have heard a great deal about **core competencies**. They are an excellent place to start the search for charter arena definitions. Marketers narrow their focus by targeting and segmentation. Technical people, fenced in by time, limited facilities, and money, don't relish yet another focus mechanism. But the idea of a new products arena, or area of focus, is necessary. Focus is generally achieved by

---

[26]Chris Bart and Ashish Pujari, "The Performance Impact of Content and Process in Product Innovation Charters," *Journal of Product Innovation Management*, 24(1), January 2007, pp. 3–19.

[27]Abbie Griffin, "PDMA Research on New Product Development Practices: Updating Trends and Benchmarking Best Practices," *Journal of Product Innovation Management*, 14(6), November 1997, pp. 429–458.

[28]Roger J. Calantone, S. K. Vickery, and Cornelia Droge, "A Business Performance and Strategic New Product Development Activities: An Empirical Investigation," *Journal of Product Innovation Management*, 12(3), May 1995, pp. 214–223.

the use of four types of strengths or leverage capabilities: *technology* (such as Kimberly-Clark's paper-processing technology), *product experience* (Anheuser-Busch's choice to focus on the beer business), *customer franchise* (Stanley Tools' hold on the woodworker), and *end-use experience* (Chase Manhattan's international division). **Licensing** or **acquisition** to acquire technologies or market strengths are also fair game for inclusion in strategies. The original *Star Wars* creator, George Lucas, opened bids from toy manufacturers for licenses when planning *Episode 1*. Some of them approached $1 billion.[29]

Relying solely on a technology is risky, as no one knows whether the technology-based product is something customers want (Google Glass, for example, or the Iridium satellite-based telephone, are examples of new technology-based products that did not catch on). Likewise, letting customers' stated wants drive product innovation is unlikely to work well, except in a market with enormous unmet needs and very slow reacting competitors. One recent report told how two personal computer makers differed on drivers. One, Fujitsu, bet on technology and lost, while NEC bet on customer needs and won.[30] Gambles like this are too expensive today. So consumer giants Frito-Lay and P&G have major laboratory research facilities, and technology-driven Hewlett-Packard has announced that it wants a strong market commitment behind every new product program. These firms have realized that the best option is a balanced, or **dual-drive**, strategy. Let's explore technology and market drivers separately, then see their value when taken in combination.

Technology Drivers

The most common technological strengths are in the *laboratories*. Corning used to say it would develop those products—and only those products—that exploited the firm's fabulous glass technology. Today's global competition makes it tougher for Corning (and others) to hold a superior position in a technology defined so broadly.

Many times, a firm finds it has a valuable *non*laboratory technology. Avon has an efficient small-order-handling technology. Other operations technologies include soft drink distributed bottling systems and White Consolidated's efficient appliance production lines. Big business consulting firms have built new services around capabilities of analysis and interpretation of financial information. For a firm with superior technical skills, applying the dual-drive idea means turning technical specifications into product features that satisfy market needs. Consider a firm that manufactures semiconductors and has developed the capability to produce smaller-size, highly efficient, higher-resistance semiconductors (the technical specifications). These specifications by themselves may mean little to customers or end users, but they do provide capabilities and features, such as longer battery life, lower temperature operation, or lower manufacturing or maintenance costs, that might provide useful benefits to

[29]Lisa Bannon and Joseph Pereira, "Toy Makers Offer the Moon for New 'Star Wars' Licenses," *The Wall Street Journal*, August 19, 1997, p. B1.

[30]David T. Methé, Ryoko Toyama, and Junichiro Miyabe, "Product Development Strategy and Organizational Learning," *Journal of Product Innovation Management*, 14(5), September 1997, pp. 323–336.

customers. The firm will need to think first of what products might be developed from the basic technology, such as a chip for use in smartphones, laptops, or electric motors. Then, what particular market segments would be interested in such products? Here, the firm will need to match these products, offering these features and benefits, to unmet market needs—smartphone or laptop users who require longer and more dependable battery life, possibly, or electric motor users who need lighter-weight, lower-cost units that run at lower temperatures. This procedure of converting technical specifications to product features and benefits, to market needs, has sometimes been called the **T-P-M linkage**.[31]

Even harder to see are the technologies in marketing. For example, some packaged goods firms view their product management departments as technologies. Other examples include physical distribution systems, customer technical service, or creative advertising departments.

Market Drivers

The other half of the dual-drive strategy also comes from two market sources: *customer group* and *end-use*. The best new product ideas are based on customer problems, and these problems serve as the heart of the concept generation process described in Chapter 4.

The Hoover Company once had a strategy of developing new vacuums for people who already had one—the two-vacuum-home concept. Other firms have relied on demographic dimensions for focus—concentrating on serving young couples in their first homes, perhaps, or on small businesses with their particular needs. As examples of more abstract dimensions, Hallmark famously concentrates on "people who care enough to send the very best." Welch Allyn, maker of high-tech medical devices that are used in doctors' offices and hospitals, once said, not jokingly, if you have a cavity we want to see it, and if you don't have a cavity but need one we will make it. The latter part of that strategic focus brought about their device for doing noninvasive gall bladder removal.

Firms producing services find customer-focus comfortable, since many of their operations involve the customer as an actual **coproducer** of the service. The logic of this arrangement has led many service firms, in all industries, to involve the customer as an integrated partner in the new product development process.

Occasionally, a firm can concentrate on one single customer; for example, an auto parts firm may build new items for Ford or for General Motors. A variation on the single-customer focus is **mass customization**—where we offer all customers a product of their individual choice. Marriott's Courtyard, for example, has made this successful in the hotel business. We will see more of mass customization in upcoming chapters.

The second way of focusing on the market side is on a particular *end-use*, such as sports or skiing. For example, focusing on skiers or skiing would both provide new equipment, but skiing would also lead to new lodges, new slopes, new travel

---

[31]Stephen K. Markham and Angus I. Kingon, "Turning Technical Advantage into Product Advantage," in P. Belliveau, A. Griffin, and S. M. Somermeyer, *The PDMA Toolbook 2 for New Product Development* (New York: John Wiley, 2004).

packages, and services for lodge owners (who may not even be skiers). Industrial firms make great use of end-use. You may say, but how do we know when to focus on the customer, and when on the end-use? The answer lies in the opportunity analysis that took place earlier—you studied markets, people in them, and activities they engage in. You selected a given opportunity because you thought its needs fit the firm's capabilities.

A variation on market drivers is the *distributor*—when a producer develops new products to meet the needs of, or capitalize on the franchise of, resellers. Hallmark's line of small gift items, for example, was originally developed to help their card shop franchisees make more money.

Combinations: Dual-Drive

Now, putting one technical driver together with a market driver yields a clear and precise arena focus. University Microfilms International has been using the *technology of microfilming* and the *market activity of education* as their original mainstay, but later added *photocopiers* for schools and microfilm readers for *law offices*. Penn Racquet Sports switched species of markets, putting their *tennis ball technology* to work making a line of ball toys for dogs.[32] Toro had years of success with a series of dual-drives, one of which is *global-satellite technology* and *golf course superintendents*.[33]

The Signode Corporation set up a series of seven new product venture operations and asked each group to select one company technology and one market opportunity that matched that company strength. The first team chose *plastics extrusion* (from Signode's primary business of strapping materials) and *food manufacturing*. This team's first new products were plastic trays for packaged foods designed to be heated in microwave ovens.

Goals and Objectives Section of the PIC

Anyone working on product innovation ought to know the purpose, because work can change in so many ways if the purpose changes. The PIC uses the standard definition that **goals** are longer-range, general directions of movement, whereas **objectives** are short-term, specific measures of accomplishment. Thus, a PIC may aim for market dominance (as a goal) and 25 percent market share the first year (as an objective).

Both goals and objectives are of three types: (1) *profit*, stated in one or more of the many ways profit can be stated; (2) *growth*, usually controlled, though occasionally a charter is used defensively to help the firm hold or retard a declining trend; and (3) *market status*, usually increased market share. Many (though not all) senior managers insist that new product teams entering new markets should plan to dominate them. There has been much criticism of market share as a new product goal, but it is still a popular objective. Wendy's, Burger King, Dunkin', and Starbucks all rolled out

[32]Dennis Berman, "Now, Tennis Balls Are Chasing the Dogs," *BusinessWeek*, July 13, 1998, p. 138.

[33]Richard Gibson, "Toro Charges into Greener Fields with New Products," *The Wall Street Journal*, June 22, 1997, p. B4. This article gives lots of details on a very sophisticated use of the dual-drive system of defining an arena.

breakfast menus in recent years in order to capture a larger share of the enormous breakfast market that has been dominated by McDonald's.[34]

Special Guidelines Section of the PIC

Up to this point, we have filled out three sections of the PIC form. We know the team's arena or focus and we know what they are supposed to accomplish there. But research shows that almost every new product strategy has a fourth section—some guidelines or rules of the road. They may be managerially imposed, or the consensus thinking of team members. They are certainly strategic. We have no research study that shows what such guidelines *should* be, but we do have much research showing what firms put into this section, right or wrong.

Degree of Innovativeness

How **innovative** does a management want a particular group to be? The options range from first-to-market (whether a synthetic fiber or a Frisbee) to strict imitation.

First-to-market is a risky strategy. It goes by several other names, including *pioneering*. There are three ways to get it, the first of which is by *state-of-the-art breakthrough*. Pharmaceutical firms use that route most of the time. Other products that came from such programs include bubble memory, the pacemaker, compact discs, and television. But most first-to-market products do not extend the state of the art; instead they tweak technology in a new way. This second way, sometimes called *leveraged creativity*, constitutes the most common first-to-market category. For example, DuPont researchers find the special properties (such as durability or oil and grease resistance) of synthetic materials such as Surlyn and Kevlar, then they think up creative applications to arrive at new products. Surlyn's grease resistance led to its application in the meat packing industry. The third way to be first is *applications engineering*, where the technology may not be changed at all, but the use is totally new. Loctite has done this dozens of times, for example, by using glue to replace metal fasteners in electronics and automotive products.

Far more common than pioneering is the strategy of developing an **adaptive product**, that is, taking a competitor's pioneering product and improving it in some way. This strategy is sometimes called a *fast-follower* or *second but best* strategy. Maytag followed this strategy for many years, often making major improvements over competitive products. Harris Corporation, on the other hand, entered markets where others had pioneered and used its great technical know-how to create a niche with only a slightly improved product. The firm's chairperson said Harris tried to be strong in technology and to enter a product in a timely manner.

Adaptation alone is risky. The pioneer often obtains a permanent advantage; other things being equal, the first product in a new market gains an average market share of

[34]For more on goals and objectives used by business, see Abbie Griffin and Albert L. Page, "PDMA Success Measurement Project: Recommended Measures for Product Development Success and Failure," *Journal of Product Innovation Management*, 13(6), November 1996, pp. 169–195. For developments in the fast-food industry, see Bruce Horovitz, "Fast-Food Rivals Suit Up for Breakfast War," *USA Today*, February 20, 2007.

around 30 percent. But the second firm can take over the market and win the category if its adaptation is clearly superior. Often, the firm that enters first-to-market will follow the successful entry with less innovative adaptive extensions or even straight imitations, opening up an opportunity window for competitors.

The third level of innovativeness is **imitation**, or **emulation**. Firms such as Cooper Tire & Rubber, Matsushita, and White Consolidated (appliances) deliberately wait to see winners emerge from among the pioneers and early adopters. Imitation has its risks, too: A firm cannot wait too long to enter the market, by which time the earliest firms to enter have well-established, loyal customer bases and ties to the supply networks and distribution channels. Furthermore, an incumbent firm may take an innovator to court over alleged patent, trademark, or copyright infringement (we return to trademark protection in Chapter 14).[35] In sum, first-to-market or fast-follower strategies have a competitive advantage over later followers. This finding was supported by the CPAS study results: the best firms in the study were much more likely to use these two strategies and less likely to be a late follower.[36]

Miscellaneous Guidelines

Innumerable specialized guidelines can be found in product innovation charters. Some firms may spend a fortune on R&D with the intention of always being first to market; others prefer to use a fast-follower strategy. Some of these guidelines come about because management recognizes, and has to work around, the firm's weaknesses. For example, a large mining machinery firm told its product innovators to come up with products that *did not* require strong marketing; the firm didn't have it and didn't want to invest in getting it. A pharmaceutical firm said, "It must be patentable." A small computer firm said all new products must be parts of systems, while an even smaller computer firm said, "Nothing that must be part of a system!" A food firm said, "Don't put anything in a can that Frito-Lay can put in a bag." Another miscellaneous guideline is **product integrity**, meaning that all aspects of the product are internally consistent. An example: Honda was very successful using the new four-wheel steering system because it put the innovation into a two-door coupe with a sporty image, whereas Mazda failed when putting it on a five-door hatchback that was positioned for safety and durability.

How to Prepare a Product Innovation Charter

The process for developing a PIC lies in its contents. *First*, we are always looking for opportunities, inside the firm or outside it. Each strategy can be traced to a strength of the company involved. No one firm can be strong in everything. *Second*, we have to

[35]For a discussion of pioneering benefits and risks, see M. B. Lieberman and D. B. Montgomery, "First-Mover (Dis)advantages: Retrospective and Link with the Resource-Based View," *Strategic Management Journal*, 19(12), 1998, pp. 1111–1125. Information on several later entrants who overtook pioneers can be found in Steven P. Schnaars, *Managing Imitation Strategies* (New York: Free Press, 1994).

[36]Stephen K. Markham and Hyunjung Lee, "Product Development and Management Association's 2012 Comparative Performance Assessment Study," *Journal of Product Innovation Management*, 30(3), 2013, pp. 408–429.

FIGURE 3.7
Market and
Technology
Opportunities

Market Opportunities	Technology Opportunities
User (category)	Product type
User (for our product)	Specific product
Customer (buyer)	Primary packaging
Influencer	Secondary packaging
Potential user	Design process
Nonuser	Production process
Demographic set	Distribution process
Psychographic set	Packaging process
Geographic set	Patent
Retailer	Science
Wholesaler	Material
Agent	Individual
Use	Management system
Application	Information system
Activity	Analytical skill
Franchise	Expert system
Location	Project control
Competitor	Quality attainment
Regulator	Project design

evaluate, rate, and rank them. *Third,* we simply begin filling out the PIC form—focus, goals, and guidelines. Usually, there is no shortage of suggestions for all the sections—not unlike any marketing situation analysis.

Consider first the opportunity identification step. Potentially fruitful options in technologies or marketplaces may seem hard to find, but we are surrounded by them. Figure 3.7 shows a partial list. Every one of these has been the basis for a team's new product assignment, at least once.

The second step, evaluating and ranking the opportunities, is extremely difficult. In fact, one of the most valuable creative skills in product innovation is the ability to look at a building, an operation, a person, or a department and visualize how it could be used in a new way. This skill can be developed and should be practiced. Not only is there no ready quantitative tool for measuring, say, the strength of the pharmaceutical chemistry department of a small drug manufacturer, but there is also politics, because people are involved. And, unfortunately, it is much easier to see the potential in some technology or market *after the fact.* Consider Amazon.com. Thousands of people have said how obvious was their idea of selling books on the Internet, but where were they when Amazon.com stock was selling for $10 a share?

Product Portfolio Analysis: The New Product's Strategic Fit

Now that a new products manager has written a PIC, is that it? Not at all. Upper management must approve it. Importantly, the newly chartered product must fit as part of the firm's overall business strategy. It should provide an appropriate balance to other products already being offered before any scarce financial resources are allocated to it. Many firms use a product-portfolio approach in which management allocates R&D and other scarce resources across several categories defined by strategic as well as financial dimensions.[37]

As noted in Chapter 1, virtually all firms consider financial criteria when selecting which products to add to their portfolio. But the best-performing firms also include strategic criteria in their evaluations. This can be tricky: the product team can use standard accounting criteria, such as return on investment, payback period, or net present value, for financial evaluation. But there is no one correct way to do strategic evaluation, which will depend on what is prioritized in the firm's PIC. While no means an exhaustive list, some common strategic criteria might include

- Strategic goals (defending current base of products versus extending the base)
- Project types (balancing fundamental research, process improvements, and maintenance projects)
- Short-term versus long-term projects
- High-risk versus low-risk projects
- Market familiarity (existing markets, extensions of current ones, or totally new ones)
- Technology familiarity (existing platforms, extensions of current ones, or totally new ones)
- Geographical markets (balancing sales or profits in North America, Europe, and Asia)

Forthcoming examples show the wide range of possibilities for strategic criteria. Current spending within each of the categories is assessed and compared to desired spending (which may be expressed as a dollar amount or as a percent), and adjustments are made. Thus, a firm would not allocate funds to yet another close-to-home, low-value-product project when it would be strategically more advisable to take on a riskier, higher-potential-return project.

Whatever criteria are used, the objectives of developing the product portfolio remain the same:[38]

- Strategic alignment: most importantly, the portfolio ensures that the mix of products reflects the PIC. Any new projects should be "on strategy" (they support the firm's innovation strategy and/or are critical to the strategy).
- Assessing portfolio value: projects should be selected so that the commercial value of products in the pipeline is maximized. The familiar metrics such as net present value or return on investment can be used.

---

[37]For discussions of the portfolio approach, see Robert G. Cooper, Scott J. Edgett, and Elko J. Kleinschmidt, *Portfolio Management for New Products* (Hamilton, Ontario: McMaster University, 1997), pp. 59–69; and Robert G. Cooper, Scott J. Edgett, and Elko J. Kleinschmidt, "Portfolio Management: Fundamental to New Product Success," in P. Belliveau, A. Griffin, and S. Somermeyer (Eds.), *The PDMA Toolbook for New Product Development* (New York: John Wiley, 2002), pp. 331–364.

[38]Scott Edgett, "Portfolio Management for Product Innovation," in K. B. Kahn, S. E. Kay, R. J. Slotegraaf, and S. Uban (Eds.), *The PDMA Handbook of New Product Development* (Hoboken, NJ: Wiley, 2013), Ch. 9, p. 156.

- Project balance: the portfolio should make it easy to select projects that complement the existing product line; for example, too many high-risk projects can be balanced by selecting a couple of lower-risk ones. There should be a nice mix of new-to-the-world products, improvements and revisions, cost-reducing innovations, and so forth.

- Number of projects: one must also consider the number of products in the pipeline, as resource commitments to too many projects inevitably lead to underfunding and gridlock. Resources required by the portfolio should be in balance with the amount of resources available.

As an interesting example of project balance, consider the Keurig coffee system. When first launched in 1998, Keurig machines and coffee were designed for use in business offices. Market research showed that there was a vast untapped market: home coffee drinkers. By 2003, Keurig had a new, lower-priced, streamlined system for home use; by 2006, the company was purchased by Green Mountain Coffee Roasters, and retail distribution through department stores was increased to further penetrate the home user market. Essentially, Keurig expanded its portfolio from an initial business-to-business focus by adding new machines and coffee products aimed at the consumer market, with profitable results.[39]

Managing a strategic product portfolio in order to maintain a dependable, continuous flow of products is a reality in most industries. Consider pharmaceuticals, agrochemicals, or other highly regulated industries. Product managers face incredibly difficult challenges: low likelihoods of success, high development and regulatory costs, limited financial and human resources, even the sheer difficulty of coming up with a good new product idea! Add to this the need to time product launches with marketplace demand, and it's easy to see why managers in such industries resort to complex decision models to help them manage their product portfolios.[40]

According to Robert Cooper, portfolio analysis is critical because it provides strategic direction to product project selection. His research suggests three portfolio management goals when selecting from among potential projects:

- *Strategic fit:* Does the proposed project fit with the technology and/or market focus as specified in the PIC? Is the project consistent with new product strategy?

- *Strategic contribution:* Does the proposed project help to achieve any of the targeted strategic criteria as listed earlier (such as extending the current base of products, entering into new markets, or developing totally new technology platforms)?

- *Strategic priorities:* Does the proposed project live up to the guidelines listed in the PIC (does management want the firm to be a technological leader or a fast follower)?[41]

---

[39]Anonymous, "The History of Keurig," *blog.crosscountrycafe.com*, January 2, 2014.

[40]Gary E. Blau, Joseph F. Pekny, Vishal A. Varma, and Paul R. Bunch, "Managing a Portfolio of Interdependent New Product Candidates in the Pharmaceutical Industry," *Journal of Product Innovation Management*, 21(4), July 2004, pp. 227–245.

[41]This is adapted from Robert G. Cooper, Scott J. Edgett, and Elko J. Kleinschmidt, *Portfolio Management of New Products*, 2nd ed. (New York: Perseus Books, 2001).

FIGURE 3.8
Strategic
Portfolio Model
for One SBU in
Exxon
Chemical

	Low Market Newness	High Market Newness
Low Product Newness	Improvements to Existing Products (35%)	Additions to Existing Product Lines (20%)
Medium Product Newness	Cost Reductions (20%)	New Product Lines (15%)
High Product Newness	Repositioning (6%)	New-to-the-World Products (4%)

Source: Adapted from Robert G. Cooper, Scott J. Edgett, and Elko J. Kleinschmidt, *Portfolio Management for New Products*, McMaster University, Hamilton, Ontario, Canada, 1997, p. 63.

Many companies use a **strategic buckets** approach for new product portfolio analysis. Figure 3.8 shows how an SBU within Exxon Chemical applied this approach. The business unit has defined two strategic dimensions (product newness and market newness) and has decided on the level of resources to be spent on the product portfolio. Figure 3.8 shows the ideal amount of resources to be allocated to each of the six strategic buckets. If current allocations to, say, improvements to existing products total much more than the desired 35 percent, another product project of this type would be less likely to be funded. The SBU would rather invest in a project of higher product and/or market newness. Both Eastman Chemical and Dow Corning are among the firms that use similar dimensions of technology and market newness to define their strategic categories.[42] As another example, Allied Signal has three strategic categories: platform projects, new products, and minor projects, and it maintains a portfolio within each category.[43]

Senior management can also check strategic balance using a **bubble diagram**. A wide variety of dimensions can be used to construct the diagram, and the example in Figure 3.9 (similar to one used by a division of Hewlett-Packard) uses *extent of product change* and *extent of process change*. Incremental change on both dimensions leads to enhancement products; major change on the product dimension leads to breakthrough (or really new) products. Next-generation products and new product platforms are also represented in the diagram. Too many products in any one region of the diagram represents an imbalance that would have to be rectified.[44]

Another format is given in Figure 3.10, which is a portfolio evaluation model proposed by the Strategic Decision Group (SDG).[45] This method uses expected

[42]The examples are from the Cooper et al. book, pp. 62–63.

[43]Robert G. Cooper, Scott J. Edgett, and Elko J. Kleinschmidt, "New Products, New Solutions: Making Portfolio Management More Effective," *Research-Technology Management*, March—April 2000, pp. 18–33.

[44]Randall L. Englund and Robert J. Graham, "From Experience: Linking Projects to Strategy," *Journal of Product Innovation Management*, 16(1), January 1999, pp. 52–64.

[45]See Robert G. Cooper, *Winning at New Products: Accelerating the Process from Idea to Launch*, 2nd ed. (Reading, MA: Addison-Wesley, 1993), pp. 184–185.

FIGURE 3.9
A Sample
Bubble
Diagram

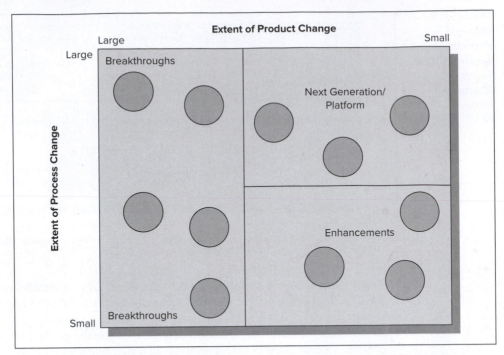

Source: Adapted from a real bubble diagram used by a division of Hewlett-Packard, as reported in Randall L. Englund and Robert J. Graham, "From Experience: Linking Projects to Strategy," *Journal of Product Innovation Management* 16, no. 1, January 1999, pp. 52–64.

commercial value (ECV), measured as the net present value of the future earnings stream, and probability of technical success to build the grid that appears in Figure 3.10. As shown in the grid, four categories emerge. *Oysters* and *Pearls* are projects with high ECV. Pearls are projected to have high technical success as well and are therefore highly desirable. Oysters are currently assessed to have a lower likelihood of technical success but potentially are highly profitable; with additional investment, the firm can "cultivate" some of these into Pearls. On the other side of the grid are the projects with lower ECV. The *Bread and Butter* projects are low risk but low ECV, and typically include incrementally new projects such as extensions and product modifications. *White Elephants* have low ECV and low probability of success and should be avoided. This portfolio model stresses balance between the three desirable categories. As with other portfolio models, the SDG model alerts the firm if it is investing too heavily in incremental Bread and Butter projects, or if it has taken on too many risky Oyster projects.

Finally, a multiple-objective strategic portfolio model, recommended by product portfolio expert Scott Edgett, is shown in Figure 3.11. This one is a kind of extension of the model of Figure 3.8 in that it includes additional objectives to be considered in project selection. In Figure 3.11, a hypothetical SBU will allocate about 18 percent of its resources to disruptive projects: these should number about 10 percent of all projects and will result in about 22 percent of incremental sales. That is, disruptive projects will be a little more expensive on average but will also have higher-than-average payoffs in

FIGURE 3.10
Strategic
Decision
Group
Portfolio
Evaluation
Model

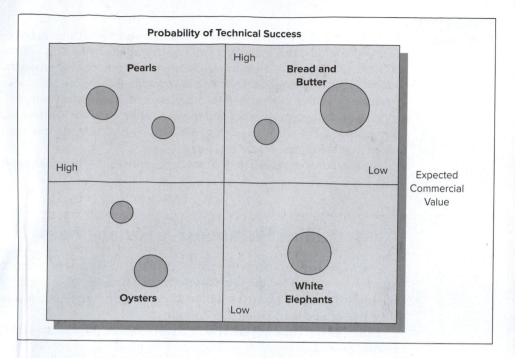

terms of sales. The percentages are interpreted the same way as in Figure 3.8: they are targets for the SBU in making project selection decisions, and if the number of disruptive projects in the pipeline falls below 10 percent, they should be prioritized.

Persistence in applying portfolio techniques is rewarded: Many firms report that their portfolio efforts are weakly implemented, resulting in an unhealthy preference for incremental projects and inefficient resource allocation.[46]

FIGURE 3.11 Portfolio of Product Types

	DISRUPTIVE INNOVATION (New-to-world or new-to-firm)	TECHNOLOGY UPGRADE (Next-generation)	PRODUCT LINE EXTENSION (Additions to product line)	INCREMENTAL INNOVATION (Improvements to existing products)
Number of Projects	10%	12%	32%	46%
Resource Allocation	18%	22%	25%	35%
Incremental Sales	22%	40%	15%	23%

Source: Adapted from Scott Edgett, "Portfolio Management for Product Innovation," in K. B. Kahn, S. E. Kay, R. J. Slotegraaf, and S. Uban (Eds.), *The PDMA Handbook of New Product Development* (Hoboken, NJ: John Wiley), 2013, Ch. 9, p. 162.

[46]Robert G. Cooper, Scott J. Edgett, and Elko J. Kleinschmidt, *Improving New Product Development Performance and Practices, Benchmarking Study* (Houston, TX: American Productivity and Quality Center, 2002).

Summary

Chapter 3 has dealt with the most important and difficult step in the entire new products process: developing a sound strategy to guide the company within the company—the subset of people and resources charged with getting new products. Strategy turns such a group into a miniature firm, a microcosm of the whole. We looked at what such strategic guidance might be—a format here called a product innovation charter. We then studied the opportunities and mandates that yield the charters and how the charters can vary. The chapter ended by looking at some important issues that often arise when discussing new product strategy.

We can now begin the study of concept generation—the subject of four chapters in Part II.

Case: Adidas Ultraboost X Parley Shoes[47]

One of today's major environmental concerns is the volume of pounds of plastic entering the oceans and threatening biodiversity. To address this growing problem, one of the most intriguing initiatives is to reclaim plastic from the oceans and recycle it into fiber that can be used for various purposes.

Parley for the Oceans (Parley) is a nongovernmental association (NGO) dedicated to raising awareness of ocean pollution and to initiating projects to combat the destruction of the oceans. Parley has been a leader in the development of plastic made from upcycled waste from beaches and shore communities. Their product, Parley Ocean Plastic, can be made into a kind of plastic thread.

German sport shoe manufacturer Adidas is a partner and founding member of Parley. Adidas has a healthy corporate social responsibility (CSR) culture and is devoted to meeting CSR obligations. Collaboration with Parley led to the idea of using ocean plastic fibers in the manufacture of running shoes. The Adidas Ultraboost X Parley, whose launch was announced for late 2016, is the first product developed from this collaboration and contained Parley Ocean Plastic fibers and recycled polyester.

Adidas is committed to the recycling and repurposing of ocean-reclaimed plastic material. Seabirds, whales, and other ocean wildlife eat plastic they find in the ocean or get entangled in plastic debris. Adidas management views reclaiming ocean plastic as a cause that they can get behind and make a credible positive environmental impact.

The launch of the Adidas Ultraboost X Parley line is a win-win proposition for both parties. Adidas has decades of experience in designing and manufacturing running shoes and other athletic wear and is a globally recognized brand name. Parley has access to the raw plastic reclaimed from the sea and the ability to produce the plastic fiber required for shoe production. The reclaimed materials are gathered from locations such as the Maldives, then shipped to a Taiwanese supplier for conversion into yarn fiber.

[47]This case was based on Parley's Web site, www.parley.tv, Adidas' Web site, www.adidas.com/us/parley, Adidas' 2015 Sustainability Progress Report available at www.adidas-group.com, and other public sources.

In addition, Adidas did not view this product launch as a one-time deal. Adidas sees the launch of this product as the first step of a long-term commitment to the development of shoes and other athletic apparel based on recycled plastics and polyester in order to establish itself as a leader in eco-friendly athletic products. No other large athletic shoe brand had yet introduced eco-friendly apparel, and this was seen as a very desirable long-term opportunity for Adidas. In fact, Adidas was targeting annual sales of 5 million pairs of shoes from recycled materials within the first couple of years and, eventually, making all of their shoes from recycled material.

In fact, sustainability is a major part of Adidas corporate strategy. The CEO of Adidas Group, Herbert Hainer, noted in the company's 2015 Sustainability Progress Report that Adidas is dedicated to sustainability efforts not only in apparel manufacture but also at the retail level (for example, elimination of plastic bags) and in other ways as well (water reduction, minimal paper use, and so on).

For more background information on Parley, check their Web site at www.parley.tv.

Based on what you have read in this case and what you already know about Adidas and its competitors in athletic wear, reconstruct the PIC that would have driven Adidas in the development of the Adidas Ultraboost X Parley. Do a brief strategic assessment and summarize it into a Background statement. Write out the Focus, being sure to address both the technical and the marketing components, and illustrating how these match and have good potential. What are Adidas' Goals? Also try to infer some of the Guidelines that may have driven this product.

Finally, assuming Adidas is successful with the Adidas Ultraboost X Parley, what new product opportunities would you recommend they pursue next? Justify your choices.

Case: The Honda Element[48]

Honda, like most automakers, is an expert in the use of product platforms. This case takes you through all new products process phases, highlighting how Honda applied its expertise in product platforms to develop a cost-efficient new light truck, the Element, that was highly appealing to the targeted market segment.

The development of the Element began in 1998 with an idea for a new kind of light truck. At the time, Honda was already producing several lines of light trucks and sport utility vehicles (SUVs), including the CR-V, Pilot SUV, and Odyssey minivan. At that time, a new cross-functional team was charged with developing a new light truck to add to this line, targeting a different customer segment and usage situation. In particular, the target was Generation Y males (aged 19–29) about to buy their first car. Gen Y was a potentially lucrative market: It was a sizeable segment, almost as large as the "baby boom" (individuals born between 1946 and 1964). Also, 52 percent of first-time car buyers were in this demographic. In the original business model, Element sales were forecasted to reach about 50,000 units in the first year. This number was based on comparison against CR-V sales, which reached about 100,000 per year in North America.

[48]This case was derived from Marc H. Meyer, "Perspective: How Honda Innovates," *Journal of Product Innovation Management*, 25(3), May 2008, pp. 261–271.

Senior salespeople at Honda recognized that several of their cars and light trucks were popular with young women or with families, but nothing appealed to young men. Honda also knew that several competitors had SUVs in the $20,000 price range that appealed to this segment. Getting loyalty at an early age has always been a strategy of automakers, as they expect that customers will trade up to more expensive or luxurious cars in the line as they become more affluent. For example, an Element buyer might trade up to an Accord, then an Odyssey, through time. Honda was clearly using demographics as a segmentation base and identifying a segment with very high growth potential.

The original charge of the product team was to develop a compelling new design that target users would respond to, while keeping the retail price affordable. Therefore, the first task was to try to understand the core values and beliefs of this unfamiliar segment. Ethnographic "fly-on-the-wall" research was conducted at the X-Games, featuring competitions in extreme events such as hot-dog skiing, snowboarding, and dirt-course motorcycle racing. Researchers with camcorders watched X-Games participants and spectators before, during, and after competitions. Later analysis of the videos provided a clear picture of the young males in the target market: They exhibit strong cohort identification, support social and environmental causes, are well educated, and tend to be less career driven than older segments. These observations provided clues to Honda designers on what features would need to be built in to appeal to this target. For example, typical users of this age group would need a vehicle that provided flexibility: it should be able to easily carry sporting equipment, dorm room furniture, or plenty of friends, and could even serve as sleeping quarters for weekend trips.

Product planners recognized that the light trucks currently in the line each had a clear positioning statement. The CR-V was for single, active individuals or small families; the Pilot was for larger families; and the Odyssey appealed to more settled families. The Element could fill a gap in the positioning map: the light truck for the single individual with an unconventional lifestyle.

Designers realized they would have to build flexibility into the Element's design. It would need a unique appearance and would also have to provide a fun driving experience. In all, four design themes were identified for the Element: adaptability/modularity, authenticity, functionality, and attitude/expression. These were added to the three design themes that drive development of all Honda cars—performance, safety, and value—to get the seven design themes that guided designers and engineers working on the Element.

Several different activities were then conducted simultaneously. Designers sketched several new versions of a bold new exterior appearance. Meanwhile, engineers worked on building in adaptability, focusing on fold-away seats that provided plenty of cargo or sleeping space when folded. Side doors were attached in such as way as to permit easier entry and exit, and the tailgate was also redesigned in a "clamshell" shape to improve access. A removable moon roof would allow the user to carry a tall piece of furniture vertically, with the top part sticking out. Armed with sketches of their progress so far, team members (both engineers and marketers) visited several universities and met with male students at frat houses. After obtaining feedback, they made adjustments and were able to achieve many "quick-turn" improvements.

To get top management support for the Element, the product team invited Honda executives to San Onofre Surfing Beach in California, together with several Gen Y university students, for a weekend camping trip. The group discussed Gen Y lifestyle as well as car issues. The team felt that top management would support the project if they "lived the life" of the target user. It worked. The top executives were convinced of the value of the Element to the Honda car line, and the project got approval. A launch date of late 2003 was chosen.

Once the project was approved, stylists updated their sketches, quarter-size clay models were built, and eventually full-size prototypes were created and submitted to top executives for approval. At the same time, a user group was selected of 30 men in the target age group, all living near Honda's Design Center in Torrance, California. They also reviewed sketches and prototypes, and gradually a design that this group found really interesting was finalized.

Here is where Honda's platform experience was put to use. New car product development is usually broken down into subsystems. In the case of the Element, four subsystems were used: exterior, interior, suspension, and power train. For each, a design strategy was created, and work progressed with periodic review by top management. The exterior subsystem consists of frame, bumpers, windshield, sunroof, tailgate, and so forth. Many of these components were specifically designed for the Element target segment, such as the unique side doors and the clamshell tailgate. The exterior panels were also designed with extra durability. In short, the Element's exterior was different enough from other Honda autos that it had to be designed uniquely, from the ground up. Similarly, the interior was a unique design. The driving principle behind the Element's interior design was the flexibility in cargo storage. The seats could be easily reconfigured into many different positions, or removed entirely. It was also expected that sand or mud would likely find its way into the storage area, so easy cleaning would be required. The flooring was urethane-coated, and electronics were located above the floor or put into waterproof barriers. Even waterproof seat fabric was used.

There was little need to develop a totally unique suspension for the Element, however. The ride needed to be maneuverable, sporty, and fun, and the current CR-V suspension would not have delivered the desired benefits. Honda engineers solved the problem by combining the basic CR-V chassis with the power steering gearbox used in the CR-V, MDX, and Pilot, making the Element wider and lower to the ground, and adding wider tires. Finally, for the power train, they used the existing 2.4 liter VTEC (variable valve timing and emissions control) engine, specifically adapted for the Element to deliver 160 horsepower at 5,500 RPM—plenty of power for the target customer. This engine also provided 26 miles per gallon (highway rating) and met all California emission standards. Since the power train accounts for about 20 to 30 percent of each car's cost of goods, Honda has historically invested in excellent power trains; product teams such as the Element team are actually not authorized to design new power trains but indeed must work with Honda's central Power Train Group. This same engine was used in the 2002 CR-V and Acura RSX, as well as the 2003 Accord. Together with the Element, four different products were supported by the same engine, and any advances made by the Power Train Group benefited all of these products.

In summer 2003, initial manufacturing runs began and early versions of the Element were delivered to dealerships. Marketing worked on finalizing the brand name;

"Element" was the favorite of the user panel and also in research studies with prospective buyers. Communications had to be carefully chosen, given Gen Y's notorious aversion to traditional advertising. Honda selected a more grass-roots approach, creating buzz in auto enthusiast groups, at auto shows, and at colleges. Honda sponsored surf events and tailgate parties at universities, highly unusual for an automaker. More traditional television advertising used a lifestyle theme, showing groups of young Gen Y friends going to the beach or to a party.

The product team's hard work paid off. The Element was named *Automobile Magazine*'s small SUV of the year for 2003, and sales have been good—2004 sales reached 75,000 cars, substantially above the forecast. The biggest surprise was that the Element proved popular across all age groups: 40 percent of Element buyers were in their mid- to late-30s, and baby boomers also bought the Element in large numbers. Still, the buyers were mostly (not totally) male, and lived more active lifestyles than typical Civic buyers. Older buyers seemed to like the fact that it was clearly a young person's car.

Comment on the factors leading to the success of the Element. Include Honda's platform strategy as well as any other aspects of the new products process that you feel are relevant. In your answer, try also to work out what the PIC might have been for the Element. What tangible benefits resulted from bringing in the voice of the customer? What could be learned from this case for firms in industries other than automobile manufacture?

FIGURE II.1

Concept Generation

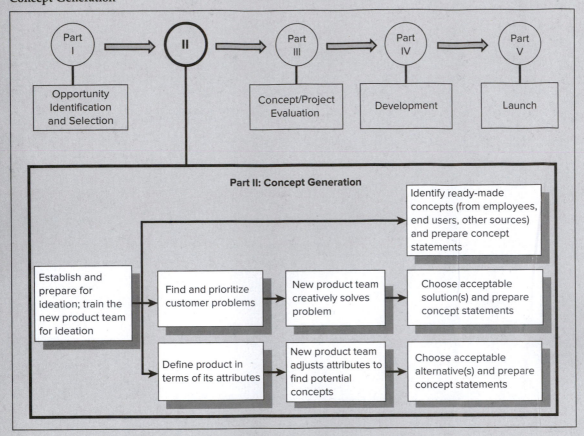

PART TWO

Concept Generation

In Chapters 1 and 2, we saw the overall new products process and learned that the first phase is all about strategic planning—the rationale being that one should seek new products that are best for the particular firm.

Ideation goes on constantly. Many employees of every organization come up with new product possibilities, and the act of creativity could never be constrained into a diagram. But there are common patterns, and we manage those.

Look at Figure II.1. Starting from the left, we see "establish and prepare for ideation," the topic of Chapter 4. People inside and outside the firm don't hold up ideating until we "prepare," of course, but managed creativity is much more successful if we assign much of the task to people with strong creative capabilities. Then, early on, we want to focus on problems and needs. So, by various means, we try to identify and clarify one or more specific problems that creativity can focus on. Identifying problems and finding creative ways to solve them are the subject of Chapter 5. Most of what follows in Part II does just that, but there still is a lot of freelance ideation going on.

In the meantime, as shown in Figure II.1, the new product team (and whoever else is working on this project) is also discovering what "surprise" products can be identified by making adjustments to the attributes of existing products. This is the topic we pursue in Chapter 6. These products, of course, are not problem-driven, so the new product team must find out if someone has a problem that fits the solution. While all of this is going on, people everywhere are telling us about their ideas: employees throughout the organization, their families, even complete strangers. These suggestions will make up another source of concepts, identified in Figure II.1 as ready-made concepts. The consequence of all of this activity is a pool of concepts, and filling this pool is the subject of Chapters 4 to 6. We will take up the issue of evaluating and refining these concepts in Part III of the book.

The Product Concept and Ready-Made New Product Ideas

Setting

This chapter takes us through several topics. First, to managers comes the task of preparing the firm for ideation—the first step in Figure II.1.[1] This means getting the right people, putting them in the correct environment, and generally getting them ready for the ideation process. Second, a creative person needs to know what is being searched for—that is, what is a concept and how is it typically found and identified? Third, you will explore a specific system of active (not reactive) concept generation, including approaches that seem to work. One part of that system—using employees and nonemployees in a search for ready-made ideas—will be discussed in this chapter, and the others will follow in Chapters 5 and 6.

Preparation

Many people think of product innovation beginning with a new product idea. But Chapter 3 showed that it is far better to select a playing field and some rules (have a strategy) before starting the game.

The Product Innovation Charter

Think about these items from a hypothetical charter (Chapter 3) in a firm making bathtubs:

- Our new product concepts should be useful to older people and others with physical handicaps.
- New products coming from these concepts must make use of the firm's strong design capabilities, as well as copper metal.

[1]Anonymous, "Inspiring Innovation," *Harvard Business Review*, August 2002, pp. 39–49.

Assuming the product innovation charter (PIC) work was well done, any person trying to come up with new bathtub ideas for this firm had better know the game plan, or many ideas created will simply be wrong. In a case like this, having a strategy helps.

Creativity and Innovation

Creativity has been described by Craig Wynett, a senior manager at Proctor & Gamble (P&G), as "the everyday task of making nonobvious connections." Firms like P&G that are known for their innovative product programs are also known for being staffed with highly creative people—those that get original ideas with a high degree of usefulness. One such highly creative person was Harry Coover, the discoverer of superglue (cyanoacrylate adhesives). He was working on plastics from which to cast precision gunsights. He noticed that the plastic he was working with stuck to everything and ruined a refractometer he was using to study it with. He also was the first to get the idea that superglues could be used by doctors as an adhesive for human tissues.[2] Harry Coover's example demonstrates that originality and usefulness are both important characteristics of creative ideas.

It is important to understand that creativity and innovation are related but are not synonymous. Creativity is usually defined as an activity at the individual level (such as previously mentioned Mr. Coover), whereas innovation refers to the implementation of a new product or technology at the group or organizational level.[3] Innovations can be based on ideas that are not that creative but are somehow superior. Online banking systems, for example, were based on available Internet technology and not necessarily unexpected or that creative; yet they were considered innovative due to the extent they disrupted the banking industry.[4] The lesson is that creativity at the individual level does not necessarily result in innovation, but it is still a main driver of innovation and, ultimately, the firm's ability to provide value to customers.

Most people think reproductively—solve problems in ways that have worked for us in the past. Creative geniuses think productively, rethinking how to visualize the problem. Nobel Prize–winning physicist Richard Feynman called it "inventing new ways to think." For example, what is half of 13? Most of us would say 6½. But by redefining the problem, we can identify other solutions:

- One half of "thirteen" is "thir."
- One half of "1-3" is "1."
- Cutting XIII horizontally through the middle gives VIII.

[2]Harry W. Coover, "Discovery of Superglue Shows Power of Pursuing the Unexplained," *Research-Technology Management*, September–October 2000, pp. 36–39.

[3]T. M. Amabile, "How To Kill Creativity," *Harvard Business Review*, 76(5), 1998, pp. 76–87; J. Zhou, "When the Presence of Creative Coworkers is Related to Creativity: Role of Supervisor Close Monitoring, Developmental Feedback, and Creative Personality," *Journal of Applied Psychology*, 88 (2003), pp. 413–422.

[4]Drew Boyd and Jacob Goldenberg, "Taming the Creative Spark: Insights from Research on Creativity in New Product Development," in Peter N. Golder and Debanjan Mitra (editors), *Handbook of Research on New Product Development*, Cheltenham, UK: Edward Elgar, 2018, pp. 13–36.

FIGURE 4.1   **Genius Thinking Strategies**

1. Geniuses find many different ways to look at a problem. Einstein, for example, and da Vinci were well known for looking at their problems from many different perspectives.

2. Geniuses make their thoughts visible. Da Vinci's famous sketches and Galileo's diagrams of the planets allowed them to display information visibly rather than relying strictly on mathematical analysis.

3. Geniuses produce. Thomas Edison had a quota of one invention every 10 days. Mozart was among the most prolific composers during his short life.

4. Geniuses make novel combinations. Einstein found the relationship between energy, mass, and the speed of light (the equation $E = mc^2$).

5. Geniuses force relationships. They can make connections where others cannot. The scientist August Kekulé dreamed of a snake biting its tail, immediately suggesting to him that the shape of the molecule he was studying (benzene) was circular.

6. Geniuses think in opposites. This will often suggest a new point of view. Physicist Neils Bohr conceived of light as being both a wave and a particle.

7. Geniuses think metaphorically. Bell thought of a membrane moving steel, and its similarity to the construction of the ear; this led to the development of the telephone earpiece.

8. Geniuses prepare themselves for chance. Fleming was not the first to see mold forming on a culture, but was the first to investigate the mold, which eventually led to the discovery of penicillin.

Source: From Michael Michalko, "Thinking Like a Genius," *The Futurist*, May 1998, pp. 21–25.

Can you think of others? The key here is to keep looking, even after you have found a solution![5] Several thinking strategies seem common to creative geniuses in all walks of life (see Figure 4.1).

A common stereotype is that creative persons are eccentric. While this may not always be the case, creative individuals do announce themselves by leaving a lifetime trail of creative accomplishments. They are creative as children and never become uncreative. This is the bottom line for us, since people being considered for new product team assignments can be evaluated on their past.

Management's Role in Creativity

Certainly, management has a role in getting the best out of its "ideas people." Some firms, like General Electric (GE), seem to truly embrace new ideas, treating them like corporate initiatives, organizing learning sessions, and importantly, sticking with them—rather than moving on to the "next big thing." This stress on business innovation allows GE to gain advantage over competitors who focus solely on financial results.[6] Recent work on idea generation in large organizations suggests that top managers

[5]Michael Michalko, "Thinking Like a Genius," *The Futurist*, May 1998, pp. 21–25. For dozens of problems of this type, try thinks.com/brainteasers. Good luck finding creative solutions!

[6]Thomas H. Davenport and Laurence Prusak with H. James Wilson, *What's the Big Idea? Creating and Capitalizing on the Best Management Thinking* (Cambridge, MA: Harvard Business School Press, 2003).

FIGURE 4.2   Obstacles to Idea Generation

Groupthink: We think we are being creative, when in reality we are only coming up with ideas that our group will find acceptable. Remember that we are not trying to find the "conventional wisdom," but truly original ideas.

Targeting error: We keep going back to the same simple demographic targets (for example, the under-35 or under-50 markets). Great new product opportunities may be missed as a result.

Poor customer knowledge: Despite the money spent on market research by the top firms, the reality is that little is understood about prospective customers. Lavish research spending doesn't guarantee that it was done well.

Complexity: Creative types within organizations, as well as senior management, often think that the more complex the idea, the better it is (or the smarter and more promotable they seem). Complexity, however, is a major barrier to new product adoption (see discussion in Chapter 8).

Lack of empathy: These same managers are also well-educated, high-income individuals accustomed to an upscale lifestyle. They may simply not understand the "typical" customer they are trying to sell to.

Too many cooks: A small new product team works fine, but large companies especially are prone to internal competition for power and influence. This is not a healthy climate for a new product in the earliest phases of development.

Source: Jerry W. Thomas, "In Tough Times, 'Hyper-Creatives' Provide an Advantage," *Visions*, 33(3), October 2009, 24–26.

should keep control over innovative projects while at the same time allowing the employees to do as much of the work as possible. In short, top management must stay involved, and participants who had a hand in the design of the innovation will be more likely to adopt it.[7]

Newly born ideas are extremely fragile, quite the opposite of the strong and almost unstoppable concepts that are 80 percent of the way through the process. By then, many ideas have picked up one or more powerful owners. So, if we give these people a hard time, show no appreciation for their ideas, and offer no particular encouragement, they simply let the ideas slide by, vowing to "not waste my 'genius babies' on those idiots." Figure 4.2 shows the kind of roadblocks that exist within firms and keep them from generating creative new ideas: not knowing the customer, not being empathetic to customers' needs, preferring ideas that everyone agrees with rather than the truly creative ones, and so on.

Management therefore has two packages of activity, one designed to encourage the creative function and the other to remove roadblocks that thwart it. Managers can spark a sense of excitement among their creative people by their attitude toward failure. Innovative types must work in an environment where they are not afraid of failure; if they fail, they learn from these mistakes and keep moving forward.[8]

Activities to Encourage Creativity

Today's managers recognize that innovators are apt to be different and need special treatment. Innovators can't be allowed to violate rules at will, but it's good to recognize individuality, be tolerant of some aberrations, and be accommodative and supportive.

[7]Davenport et al., 2003, p. 171.
[8]"Inspiring Innovation," op. cit.

Also, management should allow innovators freedom to associate with others in similar positions. This freedom extends to all functional areas and to outside the firm as well—no locked cells. Management should also permit innovators to help select projects for development, though this is often difficult. Job assignments should be challenging. Creative people don't lack confidence and, in fact, often consider their present assignments a waste of time. This means *they* will determine whether an assignment is worthy—no one can tell them.

Some firms, such as Google, offer their researchers free time to work on whatever creative projects they want to. Google's Gmail service was one innovative product that sprang from a free time project. Another was 3M's Post-It Notes; 3M is a longtime believer in free time for its employees.[9] A former 3M chairperson once said, "We do expect mistakes as a normal part of running a business, but we expect our mistakes to have originality."[10] Flextime is a similar tool, but for creative types it means letting employees take work home or stay in their workplaces and work all night if they want. Transferring creative personnel also helps. Creative people like novelty and want to change situations occasionally.

One very creative product design firm, IDEO of Palo Alto, California, takes several specific steps to create a culture of creativity and innovation. They seek individuals who love product design; set up offices in cities like Chicago, San Francisco, Boston, and Tokyo that attract creative types; and permit employees to swap positions and locations frequently. IDEO is known for its "deep dive" approach to ideation. In this approach, IDEO personnel from a wide variety of backgrounds work together to better understand a problem, generate multiple solutions, create early working prototypes, get customer feedback, rework, and re-prototype. This iterative and chaotic process continues until a highly creative solution to the original problem is obtained. A video is available, documenting IDEO's development of a new shopping cart, which solves many problems with existing carts (durability, maneuverability, safety for children, ease of use in store, etc.) and creates a very different experience for the shopper. There are many unexpected ways by which shopping carts can be improved![11]

Creative firms often use a computerized database, or *idea bank*, to store and document ideas from earlier, unused new product projects for reuse later. These ideas can come from market research or test market results, project audits, design plans, engineering notes, and elsewhere. To help transfer information, managers that worked on the earlier project can be assigned to the project where the idea might be reused.[12] Guinness Breweries, for one, periodically reviews its idea bank, viewing it as an important component of the concept generation phase of its new products process. Oce, a

[9]Ray Boyer and Rishu Mandolia, "Has the Recession Changed Innovation? Varied Perspectives from Those on the Front Lines of NPD," *Visions*, 34(1), 2010, pp. 6–7.

[10]L. W. Lehr, "The Role of Top Management," *Research Management*, November 1979, pp. 23–25.

[11]For a few of the creative shopping cart ideas imagined by IDEO, check the video at www.youtube.com/watch?v=M66ZU2PCIcM.

[12]Sarah J. Marsh and Gregory N. Stock, "Building Dynamic Capabilities in New Product Development through Intertemporal Integration," *Journal of Product Innovation Management*, 20(2), March 2003, pp. 136–148.

computer peripheral manufacturer, calls this database their "refrigerator of ideas."[13] In general, creative operations should be in areas conducive to exchange of ideas; office arrangements should make people comfortable; and distractions should be held to a minimum. The offices of the Internet startup factory Idealab!, and also IDEO, are laid out such that employees can hear each other's problems and interact with each other as much as possible.[14]

Working with innovation centers is another way to access customer data. The Tmall Inovation Center (TMIC) is the Research and Development (R&D) and innovation unit of Tmall (formerly Taobao Mall), initiated by Alibaba founder Jack Ma. TMIC has access to data on 600 million customers using Alibaba, as well as data on logistics and delivery. Dozens of companies, including P&G, Johnson & Johnson, and Samsung, have partnered with TMIC to obtain customer and market insights that assist them in product development. TMIC has also partnered with worldwide market research firms, including Neilsen and Euromonitor International. TMIC's partners have reported resulting in substantial cuts in time to market. As one example, Mars Inc. developed a spicy Snickers bar specifically for the Chinese market thanks to its partnership with TMIC.[15]

Special Rewards

There is no question about the value of recognizing creative achievement. But creative people are usually unimpressed by *group* rewards. They believe group contributions are never equal, especially if the group is company employees, for many of whom creatives have great disdain. This is unfair; large portions of successful creativity are now set in groups, and we know more now about how to make group judgments work. But creatives do like personal accolades—preferably immediately. The famous Thomas Watson of IBM commonly carried spare cash in his pockets so he could reward persons with good ideas when he heard them. Campbell Soup has Presidential Awards for Excellence. Many firms have annual dinners to recognize employees who obtained patents during the year. At IDEO, there are no organization charts or job titles: Parties and trophies, rather than job promotions, are the rewards for a job well done. In one of the most dramatic reward systems, Toyota and Honda have their champions follow the new product out the door and take over its ongoing management.[16]

The Removal of Roadblocks

As seen in Figure 4.2, some organizations set up roadblocks, perhaps unintentionally, that stop new product concept creativity. Managers will say that the concept "simply won't work," or "it's against policy," or "we don't do things that way." These statements

---

[13]Robert G. Cooper, Scott J. Edgett, and Elko J. Kleinschmidt, "Optimizing the Stage-Gate System: What Best-Practices Companies Do—I," *Research-Technology Management*, September–October 2002, pp. 21–27; Tekla S. Perry, "Designing a Culture for Creativity," *Research-Technology Management*, March–April 1995, pp. 14–17; and Zien and Buckler, op. cit.

[14]Hargadon and Sutton, op. cit.

[15]Asha McLean, "Alibaba's Tmall Innovation Center Uses Data to Help Sellers Develop Products," *ZDNet*, November 12, 2018.

[16]These ideas and many more are discussed in Tekla Perry, "Designing a Culture for Creativity," op. cit.

FIGURE 4.3 **Barriers to Firm Creativity**

1. *Cross-functional diversity.* A diverse team means a wide variety of perspectives and more creative stimulation, but also can lead to difficulties in problem solving and information overload.

2. *Allegiance to functional areas.* The team members need to have a sense of belonging and to feel they have a stake in the team's success. Without this, they will be loyal to their functional area, not to the team.

3. *Social cohesion.* Perhaps a little unexpectedly, if the interpersonal ties between team members are too strong, candid debate might be replaced by friendly agreement, resulting in less innovative ideas.

4. *The role of top management.* If senior management stresses continuous improvement, the team might stick with familiar product development strategies and make only incremental changes. Top management should encourage the team to be adventurous and try newer ideas.

Source: Exhibit from "How to Kill a Team's Creativity," by Rajesh Sethi, Daniel C. Smith, and C. Whan Park, August 2002.

are often well intentioned, and they may be accurate statements of the status quo. But they are extremely discouraging to fragile ideas, and only conscious effort by managers can help scare them away.

Some organizations use a technique called **itemized response**. All client trainees must practice it personally. When an idea comes up, listeners must first cite all its advantages. Then they can address the negatives, but only in a positive mode. The recommended language for bringing up a negative is "OK. Now—let's see what would be the best way to overcome such-and-such a problem." Note that this constructive comment assumes the problem can be overcome, and the listener offers to help. To encourage creativity, some firms deliberately encourage conflict by putting certain employees together on the same team—for example, a blue-sky creative person and a practical type. This technique is sometimes called *creative abrasion.*[17]

The bottom line here is that managers need to be aware of the barriers to group creativity. New product teams are, by definition, cross-functional, which means a greater variety of perspectives but also potential difficulties in reaching a solution acceptable to all. Further, if the team members share strong interpersonal ties, the creative abrasion might be lacking: Team members may simply reach friendly agreements. Figure 4.3 describes these and other barriers to overcome in stimulating group creativity.

The Product Concept

Given creative and exciting people, just what is it we want them to produce? What is this thing called concept? How does it differ from a new product? When does it come about?

Let's start with the end point, the successful marketing of a new product, and back up. A new product only really comes into being when it is *successful*—that is, when it meets the goals/objectives assigned to the project in the PIC. When launched, it is still in tentative form, because changes may still be required to make it successful.

[17]James Krohe Jr., "Managing Creativity," *Across the Board*, September 1996, pp. 16–22.

But going back, before technical work was finished, the product existed solely in concept form. Think back to Figure 2.3, which traced the evolution from concept to product. Very early on, we had "idea concepts," or simply "ideas." We may have hundreds or even thousands of these, and Chapters 4 through 6 discuss methods by which these ideas are generated. These are, simply, starting points, and many of them won't be of any interest—does not fit the PIC, not original enough, not realistic, requires know-how we do not have, and so on. Many of these are screened out quickly. The most promising ones, however, are developed further into concepts, to the point where they can be described to potential customers and early assessments of the concept viability can be made. Back in Chapter 1, we noted that concepts were more fully formed ideas. We will define concepts and the product concept statement more precisely later in this chapter. But for now, let's examine the process by which an idea develops into a concept.

A starting point is to consider three kinds of ideas, which serve as inputs required by the creation process.

- **Form:** This is the physical thing created, or in the case of a service, it is the sequence of steps by which the service will be created. Thus, with a new steel alloy, form is the actual bar or rod of material. On a new mobile phone service, it includes the hardware, software, people, procedures, and so on, by which calls are made and received.

- **Technology:** This is the source by which the form was attained. Thus, for a steel alloy it included, among others, the steel and other chemicals used for the alloy, the science of metallurgy, product forming machines, cutting machines, and more. In most cases, there is one clear technology (or sometimes two) that is at the base of the innovation, the one that served as the technical dimension of the PIC's focus.

- **Need/Benefit:** The product has value only as it provides some benefit to the customer that the customer sees a need for, or has a desire for.

In sum, *technology permits us to develop a form that provides the benefit*. Nevertheless, the innovation process can start with any one of the three dimensions and can vary in what happens second (see Figure 4.4). Here are the primary ways (which we will illustrate with the Designer Decaf example later in this chapter):

The customer has a NEED, which a firm finds out about. It calls on its TECHNOLOGY to produce a FORM that is then sold to the customer.

A firm has a TECHNOLOGY that it matches with a given market group and then finds out a NEED that group has, which is then met by a particular FORM of product.

A firm envisions a FORM of a product, which is then created by use of a TECHNOLOGY and then given to customers to see if it has any BENEFIT.

Any of the three can start the process, and in each case either of the other two can come second. Now, you may say, so what is the difference? The difference is too often that which is between success and failure. Putting benefit last is very risky, since it comprises a solution trying to find a problem. Google invested in the form and technology for Google Glass (a smart wearable device in glasses form), and though the technology might be used in some product in the future, the original concept never went past protoype and was terminated in early 2015. Even though it worked as

FIGURE 4.4
The New
Product
Concept

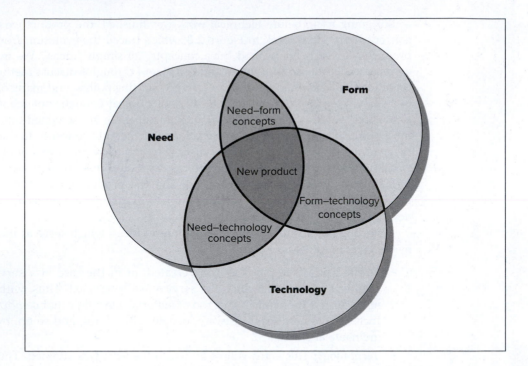

promised, potential customers did not see the added benefit, especially considering the $1,500 retail price. Therefore, we often put benefit first. Even technology-driven scientists actually put benefit first in most cases because they have some idea of need that is leading them in their efforts. For example, a pharmaceutical chemist seeking a new compound for lowering blood pressure knows how widespread that problem is.

Think about improving the convenience of using toilet brushes. Old-fashioned brushes do the job, but one could imagine someone (a thoughtful customer, perhaps, or a research chemist at a detergent company) having the idea that a new, improved brush that somehow makes toilet cleaning easier would be a big seller. Note that we said "idea" here and not "concept," as all we have so far is a need: a new brush that offers the benefit of convenience. What does that mean? Longer handle? Disposable bristles? Probably not. How about a brush that contains detergent, which is refillable and easy for the customer to attach to the brush? Now we have something resembling a simple product concept, as we have a need (convenient brush) based on use of a technology (detergent suitable for toilet scrubbing). Apparently at least three companies hit upon that concept at about the same time a few years back. But these companies developed and launched products whose forms are very different. Reckitt Benckiser produced the Lysol Ready Brush: An aerosol can of cleanser is mounted into the brush. The can is replaced when empty; the brush is not disposable. SC Johnson's entry is the Scrubbing Bubbles Fresh Brush: Here, a disposable pad containing Scrubbing Bubbles cleaner is attached to the end of the brush. The Clorox Toilet Wand is much like the Fresh Brush, but with a round, disposable sponge instead of a pad. Think of this as a kind of translation process: In each case, the idea was developed into a concept, but the concept was translated three different ways, resulting in three different products (that offer pretty much the same benefit to customers).

This simple example suggests that the product concept is very flexible, especially now during the front end of the innovation process. Any one concept can be used to generate additional concepts, by making changes to need, form, or technology. Think of the components shown in Figure 4.4 as building blocks, and that replacing one block with another creates a product concept that might even be better than the original one. For example, start with the Scrubbing Bubbles Fresh Brush, change the form (replace pad with sponge), and you have the Clorox Toilet Wand. Change the technology (replace the detergent in the sponge with air freshener) and you have a brush that performs a different task. Or, if you designed a brush that scrubbed bathtubs and tiles instead of toilet bowls, you would be meeting a different customer need. In this way, dozens more concepts could be identified by replacing one or more of these building blocks.

Let's put this all into a simple case, and maybe the issues will become clearer.

The Designer Decaf Example

Many years ago, coffee was, well, coffee. One went to a favorite restaurant, diner, or food truck in the morning or at lunch and ordered an inexpensive "regular." Typically, coffee sold in North America contained a blend of cheaper coffee beans, and that was that. With the emergence of Starbucks and competitors, the North American coffee-drinking culture changed abruptly. Fancy coffee bars, based on the Italian coffee bar model, sprang up everywhere, and Italian-style espresso soared in popularity. Espressos, cappuccinos, and lattes, often selling for three to four times the price of restaurant coffee, became big sellers overnight. Let's imagine we worked at a major coffee roasting company at about this time. Imagine also three different people walked into the new product office one week, at different times, each with an idea for a new product. Each was unaware the others were coming in.

One person said, "Our most recent customer satisfaction report showed that customers would like a decaffeinated espresso coffee that tastes identical to regular espresso and can deliver a full-flavored cappuccino. No current decafs offer this *benefit*." The second person was a product manager who said, "I was thinking last week about our coffees and our competitors, and noticed they were all about the same color and thickness. I wonder if we could mass-produce a darker espresso that actually pours out thicker, something like Turkish coffee" (*form*). The third person was a scientist who had just returned from a technical forum and said, "I heard discussion of a new chemical extraction process that can isolate and separate chemicals from foods cheaply and effectively; maybe it could be applied to taking caffeine out of coffee" (*technology*).

Each of these people had a germ of an idea, but as a concept each suggestion wasn't really very useful. The first person had something on a par with a cancer cure—benefit, but no way to supply it. The product manager had no idea whether consumers would like darker, thicker espresso or how it might be made. The scientist didn't know whether the technology would work on coffee or even whether consumers wanted a change.

A new product concept would result if the first person met with either the second or the third. If the second, they would ask the lab for a technology that would produce the sought form and benefit. If the third, they would undertake lab work to find the exact form of the new technology (for example, should all or only some of the caffeine be extracted; if darker or thicker in appearance, how dark or thick). What might best sum up the point that a concept is evolving from its creation until it metamorphoses into a new product is the saying of one manager: "Don't waste your time trying to find a *great* new product idea; it's our job to take a rather ordinary idea and *make it* into a successful new product."

The Product Concept Statement

Figure 4.4 showed that any two of the three types of ideas (form, benefit, technology) can come together to make a concept, a potential product. All three together produce a new product that may or may not be successful. Often, there is little difference. For example, inventors frequently call on companies with a prototype in hand. This is a concept that is virtually finished—it has form, based on a technology, and you can be sure the inventor knows a benefit it provides. Of course, firms know from experience that the inventor usually overstates the benefit; the technology will have drawbacks that make it impractical to use in a plant; and the form is very tentative, based primarily on tools and space in a crude workshop.

At the other extreme, the very first thought about a new product may be so incomplete that nothing can be done with it as is. For example, the scientist returning from the technical forum had only capability—nothing that had value to anyone in the coffee roasting company.

A key difference, then, between an idea and a concept is that the concept is developed to the extent that it can be tested with potential customers. We explore concept testing in Chapter 7, and a required input to this test is the **product concept statement**. Technical people and intended customers must tell us the concept is worthy of development. Their review of the concept statement allows this *if* the concept tells them what they need to know to make that judgment. A concept statement will usually do this if it has two of the three basic essentials (technology, form, benefit).

If you were asked, "How would you like zero-calorie ice cream?" you could not really answer. You probably already find yourself thinking, what will it taste like, what is it made of, what's the catch? To do concept testing, we need a concept statement that meets these information needs. What if you wanted to design a fork that would help people eat more slowly, which would reduce digestive problems, minimize gastric reflux, and (importantly) help people lose weight? What we have at this point is a concept, of course, since we have the form (a fork) and a customer benefit (weight loss and other positive health outcomes). Now, if there is customer interest in this concept, the firm can add the technology component: the R&D people can develop the technical specifications and begin making prototypes. In this case, it would require developing software that keeps track of a person's eating habits (as well as other metrics such as time spent on exercise or sleep), as well as an indicator that flashes or vibrates if the person is eating too fast. The technical side is likely to be challenging and possibly costly, so it is good to know at this early stage if the concept is not likely to be popular and time and effort is not wasted. (This product exists and is sold under the name Hapifork.)[18]

---

[18]See www.hapifork.com for details on the Hapifork and its manufacturer, Hapilabs. For a review of this product, see this video: www.youtube.com/watch?v=7ih2dArEl3E.

FIGURE 4.5   **Why Do You Need At Least Two Inputs?**

The customer needs to be able to judge whether the concept is worthy of development into a product.

If you just have an idea (the benefit, the form, or the technology), potential customers do not have enough information to judge its worthiness and will be unable to state how much they like the product or their purchase intentions.

The product concept statement (providing benefit, form, and technology, or at least two of these) gives potential customers the required information. One can get a rough but useful early read on customer liking and purchase intention based on their reactions to the product concept.

An idea: "Would you buy our great new office printer? It prints 120 pages a minute!" On a 5-point scale, how likely would you be to buy this printer?

- Very likely
- Somewhat likely
- Not sure
- Somewhat unlikely
- Very unlikely

You can't answer this! You will no doubt wonder how much it costs, how big it is, whether the pages print neatly, whether it jams up, or even if the claim is believable!

A product concept statement, then, is *a claim of proposed customer value*. It takes the form of a *verbal and/or prototype expression that describes need, form, and technology (at least two of these), and how the customer stands to gain (and lose)*. It should clearly relate the product's features (form and technology) to the customer benefit delivered. The statement could be simply a written description, or it may include a sketch, picture, or (increasingly) a 3D printed model of the concept. Early on, the information is quite incomplete, but when marketed, the concept is (hopefully) complete. Anything that doesn't communicate gain and loss to the intended buyer is still just an idea that needs work. The distinction between idea and concept is illustrated in Figure 4.5.

The importance of these three dimensions varies by industry. In most industries, one of the three often needs no attention because of general knowledge within the industry. Pharmaceutical researchers do not have to check out the desirability of a new drug that eliminates cancer. Furthermore, pharmaceutical expertise is available to manufacture virtually any new drug, so technology is the only unknown and thus the focus of attention. On the other hand, the leading food companies presume the kitchens and factory can put together anything the customer wants, so benefit (ascertained through taste tests, for example) becomes the prime variable. In the automobile industry, car manufacturers so dominate the new products process that components suppliers are told what benefit is wanted and then work with either technology or form for its innovation.

In these three different industry situations, discussion with new products people quickly indicates the critical avenue of innovation for *their* firm or industry. And the distinctions are not moot—they provide the direction for the idea stimulation process. Still, it takes all three. If a project aborts, it may be the fault of the department with the easy task. For example, Apple's marketing research may show that consumers want a phone that is lighter, thinner, and more durable. This research engenders the idea for the new product, so the process would be demand-induced. But, in reality, the technical side of the business has the toughest task. Choosing different materials to make the phone lighter and thinner might make it less durable or even lead to unforeseen problems (the phone bends if you have it in your back pocket and sit down on it).

Approaches to Concept Generation

Now that we have a clear definition of the product concept, how should we go about generating new product concepts? The diagram given in the figure at the start of Part II showed five routes—technology, end user, the product team, other insiders, and other outsiders. To manage these different sources, it is useful to think in terms of three concept generation approaches. Some concepts are "ready-made:" they exist in the minds of employees, managers, customers, partner firms, and so on, and our job is to identify these. We can add to this pool of concepts by getting customers to identify problems and thinking creatively about how best to solve them (the problem-find-solve approach) or by thinking about existing products and how we might alter them (the analytical attribute approach). In this chapter, we will discuss ready-made concepts; Chapters 5 and 6 examine the other approaches in turn.

Some manufacturers have employee and customer idea contests. In the food industry, Pillsbury runs an annual Bake-Off Contest to capture thousands of new recipes for their possible use. Google, Merck, and Michelin are among many firms that have grassroots initiatives to encourage employees to generate innovation. A famous example is Dell's EmployeeStorm, which permits employees to suggest and vote on ideas using an internal social media platform. A benefit of such programs is that it makes employees feel appreciated and encourages communication.[19] Another approach is to work closely with university labs or other research facilities. Microsoft is building an innovation hub in Durham, North Carolina (home of Duke University), designed to let university faculty and students use its cloud computing platform and to work closely with Microsoft personnel to create innovative technology.[20]

One thing we know for sure, concept generation should be an *active*, not *reactive* process. This is no time to be thinking like the Maytag repairman, waiting for something to happen.

Important Sources of Ready-Made New Product Ideas

Experience in the field of product innovation suggests that a large percentage of new product ideas are of the ready-made variety, coming from a wide variety of sources (see Figure 4.6). These include **inside sources**, or employees from all levels of the organization. Sometimes it is the chief operating officer (CEO) whose vision spearheads innovation wthin the organization; Richard Branson or Elon Musk come to mind.

Many firms are turning to formal methods to tap into ideas from customers and external stakeholders, such as suppliers. *User toolkits, crowdsourcing,* and *lead user analysis* are

[19]Elio Keko, Gert Jan Prevo, and Stefan Stremersch, "The What, Who and How of Innovation Generation," in Peter N. Golder and Debanjan Mitra (eds.), *Handbook of Research on New Product Development*, Cheltenham, UK: Edward Elgar, 2018, pp. 37–59.

[20]Ben Graham, "Microsoft Partnering with Duke in Downtown Durham," *bizjournals.com*, July 10, 2018.

FIGURE 4.6
Sources of
Ready-Made
New Product
Concepts

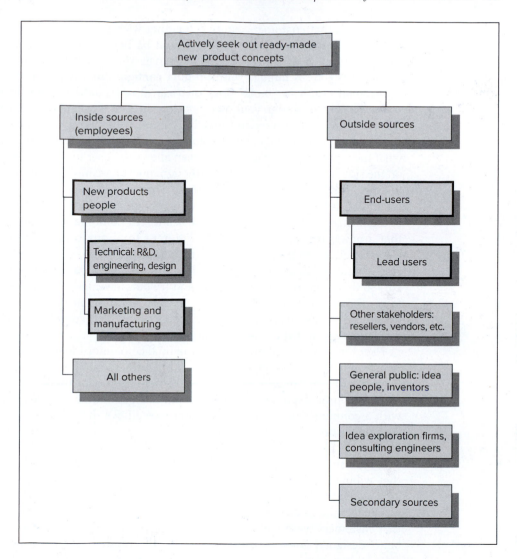

valuable ways to source customer ideas; many companies have adopted an *open innovation* framework to source from a wide range of external partners. Let's examine each of these methods in turn. For information on many other common sources of ready-made ideas, please see the brief discussion in Appendix A, at the end of this book.

User Toolkits and Customization

Some firms are turning to **user toolkits**, a method that formally turns the innovation task over, to some extent, to the users themselves.[21] A toolkit is a user-friendly set of

[21]Eric von Hippel, "Toolkits for User Innovation," in P. Belliveau, A. Griffin, and S. M. Somermeyer, *The PDMA Toolbook 2 for New Product Development* (New York: John Wiley, 2004).

design tools that customers can use, together with their understanding of their own needs, to customize a product that would be best suited to them. The customer-designed product can then be directly transferred to manufacturing or production. Almost everyone is familiar with **product configurators**, which are a simple kind of user toolkit. You can "build" your own car at www.fiat.com or your own laptop at www.dell.com, or design your own running shoes at www.nike.com. These configurators allow the user to mix and match different components (for a car, this might be engine size, interior and exterior colors, hubcaps, audio system, and so forth) and see what the retail price would be. Nike even allows the user to select a message to appear on the sides or tongues of the shoes (though, not surprisingly, the user is not permitted to enter "Buy Adidas"). In essence, these firms are practicing **mass customization**, at least to some extent, in which the user is a "segment of one." The Fiat webpage once boasted there were more than 500,000 different combinations, almost guaranteeing that a newly ordered car would be different from any other. (The cereal franchise Cereality claims to have a "gazillion" combinations of cereals and toppings on its Web site, www.cereality.com.) Coca-Cola has hundreds of soda machines with several flavors so that customers can mix them and try out new combinations. Not only is this a form of mass customization (customers can pick unique flavor combinations), but Coca-Cola tracks customer selections, observes which combinations seem popular, and gets ideas for future new products.[22]

User toolkits are not only for getting final consumer ideas. Figure 4.7 shows how two companies use user toolkits in a business-to-business setting: International Flavors and Fragrances provides an Internet-based user toolkit to design specialty flavors for processed foods; 3M's Telecom Enclosure division provides its customers with a computer-aided design program that allows them to design their own telecom enclosure, which is then reworked with the assistance of 3M until an ideal design is achieved.

Do consumers like being able to design their own products and services? And are they willing to pay a modest increase in price to do so? It seems the answer is yes, so long as the toolkit is fun to use and easy to learn, as is the case with most consumer product configurators. Product researcher Nikolaus Franke and his colleagues found that customers were willing to pay more for user-designed watches (not necessarily better-designed ones) than for comparable off-the-shelf ones, because they are more suited to the customer's unique preferences. Another study by Franke, which involved user-designed scarves, showed that the willingness to pay was higher if customers really enjoyed using the configurator. In addition, the more customers thought the scarf design was a success, the more they felt a sense of accomplishment.[23] On the

[22]Gary R. Schirr, "User Research for Product Innovation: Qualitative Methods," in K. B. Kahn, S. E. Kay, R. J. Slotegraaf, and S. Uban (eds.), *The PDMA Handbook of New Product* Development, Hoboken, NJ: Wiley, 2013, Ch. 14, pp. 239–240.

[23]The watch example is from N. Franke and F. Piller, "Value Creation by Toolkits for User Innovation and Design: The Case of the Watch Market," *Journal of Product Innovation Management*, 21(6), 2004, pp. 401–415; the scarf example is from N. Franke and M. Schreier, "Why Customers Value Self-Designed Products: The Importance of Process Effort and Enjoyment," *Journal of Product Innovation Management*, 27(7), 2010, pp. 1020–1031.

FIGURE 4.7   Two Examples of Toolkits for User Innovation*

International Flavors and Fragrances (IFF)

This company makes specialty flavors added into processed foods. Typically, a customer would place a requirement, such as a "meaty flavor to add to a soy product," and IFF starts working. A sample might be shipped back to the customer within a week. The trouble is that the customer firm may not be entirely happy, but finds it difficult to define exactly what it wants (e.g., "make it 'gutsier'"). Several iterations might need to occur between IFF and the customer before the latter is satisfied. This is especially problematic to IFF since customers typically expect they will get it right the first time.

To respond to this problem, IFF created an Internet-based user toolkit that provides a huge database of flavor profiles as well as design rules used in combining or modifying these. The actual chemical formulations are not provided in the toolkit, of course, in order to protect IFF's intellectual property. The customer firm now can design its own flavor and send it directiy to a machine that will make up a sample within a few minutes. The customer can easily make adjustments, using the easy-to-understand customer interface appearing on the computer screen, until the desired flavor is obtained.

3M Telecom Enclosure Division

This 3M division makes enclosures for telecom firms like Verizon, used in mounting external equipment. In the past, a telecom customer firm would give 3M the equipment about to be installed in a customized enclosure, and 3M would design the appropriate enclosure using a CAD program. The customer checks the design, and may at that point rethink the required equipment or some other part of the specification. As in the above example, numerous iterations might occur.

3M's solution is to provide the customer with a simple-to-use version of its own CAD program. (As above, intellectual property rights are protected by providing customers with only the customer-interface parts of the program.) The customer inputs the required equipment and other specifications, and allows the program to do its work. It can make whatever adjustments are necessary until satisfied, then sends the complete design back to 3M that can then put it right into production.

Source: Examples are from Eric von Hippel, "Toolkits for User Innovation," in P. Belliveau, A. Griffin, and S.M. Somermeyer, *The PDMA Toolbook 2 for New Product Development*, John Wiley & Sons, Inc., 2004.

other hand, there are some situations where customers value professional design over user design, such as luxury fashion brands.[24]

All of the above are examples of simple consumer products; we know less about other applications. Often, customizing business-to-business products with user toolkits is more challenging to the user. Learning to use the flavor toolkits in Figure 4.7, for example, is hard work, and if proper training is not provided, that positive sense of accomplishment (and higher willingness to pay) might be replaced with negative feelings of "too stressful" or "too difficult." We are also learning more about the value that consumers get from the toolkit. New research suggests that it may be better to make the toolkit a "learning instrument" so that consumers can interact with the toolkit and learn insights about their preferences.[25] We do not have all the answers yet, but manufacturers of business products can learn from the consumer product examples shown here.

[24]Christoph Fuchs, Emanuella Prandelli, Martin Schreier, and Darren W. Dahl, "All That Is Users Might Not Be Gold: How Labeling Products as User Designed Backfires in the Context of Luxury Fashion Brands," *Journal of Marketing*, 77(3), 2013, pp. 75–91.

[25]Nikolaus Franke and Christoph Hader, "Mass or Only 'Niche Customization'? Why We Should Interpret Configuration Toolkits as Learning Instruments," *Journal of Product Innovation Management*, 31(6), 2014, pp. 1214–1234.

Virtual reality is also a possibility in product customization. Audi allows car buyers to customize their own car and visualize it in realistic lighting conditions, using Oculus Rift technology set up at dealerships worldwide. Using Oculus for Business (which contains Oculus Rift, touch controllers, sensors, and facial interfaces), customers can change exterior and interior colors, change engine specifications, or add options to build their dream car and then visualize it in a familiar setting, including realistic lighting conditions. In addition to being fun and exciting for car buyers, it also provides them with plenty of information that can help them make a purchase decision.[26]

Crowdsourcing

Many firms will attempt to obtain product ideas from large groups of customers. This open idea solicitation is known as **crowdsourcing**.[27] While the idea of sending out an open call for suggestions is not new, this technique has become prevalent since the advent of online crowdsourcing.

Dell's IdeaStorm initiative encouraged customers to submit ideas for new products and improvements to existing products online. Over 10,000 ideas were obtained from sources around the world.[28] It was reported that Apple made use of crowdsourcing in generating ideas for the iPad. Apple monitored reviews and customer blogs, and also obtained voice of the customer data, to understand the most pressing needs of potential users, not just of the iPad tablet itself but also of related devices such as the iPhone.[29]

Crowdsourcing has rapidly caught on, and with good reason, since it provides input on customer needs directly from the customers themselves. Starbucks set up a community Web site in 2008, My Starbucks Idea, allowing members to share, discuss, and vote on ideas and to provide feedback on implemented ideas. Starbucks claims to have received over 70,000 user-generated ideas and has implemented hundreds of ideas, including free Wi-Fi in stores, free drink reward coupons, and innovative coffee flavors.[30] As another example, Ford set up the "City of Tomorrow Challenge," which used crowdsourcing to identify creative ideas to minimize traffic congestion in urban settings, focusing initially on Grand Rapids, Pittsburgh, and Miami. The best ideas are feasible within the existing transportation system and can be quickly implemented. A sample idea: using artificial intelligence to synchronize traffic lights and improve efficiency. The cities benefit from improved quality of life for residents and a

---

[26]Rebecca Hills-Duty, "Auto Dealerships Launch VR Experiences," *VR Focus*, August 31, 2017; Rebecca Hills-Duty, "Customize Your Car With Oculus Rift," *VR Focus*, October 12, 2017.

[27]A source on crowdsourcing is Gary P. Pisano and Roberto Verganti, "Which Kind of Collaboration Is Right for You?" *Harvard Business Review*, 86(12), 2008, pp. 78–86.

[28]B. L. Bayus, "Crowdsourcing New Product Ideas Over Time: An Analysis of the Dell IdeaStorm Community," *Management Science*, 59(1), 2013, pp. 226–244.

[29]Reena Jana, "Apple iPad Product Development Approach," The Conversation blog, *Harvard Business Review*, January 27, 2010.

[30]Elio Keko, Gert Jan Prevo, and Stefan Stremersch, "The What, Who, and How of Innovation Generation," in Peter N. Golder and Debanjan Mitra (eds.), *Handbook of Research on New Product Development*, Cheltenham, UK, Edward Elgar, 2018, pp. 37–59.

more hospitable setting for businesses. At the same time, Ford learns about, and can prepare for, the future of urban transportation.[31]

As a further example of crowdsourcing, Threadless invites users to submit designs for T-shirts to its Web site, www.threadless.com, and encourages users to vote on their favorite designs, which the company then produces and sells. Since awareness of new offerings is done totally on the Web site, the online community also has a big part in the marketing of the T-shirts as well. Another crowdsourced initiative familiar to everyone is Wikipedia, which depends on its contributor community to create and maintain its online encyclopedia.[32]

Crowdsourcing also occurs in business-to-business markets. Innocentive provides technical crowdsourcing for large pharmaceutical firms, including Eli Lilly (which was a financial backer), as well as many consumer-goods firms such as P&G. Innocentive offers a fee to the technical expert that can identify the best solution. Netflix tried the crowdsourcing route by holding a contest when it needed a better algorithm to select movie recommendations based on previous viewing behavior.[33] We will further explore the use of online communities in idea generation in the next chapter.

Crowdsourcing has advantages over other techniques, such as lead users, due to the "wisdom of the crowds." That is, the sheer number of participants makes it more likely that at least a couple of fantastic ideas emerge. The best idea from a crowd of 1,000 average customers may outshine the best idea of 10 lead users. In a real-life application, crowdsourced ideas for new baby products had higher novelty and offered more customer benefits than ideas that came from new product professionals.[34] Nevertheless, it is most helpful if the solution can be obtained relatively easily, since the respondents receive little or no guidance from the sponsoring company. For more difficult or specific tasks, or those that require interaction between manufacturer and solution provider, lead users will be a more useful approach.[35] When left to their own devices, crowdsourcing can lead to misleading results, since a less desirable or even useless idea may pick up crowd support. A 2016 crowdsourcing competition was held by the U.K. Natural Environment Research Council to name a new polar research vessel, and the overwhelming winning name was "Boaty McBoatface."[36]

[31]Anonymous, "Ford Launches Crowdsourcing Platform to Improve Mobility in Grand Rapids," *csengineermag.com*, June 28, 2018.

[32]Elio Keko, Gert Jan Prevo, and Stefan Stremersch, "The What, Who, and How of Innovation Generation," op. cit.

[33]The Threadless, Innocentive, and Netflix examples are from Gary R. Schirr, "User Research for Product Innovation: Qualitative Methods," op. cit., p. 237; see also A. Afuah and C. L. Tucci, "Crowdsourcing as a Solution to Distant Search," *Academy of Management Review*, 37(3), 2012, pp. 355–375.

[34]Marion K. Poetz and Martin Schreier, "The Value of Crowdsourcing: Can Users Really Compete With Professionals in Generating New Product Ideas," *Journal of Product Innovation Management*, 29(12), 2012, pp. 245–256.

[35]Nikolaus Franke, "Lead User Analysis," in Praveen Gupta and Brett E. Trusko (eds.), *Global Innovation Science Handbook*, New York: McGraw-Hill, 2014, pp. 303–320.

[36]Valentina Zarya, "'Boaty McBoatface' Is What Happens When You Ask the Internet to Name Your Ship," *Fortune*, March 21, 2016.

Crowdsourcing is most likely to generate modest product improvements rather than new-to-the-world products. In such cases, the expertise provided by lead users will be more helpful. Also, the typical user is less likely to come up with ideas that are easily developed into real products: Product development professionals (or more experienced users) will have a more realistic view of what is and is not feasible.[37] The role of the end user also depends on the industry. For example, manufacturers of scientific instruments and plant process equipment report the *majority* of their successful new products came originally from customers. In other industries, such as engineering polymers and chemical additives for plastics, customers may provide less help.

Lead Users

Lead users are customers who currently are experiencing needs that are not yet common in the marketplace but may be in coming months or years.[38] They are, by definition, at the front edge of a current trend, have the best understanding of the problems faced, and expect to gain significantly from solutions to those problems. Lead users can often be easy to identify: a cutting-edge research hospital may require measurement equipment with much more accuracy than what is commercially available for a new procedure they are researching. If this procedure is accepted in the medical community, there will be need for a highly accurate device at countless hospitals and clinics around the world in a matter of years. For this reason, lead users can help a company anticipate future customer needs. In fact, the research hospital staff, finding no suitable device available, may even have built their own prototype or otherwise improvised a solution. As another example, when carmakers needed to find lighter and stronger materials for car manufacture in order to boost efficiency, they looked to aerospace researchers who had already faced and overcome similar efficiency issues.[39] Lead users are therefore doubly valuable for product developers to partner with: they not only help identify upcoming customer needs, but they may also have already begun the process of solving these needs. Since the trends is still evolving, the product developer can work with the lead user to anticipate the next need and further develop the product.

One issue in lead user analysis is identifying lead users. While this will certainly depend on the product in question, it is possible that the lead users may display key

[37]Per Kristensson, Anders Gustafsson, and Trevor Archer, "Harnessing the Creative Potential among Users," *Journal of Product Innovation Management*, 21(1), January 2004, pp. 4–14. For an excellent resource on the importance of establishing a dialogue with customers, see C. K. Prahalad and Venkat Ramaswamy, *The Future of Competition: Co-Creating Unique Value with Customers* (Cambridge, MA: Harvard Business School, 2004).

[38]The best summaries regarding lead user analysis are Eric von Hippel, *The Sources of Innovation* (New York: Oxford University Press, 1988); and Lee Meadows, "Lead User Research and Trend Mapping," in P. Belliveau, A. Griffin, and S. M. Somermeyer (eds.), *The PDMA Toolbook for New Product Development* (New York: John Wiley, 2002), pp. 243–265.

[39]Eric von Hippel, *Democratizing Innovation*, Cambridge, MA: MIT Press, 2005; G. L. Lilien, P. D. Morrison, K. Searls, M. Sonnack, and E. von Hippel, "Performance Assessment of the Lead User Idea-Generation Process for New Product Development," *Management Science*, 48(8), 2002, pp. 1042–1059.

characteristics. In a study of product development in kite surfing, Nikolaus Franke and his coauthors found two characteristics that could identify lead users: high expected benefits and being "ahead of the trend." These characteristics identified people who were more likely to come up with commercially attractive innovations.[40]

For example, suppose your firm makes snowboards for use by extreme athletes in competitions such as the X-Games. Where should you look for product ideas? While there are always improvements in equipment for established sports such as football or golf, there are many, many more uncertainties in designing products such as high-performance snowboards. The top athletes are even today still creating new moves and pushing the boundaries of the sport. So what should your next generation of snowboard be like? Shorter? Longer? Lighter? Heavier? Wider? More aerodynamic? More flexible? How would you know, and whom should you ask? It is those very same top athletes who would know—they are your lead users. They may care little about the appearance of the board, as they are most concerned about improving high-level performance. By partnering with these athletes, your firm would be able to develop radical new snowboards that address these rapidly emerging needs. What is more, these same athletes are also quicker to adopt new products than ordinary users and are therefore also influential in speeding adoption of your new product in the marketplace.[41]

Open Innovation[42]

Many firms have adopted the *open innovation* model. Open innovation has been defined as "the use of ... inflows and outflows of knowledge to accelerate internal innovation, and expand the markets for external use of innovation."[43] This defnition shows that open innovation works in two directions. *Inbound open innovation* refers to working with external partner firms to develop or obtain required technology or know-how and thereby speed up product innovation. *Outbound open innovation* refers to monetizing innovation through external partners (for example, selling intellectual property or finding licensees for patents that would otherwise not be exploited).[44]

The first advocate of open innovation was Henry Chesbrough, who viewed it as a new paradigm for innovation in which the firm makes a strategic commitment to use

[40]Nikolaus Franke, Eric von Hippel, and Martin Schreier, "Finding Commercially Attractive User Innovations: A Test of Lead-User Theory," *Journal of Product Innovation Management*, 23(4), July 2006, pp. 301–315.

[41]Martin Schreier and Reinhard Prügl, "Extending Lead-User Theory: Antecedents and Consequences of Consumers' Lead Userness," *Journal of Product Innovation Management*, 25(4), 2008, pp. 331–346.

[42]Much of this section was derived from Henry Chesbrough, *Open Innovation: The New Imperative for Creating and Profiting from Technology* (Boston, MA: Harvard Business School Press, 2003); Henry Chesbrough, "Why Companies Should Have Open Business Models," *Sloan Management Review*, 48(2), Winter 2007; and Henry Chesbrough and Melissa M. Appleyard, "Open Innovation and Strategy," *California Management Review*, 50(1), Fall 2007.

[43]O. Gassmann, E. Enkel, and H. Chesbrough, "The Future of Open Innovation," *R&D Management*, 40(3), 2010, pp. 213–221.

[44]Roger J. Calantone and Hang T. Nguyen, "Open Innovation in the Brand Management Context," in Peter N. Golder and Debanjan Mitra (eds.), *Handbook of Research on New Product Development*, Cheltenham, UK, Edward Elgar, 2018, pp. 250–263.

the knowledge in the external environment to improve innovation performance. That is, open innovation should be thought of not as a single technique for product development but as a whole new way of thinking about how to compete in today's business climate.[45]

For years, firms have sought to externally acquire technologies that they lack, but on an as-needed basis. Outsourcing is common, for example, in the pharmaceutical industry, where top firms such as Eli Lilly and GlaxoSmithKline outsource a substantial amount of their new product research due to the enormous costs involved in new drug product discovery, development, regulatory approval, and launch.[46] Under an open innovation policy, firms start with the understanding that much, if not most, of the knowledge they could use resides outside the firm (that is, "not all the smart people work for us"). They systematically and intentionally set out to acquire knowledge from external resources to complement their own internal resources and accelerate innovation. Accessing this innovative pool is critical, even more so as global competition heats up. The result, ultimately, is improved joint value for all partners. And, as noted earlier, open innovation does not stop with inflows of knowledge. Inevitably, a firm will have invested in innovations that they ultimately don't use: They may no longer fit their business model, for example. Through outbound open innovation, a firm could spin off this innovation (sell outright to a willing buyer), offer it under license, form a joint venture with a partner, or otherwise profit from it.[47]

Open innovation does not mean that the firm outsources its R&D. Rather, the firm's goal is to reach out beyond its familiar research partners and to access R&D carried out globally, so that it will complement the know-how it develops internally. By partnering with an outside firm, the innovating firm leverages and supports its *own* R&D and product development staff. In a sense, intellectual property (IP) in open innovation is like building blocks that allow the firm to build and execute its business model. A firm can acquire IP from a partner if it supports its business model; and it can profit from an unused IP building block if another firm has a use for it. Aside from these obvious leverage advantages, the firm benefits in other ways: It has a much larger pool of innovative ideas from which to draw; it speeds up its new products process by linking with partners that have required technology; and it obtains access to its partner's IP with lower risk.

A key to making open innovation work is to select the best partner or partners. Some researchers have suggested that the innovating firm evaluate prospective partners in terms of their technological, strategic, and relational characteristics. A high level of trust between the partners is also critical to success.[48]

[45]Larry Huston and Nabil Sakkab, "Connect and Develop: Inside Procter & Gamble's New Model for Innovation," *Harvard Business Review*, March 2006, pp. 58–66.

[46]Roger J. Calantone and Michael A. Stanko, "Drivers of Outsourced Innovation: An Exploratory Study," *Journal of Product Innovation Management*, 24(3), May 2008, pp. 230–241.

[47]Michael Docherty, "Primer on 'Open Innovation,' Principles, and Practice," *Visions*, April 2006, pp. 13–17.

[48]Zeynep Emden, Roger J. Calantone, and Cornelia Dröge, "Collaborating for New Product Development: Selecting the Partner with Maximum Potential to Create Value," *Journal of Product Innovation Management*, 22(4), July 2006, pp. 330–341.

FIGURE 4.8 Open Innovation in Action: Two Success Stories

Clorox and Procter & Gamble may be fierce competitors in the cleaning-products arena, but are also open innovation partners elsewhere. P&G had the intellectual property for plastic technology, in particular strong plastic film, which is the technology used in two Clorox products: Glad Press'n Seal and also Glad ForceFlex plastic garbage bags. P&G also brought its global marketing expertise to the table, while Clorox contributed the Glad brand equity, its R&D knowhow in plastics and resins, and its organizational structure suited to marketing plastic film products. Due to this open innovation partnership and the key contribution of P&G to the plastics technology, Glad sales doubled within four years, and Glad has become the second billion-dollar brand at Clorox.

Kraft Foods sought open innovation partners for its planned Tassimo Beverage System. While they had the food knowhow, suppliers, and distribution channel, they needed assistance in the development and manufacture of the coffee maker. They assessed different home appliance manufacturers for manufacturing and R&D capabilities and competence in the appliance product category, and also for brand value compatibility, cultural fit, and compatibility of business strategies. In particular, they sought a manufacturer that shared Kraft's attitudes toward quality, convenience, and responsibility. Ultimately, they selected the Bosch and Siemens Home Appliance Group.

Source: Jacquelin Cooper, "How Industry Leaders Find, Evaluate and Choose the Most Promising Open Innovation Opportunities," *Visions*, 36(1), 2012, pp. 20–23.

Open innovation is seen as a valuable counterpoint to traditional closed innovation models. The closed innovation model allows for inputs to come from internal sources (marketing or strategic planning inputs) as well as external ones (such as customer inputs or market information). Under open innovation, firms at the front end of product innovation are now no longer looking externally only for inputs such as unmet needs or unsolved problems. Now, inventors, startup companies, or various sources or technology (such as independent, government, or industry labs) are all actively sought out as possible joint venture partners, or as the basis for leveraging internal product development skills. An established firm with commercialized products can also benefit from open innovation by accessing technologies that allow it to more easily move up by emerging product generation.

A prominent example of open innovation in packaged goods is P&G. The company had a long history of acquisition of external technologies and transforming these into successful products, such as Tide, Crest, and Bounce. In 2000, the incoming CEO, A. G. Lafley, announced a corporate-level commitment to open innovation. Under this new program, known as Connect and Develop, no fewer than 50 percent of new initiatives had to include at least one external partner. The goal of Connect and Develop was to ensure a flow of external ideas and also to better focus the firm's internal R&D efforts. P&G embraced the "not all the smart people work for us" mindset: they employed about 7,500 people but realized that about 1.5 million people who do not work for P&G might be potential external idea sources. The results soon emerged: P&G worked with a French partner involved in wound-care R&D to jointly develop Olay Regenerist, an antiwrinkle cream. Pringles Stix originated with an innovation by a Japanese partner firm. P&G licenses the Mr. Clean trademark to partner firms that make cleaning gloves, mops, and car-cleaning kits.[49] For detailed open innovation success stories, see Figure 4.8.

[49]The P&G example is drawn from www.pgconnectdevelop.com and Huston and Sakkab (2006), op. cit.

Janssen (a pharmaceutical company owned by Johnson & Johnson) also benefits from open innovation. Faced with intense competition and new, emerging competitors, they built JLABS facilities in several cities around the world, designed to support creativity in life science research. JLABS are located near top research universities such as Penn and MIT, allowing for easy collaboration with university researchers. JLABS also allow entrepreneurial researchers and their startup companies to conduct research at their facilities and to interact with Janssen researchers. Innovative new medical and health-related products have been successfully developed in JLABS due to the collaboration between company scientists, university researchers, and entrepreneurs and the availability of sufficient lab space to do the work.[50]

LEGO implemented an open innovation system to generate ideas from customers. Company management had identified a new robotics building-blocks system as a high-potential new product. Relying on the high brand equity and reputation for reliability and quality associated with its name, LEGO was able to identify and attract knowledgeable lead users and offer them the opportunity to play the role of co-creators of the new robotics offering for little more than the cost of supplying them with early versions of the product. LEGO used inexpensive but effective ways to keep in touch with their lead user community: a closed Web forum, Web sites, and blogs, in which participants could share and improve ideas and even purchase them. The company also invited the participants to tour the actual production facilities, which raised their excitement level and stimulated very positive word-of-mouth. The result: a solid, highly engaged online community that helped LEGO make its Mindstorms NXT robotics system its most successful product ever.[51]

Nike co-created Nike+ with customers, with the participation of Apple in an open innovation framework. Nike+ allows the runner to monitor performance, set objectives and workout targets, and challenge other runners, using expertise gained from Apple as an open innovation partner. Some Nike+ runners also acted as lead users by learning to track their runs using Google Maps; Nike added map tracking to its Nike+ offerings in response. Nike claims an increase in running-shoe market share of 10 points worth over $500 million.[52]

Amazon understood the potential in its Alexa voice service technology and worked closely with other companies who expressed an interest in incorporating this technology innovatively into their own businesses. In one of many such examples, the Mars Agency wanted to use voice service technology to provide customers in a local New York wine store with personalized recommendations. The store, Bottlerocket, saw a 20 percent increase in sales within two months, and the Mars Agency was seeking to expand this service to other retail stores. Working with these partner companies has obvious benefits for Amazon; internally, it would simply not be possible to come up with all the potential uses of Alexa.[53]

[50]The Janssen example is from Richard Staines, "Revolutionary Thinking," *pharmaphorum.com*, accessed January 12, 2019. See also the JLABS Web site, *jlabs.jnjinnovation.com*; and Jacquelin Cooper, "How Industry Leaders Find, Evaluate and Choose the Most Promising Open Innovation Opportunities," *Visions*, 36(1), 2012, pp. 20–23.

[51]Jennifer Dominiquini, "Dispelling the Myths About Product Innovation," at *www.prophet.com* (undated).

[52]Mark Deck, "Co-Creation: A Big Idea with Major Implications," *Visions*, 35(2), 2011, pp. 32–35.

[53]Andria Cheng, "What Amazon Is Doing to Keep Alexa in the Lead," *Forbes.com*, July 26, 2018.

These examples mostly illustrate inbound open innovation, but some companies such as IBM have profitably executed outbound open innovation. Blessed with strong internal R&D, IBM collaborates with their customers to help solve customer problems, in the First-of-a-Kind (FOAK) program. Each selected customer initiative is staffed by a few IBM researchers who solve the customer's problem. The customer benefits from IBM know-how, while IBM retains ownership of the intellectual property. Between 2002 and 2007, FOAK projects generated $400 million of revenue from the reuse of FOAK assets and another $4 billion from adaptation of these assets to other businesses.[54] Open innovation can also be in both inbound and outbound directions among firms within a kind of network; this arrangement is called a *coupled process*. As an example, BMW developed its car control mechanism, iDrive, by cooperating with several companies in different industries. Most notably, iDrive uses a joystick technology, developed by video game manufacturers, to permit the driver to control hundreds of navigation, communication, entertainment, and innovation functions.[55]

One interesting approach to open innovation is taken by the Dutch electronics company Philips, which created a specialized facility in Singapore known as the InnoHub.[56] This facility provides several realistic environments simulating an apartment, a fashion store, and a hospital ward, as well as office and workshop areas. In these environments, end users, product developers, and other partners work together to develop new ideas for breakthrough innovations. As an example, a mirror display in the fashion store triggered a couple of ideas: shoppers viewing videoclips of products at home via the Internet, then ordering online; or sending images of themselves wearing different outfits to their friends via multimedia messaging. In its first four years, over 4,000 people involved in innovation visited the InnoHub; visitors interact spontaneously to the concepts they see and often generate even more ideas.

Finally, another form of open innovation is the completely online system. One of these is InnoCreative, which describes itself on its Web site as a Web community that exists to match scientists to the research challenges of global firms.[57]

One of the complicated issues a firm must manage in an open innovation policy is intellectual property protection. Without careful partner selection, the firm opens itself up to the possibility that intellectual property could be accidentally disclosed by a partner, or worse, deliberately used illegally or given to competitors. Leading product consultants suggest that it is up to the firm to do its due diligence on prospective partners early and to make sure that all of the legalities are handled correctly, including letters of intent, memoranda of understanding, and detailed contracts.[58] Some general advantages and risks of open innovation are found in Figure 4.9.

[54]Frost and Sullivan, "Collaborative Innovation Process," available at ww2.frost.com.

[55]R. J. Calantone and H Y. Nguyen, op. cit.

[56]Elke den Ouden, Darren Ee, and Nicky Goh, "The Philips InnoHub—Generating Breakthrough Innovation in an Open Innovation Setting," *Visions*, Vol. 32, No. 1, March 2008, pp. 20–21.

[57]See www.innocentive.com; see also description in Mariann Jelinek, "Open Innovation," in V. K. Narayanan and Gina C. O'Connor (eds.), *Encyclopedia of Technology & Innovation Management* (Chichester, UK: John Wiley, 2010), Chapter 18.

[58]Robert Cooper, "What Leading Companies Are Doing to Reinvent Their NPD Processes," *Visions*, Vol. 32, No. 3, September 2008, pp. 6–10.

FIGURE 4.9   **Advantages and Risks of Open Innovation**

- Importing new ideas multiplies innovation building blocks—ideas and expertise, resulting in more total sales generated from new products.
- Exporting ideas raises cash (IBM gets about $2 billion per year in patent royalties), and improves employee retention, since creative types know that good ideas will be exported and not buried.
- Exporting signals the true worth of an innovation. Eli Lilly offers pharmaceutical licenses, but if outsiders don't bite it suggests the value of the new drug is perceived to be low.
- Exporting clarifies core business: Boeing sticks with design and systems integration, and often finds partners for manufacturing.
- Risk: the deal is not structured in a way that captures the financial value of your innovation—ask Xerox!
- Proprietary secrets can be lost to a partner, even inadvertently.
- Theft of technology, or poaching of top researchers, is a concern.

Source: Darrell Rigby and Chris Zook (2002), "Open-Market Innovation," *Harvard Business Review*, 80(10), 2002, pp. 80–89; and Mariann Jelinek, "Open Innovation," in V. K. Narayanan and Gina C. O'Connor (eds.), *Encyclopedia of Technology & Innovation Management*, Chichester, UK: John Wiley, 2010, Chapter 18.

Firms such as P&G and Kimberly-Clark that have committed to open innovation have adjusted their new products process accordingly. In short, the new products process must be able to incorporate externally developed ideas, intellectual property, technology, and/or commercialized products. To accomplish this, changes in the new products process can be made at any or all of the phases. In the concept generation and evaluation phases, these firms actively seek inventors, new start-ups, entrepreneurial firms, and other possible open innovation partners and assess the potential value of joint product development. During the development phase, firms may be looking for technical assistance from scientists and other individuals outside the firm or may seek to acquire externally developed innovations or intellectual property that can push the project along. As would be expected, this is also an opportune time for the firm to find a licensee for intellectual property not currently being used. Finally, at the time of launch or commercialization, firms may look to sell or license newly commercialized products if this provides good value, or they may acquire products already launched elsewhere to obtain immediate growth potential.[59]

Summary

Chapter 4 has introduced concept generation for new products. First, we noted that management has the task of preparing an organization for concept generation. This includes applying the strategic guidance of a product innovation charter, finding and training creative people, and then creating an environment for them to work in where they can be motivated to produce.

[59]Robert G. Cooper, "Perspective: The Stage-Gate® Idea-to-Launch Process—Update, What's New, and NexGen Systems," *Journal of Product Innovation Management*, 25(3), May 2008, pp. 213–232.

Next came a look at the concept itself, what it is, what it isn't, and how it comes into existence. The concept is built around ideas of technology, form, and benefit and is tested by whether it can communicate to an intended buyer what the proposed product is all about and whether it appears useful.

After noting that there are two broad categories of approaches to getting good new concepts, we explored the one that involves looking for ready-made concepts. Many firms use this approach heavily, and all should make at least some use of it. There are legal problems here, of course, and the chapter concluded by outlining the steps to follow in handling ideas that come from end users, lead users, employees outside the new products loop, and so on.

This prepares us to look at the most difficult, but by far the best method for creating new product concepts: problem-based ideation. This is the subject of Chapter 5.

Case: Google Glass[60]

Google announced plans to develop a new hands-free wearable device, Google Glass, in 2012. Google Glass resembled a pair of glasses; however, it offered an interactive display much like that found on smartphones, functioned on voice command, and supported Bluetooth and Wi-Fi connectivity. Google Glass was powered by Android and was compatible with devices using either the Android or Apple operating systems.

Google Glass was designed to be the next logical device in the evolution of the smartphone—a hands-free wearable that provides all the functionality of a smartphone but does not even require the user to look down at it to use it. The display is in the user's field of vision, while not obstructing vision. Wearing Google Glass, the user can do any of the familiar functions available on smartphones: send messages, take pictures and videos, make phone calls, access the Internet, navigate, and so on.

In early 2013, Google announced a Twitter campaign, #ifihadglass, and identified 8,000 highly interested participants, whom they called Glass Explorers. Explorers had the opportunity to purchase a beta-test version of Google Glass. In 2014, to expand the number of Explorers, Google announced a one-day-only public sale allowing any consumer in the United States to buy Google Glass.

Google Glass was slated to enter the market at a retail price of $1,500. There were a few competitors offering similar products. The Meta Pro retailed for almost $3,000, while other products such as Visix Smart Glasses, Recon Jet, and Optivent Ora-S AR all retailed for under $1,000. Though Google Glass had a higher price tag than any competitors (other than Meta Pro), the other devices did not have the range or features nor the big brand name with enormous brand equity.

An ad that was used to promote the original Google Glass is available on YouTube at: www.youtube.com/watch?v=YAXTQL3jPFk.

---

[60]This case was based on Jared Newman, "Google's 'Project Glass' Teases Augmented Reality Glasses," *PC World*, April 4, 2012; Nick Bilton, "Behind the Google Goggles, Virtual Reality," *The New York Times*, February 23, 2012; Vlad Savov, "Google Glass is Back From the Dead," *The Verge*, July 18, 2017; and other published sources.

Despite very positive forecasts for both the business-to-business and mainstream consumer market, Google ended the beta test of Google Glass in January 2015, and the product never made it to full launch. The company had no intention to bring the product back in any form for at least two years.

Briefly state the PIC for Google Glass. Is this a solid PIC? To what would you attribute the failure of Google Glass? Based on the promotional video and what you may know about Google Glass, what do you think of this product? Do you personally think it offers any desirable benefits? If not, do you think there are market segments that might benefit from Google Glass? Specifically, how would they benefit?

Assume the original Google Glass prototype has just been discontinued. Using the definition of product concept as illustrated in Figure 4.4, specify the need/benefit, form, and technology of the original Google Glass. Then, using the "building blocks" idea discussed in the chapter, develop at least five viable new product concepts by replacing either the need/benefit, form, and/or technology with a new one. For each concept, state who the target customer would be and justify how this would be a more desirable product with greater potential than the original Google Glass.

Case: Indiegogo[61]

Crowdfunding platforms are a popular way for new startups to obtain financial support. Recently, many large companies have discovered the benefits of crowdfunding, as a way to gauge customer opinion on product concepts and even to generate financial support for development. Founded in 2008, Indiegogo was one of the first crowdfunding platforms, along with Kickstarter. By 2018, Indiegogo had worked with about 50 of the Fortune 500 companies, including global firms such as Coca-Cola, in addition to thousands of startups. In fact, one Indiegogo offering, The Enterprise Program, originally designed to provide assistance to General Electric, is devoted to big corporate clients. According to David Mandelbrot, a senior executive at Indiegogo, the corporate giants "just started putting products that they had in their pipeline on Indiegogo" instead of relying on familiar methods such as focus groups and surveys.

In September 2018, Danish toymaker LEGO contacted Indiegogo to determine if consumers would be interested in a new product called LEGO Forma—mechanical animal models designed as a fun, stress-reducing, creative building kit for adults. LEGO Forma kits contain approximately 300 pieces that can be built into a moving model. A LEGO Forma koi fish kit was placed on Indiegogo's international crowdfunding site, at a price of $45; four different replacement skins ($15 each) allow the user to change the fish's color or change its appearance into a shark. According to Kari Vinther Nielsen, senior marketing manager and head of creative play lab pilots at the Denmark-based toy maker, "Normally, LEGO would use a traditional research and

[61]This case is based on: Mike Snider, "Indiegogo Is Selling LEGOs for Adults and They're Quite the Catch," *www.usatoday.com*, September 28, 2018; Adrianne Pasquarelli, "LEGO, Coke and Other Big Brands Are Turning to Crowdfunding for R&D," *www.adage.com*, October 12, 2018; Harry Drnec, "Sober Up ® Exceeds Initial Funding Goal on Indiegogo," *www.prnewswire.com*, October 17, 2018; and Anonymous, "Saigo Launches First Sport Utility Bike on Indiegogo," *www.businesswire.com*, October 10, 2018.

development process [for a new product of this type] and then do a global launch. But before even doing a global launch, we wanted to pilot it to see if there was an appetite." The company was not disappointed. LEGO set an Indiegogo sales goal of 500 units; within the first three months, it had reached five times that level.

Indiegogo has provided useful customer research on thousands of products, and for small startups as well as large firms. SoberUp, a drink that reduces the effects of alcohol in the body and minimizes hangover symptoms, was crowdfunded on Indiegogo in October 2018 and exceeded its fundraising goal by 148 percent within its first few days online. At about the same time, Saigo launched a sport-utility bike (SUB) on Indiegogo. Designed to be convenient and rugged, the SUB can be used as a regular bike or the rider can use a 500W electric motor to improve mileage. Users can also monitor mileage through an app or can pay for an upgraded battery that will find the bike's location remotely.

Indiegogo and other crowdfunding sites allow consumers to pay to get early access to products. They can also provide feedback, which makes them feel involved in the development process while giving valuable research information regarding product viability at low cost. For LEGO, crowdfunding has become an effective yet inexpensive product testing method, especially at a time when its traditional product line (plastic building blocks) is losing sales.

Discuss the pros and cons of crowdfunding. In any of the cases mentioned above, would you recommend any other kinds of testing before product rollout? Can crowdfunding produce misleading results? Why, and how could you avoid this problem?

Case: Aquafresh White Trays[62]

This case details how GlaxoSmithKline (GSK) entered into an open innovation relationship with a small manufacturing company, Oratech LLC, to get into the teeth whitening market with Aquafresh White Trays. In one sense, the partnership seems to be a perfect match, a textbook example of open innovation in action. GSK noted the rapid growth in teeth whitening products and was experienced in product marketing, sales, and distribution. Also aware of the potential in this category, Oratech had already developed the product, owned the patents, and could handle manufacturing. But the road was not as smooth as expected.

The first successful teeth whitening product was P&G's Crest Whitestrips, launched in 2001, followed by several competitors. While the market showed great interest in these products, there were frequent customer complaints. Most notably, customers found the first few products difficult to use, foul-tasting, and messy. This suggested to GSK a market opportunity based on improved customer value. By offering better teeth whitening properties, and at the same time delivering a product that was tastier and easier to use, GSK could capture a share of this market. GSK was already in the oral care business with its Aquafresh toothpaste line; GSK management felt that only a product that offered superior customer value would be worthy of carrying the

[62]This case is drawn from Scot Andersen, Kevin Foley, and Lee Shorter, "A Story of What Happens When Opposites Attract—Hint: It's Something to Smile About," *Visions*, 31(4), December 2007, pp. 16–17.

Aquafresh name. They also recognized that the most efficient way to enter this market was with a partner that had the required technology know-how.

Oratech, a small private-label manufacturer, was already making a teeth whitening tray and selling it to dentists and other professionals. They too recognized the growth potential in the consumer market, but they needed a partner who owned the requisite marketing skills and brand equity. Oratech identified a small number of potential partners and soon chose GSK due to their marketing and R&D capabilities, in addition to competency in working with regulatory agencies.

Some problems arose in the early going, due to differences in corporate culture. Oratech was initially surprised by the complexity of development and regulatory standards, which were second nature to a huge global corporation like GSK. Perhaps more unexpectedly, the new products processes employed by the two firms were somewhat different as well, with Oratech's version of the process being a little simpler and somewhat more streamlined, typical of a smaller manufacturing firm.

The partnership went well, taking only about 18 months to get the new product ready for launch. GSK ran into some development challenges, which required that they make some decisions typical of late-phase product development: Do we sacrifice quality, or slow down time-to-market? Despite this slight setback, there was really never any doubt at GSK: The commitment to bring the best-quality product to the consumer under the Aquafresh name was the number-one priority. Oratech managers were quite impressed with how seriously this commitment was taken by GSK, who brought in consultants to try to fix the development problems and not slow down development time too much. Scot Andersen, VP of marketing and sales at Oratech, said that the "level of sophistication with which GSK treats its own brands resulted in an improvement in our own processes."

Aquafresh White Trays were launched in early 2007, beating all sales forecasts and going on to be a top player in the teeth whitener category. Executives from both companies agreed that a key factor leading to this success was open communication throughout the new products process. As it turned out, if one partner ran into a manufacturing problem, the other was able to find a solution. A good example of this was the manufacturing process for the trays themselves. GSK preferred individual molding of the trays, but they knew that this would run up production time and cost; the alternative was to vacuum-form and cut them, which led to imperfections at the edges. With its technical and manufacturing expertise, Oratech figured out a way to trim the edges, resulting in a desirable finished product. In turn, Oratech was very surprised to see how accessible GSK employees (and even senior management) were throughout the new products process; they were not expecting such a close relationship, given GSK's size.

What accounts for the market success of the Aquafresh product? Keep in mind that as large and knowledgeable as GSK is, both P&G and Colgate already had similar products on the market, and both could easily defend themselves against the competitive launch of Aquafresh. More generally, what can be learned from GSK's perspective, and also from Oratech's perspective, about making open innovation work?

New Product Ideas: The Problem Find-Solve Approach

Setting

Chapter 5 will be devoted to the most productive concept-generating system that we know—the problem-based approach of finding and solving customers' problems. It seems obvious and easy: Ask customers what their problems are and have a scientist put together the solution! But it's not always so simple.

Just getting customers involved is often difficult. Learning their toughest problems is more difficult, partly because they often don't know their problems very well. Many departments of a firm may be involved, not just the technical ones. You might want to glance back at Figure II.1 in the introduction to Part II, which briefly depicts the problem-based approach to generating concepts, and see how problem-based ideation fits in with other methods for gathering new product concepts.

But ask product managers, and you'll find that they are passionate about identifying customer problems and figuring out how to best solve them—for them, this is fun and exciting work! Think about toy companies. The most innovative ones recognize that one cannot just ask young children what problems they experience with existing toys. But watch them playing in a room with a variety of toys and observe what appears to be missing to them and what they do about it (for example, using the box a toy car came in as a garage), and you may be on to something!

The Overall System of Internal Concept Generation

Every ideation situation is different and varies by the urgency, the skills of the firm and its customers, the product, the resources available, and so on. But one general approach, that of problem-based ideation, works best and can be modified to fit virtually every situation. The steps are diagrammed in Figure 5.1.

The flow essentially is from the study of the situation, to use of various techniques of problem identification, to screening of the resulting problems, and to development of *concept statements* that will then go into the evaluation phase. The whole system is

FIGURE 5.1
Problem-Based Concept Generation

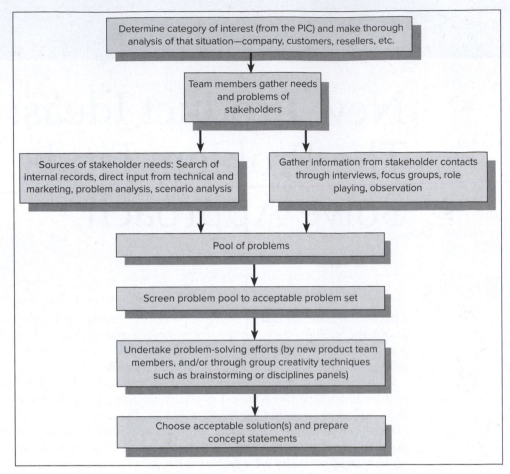

Determine category of interest (from the PIC) and make thorough analysis of that situation—company, customers, resellers, etc.

Team members gather needs and problems of stakeholders

Sources of stakeholder needs: Search of internal records, direct input from technical and marketing, problem analysis, scenario analysis

Gather information from stakeholder contacts through interviews, focus groups, role playing, observation

Pool of problems

Screen problem pool to acceptable problem set

Undertake problem-solving efforts (by new product team members, and/or through group creativity techniques such as brainstorming or disciplines panels)

Choose acceptable solution(s) and prepare concept statements

based on close involvement with parties who have information to help us, primarily stakeholders, which include end users, of course, but also advisors, financiers, consultants, maybe architects, physicians, or other professional groups, possibly resellers—even current nonusers certainly have information that may be useful to us!

Recall from Chapter 2 that the leading cause of new product failure is the absence of a perceived need by the intended end user. If our development process begins with a problem/need the end user has and agrees is important, then we have answered the toughest question. Fortunately, organizations today are getting close to their stakeholders. But stakeholder integration is especially tough on high-security *new product* matters. So we figure out how to do it, just as customer satisfaction managers have.

Gathering the Problems

Figure 5.1 showed four sources for needs and problems of stakeholders: internal records, direct inputs from technical and marketing departments, problem analysis, and scenario analysis. Let's explore each of these.

Internal Records

The most common source of needs and problems comes from an organization's routine contacts with customers and others in the marketplace. Daily or weekly sales call reports, findings from customer or technical service departments, and tips from resellers are examples. Sales files are peppered with customer (and reseller) suggestions and criticisms. Warranty files will show where problems are. In addition to these routine contacts, a firm may conduct formal marketing research to gather information on customer satisfaction. Studies of this type are useful, as are the files of the groups working on total quality management.

Industrial and household consumers sometimes misunderstand products and erroneously project into their use of products what they are *seeking*. A complaint file thus becomes a psychological projective technique. One approach to handling user complaints is the toll-free complaints number or complaints Web site. It helps defuse criticism and can lead to new products. Engineers or other employees may be collocated (sent to work at customer sites) to observe customer problems firsthand.

Information gained through routine market contacts can be profitably combined with other methods, such as the problem-solving technique or customer surveys. A consumer study commissioned by the SC Johnson Company in 2006 found that about one-third of homeowners cleaned the shower only once a month or less, and that a common reason was that they thought this job was difficult and took a long time to do. Over half of the respondents said that they waited until there was visible scum or dirt on the shower before they attempted to clean it! A couple of years later, another survey commissioned by the Soap and Detergent Association found that having a "sparkling shower" was one of the most satisfying cleanup jobs in the house. Since most people in the same survey said they would not employ a housekeeper or cleaning service, this job would have to be done by the homeowner him- or herself. Putting the results of the internal consumer study and the industry association study together, management identified a potentially huge unmet need: a shower cleaner that made the job easy. The result was the Scrubbing Bubbles Automatic Shower Cleaner: attached to the shower head; it sprays cleaning solution throughout the tub/shower area effortlessly by pushbutton. The product was a natural extension of SC Johnson's popular Scrubbing Bubbles bathroom cleaners and sprays and became quite popular.[1]

Direct Inputs from Technical and Marketing Departments

Understanding about end users and other stakeholders also lies in the minds of marketing and technical people.[2] Most of them have spent time with customers and end users, sometimes many years of it. Team representatives from these two functions should canvass their colleagues, seeking out every piece of evidence on problems. They have to take the initiative on this because most of these people are busy, and opportunities may be missed because no one reaches outside their functional area to share the idea.

---

[1] From an SC Johnson press release dated March 16, 2006.

[2] A good reference on using firm employees as sources of new product ideas is Christine Gorski and Eric J. Heinekamp, "Capturing Employee Ideas for New Products," in P. Belliveau, A. Griffin, and S. Somermeyer (eds.), *The PDMA Toolbook for New Product Development* (New York: John Wiley, 2002), pp. 219–241.

It's good to remember that technical people may be found anywhere in the business, not just in R&D or engineering—especially in manufacturing, technical service, and regulatory affairs. Salespeople may not be considered in marketing, and thus are sometimes overlooked.

The only real problems with using in-house people to report on customer problems are (1) each suggestion is usually someone's *perception* of what the customer problem is, and (2) there is usually a solution given with each suggestion. In fact, sometimes we have to ask what new product customers are asking for and then ask why; the "why" is what we want to know at this time.

These problems, including the time and difficulty of actually gathering memories, lead us to depend more on *active* searching for stakeholder problems. That is, making direct contact with all relevant stakeholders, asking *them* what their problems and needs are. And, although all of the above market contacts and searches around the firm help us compile useful problems, the methods of direct user contact are what we usually mean when we say problem analysis.

Problem Analysis

It seems that every history of an industry, a business firm, or a famous businessperson cites some key time when a new good or service capitalized on a problem that others didn't sense or appreciate. But problem analysis is much more than a simple *compilation* of user problems. Although the term problem *inventory* is sometimes used to describe this category of techniques, taking the inventory is only the beginning—analysis is the key.

As an advertising agency executive once said: If you ask people what they want in a new house and also ask them what are their problems with their current house, you will get distinctly different subject matter on each list. If you then observe their subsequent behavior, it becomes clear their problem list is a far better predictor than the want list. Users verbalize their wants in terms of current products, whereas problems are not product specific. Thus, if you ask what a person needs or wants from a shampoo, the answers will be clean hair, manageable hair, and so on—replies reflecting recent promotions of product benefits. But if you ask, "What problems do you have with your hair?" the answers may range into areas (for example, style or color) unrelated to shampoo. See Figure 5.2 for an example of what we are looking for in problem analysis, as applied to smartphones.

Several recent award-winning product designs have resulted from the application of problem analysis. In one case, homeowners reported several problems with smoke and carbon monoxide detectors: ugly designs, too hard to shut off (without climbing up on a chair), nuisance alarms, poor instructions on what to do in case of an emergency. Coleman developed its line of Safe Keep Monitors to be aesthetically pleasing in appearance and added a broom button for easy reach. The carbon monoxide monitor comes with a door that opens to reveal instructions when activated (thus eliminating the need to hunt for a manual during an emergency). By being designed to solve real customer problems, the Safe Keep line has done well in terms of sales.[3] In a

[3]Examples are from Bruce Nussbaum and contributing writers, "Winners: The Best Product Designs of the Year," *BusinessWeek*, June 2, 1997, pp. 94–111.

FIGURE 5.2
Problem Analysis Applied to the Smartphone

Here are several smartphone problems that came up in a consumer study. See if you can generalize to a smaller number of problems. Then select the one big problem that sounds most productive for smartphone new products people.

Keeping the phone clean.
Breaks when I drop it.
Battery doesn't stay charged long enough.
Hard to surf the Web.
Printing on Web pages is too small.
Keyboard "buttons" too small so it's hard to text.
Internet connection is slow.
Hard to download apps.
Hard to find apps on the screen.
Finding it in the dark.
Not enough choice of colors or styles.
Battery dies when I am in the middle of a conversation.
Who "out there" can hear me?
Dropped calls (line goes dead for no reason).
Difficulty in looking up numbers.
Other party's voice fades in and out.
I've heard about health risks—are they true?
Can't cradle it between ear and shoulder.
My arm and ear get tired.
Ringing is usually too loud, but sometimes I can't hear it.
It is a very disruptive instrument.
I can't see facial or body language.
Getting flustered making emergency calls.
People who call the wrong number in the middle of the night.
The call doesn't go through.
Fear of what the ringing might be for.
Avoiding "If you want sales, push 1," etc.
Knowing when is the best time to call people.

business-to-business application, Cemex (a large Mexican cement company) conducted customer research and discovered a previously hidden problem: Customers were unhappy with late supply arrivals at the project site. Cemex seized the opportunity and repositioned itself as the on-time supplier—a virtual "Domino's Pizza" of the cement industry![4]

Problem analysis was, at least informally, used by James Dyson in the development of the Dual Cyclone bagless vacuum cleaner (which you saw at the beginning of Chapter 1). Existing vacuum cleaners were unsatisfactory in terms of performance, maneuverability, and ease of disposing of dirt, and Dyson set out to create a better vacuum. In later years, Dyson produced a powerful hand dryer, the Airblade,

[4]Erika B. Seamon, "Achieving Growth through an Innovative Culture," in P. Belliveau, A. Griffin, and S. M. Somermeyer (eds.), *The PDMA Toolbook 2 for New Product Development* (New York: John Wiley, 2004).

sold to the business market, and by 2009 adapted the technology behind the Airblade to create a better fan. Like vacuums, regular household fans have remained quite unchanged in design for decades. Dyson's innovation was guided by a quick but thorough problem analysis that identified several points of improvement. As Dyson said, conventional fans have "spinning blades [that] chop up airflow, causing annoying buffeting. They're hard to clean, and children always want to poke their fingers through the grille."[5] One could add a few more problems: Fans can tip over and are not very energy efficient. The Air Multiplier, as it was called, was purported to address many of the problems. It was bladeless, increasing safety and ease of cleaning, as well as creating a smooth stream of air. The Airblade technology provided for effective and efficient cooling, and its low center of gravity prevented dangerous tipping. It featured functional and "attractive" design elements associated with the other Dyson products. The product was successfully developed and launched in late 2009, at a price point significantly above conventional fans (about $300), but within reach of customers who appreciate good design and substantially improved performance.

Note that in this and the earlier examples, it is up to senior management to encourage new product teams to look beyond their normal boundaries when they explore customer problems.

Problem Analysis Procedure

There are several variations in problem analysis. But one commonly used procedure is **reverse brainstorming**. In this procedure, participants generate a list of key problems with the product currently in use, then group and prioritize these such that product development can focus on addressing the most important problems.[6] The general approach is the following:

Step One Determine the appropriate *product or activity category* for exploration. This has already been done if the product innovation charter has a use, user, or product category dimension in the focus statement.

Step Two Identify a group of *heavy product users* or activity participants within that category. Heavy users are apt to have a better understanding of the problems, and they represent the bulk of the sales potential in most markets. A variation is to study non-users to see if a solvable problem is keeping them out of the market.

Step Three Gather from these heavy users or participants a set of *problems* associated with the category. Study the entire system of product use or activity. This is the inventory phase mentioned earlier, but far more is involved than just asking respondents to list their problems. A good method of doing this is asking respondents to rate (1) the benefits they *want* from a set of products and (2) the

---

[5]Rebecca Smithers, "Latest for the Dyson Touch: The Fan Without Blades," *The Guardian*, October 13, 2009.

[6]Robert G. Cooper, Scott J. Edgett, and Elko J. Kleinschmidt, "Optimizing the Stage-Gate Process: What Best-Practice Companies Do—I," *Research-Technology Management*, September–October 2002, pp. 21–27.

FIGURE 5.3
The Bother-someness Technique of Scoring Problems

The following is an abbreviated list of pet owners' problems found by manufacturers of pet products.			
	A **Problem Occurs** **Frequently**	**B** **Problem Is** **Bothersome**	**C** **A × B**
Need constant feeding	98%	21%	.21
Get fleas	78%	53%	.41
Shed hairs	70%	46%	.32
Make noise	66%	25%	.17
Have unwanted babies	44%	48%	.21

Source: From Burton H. Marcus and Edward M. Tauber, *Market Analysis and Decision Making*, Little, Brown, 1979, p. 225.

benefits they are *getting*. The differences indicate problems. Complaints are common and often taken as requests for new products. But they are apt to be just the result of *omniscient proximity*, meaning that users face a minor problem frequently, so it is the first one mentioned. Some firms have had success *observing* consumers or business firms actually using products in a given category; for example, observing skiers as they shoot down a hill or office workers handling a mailing operation.

Step Four   *Sort and rank* the problems according to their severity or importance. Various methods can be used for this, but a common one is shown in Figure 5.3. It uses (1) the extent of the problem, and (2) the frequency of its occurrence. This *bothersomeness index* is then adjusted by users' awareness of currently available solutions to the problem. This step identifies problems that are important to the user and for which the user sees no current solutions.

Methodologies to Use

The generalized structure of problem analysis still contains the question of how to gather the list of customer problems. Many methods have been used, but the task is difficult. The customer or user often does not perceive problems well enough to verbalize them. And, if the problems are known, the user may not *agree* to verbalize them (for many reasons, including being embarrassed). Much of the sophistication in newer technologies was developed specifically to deal with these problems and will be discussed in Chapter 6.

Experts   We have already mentioned going to the experts—using them as surrogates for end users based on their experience in the category under study. Such experts can be found in the sales force, among retail and wholesale distribution personnel, and in professionals who support an industry—architects, doctors, accountants, and the staffs of government bureaus and trade associations.

Published Sources   Also as mentioned earlier, published sources are frequently useful—industry studies, the firm's own past studies on allied subjects, government reports, investigations by social critics, scientific studies in universities, and many others. For example, a GlobalData consumer survey discovered that more people snack throughout the day (millennials are most likely to snack instead of getting breakfast), and that traditional mealtimes are becoming much less prevalent for many families. Other studies reveal that consumers care about eating healthy yet convenient snacks. Responding to these trends, food manufacturers have come up with innovations such as yogurt with crunchy toppings to mix in and snack packs containing pretzels with cheese and/or meat.[7]

Stakeholder Contacts   The third, and most productive, is to seek out the voice of the customer (VOC)—that is, we will ask household or business/industry customers directly, via interviewing, focus groups, direct observation, or role playing.

- **Interviewing** The most common method by far is direct, one-on-one interviewing. Sometimes this is a full-scale, very formal, and scientific survey. Other times the discussion is with lead users, an idea-generating method discussed in Chapter 4; lead users often are the first to sense a problem, and some go on to respond to it themselves. Still other times, it may be no more than conversations with some key customer friends at a trade show, because a problem statement may come from only one person and yet be very significant for us. Phone interviews have been shown to be a quick and effective way to get useful new product ideas and help to ensure that the targeted respondent (for example, a professional or a senior manager at a customer firm) actually responds, rather than a last-minute fill-in.[8] Because many end users don't think that much about the products they use and often just accept them as parts of living, even very informal discussions with individuals at a trade show or over the telephone can reopen thinking, bringing to mind things forgotten.

- **Focus Groups** The **focus group** is designed to yield the exploratory and depth-probing type of discussion required, and it *can be* easy and inexpensive to set up and use. If done wrong, it only *appears* that way. Granted, in this case we are not seeking facts or conclusions, just genuine problems, and the focus group method works well by stimulating people to speak out about things they are reluctant to mention when in one-on-one interview situations. It's much easier to talk about one's problems when others in the group have already admitted they have problems, too.

But, even in a single focus group, the costs are deceptive. Sessions can be expensive, and if a series of four two-hour, 12-person focus groups yields only five or six good ideas, those are costly ideas indeed!

Although the focus group technique is common, the outcome is not always, or even usually, successful. The focus group is a **qualitative research** technique. Unlike the

---

[7]Nico Roesler, "Snack Mashups Driving Product Innovation," *Food Business News*, December 18, 2018.

[8]For more on telephone interviews and qualitative interviewing in general, see George Castellion, "Telephoning Your Way to Compelling Value Propositions," in P. Belliveau, A. Griffin, and S. Somermeyer (eds.), *The PDMA Toolbook for New Product Development* (New York: John Wiley, 2002), pp. 63–86.

traditional survey, it depends on in-depth discussions rather than the power of numbers. A problem analysis focus group should be asked:

What is the real problem here—that is, what if the product category did not exist?

What are the current attitudes and behaviors of the focus group members toward the product category?

What product attributes and benefits do the members of the focus group want?

What are their dissatisfactions, problems, and unfilled needs?

What changes occurring in their lifestyles are relevant to the product category?[9]

In a typical example, Nissan conducted focus groups of American children between the ages of 8 and 15 to get ideas for storage, cup holders, and other features as part of the design of its full-size minivan.[10]

Other suggestions for helping guarantee the usefulness of focus group findings are to invite scientists and top executives to the sessions and to avoid what some people call *prayer groups:* Managers sit behind the mirror and pray for the comments wanted rather than really listening to what users are saying. Be sure the focus groups are large enough for the interactions and synergy that make them successful, and don't expect focus group members to like your products! Focus group moderators know not to begin the session cold, but instead to let people get comfortable and introduce themselves—a rule of thumb is to treat participants as one would treat strangers at a party. The best moderators genuinely like people and generate openness and trust by asking ice-breaker questions and by contributing personal experiences and practices.[11]

- **Ethnographic Market Research** Ethnographic market research methods are rooted in sociological studies, and involve watching customers (or noncustomers) using products in their own environments. Video recordings or photos are sometimes used to record observational data. The new product team observes the data carefully for actions, body language, and so on and tries to identify customer needs and wants, and new product ideas that might satisfy these needs.[12]

Ethnographic studies can be conducted *on-site* or *in-home*. On-site research takes place at the location where the customer uses the product, such as at the office, on vacation, or in the car. The researcher observes the product in use while interviewing

[9]"When Using Qualitative Research to Generate New Product Ideas, Ask These Five Questions," *Marketing News*, May 14, 1982, p. 15.

[10]Norihiko Shirouzu, "Tailoring World's Cars to U.S. Tastes," *The Wall Street Journal*, January 15, 2001, pp. B1, B6.

[11]Joseph Rydholm, "Respondent Collages Help Agency Develop Ads for New Pontiac," *Quick's Marketing Research Review*, March 1995, p. 7; and Tim Huberty, "Sharing Inside Information," *Quick's Marketing Research Review*, March 1995, p. 10.

[12]Dorothy Leonard and Jeffrey F. Rayport, "Spark Innovation through Emphatic Design," *Harvard Business Review*, 75(6), November–December 1997, pp. 102–113. For a look at how the design firm IDEO uses observation, brainstorming, and rapid prototyping to identify and refine product concepts, see Bruce Nussbaum, "The Power of Design," *BusinessWeek*, May 17, 2004, pp. 86–94, or check the IDEO Web site, www.ideo.com. (We explore prototyping issues in Chapter 13 of this book.)

the respondent to seek out further information. In-home research requires a lengthy home visit where the interviewer may spend hours interviewing several family members, making observations, and taking photos. The idea here is to gain insights on how a product is actually used and how customer needs may be changing or evolving.

A laptop manufacturer may test a new prototype with potential customers in a focus group and gain valuable information. But by making a home visit, insights may be obtained that would never have emerged from a controlled focus group. The home visit may reveal that the owner uses the laptop in a dimly lit room or on a desk cluttered with paper, or likes to drink coffee while working and occasionally spills some on the keyboard. Any one of these observations might suggest an unmet need that could be addressed.

When redesigning its popular Explorer sport utility vehicle (SUV), Ford sent a team of designers out to parking lots in order to watch how people used their cars. The researchers' duties were not unlike those of zoologists watching animals in their natural habitat—in fact, the work was colloquially known internally as "gorilla research." Among other ideas, the research suggested ways that the Explorer could be made easier to get into.[13] Similarly, Honda engineers and executives visited the homes of U.S. families who owned Ford SUVs and noted, to their surprise, how many parents put their children and their neighbors' children in the first two rows and the dogs in the third row. Had the research been conducted only in Japan, the researchers would have entirely missed the American love affair with dogs and might consequently have made the passenger compartment too small.[14]

- **Customer Site Visits** These are a variant of ethnographic research often used for business-to-business products that involves visiting a business customer's site. Using a site visit team, which comprises marketing as well as technical personnel, leads to better understanding of customer requirements and better cross-functional teamwork. The site visit team can initiate the research process by asking the customer to list the problems they are facing and what solutions they have in mind, if any.

In developing a revolutionary new hand-held instrument for the chemical industry, Fluke Corporation visited chemical industry trade shows and customer plants, talking informally with end users (the instrument engineers). Internally, this technique was known as *fly on the wall* or *day in the life* research. The researchers discovered two specific problems encountered by the engineers using their calibration instruments onsite: the need to carry many calibration instruments to the site and the need to transcribe readings onto a clipboard to be manually entered into a computer. These two insights led to the development of universal calibration gauges that could be used in numerous settings and applications. The new devices could also record the readings electronically, and these could be easily downloaded to a computer at a later time.[15]

[13]Al Haas, "Spying Helps to Improve Explorer," *Philadelphia Inquirer*, December 24, 2000, p. G1.
[14]Norihiko Shirouzu, op. cit.
[15]R. G. Cooper, "From Experience: The Invisible Success Factors in Product Innovation," *Journal of Product Innovation Management*, 16, pp. 115–133, 1999.

Role Playing   Though role playing has long been used in psychology to enhance creativity, there is little evidence of its successful use in generating ideas for new products. Presumably, it would be valuable in instances where product users are unable to visualize or verbalize their reactions. It should also be valuable where consumers are emotionally unable or unwilling to express their views—for example, in areas of personal hygiene.

Unfortunately, though users are the best place to begin the ideation, and problem analysis is widely used in one form or another, most firms still do not have organized systems to exploit this source. One must wonder why not, since one's own customers should be a rich source of ideas. Consider that Levi Strauss got the idea for steel-riveted jeans from a Nevada user as far back as 1873!

An alternative way to generate concepts is based on **product function analysis**. A product can be expressed in two words, a verb and an object (for example, toothpaste "cleans teeth"). Thinking of new combinations of verbs and objects can suggest new product functions. In this method, hundreds of these two-word mini-concepts can be generated and shown via computer to respondents, who rate them in terms of likely interest. The highest scoring concepts are identified and in-depth interviews are conducted to explore feelings and ideas further. In an application in the food processing industry, several novel mini-concepts emerged (have fun with food, touch food), while several others fared poorly (sponge food, vaporize food). To develop these concepts further, one would need to examine why these mini-concepts were liked.[16]

Problem Analysis in Action

One unmet need that had existed for years was the noisy candy wrapper in the theater. Years ago, TV personality Gene Shalit complained one morning on the air about crackling candy bar wrappers. An expressway-commuting executive from Hercules Inc. overheard his comment and asked the laboratory for a silent candy wrapper. Polypropylene provided the answer, though not without much effort to overcome issues in heating, waterproofing, and airproofing.

Toyota, Mitsubishi, and other carmakers redesigned their SUVs to appeal more to the U.S. marketplace demand. Often, these changes come about after disappointing sales with early SUV versions. The Toyota T100 pickup had disappointing sales in the United States; consumer research suggested that the reason was that it was viewed as too small. The full-size Tundra comes complete with a V8 engine and a passenger compartment reportedly large enough for "a passenger wearing a ten-gallon cowboy hat."[17]

Finally, ongoing problem analysis is critical to identification of newly emerging problems and continued improvement. Consider Domino's Pizza. Decades ago, Domino's founders identified a real unmet need in the market: quick, reliable pizza delivery service. Late-night customers, in fact, were satisfied with an average-quality pizza,

[16]Jeffrey F. Durgee, Gina Colarelli O'Connor, and Robert W. Veryzer, "Using Mini-Concepts to Identify Opportunities for Really New Product Functions," *Journal of Consumer Marketing*, 15(6), 1998, pp. 525–541.

[17]Norihiko Shirouzu, "Tailoring World's Cars to U.S. Tastes," *The Wall Street Journal*, January 15, 2001, pp. B1, B6.

as long as it was delivered fast and hot. Generations of customers knew Domino's promise: "thirty minutes or it's free." But by 2009, competition in the pizza business had heated up; major delivery competitors such as Papa John's had achieved immense success and even the traditional-restaurant Pizza Hut chain was getting into the delivery business. Fast and hot was no longer enough. Domino's focus groups found that customers had lots to say about the taste, most of it negative. Company president Dan Boyle decided to respond to the threat by assigning a product team to develop a new, better-tasting pizza. Marketing employees used focus groups and other research methods to capture the voice of the customer; the food engineers developed a totally new recipe to meet the specifications. Over a dozen different sauces and crusts were tried, as well as dozens of types of cheese. Despite the risks of such a dramatic strategy (what if it were New Coke all over again and customers demanded the old product back?), the new pizza was just what the market ordered. We will revisit the Domino's case in Chapter 7.[18]

Scenario Analysis

So far, we have talked about going to technical and marketing people within the firm for ideas on customer problems, about searching the many files and recordkeeping places where customer concerns can be found, and about problem analysis. The fourth general source of stakeholder needs shown in Figure 5.1—**scenario analysis**—comes into play because the ideal problem for us to find is one that customers or end users don't know they have at this time. As hockey star Wayne Gretzky said, "I don't skate to where the puck is. I skate to where it's going to be." Similarly, we have to stay one step ahead of the customers by anticipating their problems.[19]

A future problem is a good problem because most problems we find in interviews and focus groups have already been told to competitors and anyone else who will listen. Providers of the goods and services have been working on them for many years, for example, flimsy music stands and steam on bathroom mirrors. We have time to solve a *future* problem and have that solution ready to market when the time comes.

Unfortunately, end users usually don't know what their future problems will be. And they often don't really care, at least not right now. So they are not much help in interviews. This is where scenario analysis becomes valuable. Here's how it works.

If we were to describe apartment life 20 years from now, we would probably see lots of windows and sunlight coming in. If a furniture manufacturer were doing this scenario analysis, an analyst could immediately see problems, such as: Those apartment dwellers will need (1) new types of upholstery that are more resistant to the sun, and (2) new types of chairs that will let them continue such activities as conversing and eating but also let them gain exposure to all that sunlight.

The scenario analysis procedure is evident: First, paint a scenario; second, study it for problems and needs; third, evaluate those problems and begin trying to solve the

[18]Anonymous, "New Domino's Pizza Recipe Doubles Quarterly Profits," nydailynews.com, March 2, 2010; Domino's Pizza 2009 Financial Results.

[19]Mark Henry Sebell, "Staying Ahead of Customers," *U.S. Banker*, October 1997, p. 88.

most important ones. The ideal scenario is a "stylized narrative"—that is, it should be like a story: painting a clear picture of the future state, containing a "plot" or sequence of believable events. Painting a scenario does not yield a new product concept directly; it is only a source of problems, which still must be solved. In fact, it is often valuable for concept generation if several future states are described. Creative people can then choose to focus on the most likely scenario, or possibly attempt a *multiple coverage strategy* in which a separate strategy is pursued for each of several possible scenarios. A carmaker might develop several different alternative engine technologies (gas/electric hybrid, hydrogen cell, etc.) in parallel if it is unclear which of these will be dominant in the future.[20]

Scenarios take several different forms. First, we distinguish between (1) *extending* the present to see what it will look like in the future, and (2) *leaping* into the future to pick a period that is then described. Both use current trends to some extent, of course, but the leap method is not constrained by these trends. For example (hypothetically), an extend study might be: Currently, homeowners are converting from individual housing to condominium housing at an annual rate of 0.9 percent. If this keeps up for 20 years, there will be 7 million condominium units in use, which will present a need for 250,000 visitors' motel units in major condominium areas to house visitors who cannot stay in the smaller units with their hosts. The thinking of the utopian school is sometimes used. By contrast, a leap study might be: Describe life in the year 2030 in a major urban area of Germany contrasted with life in a similar setting in France.

Leap studies can be *static* or *dynamic*. In dynamic leap studies, the focus is on what changes must be made between now and then if the leap scenario is to come about—the interim time period is the meaningful focus. In static leaps, there is no concern about how we get there. Figure 5.4 shows a dynamic leap period in which the auto dealer service problem no longer exists. The time between now and then is broken down to yield the technical breakthroughs needed soon to reach that ideal condition. As another illustration, one professional forecaster made several rather bold predictions regarding technologies and our lifestyles in the future (see Figure 5.5). Any of these could be viewed as a leap scenario into some time in the not-too-distant future: These scenarios (if not too farfetched) might suggest opportunities for several new products. (Which do they suggest to you?)

Scenario analyses lead to great learning and insights, but are hard to do well. Several guidelines have been suggested for conducting a good scenario analysis:

1. *Know the now.* The participants must have a good understanding of the current situation and its dynamics, otherwise the future they envision will not be realistic or useful for idea generation.

2. *Keep it simple.* Participants will likely have difficulty understanding really complex scenarios.

3. *Be careful with selecting group members.* A group of about six, with contrasting or complementary viewpoints and prior experiences, works best.

---

[20]For more on using scenarios, see Steven Schnaars and Paschalina (Lilia) Ziamou, "The Essentials of Scenario Writing," *Business Horizons*, July–August 2001, pp. 25–31.

FIGURE 5.4
The Relevance Tree Form of Dynamic Leap Scenario

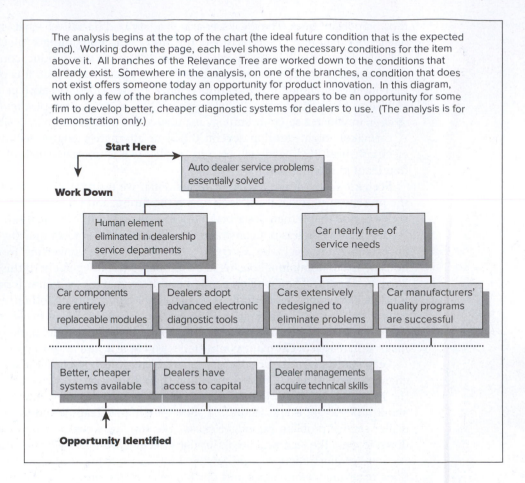

The analysis begins at the top of the chart (the ideal future condition that is the expected end). Working down the page, each level shows the necessary conditions for the item above it. All branches of the Relevance Tree are worked down to the conditions that already exist. Somewhere in the analysis, on one of the branches, a condition that does not exist offers someone today an opportunity for product innovation. In this diagram, with only a few of the branches completed, there appears to be an opportunity for some firm to develop better, cheaper diagnostic systems for dealers to use. (The analysis is for demonstration only.)

Start Here

Work Down

Auto dealer service problems essentially solved

Human element eliminated in dealership service departments

Car nearly free of service needs

Car components are entirely replaceable modules

Dealers adopt advanced electronic diagnostic tools

Cars extensively redesigned to eliminate problems

Car manufacturers' quality programs are successful

Better, cheaper systems available

Dealers have access to capital

Dealer managements acquire technical skills

Opportunity Identified

4. *Do an 8- to 10-year projection.* Too far out, and the participants are guessing. Not far enough out, and the respondents will just extend whatever is going on now.

5. *Periodically summarize progress.* This keeps the group on track and avoids contradictions.

6. *Combine the factors causing changes.* Scenarios should not be determined by just one factor.

7. *Check fit* or consistency at the end.

8. Once you have done the scenario analysis, *plan to use it several times.* These can be expensive.

9. *Reuse the group.* The more scenario analyses they do, the more they enjoy the task, and the better they get at it.[21]

FIGURE 5.5 **One Professional Forecaster's View of the Future**

Graham Molitor is a professional forecaster who relies on a variety of sources to develop his forecasts: census documents, government statistics, trade journals and similar publications, weekly newsmagazines, and his own 40 years of experience. Here are a few of the trends and forecasts he envisions for the 21st century:

1. Investment in communication will allow more people to work at home; by 2020, telecommuting and videoconferencing will have largely replaced in-person business meetings.

2. Internet use will continue to increase rapidly, and Americans will spend more on computers than on televisions. Handheld videophones will be a commercial hit by 2025.

3. Medical technology breakthroughs will continue to happen: Improved cloning technology will extend human life, and computerized health monitors will be of wearable size.

4. Ethical and social issues related to health and lifestyle will continue to be prevalent: These will include euthanasia, cloning, genetic manipulation, and biological engineering.

5. The traditional "nuclear family" will continue to become a thing of the past; by 2020 the average household size will be down to 2.35 persons.

6. By 2050, over a quarter of the U.S. population will be over 65. Large-type and recorded books, and cars that can be operated by people with reduced dexterity, will become popular.

7. By 2100, Americans of European descent will be in the minority (that is, less than 50 percent of the population). Continued diversity and multiculturalism will be stimulated by increased immigration.

8. In the far future (2200 to 2500), biotechnology and related life-science industries will have replaced tourism as a key employer in the U.S.

9. Greater globalization of manufacturing industries, more outsourcing of capital-intensive functions, and more electronic commerce, will mark business and industry.

10. Supplies of petroleum will shrink and prices will rise; by 2050, electricity demand will multiply by a factor of four.

What new products do each of these forecasts suggest? Do any of them suggest any changes in the new product development process? Do any of them seem too far-fetched to believe?

Source: Graham T. T. Molitor, "Trends and Forecasts for the New Millennium," *The Futurist* , July–August 1998, pp. 53–59.

Solving the Problems

Once an important user problem has been identified, we can begin solving it. Most problem solving is probably done by members of the new products group that has been leading the concept generation work so far. They do it instinctively, from the moment they hear of a problem. There is no way we can quantify or describe the methods they use, most of it being intuitive. It is probably best for the group to attempt to solve one problem at a time, however—taking on too much in the real world can be confusing and may foster communication difficulties.

Many problems are sent into the technical areas for more systematic attempt at solution. Here science and intuition rule, side by side. Some firms have it as strategy that problem solutions must come from R&D or engineering, with the solution itself being found in the application of some specific technology. A bus line wants travel problems solved by buses, and a bank probably wants problems solved by borrowing money. Besides technical people, the creative talents of marketing people are often used as well.

Note that the problem has to be carefully specified in order to find a good, creative solution. Proctor & Gamble (P&G) product developers reportedly spent months trying to solve the problem, "How can we make a green striped soap that will draw sales from Irish Spring?" It was only when they focused their attention on a new problem, "How can we make a soap that connotes freshness in its appearance, shape, and color better than Irish Spring?" that Coast (a soap with blue and white swirl patterns and a more oval shape) was developed and was ultimately successful.[22]

Group Creativity

New products people use individual problem-solving effort, but many think that **group creativity** is more effective. Some scientists protest loudly that this is not true, that the synergism of groups is way overplayed. Generally, individuals can handle really *new* ideas and find *radical* solutions to problems better than groups can. Some feel that one reason small firms are more innovative than large firms is that they do not often use group creativity.

Back in 1938, advertising executive Alex Osborn was one of the first to popularize the technique of **brainstorming**. All of the group ideation techniques developed since that time are spin-offs of his process and embody one idea: One person presents a thought, another person reacts to it, another person reacts to the reaction, and so on, until a large number of ideas has been generated. This presenting/reacting sequence gives group creativity its meaning, and the various techniques developed simply alter how ideas are presented or how reactions take place.

Brainstorming

Because brainstorming techniques have been around so long, they are widely misused. Left unchecked, a singular focus on quantity of ideas may lead to a large number of bad, mediocre, or non-creative ideas, so some guidance in brainstorming is required.[23] Thomas Kelley of the design firm IDEO laid out several rules for making brainstorming sessions more effective. These include: *mind the rules* (go for a large quantity of ideas, defer judgment, no snickering allowed); *number the ideas* (can you hit 100 ideas per hour?); *jump and build* (when the group hits a plateau, the facilitator suggests a new direction); and *get physical* (by using odds and ends to build models and prototypes).[24]

The biggest change in the practice of problem solving over the past 20 years is to use brainstorming combined with other tools of creativity. We still try to avoid the *bazooka*

[22]Peter Wilson, "Simplex Creative Problem Solving," *Creativity and Innovation Management,* 6(3), September 1997, pp. 161–167.

[23]A. T. Stephen, P. B. Zubcsek, and J. Goldenberg, "Lower Connectivity Is Better: The Efforts of Network Structure on Customer Innovativeness in Interdependent Ideation Tasks," *Journal of Marketing Research*, 53(2), 2014, 263–279.

[24]Tom Kelley, *The Ten Faces of Innovation* (New York: Currency Books, 2005).

effect (state an idea only to have someone shoot it down), but also to avoid the scores of easel sheets with hundreds of ideas scribbled on them. Instead, we aim for group delib-erations that are exploratory, evaluative in a constructive way, hours long (versus the 20-minute brainstorming session), and built toward a few specific solutions that appear operational. IDEO uses brainstorming in combination with "lickety-stick" prototype development (see Chapter 2) to speed up innovation.[25]

There have been many attempts to stick with the basic idea of brainstorming, but to tweak it in some way to overcome the problems. In *brainsketching*, participants draw their ideas rather than expressing them in words. Some evidence shows that brainsketching helps participants draw more connections with earlier ideas when coming up with new ideas.[26] Another emerging technique is called *speedstorming*. It is described as a round-robin format, similar to speed-dating, in which participants pair off (at random, or with some pattern in mind such as that the two participants must be from different functional areas) and discuss a topic for a three- to five-minute round. The goal of each round is to come up with ideas that can be pursued by the new product team. After each round, partners switch around and another round begins. At the end of the session, numerous new ideas have been generated, and participants have identified which partners they seem to collaborate with the best. For this reason, the proponents of speedstorming claim that it is particularly good at overcoming the communication difficulties typical of cross-functional teams.[27]

Some other common techniques are described in Appendix B.

Electronic Brainstorming and Computer-Assisted Creativity Techniques

Despite its popularity, brainstorming has several drawbacks. Only one person can talk at a time, and social loafing may occur (average work intensity may be lower in a group set-ting). Further, some individuals may still fear being criticized for having unpopular ideas. **Electronic brainstorming**, a form of brainstorming assisted by **group support systems** (or **GSS**) **software**, is said to overcome these limitations of traditional brainstorming, as it allows participants to all answer at once, and also to answer anonymously.

A GSS-assisted brainstorming session may take place in a room set up with a net-work of computer terminals. Participants sit at the terminals and respond to questions provided by the moderator, who runs the GSS software. The GSS software gathers the participants' responses and projects them onto a large screen at the front of the room or on the participants' monitors. Seeing the responses stimulates even more ideas and encourages follow-up discussion. The GSS also automatically takes electronic notes of all the proceedings, so nothing is lost or erroneously transcribed.[28]

[25]Bruce Nussbaum, op. cit.

[26]Remko Van Der Legt, "Brainsketching and How It Differs from Brainstorming," *Creativity and Innovation Management*, 11(1), 2002, pp. 43–54.

[27]Caneel K. Joyce, Kyle E. Jennings, Jonathan Hey, Jeffrey C. Grossman, and Thomas Kalil, "Getting Down to Business: Using Speedstorming to Initiate Creative Cross-Disciplinary Collaboration," *Creativity and Innovation Management*, 19(1), 2010, pp. 57–67.

[28]An assessment of GSSs is found in Robert O. Briggs and Gert-Jan De Vreede, "Meetings of the Future: Enhancing Group Collaboration with Group Support Systems," *Creativity and Innovation Management*, 6(3), June 1997, pp. 106–116.

One is not restricted to a single location, either. GSSs can facilitate activity at many sites simultaneously (through computer linkups or videoconferencing) and handle group sizes into the hundreds.

GSSs have become very popular in facilitating meetings, and there is some evidence that electronic brainstorming outperforms traditional brainstorming in terms of productivity and output of unique ideas.[29]

An increasing number of firms are using computer programs such as Mindlink, Mindfisher, and NamePro to assist their creative efforts in idea generation and management, and also to help out in other creative tasks such as brand name generation and selection. While they come in many forms, many of these work by drawing from large databases of words, phrases, or even pictures, encouraging the user to *think laterally* (gather unrelated thoughts, then try to associate them with the problem at hand). Most are straightforward and stimulating to use.[30] Also, many are adaptable to use in a GSS setting.

Online Communities[31]

Online communities (or *virtual communities*) have revolutionized customer information gathering. An online community can be defined as any group that interacts using a communications medium such as online social networking. Numerous firms, including P&G, Kraft Foods Group, Dell, and Hewlett-Packard, use online communities as a key part of their voice of the customer efforts and, indeed, throughout their new products process. Familiar online communities such as Facebook, Twitter, or LinkedIn are open to everyone and widely popular. But there are alternatives, some of which are much less well known. Some online communities such as tivocommunity.com are set up by lead users with an interest in a particular product or service; some such as Johnson & Johnson's babycenter.com are launched by firms. In addition, service providers like MarketTools or Vision Critical obtain rich customer insights by setting up *private online communities* of 500 or fewer carefully selected members. Firms can also access *proprietary online panels (POPs)*, which may contain hundreds of thousands of individuals who are statistically representative of a target market. These panels can be used to supplement online communities in a number of ways. For example, POPs can validate promising ideas or insights generated from a private online community.

Firms may have a range of objectives when initiating an online community. As a VOC technique, online communities provide a listening function: They allow firms to obtain new ideas from customers and get feedback on new concepts. Working with a

[29]Keng L. Siau, "Group Creativity and Technology," *Journal of Creative Behavior,* Third Quarter 1995, pp. 201–217.

[30]Tony Proctor, "New Developments in Computer Assisted Creative Problem Solving," *Creativity and Innovation Management*, 6(2), June 1997, pp. 94–98; and Mark Turrell, "Technology Spotlight: Unfuzzing the Front-End with Web-Based Idea Management," *Visions*, 27(1), January 2003, pp. 18–21. For a critique of several of these computer programs, see Arvind Rangaswamy and Gary L. Lilien, "Software Tools for New Product Development," *Journal of Marketing Research* 34, February 1997, pp. 177–184.

[31]Much of this section derives from Claire-Juliette Beale, "How Online Communities Are Changing the NPD Landscape—An Introduction to the Value of This New Tool," *Visions*, 32(4), December 2008, pp. 14–18.

service provider like MarketTools, firms can monitor public communities and blogs to spot new customer trends and emerging opportunities. Online communities are also a way to establish rapport with customers, enable customer support, and build emotional bonds between customers and the firm.

Del Monte Foods (makers of many pet food brands such as Kibbles 'n Bits, Milk-Bone, Meow Mix, and 9 Lives) used online communities extensively to get a better understanding of changes in its consumer market, identifying opportunities early and quickly developing products. In 2006 they joined forces with MarketTools and brand monitoring agency Umbria to start the I Love My Dog initiative. By analyzing data from millions of blogs, user forums, and message boards, Del Monte was able to identify the things that pet owners cared about and wrote about the most. In fact, a new customer segment of dog lovers (named the "Dogs Are People, Too" segment) was identified. Next, an online community was created to encourage innovative solutions from consumers within this segment. A community of 500 consumers was contacted and asked to enter a by-invitation-only, password-protected site that encouraged interaction and mutual understanding among participants. The community generated and refined ideas for a new breakfast product, which was immediately put into development by Del Monte. During the development process, Del Monte contacted community members, either individually or in group format, about a dozen times. By summer 2007, the new product, Snausage Breakfast Bites, was launched. The process from idea to launch took only six months, half the normal time for a product in this category. Since then, Del Monte has continued to explore ways to exploit online communities. In 2008, the firm partnered again with MarketTools; this time to tap into the latter's Moms Insight Network and quickly identify cat owners. The newly created cat owner community, named Meow Mixer, is used by Del Monte to generate ideas, develop concepts, sample new products, and obtain packaging and marketing suggestions.

Like anything else, online communities take work, and the firm seeking to institute an online community must be aware of the drawbacks.[32] Building and managing an online community requires hiring moderators and facilitators, and can take time—a good-sized community may take more than a year to mature. Also, the longer the community is in operation, the more difficult it becomes to organize the content and make it easy for participants to find their way around. There are also legal issues, such as member privacy, confidentiality of statements, and content ownership, that would need to be considered. Usually, participants would be expected to sign a service agreement so that the sponsoring firm could avoid legal problems down the road. Despite the drawbacks, it is likely that online communities will be a major source of customer input for years to come.

Disciplines Panel

Several of today's leading new products consulting firms believe creativity groups should actually work on a problem, not just talk about it, particularly in situations calling for significant innovation. Their approach is to assemble experts from all

---

[32]Claire-Juliette Beale, "Creating Your Own Online Community—How to Avoid the Pitfalls," *Visions*, 33(1), March 2009, pp. 15–19.

relevant disciplines and have them discuss the problem as a **disciplines panel**. A panel on new methods of packaging fresh vegetables might include representatives from home economics, physics, nutrition, medicine, ecology, canning technology, marketing, plastics, chemistry, biology, industrial engineering, agriculture, botany, and agronomy. The panel may also include outside experts.

One panel working in the shampoo industry was focusing on a consumer need: to put on hair conditioner that actually sought out split ends and went to work there. An R&D person on the panel noted that the products available at the time already did that! This surprising comment led to a new product that made the claim others had overlooked, and which turned out to be very successful.

Concept Generation Techniques in Action

This chapter provided several **creativity-stimulating techniques** that can be used to generate concepts; Appendix B provides many more. Throughout the chapter, we have provided examples of firms that have successfully applied these techniques. Here are a few additional recent examples that illustrate the successful use of some other, perhaps less common, techniques.

1. *Using Props.* Life Savers Company wanted to develop new flavors. They hired a consultant who filled a room with samples of fruits, varieties of perfumes, and lists of dozens of ice cream flavors. Life Savers' Fruit Juicers line came out of the session. P&G's Duncan Hines Pantastic party cakes came from an idea stimulation session where greeting cards were among the props used.

2. *Role Playing.* Bausch and Lomb's Polymer Technologies Division came up with the idea of cushioning material bonded to the lens surface by getting pairs of executives to play the roles of eyeball and contact lens. The actors had to think of ways the lens could stop hurting the eyeball while role playing.

3. *Imitating Nature.* Goats eat waste and emit it in the form of small pellets. This idea inspired Whirlpool in its development of the Trash Smasher compactor.[33]

Summary

Chapter 5 began our study of the many specific techniques developed by concept creators to aid them in their work. The most common approach is based on the paradigm of "find problem, solve problem," requiring participation by many people in the firm, plus stakeholders and others outside the firm. Then, we looked at the many techniques developed to spot problems. These included (1) inputs from technical and marketing departments; (2) search of internal records from sales calls, product complaints, customer satisfaction studies, and more; (3) problem analysis as a way of involving end users and other stakeholders; and (4) scenario analysis as a way of learning about future problems. Once problems are discovered, efforts at solution can begin; most

[33]Bryan Mattimore, "Eureka: How to Invent a New Product," *The Futurist*, March–April 1995, pp. 34–38.

efforts are individual thinking and analysis, whether in the office or in the lab. One major group of techniques uses the label of group creativity; it includes a great variety of approaches, but most are variations of brainstorming.

Next we will turn to some methods called analytical attributes, created over the years to aid marketing managers in seeking improvements while they are waiting for the approach of problem find-solve to bear fruit. This is the approach where we start with form, then see if there is a need, and if so, then develop the necessary technology.

Case: Creative Customer Problem Solving

In Appendix B of this text, you will find many different ideation techniques that can be used to generate creative solutions to customer problems or to address emerging customer needs. These techniques are designed to provide a free-flowing source of ideas where quantity dominates quality: we can always weed out weaker ideas and focus on further developing the stronger ideas later. At this early stage, the goal is to approach the problem in ways we might never have otherwise tried, and perhaps identify unique solutions as a result.

Some of these techniques you have met already in the chapter, such as brainstorming and similar techniques. Here also, quantity of ideas is most important, and participants are encouraged to build on ideas and generate even more. The techniques highlighted in this short case can be used effectively as an alternative to familiar brainstorming to generate even more ideas.

All of the following approaches to creative problem solving are **lateral search techniques**, which work on the principles of divergence and convergence. The reason we sometimes can't come up with novel solutions to customer problems is that we tend to approach our problem from the same, tried-and-true direction. These techniques all require participants to think divergently (use stimuli to generate out-of-the-box ideas) and then convergently (relate some or all of these ideas back to the original customer problem). That is, participants step away from the problem, think creatively, then focus back on the problem with new insights.

First, we have to gain agreement among participants on what the customer problem is that must be solved or the customer need that must be addressed. Imagine that you are working for a big electronics company, well known worldwide for innovative consumer electronics such as TVs, phones, laptops, and so forth. Let's say that you have brainstormed with your colleagues, under the supervision of a creativity specialist, and you have settled on the following problem to solve:

"How can we make television viewing more realistic for the home viewer?"

Use each of the following three techniques described in Appendix B to develop at least five creative insights to solve this problem:

- Creative Stimuli (using random pictures as the stimuli)
- Use of the Ridiculous
- Stereotype Activity

Note that you do not need to generate full product concepts. At this point, you are still doing ideation, so you might settle on something that technology could focus on (such as, for example, better sound). Remember, there are no wrong or dumb answers.

Here are some suggestions for applying these techniques:

Creative Stimuli: Select a few random interesting pictures online. (Different students should get different pictures, if conducted in a group setting.) Take a piece of paper and make two columns: Stimulus and Connection. Look at the picture for about 5 minutes. In the Stimulus column, write down whatever comes to mind when considering your picture. Try to list at least five stimuli. Then, take about 10 minutes and try to relate each stimulus back to the problem (in this case, making television viewing more realistic). These you will list in the Connection column. You may not think of a connection for each of your stimuli, but try to match up at least a few of the stimuli with a connection. If working in a group, share what you found and try to build on each other's ideas to develop a full list of insights.

Use of the Ridiculous: This works best as a kind of competition. Working in groups, one person should come up with a ridiculous idea. (So, for realistic television viewing, someone might say that the actors speak directly to viewers and call them by name.) Then the goal is for the next person to think of something even more ridiculous. One participant keeps a list of all ideas. The task often becomes a friendly competition that most participants enjoy. After about 10 contributions, stop the discussion, look at the list, and discuss how each of the ridiculous ideas might be converted to an idea that is, in fact, quite promising and not ridiculous.

Stereotype Activity: Think of a few celebrities from the entertainment, sports, or political world. Narrow the list down to about six names. Then, ask how each of these people would think or behave (in this case, what would they be looking for in realistic television viewing). For example, what kind of TV would Arnold Schwarzenegger have? Tiger Woods? Angelina Jolie? Have fun with it, but be sure to keep a list of the ideas you generate. Again, after about 8 or 10 contributions, look at the list and see if any of these ideas are promising.

CHAPTER SIX

New Product Ideas: Analytical Attribute Approaches

Setting

In Chapter 5, we studied an approach to concept generation that involves identifying users' problems and finding solutions to them. The problem-based approach is very useful because product concepts found by this route are most likely to have value for the user.

This chapter introduces a different set of techniques that are commonly used in the problem-solving phase (see Figure II.1 at the beginning of Part II). Everyone involved with the creation and sale of goods and services can make use of these techniques, including some who don't even know they are doing formal concept generation. What these techniques do is create views of a product different from the usual ones—the differences come from making adjustments to the product's attributes. The resulting product concepts can appear to be strictly fortuitous or lucky when they work, and they have indeed worked—many times, as you will see in this chapter. But actually, they are quite deliberate and purposeful, allowing discovery—serendipitous findings that come to people who know what they are looking for. We refer to these techniques as analytical attribute techniques, and they are our concern in Chapter 6.

Understanding Why Customers Buy a Product

Products Are Groups of Attributes

What is a **product attribute**? Figure 6.1 shows the set of them. A product is really nothing but attributes, and any product (good or service) can be described by citing its attributes.[1] Attributes are of three types: **features** (what the product consists of),

---

[1] For a useful perspective on how to conduct research on identifying what attributes are most valued by customers, see Charles Miller and David C. Swaddling, "Focusing NPD Research on Customer-Perceived Value," in P. Belliveau, A. Griffin, and S. Somermeyer (eds.), *The PDMA Toolbook for New Product Development* (New York: John Wiley, 2002), pp. 87–114.

FIGURE 6.1
A Typology of Attributes

A. Product attributes (for our purposes) are of three types:

Features	Functions	Benefits

Features can be many things:

Dimensions	Esthetic characteristics	Components
Source ingredients	Manufacturing process	Materials
Services	Performance	Price
Structures	Trademarks	And many more

Benefits can be many things:

Uses	Sensory enjoyments	Economic gains
Savings (time, effort)	Nonmaterial well-being	And many more

Benefits are either direct (e.g., clean teeth) or indirect (e.g., romance following from clean teeth).

Functions are how products work (e.g., a pen that *sprays* ink onto the paper). They are unlimited in variety, but are not used nearly as often as benefits and features.

B. Analytical attribute approaches use different attributes:

Dimensional analysis uses features
Checklists use all attributes
Trade-off analysis also uses determinant attributes
Several methods in Appendix B use functions and benefits

functions (what the product does and how it works), and **benefits** (how the product provides satisfaction to the user). Benefits can be broken down in an almost endless variety—uses, users, used with, used where, and so on. Concept generation is a creative task, so great liberty has been taken with definitions in its activity. The classification system used in this book is an attempt, and no more than that, to arrange them for study. It is important here to recognize that it makes sense for us to define attributes broadly. A pair of shoes can be thought of as a group of attributes; a person may buy a given pair because she likes the appearance of the leather (*feature*), because they are excellent walking shoes (*function*), or because they are very comfortable (*benefit*). (And if you disagree with the classification of these attributes as features, functions, or benefits, that's OK, too!)

A spoon is a small shallow bowl (*feature*) with a handle (another *feature*) on it. The bowl enables the spoon to *function* as a holder and carrier of liquids. The *benefits* include economy and neatness of consuming liquid materials. Of course, the spoon has many other features (including shape, material, reflectiveness, and pattern), not to mention other functions (it can pry, poke, be used as a catapult) and benefits (such as pride of ownership, status, or table orderliness).

Theoretically, the three basic types of attributes occur in sequence. A feature permits a certain function, which in turn leads to a benefit. A shampoo may contain certain proteins (feature) that coat the hair during shampooing (function), which leads to more shine on the hair (benefit). A new tire may have very deep treads (feature), which make it handle better in rainy or snowy conditions (function), providing a safer ride for passengers (benefit).

Analyzing Product Attributes for Concept Generation and Evaluation

Analytical attribute techniques allow us to create new product concepts by changing one or more of its current attributes or by adding attributes, and to assess the desirability of these concepts if they were to be developed into products. That is, these techniques can be used in concept generation (which will be approached in this chapter) and also in concept evaluation and even further along in the new products process, as you will see in succeeding chapters. If we were to change current product attributes in all the ways they could be changed, or to think of many additional attributes that could be built into the product, we would eventually discover every change that could ever come about in that product. In addition to adding attributes, one could reduce or even eliminate attributes, resulting in even more products. All these techniques work, as you will see—they have been used in all product categories from new car lines at Ford or Toyota to new eyeglass styles and cereal brands.

There are a variety of quantitative and qualitative **attribute analysis** techniques available. In this chapter, we explore one common quantitative technique: **perceptual gap analysis**. After an introduction to determinant gap maps, we will show how perceptual mapping techniques such as factor analysis can be used to generate perceptual gap maps. These techniques are frequently used in concept generation, and indeed, throughout new product development, during launch, and even beyond. We shall be returning to them from time to time as we proceed through the new products process. We also examine another common quantitative technique, conjoint analysis, and several other qualitative techniques.

Gap Analysis

Gap analysis is a statistical technique with immense power under certain circumstances. Its *maps of the market* are used to determine how various products are perceived by how they are positioned on the market map. On a geographical map, New York City is much closer to Pittsburgh than it is to Los Angeles. But on a *nearness-to-the-sea* map, New York City would be right next to Los Angeles. On any map, the items plotted tend to cluster here and there, with open space between them. These open spaces are gaps, and a map that shows gaps is, not surprisingly, called a **gap map**.

Gap maps can be developed simply using *managerial expertise and judgment* to plot products on a map and make a **determinant gap map**. Alternatively, research into customer perceptions can be used to generate a **perceptual gap map** based on attribute ratings provided by customers. We will explore each of these methods here.

Determinant Gap Maps

Figure 6.2 shows a map of snacks prepared by members of a new products team seeking to enter the snack market. The map consisted of two dimensions (they personally thought crunchiness and nutritional value were important in snacks). Scales ran from low to high on both factors. Each brand then in the market was scored by the managers on each of the two factors.

FIGURE 6.2
Gap Map for
Snack Products

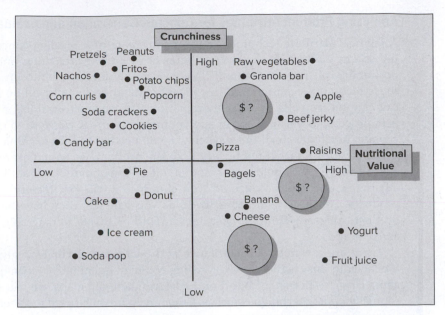

While the scoring may seem arbitrary and subject to managerial error, determinant gap maps are often a good place to start. Remember, concept generation takes place *after* strategy (the product innovation charter [PIC]) has targeted a market or user group on which to focus. Either the firm had experience in this market (a strength) or the market was researched. Each brand was then entered on the diagram (Figure 6.2) according to its scores. The result was a map of the brands, each in relationship to all others, on these two factors. Many maps could have been prepared, each with a different pair of attributes. They can also be three-dimensional. But the managers providing inputs to the determinant gap map are not new to this industry; they would have valuable and useful beliefs and judgments that may be very helpful in guiding concept generation. (Of course, they can still be wrong. Do you disagree with any of the assigned positions in Figure 6.2? Look closely!)

Attributes used in gap analysis should normally be *differentiating* and *important*. Consumers differentiate snacks on their crunchiness and on their nutritional value. And these attributes are important in buying snacks. Snacks also have different shape aesthetics, but these are not often used to differentiate one from another. Even if they were, most people would probably not find them important.

Attributes that both differentiate and are important are called **determinant attributes**, because they help determine what snacks are bought. In an industrial study of vinyl siding, some of the determinant attributes identified were appearance/status, maintenance/weathering, application/economy, and dent resistance.[2] The reason it is important to use determinant attributes in making the maps is that our purpose in this

[2]Steven A. Sinclair and Edward C. Stalling, "Perceptual Mapping: A Tool for Industrial Marketing: A Case Study," *Journal of Business and Industrial Marketing*, Winter/Spring 1990, pp. 55–66.

method is to find a spot on the map where a gap offers potential as a new item, one that people might find different and interesting.

For example, on the snacks map in Figure 6.2 the circles marked "$?" are gaps and thus offer new product possibilities. Note that the large number of snacks makes our gaps few and small—for example, the gap of semi-high crunchy and semi-high nutritional is close to the granola bar, the apple, beef jerky, and soda crackers.

Determinant gap maps are speedy and cost-efficient but have the weakness of being driven by only managerial judgment. Customer perceptions may indeed be quite different. Plus, brand perceptions might be more difficult for managers to judge correctly. In Figure 6.2, we might all agree that potato chips have lower nutritional value than granola bars, but how do customers perceive different brands of granola bars? Do they really think Nature Valley bars are the most nutritious, best tasting, or lowest in calories? And how important are each of these attributes to customers when they form preferences? Techniques that gather customer perceptions use them to develop gap maps that can provide important (and perhaps surprising) insights to the manager. We now explore two commonly used types of perceptual gap maps.

Perceptual Gap Maps

Unlike the determinant gap map method, a perceptual gap map based on attribute ratings (or simply, a *perceptual map*) positions brands into customer perceptions based on market research into customer perceptions of the different brands. (While we are gathering customer perceptions of the various brands, we also obtain customer preferences, which allows us to assess whether benefit segments exist; but we will come back to this point later.) Usually the two most important attributes are used to present the relative perceived positions of brands. For example, Figure 6.3 shows a hypothetical perceptual map for five top brands of swimsuits, according to customer perceptions of each brand on comfort and fashion. The map shows Aqualine is perceived as the most comfortable and Sunflare as the most fashionable. The other choices occupy intermediate positions in perceptual space. Note that perceptual maps are based on customer perceptions of reality, which may be very different from the engineered position! Splash may indeed be one of the most fashionable and comfortable brands on the market, but its relatively poor position indicates that it is not perceived that way. Advanced data analytical techniques, such as *factor analysis*, can be used to generate perceptual maps like Figure 6.3 from customer perception data.

The perceptual map we just built resembles the snack map of Figure 6.2, and the search for gaps can proceed as before. Because the perceptual map was built using actual customer perceptions, any gaps found are more likely to interest the potential users.[3] For example, the perceptual map suggests that customers perceive some swimsuits to be comfortable and others to be fashionable but none offers both high comfort and high fashion (Gap 1 in Figure 6.3). Congratulations—you've just uncovered a gap!

---

[3]For more information on the use of factor analysis in new products, see Uwe Hentschel, "On the Search for New Products," *European Journal of Marketing* 5, 1976, pp. 203–217.

FIGURE 6.3
AR Perceptual
Map of
Swimsuit
Brands

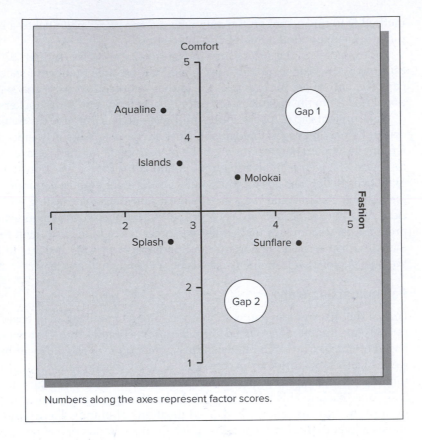

Numbers along the axes represent factor scores.

Comments on Gap Analysis

There are some issues to consider when using gap analysis for concept generation. The input data come entirely from responses to questions about how the choices differ. Nuances and shadings are necessarily ignored, as are interrelationships and synergies. Creations requiring a conceptual leap are missed. In the early 1900s, for example, gap analysis might have led to breeding faster horses or to wagons with larger wheels, but it probably would not have suggested the automobile.

One troublesome aspect is that gap analysis discovers gaps, not necessarily demand. Gaps often exist for good reasons (e.g., fish-aroma air freshener or aspirin-flavored ice cream). New products people still have to go to the marketplace to see if the gaps they discovered represent things people want.

Returning to Gap 1 in Figure 6.3, we do not know yet whether the market wants a very comfortable, very fashionable swimsuit. Inspection of Figure 6.3 also suggests there is a gap at medium fashion, low comfort (Gap 2). Maybe this is a better bet for a new concept. To answer this question, we need to gather data on customer preferences, which (as we noted earlier) is collected at the same time as gathered perceptual data. We will explore this issue further in Chapter 7 when we analyze customer preferences and identify benefit segments.

And, as in all ideation of new products, people must avoid being bound by what is now impossible. For example, for years gap maps on analgesics showed a big gap where strength was paired with gentleness. The strong/gentle part of the map was always empty, and everyone knew why—an over-the-counter analgesic that was potent yet didn't irritate the stomach could not yet be made. It made sense for pharmaceutical companies to do research to develop analgesics that had both desired attributes. Of course, Extra-Strength Tylenol and later products such as Aleve were eventually developed that filled this gap, offering both strength and gentleness.

Trade-Off Analysis

Trade-off analysis (often called **conjoint analysis**) is another commonly used technique for generating high-potential concepts. It is also frequently used in concept evaluation, so we will meet it again in Chapter 7. The terms "trade-off" and "conjoint" are not interchangeable. Trade-off analysis refers to the analysis of the process by which customers compare and evaluate brands based on their attributes or features. Conjoint analysis is the name of one of the most common analytical tools used to assess trade-offs (much like factor analysis is a tool that is used to develop perceptual maps). Trade-off analysis is thus the broader term. In this text, we will use "conjoint analysis" when we are specifically referring to that technique for assessing trade-offs.

Recall that after finding the determinant attributes (important attributes on which the available products differ), gap analysis plots them on maps. In using conjoint analysis, we assume we can represent a product as a set or bundle of attributes. Conjoint analysis puts all of the determinant attributes together in new sets and identifies which sets of attributes would be most liked or preferred by customers. In fact, gap analysis output can be used to select the attributes used in conjoint analysis.

Using Trade-Off Analysis to Generate Concepts

Let's say you are developing a new salsa product for a small, national food company. To keep the example simple, assume that there are only three important attributes to salsa: thickness, spiciness, and color. Also for simplicity's sake, we can assume that there are only three levels of thickness (regular, thick, and extra-thick), three levels of spiciness (mild, medium-hot, and extra-hot), and two color choices (red or green, depending on whether tomatoes or tomatillos are used). Figure 6.4(a) shows these three attributes and the different levels available for each attribute. There are a total of 18 available combinations, or options (3 thicknesses × 3 levels of spiciness × 2 colors). Conjoint analysis estimates the relative importances of the three attributes and identifies which levels are the most preferred by examining the ways customers rank the available options.

You can visualize what conjoint analysis does in this simple example. Suppose you really preferred mild salsa over all other kinds. If you were given each possible option and rank ordered them, one would see a pattern in your responses that reflects your preferences—the mild ones would tend to be ranked high, and spicy ones would be ranked lower. Similarly, if you really didn't care whether the salsa was red or green, there would be no such pattern in the rankings. Basically, you are trading off other attributes to get what you desire—that is, the mild salsa. Conjoint

FIGURE 6.4   Conjoint Analysis Output—Salsa Data

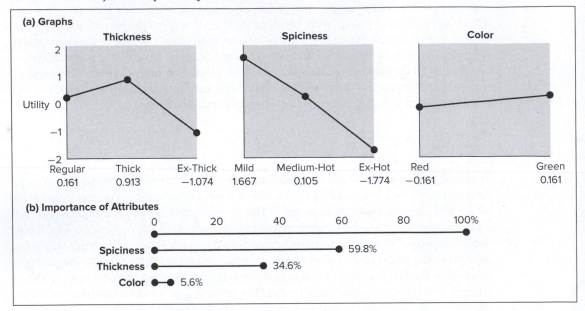

analysis essentially finds patterns like this to estimate customer preference for each level of each attribute separately, so that overall favorite products can be identified. Assuming that the results shown in Figure 6.4(a) are representative of the average targeted customer, the highest-rated product would be the one that combines the best levels of each attribute: a thick, mild, green salsa. Unless this particular combination was already on the market, we would have a new product concept. Other high-potential concepts are also suggested in the figure; for example, thick, mild, and red salsa might not be a bad idea.

Figure 6.4(b) also shows the relative importances of the three attributes as derived from the conjoint analysis.[4] As can be seen, spiciness is most important, followed by thickness; the respondent seems to be almost indifferent to color. One should keep in mind that these results are very dependent on the levels actually selected for the conjoint task. The respondent might not have been indifferent to color if the options were red, green, and shocking pink.

One must also consider segments within the market. It may be that about half the market likes mild salsa and about half likes extra-hot. If we only examined the average, we might conclude that medium-hot is best, though in reality nobody may like it! Thus, the next analytical step is to identify benefit segments. This will be discussed later in Chapter 7.

[4]These are estimated by looking at the ranges of utilities of the three attributes (that is, the gap between the highest and lowest utilities). As seen, the range for spiciness is 3.441. The ranges for thickness and color can be calculated as 1.987 and 0.322. Summing the three ranges yields a total of 5.750, and each range is divided by this amount to get its relative importance. For spiciness, 3.441/5.750 = 59.84 percent.

FIGURE 6.5

Form versus
Function and
Ergonomic
Trade-Offs in
the Car
Industry

According to Raj Echambadi, a professor at the University of Illinois at Urbana-Champaign, automakers need to consider trade-offs between form, function, and ergonomics when designing cars. His research finds that prioritizing investment in function and ergonomics leads to higher market share, while investment in form design is better for retaining market share through time.

Prof. Echambadi distinguishes between "design for delight" (investing in improving form) and "design for satisfaction" (investing in function or ergonomics). He explains that form, or appearance, is conspicuous and universal, but function, or ergonomics, are more personal. To explain: the distinctive shape of a Corvette, VW Beetle, or BMW sedan is obvious to everyone and provides status, "cool factor," or luxury. By contrast, function is more about product performance or smoothness, and ergonomics is about the product-user interface: these will vary from person to person. As Prof. Echambadi says, "What is comfortable for you might not be comfortable for me."

The trade-off, then, is whether the car designers should more heavily weight customer delight or satisfaction. Prof. Echambadi elaborates: "Anyone can produce a 365-horsepower engine. But when you talk about the unique form design of a Lexus RX 350 or a Chrysler 300, well, that's much more difficult to imitate."

His research shows that high form design leads to better market share retention for older models than high functional or ergonomic design. The strategic implication is that an older form may be extended longer, and form may not need to be rethought every two or three years. Thus, it makes sense to make quicker changes to function or ergonomics—for example, to boost engine performance or rider comfort. But if a car is well known for superior form design, it might not want to make extreme investments in function or ergonomics, as this might be perceived as costly overdesign by customers.

Prof. Echambadi concludes, "If you need to invest [in design], invest in either functionality and ergonomics, or in form—one or the other. This is the strategic capability tradeoff." He does caution, however, that the car should be at least average in all three (form, functionality, and ergonomics) in order to have respectable market share growth, and that the trade-off will depend on whether the car is competing in the luxury or economy market. Given that a fraction of a percentage point of market share translates into over half a billion dollars of sales revenue, automakers are keen on making the right strategic trade-offs.

Source: Ciciora, Phil. 2016. Strategic Trade-Offs in Automobile Design Affect Market-Share Value. phys.org, August 3, 2016.

Though our first example centered on consumer goods, trade-off techniques are very versatile and can be used in many different situations. In fact, because business buyers tend to make a more rational analysis of product features, trade-off analysis has become quite valuable in industrial product innovation. Applications include snowmobiles, health care systems, aircraft, lift trucks, hotel rooms, and computer software, as well as business services of all kinds.[5] Conjoint analysis was also used by Marriott Corp. when designing and developing the Courtyard chain to build in the most desired needs and wants of both business and leisure customers. Figure 6.5 illustrates the strategic implications of trade-offs among form, function, and ergonomic attributes in the car industry.

[5]For details on usage of the trade-off technique, see Dick R. Wittink and Philippe Cattin, "Commercial Use of Conjoint Analysis: An Update," *Journal of Marketing*, July 1989, pp. 91–96; Dick R. Wittink, Marco Vriens, and Wim Burhenne, "Commercial Use of Conjoint Analysis in Europe: Results and Critical Reflections," *International Journal of Research in Marketing*, January 1994, pp. 41–52; and Gary L. Lilien, Arvind Rangaswamy, and Timothy Matanovich, "The Age of Marketing Engineering," *Marketing Management*, Spring 1998, pp. 48–50.

Is Conjoint the Right Method?[6]

Does conjoint analysis produce valid results? A study of a simple product line extension (a baking soda toothpaste) suggested that conjoint results obtained when customers were only exposed to the product concept were very similar to those obtained if customers were actually allowed to try the product.[7] Thus, conjoint results are a valid early indicator of ultimate product success, at least for product line extensions. Of course, conjoint analysis and perceptual mapping, as well as product trial, will be rich sources of customer information later in the new products process. In the case of major innovations (such as the first tablet device or smartphone), however, customers without a high level of expertise in the product category may be unable to assess the innovation's benefits, and concept test results may not validly predict how well the actual product will be received. Some have advocated using only customers with at least moderate levels of expertise, even for minor innovations.[8]

Despite its usefulness in product research, conjoint analysis can be misused. First, one should be able to break down the product into discrete attributes (such as spiciness, thickness, and color in the salsa example). Conjoint analysis assumes that customers combine these features rationally when evaluating brands, and there are cases where this is not a realistic assumption. A young consumer may reveal in conjoint analysis that she prefers thick, mild, green salsa, but she will actually choose an extra-thick, spicy brand because that's the brand her mom used to buy. Or a car buyer might say he likes large trunk space and a high-powered engine, yet he will buy a Smart Car because he thinks it's eye-catching or he will look cool driving it. A further problem encountered with complex products such as cars is that there are so many hundreds or even thousands of attributes that one might consider, but the average customer can only handle about 10 of these in a given conjoint study, at most. The researcher must be certain that all the important ones are included. For example, if the researcher did not include "ease of parking" in a conjoint analysis for cars, the popularity of the tiny Smart Car might have been underestimated, especially among city residents.

Other issues are just not handled by conjoint analysis. Purchase occasion is not included (the young consumer may buy extra-thick, spicy red salsa for herself but thick, mild green salsa for her children or her guests); variety-seeking behavior is not considered (every once in a while, she will buy the medium-thick, mild red salsa just to try something different); and decisions made jointly may pose difficulties (the husband may care about legroom while the wife cares about trunk space, and it is unknown who has the ultimate decision or how they resolve differences in their car purchase decision).

[6]Steve Gaskin, "Navigating the Conjoint Analysis Minefield," *Visions*, 37(1), 2013, pp. 22–25.

[7]John R. Dickinson and Carolyn P. Wilby, "Concept Testing With and Without Product Trial," *Journal of Product Innovation Management*, 14(2), March 1997, pp. 117–125.

[8]Jan P. L. Schoormans, Roland J. Ortt, and Cees J. P. M. de Bont, "Enhancing Concept Test Validity by Using Expert Consumers," *Journal of Product Innovation Management*, 12(2), March 1995, pp. 153–162.

Additional guidelines for conjoint analysis would include the following:

1. One should know what the determinant attributes are before doing the conjoint analysis. Perceptual gap mapping or one of the qualitative techniques can be helpful in this regard.
2. Respondents should be familiar enough with the product category and the attributes to be able to provide meaningful data on preference or purchase likelihood. Conjoint may be less useful for new-to-the-world products.
3. The firm should be able to act on the results; in other words, actually develop a product that delivers the combinations of attributes preferred in the conjoint analysis.[9]

Finally, we should reiterate that trade-off (conjoint) analysis is commonly used in concept evaluation, and we will pick up the discussion of this technique in Chapter 7.

Alternatives to Full-Profile Conjoint Analysis

The salsa example illustrated *full-profile* conjoint analysis, meaning that all of the possible combinations were included in the study. The ranking task was relatively easy in this simple case, as there were only 18 options to rank order. Of course, in most settings there are many more attributes and/or levels to consider. Even for a simple product like salsa, one might need to consider type of container (glass jar versus plastic bucket), size of container (10 ounces versus 16 ounces), type of ingredients (organic versus not organic), and three different potential brand names, in addition to the three attributes listed above. That is $3 \times 2 \times 3 \times 2 \times 2 \times 2 \times 3 = 432$ different options. No respondent, however well intentioned, will have the patience to put these in rank order. More advanced versions of conjoint analysis, such as choice-based conjoint or adaptive choice-based conjoint analysis, are capable of handling far more complex decision scenarios. These are available through commercial sources such as Sawtooth Software.

Prototypes in Concept Testing

Early prototypes and virtual prototypes can be used in concept testing as well. The fastest-growing technique is to use 3D printing to make a simple, nonworking or partially working prototype, as an illustration of the product concept statement. For example, a medical supply company may be designing a new weekly pill box for elderly patients who have trouble remembering to take their medication. They have developed two early pill box prototypes: one with a screw-off cap much like an aspirin bottle and one with a small sliding door on the side. They can use a 3D printer to make life-size plastic replicas of both of these, and could even make them more realistic by making the screw top and sliding door actually work. These can be handled by respondents and/or passed around in a focus group, and realistic statement of product like/dislike and purchase intention can be obtained. Alternatively, the prototype can be virtual: respondents may go online and view a static picture, PowerPoint presentation, or video clip that simulates the product in action. These virtual prototypes are, of course, far less costly to produce and test than actual physical prototypes, allowing the firm to test a wide range of concepts quickly

[9]Adapted from Robert J. Dolan, *Managing the New Product Development Process: Cases and Notes* (Reading, MA: Addison-Wesley, 1993), p. 125.

and cheaply.[10] Finally, improvements in **virtual reality** computer and video technology are providing marketers with many exciting new ways to test concepts with customers.

Qualitative Techniques

We have seen several quantitative techniques that can be used to incorporate customer input into concept generation. As noted at the beginning of this chapter, however, these techniques have natural complements: namely, a collection of qualitative techniques, which we will now explore.

Dimensional Analysis

Dimensional analysis uses any and all features, not just measurements of dimensions (such as spatial—length, width, and so on). The task involves listing *all* of the physical features of a product type. Product concept creativity is triggered by the mere listing of every such feature, because we instinctively think about how that feature could be changed. Rarely is anything worthwhile found in dimensional analysis until the list is long. It takes a lot of work to push beyond the ordinary and to visualize dimensions that others don't see.

Some of the most interesting features are those that a product doesn't *seem* to have. For example, a spoon may be described in terms of its aroma, sound, resilience, bendability, and so on. Granted, the aroma may be hard to detect, the sound (at the moment) may be zero, and the resilience may be only when pushed by a vise. But each feature offers something to change. How about spoons for children that play music when used? How about spoon handles that light up or glow in the dark? How about spoons that smell like roses? Or monitor how quickly you eat (like the Hapifork you saw back in Chapter 4)?

Listing hundreds of features is not uncommon. Figure 6.6 shows a shorter list, but perhaps it suggests what must be done. Successful users claim that just citing a unique dimension sparks ideation, and that the technique has to be used to be believed.

Checklists

From early forms of dimensional analysis evolved one of today's most widely used idea-generating techniques—the **checklist**. The most widely publicized checklist was given by the originator of brainstorming:

Can it be adapted?	Can something be substituted?
Can it be modified?	Can it be magnified?
Can it be reversed?	Can it be minified?
Can it be combined with anything?	Can it be rearranged in some way?

These eight questions are powerful; they do lead to useful ideation.

---

[10]Ely Dahan and V. Srinivasan, "The Predictive Power of Internet-Based Product Concept Testing Using Visual Depiction and Animation," *Journal of Product Innovation Management*, 17(2), March 2000, pp. 99–109.

FIGURE 6.6 Dimensional Attributes of a Flashlight

Using dimensional analysis, here are 80 dimensions. There were almost 200 in the analyst's original list. A change in any one of them may make a new flashlight.

Overall unit:
Weight
Rust resistance
Balance
Gripability
Shock resistance
Shear force
Heat tolerance
Insulation material
Automatic flasher
Manual flasher
Distance visible
Length
Hangability
Stain resistance
Cold tolerance
Flexibility
Insulation color
Translucence
Focus of beam
Closure type
Lining material
Buoyancy
Flammability
Malleability
Compressibility
Reflectiveness
Surface area/color
Closure security
Material of case
Color

Number of body seams
Water resistance
Diameter
Washability
Weight of metal
Explosiveness
Smell of unit
Number of tags
Snagability
Sealant material

Lens:
Material
Opacity
Color
Strength
Texture

Springs:
Number
Material
Length
Strength
Style

Switches:
Number
Pressure
Noise
Type
Location

Bulb:
Number
Shape
Size
Gas type
Thread strength
Length of stem
Filament shape
Thread size
Filament material
Shatter point
Thread depth
Amperage

Batteries:
Number
Size
Terminal type
Direction
Rechargeability

Reflector:
Depth
Diameter
Shape
Durability
Surface
Color
Temperature limit

Business and industrial goods analysts use such features as source of energy, materials, ease of operation, subassemblies, and substitutable components. (See Figure 6.7 for an abbreviated list of such industrial checklist questions.)

Checklists produce a multitude of potential new product concepts, but most of them will be worthless. Much time and effort can be spent culling the list. A *creativity template* might be used to generate new concepts efficiently (see Figure 6.8). For example, *attribute dependency* can suggest a new concept. You have no doubt seen coffee cups with designs that change color when hot liquid is added. By making the color dependent on the cup's contents, a new concept emerged (cups that warn you if the liquid is too hot). The same concept can be extended to baby bottles or sippy cups that change color when hot. One more conceptual leap takes us to infant bath mats that

FIGURE 6.7
Checklist of Idea Stimulators for Industrial Products

Can we change the physical, thermal, electrical, chemical, and mechanical properties of this material?
Are there new electrical, electronic, optical, hydraulic, mechanical, or magnetic ways of doing this?
Find new analogs for parallel problems.
Is this function really necessary?
Can we construct a new model of this?
Can we change the form of power to make it work better?
Can standard components be substituted?
What if the order of the process was changed?
How might it be made more compact?
What if it was heat-treated, hardened, alloyed, cured, frozen, plated?
Who else could use this operation or its output?
Has every step been computerized as much as possible?

FIGURE 6.8
Templates for Creativity

Goldenberg and Mazursky present several "Creativity Templates" that can be used to manipulate the existing knowledge base encoded in product attributes to discover innovative new products. Procedure: Begin by identifying the determinate attributes, then manipulate these according to the four creativity templates. The templates are:

1. *Attribute Dependency Template:* Find a functional dependency between two independent variable attributes. The interaction may suggest a creative new product. Example: the color of the ink on a coffee cup is dependent on the contents, and a warning message can be revealed if the beverage is too hot.
2. *Replacement Template:* Remove one of the components of the product and replace it with one from another environment. The function the removed component performed is done by another component. Example: the antenna on a Walkman is replaced by the headphone cord.
3. *Displacement Template:* Remove an intrinsic component and its function, in such a way as to functionally change the product. This may create a new product for a new market. For example: removing floppy and CD drives on laptop PCs resulted in the ultra-thin PCs.
4. *Component Control Template:* Identify and create a new connection between a component internal to the product and one that is external to the product. Examples: Toothpastes with added whiteners, or suntan lotions with added skin moisturizers.

Source: From Jacob Goldenberg and David Mazursky, *Creativity in Product Innovation*, Cambridge University Press, 2002.

signal if the bath water is too hot. As an example of the replacement template, Apple removed the input jack from the iPhone 7, requiring users to try wireless headphones (or plug headphones in through the charging port using a dongle). One port (used for both the charger and headphones) thus takes the place of two. Other examples are given in Figure 6.8.

Analogy

We can often get a better idea of something by looking at it through something else—an **analogy**. Analogy is so powerful and popular that it is used heavily as part of the problem-solving step in problem-based methods (Chapter 5). Just think of how many analogies are involved in computing terminology: cut-and-paste, recycle bin, browsing, surfing, briefcase, folder, and so many other terms are familiar to us in noncomputer contexts, and the use of these terms in computer settings is intuitively obvious to computer users.

A good example of analogy was the study of airplane feeding systems by a manufacturer of kitchen furniture and other devices. Preparing, serving, and consuming meals in a plane is clearly analogous to doing so in the home, and the firm created several good ideas for new processes (and furniture) in the home kitchen. Amusement park designers watched cattle being herded and came up with the idea of queues for those waiting to go on popular rides! An analogy for bicycles might be driving a car, airplane travel, skating, or even running in a maze like a mouse.

Goodyear Tire management wondered how to make the tire purchase and installation process more convenient and efficient for consumers, with a particular focus on growing traditionally weaker market segments (millennials and women). The result was the Roll By Goodyear concierge tire shopping and installation service. Goodyear got ideas for their showrooms by analogy with other retailers popular with their target market, such as coffee shops. The Roll By Goodyear showrooms, first launched in Washington, D.C., are bright and trendy-looking, appearing more like a coffee shop or hair salon than a tire store. To increase customer convenience, the service included offering vehicle pickup and delivery by a Goodyear employee, or driving a van out to the consumer's location to change tires on site. The redesigned showrooms proved popular with the target audience: 79 percent of millennial females indicated they would go to a Roll By Goodyear the next time they bought tires.[11]

Analogies that offer the most creative potential are those that balance remoteness and familiarity—different enough to identify unique solutions but also similar enough to suggest recognizable solutions. That is, a balance is struck between connection and disconnection.[12] The goal is to get the new product team to avoid preconceptions about the product. For example, bike designers might effectively think about the similarities and differences of car or airplane travel as compared to bike travel.

Analogy is used in several of the specialized techniques in Appendix B.

Value Curve Creation

The *value curve creation* approach, proposed by W. Chan Kim and Renée Mauborgne, focuses on adjusting key attributes of current products in order to create customer value systematically.[13] Adjustments can be to strengthen or reduce current attributes, add new attributes, or delete current attributes. Any of these adjustments can result in a creative new concept. Specifically, four basic questions drive this model:

Reduce: Can we reduce any attributes to levels that are below industry standard?

Eliminate: Can we totally eliminate any attributes that are currently industry standard?

---

[11]Kate Taylor, Goodyear Is Testing a Special Tire Store for Millennial Women That Looks Like a Trendy Hair Salon," *Business Insider*, October 15, 2018.

[12]L. Zuo, "Creativity and Aesthetic Sense," *Creativity Research Journal*, 11(4), 1998, pp. 309–313; and D. W. Dahl and P. Moreau, "The Influence and Value of Analogical Thinking During New Product Ideation," *Journal of Marketing Research*, 39(1), 2002, 47–60.

[13]The examples are drawn from W. Chan Kim and Renée Mauborgne, "Creating New Market Space," *Harvard Business Review*, January–February 1999, pp. 83–93.

Raise: Can we increase any attributes to levels above industry standard?

Create: Can we create any new attributes that are not currently industry standard?

Some examples of value curve creation in action demonstrate how customer value can be created by clever adjustment of key attributes:

- The first tax preparation software products were expensive and encyclopedic. Intuit realized that the average tax preparer wanted something that was easier to use, offered just the basic features, was jargon-free, and cost far less. It launched its Quicken software product at a much lower price and redefined the market for tax preparation software.

- Years ago, Sony took its existing cassette tape recorder, stripped out the recording mechanism (so it could play prerecorded sound but not record), and also stripped out the speakers (so the user needed to wear headphones). Removing these attributes made the device smaller and more portable. The resulting product was, of course, the Walkman, which was hugely successful.

- Barnes & Noble succeeded in the bricks-and-mortar bookselling business by improving on several attributes: knowledgeable staff, pleasant store ambience, classical music, convenient store hours, and a café and lounge area. They transformed the bookstore into a relaxing place to browse, read quietly, or meet people.

- Body Shop created new attributes never before seen in cosmetics retailing: a focus on natural ingredients and healthy lifestyle, and notably no emphasis on the industry standard attributes (high-tech cosmetics, packaging, heavy advertising, and glamour).

Product Enhancements[14]

Another way to think about product attributes is in terms of *product enhancements*: modifications to the core product that provide new benefits to customers. Steven Shugan distinguishes between four different kinds of enhancements:

- *Upgrades:* Improve the quality of the core product for certain customer segments who are willing to pay the extra price (a hotel may offer upgrades such as a suite, a room with a better view, or a breakfast).

- *Add-ons:* Add extra products in order to customize or provide variety (a cruise ship may offer a choice of a nature tour, city tour, or beach day at one of its ports of call).

- *Extras:* Add features that appeal to customers depending on their usage rate (a hotel may offer an hourly or daily rate for valet parking).

- *Accessories:* Provide stand-alone complementary products (Apple might make a phone carrying case that is especially designed for Apple but might also be used with other phones).

---

[14]Much of this section derives from Steven A. Shugan, "Strategic Use of Product Enhancements: Upgrades, Add-Ons, Extras, and Accessories," in Peter N. Golder and Debanjan Mitra (eds.), *Handbook of Research on New Product Development* (Cheltenham, UK: Edward Elgar, 2018), pp. 207–226.

There are subtle differences among the categories of enhancements. Upgrades effectively segment the market vertically (price-sensitive customers versus those who see the value in paying for the upgrade). "Freemium" apps are designed this way: one can use the Amazon site for free or become an Amazon Prime member for added benefits. Spotify and other music services allow for free membership, but one can upgrade to avoid commercial interruptions.

By contrast, add-on enhancements segment the market horizontally. The cruise ship that offers a wide range of activities allows satisfying different target segments according to preference. Extras, such as discounted parking for high-use clusters, segment the market according to usage range. And adding accessories may create a product system and contribute to increased switching costs.

TRIZ[15]

TRIZ is a method that has been successfully used by firms such as Samsung, Hyundai, and many others to develop ideas for new or improved products. The name TRIZ derives from the Russian acronym for "Theory of Inventive Problem Solving," a method developed by G. S. Altshuller and colleagues. The idea behind TRIZ is that there are general patterns of problems and solutions, which can then be applied to specific problems. In a product innovation setting, TRIZ problem-solving principles often can suggest products with surprising and creative changes in their attributes.

Having studied hundreds of thousands of patents, Altshuller discovered 40 inventive principles underlying almost every one. TRIZ suggests that any problem one might face can be expressed in terms of its implicit contradictions. Once these contradictions are identified, one or more of those 40 tried and true inventive principles can be applied to eliminate the contradiction and solve the problem. Karl Ulrich and Steven Eppinger provide a simple example: a toolmaking company wants to design a better tool for driving nails.[16] One inherent contradiction in this design is that a more powerful nailer (power being desirable) would probably also be heavier (excess weight being undesirable). Now turning to the 40 inventive principles, we see that one is *periodic action* (replace a single continuous action with periodic, repeated actions). This suggests one possible solution: a nailer that makes several small strikes to drive the nail rather than one powerful blow. Another principle is *the other way round* (making something fixed movable, or making something movable fixed). The nailer might be more effective if it twisted and pushed the nail into place rather than simply driving it.

There are many other inventive principles that product developers might find useful for stimulating concepts. Here are a few, including illustrative examples:

- *Segmentation* (make an object easy to disassemble): trucks replaced by truck-trailer combination; IKEA-style furniture shipped in unassembled form; modular living room furniture.

---

[15]For a fuller description of TRIZ and an extended example, see Ik Cheol Kim, "TRIZ Develops New Product Concepts," *The TRIZ Journal*, https://triz-journal.com/use-triz-for-new-product-concept-development, December 3, 2007.

[16]Karl Ulrich and Steven Eppinger, *Product Design and Development*, 2nd ed. (New York: Irwin/McGraw-Hill, 2000), pp. 121–123.

- *Local quality* (object's structure changes from uniform to nonuniform): plastic food containers with hot and cold compartments, or separate liquid compartments.
- *Universality* (object can perform multiple functions): a lawn mower that is also a mulcher; a child car seat that is also a stroller; a vinyl record player that makes digital recordings of the songs being played.
- *Nested doll* (objects are located inside other objects): coffee shops inside bookstores; fast-food restaurants inside discount stores.
- *Another dimension* (add a dimension or adjust along a dimension): squeezable body wash bottles that stand on their lids for easier use).[17]

Summary

In this chapter, we have presented a review of several analytical attribute techniques. Qualitative techniques included the very simple yet challenging dimensional analysis and other methods such as checklists and analogies. Quantitative approaches included gap analysis and trade-off analysis. These can be used in complementary fashion: the qualitative methods can be used prior to the more numbers-oriented models (to specify or double-check the attributes included in the analysis) or after the fact (to help interpret results).

The essence of attribute analysis, in every case, is to force us to look at products differently—to bring out new perspectives. We normally have fixed ways of perceiving products, based on our sometimes long-term use of them, so forcing us out of those ruts is difficult. Anyone reading this in preparation for a specific ideation activity is encouraged to scan the many other techniques given in Appendix B.

We are now finished with concept generation and hope to have several good concepts ready for serious review and evaluation before undertaking costly technical development. We meet evaluation in Part III, Chapters 7–10, entitled Concept/Project Evaluation. We will also find that several of the analytical techniques we encountered in these chapters will be of assistance in assessing customer preferences, specifying product design characteristics, and even beyond in the new product development process.

Case: Comparing Smartphones (A)[18]

The smartphone, or mobile phone with advanced computing capability and connectivity features, is a part of daily life for an increasing number of people, and needs no introduction.

---

[17]For a list of all 40 principles and more illustrative examples of each, see TRIZ40 by Solid Creativity, at www.triz40.com/aff_Principles_TRIZ.php.

[18]Sources: Definition of smartphones is from wikipedia.com; ratings are from mobilevillage.com (March 2018). A few entries were unavailable and are estimates for the case illustration. The case is meant to provide a simple illustration of positioning maps and includes phones that are commonly rated as superior quality.

Of the hundreds of different smartphone models available on the market, six are commonly listed as the most popular or most feature-rich. These are the top-of-the-line models produced by six leading manufacturers of smartphones. In no particular order, these are the Samsung Galaxy S9 Plus, the iPhone X, the Google Pixel 2XL, the LG V20S ThinQ, the Sony Xperia XZ2, and the HTC U11 Plus. Each has its particular strengths, and purchasing the best smartphone is always a trade-off between various features and price.

The following table provides a direct comparison of all of these phones on common attributes: weight, price, screen size (measured diagonally), resolution (for improved picture), battery life, amount of internal storage and RAM, processor speed, and quality of the front and rear cameras (measured in megapixels).

	Samsung Galaxy S9 Plus	iPhone X	Google Pixel 2L	LG V30S ThinQ	Sony Xperia XZ2	HTC U11 Plus
Price ($)	840	999	849	930	799	750
Weight (grams)	190	172	177	159	200	186
Screen (inches)	6.2	5.8	6.0	6.0	5.7	6.0
Resolution (pixels)	2960 × 1440	2436 × 1125	2880 × 1440	2880 × 1440	2160 × 1080	2880 × 1440
Battery Life (hours:minutes)	8:05	8:41	8:57	9:34	8:30	7:32
Internal Storage (GB)	64	64	64	128	64	64
RAM (GB)	6	3	4	6	4	4
Processor Speed (GHz)	2.80	2.49	2.35	2.45	2.70	2.45
Front Camera (Megapixels)	8	7	8	5	6	8
Rear Camera (Megapixels)	12	12	12.2	16	19	12

Pick two of the *nonprice* attributes that you consider to be most important in choosing a smartphone. Using these two attributes, construct a positioning map for this industry using the information presented in the case. (Alternatively, you can try a "per-dollar map": divide the ratings on each attribute by price before constructing the map. Per-dollar maps give you an idea of how much of the attribute you get per dollar spent and improve the relative position of lower-price products.) Then, pick two other attributes and do the same (you will have constructed two positioning maps).

Discuss the relative positions of the iPhone X and its major competitors on the selected attributes. Do you think the iPhone is well positioned with respect to its competitors? Which competitor(s) should the iPhone be the most concerned about? Why? What additional information might you want to have about the competitors and/or about the marketplace at this point? What factors accounting for the iPhone's continued success are not considered in a positioning map such as this one? How might a seemingly "weaker" competitor (i.e., outpositioned by the iPhone) on key attributes make a dent in the iPhone's sales share?

Case: Ray-Ban[19]

Chances are you have seen photos of Tom Cruise, Mark Zuckerberg, Beyoncé, or the Blues Brothers wearing sunglasses, and if so, they were probably wearing Ray-Bans. The popular brand of sunglasses first emerged in the years preceding World War II, when the U.S. Air Force requested the Bausch & Lomb company to produce glare-reducing eyewear for its pilots. While the Ray-Ban name may be quite high-profile today, they had faced hard times due to changes in fashion preferences. During the 1980s, Tom Cruise prominently wore Ray-Bans in two blockbuster movies, *Risky Business* and *Top Gun*, boosting popularity and the brand's stylish image. Still, by 1999, the brand was in poor shape. Ray-Bans were being sold at gas stations and convenience stores for $19; product tooling was poor and materials for frames and lenses were low quality. At this time, the Italian eyewear company Luxottica bought the brand, committing to reinventing the Ray-Ban name and fostering a culture of continuous improvement.

Stefano Volpetti, Chief Marketing Officer of Luxottica, commented on the reasons for Ray-Ban's remarkable turnaround. Within a couple of years of the acquisition, Ray-Bans were removed from 13,000 points of sale (including most low-end distributors such as gas stations and convenience stores). By 2000, the price for a pair of Ray-Ban Aviators had increased to $79. By 2009, investments had been made in better, carbon-fiber frames and improved lens technology, pushing the retail price to $129 and up.

An important change effected by Luxottica was the entry into prescription lenses. When the brand was acquired, all Ray-Bans were nonprescription sunglasses. Prescription lenses, by contrast, are higher in price and profit per unit. By 2015, prescription glasses accounted for 20 percent of Ray-Ban revenues. In addition, major expansion occurred online. In 2013, Ray-Ban announced Re-Mix, a product configurator allowing users to mix and match frames, materials, and styles to suit their preferences. Within a few years, Re-Mix accounted for 40 percent of online revenue.

Looking to the future, Ray-Ban will continue to position its product offerings as good-looking (classic, and not so fashion-forward as to go out of style), as well as high-tech (lenses and frames will be based on the latest technical advances). According to retail industry analyst Joe Jackman, "as long as the brand continues to balance those two dimensions, technical innovation and counterculture stylishness, it's going to be fine."

[19]This case is based on Anonymous, "How a Pants-Free Tom Cruise Rescued Ray-Ban," CBC Radio One, April 18, 2018; Phil Wahba, Re-Tooled: How Ray-Ban Brought Its Brand Back from the Brink," *fortune.com*, January 27, 2016; and Graham Winfrey, "3 Design Lessons From Ray-Ban Sunglasses," *inc.com*, August 12, 2014.

Discuss Ray-Ban's success in terms of analytical attribute techniques. Can you construct a perceptual map of the glasses market, and identify the gaps that Ray-Ban have filled with their innovative new products? Discuss how Ray-Ban identified one or more potentially determinant attributes and developed these into determinant attributes.

Case: Rubbermaid[20]

Rubbermaid, a subsidiary of Newell Brands, is a global company that manufactures and sells a wide range of brands worldwide. Its divisions include Tools (Lenox, Hilmor), Writing (Sharpie, Waterman, Paper Mate), Baby and Parenting (Graco), Home Solutions (Rubbermaid, Calphalon), Specialty (Mimio, Bulldog Hardware), and Commercial Products sold under the Rubbermaid name. Rubbermaid had been a successful product innovating company for years before its purchase by Newell in 1999, and as many as 200 new products per year are launched under the Rubbermaid name. The success of the Rubbermaid division is based partly on creating and producing high-quality, functional plastic products for anywhere in the house: kitchen, garage, laundry room, and bathroom, as well as closet organizers, car organizers, trash bins, and similar products. In recent years items have ranged from lunch boxes with snack compartments to stacking cereal containers, storage trunks and benches, power scrubbers, and many more. Category brands include TakeAlongs®, Lunch Blox™, Closet Helper™, and others.

The firm makes almost a half-million different items, boasts a 90 percent success rate on new products, and obtains at least 30 percent of its sales each year from products less than five years old.

The firm's new product strategy is to meet the needs of the consumer. The new product rate is high, and diversification is desired. It is market-driven, not technology-driven, although in recent years the firm has identified such technologies as recycling new plastic parts from old tires for which it is seeking market opportunities. This practice of seeking opportunities for specific technologies will increase as a fallout of the firm's current use of simultaneous product development.

For idea generation, Rubbermaid depends on finding customer problems that can be built into the strategic planning process. Problems are sought in several ways, the principal one of which is focus groups. It also uses comments and complaints from customers, an example of which came when then-CEO Stanley C. Gault heard a Manhattan doorman complaining as he swept dirt into a Rubbermaid dustpan. Inquiry determined that the doorman wanted a thinner lip on the pan, so less dirt would remain on the walk. He got it.

Each complaint is documented by marketing people, and executives are encouraged to read the complaints. One complaint by customers in small households, who found the traditional rack-and-mat too bulky to store, led to a compact, one-piece dish drainer. The firm generally finds its problems by using problem analysis in focus groups and solves them internally. They occasionally use scenario analysis to spot a problem. But scenario analysis is much less useful than problem analysis because the

[20]This case was prepared from www.rubbermaid.com and many public information sources.

lead times are so short; their new product cycles make them concentrate mainly on already existing problems. The organization is kept conducive to newly created ideas by promoting cross-functional association among workers. Problem-find-solve is encouraged at all levels.

Some other new items have been:

Bouncer drinkware was created for people who fear using glassware around their swimming pools.

A lazy Susan condiment tray and other patio furniture products came from studies of lifestyle changes.

People working at home told of problems that led to a line of home office accessories, including an "auto-office," a portable device that straps onto a car seat and holds pens and other office articles.

Generally speaking, Rubbermaid does not make much use of attribute listing and other fortuitous scan methods of ideation, including the various mapping approaches. It does find that product life-cycle models can be useful, and it closely tracks competitive new product introductions.

Rubbermaid is, however, always looking for new ways by which it can come up with good new product concepts. They know from experience, for example, that there will be new ways by which problem-find-solve techniques can be used. And perhaps the fortuitous scan methods can be of greater use than now perceived.

What would you recommend to Rubbermaid management? Should they use any of the concept generation techniques discussed in this chapter, in addition to the methods they traditionally use? Which ones, and why?

FIGURE III.1

Concept/Project Evaluation

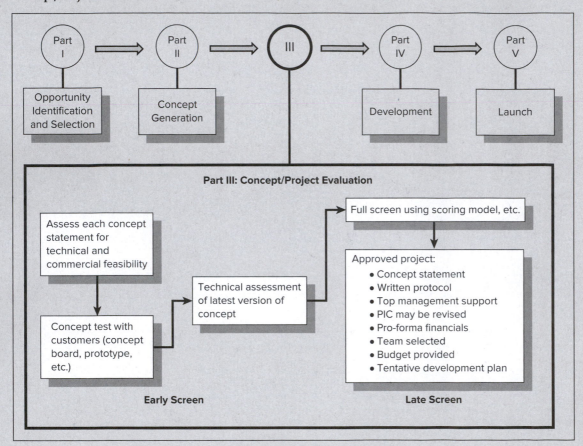

PART THREE

Concept/Project Evaluation

Part II completed our study of the various methods of generating new product concepts. The next task is to undertake evaluation of these concepts. Evaluation takes place at many different times and in different ways, by different people, for different reasons. Therefore, a *system* of evaluations is needed, an idea that will be explained in Chapter 7.

In Chapter 7, we will also be looking at the different phases in that system (see Figure III.1). Concept testing is the first major tool and will be discussed there. Chapter 8 covers the activity generally called a *full screen*, a step in which the concept is judged by how well it fits the company and its marketing strengths. Once the project has cleared the high hurdles set at the full screen, it is approved for development and ready to move into the next phase of the process. Chapters 9 and 10 focus on specific topics appearing in the last box in Figure III.1: a financial analysis, a check to make sure the project (still) fits with the product innovation charter, and the development of a protocol. At that point, development can begin, teams are assigned (if they do not exist yet), and we move to Part IV of the book.

The evaluation tools discussed in Part III are those that precede development. Once prototypes or service configurations begin to appear, evaluation begins again, first in the form of product use testing and later in market testing, and more. These are covered in later chapters. All of these efforts at evaluation are themselves major topics, so our discussions must be selective. Unfortunately, industry uses many of the tools in different ways, so they tend to blend together at the edges. When, for example, does a prototype concept test become a product use test?

Likewise, industry often combines two or even three of the tools. For example, if it is easy to prepare prototypes (even a nonworking 3D-printed full-size model), it may be possible to do an early customer survey that is part market analysis, part concept test, and part prototype test. Finally, standardized and fully accepted terminology often doesn't exist. Therefore, we have had to do some standardizing of terms, and some of our decisions won't be acceptable to all people.

CHAPTER SEVEN

Concept Evaluation and Testing

Setting

Throughout the new product development process, we are doing evaluations, and there are evaluation techniques appropriate to each of the phases in the basic new products process. Furthermore, none of these techniques is used all of the time or in all cases. Chapter 7 provides an overview of concept evaluation, presenting models such as the cumulative expenditures curve and the A-T-A-R model as ways that can help us decide which evaluation techniques to use. Later in this chapter, we begin the process of evaluating new products (goods and services) prior to undertaking technical development. In this chapter, we investigate the early part of concept testing (up to, but not including, the full screen, as shown in Figure III.1) and discuss evaluation techniques that are used at this time. Chapter 8 is devoted to a detailed examination of the full screen. All the evaluation steps shown in this chapter and Chapter 8 should be viewed as investments—the additional information provided far outweighs their cost, and cutting corners in getting important early information from customers can prove costly in the long run.

You will recall from Chapter 2 that new products fail because (1) there was no basic need for the item, as seen by intended users; (2) the new product did not meet its need, considering all disadvantages; and (3) the new product idea was not properly communicated (marketed) to the intended user. In sum, they didn't need it, it didn't work, they didn't get the message. Keep these factors in mind as you see how an evaluation system is constructed.

What's Going On in the New Products Process?

New products build up the way rivers do. Great rivers are systems with tributaries that have tributaries. Goods that appear complex are just collections of metal shapes, packaging material, fluids, prices, and so on. A good analogy is the production of automobiles, with a main assembly line supported by scores of subsidiary assembly lines scattered around the world, each of which makes a part that goes into another part that ultimately goes onto a car in that final assembly line.

If you can imagine the quality control people in auto parts plants evaluating each part before releasing it to the next step, you have the idea of a new product **evaluation system**. The new product appears first as an idea, a concept in words or pictures, and we evaluate that first. As workers turn the concept into a formed piece of metal, or software, or a new factory site preparation service, that good or service is then evaluated. When a market planner puts together a marketing plan, its parts are evaluated separately (just as minor car parts are) and then evaluated again in total after it is added to the product.

The Evaluation System for the Basic New Products Process

Although the overall purpose of evaluation is to guide us to profitable new products, each individual evaluation step task has a specific purpose, keyed primarily to what happens next. Recall Figure 2.2, which showed that different evaluation tasks were appropriate to specific phases in the new products process. Figure 7.1 presents the same information but adds the most common evaluation techniques used throughout the process. Before going any further, this is a good place to note that conducting the evaluation tasks really does improve new product performance. The Comparative Performance Assessment Study (first introduced in Chapter 1) included an analysis of the most commonly used evaluation techniques: In all cases, the Best firms were significantly more likely to use these techniques than the Rest, and they ended up with better sales and profit results from their new products.[1]

In the process of Figure 7.1, ideas become concepts; concepts get refined, evaluated, and approved; development projects are initiated; and products are launched. Throughout this process, different questions need to be asked, and different evaluation techniques provide the required answers. For example, the very first evaluation *precedes* the product concept—in fact, it takes place in Phase I, when an opportunity or threat is identified and assessed. Someone decided the firm had a strong technology, or an excellent market opportunity, or a serious competitive threat—whatever. As discussed in Chapter 3 on strategy, a judgment was made that if the firm tried to develop a new product in a given area, it would probably succeed. This early evaluation step (direction) is shown at the top of Figure 7.1. Where should we look, what should we try to exploit, what should we fight against? The tool is opportunity identification and evaluation, also discussed in Chapter 3. This tool keeps us out of development projects in which we stand a poor chance of winning; in other words, it makes sure we play the game on our home field. This direction is provided in the product innovation charter.

Now continue down Figure 7.1 to see how the evaluation tasks change as we progress through the basic new product process. In Phase II (concept generation), ideas begin to appear, and the purpose of evaluation changes: Now the goal is to avoid the big loser or the sure loser. We want to cull them out and spend no added time and money on them. This step is essential if we are to focus limited resources on the

[1]Gloria Barczak, Abbie Griffin, and Kenneth B. Kahn, "Perspective: Trends and Drivers of Success in NPD Practices: Results of the 2003 PDMA Best Practices Study," *Journal of Product Innovation Management*, 26(1), January 2009, pp. 3–23; and Stephen K. Markham and Hyunjung Lee, "Product Development and Management Association's 2012 Comparative Performance Assessment Study," *Journal of Product Innovation Management*, 30(3), 2013, pp. 408–429.

FIGURE 7.1 The Evaluation System Including Common Techniques

New Products Process Phase	Evaluation Task at End of Phase	Evaluation Techniques
Opportunity Identification and Selection	*Direction:* Where should we look?	Opportunity identification (trends and megatrends) Market descriptions Social media Customer site visits Interviews and focus groups Other qualitative techniques
Concept Generation	*Initial Review:* Does the idea pass initial screen and go on to concept development?	Product innovation charter Immediate judgment (can we make it and will they buy it) Preliminary market analyses Concept testing Lead users Ethnographic market research Customer site visits Interviews and focus groups Other qualitative techniques
Concept/Project Evaluation	*Full Screen:* Should we put the concept into development?	Checklists Profile sheets Scoring models
Development	*Technical Questions:* Have we developed the product? And if not, should we continue to try?	Prototype tests Product use tests (alpha, beta, and gamma tests) Protocol checks
	Marketing Questions: Should we market it? And if so, how?	Speculative sale Simulated test market Controlled test market Test market Informal selling
Launch	*Post-Launch Evaluation:* How are we doing relative to objectives?	Rollout tracking Sales, profit, market shares

worthwhile concepts and not get overwhelmed with the sheer number of available ideas. We will also try to spot potential big winners. Some concepts are good, but a few are great, and we want to recognize them as soon as possible. These get added effort, usually in the form of a very complete concept testing and development program. Although there is no one set screening procedure, certainly at this early stage we would be assessing the ideas in terms of the following criteria:

- Uniqueness: Is the idea original? Can it be easily copied by competitors?
- Need fulfillment: Does it meet a customer need?
- Feasibility: Do we have the capability to develop and launch it?

- Impact: How will our firm or organization be affected?
- Scalability: Can we become more efficient in production as volume increases?
- Strategic fit: Is there a good match with corporate strategy and culture?[2]

Many firms use some variant of this idea screening technique. For example, Unilever requires that a brief be written for each new idea under consideration. The brief must describe the consumer need, any technical specifications, the "idea solution" (benchmarks and standards), "must-haves" (minimum requirements or specifications), "killers" (an assessment of what might cause it to fail), a statement of what is already known, a budget, and a time line.[3]

This kind of activity leads us to Phase III (concept/project evaluation) and the decision on whether to send the concept into full-scale development. This decision, if the amounts to be spent make it an important decision, will benefit from a very thorough scoring model application. Should we try to develop it?

The decision to enter Phase IV (development) introduces the part of the process where the parallel or simultaneous technical and marketing activities are done (as seen in Figure 2.1). All through this phase, we are continually asking, Have we got what we want? Is this part ready? Is that system subset cleared for use? Does the software not only work but produce what the customer needs? A protocol check tells us whether we are ready to develop a product for serious field testing.

Sooner or later, the technical efforts yield a product that evaluators say meets the customers' request. We then enter Phase V (launch), and attention turns to launching the item. The evaluation issue now is whether the firm has proven itself able to make and market the item on a commercial scale. This is usually resolved by some form of market testing.

Product Line Considerations in Concept Evaluation

Keep in mind that any one product being evaluated is not alone. Most organizations have several products under development, sometimes scores or even hundreds of them. As we saw in Chapter 3, managers often think in terms of a portfolio of products and evaluate new product projects in terms of how well they would fit with corporate strategy. We will see how product projects are selected relative to strategic concerns (such as strategic portfolios) in more detail in Chapter 9.

Especially at the early phases (the front end) of the new product process, there are risks involved in making project selection decisions. Depending on the evaluation mechanism chosen, the firm may let through too many bad ideas or reject good ideas. There is no one right way to optimize project evaluation, but some experience can help set the best rules for a given firm or industry. For example, a firm that needs new product help fast may skip early checkpoints and narrow down to just one or two alternative formats during development. They will tend to put in one major check late in the process to make sure the marketing plan communicates and the distribution system is in place. In an industry like pharmaceuticals, a firm might bring two or more ideas

[2]Jacquelin Cooper, "How Industry Leaders Find, Evaluate, and Choose the Most Promising Open Innovation Opportunities," *Visions*, 36(1), 2012, pp. 20–23.

[3]The examples are from J. Cooper, *Visions*, op. cit.

through to development: With more potential products, there is a greater chance that one will be a winner, and the payoff for winning is large enough to offset the extra costs incurred in developing more products. Having hurdles that are too high may reduce failure rate but contribute to major, costly delays in a new product launch. If a firm makes products with very short cycle times (such as computer games), it has to control the number of products in the process queue at any given time so that products receive development funds in a timely manner.[4]

The Cumulative Expenditures Curve

As we have seen, the new product evaluation system flows with the development of the product. What evaluation occurs at any one point (how serious, how costly) depends greatly on what happens next. Figure 7.2 shows a key input to the design of any evaluation system: In the middle of that figure, a gradually upward-sloping curve represents the accumulation of costs or expenditures on a typical new product project from its beginning to its full launch.

This generalized curve, taken from various studies over the years, is just an average. It need not reflect any one firm, but it is typical of many durable consumer goods, nontechnical business-to-business products, and many services. Shown with the average curve are two others. The early expenditures curve is representative of product development in technical fields, such as pharmaceuticals, optics, and computers. Research and development (R&D) is the big part of the cost package, and marketing costs are relatively small. The lower curve in the figure shows the opposite type of firm, say, a consumer packaged goods company. Here, the technical expenditures may be small, but a huge TV advertising program is needed at introduction. These are generalizations, and individual exceptions do occur. But whoever develops a concept evaluation system needs to know what situation it is for. No evaluation decision is independent of what will be done next or how much will be spent. An old proverb says, "Spend your energy sharpening the edge of the knife, not polishing the handle."

The Risk/Payoff Matrix

Figure 7.3 applies these ideas in a **risk/payoff matrix**. At any single evaluation point in the new product process, the new products manager faces the four situations shown. Given that the product concept being evaluated has two broad ultimate outcomes (success or failure) and that there are two decision options at the time (move on or kill the project), there are four cells in the matrix.

The AA cell and the BB cell are fine; we drop a concept that would ultimately fail, or we continue on a concept that would ultimately succeed. The managerial problem arises in the other two cells. AB is a "drop error": A winner is discarded. But BA is a "go error": A loser is continued to the next evaluation point.

[4]For more on this topic, see Donald G. Reinertsen, "Taking the Fuzziness Out of the Fuzzy Front End," *Research-Technology Management*, November–December 1999, pp. 25–31.

FIGURE 7.2
Cumulative
Expenditures—
All-Industry
Average
Compared to
Occasional
Patterns

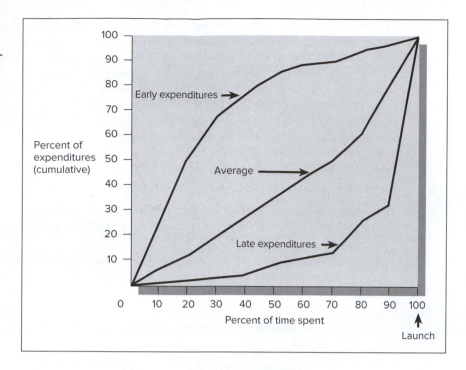

FIGURE 7.3
Matrix of Risk/
Payoff at Each
Evaluation

Decision is to:	A Stop the project now	B Continue to next evaluation
If the product were marketed		
A. It would fail	AA (no error)	BA (go error)
B. It would succeed	AB (drop error)	BB (no error)

Comment: Cells AA and BB are "correct" decisions. Cells BA and AB are errors, but they have different cost and probability dimensions.

Which error does the manager most want to avoid? The answer depends on the dollars. First, throwing out a winner is very costly, because the ultimate profits from a winning product are bound to be much greater than all of the development costs combined, let alone those in just the next step. So error AB is much worse than BA.

The exception, of course, is the opportunity cost. What other project is standing by, waiting for funding? When good candidates wait in the wings, the losses of dropping a winner are much less because the money diverted will likely go to another winner. The point is, a manager must think of these matters when deciding what evaluation to do. If the net costs of the next step in any situation are low, then a decision will probably be made to go ahead, perhaps with very little information. For example, Proctor & Gamble (P&G) supported both Febreze (an odor eliminator) and

Dryel (which lets you wash dry clean–only clothes at home) with substantial market testing, including lengthy test marketing, as they were seen as risky, new-to-the-world (and also new to P&G) products. But P&G would support a simple detergent line extension with much less extensive testing (relying on some of the alternative methods we will see in Chapter 16), as that would be considered a much less risky launch. You will read later about how Starbucks extensively tested Via instant coffee because they saw it as a potentially risky product launch and needed to mitigate these risks. Consider: Who knows more about detergents than P&G? Who knows more about coffee than Starbucks? Yet even these companies recognized that high-risk situations called for more extensive market testing.

In general, the new products team should consider four generic risk strategies:

Avoidance: Eliminate the risky product project altogether, though an opportunity cost is incurred (what if they had pushed through with the project and it succeeded?).

Mitigation: Reduce the risk to an acceptable, threshold level, perhaps through redesigning the product to include more backup systems or increasing product reliability.

Transfer: Move the responsibility to another organization, in the form of a joint venture or subcontractor, for example. The other party would be better equipped to handle the risk.

Acceptance: Develop a contingency plan now (active acceptance) or deal with the risks as they come up (passive acceptance).[5]

The Decay Curve and the New Products Process

The risk matrix decisions lead to the idea of a **decay curve**. By applying the new products process, the hundreds or thousands of ideas the company may have started with gradually get reduced. Only the best ideas are developed into concepts; only a small number of concepts are put into development, and not all of these might eventually be commericalized. The discarded ideas and concepts drop off at various times during the process, and when they drop off is primarily determined by the analysis of the risk matrix.

Planning the Evaluation System

The previous considerations help set the tone for management decisions on an appropriate evaluation system for any particular new product concept. There are four other relevant but less demanding concepts that help us decide whether to concept test, how long to run a field use test, whether to roll out or go national immediately, and how thorough a financial analysis to demand.

[5]Gregory D. Githens, "How to Assess and Manage Risk in NPD Programs: A Team-Based Risk Approach," in P. Belliveau, A. Griffin, and S. Somermeyer (eds.), *The PDMA Toolbook for New Product Development* (New York: John Wiley, 2002), pp. 187–214.

Everything Is Tentative

It's easy to imagine that building a new product is like building a house—first the foundation, then the frame, then the first floor, and so on. Product development projects, however, rarely progress in such a straightforward way. Occasionally, they do, as when a technical process dominates development, or when a semifinished product is acquired from someone else, or when legal or industry requirements exist.

We usually assume everything is tentative, even up through marketing. Form can usually be changed, and so can costs, packaging, positioning, and service contracts; so can the marketing date and the reactions of government regulators. So can customer attitudes, as companies with long development times have discovered.

This means two long-held beliefs in new product work are actually untrue. One is that everything should be keyed to a single Go/No Go decision. Granted, one decision can be critical—at times, for example, when a firm must invest millions of dollars in one large facility or when a firm acquires a license that commits it to major financial out-lays. But many firms are finding ways to avoid such commitments by transferring risk: by having another supplier produce the product for a while before a facilities commitment, or by negotiating a tentative license, or by asking probable customers to join a consortium to ensure the volume needed to build the facility.

The other fallacy is that financial analysis should be done as early as possible to avoid wasting money on poor projects. This philosophy leads firms to make complex financial analyses shortly after early concept testing, although the numbers are inadequate. Early financial analysis might kill off ideas that would have looked great after further development, when more information is available. The financial analysis is best built up piece by piece, just like the product itself. We will see later how this works.

Still another tentative matter is the marketing date. Marketing actually begins very early in the development process (for example, when purchasing agents are asked in a concept test whether they think their firm would be interested in a new item). Rollouts (discussed in Chapter 16) are now so common it is hard to tell when all-out marketing begins. In fact, marketing activity has been rolling forward gradually throughout the new products proess, picking up steam, which clearly affects the evaluation system. What results in some cases is a sort of *rolling evaluation*. The project is being assessed continuously, figures are penciled in, premature closure is avoided, and participants avoid mindsets of good and bad. This is, in a way, dealing with risk via acceptance or mitigation. We know product development projects are risky, so we evaluate, move to the next phase, if wanted, and continuously upgrade the quality of information available to us throughout the process to minimize the chances of failure (mitigation) and to expect contingencies and deal with them as they come up (acceptance). There is, nevertheless, likely to be an "I think we've got it" moment in the development phase, when marketing really begins to ramp up its activities; we will see more about this in Chapter 13.

Potholes

One critical skill of product developers is the ability to anticipate major difficulties, the potholes of product innovation. In automobile travel, potholes are always a problem, but they only become costly when we fail to see them coming in time to slow down or steer around them. The same thinking applies to new products: We should carefully scan for the really damaging problems (the deep holes) and keep them in mind when we decide what evaluating we will do. If the pothole is deep enough, the development team may have to seriously consider the risk avoidance option: Drop the project!

For example, when Campbell Soup Company undertakes the development of a new canned soup, odds are in its favor. The company knows development, manufacturing, packaging, distribution, and promotion of such products extremely well. But experience has shown two points in the process when it may fail, and if it does, the product won't sell. The first is manufacturing cost—not quality, as that's one of the company's key strengths. But there is always a question about whether the chosen ingredients can be put together to meet market-driven cost targets. The second is whether consumers think it tastes good. So the company's evaluation system is set to never overlook these two points.

A software developer said his biggest pothole was customer unwillingness to take the time to learn to use complex new products. He had several worthwhile products in the graveyard to prove it. Among the potholes faced by pharmaceutical manufacturers is the uncertainty regarding U.S. Food and Drug Administration approval; for that reason, a firm may go to the expense of taking two similar products through the approval process in the hopes that at least one of them makes it.

The People Dimension

Product developers also have to remember that they are dealing with people, and people cause problems. For example, although R&D workers are quite enthusiastic early in the life of a new product, the idea may have little support outside of R&D; it is fragile and easy to kill. Late in the development cycle, more people have bought in to the concept and are supportive because they have played a role in getting it to where it is. Consequently, the now strong proposal is tough to stop.

This means that an evaluation system should contain early testing that is supportive. In fact, concept *testing* is sometimes called concept *development* to reinforce the idea of helping the item, not just killing it off. Later in the cycle, hurdles should usually be tough and demanding, not easily waved aside. One firm designated its market research director as a manager of screens. His task was to impose absolute screens, such as, "A new food product, in home placement testing, must achieve a 70 percent preference against the respective category leaders." If less than 70 percent of the testers preferred the new item, it was stopped, period. This sounds severe and arbitrary, but it shows how difficult it sometimes is to kill off marginal products late in development. Another people problem relates to personal risk. All new product work has a strong element of risk—risk to jobs, promotions, bonuses, and so on. Consequently, some people shy away from new product assignments. We're always under the gun from someone—an ambitious boss, a dedicated regulator, an aggressive competitor, a power-hungry distributor, or an early critic who was overruled within the company. A good evaluation system, built on a thorough understanding of the road the new item will follow as it winds its way through development, protects developers from these pressures. The system should be supportive of people and offer the reassurance (if warranted) that players need.

Surrogates

The timing of factual information does not often match our need for it. For example, we want to know customer reactions early on, even before we develop the product, if possible. But we can't really know their reactions until we make some of the product and give it to them to try out. So, we look for **surrogate questions** to give us pieces of information that can substitute for what we want to learn but can't. Here are four questions to which we badly need answers and four other questions that can be answered earlier (thus giving *clues* to the real answer):

Real Question	Surrogate (Substitute) Question
Will they prefer it?	Did they keep the prototype product we gave them?
Will cost be competitive?	Does it match our manufacturing skills?
Will competition leap in?	What did they do last time?
Will it sell?	Did it do well in field testing?

Surrogates often change at different times in the evaluation process. For example, let's go back to one of the questions just above: Will cost be competitive? At different times during the project, the surrogate used might be:

Time 1: Does it match our manufacturing skills?

Time 2: Are the skills obtainable?

Time 3: What troubles are we having in making a prototype?

Time 4: How does the prototype look?

Time 5: Does the manufacturing process look efficient?

Time 6: How did the early production costs turn out?

Time 7: Do we now see any ways we can cut the cost?

Time 8: What is the cost?

Time 9: What is the competitive cost?

Only when we know our final cost and the competition's cost can we answer the original question. But the surrogates helped tell us whether we were headed for trouble.

The last tool that we use for designing an evaluation system for each new project as it comes along is based on how we forecast sales and profit on a new item. The calculation is much like a pro forma income statement, an *array* of figures allowing us to see what the profits will look like based on where we are at any one time in the development.

The basic formula, shown in Figure 7.4, is based on what is known in the marketing field as the **A-T-A-R concept** (awareness-trial-availability-repeat).

FIGURE 7.4
The A-T-A-R
Model

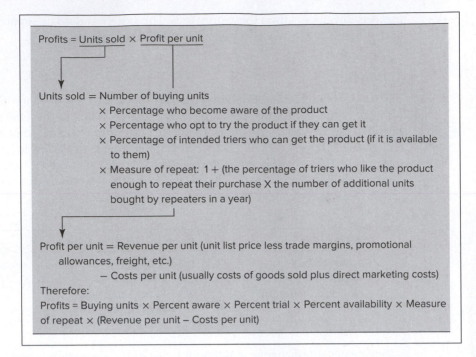

Profits = Units sold × Profit per unit

Units sold = Number of buying units
       × Percentage who become aware of the product
       × Percentage who opt to try the product if they can get it
       × Percentage of intended triers who can get the product (if it is available
         to them)
       × Measure of repeat: 1 + (the percentage of triers who like the product
         enough to repeat their purchase X the number of additional units
         bought by repeaters in a year)

Profit per unit = Revenue per unit (unit list price less trade margins, promotional
      allowances, freight, etc.)
         − Costs per unit (usually costs of goods sold plus direct marketing costs)
Therefore:
Profits = Buying units × Percent aware × Percent trial × Percent availability × Measure
of repeat × (Revenue per unit − Costs per unit)

The A-T-A-R Model

This is taken from what is called **diffusion of innovation**, which is explained this way: For a person or a firm to become a regular buyer/user of an innovation, there must first be awareness that it exists, then there must be a decision to try that innovation, then the person must find the item available to him or her, and finally there must be the type of happiness with it that leads to adoption, or repeat usage.[6]

We want to use the formula to calculate all the way to profit, so we expand it to include target market size (potential adopters), units purchased by each adopter, and the economics of the operation. But at the heart of the calculation is A-T-A-R. We use one form of this model here in predicting first-year profitability; in Chapter 9, we revisit A-T-A-R as a market share forecasting tool, and we see it again later in Chapter 16 in the context of simulated test markets.

Let's take a simple example to explain how it works. Assume our company is developing the next generation of smartphone. We presume that the product is analogous to existing smartphones with video display (that is, the new product will be

---

[6]The basic A-T-A-R sequence has been broken down further into many microsteps. One example of this extension is John H. Antil, "New Product or Service Adoption: When Does It Happen?," *Journal of Consumer Marketing*, Spring 1988, pp. 5–16. Some people use this model in abbreviated form, stopping at unit sales. They calculate market share and make conclusions on that.

comparable in many ways to these cell phones: similar price, similar target market, similar benefit provided). A rough estimate, then, of the potential for the new product is the size of the market for the analogous existing product (more about the use of analogous products in forecasting in Chapter 9). To apply the A-T-A-R model, we need the following (hypothetical) data:

- Number of owners of smartphones (who are our potential buying units for the new product): 10 million.
- Percentage of owners of smartphones we think we can make aware of our new generation phone the first year on the market: 40 percent.
- Percentage of aware owners who will decide to try the new phone during the first year and set out to find it: 20 percent.
- Percentage of customary consumer electronics retailers whom we can convince to stock the new phone during the market introduction period: 70 percent. (To keep things simple, assume that potential buyers probably will not seek beyond one store if they cannot find it there.)
- Percentage of the actual triers who will like the product enough to repeat-purchase within the first year: 20 percent.
- Number of additional units bought by these repeat buyers, on average: 1 (that is, they buy a total of two phones, possibly one for personal use and another for a family member).
- Dollar revenue at the factory, per device, after trade margins and promotion discounts: $100.
- Unit cost, at the intended volume: $50.

The profit contribution forecast, based on the A-T-A-R model as depicted in Figure 7.4, would be

$$\text{Profit contribution} = \text{Potential} \times AW \times T \times AV \times R \times \text{margin}$$
$$= 10 \text{ million} \times 0.40 \times 0.20 \times 0.70 \times 1.20 \times (\$100 - \$50)$$
$$= \$33{,}600{,}000$$

where AW = awareness and AV = availability, and R is calculated as shown in Figure 7.4 as

$$1 + (\text{percentage of repeaters} \times \text{number of additional units}) = 1 + (0.20 \times 1) = 1.20$$

What we did was prepare a mathematical formula and run it through one set of data. Since the development was almost finished when the calculation was made, the forecast was fairly solid. But the formula could have been used at the very beginning as well. Only a few figures (e.g., number of potential adopters) are known at the start, but estimates can be plugged into the other spots, and the model can be set up for use down the line.

As with the other parts of this chapter, the A-T-A-R model gives us guidance on evaluation system design. You can immediately see the importance of awareness, trial, and so on. That means tests will have to be run in which customers are checked for their interest in trying, their reactions after trying (how likely would they be to try again?), and whatever else contributes to the formula.

Two things are important about this model's sales and profit forecasts for the new smartphone:

1. *Each factor is subject to estimation,* and in every development phase we are trying to sharpen our ability to make the estimates. For example, we may be trying to check the introductory promotion's awareness-building capability or just how much price discounting we must do to motivate a first purchase of the device.

2. *An inadequate profit forecast can be improved only by changing one of the factors.* For example, if the forecast of $33,600,000 profit contribution is insufficient, we look at each factor in the model and see which ones might be changed and at what cost. Perhaps we could increase the retail margin by 5 percent and get another 10 percent of retailers to stock it. On the other hand, perhaps an increase in advertising (or a qualitative improvement in the advertising message) would produce more awareness.

A-T-A-R is a term that came from consumer products marketing. Industry has traditionally used slightly different language, so a natural question is, "Does the model apply to all types of new products, including industrial ones, and services too?" The answer is absolutely, though each term may be defined slightly differently in different settings.

See Figure 7.5 for the definitions of terms that vary. A **consumer buying unit** may be a person or a home. For office furniture, it will perhaps be a facility manager; for industrial products, it will generally be a purchasing or engineering person (part of a team); and for a consumer bank loan, it will once again be a person or a family. Product developers know what these definitions should be; the target users were selected partly because we know them well.

Without a precise definition there can be no worthwhile measurement. In each case, something about the term tells you how to define it. For **awareness**, we want to know if the buying unit has been sufficiently informed to stimulate further investigation and consideration of the trial. If it has only heard the product's name, it probably won't go any further. For **trial** of our new product, we might imagine an in-store situation where the prospective customer tries out the smartphone and sees if the product is satisfactory. For other kinds of new products (such as a new electronic security

FIGURE 7.5
Definitions Used in the A-T-A-R Model

Buying unit means purchase point; may be each person, household, or department who participates in the decision.
Aware means someone in the buying unit hears about the existence of a new product with some characteristic that differentiates it; subject to variation between industries and even between developers.
Available means the percentage chance that if a buyer wants to try the product, the effort to find it will be successful; often "percent of stores that stock it." Direct sellers have 100 percent availability.
Trial is variously defined; may be use of a sample in an industrial setting where such use has a cost associated with it; in most situations, means an actual purchase and at least some consumption.
Repeat is also varied; on packaged goods, means to buy at least one (or two or three) more times; on durables, may mean be happy and/or make at least one recommendation to others.

device to be installed on a car), you may wonder how a potential buyer could try the product, that is, try it in risky situations, waiting for a thief to challenge it. The answer is that we get as close to the perfect answer as we can, and that sometimes calls for ingenuity. Otis Elevator Company, for example, takes prospective buyers to a site where the elevator under consideration is already installed. The trial is not perfect, but it is close enough for real customer learning.

For **availability**, we want to know whether the buyers can easily get the new product if their decision is made to try it. This factor is more standard, and for consumer products it is usually the percent of those outlets where our target buyers shop where the firm has stock of the new item. If the firm sells direct, or the product is sold online, there is almost always availability (unless the factory has extended backorders). Another measure commonly used is **all commodity volume** (ACV), which is the percentage of the market that has access to the product in local distribution channels. Business-to-business often uses distributors of some type, usually under some franchise or semifranchise agreement, again ensuring availability. But many small firms cannot be sure of availability and spend much of their marketing money on trying to get it.

Repeat is easy for consumer packaged goods (usually, a repeat purchase), but it really means the trial was successful—the buying unit was pleased. For one-time purchases (industrial or consumer), we have to decide what statistic will tell us that. Some people use the direct one: "Were you satisfied?" Sometimes an indirect one—such as "Have you had occasion to recommend the product to others?"—is better. Another possibility is whether a second unit was bought by the consumer. In any case, a firm should arrive at some acceptable definition and stick with it.

Where Do We Get the Figures for the A-T-A-R Model?

The evaluation techniques shown in Figure 7.1 (primarily concept testing, product use testing, and market testing) will provide the data needed for the A-T-A-R model. You are not yet acquainted with the various tests, but they will be tied into the A-T-A-R model as they come up. Though various evaluation events can help on several of the key factors, we are usually most interested in the one event that makes the biggest contribution—noted as *Best* in the figure. And we should know which these are prior to starting the evaluation. That way, we spend our limited funds first on the best steps and then on others if funds are available. Also, if we have to skip a step (for example, the concept test), we immediately know we are leaving open the question of whether users are likely to try the item when it becomes available. If we are going to do product use testing, then it should be set up in a way that lets us go through a concept test in the process of getting people to sign up for the use testing. It's later than we wanted, but better now than not at all.

Further Uses of the A-T-A-R Model

In this chapter, we outlined the use of A-T-A-R relatively early in concept evaluation as a rough forecasting tool (i.e., what is the potential profit contribution of this product, is it satisfactory, and how could it be improved?). The A-T-A-R model is useful at this early point, as it provides an early sales and profit forecast based on estimates specific to the new product (i.e., the A, T, A, and R)—it calls for numbers that usually can be researched, and it uses them in a managerial way. We will use A-T-A-R at later phases in the new products process and therefore will return to it occasionally in this book. In Chapter 9, we will use it as the basis of a somewhat more detailed sales forecasting model. A-T-A-R is implicit throughout the discussion of market launch planning (Chapters 14 and 15): What else could be more important for the marketing effort to do than achieve awareness, trial, availability, and repeat use?[7] Finally, in Chapter 17, we visit it again, this time as a tool to assess the launch, identify where the problem areas are, and steer it back on course.

Concept Evaluation: Fit with Product Innovation Charter

The earliest evaluation that a firm makes is *of itself and its situation*. That evaluation yields a priori conclusions about new product proposals. The firm reaches these conclusions while making basic strategic decisions, as discussed in Chapter 3 on the product innovation charter (PIC). These decisions assess what types of new products fit best.

The PIC itself will eliminate many new product ideas. In advance and without knowing the concepts, the firm decides to reject ideas that violate PIC guidelines. Following the PIC should result in excluding the following kinds of ideas:

- Ideas that require technologies the firm does not have
- Ideas to be sold to customers about whom the firm has no close knowledgeï€
- Ideas that offer the wrong degree of innovativeness (too much or too little!)
- Ideas wrong on other dimensions: not low cost, too close to certain competitors, and so on

The PIC thus eliminates a large number of product ideas that would not be a good fit and should not be pursued further. Having been established at the beginning of the new products process, the PIC precludes the unfortunate practice of having unwanted proposals eat up valuable development funds before they are detected and weeded out.

Concept Testing and Development

Most major firms make frequent use of **concept testing**. It is a mandatory part of the process for makers of consumer packaged goods, and use is growing in industrial firms, which actually invented it. Business-to-business firms have always spent much time talking with users about their needs and problems, what suggestions they have, what they think about various ideas, and so on. This is indeed a basic, informal way to do concept testing.

But first, let's deal with some concerns about this activity—there are times when it doesn't help. When the prime benefit is a *personal sense*, such as the aroma of a perfume or the taste of a new food, concept testing usually fails. The concept cannot be

[7]One of our top sales forecasting experts addressed the new product situation, particularly the issues surrounding the many techniques. Robert J. Thomas, "Issues in New Product Forecasting," *Journal of Product Innovation Management*, 10(3), September 1994, pp. 347–353.

communicated short of actually having some product there to demonstrate. Try to describe the scent of your favorite cologne or perfume! Concepts embodying new *art and entertainment* are also tough to test. The American painter Whistler could not have concept-tested his idea for a painting of his mother. George Ferris, the inventor of the Ferris wheel, could not have surveyed people to ask what they thought of his rotating ride. TV shows that did well in concept tests often did not catch on, and some that tested poorly eventually became classics. These are products that simply have to be experienced personally.

If the concept embodies some *new technology* that users cannot visualize, concept testing may not yield accurate results. For example, Gillette could explain what the latest blade does and in what ways it is superior to all competitive blades, but the concept test results might be more realistic if users actually try a working prototype blade for a couple of days from an early small-batch production and actually experience the difference. As another example, physicians rejected the concept of a heart pump—they could not know the full attributes (and thus the risks) of such a product before work was completed.

There are times when firms mismanage concept testing and then blame the tool for misleading them. In one of the most famous market research flubs of all time, Coca-Cola asked their customers to taste-test New Coke in comparison to both regular Coke and Pepsi, and the new product tested very favorably. Coca-Cola took those taste test results to mean customers would buy New Coke. But customers did not have all the information (namely, they did not know classic Coke would be dropped forever if New Coke went into production) and quite reasonably assumed classic Coke would always be around. If the market research is flawed, product developers can be deceived. Another difficulty is that consumers sometimes just do not know what problems they have. The microwave oven serves as an example—customers didn't know what to do with it when it first hit the market, and they certainly could not have responded helpfully to researchers asking what they thought about the concept.[8]

Nevertheless, some new products developers have doubts about concept testing on business-to-business products and on services. Regarding the former, in situations where the customer has the ability to make judgments, those judgments are worth gathering; but major technological breakthroughs don't qualify for that, and we just have to take the risk. On services, there may be little technical development and therefore less *need* to do concept testing. If it is simple to go from concept to full service description (a form of prototype), then the services firm can proceed to what is called **prototype concept testing**. Such testing is, of course, much more reliable with a physical prototype (or at least a 3D-printed version) to talk around.

What Is a New Product Concept?

As we have seen earlier, we define a concept as something more than just an idea or a starting point for product development. Businesspeople use the term *concept* for the product promise, the customer proposition, and the real reason why people should buy. We have, of course, previously seen it in Chapter 4, where we described it as a

[8]Some of these examples are discussed in Justin Martin, "Ignore Your Customer," *Fortune*, May 1, 1995, pp. 121–128.

stated relationship between product features (form or technology) and consumer benefits (needs satisfied). That is, the product concept is a claim of proposed value to the customer.

More formally, a **product concept** is a statement about anticipated product features (form or technology) that will yield selected benefits or problem solutions relative to other products already available. Examples would include "a new electric razor whose screen is so thin it can cut closer than any other electric razor on the market" or "a copier that has twice the speed of current models."

The Purposes of Concept Testing

Recall that concept testing is part of the **prescreening** process, preparing a management team to do the full screening of the idea by providing input into the full screen just before beginning serious technical work. We look at information to help the screeners use scoring models and write out product protocols in Chapter 8.

Therefore, the *first* purpose of a concept test is to identify the very poor concept so it can be eliminated. If music lovers, for example, don't care about a new kind of compact disk that will last forever (because they subscribe to music streaming services and gave up on compact disks years ago) and thus reject it out of hand, the concept is probably a poor one.

If the concept passes the first hurdle, a *second* purpose is to estimate (even crudely) the sales or trial rate that the product would enjoy—a sense of market share or a general range of revenue dollars. A prediction based on purchase intention can be a rough but good indication of future sales and can be used to assess the worthiness of the product concept.

The buying intention question appears in almost every concept test. The most common format for purchase intentions is the classic five-point question: How likely would you buy a product like this, if we made it?

1. Definitely would buy.
2. Probably would buy.
3. Might or might not buy.
4. Probably would not buy.
5. Definitely would not buy.

The number or percentage of people who definitely would buy or probably would buy are usually combined and used as an indicator of group reaction. This is called the **top-two-boxes** score, as it is the total number of times one of the top two boxes on the questionnaire (definitely or probably) was checked.

Whether this many people actually purchase the item is not important. Researchers have usually calibrated their figures, so they know, for example, that if the top two boxes total 60 percent, the real figure will be, say, 25 percent. They do this from past experience, discounting what people tend to say in interview situations. Direct marketers can do the best calibration because they will later be selling the tested item to market groups they surveyed; they can tell exactly how actual behavior matches stated intentions. The data banks of the BASES Group, the largest supplier of concept tests and now part of A. C. Nielsen, literally let a client company calibrate all of its concept test questions by product type. For a price, BASES translates a client's raw intentions data into probable intentions.[9]

Obviously, the concept's sales potential will be closely related to how well it satisfies customer needs or offers desired benefits to the customer. Later sections of this chapter show more advanced analytical procedures that identify customer segments based on benefits sought. Knowing the benefit segments that exist in the marketplace, the firm can identify concepts that would be particularly desirable to specific segments or niches.

The *third* purpose of concept testing is to help develop the idea, not just test it. Concepts rarely emerge from a test the way they went in. Moreover, a concept statement is not enough to guide R&D. Scientists need to know what attributes (especially benefits) will permit the new product to fulfill the concept statement. Because the attributes frequently oppose or conflict with each other, many trade-offs must be made. When better to make them than when talking with people for whom the product is being developed? Near the end of this chapter, we will see how conjoint (trade-off) analysis, a technique we discussed in Chapter 6, is frequently used for this task.

Considerations in Concept Testing Research

Prepare the Concept Statement

A concept statement states a difference and how that difference benefits the customer or end user: "This new refrigerator is built with modular parts; consequently, the consumer can arrange the parts to best fit a given kitchen location and then rearrange them to fit another location." If you think this sounds somewhat like a positioning statement, you are correct. And if the interviews are with a logical target group of potential buyers, the principal parts of a marketing strategy are in place—target market and product positioning. This is consistent with the basic new products process, where we say that the product and its marketing plan are developed simultaneously.

Format

Practitioners urge that any concept statement should make the new item's difference absolutely clear, claim determinant attributes (those that make a difference in buying decisions), offer an element of familiarity by relating in some way to things familiar to the customer, and be completely credible and realistic. And be short, as short as possible, although there have been concept statements of three to five pages that worked very well in complex technical situations.[10]

This information is usually presented to potential buyers in one of several formats: a narrative (verbal) format, a drawing or diagram, a model or prototype, or in virtual

[9]BASES is only one of many concept testing suppliers that provide this service.

[10]Regarding clarity, Anheuser-Busch said consumers had difficulty understanding Bud Dry, even when it was marketed. Perhaps the reason lies in what an executive said it was: "A cold-filtered draft beer—not pasteurized—with no aftertaste, basically a full-alcohol, light beer, a cleaner beer." (So, is other beer not clean?)

FIGURE 7.6   Concept Test Format—Plain Verbal Description of the Product and Its Major Benefits

A major soft-drink manufacturer would like to get your reaction to an idea for a new diet soft drink. Please read the description below before answering the questions.

New Diet Soft Drink

Here is a tasty, sparkling beverage that quenches thirst, refreshes, and makes the mouth tingle with a delightful flavor blend of orange, mint, and lime.

It helps adults (and kids too) control weight by reducing the craving for sweets and between-meal snacks. And, best of all, it contains absolutely no calories.

Comes in 12-ounce cans or bottles and costs 60¢ each.

---

1. How different, if at all, do you think this diet soft drink would be from other available products now on the market that might be compared with it?

    ❑ Very different
    ❑ Somewhat different
    ❑ Slightly different
    ❑ Not at all different

2. Assuming you tried the product described above and like it, about how often do you think you would buy it?

	Check one
More than once a week	❑
About once a week	❑
About twice a month	❑
About once a month	❑
Less often	❑
Would never buy it	❑

Source: NFO Research, Inc., Toledo, Ohio, now part of TNS, a worldwide market information company. See www.tnsglobal.com.

reality. Early in concept testing, it apparently does not make too much difference which of these formats is used, as all yield about the same answers from the respondents.[11] All the concept testing techniques we discuss here are commonly used for business-to-business product development, though in those cases it is especially important to provide sketches, models, and/or other renditions of the concept such that meaningful, objective reactions can be obtained.[12]

Figure 7.6 shows an example of the narrative format. Some people prefer a very brief presentation, giving only the minimum of attributes and letting the respondent offer additional ones. Others prefer a full description, approaching what a diagram or prototype would provide.

---

[11]Gavin Lees and Malcolm Wright, "The Effect of Concept Formulation on Concept Test Scores," *Journal of Product Innovation Management*, 21(6), November 2004, pp. 389–400.

[12]Ronald L. Paul, "Evaluating Ideas and Concepts for New Business-to-Business Products," in M. Rosenau, A. Griffin, G. Castellion, and N. Anscheutz (eds.), *The PDMA Handbook of New Product Development* (New York: John Wiley, 1996), pp. 207–216.

FIGURE 7.7
Concept Test Format—Verbal Description plus Sketch

Aerosol Hand Cleanser
A large-size can of hand cleanser concentrate that completely eliminates those lingering unpleasant odors that come from handling fish, onions, garlic, furniture polish, etc. Not a covering odor! Just press the button and spray directly on the hands, rub for a few seconds, and rinse off under the faucet. 24-ounce aerosol can will last for months and can be easily stored. Costs $2.25.

1. How interested would you be in buying the product described above if it were available at your supermarket?

	Check one	Responses in sample (%)
I would definitely buy	☐	5%
I would probably buy	☐	36%
I might or might not buy	☐	33%
I would probably not buy	☐	16%
I would definitely not buy	☐	10%
		100% Total

Note: These hypothetical response percentages are for illustrative purposes only.
Source: NFO Research, Inc., Toledo, Ohio, now part of TNS, a worldwide market information company. See www.tnsglobal.com.

Visuals, like diagrams and sketches, comprise a second way to present concepts to respondents. Figure 7.7 demonstrates the use of a sketch. Visuals usually must be supplemented by a narrative statement of the concept. Figure 7.7 also shows what the results might look like. As shown, 5 percent of respondents said they would definitely buy the product, and 36 percent said they would probably buy it, so the top-two boxes score is 5 + 36 = 41 percent. The concept tests illustrated in Figures 7.6 and 7.7 can easily be administered online and executed with minimal difficulty.

Prototypes, or models, are a third, more expensive form of concept statement because many decisions have to be made about the new product to get it into a prototype. Whoever builds an early prototype makes lots of decisions about the item that probably should be kept open at this early date. Prototypes are useful in several situations: a consumer packaged goods company can produce a small early batch of a new soup or cola, or they may make a preliminary 3D-printed version of two or three designs for a new gum-dispensing package; then they can try these out in a focus group before beginning more extensive testing. In other cases, the concept is so complex that the buyer cannot react without more knowledge than a simple narrative would give. Here again a prototype might be required. A firm in Canada was trying to get reactions to the concept of a traveling medical examining unit that would be driven to various corporation offices where examinations would be given. The answer was to build a small model of the unit, showing layout, equipment, and so on.[13]

The fourth type of concept format, virtual reality, captures the advantages of the prototype without most of the disadvantages. Steelcase, the office supply firm, has a software system that allows them to virtually build three-dimensional images of office concepts. The interviewee can actually walk around rooms, seeing things from any angle.[14] The real question is, "What does it take to communicate to the buyer what we have in mind?" From that point on, it is a question of the cost of better displays versus the need for that information in making forecasts of buying intentions.[15]

Commercialized versus Noncommercialized Concept Statements

One decision that needs to be made here is whether to present a **commercialized** or **noncommercialized concept statement**. Compare these two concept statements:

> Light Peanut Butter, a low-calorie version of natural peanut butter that can provide a tasty addition to most diets.

> A marvelous new way to wake up your diet has been discovered by General Mills scientists—a low-calorie version of ever-popular peanut butter. As tasty as ever and produced by a natural process, our new Light Peanut Butter is a great addition to any diet!

The first is a noncommercialized concept statement (or a *stripped description*), which presents just the facts (this can even be in bullet points); the second is a commercialized concept statement (or an *embellished description*) that sounds more like how the product would actually be promoted or advertised to customers. It is not clear that one form is better than the other.[16] Due to their similarity to advertising copy, some say that commercialized statements will produce more realistic customer evaluations (that is, greater acceptance); nevertheless, good or poor advertising copywriting might bias the results. Some favor the noncommercial form; they argue, why evaluate the advertising when all we want at this time is reaction to the concept?[17]

Neither form is *better* than the other, and many managers simply go for a compromise: a gentle sell that puts advantages in language that stakeholders are used to. Some practitioners say that it is most important to keep the idea simple, to be clear and realistic, and not to oversell the concept. Also, if testing several concepts, be

---

[13]Robert G. Cooper, *Winning at New Products*, 3rd ed. (Cambridge, MA: Perseus Publishing, 2001), p. 162.

[14]Information from William Miller, director of research and business development, at a Product Development & Management Association conference in Southfield, Michigan, January 1995.

[15]Actually, Green Giant Vegetable Yogurt in four "flavors" (cucumber, beet, tomato, and garden salad) scored well on concept tests (87 percent top two boxes). But the firm couldn't deliver what the concept seemed to promise to consumers (should it be crunchy?). This one failed in the marketplace.

[16]G. Lees and M. Wright, "The Effect of Concept Formulation on Concept Test Scores," *Journal of Product Innovation Management*, 21(6), pp. 389–400.

[17]Jeffrey B. Schmidt, "Concept Selection Matrix," in Jagdish N. Sheth and Naresh K. Malhotra, *Wiley International Encyclopedia of Marketing*, Volume 5, Product Innovation and Management (West Sussex, UK: John Wiley, 2011), p. 27.

consistent: don't mix commercial with noncommercial concept statements, and don't mix radically new concepts with minor improvements.[18]

Offering of Competitive Information

Customers of all types know much less about their current products and other options than we would like. A new concept may well offer a benefit that the customer doesn't realize is new. One solution is to provide a full data sheet about each competitive product. Many new product managers, however, don't like to overload the concept statement; it diffuses the message and confuses the customer.

Price

Another issue turns on whether to put a price in the concept statement. The examples in Figures 7.6 and 7.7 both mention price. Some people object to this, saying reaction to the concept is wanted, not to its price. Yet price is part of the product (actually, a product attribute in the customer's eyes), and buyers can't be expected to tell purchase intentions without knowing price. An exception occurs for those complex concepts (for example, the Canadian medical examinations van, described earlier) requiring many decisions before the cost is known.

Define the Respondent Group

We would like to interview any and all persons who will play a role in deciding whether the product will be bought and how it might be improved. When the New Zealand Wool Testing Authority came up with a new wool testing service, it had to test the concept with three levels in its channel—brokers who sell the raw wool, scourers who scour the wool and prepare it for shipment, and exporters who sell the wool to manufacturers.[19] A cement company, which created a new concept in cement for use in construction, had to seek advice from brick makers, siding makers, architects, builders, designers, and regulators, among others, in addition to the people who would be buying the buildings. Some industrial products may involve 5 to 10 different people at each buying point, and durable consumer goods usually involve more than one person. Yet that peanut butter mentioned earlier could probably be tested with just one person in a family setting—the household member who does the buying—or could it?

The solution is to think in terms of **stakeholders**—any person or organization who has a stake in the proposed product. Our new product wastebaskets are filled with products that made sense to the end users but that could not get to them—for example, when professional sanitary engineers refuse to endorse a new system of water treatment.

[18]Brian Ottum, "Market Analytics," in K. B. Kahn, S. E. Kay, R. J. Slotegraaf, and S. Uban (eds.), *The PDMA Handbook of New Product Development* (Hoboken, NJ: John Wiley, 2013), Ch. 15, p. 260; see also Ned F. Anscheutz, "Evaluating Ideas and Concepts for New Consumer Products," in M. Rosenau, A. Griffin, G. Castellion, and N. Anscheutz (eds.), *The PDMA Handbook of New Product Development* (New York: John Wiley, 1996), pp. 195–206.

[19]Arch G. Woodside, R. Hedley Sanderson, and Roderick J. Brodie, "Testing Acceptance of a New Industrial Service," *Industrial Marketing Management* 17(1), February 1988, pp. 65–71.

Reaching this full set of influencers sounds simple, but it is complex and expensive. Some people try to seek a small number of lead users (see Chapter 4), or influencers, or large users. This approach saves some money and gets more expert advice but often fails to reflect key differences (and misunderstandings) in the marketplace. It would seem to be a technique for situations where there is a right understanding or perception or preference. Of course, we should always watch out for critics, people who have a reason for opposing the concept. A developer came up with a device that read electrocardiograms and needed the reactions of cardiologists, but the obvious conflict of interest made the interviewing tricky.

Some new products people, aware that they will first have to interest the innovators and early adopters in a market, concentrate their concept testing solely on them. If this group is interested, it's a good bet others will be also.

Select the Response Situation

There are two issues in the response situation: (1) the mode of reaching the respondent, and (2) if personal, whether to approach individually or in a group.

Most concept testing takes place through personal contact—direct interviewing. Survey samples typically run from 100 to 400 people, though industrial samples are usually much smaller. Personal contact allows the interviewer to answer questions and to probe areas where the respondent is expressing a new idea or is not clear. As shown in Figures 7.6 and 7.7, online concept testing can provide an inexpensive alternative in some cases.

Another similar technique now used in concept evaluation is to employ group support systems software (see Chapter 5) in a focus group setting and to have the participants react to different versions of products. For the aerosol hand cleanser of Figure 7.7, as an example, different spray applicators, package sizes, effectiveness levels, and price points could be tried. The group's responses can be averaged and immediately displayed at the front of the room, and good concepts can be selected. The moderator can probe for suggestions and make incremental changes to the product attributes, measuring how purchase intentions are affected, eventually arriving at a much improved concept.

The second issue concerns individual versus group. Both are widely used. Focus groups are particularly useful when we want respondents to hear and react to the comments of others and to talk about how the product would be used.

Prepare the Interviewing Sequence

Simple interviewing situations state the new product concept and ask about believability, buying intentions, and any other information wanted. The whole interview may take only two or three minutes per product concept if the item is a new packaged good and all we really want is a buying intention answer.

Usually, we want more than that. In such cases, we first *explore the respondent's current practice* in the area concerned, asking how people currently try to solve their problems, what competing products they use, and what they think about those products. How willing would they be to change? What specific benefits do they want? What are they spending? Is the product being used as part of a system?

This background information helps us understand and interpret *comments about the new concept*, which are asked for next. The immediate and critical question is, "Does the respondent understand the concept?" Given understanding, we then seek other reactions:

Uniqueness of the concept.	Does it solve a problem?
Believability of the concept.	How much they like the concept.
Importance of the problem.	How likely would they be to buy it?
Their interest in the concept.	Their reaction to the price.
Is it realistic, practical, useful?	Problems they see in use.

We are especially interested in what changes they would make in the concept, exactly what it would be used for and why, what products or processes would be replaced, and who else would be involved in using the item.

In all this interviewing, remember we are not taking a poll but, rather, *exploring what people are doing and thinking*. Only a few questions will be in standard form for tabulation. Each new concept addresses a very specific problem (or at least it should), and we need to know what people think about that problem in the context of the new concept. It doesn't pay to get too formal in the questioning, unless you are conducting many concept tests where there is a database for comparison.

Analyzing Research Results

A great number of firms rely on a simple top-two boxes score in doing concept testing. Nevertheless, more information is needed. We cannot assume all customers will have the same needs or look for the same benefits when making a purchase. In fact, through **benefit segmentation**, a firm may identify unsatisfied market segments and concentrate its efforts on developing concepts ideally suited to the needs of these segments. We now turn our attention to ways in which we can identify benefit segments in our desired market and develop products that will be most preferred by key benefit segments.[20]

Identifying Benefit Segments

Let's return to the swimsuit example of Chapter 6. When we were collecting respondents' perceptions of the existing swimsuit brands, we also used that opportunity to have them rate how important each attribute was in determining their preference among brands. These **importance ratings** can be used to model existing brand preferences and predict likely preferences for new concepts.

Suppose there were only two attributes to consider: comfort and fashion. It might be very simple to identify benefit segments on an *importance map* as in Figure 7.8. Each

---

[20]Note that, in our typology, benefits are one type of attribute (the others being features and functions). The terms "benefit segmentation" and "benefit segments" are commonly used for the procedure described in this section and should not imply that only benefit-type attributes can be considered.

FIGURE 7.8
Importance
Map Showing
Benefit
Segments

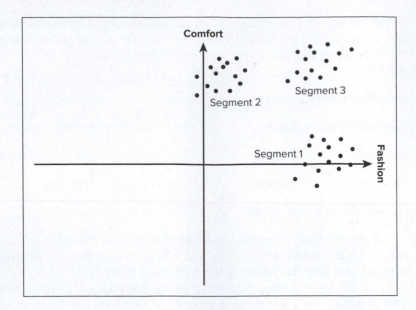

customer is indicated by a dot in this figure, according to the importance she attaches to each of the two attributes. In this simple case, three obvious benefit segments emerge of approximately equal size: customers that think comfort alone is important, those that think fashion alone is important, and those that think both are important.

We can now overlay the benefit segments onto our perceptual map (previously shown in Chapter 6). The result is called a **joint space map**, and it allows us to assess the preferences of each benefit segment for different product concepts. In this map, each of the three segments is represented by its **ideal brands**; that is, its preference as obtained from the research. (Segment 1, for example, likes the fashionable brands.)

We expect the brand that is located closest to a segment's ideal brand in the joint space map will be preferred by that segment. In Figure 7.9, Segment 1 is likely to prefer Sunflare, while Segment 2 seems to be satisfied with either Aqualine or Islands. The brand nearest to Segment 3's ideal point is Molokai, but none of the brands is really that close. Thus, a new brand high in both fashion and comfort has a chance to draw substantial market share from competitors.

Figure 7.10 provides a fully worked-out benefit segmentation of the car-driving market. At the left are four benefits identified through factor analysis: need to haul people and belongings, good performance, practical, and safe. The figure shows that five segments were identified:

1. *Experience Seekers:* While performance and safety are important, they really care about hauling lots of stuff.
2. *Pragmatic:* They care mostly about practical transportation.
3. *Performance Seekers:* They seek high-performance cars only.
4. *Affordable Performance:* They care about performance but also about practicality.
5. *Safety Conscious:* Only the safety benefit is important.

FIGURE 7.9
Joint Space
Map Showing
Ideal Points

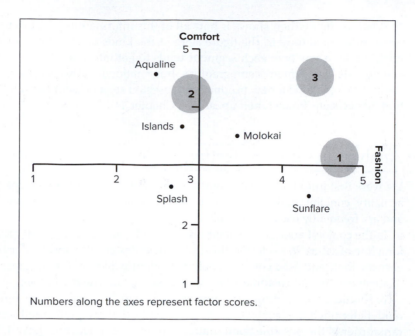

Numbers along the axes represent factor scores.

FIGURE 7.10   **Benefit Segment Profiles**

	Segment				
Benefits	**Experience Seekers**	**Pragmatic**	**Performance Seekers**	**Affordable Performance**	**Safety Conscious**
Need to haul people and belongings	**				
Good performance	*		**	*	
Practical		**		*	
Safe	*				**
Preferred Vehicle	SUV	Hybrid	Luxury Performance	Performance	Sedan
Preferred Way to Seek Car Information	Visit dealerships	Read *Consumer Reports*	Visit dealerships	Web and dealerships	Web
Male/Female	50/50	35/65	75/25	65/35	35/65
Median Age	40	49	42	33	40
Children	80%	60%	30%	20%	50%
Median Income	$70K	$60K	$85K	$35K	$60K

Note: **This cluster's factor score is *very* high for this benefit.
*This cluster's factor score is *relatively* high for this benefit.
Source: Adapted from Brian Ottum, "Segmenting Your Market So You Can Successfully Position Your New Product," in A. Griffin and S. M. Somermeyer, *The PDMA Toolbook 3 for New Product Development*, John Wiley & Sons, Inc., 2007, Ch. 7.

What the figure then shows is how all of this information is put to use by management. Additional rows in the figure suggest the kinds of cars each of these segments might prefer, show how each segment tends to get information about car purchases, and provide key segment demographics. Information like this is very useful to managers in developing ideal new products for targeted segments and also for making positioning decisions (to be taken up later in Chapter 14).[21]

Conjoint Analysis in Concept Testing

We were first introduced to conjoint analysis in the context of concept generation. In actuality, conjoint analytic techniques are extremely useful in concept testing as well and are frequently used at this point.

In the conjoint analysis of Chapter 6, you had assumed the role of product manager for a line of salsas. We selected three key attributes of salsa and two or three levels for each attribute and used conjoint analysis to identify high-potential gaps: combinations of attributes that (a) customers like and (b) are not on the market yet.

It should be clear how conjoint analysis can be used at concept testing. The model identified the levels of the key attributes that are preferred by customers and rank ordered the possible combinations from most to least preferred. Each of these combinations could be thought of as a concept, and the top-ranking concept or concepts are the ones that hold the highest potential and should be considered for further development. Of course, the model also identified the real losers! Overall, conjoint analysis is extremely useful in concept testing because of its ability to uncover relationships between attributes (features, functions, benefits) and customer preferences, as illustrated in the salsa example.

We had used attribute statements as the stimuli in our salsa example, since we were at the very earliest phases of the new products process. Note, however, that conjoint analysis can easily use concept statements in other forms as stimuli. At concept testing, we may have concept statements in any of the forms discussed earlier in this chapter (verbal narratives, visuals, 3D-printed models or prototypes, even virtual-reality representations). The analysis would proceed in the same way regardless of the stimuli used.

Benefit segments can also be identified in conjoint analysis. Recall that conjoint analysis identifies each customer's value system, that is, the relative importance of the attributes to each customer and the preferred levels of each attribute. We took a shortcut in Chapter 6 by assuming that all customers had about the same value system, so we identified the medium-hot green salsa as the best combination.

---

[21]The car example is adapted from Brian Ottum, "Segmenting Your Market So You Can Successfully Position Your New Product," in A. Griffin and S. M. Somermeyer, *The PDMA Toolbook 3 for New Product Development* (New York: John Wiley, 2007), Ch. 7.

Conclusions

The advantages of concept testing and development prior to full screening are many. It can be done quickly and easily, gives the screeners invaluable information for the sorting out of less-valuable concepts, proves market research technology exists, is reasonably confidential, helps us learn a lot about buyer thinking, and enables segments and positionings to be developed in tandem with the concept. Unfortunately, some developers (especially industrial designers) still refuse to do concept testing. Herman Miller, for example, was unable to market successfully a Hygiene System that incorporated a toilet, sink, and tub. It had not been concept tested, and after it failed, the designer claimed that industry people still did not understand it.

Nevertheless, concept testing can be treacherous—mistakes are easy and can be costly. It is not a tool for amateurs. There have been classic flops, most of which passed concept tests—dry soups, white whiskey, and many others. The original chewable antacid tablet floundered because the concept test missed the idea that people then wanted water with antacids. One firm studied executions of a single new product idea by three copywriters and found that the most important determinant of high scores in the concept test was the skill of the copywriter.

People find reacting to entirely new concepts difficult without a learning period; the stimulus of a concept statement is very brief; many situation variables will change by the time the product is marketed; and certain attributes cannot be measured in a concept test—for example, rug texture, shower nozzle impact, and what color will be trendy next season. Perhaps most troublesome, the technique has just enough slippage in it that persistent product champions often argue successfully against its findings.

Summary

This chapter covered the tools used to evaluate new product proposals. Because evaluation actually begins prior to ideation (that is, deciding where to seek ideas), we first looked at the product innovation charter. By focusing the creative activity in certain directions, the charter automatically excludes all other directions and thus, in effect, evaluates them negatively.

Once the strategic direction is clear, most firms undertake a market analysis of the opportunity described by it. The customer should be a major input to any product innovation program, and immediately after strategic decisions have been made is an excellent time to seek this input. Then, as the ideas begin to roll in, an initial response is made—highly judgmental, quick, and designed primarily to clean out the worthless ideas. Once an idea passes that test, more serious evaluation begins. The tool at this point is concept testing, or concept development, which now has a lengthy history of successful use. The chapter gave the overall procedure for concept testing, including its purposes, options in concept format, respondent selection, and the interviewing procedure. An immediate benefit of concept testing is that it gives management the information needed to make the judgments required by the scoring models used in the following step: the full screen of the concept, which is the subject of Chapter 8.

Case: Concept Evaluation at Amazon[22]

Amazon is consistently rated by Forbes as one of the "Most Innovative Companies." Amazon Web Services releases over 500 innovative new products annually. How does it maintain this level of innovativeness? One clue might be the process used internally to create, and then evaluate, product concepts. Before the product is created, Amazon product developers must write a one-page press release and a six-page FAQ document for the hypothetical product. This process helps to clarify the product and its potential value to customers. The documents may be coupled with a mock-up screen display, a tangible prototype, or other visuals, if desired. The idea here is that if the developer cannot create a marketable and intriguing press release, the product probably would not succeed. Amazon Web Services CEO Andy Jassy calls the process the "working backwards" approach, as it requires serious discussion of the concept's objective and value proposition at the earliest stages.

Amazon Web Services insists on clear documentation: if the engineering department happened to come across the press release, they should be able to start product development work right away. The press release and Q&A document should make it easy for Amazon product developers to determine the capabilities in which it will need to invest. Mr. Jassy and other executives receive and review over 100 e-mails of this type every year.

Once the press release gets management approval, it becomes the blueprint for developing the concept into a final product. A "single-threaded leader" is assigned to an approved concept, who may be the developer who created the press release or someone else identified to serve as project manager. The project manager is given full responsibility for product development, assigned full-time to the project, and removed from other projects. According to Amazon executive Dave Limp, "the best way to fail at inventing something is by making it somebody's part-time job." The project manager is permitted to add team members, usually starting with a couple of technical developers.

Company founder Jeff Bezos approached Amazon's CEO Worldwide Consumer Jeff Wilke with the "working-backwards" approach, and the latter found the idea almost too simple at first. Nevertheless, the approach gives any employee a simple procedure to create innovative ideas and introduce them to management for consideration. Amazon claims a high degree of success with this process. Mr. Wilke estimates that 50 percent of concepts generated using this approach progress through development and are launched successfully.

Discuss Amazon's concept evaluation process as described here, and compare it to concept evaluation as discussed in this chapter, or as applied in a company you know. What is unique or different about it? What do you think Amazon needs to do to make it work successfully? Can you recommend other techniques they should be using to generate and to evaluate concepts? Do you think other companies in very different

[22]This case was based on Jeff Dyer and Hal Gregersen, "How Does Amazon Stay at Day One?," *forbes.com*, August 8, 2017; Jillian D'Onfro, "Why Amazon Forces Its Developers to Write Press Releases," *businessinsider.com*, March 12, 2015; and Laura Stevens, "Jeff Wilke: The Amazon Chief Who Obsesses Over Consumers," *wsj.com*, October 11, 2017.

industries could learn from and use Amazon's concept evaluation process (e.g., a cereal company, a pharmaceutical manufacturer, a financial service provider)? Why or why not?

Case: Domino's[23]

By 2009, Domino's had a track record of nearly 50 years of fast, dependable pizza delivery and claimed to be the "World Leader in Pizza Delivery." From a single pizza store in Ypsilanti, Michigan, in 1960, founder Tom Monaghan grew the business to over 8,000 stores by 2006, about 10 percent being company owned and the remainder franchised. This total included about 3,000 international stores in over 70 countries. Domino's is one of the leading companies worldwide in online transactions as well, since instituting online ordering in 2007. It also launched a line of oven-baked sandwiches in 2008, immediately launching it into the number one position in sandwich delivery.

But not all was well within Domino's. Their promise of easy ordering and 30-minute delivery might have been their ticket to success in the early years, but by 2009 it was clear that customers were demanding something more: better taste. Customer testing at the time, including focus groups, alarmed Domino's management, who heard customers complaining that the "pizza was cardboard" or that it tasted "wet and flavorless." Lost-buyer analysis suggested that the main reason Domino's lost customers was because of the menu, and the pizza in particular. In 2008, Domino's tried an ad campaign stressing the many years of reliable delivery service: the slogan "You got 30" reminded viewers of the 30-minute delivery promise. When the campaign failed, it was clear that action was required.

Domino's senior executive J. Patrick Doyle viewed the negative customer comments and the failed ad campaign as a new product challenge. Domino's initiated the "pizza turnaround," led by Doyle and two other senior managers, Russell Weiner and Brandon Solano. The goal of the pizza turnaround was not just to improve the flavor of Domino's pizza. The CEO at the time, Dave Brandon, said that "incrementally better" would not be good enough. According to Doyle, the goal was to completely reformulate the flagship product from the ground up so that it could actually beat competitors in a taste test.

The new product team started by rethinking an unstated assumption: Domino's was viewing good quality and quick delivery as trade-offs. As Doyle said, "There is no reason that we can't deliver terrific food and do it in the same amount of time." To achieve this, however, required Domino's to rethink their platform for pizza innovation. Traditionally, pizza product development had been very incremental: new toppings, for example. But at this point, the success of the oven-baked sandwiches in the previous year was fresh in the minds of the new product team. Not only were the sandwiches a radical, new-to-the-firm innovation for Domino's, but they were also developed in record time and were successful. It was the success of the new sandwich

---

[23]This case is adapted from Greg Githens, "Domino's Pizza Reinvents Itself: The Story-Behind-the-Story of the New Product Launch," *Visions*, 34(4), 2010, pp. 10–13, and from www.dominos.com and www.pizzaturnaround.com.

line that emboldened the new product team to undertake the radical innovation needed with pizza.

It was decided to take on the challenge of completely rethinking the pizza product. Based on early consumer research, Solano says the company began asking, "Could we make a better cheese? Dough? Sauce? What made a sauce better? What characteristics of cheese made it better?" This led to further consumer tests of different combinations of attributes. Solano explains the process:

> We had three components (three crusts, three sauces, two cheeses) yielding 18 pizzas. We tested many of these combinations and modeled the ones we did not test. We had a winner coming out of this ... it was the product with all our new components. We did it!

Further testing confirmed that the favored product was viewed as not just better and different, but much better. Cost was also a consideration, according to Weiner: "The pizza had to be significantly better, but it could not cost more or take longer to make [at the store]. There were financial and operational parameters."

The new products team knew that they would need to make the case to top management. Internally, they knew there would be opposition from some managers who felt the product was just fine. Solano said that they would need to be prepared to face senior management, but that unlike many other companies, they could informally "walk right in and talk about what we just learned." When R&D personnel were shown the customer complaints, they were alarmed and recognized that this time, product development could not be "business as usual." Weiner also noted that they would need to convince franchisees. He said, "We did research pretending we were the franchisees ... for example, the sauce is spicier. [Franchisees might ask], could that make people sick after eating a lot? ... So we did a road show with franchisees. They did a blind taste test; most of them liked the new better."

A major part of the launch campaign was a four-and-a-half minute promotional "pizza turnaround" video, launched on the Web site www.pizzaturnaround.com and also available on YouTube. The video showed extremely negative customer comments and clips from focus groups, then went into detail on how the company completely redesigned the crust, sauce, and toppings. The video emphasized that some companies might hide customer criticism, but Domino's acted on it to improve the product. Doyle noted that it might have been risky to talk about negatives in their rollout promotional campaign, but as Weiner said, "we ... did a lot of testing to get the right balance of negative to positive [comments]. If we were too negative we got a poor result and if we were too positive we got a poor result."

The pizza turnaround was a stunning success. Taste was improved to the point where Domino's claims that three out of five people prefer Domino's to competitors. Soon after launch, new customers increased by 30 percent and repeat purchase was up by 65 percent, indicative of excellent customer loyalty. These figures translated into an increase of 14.3 percent in quarterly same-store sales, even during a U.S. economic slump.

What do you think caused the crisis within Domino's that led to the pizza turnaround decision? Comment on how the new product team at Domino's used attribute analysis to test various improved-pizza concepts. In your opinion, how important was this analysis to the team in selling the pizza turnaround internally? What else did the new product team do to boost their chances of success? What can be learned in general from this case about the use of analytical attribute approaches for concept testing? How could other concept testing approaches presented in this chapter have been used to guide the new product team?

Case: Comparing Smartphones (B)[24]

Refer back to the Comparing Smartphones (A) case at the end of Chapter 6. In addition to the competitive information made available there, assume that you have commissioned additional customer research. You have gathered customer preference data, and this data set was used to identify "ideal brands" and assess the number and size of customer benefit segments in the marketplace. (For this study, consider only screen size and battery life as the most important attributes.) Three segments were identified. Segment 1 (about 20 percent of the market) prefers the largest screen size and doesn't care much about battery life; Segment 2 (about 30 percent of the market) likes long battery life but doesn't care much about screen size; and Segment 3 (about 50 percent of the market) values a combination of the two attributes.

Draw a positioning map for these two attributes, using the data from case (A). Which are the most serious competitors in each segment? What are the competitive implications?

---

[24]See the Comparing Smartphones (A) case in Chapter 6 for further information. The customer preference segments are for illustrative purposes only.

CHAPTER EIGHT

The Full Screen

Setting

We know that project selection can be quite a challenge, even for top product developing firms. In a recent benchmarking study of product managers, over half of managers reported that they had too many projects in their portfolios given available resources, and almost half noted that they were managing portfolios of more than 50 products.[1] These results suggest that managers have difficulty with concept selection, resulting in too many projects getting into the pipeline.

In the last chapter, we looked at the early part of the concept evaluation phase. There, we allow ourselves some flexibility to get concept testing results and use those, drop weak concepts and improve strong concepts, and basically try to avoid killing off any good concepts that might just need some tweaking. But by now, after all this effort, we still are left with several concepts that pass the early part of concept testing: they clear all the hurdles. In the second part of this phase, we reset the hurdles much higher. Of those 3 or 4 or 10 or 20 remaining concepts, we will only have enough human and financial resources to send 1, or maybe 2, through to the development phase. And managers will agree that culling those last few concepts is a very challenging task! That last screen had better be very tough, and very reliable, because whichever concept gets through it goes directly into development—and recall from Chapter 7 that expenditures are going to really start climbing now! We are also now facing opportunity costs, because if we pick the wrong concept to put into development, we lose out on the potential of the concepts we have knocked out at this point.

In this chapter, we address this second, rigorous part of the concept selection phase chapter by introducing you to the full screen. We cannot present what any particular firm should do. That's up to the new products manager. But we can present the range of alternatives, many of which actually fit most firms. See Figure 8.1 for how screening relates to concept testing and the protocol step that follows from it.

[1] Carrie T. Nauyalis and Maureen Carlson, "Portfolio Pain Points: New Study Reveals That Companies Are Suffering from a Lack of Streamlined Product Portfolio Management Processes," *Visions*, 34(1), 2010, pp. 13–18.

FIGURE 8.1 **Flow of New Product Concepts through Screening and Protocol**

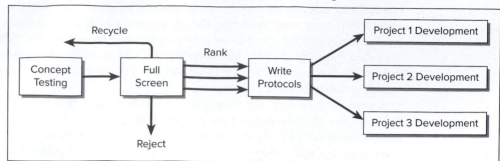

Purposes of the Full Screen

Recall where we are in the product innovation process. After the original idea emerged, we put it into concept format and then gave it a brief initial exposure for reaction by key players. In the first part of the concept evaluation phase, concept testing enabled us to add the thoughts of potential users to the set of market and other data collected since the time of the product innovation charter. Along the way, we have been compiling the inputs of key functional people in the firm—technical, marketing, financial, operational, and so on.

This work leads to the second and more rigorous part of concept evaluation, called the *full screen*. The term "full" here means that we now have as much information as we are going to get before undertaking technical work on the product. The full screen often involves the use of a **scoring model**, which is an arrangement of checklist factors with weights (importances) on them, though we will see some variations in this chapter.[2]

Why do the full screen? Actually, the full screen accomplishes three objectives. *First, it helps the firm decide whether it should go forward with the concept or quit.* Keep in mind that if a concept passes the full screen, the next phase in the new products process is development. The concept will become a new product development project and will require a serious increase in commitment of financial and human resources. The full screen helps us decide whether these resources (R&D personnel, systems design for services, engineering, and so on) should be devoted to the project, and, if so, how vigorously.

As far back as idea generation, we are screening good ideas from bad, using simple judgment calls such as "can we make it?" and "will they buy it?" By this time, however, we have worked our way through concept generation and evaluation, and we are working with detailed concept statements, not ideas scribbled on sticky notes. So we can ask the same questions (can we make it? will they buy it?) but in much more finely grained detail. This is the idea behind the full screen.

[2]For a discussion and comparison of many of the most common full screen techniques, see K. L. Poh, B. W. Ang, and F. Bai, "A Comparative Analysis of R&D Project Evaluation Methods," *R&D Management*, 31(1), January 2001, pp. 63–75.

The first of these two questions—"can we make it?"—assesses feasibility: is technology up to the task, do we have it, can we afford it? The second—"will they buy it?"—asks about whether we want to take on the project: will we get out of the project the profits, market share, or whatever it is we are doing product innovation for? Sometimes these are called *feasibility of technical accomplishment* and *feasibility of commercial accomplishment*, respectively, and assessing these two types of feasibility (often through a scoring model) is central to most full screens.

Second, the full screen helps manage the process by sorting the concepts and identifying the best ones. The best of the concepts can be rank ordered or prioritized such that we have some options on standby when an ongoing project stalls or is canceled, while some unacceptable, but possibly worthwhile, concepts get cycled back into concept development where more work may make them acceptable. Further, a record is kept of rejected concepts to prevent reinventing the wheel when a similar concept comes up again later. This latter may seem a trivial point, but to managers who screen hundreds or even thousands of new product concepts a year, it is not trivial. A good corporate memory helps settle arguments later. In firms that like to reward creativity, it helps to know who suggested what, and when.

Third, the full screen encourages cross-functional communication. Scoring sessions are peppered with outbursts like, "Why in the world did you score that ratchet idea so low on manufacturing skill required?" The screening process is a learning process, particularly in making managers more sensitive to how other functions think. And it flushes out all basic disagreements about a project (including the ever-present politics) and sets them up for discussion. These disagreements put the spotlight on "potholes" or hurdles that the concept will face during development and show where new people may be needed. Many firms have difficulty with the full screen. They either select the wrong projects or select too many projects. Inefficient screening means that financial resources and new product people are spread out over too many projects. New project approval should be made with human and financial resources and constraints in mind.[3]

Some firms bypass the full screen. Smaller firms not doing much new product work may prefer what really is an opinion poll in which one or more people make a judgment on some informal checklist.[4] In some cases, participants may have a printed list of evaluation points as memory joggers, taken from the more formal lists that follow. Some packaged goods firms whose development process is rather nontechnical (me-too products and simple variations on what is already on the market) also may skip the full screen. Technical feasibility and the firm's ability to market the product are already known, and the only issue is whether consumers will like the product if it were marketed. To compensate for the lack of a full screen, these firms may do a more complete concept test (Chapter 7) and what they call **premarket testing** sales forecasting models, which we will meet in Chapter 9. When there are major issues of technical

---

[3]Robert G. Cooper, "Your NPD Portfolio May Be Harmful to Your Business Health," *Visions*, April 2005, pp. 22–26.

[4]Even some very capable firms feel they can't answer the issues in the more complete scoring models shown later. One unit of AT&T uses: Do customers care? Do we care? Can we do it? and Can we stay ahead if we do?

feasibility (and more often than not, there are), even the packaged goods firms won't depend just on concept testing and will rely on a full screen employing a scoring model, as seen in the next section.

The Scoring Model

Scoring models are simple but powerful things. Let's look at them through the eyes of a student who has a decision to make.

Introduction to Scoring Models

Assume a student is trying to decide what social activity to undertake this weekend. The student has several options, and more options may appear between now and then.

The student could list criteria on several decisions that are personally important, specifically these:

1. It must be fun.
2. It must involve more than just two people.
3. It must be affordable.
4. It must be something I am capable of doing.

These four criteria (commonly called *factors*, but don't confuse these with the factors we discussed in factor analysis) are shown in Figure 8.2. Of course, 20 or 30 factors might be involved in this student's weekend social decisions, but let's stick with the four. These factors are not absolutes; they can all be scaled—some fun, lots of fun, and so on. Figure 8.2 shows a four-point scale for each factor.

Next, each scale point needs a number so we can rank the options. With that done, the student can proceed to evaluate each option (as indicated in Figure 8.2) and total

FIGURE 8.2 **Scoring Model for Student Activity Decision**

	Values			
Factors	**4 Points**	**3 Points**	**2 Points**	**1 Point**
Degree of fun	Much	Some	Little	None
Number of people	Over 5	4 to 5	2 to 3	Under 2
Affordability	Easily	Probably	Maybe	No
Student's capability	Very	Good	Some	Little

Student's scorings:	Skiing	Boating	Hiking
Fun	4	3	4
People	4	4	2
Affordability	2	4	4
Capability	1	4	3
Totals	11	15	13

Answer: Go boating.

the score for each. The final answer is to go boating—even though it isn't quite as much fun—primarily because it can involve lots of people, it is cheap, and the student is a capable rower.

But suppose the student protests at this point and says, "There's more to it than that. If I go hiking, I'll get more exercise; but if I go skiing, a certain person is apt to be there." Or the student may argue that affordability is more important than the other factors because without enough money, there is no need to score the other points. Or the student may say, "Having fun is really more important than skill, so let's double the points for fun." (That would be a kind of simple weighting system, in which the fun points are doubled before adding. Check: Does that make any difference in the final recommendation? Why or why not?) And then there may be many objections, such as "skiing really is not all that much fun" or "boating is more expensive than you think."

A scoring process is what we actually use in making decisions like this, whether we realize it or not. The student's objections contain the basic problems of new product scoring models, and we will see how the criticisms can be handled to fashion a system that works pretty well.

The Screening Procedure

It takes a while to develop a system, but once it is running, the fine-tuning does not require much effort.[5]

What Is Being Evaluated

In the case of the previous student, we chose to base the model on four arbitrarily selected factors. Selecting factors in real life is not that easy, and how we pick them is no accident. *First, if we could, we would use only one factor.* There is one factor that covers both technical and commercial accomplishment, a financial term called *net present value of the discounted stream of earnings from the product concept*, considering all direct and indirect costs and benefits. That mouthful is simply the finance way of saying "the bottom line on an income statement for the product, where we have included all costs (technical, marketing, and others) and then discounted back the profits into what their value is today." If we can make a reasonably good estimate of that net present value, no other factors would be needed. But we almost never can; at this early point, all financial estimates are quite shaky.

More typically, we try to assess the overall value of the concept by estimating the likelihood of technical accomplishment (whether we can create something that will do what customers want) and the likelihood of commercial accomplishment (whether we can sell it profitably). That is, "can we make it," and "will they buy it?" But, as noted above, we have a great deal of insight and information about this concept at this time and may be able to answer these questions in greater detail.

---

[5]Though quite easy when done in the mode of the scoring model example given later in this chapter, we should note that an immense body of theory lies behind all scoring decisions. For example, our scoring model is technically a linear compensatory model. For further information on this and other models, see Kenneth G. Baker and Gerald S. Albaum, "Modeling New Product Screening Decisions," *Journal of Product Innovation Management*, 3(1), March 1986, pp. 32–39.

Scoring models are based on our understanding of product success. Studies of product successes and failures have suggested that there are several important success factors, such as the following:

- Having a unique, superior product, as perceived by customers (not company engineers or management), which provides superior value to customers.
- Targeting a market with positive characteristics: it is large, growing, high-margin, or few competitors.
- Taking advantage of organizational strengths and experience, for example, in technology or marketing.[6]

The scoring model as shown in Figure 8.3 is designed to quantify these and several other factors that are related to technical and commercial accomplishment and assess how different concepts stack up with these factors. Better concepts (that is, those which are most likely to succeed) will exhibit more of the important success factors, which can be identified at this stage in the new products process.

In general, a firm should start with the list of factors in Figure 8.3, scratch out any that clearly are not applicable, insert any obviously omitted, and then use it for a few times to see how the scores set with the people involved. Over time, the list should be reduced as much as possible and always kept fluid. Nothing about this system should be set in stone; after all, it is just an *aid* to decision.[7]

A simple but realistic example is presented in Figure 8.4. A carmaker is deciding which concept car (a sedan or a subcompact) should be put into development. To simplify presentation, only three factors are included for technical accomplishment, and three for commercial accomplishment. Each factor is weighted by senior management as shown in Figure 8.4, and the two concepts are rated on each factor. Higher ratings are more favorable: the subcompact (rated 4) is judged to be a slightly easier technical task than the sedan (3). The subtotals in the figure show that the subcompact is favored on the technical factors, and the sedan is favored on commercial factors. The grand totals for the two concepts are not that different, but the technical factors are room for improvement for the sedan concept.

A useful scoring model was developed by the Industrial Research Institute on how best to determine the success of an individual technical project. The model, developed with the help of this institute's member company managers, contains two parts: a set of technical success factors and a set of commercial success factors. Each project is rated on each of these factors on a 1 to 5 scale. Importance weights for each success factor are also established. Weighted sums of the technical success

---

[6]Prominent product success and failure studies include those by R. G. Cooper and E. J. Kleinschmidt, "Winning Businesses in Product Development: The Critical Success Factors," *Research-Technology Management*, July–August 1996, pp. 18–29; R. G. Cooper, S. J. Edgett, and E. J. Kleinschmidt, *Portfolio Management of New Products*, Perseus Books, 2001; S. K. Markham and H. Lee, "Product Development and Management Association's 2012 Comparative Performance Assessment Study," *Journal of Product Innovation Management*, 30(3), 2013.

[7]For further information, especially from a more corporate management view, see Thomas D. Kuczmarski, *Managing New Products* (Englewood Cliffs, NJ: Prentice-Hall, 2002). From the consumer products view, see Larry A. Constantineau, "The 20 Toughest Questions for New Product Proposals," *Journal of Product and Brand Management*, 2(1), 1993, pp. 51–54.

FIGURE 8.3 **Scoring Model for Full Screen of New Product Concepts**

Category	Factor	Scale 1	2	3	4	5	Score	Weight	Weighted score
Technical accomplishment	Technical task difficulty	Very difficult				Easy	4	4	16
	Research skills required	Have none required				Perfect fit	5	3	15
	Development skills required	Have none required				Perfect fit	2	5	10
	Technical equipment/ processes	Have none required				Have them	.	.	.
	Rate of technological change	High/erratic				Stable	.	.	.
	Design superiority assurance	None				Very high	.	.	.
	Security of design (patent)	None				Have patent			
	Technical service required	Have none required				Have it all			
	Manufacturing equipment/processes	Have none required				Have them now			
	Vendor cooperation available	None in sight				Current relationship			
	Likelihood of competitive cost	Well above competition				Over 20% less			
	Likelihood of quality product	Below current levels				Leadership			
	Likelihood of speed to market	Two years or more				Under six months			.
	Team people available	None right now				All key ones			
	Dollar investments required	Over 20 million				Under 1 million			
	Legal issues	Major ones				None in sight			Total 210
Commercial accomplishment	Market volatility	High/erratic				Very stable	2	3	6
	Probable market share	Fourth at best				Number one	5	5	25
	Probable product life	Less than a year				Over 10 years			
	Similarity to product life	No relationship				Very close	.	.	.
	Sales force requirements	Have no experience				Very familiar	.	.	.
	Promotion requirements	Have no experience				Very familiar	.	.	.
	Target customer	Perfect stranger				Close/current			
	Distributors	No relationship				Current/strong			
	Retailers/dealers	Trivial				Critical			
	Importance of task to user	No relationship				Current/strong			
	Degree of unmet need	None/satisfied				Totally unmet			
	Likelihood of filling need	Very low				Very high			
	Competition to be faced	Tough/aggressive				Weak			
	Field service requirements	No current capability				Ready now			
	Environmental effects	Only negative ones				Only positive ones			
	Global applications	No use outside national				Fits global			
	Market diffusions	No other uses				Many other areas			
	Customer integration	Very unlikely				Customer seeks it			
	Probable profit	Break even at best				ROI > 40%			Total 240

Grand Total 450

Concept: _____

Date of screen: _____

Action: _____

FIGURE 8.4
A Scoring
Model
Illustration:
Which Car
Concept to
Develop?

	Weight	Score	Wtd. Score	Score	Wtd. Score
Technical Accomplishment:			SEDAN		SUBCOMPACT
Technical task difficulty	3	3	9	4	12
Research skills required	4	3	12	3	12
Development skills required	4	2	8	3	12
Total Technical Accomplishment Score:			**29**		**36**
Commercial Accomplishment:			SEDAN		SUBCOMPACT
Market volatility	2	4	8	4	8
Probable market share	5	4	20	3	15
Sales force requirements	4	3	12	2	8
Total Commercial Accomplishment Score:			**40**		**31**
Total Score:			**29 + 40 = 69**		**36 + 31 = 67**

Recommendation: Both are viable concepts, the sedan slightly better but it has to overcome some technical weaknesses.

and commercial success factors are calculated; projects with the highest total scores are most likely to succeed. The Industrial Research Institute's model factors are as shown in Figure 8.5.

The Scoring

Given a scoring form such as that shown in Figure 8.3 or Figure 8.5, the team members who will be doing the scoring first undergo a familiarization period, during which they get acquainted with each proposal (market, concept, concept test results). Then each scorer starts with the first factor (in this case, the difficulty of the technical task) and rates each one by selecting the most appropriate point on the semantic differential scales given in the third column. These scorings are multiplied by the assigned importance weights, and the factor totals are extended. The scorings continue for the other factors, and the ratings are then totaled to get the overall rating for that concept by each individual.

Various methods are used to combine the individual team member's ratings, an average (mean) being the most common. Some firms use the Olympic figure-skating method of dropping the highest and lowest ratings before averaging. Some firms have an open discussion (which can be virtual, with participants joining remotely) after the averages are shown, so individuals can make a case for any view that is at odds with the group.

Unusual Factors

On some factors, a bad score constitutes a veto. For example, in the case of the student seeking to decide what entertainment to pursue this weekend, a money shortage may

FIGURE 8.5   **Industrial Research Institute Scoring Model**

Technical success factors:
- *Proprietary Position:* developing a strong, defendable patent in the technology to be researched.
- *Competencies/Skills:* Available technical resources have the competencies to undertake the research project.
- *Technical Complexity:* The impact of technical complexity on product success.
- *Access to and Effective Use of External Technology:* The availability of external technology and the firm's ability to use it successfully.
- *Manufacturing Capability:* Relates to whether the firm has internal or external capabilities to manufacture the product or incorporate the process into its operations.

Commercial success factors:
- *Customer/Market Need:* Is there a ready market for the product or the process, resulting from the project?
- *Market/Brand Recognition:* The likelihood that the product will be accepted in the marketplace, due to company strengths and/or image.
- *Channels to Market:* The ease with which the product will be introduced and distributed.
- *Customer Strength:* The probability that the product will succeed or fail based upon the strength of the customer in the business area of interest.
- *Raw Materials/Components Supply:* The effect of the availability of key components and materials.
- *Safety, Health, and Environmental Risks:* The probability that any of these effects will hinder project success.

Source: John Davis, Alan Fusfield, Eric Scriven, and Gary Tritle, "Determining a Project's Probability of Success," *Research-Technology Management*, May–June 2001, pp. 51–57.

block anything costing more than $30. This problem should be faced in the beginning so no time is wasted drumming up options costing more than $30. It is the same in industry, and a key role for the product innovation charter is to point out those exclusions. These are sometimes called **culling factors**.[8]

Another problem occurs when the factor being scored has all-or-nothing, yes-or-no answers; for example, "Will this concept require the establishment of a separate sales force?" This type of factor is handled by using the end points on the semantic differential scale, with no gradations. If possible, such factors should be scaled as, for example, "How much additional cost is involved in setting up sales coverage for this concept?" Columns might be None; Under $100,000; $100,000 to $300,000; and so on.

The Scorers or Judges

Selecting the members of a scoring team is like selecting the members of a new products team. The four major functions (marketing, technical, operations, and finance) are

[8]See Rodger L. DeRose, "New Products—Sifting through the Haystack," *The Journal of Consumer Marketing*, Summer 1986, pp. 81–84. This article shows some direct connections between product strategy at Johnson Wax and the firm's new product screening; for example, its screening factors include "only safe products," "use existing capabilities," and "reflect the company's position and style."

involved, as are new products managers and staff specialists from information technology, distribution, procurement, public relations, human resources, and so on, depending on the firm's procedure for developing new products.

Top business unit managers (presidents, general managers) should stay out of the act, except, of course, in small firms. Such people inhibit the frank discussions needed when assessing the firm's capabilities (for example, in marketing or manufacturing). Some CEOs are intuitively so good at this task they can't be excluded.[9]

Screening experience is certainly valuable. So is experience in the firm and in the person's specialty. Technical people generally feel more optimistic about probable technical success, and marketers are more pessimistic.

Problems with individuals are more specific. Research indicates that (1) some people are always optimistic, (2) some are sometimes optimistic and sometimes pessimistic, (3) some are "neutrals" who score to the middle of scales, (4) some are far more reliable and accurate than others, (5) some are easily swayed by the group, and (6) some are capable but erratic. Scoring teams need a manager to deal with such problems. Some firms actually weight each evaluator's scores by past accuracy (defined as conformity with the team's scores). Dow Brands uses a computerized groupware approach primarily because they like the scorings to be anonymous.

Weighting

The most serious criticism of scoring models is their use of weights because the weightings are necessarily judgmental (an exception from new research will be discussed in a moment). Let's go back to the student seeking a weekend activity. To a money-cautious student, affordability deserves more weight than the other factors. But how much more? Should it be weighted at 2 and the other factors at 1? Because of weighting's importance, some firms measure its effect using **sensitivity testing**. Scoring models are actually just mathematical models or equations, so an analyst can alter the scorings or the weightings to see what difference the alterations make in the final score. Spreadsheet programs handle this easily, and so does most groupware.

Profile Sheet

Figure 8.6 presents an alternative preferred by some firms for its graphic capability. The **profile sheet** graphically arranges the 5-point scorings on the different factors. If a team of judges is used, the profile employs average scores. The approach does indeed draw attention to such patterns as the high scores given near the bottom of the profile (in Figure 8.6) compared to those near the top.

---

[9]One leading packaged goods firm's CEO was such an expert at selecting among product manager job applicants that other evaluations were considered unnecessary.

FIGURE 8.6
The Profile of a
New Product
Proposal

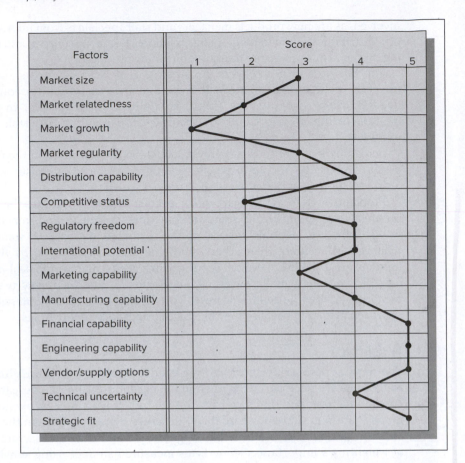

The Analytic Hierarchy Process

Another technique for product project screening and evaluation is the **Analytic Hierarchy Process (AHP)**.[10] AHP, developed in the 1970s by Thomas Saaty, is a general technique that systematically gathers expert judgment and uses it to make optimal decisions. It has been used in dozens of business and nonbusiness settings over the years and can be applied in full screening as a way to prioritize and select new product projects. When used as a full screen technique, AHP gathers managerial judgment and expertise to identify the key criteria in the screening decision, obtain scores for each project under consideration relative to these criteria, and rank the projects in order of desirability. Commercially available software such as Expert Choice makes AHP very easy to use.[11]

[10]For a full treatment of AHP, see Thomas L. Saaty, *The Analytic Hierarchy Process* (New York: McGraw-Hill, 1980).

[11]Expert Choice is presented in Arvind Rangaswamy and Gary L. Lilien, "Software Tools for New Product Development," *Journal of Marketing Research* 34, February 1997, pp. 177–184. Expert Choice has a simple online AHP tutorial on its Web site, www.expertchoice.com, and also allows the user to download a small trial version of AHP from the Web site.

The product manager begins by building a hierarchical decision tree. The tree will show the manager's ultimate goal (in this case, choosing the best new product project) at the top. The next level below will include all the *primary criteria* the manager considers important in reaching the goal. There may be several levels of criteria (secondary, tertiary, etc.) under the primary criteria in the tree. Lastly, the choices (new product projects under consideration) are placed at the bottom of the tree.

Next, the manager provides comparison data for each element in the tree with respect to the next higher level. That is, the criteria are compared in terms of their importance in reaching the goal, and the choices are compared in terms of their ratings on each criterion. The AHP software takes over from this point. It converts the comparison data into a set of relative weights, which are then aggregated to obtain composite priorities of each element at each level. Ultimately, the available choices (new product projects) are rank ordered in terms of their preferability to the manager.

A sample, real-life application of AHP in a new automobile project screening setting is provided in Figure 8.7.[12] In this case, the product manager for one of the Big Three U.S. automakers screens projects with respect to four primary criteria: fit with core marketing competencies, fit with core technical competencies, total dollar risk profile of the project, and managerial uncertainty about the project's outcomes. (As always, both financial and strategic criteria are considered, though the criteria used here are specific to the auto industry.) As shown in the figure, each of these primary criteria can be assessed in terms of several secondary criteria. For example, market fit considers the new product's expected fit with the existing product line, distribution channel, distribution logistics, market timing strategy, price, and sales force. Finally, there are four new automobile projects under consideration (a sedan, a subcompact, a sporty two-seater, and an SUV); these are placed at the bottom of the decision tree.

After the decision tree is built, paired comparisons are obtained. Usually, this is done by asking the manager first to rate the relative importance of the primary criteria in pairwise fashion on a scale of 1 through 9 (for example, "how much more/less important is fit with marketing competencies as compared to fit with technical competencies?"). Expert Choice allows several other ways for the paired comparisons to be entered by the respondent. Next, the relative importance of the secondary criteria are obtained (for example, "how much more/less important is fit with product line as compared to fit with distribution channel?"). Finally, comparisons of the new product projects with respect to each secondary criterion are made.

Using these data, the AHP software calculates overall global weights for each new product project. These weights can be interpreted as the relative contribution of each alternative to the overall goal. The AHP output, shown at the bottom of Figure 8.8, clearly shows the sedan to be the preferred project, having the highest overall global

---

[12]Roger J. Calantone, C. Anthony Di Benedetto, and Jeffrey B. Schmidt, "Knowledge Acquisition in New Product Project Screening with the Analytic Hierarchy Process," *Journal of Product Innovation Management*, 16(1), January 1999, pp. 65–76.

FIGURE 8.7   **An Application of the Analytic Hierarchy Process (AHP)**

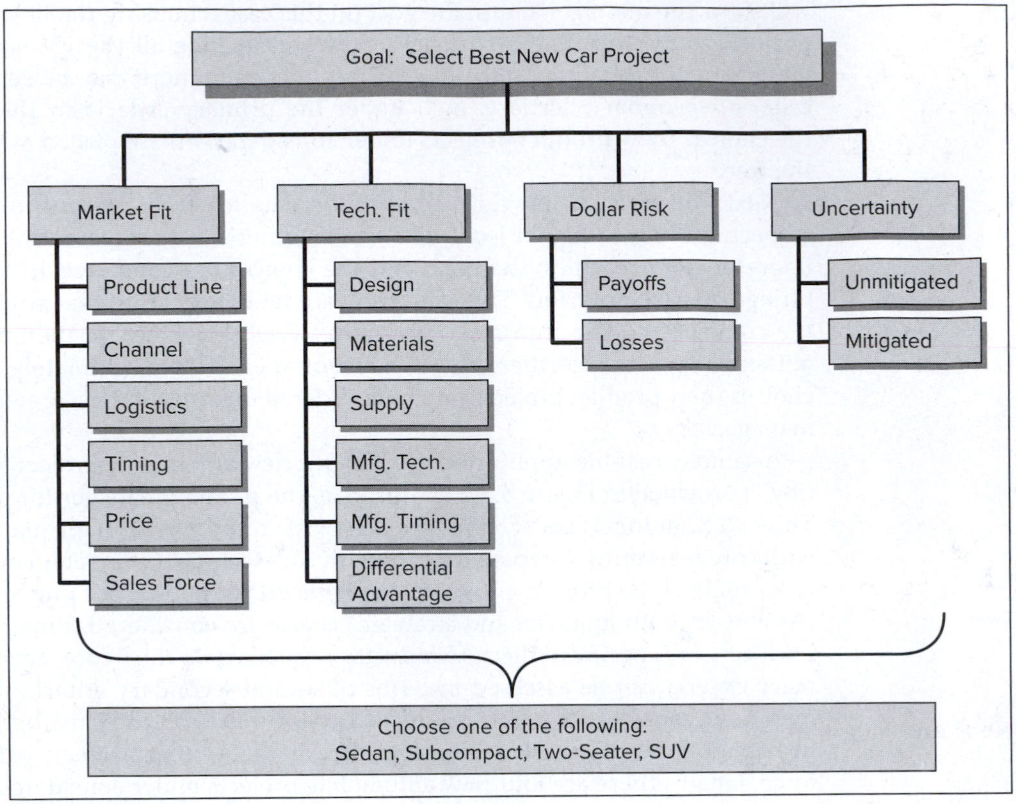

weight (0.381). The subcompact is second best at 0.275, while the other two choices are also-rans.

While all the AHP results cannot be shown here, Figure 8.8 summarizes some of the key findings and provides some insights on how the sedan came to be the top choice. The Level 1 weights indicate the relative importance of the primary criteria. This manager views dollar risk to be the most important criterion, followed by market fit, technical fit, and uncertainty. Similarly, the Level 2 weights indicate how important each of the secondary criteria are to this manager. For example, under market fit, timing and price are rated more important than sales force or product line fit. The last column shows the project that was ranked highest on each secondary criterion. The sedan was ranked highest on most of the secondary criteria and almost all of the really important ones (as judged by the Level 2 weights). The subcompact tended to do a little better on several of the technical fit criteria, but technical fit is less important to this manager than dollar risk or market fit. So it is not surprising that the sedan comes out ranked first, with the subcompact in second place.

FIGURE 8.8   AHP Results and Overall Project Selection

	Level 1 Weights	Level 2 Weights	Highest Ranked Project
Dollar Risk	0.307		
Payoffs		0.153	Sedan
Losses		0.153	Sedan
Market Fit	0.285		
Timing		0.094	Sedan
Price		0.064	Subcompact
Logistics		0.063	Sedan
Channel		0.036	Subcompact
Product line		0.014	Sedan
Sales force		0.014	Subcompact
Technical Fit	0.227		
Differential advantage		0.088	Sedan
Manufacturing timing		0.047	Subcompact
Design		0.032	Subcompact
Materials		0.027	Subcompact
Manufacturing technology		0.023	Subcompact
Supply		0.010	Sedan
Uncertainty	0.182		
Unmitigated		0.104	Sedan
Mitigated		0.078	Sedan

Ranking of Alternatives:

Project	Overall Weight	
Sedan	0.381	xxxxxxxxxxxxxxxxxxxxxxxxxxxxxxxxxxxxxxxx
Subcompact	0.275	xxxxxxxxxxxxxxxxxxxxxxxxxxxxxx
Two-Seater	0.175	xxxxxxxxxxxxxxxxxx
SUV	0.170	xxxxxxxxxxxxxxxx

Special Aspects

A few other aspects round out our discussion of scoring models. One concerns the product champion (discussed fully in Chapter 12). Champions are sometimes needed to push past normal resistance to change and to see that the concept gets a fair hearing at all turns. They try to give the scorers all favorable information and may argue that standard forms don't fit their special situations.

Last, experience shows that management sometimes misuses scoring models. One consumer products manufacturer threw out a scoring model system because it

1. Was rejecting products that would help round out the line.
2. Was rejecting products that would help forestall competitive entry into the market.
3. Was rejecting too many products, according to the sales department.

The first two problems arose from either faulty factor selection or faulty factor weighting and were easily solved. The third arose because the cutoff score was set too high. Scoring models require competent management.

Summary

If an idea progresses through early concept testing and development to the point where it is a full-blown concept ready for technical workup, it must then be screened. Screening is commonly done with scoring models, whereby the firm's ability to bring off the required development and marketing is estimated. If the concept scores well by whatever criteria the firm uses, it is sent into technical development.

Just prior to that, however, some firms try to spell out a protocol—an agreed set of benefits and other requirements that the technical development and marketing phases must deliver. And once the team feels the product parts of the protocol have been achieved, the concept is in prototype form. It can be taken to the field for further concept testing. The concept test is much more productive when the concept is in prototype form, though it may be more expensive because substantial technical expenditures have already been made. These matters of protocol and prototype testing will comprise Chapter 10.

Tesla (A)[13]

Tesla CEO Elon Musk was pursuing a lofty goal with the development of the Tesla electric car: to make the world cleaner and safer. In the early days of Tesla, the company did not have the engineering to sell a mass-produced electric car at a low price. Competitive electric cars at the time were lower-priced vehicles such as the Nissan Leaf, known more for fuel efficiency than performance. Tesla's solution: the first Tesla to be launched, named the Model S, was released in 2012, at a base price of $72,000 (with add-ons, purchase price could easily exceed $100,000).

Obviously, Tesla was not pursuing the price-sensitive car buyer segment with the Model S. In fact, the Model S has one of the fastest 0–60 mph acceleration time of any car, and it became known as a high-performance car that happened to be electric, redefining the popular conception of an electric car as a practical and economic alternative to combustion engines. Despite selling only about 100,000 units in its first three

---

[13]This case is drawn from the following: Elon Musk, "The Tesla Approach to Distributing and Servicing Cars," *tesla.com*, October 22, 2012; Jeff Dyer and David Bryce, "Tesla's High End Disruption Gamble," *Forbes*, August 20, 2015; Yonatan Levy, "The Genius of Tesla's Product Launch Strategy," *medium.com*, January 4, 2018; and other sources.

years, the Model S solidified Tesla's competitiveness in the auto industry: The Model 3 had won numerous awards, including Motor Trend's Car of the Year, and Tesla was named the Most Innovative Company in 2017 by Forbes.

One reason Nissan could mass-produce an electric car, while Tesla was unable to with its first launch, is that the Nissan Leaf is built on an existing car platform—the battery is added as a module replacing the combustion engine. By contrast, the Model S is built on a totally different car architecture. The drive train and other systems are engineered from the ground up around the battery; some of the subsystems such as traction control were not existing technologies borrowed from similar cars but were engineered using totally new and different technologies. In short, mass-produced electric cars used existing car architecture; Tesla was essentially using an innovative new architecture. This product architecture decision made it possible for Tesla to protect its battery technology lead against competitors, even though Tesla gave competitors access to its technology patents. Another competitive advantage is the Supercharger battery charger, which allows for free, high-speed charging, but it only works on Tesla cars.

The distribution strategy Tesla uses should also be mentioned. Instead of distributing through existing franchised car dealers (which would seem the cheapest and quickest way to get distribution), Tesla has a series of company-owned stores and galleries, in malls, on busy shopping streets, or in other high-traffic areas. This strategy provides a couple of important benefits to the company. First, the high-visibility stores are designed to get potential customers curious and encourage a visit and a meeting with a product specialist. While car salespersons often work on commission, Tesla product specialists are not on commissions and do not pressure customers to buy. Mr. Musk himself has said that the most important metric for the product specialist is how much the customer enjoyed visiting the store and looks forward to coming back. Tesla feels that this strategy gives the product specialists a better opportunity to educate potential customers about this unique car than if they were operating in a typical franchise dealership. Another reason supporting the unusual distribution strategy: existing franchise dealerships sell mostly gasoline-powered cars, so they would be less likely to give proper support to the Tesla, which could cannibalize their existing business.

You are advising Tesla on the market potential of the Model S, prior to their commitment to develop this car. Use the Industrial Research Institute Scoring Model described in this chapter to assess the viability of the Tesla Model S. Briefly discuss how you would rate this car project on each of the technical and commercial success factors. Where are the strengths, and how can Tesla overcome the weaknesses? Use this analysis to justify Tesla's development of the high-priced, high-performance Model S, instead of (1) an affordable luxury electric car and (2) a low-priced electric car competitive to the Leaf and other currently available electric cars.

CHAPTER NINE

Sales Forecasting and Financial Analysis

Setting

Now that we have finished the full screen, we know the product concept meets our technical capabilities (present or acquirable) and that it meets our manufacturing, financing, and marketing capabilities as well. Also, we know it offers no major legal problems, and so on. So we are ready to charge ahead.

Or are we? Most managers don't think so—they are very interested in the financial side of this proposition. In fact, they have been interested in money from the very start of a project—think back to the product innovation charter where we talked about the size of potential markets and objectives on market shares and profits. And they will still be interested in money when they look back and total up whether the whole project was worthwhile. In addition, knowledgeable managers have learned that looking at the financial projections is not enough. To make the best possible choices from all projects being considered, one needs to keep in mind how well each project fits with the organization's strategic goals and competencies. Indeed, one of the biggest problems facing firms at this phase is that they commit to too many projects, spreading human and financial resources out too thin. That is, firms need to improve their project selection procedure—for many, that means considering strategic fit to a greater extent than previously.[1]

Now is a good time to take a closer look at the *managerial* side of analysis. How should we select and manage a new product project such that it achieves reasonable financial goals and is in keeping with the PIC? In this chapter we focus our attention on the financial analysis and in particular on the sales forecast, which is usually one of marketing's most critical contributions to the financial analysis. We then reconsider the product innovation charter to determine whether the project(s) under consideration are consistent with the firm's strategy for innovation. These activities make up part of the last box in Figure III.1: They are part of the project approval process. In the next chapter, we will develop a written protocol for the project—at that point, we are ready to move forward to the development phase.

[1]Robert G. Cooper, "From Experience: The Invisible Success Factors in Product Innovation," *Journal of Product Innovation Management,* 16(2), March 1999, pp. 115–133.

Sales Forecasting for New Products

We begin the financial analysis with the **sales forecast**. As noted above, this is typically the responsibility of the marketing person on the new product team. Once sales have been projected over the next several planning periods, we can assess costs, make profit projections, and calculate key financial benchmarks such as net present value or internal rate of return. Other participants on the team (such as manufacturing engineers, R&D people, financial and accounting specialists, etc.) have a greater input in providing the costs and other data that will make up the financial analysis.

One of the hardest challenges in financial analysis is developing a reasonable sales forecast, especially for a very new product based on rapidly advancing technology. In 2000, forecasters were predicting that by 2007 there would be 36 million satellite radio subscribers; a year later this forecast was reduced to about 16 million. The actual number achieved by the end of 2006 was about 11 million, and revenues to Sirius and XM Satellite have been much lower than expected.[2] See Figure 9.1 for some other

FIGURE 9.1 **What the Future Looked Like in 1967**

In 1967, noted authorities in science, computers, and politics made a series of long-term forecasts about the coming 30 years. Many of these turned out to be highly accurate:

- We would have artificial plastic and electronic replacements for human organs by 1982, and human organ transplants by 1987.
- Credit cards would virtually eliminate money by 1986.
- Lasers would be in common use by 1986.
- Many of us would be working at home by the 1980s, using remote computer terminals to link us to our offices.
- By 1970 man would have walked on the moon.
- By 1986 there would be explosive growth in expenditures on recreation and entertainment.

While about two-thirds of the forecasts were remarkably accurate, about a third were just plain wrong. Samples:

- Manned planetary landings by 1980, and a permanent moon base by 1987.
- Private cars banned from city centers by 1986.
- 3D television globally available soon.
- Primitive life created in the laboratory by 1986.

What can we learn from the correct, and from the incorrect, forecasts? Firstly, forecasts do not have to be absolutely perfect to be used for planning. Recall that old-time ship captains used maps that contained inaccuracies, but still got where they wanted to go. Secondly, incorrect forecasts seemed to fit into two categories: underlying factors driving the projections changed or the forecaster was overly optimistic in the speed of development. Space funding was substantially cut back after the 1969 moon landing, throwing off forecasts about future space exploration. 3D television may indeed be big a couple of decades from now—of course we were saying that about video phones back in the 1960s.

Source: From Edward Cornish, "The Futurist Forecast 30 Years Later," *The Futurist,* January–February 1997, pp. 45–58.

[2]See Sarah McBride, "Until Recently Full of Promise, Satellite Radio Runs into Static," *Wall Street Journal,* August 15, 2006, pp. A1, A9.

forecasts—good and bad—about today's society and products made by a panel of futurists a few decades ago. What the figure suggests, however, is that expert forecasters often do quite a good job predicting how advancing technologies will result in new products, even 30 years or more into the future, provided they keep a level head.

We must keep in mind several considerations when developing the sales forecast. First, a product's *potential* may be extremely high, but sales may not materialize due to insufficient marketing effort. Advertising may not adequately create awareness, or inadequate distribution may make the product unavailable to much of the market. The A-T-A-R model we discussed in Chapter 7 will help us adjust sales forecasts based on awareness and availability. Second, sales will grow through time if we successfully get customers to try the product and convert many of these customers into repeat purchasers, if they pass along favorable word of mouth to their friends, if greater demand encourages more dealers to stock the product, and so on. After this growth period, sales will eventually stabilize. Thus, we will be interested in developing projections of long-run sales or market shares. Third, we should recognize that our product's sales will depend on our competitors' strategies and programs as well as our own.

Forecasting Sales Using Traditional Methods

Many standard techniques, such as those shown in Figure 9.2, can be taken to forecast a new product's sales at this early phase in the new products process.[3] In addition to the considerations of time and cost, one should also consider product and

FIGURE 9.2 **Commonly Used Forecasting Techniques**

Technique	Time Horizon*	Cost	Comments
Simple regression	Short	Low	Easy to learn
Multiple regression	Short-medium	Moderate	More difficult to learn and interpret
Econometric analysis	Short-medium	Moderate to high	Complex
Simple time series	Short	Very low	Easy to learn
Advanced time series (e.g., smoothing)	Short-medium	Low to high, depending on method	Can be difficult to learn but results are easy to interpret
Jury of executive opinion	Medium	Low	Interpret with caution
Scenario writing	Medium-long	Moderately high	Can be complex
Delphi probe	Long	Moderately high	Difficult to learn and interpret

*Generally, a short time horizon means under three months; medium time horizon means up to two years; and a long time horizon means over two years. For more details on these and other forecasting techniques, please consult any good forecasting textbook.
Source: Adapted from Spyros Makridakis and Steven C. Wheelwright, "Forecasting: Framework and Overview," in *Forecasting,* S. Makridakis and S. C. Wheelwright (editors), *Studies in the Management of Sciences,* Vol. 12, Amsterdam: North-Holland, 1979.

[3]For an excellent resource, see Kenneth B. Kahn, *New Product Forecasting: An Applied Approach* (Armonk, NY: M. E. Sharpe, 2006). Also see Kenneth B. Kahn, "Using Assumptions-Based Models to Forecast New Product Introduction," in A. Griffin and S. M. Somermeyer, *The PDMA Toolbook 3 for New Product Development* (New York: John Wiley, 2007).

FIGURE 9.3 **New Product Forecasting Strategies**

	Current Product Technology	**New Product Technology**
Current Market	Type of innovation: cost reductions and process improvements Type of forecasting: sales analysis	Type of innovation: line extension Type of forecasting: product line analysis, life cycle analysis
New Market	Type of innovation: new market or new product uses Type of forecasting: customer analysis, market analysis	Type of innovation: new-to-the-world or new-to-the-firm Type of forecasting: scenario or "what-if" analysis

Source: Adapted from K. B. Kahn, "Forecasting New Products," in K. B. Kahn, S. E. Kay, R. J. Slotegraaf, and S. Uban (Eds.), *The PDMA Handbook of New Product Development* (Hoboken, NJ: John Wiley), 2013, Ch. 16, p. 276.

market newness when selecting the most appropriate forecasting model (see Figure 9.3). The most straightforward kind of forecast to conduct is a sales analysis, used for current technologies being sold into current markets (for example, Kellogg's assessing how many boxes of corn flakes it will sell next year if it can reduce costs per package by 5 percent). Time series and regression forecasts are useful here. For selling a new technology into a current market (the new generation of HP printer replacing the old model), a product line or life cycle analysis is recommended. Despite some technology uncertainty, reasonable forecasts can be obtained by analogy: the new generation's life cycle curve would be forecasted as similar to that of the current generation. For example, current printer sales might have been slow in the first couple of months, but peaked at months 7 and 8. This pattern might repeat for the new printer.

The situation is reversed if a current technology is being sold into a new market (for example, the current HP printer being sold into foreign markets). In this case, customer and market analysis would be required to minimize the uncertainty surrounding the behavior of the new market. Finally, for new-to-the-world or new-to-the-firm products, the best forecasting methods would be scenario or "what-if" analyses. No data exist on past sales or even on whether the new technology would be accepted, so more subjective techniques are required here. The forecasting task is obviously a lot more difficult in this latter case, and some might think it to be almost impossible. Yet, Professor Kahn notes that accuracy rates of 40 percent for new-to-the-world products are achieved, on average, over a forecast time horizon of 36 months. By comparison, accuracy rates for simpler forecasting tasks, such as for cost reductions, product improvements, or line extensions, are in the 63–72 percent range, with a shorter time horizon of about 21 months.[4]

[4]K. B. Kahn, "Forecasting New Products," in K. B. Kahn, S. E. Kay, R. J. Slotegraaf, and S. Uban (Eds.), *The PDMA Handbook of New Product Development* (Hoboken, NJ: John Wiley, 2013), Ch. 16, pp. 276–278.

Forecasting Sales Using Purchase Intentions

Think back to concept testing (Chapter 7). Among other things, we gathered purchase intentions from respondents. When presented with a concept, they were asked (typically using a 5-point scale) to state their likelihood of purchasing that product if it were made available. As mentioned at that time, it is common to look at the top-two-boxes totals (the number of customers who stated they would either definitely or probably buy the product). This measure can be refined and calibrated through experience.

As an example, recall that in our example of a concept test for an aerosol hand cleanser (Figure 7.7), we found that 5 percent of the respondents would definitely buy it, and 36 percent would probably buy it. Based on averages from data collected on similar products launched in the past, about 80 percent of those people who say they would "definitely" buy actually buy the product, and 33 percent of those who say they would "probably" buy actually buy. From this information, our first estimate of the percentage of potential purchasers would be $(0.05)(0.80) + (0.36)(0.33) = 16\%$. This estimate assumes 100 percent awareness and availability, and so it would have to be adjusted downward. If we expect that 60 percent of the market will be aware of the product *and* have it available to them at a nearby retail outlet, our predicted percentage of actual purchasers would be $(0.16)(0.6) = 9.6\%$. As a refinement to this method, we could also vary the concept and get separate purchase intentions for each variation. For example, we might have asked respondents to state their purchase intentions for an aerosol hand cleanser that disinfects as well as cleans, using the same 5-point scale. As another example, consider satellite radio again.[5] In 2000, there were roughly 213 million vehicles in the United States. Let's assume 95 percent availability (due to heavy distribution at satellite outlets) and 40 percent awareness (attributed to heavy promotion by Sirius and XM Satellite). Market potential adjusted for awareness and availability is (213 million) $\times (0.40)(0.95) = 81$ million. Market research suggests that half of this market could afford satellite radio; the forecast now becomes 81 million $\times 0.5 = 40.5$ million. Of these, what percentage actually intends to subscribe to satellite radio? One way to estimate this is to estimate the percentage of customers who are among the first to try a new technology. If this percentage is estimated at 16 percent, then the forecast becomes 40.5 million $\times 16\%$, or a little over 6.4 million. Let's take this as first-year (i.e., 2001) subscriptions and project yearly effective growth rate at 10 percent. (Effective growth rate means that we are considering new subscriptions as well as defectors.) By the end of 2006, we would project a little over 10 million subscribers—below the actual number attained but much closer than the industry estimate of 36 million! Indeed, the two rivals (Sirius and XM Satellite) agreed to merge in early 2007.

[5]The satellite radio example is adapted from Kenneth B. Kahn, "Using Assumptions-Based Models," op. cit.

Forecasting Sales Using the A-T-A-R Model

In Chapter 7 we worked through a simple example of the A-T-A-R model in action and briefly mentioned where some of the data could be obtained. This simple model can be used to construct a sales or profit forecast, and market researchers long ago pushed the early, simple models into far more powerful forecasting devices. These advanced research models are used largely on consumer packaged goods, where firms have lots of new product experience on which to develop model parameters and to calibrate the raw percentages they get from consumers.

The A-T-A-R model is the basis of many of the simulated test markets we will encounter in Chapter 16. This is one of the pseudo sale market testing methods used later in the new product process, typically when the physical product is available for the consumer to take home and try. Post-trial data are then collected from the consumer and used as input to the A-T-A-R model. At this early stage in the new products process, before product design and prototype manufacture, the A-T-A-R model can still be applied using data from other sources, and even assumptions. Trial and repeat rates that need to be achieved to reach sales or profit projections can be estimated early and adjusted as the product goes through later stages and more information becomes available.

Here we are using a form of A-T-A-R that is commonly used in forecasting market shares. First-time product trial might be estimated using the purchase intention method described above. For frequently purchased consumer packaged goods, it is critical to get a good estimate of repeat purchase as well as trial, since long-run market share can be expressed as

$$MS = T \times R \times AW \times AV$$

where T =   ultimate long-run trial rate (the percentage of all buyers who ultimately try the product at least once)

R =   ultimate long-run repeat purchase rate (share of purchases of the product among those who tried the product)

AW =   percent awareness

AV =   percent availability

Repeat purchase rate, R, can be obtained by analogy to similar products for which such data are available. It can also be calculated using a switching model.[6] We can define R_s as the proportion of customers who will switch to the new product when it becomes available, and R_r as the proportion of customers who repeat purchase the

---

[6]This switching model is an application of a Markov model (a form of model used to determine equilibrium states) in which the long-run repeat purchase rate is the equilibrium state. Details on the switching model are given in Glen Urban, "PERCEPTOR: A Model for Product Positioning," *Management Science*, 21(8), 1975, pp. 858–871.

FIGURE 9.4
A-T-A-R
Model—Results
in Bar Chart
Format

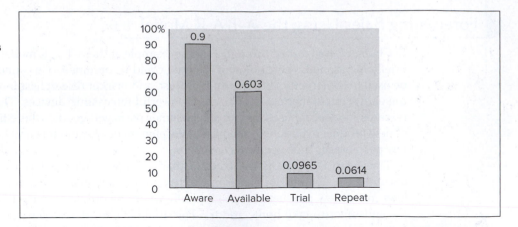

product. The switching model estimates long-run repeat purchase rate, R, as $R_s/(1 + R_s - R_r)$. If R_s and R_r are estimated as 0.7 and 0.6, respectively, repeat purchase is estimated as $0.7/(1 + 0.7 - 0.6) = 0.636$. If awareness and availability are 90 percent and 67 percent, respectively, and 16 percent of the market that is aware of the product and has it available to purchase tries it at least once, long-run market share is calculated as

$$MS = 0.16 \times 0.636 \times 0.90 \times 0.67 = 6.14\%$$

Furthermore, if the total number of purchases in this product category is known, this market share can be converted into long-run sales. If total number of purchases is 1,000,000 units, the firm's long-run sales are estimated to be $1,000,000 \times 6.14\% = 61,400$ units. The process of calculating market share is illustrated in the bar chart in Figure 9.4. The y-axis represents the total market (100 percent). The figure shows that 90 percent of the market is aware of the product; 67 percent of the "aware" market ($67\% \times 90\% = 60.3\%$) also has the product available to them; 16 percent of the "aware" market that has the product available tries it at least once; and 63.6 percent of the latter become repeat purchasers.

As stated above, the accuracy of forecasts obtained using these methods depends on the validity of the measures. When building the forecasting models, one must also consider data availability, and also data precision. In the above example, we had assumed availability of 67 percent, but this might not be very precise; actual availability may be as low as 40 percent or as high as 80 percent. In such a case, it makes sense to do a **what-if analysis**. Substituting these values into the market share calculation, we see that the market share forecast falls into a range of 3.66 percent to 7.33 percent, representing the worst- and best-case scenarios.[7]

We shall return to A-T-A-R models of this type when we have a product prototype we are ready to test with customers, a little later in the new products process.

[7]See Kenneth B. Kahn, "Using Assumptions-Based Models," op. cit.

Techniques for Forecasting Product Diffusion

Diffusion of innovation refers to the process by which an innovation is spread within a market, over time and over categories of adopters. The adopter categories, which we will look at more closely in Chapter 14, are often called *innovators, early adopters, early and late majority,* and *laggards.* In theory, individuals in the earlier adopter categories influence the purchase behaviors of later ones through word of mouth and other influence processes. The rate of diffusion of a product can be difficult to assess, especially at this early stage in the new product process, since it is unknown how influential the earlier adopter categories will ultimately be. We have already seen, in the satellite radio example, how important it is to get an estimate of the number of innovators and early adopters (i.e., those users who will be among the first to try the product).

To get a handle on the growth potential of an innovative product, we can use an analogous existing product as a guideline. If we are assessing the market potential of a new kind of automobile tire (that could, say, run safely for 100 miles after being punctured), we could reasonably use common radial tires as an analogy. They are sold to the same populations (car manufacturers and service centers) and provide basically the same benefit. Thus, as a rough estimate, long-run market potential for our new tire is probably similar to the sales level achieved by radial tires. Managerial judgment regarding our new product might suggest that actual market potential be somewhat higher or lower than this initial estimate.

Quantitative innovation diffusion models can also be used in predicting future product category sales based on historical product sales levels. A diffusion model commonly used for durable goods is the **Bass model**,[8] which estimates the sales of the product class at some future time t, $s(t)$, as:

$$s(t) = pm + [q - p]\,Y(t) - (q/m)\,[Y(t)]^2$$

where p is initial trial probability,

q is a diffusion rate parameter,

m is the total number of potential buyers,

$Y(t)$ is the total number of purchases by time t.

The Bass diffusion model is based on the diffusion curve of new products through a population. The initial diffusion rate (growth in total number of purchases) is based on adoption by innovators. Following these early purchases, the growth rate accelerates as word-of-mouth helps to promote the product and more of the market adopts the product. Eventually, however, we reach the point where there are not that many potential purchasers left that have not yet tried the product, and growth rate slows.

---

[8]The model was originally published by Frank Bass, "A New Product Growth Model of Consumer Durables," *Management Science*, 15(1), January 1969, pp. 215–227, and has since been extended in dozens of research articles. This stream of literature is reviewed in Vijay Mahajan, Eitan Muller, and Frank M. Bass, "New Product Diffusion Models in Marketing: A Review and Directions for Research," *Journal of Marketing*, 54(1), January 1990, pp. 1–26.

Managerial judgment, or standard procedures for market potential estimation, can be used to estimate m, the number of potential buyers. If the product category has been around for a while and several periods of data exist, one could use past sales to estimate the size of p and q. To set these values for a recent innovation, one might look at similar (analogous) products for which these values are known or rely on judgment or previous experience with this kind of model. Previous studies suggest that p is usually in the range of about 0.04, and q is typically close to 0.3, though these values will vary depending on the situation.[9]

A desirable feature of this growth model is that, once p and q are estimated, the time required to reach the sales peak (t^*) can be predicted, as can the peak level of sales at that time (s^*). These are given as:

$$t^* = (1/(p + q)) \ln(q/p)$$

$$s^* = (m)(p + q)^2/4q$$

Let's say you are working for a company that is assessing the viability of a new product category: a combination cappuccino maker–miniature convection oven. You believe the long-run potential for this product is in the area of 25,000,000 households. For similar small household appliances your company has sold in the past, innovation and imitation rates have tended to be in the area of 2 percent and 12 percent. Figure 9.5 presents a sales forecast derived for this new product category, based on applying the Bass model to these estimates. This preliminary forecast suggests that peak sales will occur about four years from now, and that total product category sales during that year will be a little over 4 million units. If these sales projections are combined with price, cost, and market share projections, the product's potential

FIGURE 9.5
Bass Model Forecast of Product Diffusion

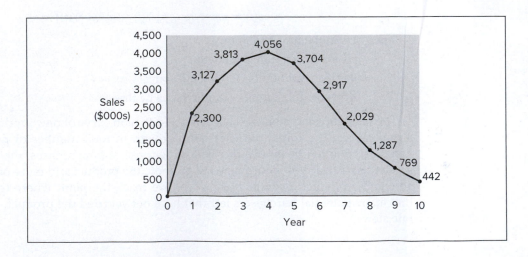

[9]Parameter estimation issues are discussed in Vijay Mahajan and Subhash Sharma, "Simple Algebraic Estimation Procedure for Innovation Diffusion Models of New Product Acceptance," *Technological Forecasting and Social Change*, 30, December 1986, pp. 331–346; and Fareena Sultan, John U. Farley, and Donald R. Lehmann, "A Meta-Analysis of Applications of Diffusion Models," *Journal of Marketing Research*, 27(1), February 1990, pp. 70–78.

projected contribution to profit can be assessed. The Bay City Electronics case at the end of this chapter shows a set of sales projections for a new product (derived using Bass or some similar model) and takes you through these steps, finishing with an NPV analysis.

Bass showed that, despite its simplicity, his model did a good job at predicting the time and magnitude of the sales peak for many durable consumer goods, including clothes dryers, television, coffee makers, irons, and many others. Later researchers have used the Bass model to forecast the diffusion of many high-tech product categories such as satellite TV or music CDs.[10] Interestingly, it has also been used to predict the growth of Internet communities such as Facebook. The similarities to durable goods diffusion are striking: One is either a member of Facebook or is not; and some people will be the innovators and join right away. The more influential these innovators are in encouraging others to join, the faster the new community will grow.[11] Other extensions of the Bass model have shown how it can be applied to nondurable goods where repeat sales need to be considered.[12] Many other extensions have included more variables and better estimation techniques, resulting in even more accurate sales forecasts.[13]

Observations on Forecasting Models

Model makers are rapidly accumulating experience and sharpening their models, which are now readily available to consumer packaged goods innovators, are quite inexpensive compared to test markets and rollouts, and allow diagnostic output as well as sensitivity testing.

Unfortunately, they also require massive amounts of data to work well, are built heavily on assumptions, and are so complex that many managers are wary of them. Having been developed initially in the 1950s and 1960s, they often incorporate assumptions no longer valid—for example, reliance on mass advertising and easy-to-get distribution. But they are now a mature industry, a large and profitable one.

---

[10]C. van den Bulte, "Technical Report: Want to Know How Diffusion Speed Varies Across Countries and Products? Try Using a Bass Model," *Visions,* 26(4), October 2002, pp. 12–15.

[11]D. R. Firth, C. Lawrence, and S. F. Clouse, "Predicting Internet-Based Online Community Size and Time to Peak Membership Using the Bass Model of New Product Growth," *Interdisciplinary Journal of Information, Knowledge, and Management,* 1, 2006, pp. 1–12. See discussion of this topic in C. Anthony Di Benedetto, "Diffusion of Innovation," in V. K. Narayanan and Gina C. O'Connor (eds.), *Encyclopedia of Technology & Innovation Management* (Chichester, UK: John Wiley, 2010), Chapter 16.

[12]See Vijay Mahajan, Eitan Muller, and Frank M. Bass, "New Product Diffusion Models in Marketing: A Review and Directions for Research," *Journal of Marketing,* 54(1), January 1990, pp. 1–26.

[13]A brief discussion of this literature is in Deepa Chandrasekaran and Gerard J. Tellis, "A Summary and Review of New Product Diffusion Models and Key Findings," in Peter N. Golder and Debanjan Mitra (eds.), *Handbook of Research on New Product Development,* Cheltenham, UK, Edward Elgar, 2018, pp. 291–312.

It is interesting that the most successful firm by far uses the simplest methodology and requires the least data. In BASES II, Burke (a division of Nielsen) combines a concept test and a product use test, calibrates the trial and repeat percentages from their massive files of past studies, and uses a set of experience-honed heuristics (rules of thumb) to translate those percentages into market shares.

But product innovators outside of consumer packaged goods still most often use the simple version of the A-T-A-R model in Chapter 7, if they use any forecasting model at all. Research continues toward improving all of the sales forecasting models.[14]

Problems with Sales Forecasting

Doing the sales forecasts poses no problem as such. We have an immense arsenal of forecasting methodologies, as seen above in Figure 9.2. We know, based on the A-T-A-R model we encountered in Chapter 7, what makes for sales. This model does an excellent job and serves as the basis for some very advanced mathematical systems used by sophisticated new product marketers. And every firm has people who can make an income-statement-based net present value (NPV) or internal rate of return (IRR) calculation (using discounted cash flow methods),[15] as illustrated in the Bay City case at the end of the chapter. The real problems are getting the required information to do the financial analysis and not ignoring strategic issues when considering new product projects.

One can use A-T-A-R to assist in building the sales forecast for the financial analysis. A-T-A-R, however, requires a solid estimate of how many people/firms will become aware of our new item, how many of those will opt to try the item in one way or another, and so on. Each of these figures, however, is very difficult to estimate. For example:

- The folks at Google or Twitter did not *know* their Web sites would become that popular.
- Apple did not *know* so many of us, even dyed-in-the-wool Windows users, would buy iPads or iPhones.
- Amazon.com did not *know* we would buy millions of items of all types over the Internet.
- Samsung did not *know* that the Galaxy smartphones would become all the rage.

Also, the financial model requires product cost, prices, the current value of money, probable taxes on the future income, the amount of further capital investments that

[14]For a discussion of the use of forecasting techniques used in new product development, see Kenneth B. Kahn, "An Exploratory Investigation of New Product Forecasting Practices," *Journal of Product Innovation Management*, 19(2), 2002, pp. 133–143; and Kenneth B. Kahn, *New Product Forecasting*, op. cit.

[15]While we use NPV analysis in this chapter, some analysts suggest internal rate of return (IRR) instead for financial evaluation of projects since the latter tends to select the largest projects, not necessarily the highest-return projects! See Carey C. Curtis and Lynn W. Ellis, "Satisfying Customers While Speeding R&D and Staying Profitable," *Research-Technology Management*, September–October 1998, pp. 23–27.

will be required between now and when we close the books on the product, and much more.

These will never be certain, even after living out the product's life cycle. Sales will be known, but we might have had a better marketing strategy. Costs are always just estimates. We will never know the true extent to which a new item cannibalized sales from another product. If we had not marketed the new item, a competitor probably would have. The fact is, we rely on estimates. Management's task is to make the estimates as solid as we can and then manage around the areas of uncertainty in such a way that we don't get hurt too badly. On minor product improvements, we generally can estimate quite well, but for really new products, using technologies never applied before, there is much more uncertainty and estimation is more of a challenge.

Summary of the Problems

What makes forecasting so difficult? For one thing, target users don't always know what the new product will actually be, what it will do for them, what it will cost, and what its drawbacks will be, nor will they have had a chance to use it. And if they do know, they may want to keep some information from us or offer outright falsehoods. Complicating this problem is that market research on these potential users is often poorly done—there is no lack of horror stories about focus groups.

At the same time, competitors don't sit still. In fact, they are trying very hard to ruin our data, just as we do to theirs. Resellers, regulators, and market advisers are in a constant flux.

Information about marketing support—what kind of service will be available in the firm, for example—may be lacking. No sales manager can make promises a year ahead about sales time and support. Internal attitudes can be biased, and politics are always present. Many new products managers will not be ready to show just how good the new item is for some time, so they try to delay official forecasting.

In their excitement to get to market, new products managers sometimes get themselves into trouble by rushing their products out, without stopping to field-test the new item. Steelcase management, responding to some disappointments, now demands that new office furniture systems be *thoroughly* tested in *end-user offices*.

Finally, most common forecasting methods are extrapolations and work well on established products. New products don't have a history. Even forecasting methods that seem free of history (use of leading indicators and causal models) use *relationships* established in the past.

Actions by Managers to Handle These Problems

Given that we badly need financial analyses and that good analyses are difficult to make, what is a manager to do?

Improve the New Product Process Currently in Use

Most of the horror stories given earlier from the trade press are embarrassing to their managers. In most of them a key step was skipped. In an effort to hurry, or to capitalize on the conviction of someone working in or around the project, a bad assumption was made. In Chapter 7, you read the story of New Coke. A market test might have revealed the emotional backlash that Coca-Cola faced when it became known that regular Coke would be immediately dropped (and eventually brought back as Classic Coke). Top new product professionals today know good new products process, but many others don't. They lack information and don't realize it. All the standard forms will not make up for omissions of key data pieces.

Use the Life Cycle Concept of Financial Analysis

Firms sometimes err by focusing their financial analysis at one particular point—perhaps a stage in a phased system. That point is often right where we are in this book, at full screen. Another popular time is later, near where some major financial commitment must be made—for example, building a plant or releasing an expensive marketing introductory program. Managers talk about a point of no return. It is indeed a phase, a hurdle, and new product managers may spend weeks getting ready for the meeting.

But both instances are exaggerated. Technical work can begin without committing the firm to a huge technical expenditure. Building a plant can often be avoided by contracting out early production or by building a large pilot system for trial marketing in a restricted rollout.

It is far better for managers to see their project as a living thing—a bottom line that is created gradually, over the life of the project, never being completely accurate, even well after the item is launched (see Figure 9.6). A product innovation charter is accepted only because the management believes the combined technologies and market opportunities fit well with each other and with the firm. A PIC describes a home field where we can't ever be sure of the final score, but where we should be able to win. A concept test result doesn't ensure financial success either, but it can say we are one step further along—the intended user agrees there is a need

FIGURE 9.6
Financial
Analysis as a
Living Thing:
The Life Cycle
of Assessment

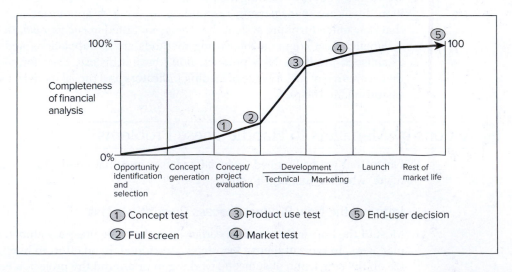

for something like our concept and wants some to try out. An early field use test with a prototype also won't ensure success, but it can say intended users like what they see. An advertising agency or a sales manager cannot guarantee success either, but they can assess whether the new item will be brought to the attention of potential end-users and that it will be tried. If it delivers, it will sell, and if manufacturing is able to do what it felt it could, there will be profit in the item. And so on. The best we can do at any point is to ask whether progress to date is consistent with a successful life cycle.

It is the same with financial analysis—where are we today, is what we know at this time consistent with profit goals, is there reason to change our past projections? Some financial analysts now prefer to set up with full financial sheets at the beginning and then compare progress against those spreadsheets. Many boxes are blank in the beginning, but will be filled in when we know them. But the profit figures at the bottom of the page are not current *forecasts*, just current *goals*. As long as current progress is consistent with those goals, we proceed. A successful cola taste-test is not a reliable indicator of consumers' ultimate trial. If we get to trial, the taste-test says the chances are we will get repeat business.

The life cycle concept of financial analysis enables us to avoid setting up systems where make-or-break decisions rest on one sales forecast or one cost forecast.

Reduce Dependence on Poor Forecasts

If it is difficult to make sales and profit forecasts, are there ways of avoiding having to make them? Yes, several, and many firms use them, though with precaution.

Forecast What You Know

This is actually an attitude toward forecasting. Why try to forecast what people in the marketplace will do, if there is no reasonable way we can do so? A blank in a spreadsheet can be filled in with a range of estimates to see where the failure point is. If that is very unlikely, then go ahead.

Approve Situations, Not Numbers

This is a variation on what was mentioned earlier. Analyze to find what the success factors are, and then look to see if the situation offers them. If so, go ahead, knowing that success should come even though we don't know just how much. An extreme example of this occurred once when a marketing vice president was asked to predict what he would do if he could get a license to use the Coca-Cola trademark on a line of new products. His answer was, right now I don't know, but with that trademark it's only a matter of how much, not whether.

One way of betting on a situation has a parallel in horse racing; some betters bet on the jockey, not the horse (about whom they may be able to learn very little). Many firms "bet" on a top-notch scientist, sales force, trademark, or reputation.

Another situation variable is *leadership*. Some firms encourage the *champion system*. They expect champions to force their way past a restrictive financial system. This makes for a strange but very workable practice of evaluating teams and their leaders, rather than the ideas they come up with. These firms don't seek great new products; they seek concepts that they can *manage* into great new products. You may have heard about the movie producer who builds a staff of outstanding creative people and depends on them to work miracles with ordinary scripts. A competitor invests in top scripts instead. But both were avoiding the necessity of relying on complex forecasts and financial analyses.

People who love to fish do this all the time; they spend lots of money to find and reach top trout streams. They know they are likely to succeed as long as they have good skills, a good location, and good fishing equipment. It is much the same for new products. A firm must know what the success factors are in any situation. One of those two movie producers may be wrong. Notice how, in the fishing example, you needed to consider the stream, the fisherman's skill, *and* the good equipment.

Recall from Chapter 7 the two potholes to success identified by Campbell Soup: the taste of the soup and the manufacturing cost. Their name and skills could overcome any other limitations. Precise forecasting wasn't necessary under this strategy, but being sure on taste and cost was.

Commit to a Strategy of Low-Cost Development and Marketing

There are times when a company can do the type of product innovation that some call temporary products. Develop a stream of new items that differ very little from those now on the market, insert them into the market without great fanfare, and watch which ones end users rebuy. Drop those that don't find favor. Japanese and South Korean makers of electronics goods do this regularly, with Sony and Samsung introducing several hundred new items in a year; there even are cities in Japan where firms introduce their food and since consumers know this, marketing costs can be kept low.

Go Ahead with Sound Forecasts But Prepare to Handle the Risks

This strategy especially appeals to managers who feel business is suffering from "paralysis by analysis." There are lots of ways to put risk back into product innovation while managing it well. One approach is to isolate or neutralize the in-house critics (a strong reason for setting up project matrixes and spinouts).

Another approach defers financial analysis until later in the development process. One firm realized it was consistently killing off good new product ideas by demanding precise financial analyses at the time of screening. It didn't have the data. Another strategy is to use market testing rollouts (see Chapter 16). If a financial analysis looks weak, but the idea seems sound, try it out on a limited scale to see where the solution might lie. This thinking may violate several popular management theories (e.g., empowered teams), but it may be necessary at times.

Managing risk is a major field in itself today, since we know business needs risk as a source of profits. Figure 9.7 shows the risk situation new product managers face in their evaluations—they know their product will bring more risk than the average risk of the firm, but how much? Conceptually, Figure 9.7 suggests that the riskier the new project is expected to be, the higher the **required rate of return** should be, but in practice it can be difficult to put real numbers into the diagram.

Product managers can borrow from options-pricing theory to make early decisions on product concepts. **Real-options analysis** may be used to estimate the net present

FIGURE 9.7
Calculating the
New Product's
Required Rate
of Return

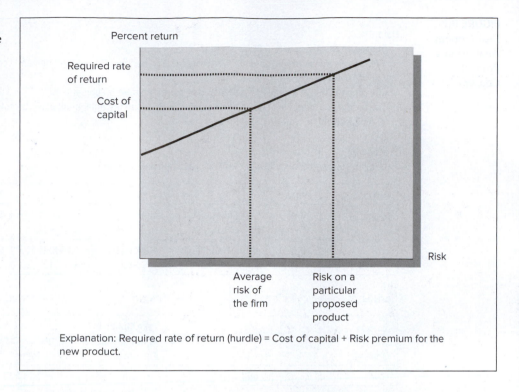

Explanation: Required rate of return (hurdle) = Cost of capital + Risk premium for the
new product.

value of a new product when it is still in the concept stage. It accounts for the fact that
there still are unknowns at this early stage, and that the firm may need to abandon the
project at some time in the future as more information is obtained, and uncertainty is
reduced.[16] Consider the example detailed in Figure 9.8. A product concept under consideration would incur startup costs of $70,000. Demand is still uncertain; let's assume
a 50-50 chance of generating a cash flow of either $40,000 or $10,000 per year for the
next four years, depending on whether demand turns out to be high or low. In the
case of low demand, the firm has the option of abandoning the project at the end of
the first year and selling the equipment for an estimated $38,000. Assume a discount
rate of 12 percent.

As shown in Figure 9.8, the way to begin is to calculate net present values as of the
end of Year 1, which is when the option would be exercised. The figure shows that, as
of the end of Year 1, the NPV is over $136,000 if demand is high, but is only about
$34,000 if demand is low. If the firm exercises the option and abandons the project, the
NPV increases to $48,000, so the firm will indeed choose to abandon the project one
year from now if demand turns out to be low.

With this information, we can now go back and calculate the expected value of the
concept to the firm. The last part of Figure 9.8 shows that there is a 50 percent chance

[16]For a good discussion of real-options analysis in financial evaluation of product concepts, see
Edward Nelling, "Options and the Analysis of Technology Projects," in V. K. Narayanan and Gina C.
O'Connor (eds.), *Encyclopedia of Technology & Innovation Management* (Chichester, UK: John
Wiley, 2010), Chapter 8.

FIGURE 9.8
Real-Options
Analysis of a
Product
Concept

Data:
Startup costs in Year 0: $70,000.
The cash flows for Years 1 through 4 are estimated to be $40,000 in a high-demand scenario,
or $10,000 in a low-demand scenario.
The probabilities of a high- or low-demand scenario are both 50 percent.
The product concept could be abandoned after Year 1, and the equipment could be sold
for $38,000.
Discount rate = 12%.

Procedure:
Begin by assessing cash flow in Year 1 for each demand scenario.

Demand	Year 1	Year 2	Year 3	Year 4	Total
High	40,000	$40,000/(1.12)$ $= 35,714$	$40,000/(1.12)^2$ $= 31,888$	$40,000/(1.12)^3$ $= 28,471$	$136,073
Low	10,000	$10,000/(1.12)$ $= 8,929$	$10,000/(1.12)^2$ $= 7,972$	$10,000/(1.12)^3$ $= 7,118$	$34,018

Next, assess cash flow for Year 1 if the option to abandon the project is taken and the equipment is sold:

Demand	Year 1	Take Option to Abandon and Sell Equipment	Total
Low	10,000	38,000	$48,000

Since $48,000 > $34,018, management will choose to abandon the project after Year 1.
Next, go back to the present (Year 0) and assess NPV for each demand scenario, with the knowledge
that management will choose to abandon the project after Year 1 if demand is low.

Demand	Year 0	Year 1	Year 2	Year 3	Year 4	Total
High	−70,000	$40,000/(1.12)$ $= 35,714$	$40,000/(1.12)^2$ $= 31,888$	$40,000/(1.12)^3$ $= 28,471$	$40,000/(1.12)^4$ $= 25,421$	$51,494
Low	−70,000	$48,000/(1.12)$ $= 42,857$				−$27,143

Since each scenario is equally likely to occur, the expected value of the investment is:
(0.5)($51,494) + (0.5)(−27,143) = $12,176, and since this expected value is greater than zero, the firm
should make the investment.

Source: Edward Nelling, "Options and the Analysis of Technology Projects," in V. K. Narayanan and Gina C. O'Connor (eds.), *Encyclopedia of Technology & Innovation Management*, Chichester, UK: John Wiley, 2010, Chapter 8.

that demand will be high, and the product will generate an NPV of over $51,000. There is also a 50 percent chance that the demand will be low, in which case the project will be abandoned and the current NPV would be a loss of about $27,000. The expected value of the product concept's NPV is therefore a little over $12,000. Since this is positive, the firm should go ahead with the investment. The possibility that the project loses money is offset by the firm's ability to recover some of the investment should the project be abandoned.

Use Different Methods of Financial Analysis on New Products, Depending on the Situation

Most product innovation (in terms of sheer numbers of items) is singles, not home runs—product improvements and close line extensions. This innovation is managed deep within the ongoing operation, no empowered teams, no huge technical break-throughs. The item is often demanded by a key customer or key channel, and the decision to develop it is not based on item profitability at all. The risks are relatively small; sometimes the development is in a partnership with a customer who will provide profitable volume.

But home runs are something else entirely. They involve big risks and potentially big gains. They need much attention and cannot be handled easily with methods such as those in the previous section. Here, the best approach is to have *two* systems of financial analysis, one for singles and one for home runs. Alternatively, some firms have no standard system at all, but develop a *financial analysis for each project*, keying the information to those issues where the risks really lie and unknowns prevail.

Improve Current Financial Forecasting Methods

For example, marketing people sometimes make use of mathematical sales forecasting models (such as A-T-A-R or something similar). Although many of these models were developed for use on consumer packaged goods, efforts continue to make them work better on durable goods.[17] Some firms analyze their own past efforts as well. More progress will come when firms systematically study their most recent 50 (or 25, or whatever) new products to summarize what financial methods were used and how well they forecast the actual outcomes. This is what we now call success/failure analysis, and the idea is that learning from the past will lead to best practices in the future. There have also been some improvements in accounting methods. Lastly, some new products managers make a general plea that all financial analysis should be advisory—not fixed hurdles and mandates but flags that warn of potential problems. Of course, hurdle rates can be *managed* in the sense of being situational (see Figure 9.9).

FIGURE 9.9 Hurdle Rates on Returns and Other Measures

Product	Strategic Role or Purpose	Hurdle Rates		
		Sales	**Return on Investment**	**Market Share Increase**
A	Combat competitive entry	$3,000,000	10%	0 Points
B	Establish foothold in new market	$2,000,000	17%	15 Points
C	Capitalize on existing markets	$1,000,000	12%	1 Point

Explanation: This array shows that hurdles should reflect a product's purpose, or assignment. For example, combating a competitive entry will require more sales than would establishing a toehold in a new market. Also, we might accept a very low share increase for an item that simply capitalized on our existing market position.

[17]See Glen L. Urban, John S. Hulland, and Bruce D. Weinberg, "Premarket Forecasting for New Consumer Durable Goods; Modeling Categorization, Elimination, and Consideration Phenomena," *Journal of Marketing*, April 1993, pp. 47–63.

Return to the PIC

So far in this chapter, we have focused on financial analysis for a new product project. Before leaving this topic, we should note that many of the very successful product developing firms have realized that financial analysis is not enough. One must also reconsider the PIC and the strategic criteria it implies: For example, does the new product project technology create a new market opportunity or reshape an existing one?[18] Firms are increasingly using a combination of financial analysis and PIC considerations when making the tough decisions on which new product projects to commit to. That is, projects need to be considered on how well they fit the firm's strategy for innovation.

As noted above, many firms report that too many new product projects get approved, and the human and financial resources end up getting spread too thin. This can happen for several reasons. Too many projects clear simple financial hurdle rates (such as minimum NPV), and all get approved; resource constraints are not included in the NPV calculations so trade-offs are not made; or low-quality work at the fuzzy front end reduces the quality of information available to managers making Go/No Go decisions. Furthermore, the wrong mix of projects may be undertaken: Management approves several small, quick-hit projects while passing up the opportunity to develop a significant new product platform or technology.[19] These problems may stem from the firm's reliance on only financial projections when selecting projects. These projections may be unreliable (especially at this early stage in product development) and obviously do not provide any information about how well the project fits the firm's product innovation charter.[20] Recall from earlier discussions that firms that use both strategic and financial criteria in project selection tend to outperform those relying mostly on financial projections.

In Chapter 3, the strategic portfolio model for portfolio management was presented. It is typical of a **top-down** strategic approach—that is, the firm or SBU lays out its strategy first, then allocates funds across different kinds of projects. This approach can clearly be used in project selection. For example, if the firm is already involved in plenty of quick-hit projects, strategic portfolio considerations would indicate that new funding would be better routed to a long-term, major technology development.

Management can also take a **bottom-up** approach to strategy development by building strategic criteria into their project selection tools. The top-performing firms, in fact, often use a combination of top-down and bottom-up approaches and consider

---

[18]Edward U. Bond, III and Mark B. Houston, "Barriers to Matching New Technologies and Market Opportunities in Established Firms," *Journal of Product Innovation Management*, 20(2), 2003, pp. 120–135.

[19]See Robert G. Cooper, Scott J. Edgett, and Elko J. Kleinschmidt, "New Products, New Solutions: Making Portfolio Management More Effective," *Research-Technology Management*, March–April 2000, pp. 18–33.

[20]Randall L. Englund and Robert J. Graham, "From Experience: Linking Projects to Strategy," *Journal of Product Innovation Management*, 16(1), January 1999, pp. 52–64.

FIGURE 9.10
Hoechst-U.S.
Scoring Model

Key Factors	Rating Scale (from 1–10)						
	1	...	4	...	7	...	10
Probability of Technical Success	<20% probability						>90% probability
Probability of Commercial Success	<25% probability						>90% probability
Reward	Small						Payback < 3 years
Business-Strategy Fit	R&D independent of business strategy						R&D strongly supports business strategy
Strategic Leverage	"One-of-a-kind"/ dead end						Many proprietary opportunities

Source: Adapted from Robert G. Cooper, Scott J. Edgett, and Elko J. Kleinschmidt, *Portfolio Management for New Products,* McMaster University, Hamilton, Ontario, Canada, 1977, pp. 24–28.

strategic as well as financial criteria when selecting projects, while the worst performers tend to rely only on financial criteria.[21]

Robert Cooper and his colleagues use Hoechst-U.S.'s scoring model as an example of how to balance strategic and financial concerns (see Figure 9.10). Of the five factors shown in the figure, two are clearly full-screen feasibility factors similar to those in Figure 8.5 (Probability of Technical and Commercial Success), one is a financial criterion (Reward), and two are strategic factors related to the firm's PIC (Business-Strategy Fit and Strategic Leverage). Similarly, Specialty Minerals, a spin-off of Pfizer, uses a 7-point scoring model that shows a similar combination of financial and strategic considerations:

- Management interest
- Customer interest
- Sustainability of competitive advantage
- Technical feasibility
- Business case strength
- Fit with core competencies
- Profitability and impact

As another example, the screening criteria used by a real manufacturing company (whose identity was not revealed) included:

- Net Present Value
- Internal Rate of Return
- Strategic Importance of Project (how the project aligns with business strategy)
- Probability of Technical Success

[21]See Robert G. Cooper, "Portfolio Management: Results of New Product Portfolio Management Best Practices Study," in L. W. Murray (ed.), *Maximizing the Return on Product Development*, Proceedings of the 1997 PDMA Research Conference, Monterey, CA, pp. 331–358.

FIGURE 9.11
A Tool for
Concept
Evaluation

Dimension	Sample Questions
Strategic Fit	Does the concept fit with corporate vision?
	Does the concept fit with our sales force?
Customer Fit	Does the concept allow the customer to better meet consumer needs?
	Does the concept have a good value as perceived by the customer?
Consumer Fit	Does the concept satisfy an unmet or latent consumer need?
	Will consumer loyalty be increased?
Market Attractiveness	Is the concept unique relative to the competition?
	Could our firm be a Number 1 or Number 2 competitor?
Technical Feasibility	Is the concept feasible?
	Is the concept protectable?
Financial Returns	Will the project break even soon?
	Will the project achieve required earnings in the desired time?

Source: Seamon, Erika B., "Achieving Growth Through an Innovative Culture," in P. Belliveau, A. Griffin, and S. Somermeyer (eds.), *The PDMA Handbook 2 for New Product Development* (Hoboken, NJ: John Wiley & Sons, Inc.), 2004, Chapter 1.

Again, one criterion (the third) is clearly a measure of fit with PIC (albeit using slightly different terms), while the others are related to technical feasibility or financial expectations.[22] Research into this subject continues, but so far the results are suggesting that consideration of strategic as well as financial criteria is important when assessing new product projects.

Finally, Figure 9.11 presents the advice of Erika Seamon of Kuczmarski and Associates, a well-respected consultant group. This consultancy clearly also advocates that firms should consider both strategic and financial criteria when deciding which concepts to move into prototype development: their concept evaluation tool includes several ways to assess strategic fit and market attractiveness, and also considers financial performance.

Summary

This chapter has dealt with the matter of how to make judgments on the financial merits of new products. It has also explored in depth the issue of sales forecasting, since this is one area where the new product team usually relies heavily on the expertise brought in by the marketing representative. There are good basic methods for doing financial analysis (net present value calculations using discounted cash flow) and for doing sales forecasting. Most firms use these daily. However, new products managers know they often do not have the data these sophisticated methods require. So they may also need to use "risk-reducers"—actions that give them nonquantitative guides to probable success.

[22]The Hoechst, Pfizer, and manufacturing firm examples are from Robert G. Cooper, Scott J. Edgett, and Elko J. Kleinschmidt, *Portfolio Management for New Products* (Hamilton, Ontario: McMaster University, 1997), pp. 22–29.

The method of making financial analyses is given in the Bay City case found below. The case offers data for a new electronics product and gives the opportunity as well to look at some nondata issues involved in financial analysis.

At this point in the new product development process, we are ready to begin Phase IV (development).

Case: Bay City Electronics[23]

Financial analysis of new products at Bay City Electronics had always been rather informal. Bill Roberts, who founded the firm in 1970, knew residential electronics because he had worked for almost seven years for another firm specializing in home security systems. But he had never been trained in financial analysis. In fact, all he knew was what the bank had asked for every time he went to discuss his line of credit. Bay City had about 45 full-time employees (plus a seasonal factory workforce) and did in the neighborhood of $18 million in sales. His products all related to home security and were sold by his sales manager, who worked with a group of manufacturers' reps, who in turn called on wholesalers, hardware and department store chains, and other large retailers. He did some consumer advertising, but not much.

Bill was inventive, however, and had built the business primarily by coming up with new techniques. His latest device was a remote-controlled electronic closure for any door in the home. The closure was effected by a special ringing of the telephone: For example, if a user wanted to leave a back door open until 9:00 p.m., it was simple to call the house at 9:00 and wait for 10 rings, after which the electronic device would switch the door to a locked position. A similar call would reopen the door.

The bank liked the idea but wanted Bill to do a better job of financial analysis, so the loan officer asked him to use the forms shown in the Bay City Appendix as Figure 9.12 and Figure 9.13. After some effort, Bill was able to fill out the key data form, Figure 9.12, and his work is reproduced here. To date, Bay City had spent $85,000 in expense money for supplies and labor developing the closure and had invested $15,000 in a machine (asset). If the company decided to go ahead, it would have to invest $50,000 more in a new facility, continue R&D to validate and improve the product, and—if things went according to expectations—invest another $45,000 in year 3 to expand production capability.

He also had to fill out the financial worksheet, Figure 9.13; for this he used a friend of the family who had studied financial analysis in college. The friend had relied on a summary of how to do this, and this summary is attached. He also warned Bill that there were lots of judgment calls in that calculation, "so don't get into an argument with the people at the bank about details."

[23]This is a realistic, but hypothetical, situation.

FIGURE 9.12 **Key Data Form for Financial Analysis, Part A**

Financial Analysis Proposal: *Bay City Electronics Closure**
Date of this analysis: _____ Previous analysis: _____

1. Economic conditions, if relevant:
   Corporate scenario OK

2. The market (category): | 3. Product life *5* years
   Stable-5% growth |

4. List price: *$90* | Other discounts:
   Distributor discounts: *$36* | Promotion: *$1*
   Net to factory: *$54* | Quantity: *$1*
   | Average dollars per unit sold: *$52*

5. Production costs:
   Explanation of any unique costing | Applicable rate for indirect
   procedures being used: | manufacturing costs: _____
   None. Experience curve effect. | *20% of direct costs*

6. Future expenditures, other capital investments, or extraordinary expenditures:
   Build production facilities: $50,000
   Ongoing R&D: $15,000; $10,000; $15,000; $10,000 for first four years after intro
   Special UL test during the 2nd year will cost $5,000
   Expand facilities in 3rd year for $45,000

7. Working capital: *35* % of sales | 8. Applicable overheads:
   10% inventory; recover 80% in period 5 | Corp.: *10* % of sales
   15% receivables; all recovered in period 5 | Division: *-* % of sales
   10% cash, all recovered |

9. Net loss on cannibalized sales, if any, expressed as a percent of the new product's sales: *10* %

10. Future costs/revenues of project abandonment, if that were done instead of marketing: *Abort now would net $3,000 from sale of machine.*

11. Tax credits, if any, on new assets or expenditures: *1% of taxes due to state and federal, based on positive environmental effect.*

12. Applicable depreciation rate(s) on depreciable assets: *25% on orig. plant and machines; 33 1/3% on expansion facilities*

13. Federal and state income tax rate applicable: *34* %
    Comments:

14. Applicable cost of capital: *16* %
    ±Premiums or penalties: *high-risk project 8* %
    _____ _
    Any change in cost of capital anticipated over life of product? *No*

*This key data form is filled in with demonstration data for the Bay City Electronics case.

FIGURE 9.12 **(CONCLUDED)** **Key Data Form for Financial Analysis, Part A**

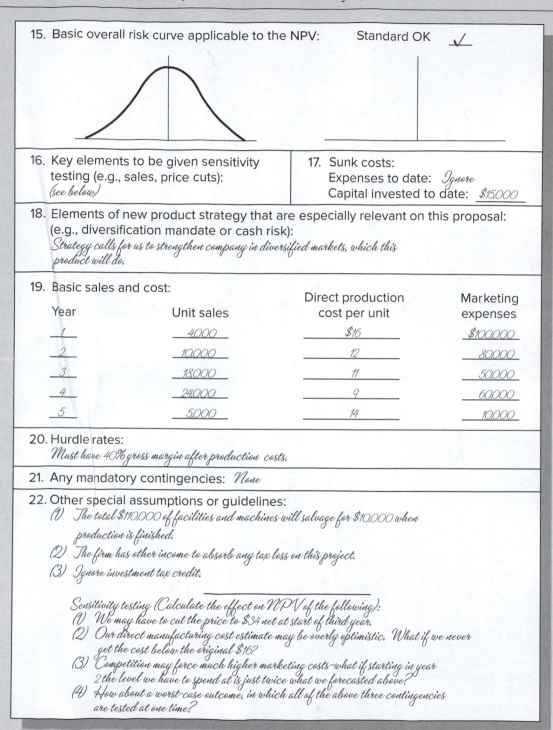

15. Basic overall risk curve applicable to the NPV: Standard OK ✓

16. Key elements to be given sensitivity testing (e.g., sales, price cuts): *(see below)*

17. Sunk costs:
Expenses to date: *Ignore*
Capital invested to date: *$15,000*

18. Elements of new product strategy that are especially relevant on this proposal: (e.g., diversification mandate or cash risk):
Strategy calls for us to strengthen company in diversified markets, which this product will do.

19. Basic sales and cost:

Year	Unit sales	Direct production cost per unit	Marketing expenses
1	*4,000*	*$16*	*$100,000*
2	*10,000*	*12*	*80,000*
3	*18,000*	*11*	*50,000*
4	*24,000*	*9*	*60,000*
5	*5,000*	*14*	*10,000*

20. Hurdle rates:
Must have 40% gross margin after production costs.

21. Any mandatory contingencies: *None*

22. Other special assumptions or guidelines:
(1) The total $110,000 of facilities and machines will salvage for $10,000 when production is finished.
(2) The firm has other income to absorb any tax loss on this project.
(3) Ignore investment tax credit.

Sensitivity testing (Calculate the effect on NPV of the following):
(1) We may have to cut the price to $34 net at start of third year.
(2) Our direct manufacturing cost estimate may be overly optimistic. What if we never get the cost below the original $16?
(3) Competition may force much higher marketing costs—what if starting in year 2 the level we have to spend at is just twice what we forecasted above?
(4) How about a worst-case outcome, in which all of the above three contingencies are tested at one time?

FIGURE 9.13   Financial Worksheet, Bay City Electronics

Product Proposal: Electronic Closure   Date:

			Years of the Market			
	0	1	2	3	4	5
Unit sales	0	4,000	10,000	18,000	24,000	5,000
Revenue per unit	0	52	52	52	52	52
Dollar sales	0	208,000	520,000	936,000	1,248,000	266,000
Production costs:						
Direct	0	64,000	120,000	198,000	216,000	70,000
Indirect	0	12,800	24,000	39,600	43,200	14,000
Total	0	76,800	144,000	237,600	259,200	84,000
Gross profit	0	131,200	376,000	648,400	988,000	176,000
Direct marketing costs	0	100,000	80,000	50,000	60,000	10,000
Profit contribution	0	31,200	296,000	648,400	928,800	166,000
Overheads (excluding R&D):						
Division	0	0	0	0	0	0
Corporate	0	20,800	52,000	93,600	124,800	26,000
Total	0	20,800	52,000	93,600	124,800	26,000
Other expenses:						
Depreciation	16,250	16,250	16,250	31,250	15,000	15,000
Cannibalization	0	20,800	52,000	93,600	124,800	26,000
R&D to be incurred	0	15,000	10,000	15,000	10,000	0
Extraordinary expense	0	0	5,000	0	0	0
Project abandonment	3,000	0	0	0	0	0
Total	19,250	52,050	83,250	139,850	149,800	41,000
Overheads and expenses	19,250	72,850	135,250	233,450	274,600	67,000
Income before taxes	(19,250)	(41,650)	160,750	414,950	654,200	99,000
Tax effect:						
Taxes on income	(6,545)	(14,161)	54,655	141,083	222,428	33,660
Tax credits	(65)	(142)	547	1,411	2,224	337
Total effect	(6,480)	(14,019)	54,108	139,672	220,204	33,323
Cash flow:						
Income after taxes	(12,770)	(27,631)	106,642	275,278	433,996	65,677
Depreciation	16,250	16,250	16,250	31,250	15,000	15,000
Production facilities	50,000	0	0	45,000	0	0
Working capital: Cash	0	20,800	31,200	41,600	31,200	(124,800)
Working capital: Inventories	0	20,800	31,200	41,600	31,200	(99,840)
Working capital: Acc. Rec.	0	31,200	46,800	62,400	46,800	(187,200)
Net cash flows	(46,520)	(84,181)	13,692	115,928	339,796	492,517
Discounted flows	(46,520)	(67,888)	8,904	60,803	143,725	168,001
Net present value	$267,025					
Internal rate of return	73.7					
Payback	Nov., Year 3					

Test 1: NPV = $88,885
Test 2: NPV = $149,453
Test 3: NPV = $196,013
All 3: NPV = ($99,699)

Worst case is very undesirable, even here where indirect effects, sunk costs, and salvage were omitted.

While waiting for his appointment at the bank, Bill spent some time just thinking about his situation. Did the numbers look good? Where were the shaky parts that the banker might give him trouble on? Most of all, he was curious about whether a friend of his at the LazyBoy chair firm in Monroe had to do the same thing, and would 3M require the same type of form from his daughter, who now worked for them? Frankly, he didn't feel he personally had learned much about his situation from the exercise and was already wondering whether there weren't better ways for him to go about reassuring the bank that their loan was a good proposition.

BAY CITY APPENDIX: FINANCIAL ANALYSIS FOR NEW PRODUCTS

New products financial analysis requires two separate activities: (1) gathering the full set of data and other "givens" in the situation, and (2) using them in calculations to derive whatever final figure is sought. These two tasks are shown in Figures 9.12 (the key data form) and 9.13 (the financial worksheet).

COMPILING THE KEY DATA

Economic Conditions. Most firms have ongoing economic forecasts, but sometimes a team wishes to differ. If so, the difference should be noted here.

The Market or Category. The "market" for the new product is defined carefully, and the growth rate assumption is noted. Also, the current total market unit and dollar volumes are recorded.

Product Life. The number of years used in the economic analysis of new products is usually set by company policy, but any particular project may be an exception.

Pricing. Start with the end-user list price, work back through the various trade discounts to get a factory net, then deduct any planned special discounts and allowances. The average dollars per unit sold is the price used in worksheet calculations.

Production Costs. Is anything unusual being done on this project? Actual anticipated cost goes directly onto the financial worksheet. Cite factory burden percentage rate.[24]

Future Special Expenditures. These typically include factory facilities, licensing rights, the one-time introductory marketing cost, up-front payments to suppliers, further R&D on improvements and line extensions, and plant expansions as volume grows. These are all *investment outflows*.

Working Capital. This estimates cash, inventories, and receivables needed to support the sales volumes. How are they to be recovered?

---

[24]Factory overheads are often assigned using an activity-based costing (ABC) system. If adopted, new items have a greater chance of realistic allocations. See Bernard C. Reimann, "Challenging Conventional Wisdom: Corporate Strategies That Work," *Planning Review*, November/December 1991, pp. 36–39.

Applicable Overheads. Some firms assign only "direct" overheads—those caused by the new product (such as an expanded sales force or a new quality function). Other firms believe overheads tend to grow as functions of volume and should be included.

Net Loss on Cannibalized Sales. These are dollar sales lost as the new product steals sales from current products. This is to be deducted from revenue. Some experts believe if we don't do this a competitor will, so they omit it.

Future Costs/Revenues of Project Abandonment. Along the way, the project may have accumulated facilities, people, patent rights, inventories, and so on. If abandoned now, disposal of these will produce revenue, money that is actually a *cost of abandoning the project.* But disposing of radioactive chemicals may be expensive, thus a *revenue* of going ahead.

Tax Credits. Federal or state incentives for activity in the public interest.

Applicable Depreciation Rate. Policy question, set by management.

Federal and State Income Tax Rate. Company figure, provided.

Required Rate of Return. This one tells us the cash flow discount rate to be used and can be complex and political. Theoretically, the figure to use is the *weighted average cost of capital,* including the three sources of capital—debt, preferred stock, and retained earnings. Often it is simply the *firm's current borrowing rate.*[25] It may be the *rate of earnings from current operations.* New product managers want it low, conservative financial people may want it high. The actual rate to be used is often an arbitrary decision. Whatever the rate, the next step is to decide how the riskiness of this project compares with the rest of the firm's activities. Look at Figure 9.7, which shows that a relationship between risk and rate of return exists for every business, as discussed in the chapter. Given the current average cost of capital and the level and slope of the line, the manager can mark off the risk of the particular new product, go up to the risk/return line, and then read off the required rate of return. Except in unusual circumstances, that required level will represent a premium over the current cost of capital. The premium is entered in section 14 of the key data form.

Risk Curve. Figure 9.9 shows the typical **risk curve** of possible profit outcomes from a given new product project, as discussed in the chapter. In the B pattern, for example, chances are the project will have a lower payout, but a very high payout is also possible. Imitative competition is expected; but, if it doesn't come, the profit will be high. This risk pattern information is good to keep in mind when making the financial analysis, though few firms undertake the probability-adjusted risk analysis it permits.

Sensitivity Testing. After an analysis has been completed using original data, the analyst goes back and recalculates the profit using other figures for especially sensitive factors.

---

[25]A variation on this is to use the current market risk-free cost of capital (interest rate on Treasuries, for example). We then add a premium reflecting the general level of risk in the industry at hand.

Elements of Strategy. When evaluating new product proposals, it is important to remember the strategy that prompted them. Less-profitable products may well be warranted under certain strategies.

Basic Sales and Cost Forecasts. This section gives the primary data inputs—the number of units to be sold, the direct production cost per unit, and the total marketing expenditures.

Hurdle Rates. A company sometimes has hurdle rates on variables other than rate of return.

Mandatory Contingencies. A firm may want one or more contingencies worked into the analysis every time, not left optional.

Other Special Assumptions or Guidelines. This is the typical miscellaneous section, totally situational.

Beyond the Key Data Form: Sunk Costs. Sunk costs should not enter into this analysis. Sunk money is just that—sunk. It stays sunk whether we go ahead at this time or abandon the project.

Salvage. NPV forms sometimes call for the dollars obtained at the end of the product's life from sale of salvaged equipment. The amounts are usually small and are best omitted.

Portfolio. If the new item is playing a special role as part of an overall portfolio of projects, the value of that role should be mentioned. The new project may be high risk but still worthwhile to balance a large number of low-risk projects—or the reverse.

Case: Mercedes Benz[26]

Mercedes Benz is the top-selling luxury car brand in the world and recorded its highest quarterly sales ever in early 2018. Big sales gains on both the GLC crossover and the newly revised S-Class model accounted for much of this sales increase. A year earlier, in April 2017, Mercedes' parent company Daimler AG had initially set its 2018 sales forecasts at modest levels. When the new models were released, however, these forecasts were readjusted and the company was predicting growth in both luxury cars and SUVs, owing largely to the predicted success of these new models.

Mercedes is following a technology road map in which it plans for success with upgrades and new models in the short term (as seen with the GLC and S-Class launches in 2018), while at the same time making long-term adjustments so that it will be competitive well into the future as the car industry evolves. For example, in 2018, Daimler had a line of 10 totally battery-powered electric cars in development that would be on the market within five years. These would be sold under a new sub-brand, Mercedes EQ. The company was also planning to launch hybrid models of existing

[26]This case is based on Edward Taylor, "Daimler Lifts Profit Forecast as Mercedes' Sales Accelerate," *reuters.com*, April 26, 2017; Fred Lambert, "Mercedes-Benz Unveils EQC Electric SUV, Says It's Going 'All-In' On Electric," *electrek.co*, September 4, 2018; and the Mercedes-Benz Web site, www.mbusa.com.

Mercedes vehicles. These technological developments cost Mercedes about 2.3 billion euros in the first quarter of 2018 alone, so like any other significant investment in new car platforms, the cost would need to be absorbed over several years and several models.

As might be expected of Mercedes, the all-electric EQC class is projected to feature much impressive technology in line with the luxury car buyer's expectations. For example, the newly developed media system will respond to driver verbal commands, govern car functions, and manage charge status, energy flow, and other necessities for an electric vehicle. It will also learn over time, thereby improving driving efficiency. The initial promotion on the Mercedes Web page described the EQC class as "more than just an electric vehicle: It's a bold statement about the future of driving."

Indeed, the development of the hybrid and fully electric models is consistent with Mercedes' vision of technologies that are predicted to transform the car industry. These are known by the acronym CASE: Connected, Autonomous, Shared and Services, and Electric. These technologies will shape not just car features, but how cars and drivers interact with each other and with the environment.

- *Connected* has several meanings: The driver is connected to the car's functionality (ignition, door lock control, climate control, etc.) via an app. Drivers are also connected to other drivers (for example, to share information about accidents or slow traffic patterns).
- *Autonomous* also has several interpretations. It could mean fully autonomous driving (driverless cars), but it can also be defined more broadly. The media system described above, for example, monitors key metrics and learns through time, thus taking this responsibility to some extent away from the driver.
- *Shared and Services* has a big impact on trends in the customer market for cars. Due to the trend toward ride-sharing, car sales may shift to some extent away from consumers and toward companies that offer transportation subscriptions to customers.
- *Electric* for Mercedes clearly means battery-powered cars: either electric-combustion hybrid versions of existing cars (the most immediate solution), or fully electric cars, which are a longer-term goal. Consistent with its technology road map, Mercedes will gradually add these cars to its fleet, while phasing out older models with combustion engines.

The EQC cars are compliant with three of the four CASE technologies: by being connected and autonomous, they provide user-friendliness, and running on batteries has the benefit of protecting the environment. Of course, Mercedes drivers will get the benefits they have come to expect: elegant design and excellent driving performance. These attributes will not be compromised in the EQC series.

By the time the electric cars are launched, prototype versions will have driven millions of miles throughout Europe. These prototypes use the IONITY charging system, which is gaining acceptance as a standard in Europe; the number of IONITY charging stations is projected to ramp up significantly. Nevertheless, since the electric battery is such new a technology, soon to be commercialized for the first time by Mercedes, the company remains concerned about the potential warranty costs.

The expected launch of the first EQC model (an SUV) is in 2019. At least one car industry expert praised the design and appearance of the EQC in late 2018 but did raise a couple of concerns. The power train is similar to Audi and Tesla electric cars in terms of performance metrics (such as charging capacity), but Tesla was already on the market a year earlier and Audi is expected to launch the e-tron quattro® soon. Plus, while Mercedes is announcing a range of 230–240 miles, the effective range might be more like about 200 miles. If Mercedes sets a suggested retail price in the $50,000–$60,000 range, it might work, but if priced near Tesla and Audi at about $80,000 range, it may not be viewed as competitive.

How would you go about forecasting sales for the hybrid and electric Mercedes models? That is, what are the factors you would need to consider in advising the company moving forward? Importantly, what can go wrong? What external shocks to the system might seriously impact Mercedes electric car sales (positively or negatively)? Can anything be done to control for, or mitigate, these shocks to the system? (Think broadly about the car industry in answering this question.) What information used in developing the long-term forecast is the most uncertain?

CHAPTER TEN

Product Protocol

Setting

When a new products group finishes the full screen and the associated financial analysis, they have reached what many feel is the most critical single step in the new product's life—more critical than the market introduction and more critical than even the building of manufacturing capacity. This is the point where very important things *all around the firm* begin to happen.

Granted, some managements still use a relay race system, where one department does its work, passes the product concept to the next department, which does its work, and so on. The leading product innovators do not follow the relay race model: they use some type of **concurrent system**, one in which all of the players begin working, doing as much as they can at any time as the project rolls along. When technical work begins, process engineers are not sitting around waiting for the final prototype to be tossed to them. When process engineers are laying out the manufacturing system, procurement people are not waiting for final word about when certain components are going to be built. And while all of this technical/operations work is continuing, marketing people are not idly waiting for a hand-off that will trigger their thoughts about advertising and customer technical service.

At the most innovative firms, all product team members begin work at the same time, and in fact many have been watching the concept testing and screening to see how positive the early word is. If a concept looks like a winner, even if financial screening won't take place for a few months, these down-the-line people are already starting to do what they will *eventually* have to do. Some workers actually may be a year ahead of need, especially if there is some built-in delay in what they do.

For example, while process engineers are waiting for product specs, so they can begin ordering cost-effective components and developing appropriate manufacturing systems, packaging people have been thinking about the concept. Many products require packaging—durable, value-producing packaging, or impressive, shelf-talking promotion packaging. Packages, in turn, require product names. So purchasing cannot order new packages until brands are settled, and brands cannot be settled until product content is known and marketing strategy is settled. Marketing strategy involves price decisions, which must await costs, which must await final manufacturing systems and component costs, which is where we started at the beginning of this paragraph! Clearly, coordination of all parties involved will be critical to the success of the new product project, otherwise things can go very wrong.

The Product Protocol

What do we do? We do it all, side by side, doing what we can, when we can, making minor commitments at some risk, holding on costly commitments. All of these efforts are risky and will never work well without *something that keeps the team together*, something that allows them to make reasonable speculations.

That something currently has no standard form, no accepted name, and no established practice. But most firms are doing part of the task, a few all of it, waiting for the activity to gel. In this book we will call the activity *protocol preparation,* and the output is a **product protocol**. Other names that it goes by are *product requirements, product definition,* and *deliverables.* All terms mean the same thing—what is the final package of output from the development system, what benefits or performance will the product deliver to the customer, and what changes will the marketing program bring in the marketplace.

A protocol is, by definition, a signed agreement between negotiating parties. In a product protocol, the negotiating parties are the functions—marketing, technical, operations, and others. Signed agreement is a bit formal, perhaps, but the financial analysis that triggered this phase depended on certain assumptions—product qualities and costs, certain support facilities, certain patents, and certain marketplace accomplishments. If they are not delivered, all bets with management are off. Since most projects today involve some form of multifunctional team, the whole group is responsible for writing a protocol. Although new products do indeed require trade-offs, they are negotiated in a very positive use of the term. Even if the multifunctional team works well together, technical limitations may emerge that may make quick agreement difficult. A humorous view of the kind of challenges that can crop up at this phase is presented in Figure 10.1.

One technique used by Toyota to get cooperation across functional areas, to speed up integration, and to focus the team is the "Oobeya Room," described in detail in Figure 10.2. The Oobeya Room is conceptually very close to the idea of the product protocol: It very effectively overcomes the challenges shown in Figure 10.1 by giving the team members little choice but to work together.

FIGURE 10.1
A Marketing-R&D Conversation

MKTG: We're going to be needing a solar-powered version of our standard garage door opener, soon.

R&D: How reliable should it be? Should it be controllable from inside the house? Should we use new electronics technology? Should it be separate from the collector system already installed?

MKTG: Well, you're the technical people, make some recommendations.

R&D: In other words, you don't know what you want.

MKTG: Cripes, do we have to tell you everything? What do you do for a living? How should we know where the collectors should be located?

R&D: If we go electronic, you'll say it's too expensive. If we go electric, you'll say we're living in the '30s. Wherever we put the collectors you will say we are wrong. If we guess, you second-guess.

MKTG: OK. Put the collectors on the garage roof.

R&D: That probably can't be done.

FIGURE 10.2
The Oobeya Room

One tool used by Toyota to speed up its product development is the Oobeya Room. "Oobeya" (from the word for "room" in Japanese, pronounced oh-beya) is, indeed, a big room, set up to accommodate the entire team for one new product project (usually containing people from marketing and sales, engineering, logistics, planning, design, and production). In the center of the Oobeya room is the prototype (a model, mock-up, or drawing) that encourages communication among team members, and helps the team visualize the product and identify potential problems early. All around the room are boards that guide discussion of the product project. These would include:

An objective board (containing Toyota's version of a PIC: background, objectives, technical specifications, and project organization)

A metrics board (showing current project status and allowing for team members to determine where they are at, or behind, target)

An action board (showing the activities of all members on the team that are required to reach the objective and indicating which activities are already completed)

A decomposition board (indicating which sub-projects need the most attention)

An issue board (showing the most critical problems that have arisen, used to stimulate discussion between team leader and team members and to assign accountability)

An important part of the Oobeya Room concept is the roles of all the participants. The team leader is responsible for setting targets, assessing team member plans, negotiating with the team or with company management when the goals are not realistic, and keeping meetings under control. Team members' responsibilities include providing solutions that help the team attain desired goals, providing status reports (on target versus behind target), suggesting how to overcome obstacles, understanding the activities of other team members, and resolving key issues. Generally, at each meeting, team members are expected to make a short presentation about their areas. The more experience they have, the easier it is for team members to keep their reports under three minutes. Total meeting time, including review of main and issue boards, usually is under one hour.

The Oobeya Room concept seems rather simple, but it is in fact a powerful tool. The payoff comes from the fact that the process requires the team members to integrate their behaviors, and to work in a very efficient and structured manner. That way, more information is generated and less time is needed. Problem detection and resolution speeds up and the value of each individual meeting is increased. No one can "loaf," read reports, or send e-mails, since there are strict time constraints. To get the work done well and on time requires a real commitment to collaboration and interaction.

Source: Toshi Horikiri, Don Kieffer, Takashi Tanaka, and Craig Flynn, "A Toyota Secret Revealed: The Oobeya Room—How Toyota Uses This Concept to Speed Up Product Development," *Visions*, 33(2), July 2009, pp. 9–13.

Protocol preparation is the subject of this chapter. In prior chapters of this book, you had a chance to see the new product process from an overall perspective—how it goes from strategy to market success, how the strategy gives the process focus, how concepts are created and gathered, how concepts are then tested and evaluated, and how the evaluation process comes to a temporary conclusion with the full screen and financial analysis.

Figure 10.3 shows what happens now. In the middle of the figure lies a bull's-eye-like circle representing the **augmented product concept**. This shows that at the core of a product is end-user benefit, the real purpose for which the product was created.

FIGURE 10.3
The Integrating and Focusing Role of Protocol

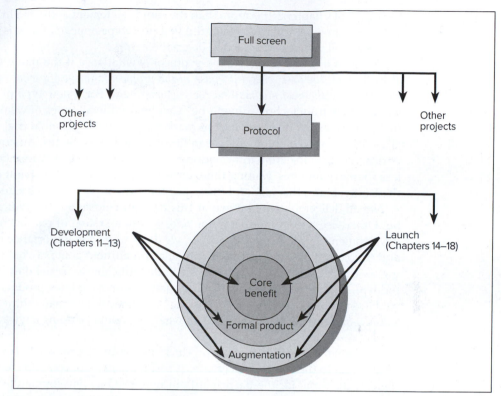

Purposes of the Protocol

This can vary from market segment to market segment and from time to time. What the customer actually buys, as depicted in Figure 10.3, consists of one or more core benefits, a formal product presentation (physical form or service sequence), *and* an augmentation of things from presale technical service to a money-back guarantee. The point here is that customers and end users buy fully augmented products, and their core benefit may partly come from the augmentations. New products managers cannot focus only on the formal product. All three of the concentric rings of the bull's-eye must be designed and executed, and both functional groups (R&D and marketing) play a role in all of them, as shown by the arrows leading into the augmented circles. Figure 10.3 also shows that the technical departments (with help from manufacturing, quality, procurement, and others) work essentially as a unit, performing the development tasks on the left side of the diagram, and marketing (with help from its allies in sales, market research, promotion, channel management, and others) does the same on the right side of the diagram. Both groups keep in close touch with each other and coordinate their efforts.

The issue is: *What do these two groups need to do their work?* The answer differs by firm and industry and situation, but whatever, it should be consolidated into a protocol statement. The protocol is, in fact, one step in the evolution of a concept, as you saw in

Figure 2.3 of Chapter 2. It is more than the simple statement approved in the screening, and less than what will exist when the first prototype appears. But it is what we need now, what all departments need to begin their work.

This idea of how others use the protocol is what gave it the name *product deliverables*. In fact, *the first general purpose of the protocol is to specify what each department will deliver to the final product that the customer buys*. For a new type of golf footwear, a deliverable from technical might be "Can be used in all types of weather and on all turf conditions." A deliverable from marketing might be personal trial use by at least 80 percent of the golf professionals in Europe, the United States, Australia, and South Africa. A deliverable from information technology might be "800 number service with less than five minutes' waiting time, covering the needs of 80 percent of callers from the United States this year and from the other markets by end of second year."

Not all deliverables are known at this time, of course, but the critical ones should be. Otherwise, we are not ready for release into a system of parallel (or concurrent) development. If, on that golf footwear, we don't know the importance of bad weather and turf conditions, the golf pro's influence on affluent golfers (what we are producing we can see will have to be expensive), the criticalness of trial (key benefits will be hidden), and the certainty of technical questions on a complex product like this, then we haven't done our homework. The fact is, protocol (like many things in use today) states requirements that force us to do what we should be doing anyway, such as good market research!

In Chapter 3, you read that the product innovation charter is used to provide clarity of direction to the new product team. A second general purpose of the protocol statement is the same for the participants in new product development. *It communicates essentials to all of the players, helps lead them into integrated actions, helps direct outcomes that are consistent with the full screen and financials, and gives all players their targets to shoot for.* Some new products people think the mere call for the document leads to early customer contacts that should always be made, but often are not.

A third purpose of the protocol relates to time through the process, or *cycle time*. As seen in Chapter 2, many firms place high priority on accelerated time to market, and better product definition can help cut development time. Consider how much development time would be wasted, and how many costly steps would have to be redone, if a new smartphone, intended to take market share away from the iPhone and Galaxy, were fully planned, designed, and in prototype production when someone noticed it was too heavy for normal use! It would have been better to specify the desired and maximum weight before undertaking development. Seemingly small decisions like this at product definition, if done wrong, can result in extremely costly fixups late in the process.

Fourth, if done right, the protocol gives requirements in words that can usually be measured. It thus permits a development process to be *managed*. It tells what is to be done, when and why, the how (if that is required by some power beyond our control), the who, and perhaps most important, the whether. That is, we know at any time whether the requirements have been met; this will automatically caution that we are not ready to market an item if there is still an open requirement, unless specifically waived. Many of the techniques we have learned in preceding chapters (perceptual gap analysis, preference mapping, conjoint analysis) will provide us with information that can be used as inputs to various "requirements" of the protocol.

Protocol's Specific Contents

You have just read what is in a protocol, in general terms. The details can vary greatly and will for some time until our practice on this new step tells just how to do it. But we should specify guidelines for product development. This might include some physical characteristics, but will at the very least include customer attributes or benefits sought (sometimes called an "I want" list). Do you recall the Hapifork from Chapter 4, which was designed to make people eat slower? The "I want" list would include:

- Same shape and weight as a regular fork; handle should not be much bigger than normal.
- Emits a signal if the person is eating too quickly.
- Washable and dishwasher safe.
- Resistant, not fragile.
- Comes in a wide variety of colors to match any décor.
- Can connect via Bluetooth or USB to other devices to record and track progress.
- Easy to use.
- Comes with information on diet and exercise.[1]

Note that some of those customer needs seem simple to say, but might require much work on the technical side. What's the power source for the fork? If AA batteries are mounted in the handle, the handle then becomes too large. What kind of signal would be best, a beeping sound or vibration, or both? And making it dishwasher safe poses its own challenges in terms of waterproofing. These are challenging but required tasks for R&D when designing the new fork. But R&D is not guessing at the specifications—they know that if they can achieve these objectives, it will result in a product customers will want. Also, not everything that we call for *must* be delivered. Some firms use the terms *Musts* and *Wants*—that is, some requirements we must have, and some are simply what we *would like* to have if feasible and practical within technology, cost, and time frames.

The following sections list items often found in protocols. An abbreviated version of a simple protocol for a new home trash disposal system is given in Figure 10.4. This figure shows the targeted customer benefits or attributes for the new system, as well as marketing, technical, financial, and corporate requirements and other items usually specified in the protocol.

Target Market

Most firms *manage* most of their new product projects using techniques we have been presenting: PICs, concept testing, screening models, protocols, and so on. Other projects are *wildcatting*—betting on a technology that hasn't yet been shown to work, betting on a new application where some end-user will partner with us to see what works, or just betting on a scientist with a good track record for coming up with saleable new products.

---

[1]See www.hapifork.com.

FIGURE 10.4 **Simplified Protocol for a Home Trash Disposal/Recycling System**

1. **Target market:**
   Ultimate: Top 30% of income group, in cities of over 100,000, with upscale lifestyle.
   Intermediate: Stakeholders in building industry for homes over $300,000, especially developers, architects, builders, bankers, and regulators.

2. **Product positioning:**
   A convenient, mess-free method for recycling items in the home.

3. **Product attributes (benefits if possible):**
   - The system must automate trash disposal in a home environment with recycling (separating trash, compacting, placing bags outside, and rebagging the empty bins and notifying user when the bag supply is running out) at a factory cost not to exceed $800.
   - The system must be clean, ventilated, and odor-free. The user will want an easy-to-clean appliance. Rodents, pets, and angry neighbors could become a problem if odors exist.
   - Installation must be simple. Distributors and other installation personnel must have favorable experience in installations.
   - The system must be safe enough for operation by children of school age.
   - The entire working unit must not be larger in cubic feet than twice a 22 cubic foot refrigerator.

4. **Competitive comparison:**
   None: First of a kind.

5. **Augmentation dimensions:**
   Financing arrangeable with us, if necessary. Generous warranty. Competent installation service, and fast/competent post-installation service. Education about recycling and about the product will be difficult and essential.

6. **Timing:**
   Being right overrides getting to market fast. But the window will not be open more than two years.

7. **Marketing requirements:**
   - Marketing announcement must be made at national builders shows and environment/ecology shows.
   - A new channel structure will be needed for the intermediate target market, but it will eventually be collapsed into our regular channel.
   - We will need a small, select sales force for this introduction.
   - To capitalize on announcement value, we need 50 installations during the first four months.

8. **Financial requirements:**
   - Development and intro period losses will not exceed $20,000,000. Break-even is expected by end of second full year on the market.
   - Ultimately, this project must achieve a five-year net present value of zero, based on 35% cost of capital.

9. **Production requirements:**
   - Once we announce, there must be no interruption of supply.
   - Quality standards simply must be met, without exception.

10. **Regulatory requirements:**
    Regulations are from many sources and vary by states and localities. There are various substakeholders here; we need to know them well. A surprise, significant holdup (after launch) cannot be allowed on this development.

11. **Corporate strategy requirements:**
    Corporate strategy is driving this project, and has personal leadership at the corporate general management level. We seek diversification of markets, enhanced reputation for innovativeness, and sustainable margins higher than those in our major markets today.

12. **Potholes:**
    This project has massive pothole potentials, because of its newness. The most worrisome ones are (1) regulatory approval of health issues, (2) accomplishing the $800 cost constraint, and (3) getting fast market approvals for early installations.

None of these is appropriate for a protocol; we just don't have the knowledge to write one, and its only effect would be to bother the developers, who, actually, will ignore it completely.

In most cases, however, we know the target market very well—first in finding their problems to solve, later in asking if our new product concept meets their need and seems reasonable to them, and still later in screening factors (e.g., do we have a sales force that can reach them or will we have to build a new one?). Perceptual and preference mapping techniques we discussed in earlier chapters can be very helpful in developing this part of the protocol, as benefit segments will have been identified and their specific needs will be understood.

The target market needs to be spelled out here, quite specifically. Some firms like to have a primary target market, selected perhaps due to size, growth rate, urgency of need, buying power, perceived ease of making competitive inroads, and so on. Typically, one or more secondary target markets will also be selected to move to after successful introduction, and at least one fall-back target market if the primary does not work out due to technical failure, regulation, competition, or other reasons.

Positioning

This is a real challenge for many firms. **Product positioning** is the concept that came out of the advertising world in the early 1970s. Essentially, it says, "Product X is better for your use than other products because . . . ." It announces the item as new and gives the end user a real reason for trying it. In the process, it shows the end user what problem it attacks and what about it makes it better than whatever they are using now. This concept will be developed more completely when we get to Chapter 14, but for now it is usually enough to state the target market and complete that sentence above. Fortunately, this should be easy because joint space mapping and other concept testing activities will have provided key information on desirable positioning options for our product. In effect, the concept test assures us stakeholders will be interested in trying an item and a positioning claim.

Technical people are often not told what the positioning of a new item will be. It's almost as though we say, develop a new item and do it in a way the customer will like. That's not management; that's abdication. Even in large packaged goods firms today, with their excellent staffs, products a bit off the beaten track often get neglected; many of these firms' R&D staffs have had to build market research departments to do concept testing on items they are originating. Misunderstandings on positioning have probably been the cause of more technical/marketing fights than anything else.

Product Attributes

As discussed earlier, product attributes define the product. They are of three types—features, functions, and benefits. Of the three, benefits are the most desirable form for a protocol to use. Information obtained from conjoint (trade-off) analysis and other concept testing techniques can be extremely useful in determining what combinations of features, functions, and specifications ought to be built into the product. An advantage of specifying the protocol in terms of benefits is that it places no (or very few) constraints on the R&D staff: They are given free rein to figure out how best to design the product so that it provides the desired benefit. Consider Built NY, which is a small design firm. A friend of the firm's owners suggested an idea for a new product: a convenient carrier for two wine bottles, which could be brought to a BYOB restaurant. The designers quickly developed a list of customer benefits for the ideal two-bottle wine carrier: protective (so the bottles wouldn't break), insulating (to maintain temperature), ergonomic (easy to carry), lightweight, reusable, inexpensive, maybe also flexible (easy to store when not in use). The challenge then was to select the material that could best deliver all these benefits. They hit upon neoprene, a synthetic material most commonly used for wetsuits. It offered all of the customer benefits, and also turned out to be easy to cut into shape and to dye into designer colors. The "Two-Bottle Tote" won awards for product design and also inspired a range of similar products, such as beer carriers and baby-bottle carriers.[2]

Function and feature attributes are also sometimes used in protocol specification. Feature attributes may originate from technical personnel, who have their input on available technologies. Function attributes may be confusing. Marketers tend to use them a lot, and they are often called performance specs, or performance parameters, or design parameters. One everyone knows is: "The car must accelerate from 0 to 60 miles per hour in 8 seconds." This requirement does not tell us what features will yield that performance. What it *does* is answer the question of how the customer achieves the benefits of exciting (or safe) start-ups.

Protocols for services are especially likely to be in performance terms since the production of a service is a performance, not a good. But protocols are also much less necessary on services because of the smaller investment in technical development. These producers can, in many cases, get to prototype very quickly, so that prototype concept testing or even product use testing can easily gain confirmation of customer need fulfillment.

Detailed Specifications

On occasions, customers make such decisions and call for products with specific features. This is dangerous. If the customers are qualified and have reason to know better than we do what features will do for them, we are wise to listen. In Chapter 4 we talked about getting finished product concepts from lead users (sometimes even a finished prototype).

Another case where features may be needed is where a firm is benchmarking competitive products. One strategy is to have the Best of the Best. Take the best features in the market, all products combined, and assemble them in your new product. This sounds great, but it means our product design is being led by competitors, not end users.[3]

Still other situations where features will appear in protocols are (1) where regulations stipulate a particular feature (e.g., prescription containers), (2) where end users own major items of equipment that impose limitations (e.g., dashboard space limitations for car entertainment centers), (3) where established practice in a customer industry is too strong for one supplier to change (e.g., for many years software makers had no

---

[2]The firm's Web site is www.builtny.com.

[3]This is explained by Milton D. Rosenau Jr. in "Avoiding Marketing's Best-of-the-Best Specification Trap," *Journal of Product Innovation Management*, 9(4), December 1992, pp. 300–302.

choice but to put MS-DOS as a feature requirement), and regrettably (4) where upper managements have personal preferences.

In general, as a conclusion to this section on attributes, it is still the best policy to write protocols in terms of benefits, using performance or specific features if that helps explain and doesn't inhibit too much. For the Hapifork, the customer probably doesn't care if the fork is made of metal or high-strength plastic, as long as it is durable and can be tossed in the dishwasher after use.

Competitive Comparisons and Augmentation Dimensions

Benchmarking has been mentioned, but there are many other competitive standards that can be put into a protocol—matching some important policy, the degree of differentiation we have to meet, and many aspects of the marketing plan (e.g., size of sales force, price, distribution availability, and more). Information on competitive comparison can be derived from perceptual maps, and the gaps appearing on the perceptual map can provide guidance on selecting an appropriate competitive position.

Just as the product itself was described in attributes above, the augmentation ring of the product can also be cited. Sometimes the product itself may be "me-too," but still is a legitimate competitive offering as it may offer the customer a new level of service, a better warranty, or better distributor support. Recall that there are three rings in the fully augmented product—ring one (core benefit) is covered in the positioning statement, ring two (the formal product) is covered in the attribute requirements, and ring three (augmentations) is covered here.

Other Components of the Product Protocol

There are several other components of the protocol that we will handle here very briefly. These are probably best illustrated through example, such as in Figure 10.4.

Timing: Most new products today must come out faster, but not all do. Some involve major technical breakthroughs that cannot be put on the clock. The distinction needs to be clear to all. And if there is a date to meet, it should be right here.

Financials: Typically, the protocol will include price level, discounts, sales volume, sales dollars, market share, profits, net present value, and many of the other financial data introduced in the previous chapter.

Production: This one is much like marketing requirements, some focusing on what the function will prepare to do and what that will accomplish—thus, plants to be built, volumes, and quality to be achieved.

Regulatory Requirements: These are highly varied, but managements today understand the need to have advanced understanding on them.

Corporate Strategy Requirements: Key ideas (such as core competencies) will have already been captured in the product innovation charter. Also, at this time, the assurance of upper management support is important.

Potholes: As we have seen before, there are potholes in product innovation, just as they are on that stretch of highway as you drive at night—and they are capable of bringing a new product down. Management that doesn't take a good look ahead deserves to hit one. We don't usually drive into *known* potholes, so listing them here helps.

Protocol and the Voice of the Customer

Hearing the Voice of the Customer[4]

Back in Chapter 2, you were introduced to the concept of the voice of the customer (VOC). We return to it here, as it plays such an important role of the development of the product protocol.

VOC has been defined as a "complete set of customer wants and needs, expressed in the customer's own language, organized the way the customer thinks about, uses, and interacts with the product . . . , and prioritized by the customer in terms of both importance and performance—in other words, current satisfaction with existing alternatives."[5] In this definition, "customer's own language" means exactly that—no scientific jargon. Printer users don't generally think in terms of edge resolution or number of pixels; rather, they think in terms of how well the letters come out, or how nice the pictures look. Just because the terms don't sound scientific doesn't mean the opinions are unimportant! Also, the customers must organize and prioritize their needs in their own way, as they see fit; this is likely to be different from the way the firm sees it.

Recall from Chapter 5 that we have several ways to access the voice of the customer: through direct interviewing, for example, or by conducting focus groups. Interviewing customers individually can provide very rich and detailed information, but might be time-consuming and costly. So, how many interviews should be conducted before one is relatively confident the VOC has been captured? Research by Abbie Griffin and John Hauser suggests a reasonable ground rule for interviews: about 30 individual interviews, each lasting about three-quarters of an hour, produce close to 100 percent of all customer needs; 20 interviews produce about 90 percent of the needs. A VOC process should be audio-recorded with verbatim transcription; this is far more accurate and detailed than having a human note-taker. Respondents should be asked for permission to be recorded; almost everyone complies, and soon forgets the recorder is on.[6]

If the VOC process was successful, the new product team should have obtained about 70–140 customer needs statements from these interviews. The customer needs statements should then be organized into 15 to 25 groups, called *affinity groupings* (preferably by the customers themselves as they will generally have a different way of organizing these than will the market researchers). These groupings can then be prioritized by importance to the customer. While this sounds like a long and involved process, cutting corners may compromise the richness of the insights or result in incorrect prioritizations of customer needs.[7]

---

[4]Much of this section derives from Gerald M. Katz, op. cit.

[5]Gerald M. Katz, "The Voice of the Customer," in P. Belliveau, A. Griffin, and S. M. Somermeyer, *The PDMA Toolbook 2 for New Product Development* (New York: John Wiley, 2002), Ch. 7.

[6]Abbie Griffin and John Hauser, "The Voice of the Customer," *Marketing Science,* 12(1), Winter 1993, pp. 1–27.

[7]Part of this section is adapted from Gerry Katz, "Nine Myths about the Voice of the Customer," *Visions*, 35(3), 2011, pp. 34–35.

The interviewer should be prepared with the right questions. One of the worst ways to elicit the VOC is to ask "What are your needs?" or "What are your requirements?" Customers are all too willing to provide a wish list of "must-haves," almost certainly taken from existing, available solutions. Innovation expert Guy Kawasaki says, "If you ask customers what they want, they will tell you, 'better, faster, and cheaper,' that is, *better sameness*, not revolutionary change." Apple co-founder Steve Jobs famously said, "It's really hard to design products by focus groups. A lot of times, people don't know what they want until you show it to them. . . . You can't just ask customers what they want and then try to give that to them. By the time you get it built, they'll want something new."[8] What should we learn from these comments? Should we forget about using focus groups or interviews to hear the voice of the customer?

The real issue here is, what kind of information can you expect to get from focus groups or interviews? To avoid "better sameness," a better way to proceed is to focus on experiences or desired outcomes, for example, by asking "What are the most difficult tasks you are trying to accomplish with the product?" "What do you like, and what do you dislike?" or "What is the best, and the worst, experience you have ever had with this product?" Consider staying overnight at a hotel. If you were asked to state your needs, what would you say? Probably a clean room, a nice bed, shower, TV, and Internet connection. But if asked what your worst experience was, what would it be? Couldn't find the plug for your razor? Bumped yourself on the shower head? Towels weren't clean? Front desk personnel were rude? The interviewer will get many more ideas for product or service improvements this way.

To go back to Steve Jobs's comment, Apple was indeed asking the right questions of customers and was listening to them. This is what he said about marketing the iPod Touch:

> Originally we weren't exactly sure how to market [it]. . . . Was it an iPhone without the phone? Was it a pocket computer? . . . What customers told us was, they started to see it as a game machine. We started to market it that way, and it just took off. And now what we really see is it's the lowest-cost way to the App Store, and that's the big draw. So . . . we were focused on [getting] the price down where everyone can afford it.[9]

So Apple *was* listening, absolutely: to customer's desired outcomes and how the product would best provide those outcomes! There is no question that the long list of successful Apple products are primarily technology-push; as Guy Kawasaki said, "The richest vein for tech startups is creating the product that you want to use . . . that's what [Apple] did."[10] But recall from the PIC that the technology dimension must match with a viable, high-potential market dimension. The iPod Touch example nicely reminds us that the value of the VOC does not come from asking customers to tell you what they want. While perhaps obvious, this point is easy to miss, and lack of success with the VOC may well be due to poor implementation.

---

[8] The Guy Kawasaki and Steve Jobs quotes are from Brad Barbera, "Steve Jobs: A Product Developer's Perspective," *Visions*, 36(1), 2012, pp. 10–15.

[9] Brad Barbera (2012), op. cit.

[10] Brad Barbera (2012), op. cit.

In obtaining the VOC, it is not enough to get the generalities, such as "I need my smartphone to be flexible," or "I need my Internet access provider to be consistent." The obvious follow-ups here are "What do you mean by flexible?" and "What do you mean by consistent?" This ensures that the VOC is clearly heard and not misinterpreted. A good rule of thumb is to keep asking why: "Why did you say that?" "Why do you feel like that?" "Why would it be better that way?" The goal, remember, is not to get technical solutions to the problems. That comes later. Rather, the customer's wants, needs, likes, dislikes, and so on must be articulated as well as possible at this point.

Figure 10.5 provides two examples of firms that did not go far enough with their customer research. While they might have known some of the generalities, they needed to dig deeper to get a precise picture of customers' desired outcomes.

Voice of the customer research can help manufacturers determine what attributes are growing in importance, which helps to focus R&D for future product generations. Consider the evolution of the smartphone. While you may have loved your first smartphone, you may have encountered some problems and developed a wish list of features that no phone had yet ("the screen cracks easily if I drop it, and I wish it were less prone to cracking," or "the phone goes dead in the middle of a call, and I wish the battery would

FIGURE 10.5
The Importance of Getting the Voice of the Customer

Kawasaki, seeking to improve its original Jet Skis, asked current Jet Ski customers for suggestions but did not go deeper and, therefore, missed the underlying problem they could have tried to solve. Most customers suggested adding padding or some other features that would make it more comfortable for the standing rider. No one suggested adding a seat, which, of course, provides the desired outcome (increased comfort). By the time Kawasaki added seats to its Jet Skis, other competitors had already done so, reducing the one-time leader to a "me-too" competitor. Ironic, since Kawasaki could have looked to the motorcycles it produced and got the seat idea!	The Tata Group learned an expensive lesson with their launch of the Tata Nano. It was company CEO Ratan Tata's vision to bring an inexpensive car to the growing Indian middle-class market, and it would be affordable enough to compete with scooters. After spending hundreds of millions of dollars on development and production, the car was launched in 2009 at a retail price of $2,000. Unfortunately, the Nano was perceived as cheap-looking and unsafe. A better understanding of the voice of the customer would have revealed that the target market was not willing to give up appearance, comfort, and safety to get a rock-bottom price.

Sources: Kawasaki example from Anthony W. Ulwick, "Turn Customer Input into Innovation," *Harvard Business Review*, January–February 2002, pp. 91–98; Tata example from Elio Keko, Gert Jan Prevo, and Stefan Stremersch, "The What, Who, and How of Innovation Generation," in Peter N. Golder and Debanjan Mitra (editors), *Handbook of Research on New Product Development*, Cheltenham, UK, Edward Elgar, 2018, pp. 37–59.

last longer"). Or a competitor might have made an advance that you find desirable ("I love my iPhone, but those Samsung Galaxy phones have big screens with beautiful displays"). These comments are helpful to the new product team as they reveal which attributes are important, including some that may not have been big considerations in the past. The iPhone X was designed with a large screen (5.8-inch diagonal), is thin (0.30 inches) and light (6.14 ounces), offers high-resolution images, and comes with a highly durable glass and surgical-grade stainless steel frame that is water and dust resistant. The phone's aesthetics follow the familiar Apple appearance: rounded edges and attractive curved design. The battery life is two hours longer than in previous models, and Face ID can be used to log in securely and use Apple Pay safely for transactions. Clearly, the designers of this phone were focused on improving performance on important attributes, while at the same time, not compromising features that iPhone's loyal customers had long desired, such as appealing appearance and secure transactions.[11]

Market researcher and consultant Gerry Katz summarizes the misconceptions about VOC that can lead to its misuse and should be avoided.

1. Many companies treat VOC as qualitative research only, whereas the real value of it comes from organizing and clustering the stated needs and prioritizing them into their relative importance. This is a quantitative process and is often overlooked.

2. Firms often focus on getting the VOC only from major customers, while much important information can be obtained from noncustomers, average customers, and customers who favor the competitor's product.

3. Managers may believe that customers don't know what they want. In fact, they are quite good at stating their needs. Not being professional engineers or R&D personnel, they are usually not able to tell what new technology needs to be developed to address those needs. It is up to the firm to match customer need to engineering characteristics. This may be accomplished through Quality Function Deployment, which we explore later in this chapter.

4. Finally, to repeat, it is tempting just to ask customers what they want and need, but that usually provides few new insights. It is better to ask what they like and dislike about current products and what outcomes they would like to see in the future.

Protocol and Quality Function Deployment (QFD)

QFD and the House of Quality

To understand the role of the product protocol in the new products process, think of this process as shown in Figure 10.6. This figure emphasizes the role of the customer, as it shows that we begin with the voice of the customer and end up with a product that satisfies the customer's needs. Through market research, sales calls, and other forms of customer contact, we are able to identify what the customer desires. The next step is a tricky one, but absolutely essential. We need to convert those customer desires into some kind of blueprint, perhaps an engineering schematic or a detailed

[11]Details on iPhone X attributes are available on the product Web site, www.apple.com/iphone-x/specs.

FIGURE 10.6
The Role of Protocol in the New Products Process

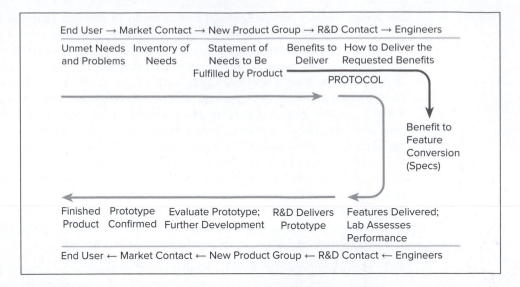

service plan, that offers the customer those desired benefits in a format that is useful for the product development team. Once we get to this point, we can take it back to the customer and conduct the appropriate tests to fine-tune the product. It is indeed the product protocol, the subject of this chapter, that helps the firm get "around the bend" of Figure 10.6, because when carefully planned, the protocol allows the firm to translate customer desires into the appropriate product form.

The importance of this translation process cannot be overstated. Suppose you work for a company that produces flat-screen TVs. You have done the VOC research and you discover that customers want "nice pictures," "bright colors," "realistic sound," and a "sleek appearance." These are the actual customer needs and wants, stated in typical, nontechnical customer terminology. Engineering can develop a next-generation TV that meets these customer needs, but engineers use different words in the development process: megapixels, number of available colors, scan rate, audio response of speakers at different frequencies, physical dimensions, and so forth. It literally is a translation process, converting the nontechnical VOC into terminology that will guide the technical personnel in their efforts.

This next section describes a technique that allows the VOC to become a driver of all later steps in the new products process.

Quality function deployment (QFD) was invented in the Japanese automobile industry years ago as a tool of project control in an industry with incredibly complicated projects. It can lead to reduced design time and costs, and more efficient communication between project team members from functional areas.[12] In fact, QFD has been

---

[12]John R. Hauser and Don Clausing, "The House of Quality," *Harvard Business Review,* 66(3), 1988, pp. 63–73; Abbie Griffin and John R. Hauser, "Patterns of Communication among Marketing, Engineering and Manufacturing: A Comparison between Two Product Teams," *Management Science,* 38(3), March 1992, pp. 360–373; and Abbie Griffin, "Evaluating QFD's Use in U.S. Firms as a Process for Developing Products," *Journal of Product Innovation Management,* 9(3), September 1992, pp. 171–187. For more information on QFD, try the Web site for the QFD Institute, www.qfdi.org.

credited with a major contribution to the U.S. automobile industry's comeback against Japanese competition. We present it here, as it is one way in which many firms have fostered the kind of cross-functional interaction mandated by the product protocol. QFD has also been successfully used earlier in the new products process, very early in the fuzzy front end in concept generation, because it can help the new products team think of novel new concepts that will satisfy customer needs.[13]

In theory, QFD is designed to ensure that customer needs are focused on all through the new product project: product engineering, parts deployment, process planning, and production. In practice, the first step of QFD has received the most attention and has been useful to the largest number of firms, and that is the so-called **house of quality (HOQ)**. The value of the HOQ to firms is in the way it summarizes multiple product aspects simultaneously and in relationship to one another. Figure 10.7 shows a sample HOQ for the development of a new computer printer.

The HOQ requires inputs from marketing and technical personnel and encourages communication and cooperation across these functional areas. Down the left-hand side of the figure appear the *customer attributes* (CAs), variously called needs, whats, or requirements. This is a critical marketing input into the HOQ. Compatibility, print quality, ease of use, and productivity were identified in this case as the most important CAs for a printer. CAs are identified through market research: focus groups, interviews, and the like. This section of the HOQ corresponds to the part of protocol relating to what the end user will get from the product. It is usually filled with benefits, though occasionally (as above), features or functions (functional benefits) are so mandatory that they are put there. The CAs in this example seem to be primary attributes; in a more complex application there may be secondary or even tertiary attributes under each. For example, ease of use might include "easy to learn how to operate," "easy to connect," "easy to replace the paper," and so on. CAs are also frequently weighted in terms of importance.

At the far right of the HOQ are the ratings of the proposed new product and its main competitors on each of the CAs, where 0 = "poor" and 5 = "excellent." This section can be interpreted as a kind of simple perceptual map of all competitive products on the key customer attributes. It identifies the strong points and areas for improvement of our new product.

The upper section of the HOQ shows *engineering characteristics* (ECs): edge sharpness, resolution, and so on. ECs are often technologies, but can also be stated in terms of performance or design parameters. This is where the customer's needs are translated into technical specifications. The project team goes through the central grid of the HOQ, identifying those ECs that will affect one or more CAs either positively or negatively. In this case, "hours of training required" is positively related to both ease of use (strongly) and productivity (less strongly); "Speed of text" is strongly related to productivity. Obviously, this step requires real cooperation between marketing and technical personnel. Objective measures are then set for

[13]Gerald M. Katz, "Practitioner Note: A Response to Pullman, et al.'s (2002) Comparison of Quality Function Deployment versus Conjoint Analysis," *Journal of Product Innovation Management,* 21(1), 2004, pp. 61–63.

FIGURE 10.7
**QFD and
Its House of
Quality**

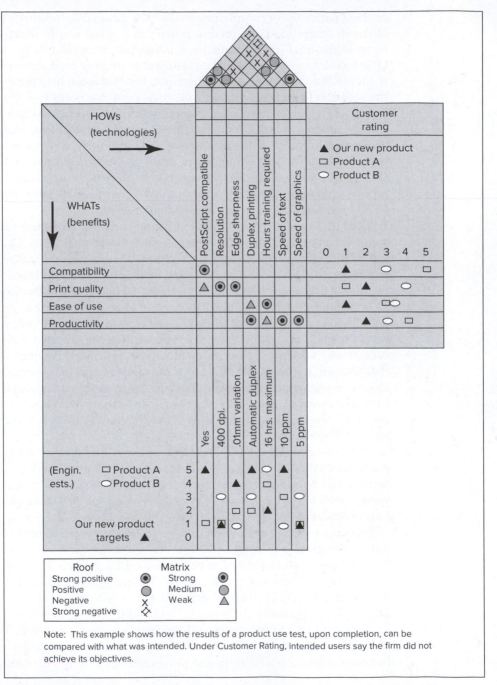

Note: This example shows how the results of a product use test, upon completion, can be compared with what was intended. Under Customer Rating, intended users say the firm did not achieve its objectives.

Source: From Milton D. Rosenau Jr and John J. Moran, *Managing the Development of New Products,* John Wiley & Sons, Inc., 1993, p. 231.

each EC (usually by engineers), and the team can now begin setting target values for the ECs based on customer need and competitive offerings. For example, speed of text can be objectively measured in pages per minute (ppm); and in this case, 10 ppm was set as the objective.

In the automobile example earlier of fast pickup speed, one CA might be "exciting driving experience." Related ECs might be a new engine (a technology), the 0–60 time (a performance parameter), or a weight switch putting more load at the point of drive-wheel contact (a design parameter). Practice varies such that we can't give instruction here, but there are other sources.[14]

Finally, the top part of the house (the peaked "roof") shows the trade-offs between ECs that the technical personnel must consider. Each diamond in the roof repre-sents the interaction between a pair of ECs, and the technical staff must identify each significant interaction. The "strong negative" hash mark (pound sign) at the crossing of "resolution" and "speed of graphics," for example, indicates that if the printer's resolution quality is boosted, it is likely to slow down speed of graphics printing. Some of these interactions are positive: A single design change may boost both speed of text printing and of graphics printing.[15]

As noted above, the HOQ is really only the first part of the full QFD procedure. Figure 10.8 shows what comes next. The HOQ, which translates CAs into ECs, is linked to a parts deployment house, which takes the ECs as inputs and converts them into parts characteristics. Subsequent houses specify the key process operations and production requirements. Nevertheless, experienced QFD practitioners will often find that 80 percent of the value of QFD can be obtained in the first HOQ matrix; consequently, few QFD projects go all the way through the process.[16]

In a very simple illustrative example, suppose we had decided on the concept of extra-hot, thick, green salsa on the basis of our conjoint analysis in Chapter 6. The CA of extra-hot might be translated to an EC such as hotness on a 10-point scale (a kind of simplified Scoville pepper scale) where habaneros, the hottest peppers we have available, are rated 10. We might aim at no more than 7 or 8 on this scale (as only the most daring would want salsa to be hotter!). Thickness could be trans-lated into a viscosity measure, and we might aim at a score of between 4 and 6 on a 10-point thickness scale (where 7 and higher would be too thick, and 3 and lower would not be thick enough). The ECs in turn suggest which parts—or, in this case,

[14]See Hauser and Clausing, "The House of Quality," for a general introduction. For applications, see John R. Hauser, "Puritan-Bennett, The Renaissance Spirometry System: Listening to the Voice of the Customer," *Sloan Management Review* 34, 1993, pp. 61–70; and Milton D. Rosenau and John J. Moran, *Managing the Development of New Products* (New York: Van Nostrand Reinhold, 1993), pp. 225–237.

[15]In a real-life application (iron ore products), increasing a metal's hardness reduces its malleability (how easily it can be formed into shapes). See Magnus Tottie and Thomas Lager, "QFD: Linking the Customer to the Product Development Process as a Part of the TQM Concept," *Research-Technology Management,* July 1995, pp. 257–267.

[16]Gerald M. Katz, "Quality Function Deployment and the House of Quality," in A. Griffin and S. M. Somermeyer, *The PDMA Toolbook 3 for New Product Development* (New York: John Wiley, 2007), Ch. 7.

FIGURE 10.8
Later Stages of QFD

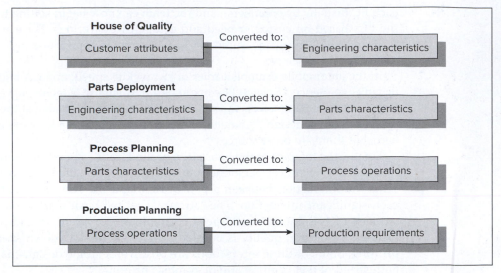

Source: Adapted from "The House of Quality," by John R. Hauser and Don Clausing, May–June 1998. The Harvard Business Publishing.

ingredients—to use: which types of hot chile peppers, how much tomato and garlic, and so on. Process requirements might specify what kind of food processing (chopping, boiling, etc.) will be involved. Related production requirements would be the settings of the food processing equipment that give the desired consistency and appearance. Using the puree setting on the chopper might make the salsa too runny.

Outcomes of QFD

There are several benefits of applying QFD. For one thing, everything—from product engineering to designing the production process—is driven by customer needs (or, more specifically, by the stated customer attributes). The likelihood that the product about to be developed is one of those better mousetraps that doesn't have a market is minimized. Furthermore, to get the benefits out of QFD, the various functional areas really do have to work together. This is especially an issue in the development of some industrial products. While consumer-good firms may routinely collect the market data used in the HOQ, industrial product developers often question why they need to do customer needs assessment (or even talk to the folks in marketing)—after all, they say they know the market! QFD has been useful in such firms in promoting dialogue between disparate groups and in encouraging product developers with technical backgrounds to see the advantages of assessing customer needs. In sum, QFD encourages cross-functional dialogue and interaction throughout the technical development process—which is precisely the kind of agreement called for by the product protocol.

When QFD was first used extensively in the United States, mixed but generally favorable results were reported. Over 80 percent of teams using QFD reported a long-term strategic benefit and an improvement in cross-functional teaming.[17] A more recent survey of QFD use in the United States and Japan finds firms in both countries having success with QFD, but in somewhat different ways. U.S. firms tend to concentrate on the HOQ matrix and collect new primary data from their customers (for example, through focus groups). Japanese firms use more of the downstream matrices and rely more on existing product data (such as complaint information and warranty data). Interestingly, U.S. firms report greater benefits in cross-functional integration and decision making through QFD than do Japanese firms, possibly because the U.S. firms had the most to learn about listening to customer needs![18]

QFD has had only mixed results in some applications. It's expensive, in both cost and employee time, due to the extensive data collection at the VOC phase. It probably is best suited to major projects such as new platform development or major process reengineering.[19]

Use of QFD by firms tends to be related to better financial performance and greater customer satisfaction. Many firms, however, use it occasionally rather than consistently, and especially for exploratory products (that is, one that will be dropped unless a customer will support it). Besides, the data requirements can be overwhelming. The term *matrix hell* has been used to describe its application, and highly trained technical personnel may not be able to resolve conflicts that arise. In some cases, the customer firm may not know what it wants, so specifying the "whats" can be difficult. Nevertheless, QFD has been experiencing a resurgence lately, probably because it is viewed as one of the most thorough and objective ways to translate customer needs to engineering specifications.[20] Its proponents say it is the best way to uncover customer wants and boost cross-functionality, while its detractors call it overly lengthy and boring, leading some participants to wonder why they are doing it.[21] In general, the better the team, the more efficient the QFD; Figure 10.9 provides some guidelines in team selection. The efficiency of QFD can also be improved by doing one or more of the following:

- Concentrate on only some of the engineering characteristics: either the apparently most critical ones or some others where improvements might be easy to accomplish.

- Organize the engineering characteristics into groups and designate responsibility for these to specific functional areas (i.e., manufacturing, product design, even marketing).

[17]Abbie Griffin, "Evaluating Development Processes, QFD as an Example," *Marketing Science Institute,* Report No. 91–121, August 1991.

[18]John J. Cristiano, Jeffrey K. Liker, and Chelsea C. White III, "Customer-Driven Product Development through Quality Function Deployment in the U.S. and Japan," *Journal of Product Innovation Management,* 17(4), July 2000, pp. 286–308.

[19]Gerald M. Katz, "Quality Function Deployment and the House of Quality," in A. Griffin and S. M. Somermeyer, *The PDMA Toolbook 3 for New Product Development* (New York: John Wiley, 2007), Ch. 7.

[20]Gerald M. Katz, "Is QFD Making a Comeback?" *Visions,* 27(2), April 2003.

[21]Gerald M. Katz, "Quality Function Deployment and the House of Quality," op. cit.

FIGURE 10.9
Criteria for
Good Team
Selection

Make sure the team is cross-functional. This means design, manufacturing, R&D, marketing, finance, technical support, and anyone else that might have a stake in the success of the product.

Appoint an administrator and an advocate for the Voice of the Customer. One person should be well informed on all customer details, and able to explain exactly what customers mean when they express their needs.

Team members should have ultimate responsibility to act on the results. If key line managers are on the team, it eliminates the need to convince them of the correctness of the analysis and the need to act.

Other criteria: Team members should have knowledge of current practice and also a historical perspective; team members should be respected by their peers; include some top-level executives; include people from a range of levels within the firm; don't shy away from those who will try some "creative abrasion" to stretch team thinking (but keep the disrupters off the team).

Source: From Gerald M. Katz, "Quality Function Development and the House of Quality," in A. Griffin and S. M. Sommermeyer, *The PDMA Toolbook 3 for New Product Development,* John Wiley & Sons, Inc., 2007, Chapter 7.

- Do a cost-benefit analysis on each engineering characteristic to identify which ones provide the greatest benefit relative to associated cost of improvement on that characteristic.[22]

Some Warnings about the Difficulty of the Protocol Process

The protocol process is very complicated. For one thing, it is fraught with politics. The departments are all in natural competition for power and budget. Key individuals are as different as night and day, being scientist, marketer, accountant, and factory manager. The situation itself is fluid and changing, seemingly never nailed down. Management senses the importance of the various projects and puts heavy pressure on them. A big winner on the product frontier can make a career, exonerate a general manager's other disappointments, award very large bonuses; and of course, a major failure can make a mess of everything close to it.

This means that people have their own agenda for incorporating into a protocol (or not incorporating into it). Most want the other people nailed down to specific accomplishment requirements with dollar signs and dates clearly attached, but with no such promises from themselves.

Given that a protocol is needed early, just prior to broad-scale work being started, many people are not yet on the scene. They have more pressing, near-term problems, so they delay the process or weaken it by their absence.

[22]For good practical discussions of QFD, see Gerald M. Katz, "Is QFD Making a Comeback?" *Visions,* October 2001; Gerald M. Katz, "After QFD: Now What?" *Visions,* 25(2), April 2001, pp. 22–24; and Carey C. Curtis and Lynn W. Ellis, "Satisfying Customers while Speeding R&D and Staying Profitable," *Research-Technology Management,* September–October 1998, pp. 23–27. For a perspective on how to overcome QFD difficulties, see Rick W. Purcell, "Should the IV House Be a Duplex?" *Visions,* 27(2), April 2003.

But, beyond the politics and pressures, we also see a hardening of the requirements in a protocol. People think they were all wise when developing the document and presume the contents are all set in concrete. But it shouldn't be seen that way. It is an *aid to management,* not a *substitute for thinking*. All protocols have to change, some of them many times. But the burden of proof is on those who want to change a requirement.

Last, most of these problems go away if preparation of a protocol is assigned to a multifunctional new products team. Technical doesn't write one, and neither does marketing. Most assuredly, top management does not write one.

Summary

This chapter has dealt with a powerful concept—protocol. As an agreement among the functions about the required output or deliverables from a specific new product program, it sets the standards for it. The purpose is to communicate the required outputs as product benefits and other dimensions, integrate the team onto the same frequency, make clear the timing importance, and make it easier to manage the process against specific targets.

You saw a simplified version of a typical protocol. At this time we are ready to blow the whistle and charge into the development activity. As seen in the new products process of Chapter 1, action will now take place in marketing and technical in parallel, so we are going to need excellent communication among marketing, R&D, production, design, and other functional areas to get us through the next phase.

Case: Product Protocol for Entrepreneurs[23]

In 2010, entrepreneur Sarah Kauss introduced the S'Well water bottle to the market. Her original idea was to cut substantially into the number of plastic water bottles that are used once and not recycled. She noted, "I started this company because I wanted people to stop using single-use plastic bottles." While long-lasting, refillable water bottles had been around for some time, they weren't ideal. They were often too large to fit neatly into a pocketbook or school bag and were bulky and unattractive. (According to Ms. Kauss, most reusable bottles "looked like camping accessories.") Meanwhile, the use of single-use plastic bottles continues unabated.

The S'Well bottle was designed, in terms of both function and aesthetics, to meet many consumer needs that were inadequately satisfied by existing bottles. It offers the following benefits:

- *Sustainability:* The bottle is reusable and BPA-free.
- *Convenient size:* Smaller bottles fit neatly into car cup holders, while the largest size can hold a bottle of wine.

[23]This case is based on the S'Well Web site, www.swellbottle.com; James Barron, "320,000 High Schoolers to Get Free Water Bottles. The Goal? 54 Million Fewer Single-Use Drinks," *The New York Times*, September 23, 2018; Lo & Sons Web site, www.loandsons.com; Anonymous, "Pop Bags Opens in Florence," *magentaflorence.com*; and the Pop Bags U.S. Web site, www.popbagusa.com.

- *Large mouth:* The bottles have a wide enough mouth to add ice easily; this benefit is particularly nice for those who want to take smoothies on the go.
- *Easy to grip:* The bottles are ergonomically designed so that even the widest ones are easy to hold.
- *Temperature-controlled:* Hot drinks stay hot for 12 hours, and cold drinks stay cold for 24 hours.
- *Stain-free:* The bottles are easy to clean, and the insides are stain-resistant.
- *No condensation:* A triple-wall design means no condensation on your hands, in your pocketbook, or all over your phone or laptop.
- *Attractive:* There is a range of stylish, sleek designs and colors to choose from.

Also available are S'Well tumblers, as well as Travelers and Roamers (bigger-sized bottles), which all share similar customer benefits.

While the product itself has many advantages that contributed to its success, the company has remained true to its environmental mission. For example, in 2018, S'Well donated 320,000 bottles to the city of New York: one for every high school student attending public or charter school. Working with New York City Hall and the Mayor's Office for Sustainability, this initiative is hoped to reduce the number of single-use plastic bottles by 54 million per year.

Plastic bottles are not the only product category where an entrepreneur with a good handle on customer needs can make a difference. Consider Helen Lo, who traveled frequently and had to make do with travel bags that were too heavy, unattractive, too expensive, or impossible to find anything in. She designed a series of travel bags in multiple sizes for men and women that provided the benefits most sought by frequent travelers: lots of convenient pockets, compartments for laptops and other devices, an adjustable sleeve to cover suitcase handles, and a sleek, simple, and attractive design. One particularly interesting model was the Seville: this is a woman's handbag for which one can buy a removable, matching shell that fastens inside. More pockets, plus a removable shell, leads to more practical travel, and no more fumbling around in a "black hole" to find keys or pens.

Another totally new idea in handbags is the modular handbag, marketed under the name Pop Bags. The Florence-based founder of J&C Jackyceline, designer Sara Lin, hit upon the idea of Italian-leather handbags made up of modular parts that snap together using attractive metal buttons. One could, for example, buy two leather pieces, one red and one blue, and snap these together to make the two sides of a unique and distinctive bag. Buying more leather pieces, one would be able to mix and match to create even more combinations. The bags are available in dozens of colors, as well as several sizes and price points. Initially, the stores were in Florence, Italy, but the company has opened distribution elsewhere in Europe and has begun opening pop-up stores in U.S. malls. It seems like a product that could only have come from Italy, a country with centuries of expertise in leather goods and a rich history of world-class design.

Think about these three examples. In each case, there was an opportunity for an innovative new product, based on inadequacy of existing products or perhaps just a brainstorm on a high-potential new product concept. It is easy to develop a simplified product protocol, essentially a list of the most important customer needs or desired benefits. In addition, good voice of the customer research would uncover some interesting surprises (for example, "sustainability" or "convenient size" would probably be mentioned as important benefits by most consumers considering a reusable water bottle; "temperature-controlled" or "no condensation" might be nice voice of the customer surprises). But remember that even if the customer benefit is obvious, the product design and engineering to deliver that benefit might require some work. For example, eliminating condensation requires using a triple-wall design, but the designer does not want to add extra weight or thickness to the bottle, so solving this problem may require an ultra-light yet durable metal for use as the liner.

For the products listed above, can you think of any other customer benefits that could be added, maybe for future additions to the product line? Think of at least one other simple consumer product like those shown here and list a few customer benefits that are not yet satisfied or are underserved. Develop this into a simplified product protocol (list of benefits that the new product must deliver). Which of these benefits might pose a real engineering challenge that you would have to overcome in order to have a successful new product? Would any desired benefits lead to engineering or design trade-offs?

Case: DuPont[24]

DuPont is a chemical company with a long and successful history of product development. Founded in 1802, it is one of the world's leading chemical companies and produces products for the food, construction, communications, and transportation industries, among others. DuPont operates in over 70 countries and employs over 58,000 people. DuPont's success with new products over the years is well documented: some of the most familiar include nylon, Teflon, Kevlar, and Lycra.

In 2007, however, DuPont senior management felt that something was amiss in the firm's new products process. After lengthy study, the company identified several problems, which are really not that uncommon. First, there was little deep customer insight, in particular at the customer segment level. DuPont was wrestling with a familiar segmentation issue: develop a product for a single customer and there is no guarantee of sales in the wider market, but a one-size-fits-all product will end up pleasing no one. Insights at the target segment level were lacking. Second, on paper the company had a voice-of-the-customer process, but it seemed to have devolved into "chat with the customer" sessions that were not generating breakthrough ideas. Finally, DuPont representatives were meeting with direct customers, but not with their customer's customers. While it is the direct customer that actually pays the bills, it is the customer's customer who has the important needs that must be met by new products. As a result, the value propositions developed by DuPont were often based on wishful thinking, not hard customer-needs data, and therefore did not inspire customers.

[24]This case is adapted from Dan Edgar and Dan Adams, "How DuPont Uses New Product Blueprinting at the Front End—And Implemented a New e-Learning Model to Teach It," *Visions*, 34(3), 2010, pp. 12–17.

Recognizing the need for a novel, innovative approach to the front end of the new products process, DuPont turned to the Institute for the Study of Business Markets (ISBM), where they met with the consulting firm AIM and discovered New Product Blueprinting, an approach especially suitable for business-to-business (B2B) product development. There are several characteristics of B2B product development that distinguish it from consumer product development, and which drive New Product Blueprinting. First, B2B customers are knowledgeable, having the education and experience to be able to provide new product guidance to their suppliers (like DuPont). Second, B2B customers want to help their suppliers because it can help them as well, in terms of lower costs or higher performance for their own products. Third, B2B customers make rational, stable decisions, and fourth, there are relatively fewer B2B customers and their decision making can be influenced by supplier actions.

New Product Blueprinting emphasizes "going deep" with customers. The mode of contact is by interview. Questionnaires are not used, since it is felt that "you will seldom get more than you ask for." It is deemed better instead to run an idea-generation interview, taking down "digital sticky notes" and displaying them on a big screen to fully engage customers and obtain their comments and feedback. In this synchronous process, supplier and customer interact, the customer can comment on and correct the supplier, and the supplier can probe the customer's comments deeply. In New Product Blueprinting, the focus is on finding the customer's desired outcomes, which allows the supplier to search for solutions. New Product Blueprinting also uses some quantitative metrics, in particular the market satisfaction gap (MSG). MSG is calculated as Importance $\times$ (10–Satisfaction), where Importance and Satisfaction (with current products) are measured on 1–10 scales. An MSG is greater than 30 signals a significant opportunity.

Initial trials of New Product Blueprinting at DuPont were successful. Three projects were initiated around this time. One was a product for the displays market in Asia; interaction with customers determined that there was little desire for any new materials and that the market segment held little value. The second was a product for the global electronics market for which much internal development was already completed. After properly specifying the desired customer outcomes, it was determined that at least five more years of development would have been required. The third was a global solar energy product for which strong customer needs were identified that met well with DuPont's capabilities. The result of New Product Blueprinting: the first two projects were terminated (thus avoiding two very costly failures), and the third was approved and became financially successful.

How is New Product Blueprinting different from traditional voice of the customer analysis? How does it complement VOC? Do you think New Product Blueprinting might work for a consumer packaged goods company such as Campbell Soup? What about for a service such as a hospital or bank? Why or why not? What might be drawbacks of New Product Blueprinting for a high-tech manufacturer like DuPont or for other kinds of firms?

FIGURE IV.1

Development

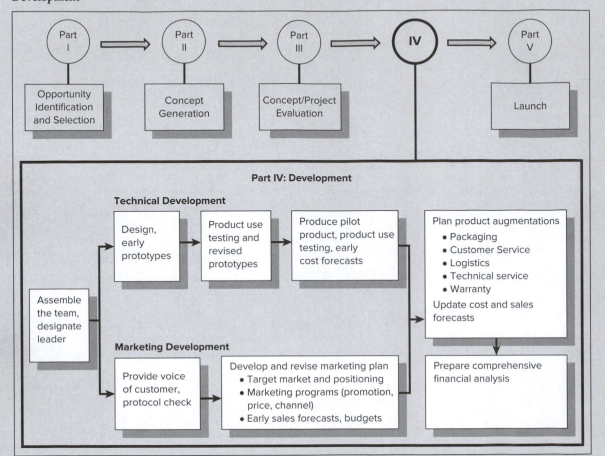

Development

Somewhere during the preceding process of creation and early evaluation, a decision was made to develop the concept being considered. The decision may have come quickly (a key customer wanted the item and was ready to help develop it) or slowly, after concept testing and extensive review of capital and operational expenditures required. A product protocol was written, and an early financial plan released funds for the development.

The question now is fulfillment of that protocol. There may be extensive technical search (for example, for a new pharmaceutical) or none (for a new service). The key problem may be in industrial design or in the very technical characteristics of the newest computer chip. Fulfillment may consist of nothing more than confirming a recipe that was used to produce new cookies for the concept testing. In cases such as the development of a new blade by Gillette, years of technical development may be necessary.

This is a point of high creativity, and there is usually a strong art form, even when dealing in scientific areas. Progress in the development phase has the attention of managers in all functions, not just the R&D people. Once the product protocol is written, the rest of the team does not sit back and wait for the engineers to produce a finished prototype. It is better to think of development as a phase that includes the creation of everything needed to *market* the product, including funding, distribution, promotion, and technical service. Look at Figure IV.1. The technical work (including design, engineering, and manufacturing) is displayed along the top of the figure; marketing and testing (among others, such as legal) are displayed along the bottom. Both continue through the launch.

Several things about that figure may surprise you.

- First, note that what we commonly think is the technical creation task is just one part of the technical (top) stream. That one part might, in turn, be broken down into thousands of steps. Many firms use a project control system called a Program Evaluation Review Technique (PERT) chart, or network diagram, originally developed for the first nuclear submarine, the *Polaris*, in the late 1950s. A network diagram uses boxes ("nodes") and connecting lines to indicate the flows of tasks in a project and how they all interrelate. In the automobile industry, a network diagram for just one assembly (e.g., the dashboard) is so complicated that it cannot even be printed out on paper.

- Note, too, the box at the far left of the figure. Getting ready to do technical development sometimes takes months—finding the people, acquiring the rights to certain materials, creating a particular culture, training the team, and, so important today, creating the information system to support the complex of activities.

- Typically there is not just one prototype. Sometimes there will be dozens or even hundreds, depending on how lucky the team is. Granted, a new Frisbee with an edge shaped to be easily grabbed by a dog in its teeth may be real progress for competitors in that sport, but hardly an afternoon's work for the designer. Edison was said to have tried hundreds of materials for the filament in the first electric light bulb before settling on the right one.

- Developers must stop frequently to have their work checked—note terms like *evaluation, check, screen, test,* and *clearance.* Generally this is good, because to advance a design with a flaw is wasteful, yet to stop at every possible turn grinds things to a halt, including morale.

- The technical side is a *rolling evolution.* Even when an early prototype looks good, it must evolve into a tested prototype, then into a process, then into a pilot product, then into a production scale-up product, then into a marketed product. This follows the same route as the life cycle of a concept that was diagrammed and explained in Chapter 2 on process. We don't really *develop* a thing so much as we *evolve* one. There are fewer "eureka moments" than people think. It's hard work, step by step.

- Note, too, how items along the top stream associate with items along the bottom. Thus, producing a prototype may start design on a package; producing a scale-up product stimulates start on a technical customer service activity; producing a marketable product means a distribution network must be in place.

But rather than try to discuss both streams simultaneously, we cover marketing's role in the technical work here in Part IV and marketing's role in the other stream in Part V. Actually, we have been working on the marketing stream from Chapter 3 on—for example, target market is usually known at PIC time and new product positioning statements are used in concept testing.

Thus Chapter 11 talks about the players involved, the essence of design, and productivity in the development process. Chapter 12 covers the creation and management of today's cross-functional teams, and Chapter 13 tells how the team finds whether the latest prototype is indeed, ready to launch—a subject we will take up in Part V of the book.

Before we get too far, let's be sure we know just what marketing's role is in the work that takes place on the technical side. There are nine important dimensions.

1. To make absolutely clear to everyone what the protocol calls for. What is the end point? How can technical groups know when they are finished?

2. To make sure that this protocol task is technically feasible and doable within the time and dollars imposed by the development budget. That is, do all technical people agree?

3. To provide an open window for industrial and systems designers to all influential forces in the marketplace. Marketing should not be a gatekeeper, but rather an enthusiastic tour guide. It is truly in their best interests, and in the firm's as well, that all development effort (technical and marketing) be based on market knowledge.

4. To provide a continuous interim of opportunity to pretest various versions of the new product. This means to cooperate in early in-house testing and in later customer use testing.

5. To be available to technical people at all reasonable times. Some marketing people seem to forget that technical work is going on. A common joke in the labs is the scientist who left for lunch with the request to an aide: "If my product manager calls, get their name."

6. To stay informed about technical progress via team meetings, lab visits, social contacts, and so forth. This is not spying. It is seeking an opportunity to pass along some market information technical people didn't know about. Well-led teams today soften this problem, but marketers have to learn how to be good team members.

7. To involve technical people in the decision making on the marketing side of the development stream—especially any changes in the givens at the start of development, target market for example. Again, teams help, but just as marketers can get distracted, so can technical people. We have to show them why we need their input on matters they may not feel are as important as the technical ones they are busy on.

8. To stay continuously alert to the project's progress and to be creative in finding ways to help. For example, in Chapter 12 you will see the benefits of cross-functional teams, one of which is to speed up a new product's development. Saving a day in marketing may be as good as saving a day in technical.

9. To flag the various ways that work in nonmarketing departments impacts marketing plans directly. This action, often called *internal marketing,* involves technical departments (for example, technical information for sales support), manufacturing (for example, cost reductions and standby production capability), packaging (for example, promotion claims made on front panel), and human resources (for example, selection of new personnel needed in the launch effort).

It is the purpose of the material in Part IV to help you perform those roles, but be aware—the technical side of the development stream is immensely more complicated than most outsiders realize. Don't take the roles lightly.

CHAPTER ELEVEN

Design

Setting

Part IV of this book explores all aspects of the development phase, which includes product design, product architecture and prototype development, and product use testing, as well as organizational and team management issues. Here in Chapter 11, we examine just what this development phase means to different companies, and we introduce design and its use as a strategic resource. We also examine the role of the product designer and the interface between design and other functions involved in the new products process.

As consumers, we have all been frustrated by poorly designed products and wonder how they ever got to market:

- Too-bulky or underpowered vacuum cleaners.
- Cereal boxes with protective packaging that rips when first opened and thus no longer protects.
- Oddly shaped spatulas that are useless for flipping pancakes.
- A coffee vending machine that does not indicate that you have to provide the cup: you learn this the first time you get hot coffee spilled on your pants.

Yet we recognize and appreciate outstanding designs—a new car, revolutionary office furniture, or even a universal screwdriver that really works—and reward the product manufacturers. The design and appearance of Apple's smart watch certainly adds to its appeal; likewise James Dyson's vacuum cleaner. In a day and age of "don't sweat the small things," it may be those very small things that determine brand preferences and that the manufacturers should focus on![1]

---

[1]Laurence P. Feldman, "But Have You Tried the Product?" *Visions*, October 1999. The examples are from this article, as well as Laurence P. Feldman, "Is Your Product 'Utility Challenged'?" *Visions*, April 2000, and from the Bad Designs Web site, www.baddesigns.com. This site features dozens of poorly or oddly designed products and includes ideas on how the design could have been easily improved.

What Is Design?

One writer defines design as "the synthesis of technology and human needs into manufacturable products."[2] In practice, however, *design* as a term has many uses. To the car companies, it can mean the styling department. To a container company it means their customer's packaging people. To a manufacturing department it most likely means the engineers who set final product specifications. Excellence in design also benefits the bottom line. Firms that are judged to be higher in design effectiveness outperform other firms in return on sales and assets, net incomes, and cash flow, as well as higher stock market returns.[3] Consider, for example, the role of design at Apple. Over the years, Apple has received much praise for the sleek, modernistic designs of its many devices. The clean, simple lines of these products can be directly traced to the 1960s-era record players and radios designed by famed German designer Dieter Rams. In fact, Apple, Samsung, and other leading firms clearly practice Mr. Rams's principles of good design, shown in Figure 11.1. In any case, design should not be considered an afterthought where industrial designers are asked to pretty-up

FIGURE 11.1 Dieter Rams's Principles for Good Product Design

Good design is:

... *innovative.* Design is not an end in itself, but innovative design is linked to innovations in technology.

... *aesthetic.* Products affect our well-being; a well-executed design can result in a beautiful product.

... *unobtrusive.* The design should be neutral and not take away from the purpose of the product.

... *long-lasting.* Even in a fashion-oriented, throwaway society, good design does not become antiquated.

... *environmentally friendly.* Good design considers resource use and total effect on the environment.

... *useful.* This includes usefulness from a psychological and aesthetic viewpoint, not just functional.

... *understandable.* Good design clarifies the product and can even make the product self-explanatory.

... *honest.* Design does not manipulate customers, nor make the product more innovative than it really is.

... *thorough down to the last detail.* Good design is careful, accurate, and respectful of the customer.

... *as little design as possible.* Less is more; concentrate on essentials and avoid the non-essentials.

Source: Adapted from Anonymous, "Ten Principles for Good Design," Design Principles FTW, July 8, 2013; retrieved from www.designprinciplesftw.com/collections/ten-principles-for-good-design.

[2]See Michael Evamy, "Call Yourself a Designer?" *Design*, March 1994, pp. 14–16. This article was part of a series in this publication, all on the matter of design definition. Useful also is Karl T. Ulrich and Steven D. Eppinger, *Product Design and Development* (New York: McGraw-Hill, 1995).

[3]Julie H. Hertenstein, Marjorie B. Platt, and Robert W. Veryzer, "The Impact of Industrial Design Effectiveness on Corporate Financial Performance," *Journal of Product Innovation Management*, 22(1), January 2005, pp. 3–21.

a product that is almost ready to be manufactured. This narrow view of design causes managers to miss the potential that design has to occasionally innovate within the organization.

Design-Driven Innovation[4]

Some writers have suggested that the traditional, dual-drive product innovation strategy (technology-driven or market-driven) neglects the potentially powerful role of design. In both technology-driven and market-driven innovation, design plays a secondary role. Technology-driven innovation starts with the technology; the role of design is to modify the product so that it can accommodate the performance characteristics. Market-driven innovation starts with the customer; here, design modifies the product so that it meets customer expectations. Design academic Roberto Verganti suggests considering a third way: **design-driven innovation**, in which it is design itself that takes on the leadership role. In his words,

> Design introduces a bold new way of competing. Design-driven innovations do not come from the market; they create new markets. They don't push new technologies; they push new meanings. Customers had not asked for these new meanings, but once they had experienced them, it was love at first sight.[5]

Verganti offers a designer teapot, designed by architect Michael Graves and sold by Italian manufacturer Alessi, as an example of design-driven innovation. Most teapots are utilitarian: they boil water, quite effectively, for maybe five minutes a day, and take up space in the kitchen for the rest of the time. The Graves design was felt to be "delightful," to the extent that it actually made the breakfast experience more pleasurable. It was attractive, its cone-shaped design with the wide bottom does not rock unsteadily on the stovetop, the handle with the grip set far back eliminates burning one's hands when pouring hot water, and a little bird on the spout whistles when the water is ready. Rather than taking up space, the teapot becomes part of the décor and is something most people would be proud to own and show off. The fact that virtually the same product was mass-produced and sold at a much lower price point through Target stores suggests the universal appeal of this high-design product. In fact, this example clearly shows that product functionality is just as important to excellent design as product appearance or aesthetics. As noted by Ken Munsch, New Product Business Development director at Herman Miller, "Sharper Image specialized in sleek, modern style and filed for bankruptcy. Beautiful is not enough. The product must be useful. Design includes the whole human interface."[6]

---

[4]This section is adapted from C. Anthony Di Benedetto, "Product Design: Research Trends and an Agenda for the Future," *Journal of Global Fashion Marketing*, 3(3), 2012, pp. 99–107.

[5]Roberto Verganti, "Radical Design and Technology Epiphanies: A New Focus for Research on Design Management," *Journal of Product Innovation Management*, 28(3), 2011, pp. 384–388.

[6]Quoted in Brad Barbera, "Steve Jobs: A Product Developer's Perspective," *Visions*, 36(1), 2012, pp. 10–15.

The Role of Design in the New Products Process[7]

Design's potential role in the new products process is sometimes underestimated. This may be because of a lack of understanding or appreciation of designers, design management, and the design function on the part of managers from other functional areas. Designers undergo rigorous training to learn how to design products that function well mechanically, that are durable, that are easy and safe to use, that can be made from easily available materials, and that look appealing. Clearly, many of these requirements will be in conflict, and it is up to the skillful designer to achieve all of them simultaneously.

Contributions of Design to New Product Goals

As proof of the importance of design, consider several ways in which design excellence can help firms achieve a broad spectrum of new product goals, as shown in Figure 11.2.

Design for Speed to Market

Ingersoll-Rand developed its Cyclone Grinder (an air-grinder power tool) in record time, thanks to an efficient cross-functional team and excellence in design. The team (composed of marketing, manufacturing, and engineering personnel) worked closely with

FIGURE 11.2
Contributions of Design to the New Products Process

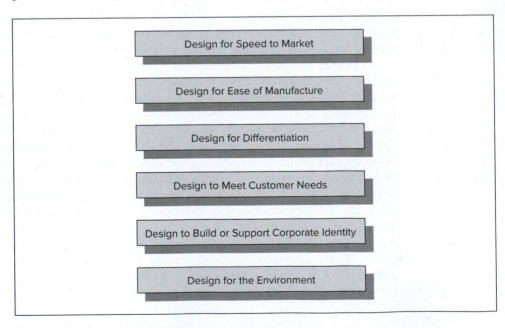

- Design for Speed to Market
- Design for Ease of Manufacture
- Design for Differentiation
- Design to Meet Customer Needs
- Design to Build or Support Corporate Identity
- Design for the Environment

[7]Much of this section is drawn from Jeneanne Marshall, "Design as a Strategic Resource: A Business Perspective," Design Leadership Program, Corporate Design Foundation, 1991; and Eric M. Olson, Rachel Cooper, and Stanley F. Slater, "Design Strategy and Competitive Advantage," *Business Horizons*, 41(2), March–April 1998, pp. 55–61. For a good view of "hot topics" among design practitioners, read the periodic newsletter *@Issue*. Current and back issues are available online on the Web site for the Corporate Design Foundation, www.cdf.org.

Group Four Design to identify customer needs. Users of traditional grinders often complained that they were difficult to hold, and that their hands would freeze (the unit became cold during use). The new grinder was ergonomically shaped (better shaped for the human body meaning, in this case, easier to hold), lighter, and made of a new composite material that was both more durable and more comfortable to hold (since it conducted less thermal energy and thus did not get cold). Furthermore, the one-piece housing design was a cost improvement over the previous version, which required assembly of seven different components.

Design for Ease of Manufacture

A classic example here concerns IBM's development of its Proprinter dot-matrix printer in the mid-1980s. At the time, the Japanese owned the worldwide market for low-end printers. It was felt, however, that the competition was vulnerable: Their printers were not well designed, and in particular had hundreds of parts including dozens of rivets and fasteners. IBM set a performance target of 200 near-letter-quality characters per second (not the current standard, but the expected standard four years into the future) and had a motto of "no fasteners": Everything had to snap together easily. Furthermore, the development time had to be compressed from the standard four years to two-and-a-half years. All of the above was achieved: The original Proprinter had only 61 parts and could be assembled in three minutes. Similarly, Swatch watches are designed for ease of manufacture, having about a third of the moving parts of a traditional Swiss watch, a plastic casing without a removable back, a plastic strap incorporated into the casing, and many other design features. Swatch watches retail at a small fraction of the price of traditional Swiss watches.

Design for Differentiation

Haworth Inc., the office furniture designer, employs an Ideation Group, responsible for exploring and assessing customer acceptance of speculative products (high-risk products without a clear-cut market). Haworth believes that "nonstandard" product development is needed for speculative products. Few of the prototypes developed by Ideation may make it to the marketplace, and those that do (like the Crossings furniture line) may end up looking quite different. Good ideas from the Ideation Group can make their way into existing lines or other future products, and more importantly, Haworth has successfully differentiated its product offerings as being more original in design. Incidentally, excellence in design seems to be important in the office furniture industry: Steelcase Inc. is a majority owner of IDEO, the design firm we have met more than once in earlier chapters.[8]

Design to Meet Customer Needs

Deep understanding of customer needs is required in order for the firm to translate a high-potential technology into a product that provides meaningful benefits to the customer. Collaboration with end users (seen in Chapter 4) and capturing the voice of

---

[8]Janis R. Evink and Henry H. Beam, "Just What Is an Ideation Group?" *Business Horizons*, January–February 1999, pp. 7–77; and Bruce Nussbaum, "The Power of Design," businessweek.com, May 17, 2004.

the customer (Chapter 10) are important ways to get this depth of understanding, now sometimes referred to as **user-oriented design**.[9]

The voice of the customer was heavily used in the design of the Ford Super Duty diesel-engine truck. The typical customer drove extensively and experienced several typical problems. The ride was often bumpy and uncomfortable, especially in long-distance driving, and diesel engines are loud, which is an annoyance for long drives and also causes difficulties at fast-food drive-throughs. The solution was to totally redesign the diesel engine so that it operated much smoother and quieter, without compromising power and durability. Ford built and tested prototypes of the new truck in realistic conditions to ensure they had addressed the needs expressed by customers. The Super Duty delivered a much quieter ride with less cabin vibration, leading to less driver fatigue, and without sacrificing toughness.[10]

Crown Equipment Corporation, a manufacturer of forklift trucks, developed its RC (Rider Counterbalance) lift truck and launched it in 2008. An age-old problem expressed by forklift truck drivers is their inability to see clearly in front, especially if they have pallets raised on the forks. In some cases, a second person would be required to guide the driver, whose sight line was obstructed by the load carried at the front of the truck. Using an ingenious counterbalance system, the RC's forks are located to the side so as to remove the driver's obstruction. Additionally, the RC had extra design elements that addressed other common user complaints and appealed to the driver: a much larger than average operator compartment, a desk-top area allowing the driver to keep papers and tools nearby, a newly designed shock absorption system that smoothed the ride, and a stylish and ergonomic appearance. The RC significantly grew Crown Equipment's market share and also won several design awards.[11]

Universal design is the term sometimes used to mean the design of products to be usable by anyone regardless of age or ability. Principles of universal design can be used to develop products for new markets based on unmet customer needs. The designer considers the abilities of real people in real-world settings when applying universal design principles. For example, some people are visually impaired, while others have temporary vision problems due to eye fatigue, recovery from surgery, or even poor lighting. Phones with extra-large buttons address permanent or temporary vision problems and can be used by anyone. Closed-captioned television, automatic garage-door openers, and automatically opening doors to grocery stores also exemplify universal design. Figure 11.3 illustrates the principles of universal design.

Design to Build or Support Corporate Identity

Many firms have established *visual equity* across the products they sell: a recognizable look or feel that they use consistently. Product design can thus help build or support

---

[9]Robert W. Veryzer and Brigitte Borja de Mozota, "The Impact of User-Oriented Design on New Product Development: An Examination of Fundamental Relationships," *Journal of Product Innovation Management*, 22(2), March 2005, pp. 128–143.

[10]The story of the Super Duty design process is shown in a video at: www.youtube.com/watch?v=uJB3nkDKFrU

[11]Bruce Nussbaum, "The Best Global Design of 2008," *Business Week*, July 17, 2008; also see the firm's Web page, www.crown.com.

FIGURE 11.3 Principles of Universal Design

Principle	Examples
Equitable Use: The design is useful to people with varied abilities.	Public phones with adjustable volume levels Powered doors to grocery stores are convenient to disabled shoppers and also people pushing carts, strollers, etc.
Flexibility in Use: The design accommodates a variety of preferences and abilities.	Phones with large buttons Scissors or knives that work left- or right-handed
Simple and Intuitive to Use: The design is easy for anyone to understand and use.	Color-coded labels on cough medicine Ikea furniture building instructions use illustrations and minimal text to avoid language barriers Newer set-top cable boxes are easier and more intuitive to program with on-screen commands
Perceptible Information: The design communicates the required information effectively to the user.	Plugs and jacks connecting devices to televisions are intuitive and simple to use Honeywell thermostats show numerical settings and also use audible click-stops when the dial is turned
Tolerance for Error: The design minimizes adverse consequences of inappropriate use.	Irons or coffeemakers that shut off if not used for five minutes Lawnmower handle that requires the user to squeeze a lever against the handle to keep the lawnmower running
Low Physical Effort: The design can be used efficiently by anyone with minimal fatigue.	Rollers and handles on luggage Angled computer keyboard easier for operator to use
Size and Space for Approach and Use: Regardless of the user's size or mobility, the product is easy to reach, manipulate, and use.	Whirlpool side-by-side refrigerator-freezers with full-length handles Copco chopping knife's handle is designed to be comfortably held in hands of any size Wide car door opening makes it easier for someone with a walker or wheelchair to get in or out

Source: From James L. Mueller and Molly Follette Story, "Universal Design: Principles for Driving Growth into New Markets," in P. Belliveau, A. Griffin, and S. Sodermeyer (Eds.), *The PDMA Toolbook for New Product Development*, John Wiley & Sons, Inc., 2002, pp. 297–326.

public perception of the firm and, ultimately, its corporate identity. Apple computers and other devices have always been designed to look user-friendly. Rolex watches all have a classic, high-prestige appearance, and Braun appliances have lines and colors that convey simplicity and quality.[12] Radically designed new BMW models, such as the latest version of the Z-class Roadster, still share familiar design attributes with classic BMWs of years ago, such as the distinctive grille.[13]

[12]Karl T. Ulrich and Steven D. Eppinger, *Product Design and Development*, 2nd ed. (Burr Ridge, IL: Irwin/McGraw-Hill, 2000), p. 219.

[13]Anonymous, "Online Extra: A Chat with Nokia's Alastair Curtis," businessweek.com, July 17, 2006.

FIGURE 11.4
Range of
Leading Design
Applications

Purpose of Design	Item Being Designed
Aesthetics	Goods
Ergonomics	Services
Function	Architecture
Manufacturability	Graphic arts
Servicing	Offices
Disassembly	Packages

Note: Design covers many areas of human activity, including new products. The new products field contributes to two classes of items (goods and services in this figure) and to all six classes of purpose listed above. One could argue that even the other four classes of items are really products to the organizations producing them.

Design for the Environment

Design for disassembly is the technique by which products can be taken apart after use for separate recycling of metal, glass, and plastic parts. Among other carmakers, BMW has designed disassembly and recycling into its cars. Used plastic parts are sorted, recycled, and made into new parts. Other components are either recycled or rebuilt, while unusable parts are incinerated to create energy.[14]

In fact, *green design* is now a driving force within many firms. The carmaker Subaru provides an example. Thomas Easterday, senior vice president, Subaru of Indiana, says that Subaru has "embraced the concepts of reduce, reuse, and recycle." He claims that Subaru has achieved zero landfill status and has attained a recycling rate of 99.8 percent (the remainder is hazardous waste that must be incinerated due to EPA regulations). Subaru works with suppliers so that they use recyclable packaging and with local companies responsible for collecting and recycling materials; the carmaker also finds markets for recycled materials. More recycling leads to less waste, and cost savings, at Subaru.[15] Apple also makes several green claims for the iPad on its Web site, noting that the display is mercury-free, there is no PVC plastic used, and the aluminum-and-glass enclosure is recyclable.[16]

Figure 11.4 shows a variety of design dimensions, using only the two criteria of Purpose of Design and Item Being Designed. Design is not just a field in which artists draw pictures of new microwaves. It blends form and function, quality and style, art and engineering. In short, a good design is aesthetically pleasing, easy to make correctly, reliable, easy to use, economical to operate and service, and in line with recycling standards. **Ergonomics** are also an important consideration; this can be defined as studying human characteristics in order to develop appropriate designs.[17] Many of the poorly designed products mentioned at the start of this chapter might have been

[14]Jacquelyn A. Ottman, *Green Marketing: Challenges and Opportunities for the New Marketing Age* (Lincolnwood, IL: NTC Business Books, 1993), p. 119.

[15]Mary G. Wojtas, "32nd PDMA International Conference Delivers Expert Insights, Knowledge, and Tools to Enhance Innovation Success," *Visions*, Vol. 32, No. 4, December 2008, pp. 22–25.

[16]The specifications are at www.apple.com/ipad/specs.

[17]Karl H. E. Kroemer, "Ergonomics: Definition of Ergonomics," National Safety Council Web site, www.nsc.org

improved with better attention to ergonomics. An excellent design can play a big role in determining how well a new product will meet the needs of customers, as well as retailers and other stakeholders, and therefore is an important determinant of success.

The role of the design in a product's ultimate acceptance by customers is easily understood. Consider a new car design. If the new style is not that different from existing cars, customers might find it uninteresting or overly conservative. On the other hand, if the new design looks as if it came from Mars, most customers are likely to find it too revolutionary or even ugly. Given that as much as $2 billion may be invested in a new car design, it seems reasonable for the car companies to spend as much as $1 million on getting just the right balance of style and shape. Focus groups may be used to get initial reactions, then full-size models (or car shapes on a computer screen) may be shown to hundreds of potential buyers. Despite careful research, however, misleading results may be obtained: Customers often don't really know what they want as far as style is concerned.[18]

Product Architecture[19]

Product architecture has been described as the process by which a customer need is developed into a product design. This is a critical step in moving toward a product design, as solid architecture improves ultimate product performance, reduces the cost of changing the product once it is in production, and can speed the product to market.

To understand architecture development, consider that a product contains *components* (a big-screen TV has speakers, an LCD or LED display, HDMI or cable ports, a power cord, and so on) that can be combined into *chunks* (the input, video system, the audio system, and the power source). A product is also composed of *functional elements* (for a big-screen TV, these might include producing realistic video and audio, adjusting picture and sound quality, obtaining content from cable or other sources, and so on). The product's architecture is how the functional elements are assigned to the chunks and how the chunks are interrelated.

A Process for Product Architecture

A stepwise process for product architecture development can be applied to make sure the product's design will be in keeping with customer needs and, ultimately, the product innovation charter.[20] The process is illustrated in simplified form in Figure 11.5. Careless product architecture results in poorly designed products that are difficult to use, not ergonomic, or not aesthetically pleasing. Although each component may work perfectly

---

[18]Tom Moulson and George Sproles, "Styling Strategy," *Business Horizons*, September–October 2000, pp. 45–52.

[19]Much of this section derives from David Cutherell, "Product Architecture," in M. D. Rosenau, A. Griffin, G. Castellion, and N. Anscheutz (eds.), *The PDMA Handbook of New Product Development* (New York: John Wiley, 1996), pp. 217–235.

[20]The stepwise process described here is based on that of Karl T. Ulrich and Steven D. Eppinger, *Product Design and Development,* 2nd ed. (Homewood, IL: Irwin/McGraw-Hill, 2000), Chapter 9.

FIGURE 11.5
Product
Architecture
Illustration

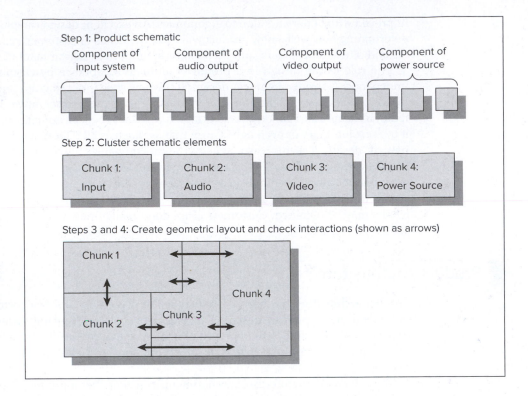

well, the way the pieces are put together makes little sense from the user's perspective, and minor rearrangement would have resulted in an intuitive, easier-to-use product.

1. *Create the Product Schematic.* The schematic shows the components and functional elements of the product and how they are interconnected. Several alternative schematics may be developed and explored at this point. For the big-screen TV, for example, a port for external speakers may be made available; a small portable version may be designed with miniature speakers; manual controls on the side of the TV could be eliminated altogether, requiring the user to adjust channel and volume by remote control only. The schematic would contain components connected with input (from cable, satellite, or some other source), video output, audio output, and power supply, among other things.

2. *Cluster the Schematic Elements.* Here, the chunks (or modules) are defined. In the figure, input, video output, audio output, and power chunks are identified. Interaction among the chunks should be simple so changes can be made easily, and one should take advantage of manufacturing capabilities wherever possible. If rapid changes are expected in some part of the product, that part should most certainly be made into a chunk. For example, if an extra-large, curved screen for use in large auditoriums is developed, one should be able to replace the current screen (video output chunk) with this new one, with minimum disruption to other chunks.

3. *Create Geometric Layout.* Here, using simulations, computer-aided design, or other techniques, the product is arranged in several configurations to determine

the "best" solutions. For example, where should the speakers be located? What about the ports? How many cable or HDMI ports should be included, and where should they be? One possible geometric layout is shown in Figure 11.5.

4. *Check Interactions between Chunks.* Understand what happens at the interfaces between chunks. In the big-screen TV, video content flows as a digital signal from the cable or other external source to the screen. If the standard screen is replaced with an extra-large curved screen, the interaction between the screen and the rest of the system may need to be adapted, but there will likely be little or no impact on other interactions.

Product Architecture and Product Platforms

Clearly, careful product architecture development is critical to a firm seeking to establish a product platform. As noted in Chapter 3, car manufacturers (with few exceptions) think in terms of designing platforms, not individual products. A successful platform can result in an initially successful car, and also lead to several other models in the future (for example, the New Beetle is built on an existing Volkswagen Golf platform).

If the architecture permits the designers to replace chunks or modules easily, several new products can be designed as technology improves, market tastes change, and manufacturing skill increases. This is how Black and Decker was able to develop those dozens of different hand-held tools on just a couple of basic motor platforms!

In the Volkswagen example, the New Beetle is referred to as a *derivative product*. This term refers to products based on the same platform as an existing product, but modified incrementally in terms of technology or customer need fulfillment (in this case, a classic Beetle-like appearance). Depending on how many features are added, the derivative product may cost about the same to manufacture (such as new designs of Swatch watches), or may cost more but offer greater value to the user. Features may also be stripped out to achieve a lower-cost derivative product. Additional cost savings can be incurred by using standardized components across many products. Whatever the case, the key is to be able to make changes to the modules while still operating on the same platform.

Assessment Factors for Industrial Design

There are several factors that can be considered by industrial designers when deciding on the appropriateness of a design. These may include quality of user interface, emotional appeal, maintenance and repair, appropriate use of resources, and product differentiation. Figure 11.6 provides an illustration of how each of these might be applied in car design. User interface refers here to ergonomics—how comfortable the driver and passengers are when traveling. Emotional appeal could include the sound of the exhaust when the car is revved up or the extremely quiet ride inside a luxury sedan. Maintenance and repair might be assessed in terms of how easy it is to do electrical or mechanical repairs or for the owner to check fuel levels him/herself. Appropriate use of resources could refer to fuel efficiency or the ability to recycle car parts after use. Finally, the appealing, distinctive aesthetic design of the car would be a differentiating factor.[21]

[21]This set of assessment questions comes from Karl T. Ulrich and Steven D. Eppinger, *Product Design and Development*, 2nd ed. (Homewood, IL: Irwin/McGraw-Hill, 2000), pp. 227–230.

FIGURE 11.6
Assessment
Factors for
Industrial
Design:
Questions in
Designing
a Car

Quality of the user interface

Will the user understand the product and its intended use? Is it safe for use? In a car dashboard design, for example, is it clear that the knobs and switches for lights, wipers, and horn are easy to locate and operate?

Emotional appeal

Is it an attractive, exciting design? Would the prospective owner be proud to own the product? Does the car make a satisfying "growl" when revved up?

Maintenance and repair

Is the procedure for maintenance obvious and easy? Can all the fluids be easily changed, and is it easy to tell which fluid goes where?

Appropriate use of resources

Does the product include unnecessary features, or does it lack key features? Were the best materials chosen, with regard to cost and quality? Were environmental and ecological factors considered when choosing, for example, types of body paint for the car?

Product differentiation

Does the design distinguish the product? Is it memorable? Does it fit with corporate identity? When prospective luxury car owners take a look in the showroom, will they say this new model really stands out?

Source: From Karl T. Ulrich and Steven D. Eppinger, *Product Design and Development*, 2nd ed., McGraw-Hill, 2000, pp. 227–230.

Industrial designers must also consider trade-offs among these factors. Bright colors on a smart watch may add to its emotional appeal but diminish perceived quality. Furthermore, many of these more aesthetic factors differ among individuals, making the designer's job more difficult.[22]

Prototype Development[23]

For most people, the word **prototype** conjures up the image of a fully functioning, full-size product essentially ready to be examined by potential customers. Industrial designers define the term more broadly. A **comprehensive prototype** would be one of these essentially complete prototypes. They also make use of what are called **focused prototypes**, which examine a limited number of performance attributes or features.

[22]Mariëlle E. H. Creusen and Jan P. L. Schoormans, "The Different Roles of Product Appearance in Consumer Choice," *Journal of Product Innovation Management,* 22(1), January 2005, pp. 63–81.

[23]Much of this section derives from Ulrich and Eppinger, op. cit., Chapter 12.

A bicycle or car manufacturer may build focused prototypes (a nonfunctioning bicycle out of foam or wood, or a wooden "frame" that very roughly simulates the layout of the seat, steering wheel, and dashboard of a new car interior) to determine customers' reactions to the product's form. The bike manufacturer may go on and develop a crude working prototype to experiment with and determine how the product might work. Recall the development of the pill box from Chapter 6. In that case, a couple of crude working pill box prototypes were 3D printed and tested with focus groups before arriving at a final prototype that customers liked.

Which type, or types, of prototypes should be built? The answer is, of course, it depends: Primarily, it depends on the intended use of the prototype. Focused prototypes are used in probe-and-learn ("lickety-stick") product development in the development of new-to-the-world products. Focused prototypes are also used in cases where the product is not so new to the world to learn about how the product works and how well it will satisfy customer needs. BMW designers, for example, built clay models of new car designs for the 3 Series and sent them to southern France to see what they would look like in the sunlight at a distance, and to determine if there were line or form defects. It is much cheaper to make required changes now, rather than later in the development process.[24]

A more comprehensive physical prototype is necessary to determine how well all the components fit together—as an additional benefit, the various members of the new product team are essentially required to cooperate to build the comprehensive prototype. Finally, more advanced prototypes can be used as milestones—the performance of the prototype can be tracked periodically to see if it has advanced to desired levels.

Once a comprehensive prototype exists, of course, it can be taken to potential users to be tested in a real usage situation, and improved and refined. This is known as product-use testing and will be taken up in Chapter 13.

Managing the Interfaces in the Design Process

New product managers have to keep in mind that product design should not be just the responsibility of the designers! Historically, in the era of powerful functional chimneys and slow, linear, stage-based development, industrial designers dominated the action in most firms making tangible products. Today, they have to share this traditional role with several other functions. Ironically, by joining the team and seeming to lose power, design stands on the verge of winning its ultimate position of influence. But it is the new product manager's task to bring this about.

There are several participants in the product design task, some in a more direct role than others, as shown in Figure 11.7. One model of how these people participate is shown in this figure. The representation there is somewhat linear, but with substantial overlapping or parallel effort.

It is easy to see how this model of operations gives people problems, particularly the designers. *Industrial designers,* trained to develop aesthetics (styling), structural

[24]C. Bangle, "The Ultimate Creativity Machine: How BMW Turns Art into Profit," *Harvard Business Review,* 2001, pp. 47–55.

FIGURE 11.7
Model of the
Product Design
Process

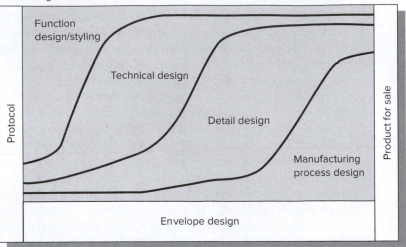

Development time scale

The members of a core team all participate in all four stages, but leadership in the first stage is often given to industrial designers, the middle two to engineering design, and the last to process design or manufacturing design. Terms in use vary widely. In chemical and pharmaceutical industries the design and engineering functions are replaced by research and development. And in some firms the term *product engineering* replaces engineering design; they want to contrast product engineer and process engineer.

For services, the same steps apply, but instead of a "thing" we are developing a service sequence and technical capability. Think of an investment service developed in a financial institution, or a cable TV system, or office design service.

Simultaneous with development (on goods *and* services) is the development of the augmented aspects of the product—pre- and postsale service, warranty, image, and so on. This activity, most often led by marketing people, is called *envelope design*, running across the bottom of the figure.

Participants in the Design Process

Direct Participants	**Supportive Participants**
Research & Development	Design Consultants
Industrial Designers and Stylists	Marketing Personnel
Engineering Designers/Product	Resellers
Designers	Vendors/Suppliers
Manufacturing Engineers and	Governments
System Designers	Customers
Manufacturing Operations	Company Attorneys
	Technical Service

integrity, and function (how the product works), directly overlap with the *design engineers,* who are technical people who convert styling into product dimensions or specifications. Technical people are not devoid of ideas on styling, and stylists are not devoid of thoughts on how the mechanics can work. This is especially true on common products (like shoes or dinnerware) where all parties have experience.

The other dimension of complexity is added by some of the supportive participants in the preceding list. Suppliers usually know their materials better than their customers do. That's why Black & Decker picked its supplier for the Snake Lite before its design was finished. Large firms like Philips have the funds to establish large central styling centers where styling skills exceed those of the typical plant stylist. Customers almost always have overriding ideas to contribute. Consequently, the styling function is a synthesis of many views beyond those of the direct participants. If we add all of the other company people listed as supportive, we get back to the list of functions usually represented on the teams discussed in Chapter 12.

The result of all this can be chaos, and in general the problems are thought to be at the heart of why some countries' producers are so often beaten by new products from Japan and Germany. In Japan, for example, product design means more than how a product looks and feels to the user; it often means engineering applications. To one observer, design in Japan "means the total-enterprise process of determining customer needs and converting them to concepts, detailed designs, process plans, factory design, and delivered products, together with their supporting services."[25] This merges a holistic view of end-user needs and a holistic structure to meet those needs. Design is seen as a vertical means of fulfillment, and individual skills are not central.

In the United States and Europe, participants end up playing musical chairs from one project to the next as roles change. Though the industrial designer is increasingly viewed as a full-fledged member of the new product team from the earliest phases, some design purists and traditionalists resist this movement. Design and marketing operate in drastically different cultures, and cultural gaps are hard to erase.[26]

In some cases, designers are taking on an expanded role as a liaison from end user to top management. Greater integration with end users can lead to better information about what design changes are desired. Designers can also serve as a conduit of information from industry, for example, making recommendations to the product development team on new materials to use.[27]

Improving the Interfaces in the Design Process

Most of the problems surrounding design have to do with concurrency, or overlapping the steps in development. It is clear from the discussion of Chapter 10 that up-front product definition (product protocol and firm prototype) is important. Several techniques are currently being used to make sure that design is integrated correctly with

[25]Daniel E. Whitney, "Integrated Design and Manufacturing in Japan," *Prism,* Second Quarter, 1993, pp. 75–95.

[26]Matthew K. Haggerty and Brian L. Vogel, *Innovation,* Winter 1992, pp. 8–13.

[27]See Michael Evamy, op. cit.; and Jeneanne Marshall Rae, "Setting the Tone for Design Excellence," *Innovation,* Fall 1994, pp. 7–9.

other functions during the development phase and that the products being designed can be manufactured in a cost-efficient way.

Important among these is **colocation** (putting the various individuals or functional areas in close proximity). The development phase can be a communications snake pit. When the different groups are not in regular contact and cooperating, there is a tendency for information to be lost (or hidden). This causes wasted work and slows the whole operation down. Further, the problems intensify in large firms with their research centers hundreds of miles from the offices of marketers and the production lines of manufacturing people. Many firms have tried colocation to shorten communication lines and increase team cohesion. Many firms such as Motorola, Ford, Honda, AT&T, and John Deere have used colocation successfully.[28]

Colocation helps integrate departments and improve information flow, and also allows the team members to identify and resolve product development problems quicker. It must, however, be carefully planned and handled. It is probably not a good idea to break up a center of technological excellence in order to colocate its members. Too-distant colocation (i.e., employees have to get in their cars and drive to another building rather than walk down the hall) might lead to team members letting their problems pile up rather than resolving them immediately. There may be an unintentional home court advantage (if the meetings are at the marketing facility, marketing team members may be perceived to be more powerful). And team members must be willing to tear down the functional walls and change their attitudes about working with individuals from other functions—otherwise, colocation facilitates social exchange, but doesn't really achieve cross-functional integration.[29]

In many firms, the effects of colocation are achieved without actual physical proximity of team members, using communications technology such as Lotus Notes or WebEx videoconferencing. This is sometimes known as **digital colocation**. Interestingly, research suggests that digital colocation and face-to-face colocation complement each other in terms of facilitating knowledge dissemination.[30]

As a final note, there is a recent increase in the use of **global teams** (that is, teams comprising individuals from at least two different countries). Improved videoconferencing technology makes global teams an increasingly feasible option. Global teams are increasingly popular in new product development, and we will take up their management in the next chapter.[31]

[28]Anthony Lee Pratt and James Patrick Gilbert, "Colocating New Product Development Teams: Why, When, Where, and How?" *Business Horizons,* November–December 1997, pp. 59–64; and Kenneth B. Kahn and Edward F. McDonough III, "An Empirical Study of the Relationships among Co-Location, Integration, Performance, and Satisfaction," *Journal of Product Innovation Management,* 14(3), May 1997, pp. 161–178.

[29]See Pratt and Gilbert, op. cit., and Farshad Rafii, "How Important Is Physical Colocation on Product Development Success?" *Business Horizons,* January–February 1995, pp. 78–84.

[30]Michael Song, Hans Berends, Hans van der Bij, and Mathieu Weggeman, "The Effect of IT and Colocation on Knowledge Dissemination," *Journal of Product Innovation Management,* 24(1), January 2007, pp. 52–68.

[31]Edward F. McDonough III, Kenneth B. Kahn, and Gloria Barczak, "Effectively Managing Global New Product Development Teams," *Proceedings,* 1998 Research Conference, Product Development and Management Association, pp. 176–188.

Other techniques are sometimes used. Some firms have sought a solution by bringing in a **produceability engineer**: an independent third party who understands both design and production and who can work in the design studios to see that production requirements are met by design decisions. Being third-party, turf battles are partially avoided. But it is not a satisfactory solution—adding another person rarely is.[32] As seen in Chapter 10, quality function deployment has also helped in getting cooperation across new product team members and in maintaining focus on customer needs and benefits. The customer's needs (counterpart of protocol) comprise an inherent part of the system and cannot be overlooked.

In addition, partnering upstream with vendors is a possibility. Of course, there are security risks, patent uncertainties, cooperation that cannot be mandated in an emergency, and the like. But most companies tell us they are doing it by using technology searches, demands that suppliers value engineer their product, and inclusion of supplier people on the new product teams. Chrysler, as an example, has cut its supplier base, establishing longer-term relationships with its suppliers, and insisted on high supplier quality in order to increase global competitiveness.[33]

It is in any vendor's best interest to be offering something an end user genuinely needs, so both parties gain from integrated activities.[34]

Computer-Aided Design and Design for Manufacturability

Another development is helping to bring people together and at the same time show the importance of all players. **CAD** (computer-aided design), **CAM** (computer-aided manufacturing), **CAE** (computer-aided engineering), **DFM** (design for manufacturability), and other variations refer to computer-based technologies that allow for very efficient product design and development.

These technologies offer lots of advantages—people have to work together to understand and use them, they force the integration of all needs into one analytical set, they are fast, and they do more than the human can do alone even if there were ample time. They also help improve the images of team players who may lack status. For example, manufacturing used to have to take a back seat to design and marketing. It was uncommon in many firms for the factory people even to be invited to meetings; they were expected to take what came from design and make it, somehow. In most firms that time is gone, and should be in all firms.

Product designers often use **design for manufacturability (DFM)** techniques to find ways to minimize manufacturing costs. On average, up to 80 percent of a product's cost is determined by the time it is designed. The idea behind DFM techniques is that an apparently trivial detail in the design phase might have huge manufacturing cost

---

[32]See Gerda Smets and Kees Overbeeke, "Industrial Design Engineering and the Theory of Direct Perception," *Design Studies*, April 1994, pp. 175–184, for ideas on how users deal with the expressiveness of products, and the impact of that on industrial design activities.

[33]Jeffrey H. Dyer, "How Chrysler Created an American Keiretsu," *Harvard Business Review*, July–August 1996, pp. 42–60.

[34]The good and the bad of this partnership are shown in Fred R. Beckley, "Some Companies Let Suppliers Work on Site and Even Place Orders," *The Wall Street Journal*, January 13, 1995, p. A1.

consequences later on, so manufacturing implications need to be considered early in product design. Another term sometimes heard is **front-loading**: identifying and solving design problems in earlier phases of the new products process.

Probably the most important DFM process is **design for assembly (DFA)**, which is concerned with checking ease of assembly and manufacture and encouraging product simplification.[35] As was shown in the classic Proprinter example given above, DFA leads to fewer components, resulting in lower materials costs as well as savings in assembly time. By programming in the manufacturing conditions and information about the particular assembly operation (for example, cars on an assembly line), the DFA program can react to any design proposal with information about its time and cost result. It also points out the major design elements contributing to slow time or high cost, so the designer can work directly on them. Unfortunately, the designer does not have comparable "design for marketing" software. Unless the protocol is very clear and accepted, or unless marketing or customer people are present during the design process, developers may be acting favorably to factory time/cost but unfavorably to customer value and usefulness.

Three-dimensional CAD mock-ups have been successfully used to front-load design problem identification. Designers of aircraft or automobiles, for example, are working within space limitations. A traditional two-dimensional engineer's drawing might not be able to identify that the designed air conditioning duct would not fit well in a new aircraft's structure. The car dashboard designers might not realize that their desired position for the audio system would protrude too far into the engine area. This sort of ill-fit can be identified and fixed readily using CAD. Similarly, Boeing used CAM in its design of the 777. They simulated climbing into the newly designed aircraft for maintenance using a computer-generated virtual human—and found that one of the navigation lights would have been hard for a real serviceperson to reach. There was no need to build an expensive prototype to find this flaw, and the fixup was easily made.[36]

Car manufacturers also use CAD techniques to improve the *decking* process. This refers to assembling the car's powertrain into the upper body (think of making a sandwich where all the parts have to fit together perfectly). Using CAD mockups, car companies such as Chrysler identify (and solve) fit problems digitally before any physical decking actually takes place. Rather than being an arduous, trial-and-error process, decking now can be completed in 15 minutes as the carmaker can usually get it right on the first or second try.[37]

Another application of CAD concerns car crashworthiness. BMW virtually "crashed" dozens of car designs using a crash simulator and was able to improve crashworthiness by about 30 percent as a result. Only two physical prototypes were actually built, crashed, and analyzed. The cost of building and physically crashing dozens of design iterations

[35]Keith Goffin, "Evaluating Customer Support during New Product Development: An Exploratory Study," *Journal of Product Innovation Management,* 15(1), January 1998, pp. 42–56.

[36]Marco Iansiti and Alan MacCormack, "Developing Products on Internet Time," *Harvard Business Review,* September–October 1997, pp. 108–117.

[37]Stefan Thomke and Takahiro Fujimoto, "The Effect of 'Front-Loading' Problem-Solving on Product Development Performance," *Journal of Product Innovation Management,* 17(2), March 2000, pp. 110–127.

FIGURE 11.8 The Impact of 3D Printing on Product Design: GE Additive

Additive manufacturing (AM) refers to the technique of building a three-dimensional (3D) object using layers of ultrathin material. GE Additive is a branch of GE devoted to AM. GE SmarTech Publishing, an industry analyst firm, has estimated total spending on 3D printers, materials, software, and services to be about $13 billion up through 2017. Yearly spend is projected to increase rapidly, to an estimated $280 billion within ten years. GE Global Innovation Barometer research found that about 9 out of 10 global executives believe AM increases creativity and speed to market. As AM technology improves, product developers will be able to make more customized parts, with a wider variety of structures and textures, resulting in improved part integration. For these reasons, GE is one of many firms investing in AM technology.

As a sample application, Optisys LLC of West Jordan, Utah, uses AM technology to manufacture metal micro-antennas and similar products for aerospace and the defense industry. Improvement in AM capability enables Optisys to provide better performance. For example, using AM allowed Optisys to reduce the number of parts in one antenna from 100 to one, while at the same time reducing weight by 95 percent, decreasing production lead time from eleven to two months, and reducing non-recurring costs by 75 percent.

AM provides several benefits for product developers. It makes small-volume or customized products cost-effective. This allows companies to use a zero-inventory policy, printing parts on demand, or permits hospitals to print customized, patient-specific implants.

GE operates Customer Experience Centers in Pittsburgh and Munich, where it can display AM capabilities to potential customers. At these centers, new product teams can learn how to optimize design and can also visualize how to ramp up from early innovation production to full-scale production. GE hopes that its early investment in AM and involvement with highly innovative companies will pay off, and that it will be viewed as a leader in innovation and manufacturing into the future.

Sources: Martin LaMonica, "Additive Manufacturing: GE, The World's Largest Manufacturer, Is on the Verge of Using 3-D Printing to Make Jet Parts," *MIT Technology Review*, 2013; also Web sites www.ge.com and www.optisys.tech.

would have been prohibitive, not to mention time consuming.[38] In sum, digital preassembly and simulation analyses are among the biggest benefits of 3D CAD to product development since they help to overcome costly and time-consuming stumbling blocks in the new products process.[39]

Finally, the advent of readily available 3D printing has had much impact on product design, and product development in general. We have already discussed the use of 3D printed product concepts used in product evaluation. But this technology can help in improving product creativity, optimizing product design, speeding up time to production, and reducing development cost. Figure 11.8 describes the impact of 3D printing on many aspects of product design.

Continuous Improvement in Design

How can one go about improving product design even further? A familiar concept in new product development—the voice of the customer—might be revisited. Too often, the basic product is designed, then a product-user interface is slapped on without

[38]Stefan Thomke, "Simulation, Learning, and R&D Performance: Evidence from Automotive Development," *Research Policy* 27, 1998, pp. 55–74.

[39]Yasunori Baba and Kentaro Nobeoka, "Towards Knowledge-Based Product Development: The 3D–CAD Model of Knowledge Creation," *Research Policy* 26, 1997, pp. 643–659.

much thought to what the customer wants. Worse yet, it may be difficult to give the customer what he or she really wants without making major changes to the basic product. By starting with the customer's needs, a better basic product would be designed in the first place. This process is sometimes called *interaction design*. For example, if a given ATM user always requests service in English and always asks for a receipt, couldn't that behavior be tracked so that after a while the machine no longer has to ask? Simple enough concept, but one that would require a substantial change to the basic product in order to give the customer what he or she wants.[40]

Summary

This chapter has dealt with the design process, the people and the activities. We have looked specifically at design process elements such as design architecture and prototype development, and explored some of the computer-aided techniques so important to design in so many firms. Design is many-faceted, however, so it will differ greatly from one industry to another. Marketing people have found it important to be flexible here, helping to shape a role for design that fits each situation and corporate policy. But in most firms, design joins manufacturing and other functions to form a working, multifunctional group (usually a team), and in Chapter 12 we will look at its structure and management.

Case: The IDEA Awards[41]

Think about the following new products:

- *The Microsoft HoloLens:* A self-contained holographic device that provides the user with an augmented reality experience through projected images.
- *The Q-Collar:* A collar to be worn by athletes to reduce the chance of brain injury. It is fastened around the neck and minimizes brain movement within the skull at the time of impact.
- *The InnoSpire Go:* A product of Philips, this is an electronic nebulizer for taking medication simply, quickly, and conveniently that can be used 30 times between charges.
- *MicroPro Grill:* Designed by Tupperware, this grill features heating technology that converts microwaves into direct heat, allowing the user to bake, sauté, or grill in their microwaves.

[40]The concept of "interaction design" and the ATM example are from Alan Cooper, *The Inmates Are Running the Asylum: Why High-Tech Products Drive Us Crazy and How to Restore the Sanity* (Indianapolis, IN: SAMS, 1999). To be fair, some systems do recall the user's preferred language, but, based on personal experiences, many still do not.

[41]The examples are taken from Megan Willett and Chris Weller, "The 22 Best Product Designs of the Year," *Business Insider*, April 21, 2016; and Chris Weller, "The Best Designed Products of 2017," *Business Insider*, December 28, 2017. Further information is on the IDSA Web site, www.idsa.org, and in particular the IDEA Awards gallery found on this site.

- *The ZEF Climatic Table:* This table contains phase-changing materials that can absorb or release heat, depending on the ambient temperature. Room temperature is thus regulated and stays comfortable, without the use of electricity.

- *Doppler Labs's Here Buds:* These earbuds allow the user to manipulate sound frequencies of their surroundings; for example, to mute that crying baby on an airplane or to set a desired level of bass at a concert.

- *Kohler's Prolific Sink:* Imagine a stainless-steel sink with an integrated cutting board, colander, racks, and wash bin. The components slide out for use when needed. The sink is also designed for easy cleanup.

- *Da Vinci Xi Surgical System:* This system combines robotics with minimally invasive surgery. The surgeon using the equipment is seated in a comfortable position and can do delicate work using the robotic arms.

- *GE's Micro Kitchen:* This is a kitchen system designed for small apartments, which houses a compact refrigerator, sink, and microwave unit, while also reducing environmental impact. The compact refrigeration, cleaning, and microwave units save space and reduce the user's environmental footprint.

What do all of the above new products have in common? All were recently cited by *Business Insider* as one of the best designed products of the year. In fact, these were all recent finalists of the International Design Excellence Awards (IDEA), a competition held annually by the Industrial Designers Society of America (IDSA). On the IDSA Web page, you can find a gallery of hundreds of products that have won IDEA awards (the direct link is www.idsa.org/awards/idea/gallery).

On its Web site, IDSA notes that IDEA award-winning products not only are well designed and profitable, but many have also truly changed people's lives and how we interact, work, and play. IDSA singles out three of the award winners: the iPhone, the Tesla Model S, and the Oculus Rift (winners in 2008, 2013, and 2016, respectively) as products that were commercially successful and also substantially disrupted industry and impacted society. In a few of the above examples, the products improve consumer health and well-being and might even save lives. While these products are marvels of technology, excellence in design plays a critical part in their ultimate, world-changing success.

Visit the IDEA awards gallery and any other Web sites listing well-designed products. Also think of any new products you have recently used, which you believe exemplify excellent product design. From these sources, compile a list of several well-designed products, and select at least two products from this list for class discussion. Present a brief report on each of your two selected products, in which you discuss how their design compares to Dieter Rams's principles of good design. In your opinion, do these products score well on most of his 10 principles? Clearly discuss and support your answer.

Looking back at the lists of best-designed products, do you disagree with any of the choices? Are there any designs that don't belong on the list? Again, use the Dieter Rams principles to support your answer.

CHAPTER TWELVE

Development Team Management

Setting

In Chapter 12, we focus our attention on the **cross-functional team**. Teams composed of individuals from various functional areas (marketing, research & development [R&D], engineering, design, manufacturing, production, and so on) and managed by a clearly identified team leader are commonly and effectively used in new product development. Yet teams differ in their composition, whom they report to, how effectively the team members work together, and how productive they are. Increasingly, the team may comprise individuals who may live thousands of miles apart. Organizing and managing product teams are real challenges. Nevertheless, as seen in earlier chapters, a well-functioning product team is critical to bringing in and using the voice of the customer, developing new product protocols, accelerating time to market while staying under budget, and in so many other ways. In this chapter, we take up the issue of product team organization and management.

What Is a Team?

Describing, building, and managing teams is complicated because there are so many different kinds of teams. Drucker made an analogy with sports teams:[1]

- *Baseball teams:* They are like assembly line teams. Their work fits together, and all the players are needed, but they generally work as individuals in their own ways. The double-play combo is a clear exception. Work is generally in a series.
- *Football teams:* These have fixed positions, but they play as a team, and everyone knows his particular responsibility for every play. Japanese car teams are of this type. Work is parallel, not series.
- *Tennis-doubles teams:* The players work with and support each other. The result is important only as the team scores a point or wins a match. Partners are dedicated. Jazz trios are another example, with each musician taking a turn improvising over solid, predictable backing by the other two.

[1]Peter F. Drucker, "There's More Than One Kind of Team," *The Wall Street Journal*, February 11, 1992, p. A16.

Baseball and football managers are quite strong, but there are no tennis-doubles managers. Some training people feel that volleyball is the best analogy for today's teams: There are more players; they develop skills at all positions; and the unique role for the manager is comparable to that of the new products team manager.

The new products team is so far from the traditional and comfortable hierarchical world that great learning is required. There is a shortage of people who know how to play the game, and performance appraisal is tough because only the team's overall performance matters. It offers the greatest risk to upper level management. Since the team members all have different backgrounds and play different roles, there is no one to "score" them against.

Structuring the Team

The new products organization can be structured in many ways. One useful listing of **organizational structure options** is shown in Figure 12.1. The options shown in this figure can be thought of as a continuum: The farther to the right, the greater is the commitment of company personnel to the new product project, and the more powerful is the project leader.[2] The term that is sometimes used is **projectization**: the farther to the right, the greater the projectization. You may also come across the terms **lightweight** and **heavyweight** teams, where heavyweight is synonymous with high projectization.[3]

On the left side of Figure 12.1 is the most lightweight option, the **functional structure**, where the work is done by the various departments with very low projectization. There usually is a new products committee or a product planning committee. The work is usually low risk and probably involves the present line of products—improvements, new sizes, and so on. The ongoing departmental people know the market and the business; they can make the necessary decisions easily and effectively. This structure does not work well for projects that require input from several functional areas and is better suited to projects that are executed within one functional area.[4]

There are some advantages associated with a lightweight team. The team leader can usually ensure relatively easily that members are informed about key issues, and communication is comparatively easy. Technical people on the team (R&D personnel and engineers) work closely with each other, focusing on their areas of expertise and

[2]New product organizational options have been expressed in scores of ways. But only one listing came from empirical research on the form and on the success or failure of actual new product projects. It was originally stated in David H. Gobeli and Eric W. Larson, "Matrix Management: More Than a Fad," *Engineering Management International*, 1986, pp. 71–76. The only change is that what the authors called *project team* is here called *venture* to reflect recent preferences. The same authors also later published a much larger empirical study on the same subject: Erik W. Larson and David H. Gobeli, "Organizing for Product Development Projects," *Journal of Product Innovation Management*, 5(3), September 1988, pp. 180–190.

[3]Gloria Barczak, "Innovation Teams," in V. K. Narayanan and Gina C. O'Connor (eds.), *Encyclopedia of Technology & Innovation Management* (Chichester, UK: John Wiley, 2010), Chapter 32.

[4]Eduardo Armando and Eduardo Vasconcellos, "Organization for Innovation," in Praveen Gupta and Brett E. Trusko (eds.), *Global Innovation Science Handbook*, New York: McGraw-Hill, 2014, pp. 659–680.

FIGURE 12.1
Structures in
New Products
Organization

	Options			
Functional	**Functional matrix**	**Balanced matrix**	**Project matrix**	**Venture**
With or without committee				Inside Outside
0%_____20%_____40%_____60%_____80%_____100%				
	Degree of projectization*			

*Defined as the extent to which participants in the process see themselves as independent from the project or committed to it. Thus, members of a new products committee are almost totally oriented (loyal) to their functions or departments; spinout (outside) venture members are almost totally committed to the project.

minimizing duplication of effort.[5] The functional area managers (R&D managers, marketing managers, and so on) are strong and can dominate the project leader, weakening his or her effectiveness.[6]

At the opposite end of Figure 12.1 is the **project structure**. This option is characterized by high projectization and is most useful for new-to-the-world or new-to-the-firm products, and the project is sometimes called a **venture**. Team members are pulled out of their departments and put to work full time on the project. High projectization encourages team members to develop a wide range of skills, and the team is typically very flexible and able to adapt to environmental changes quickly. This is a heavyweight team whose project leader has substantial organizational power. Directed by the project leader, the multifunctional team works together until they complete the project, at which time they may be relocated back to their original functional area.

A *skunkworks* environment, designed to identify new ideas or solutions to new product-related problems, is one type of venture. The venture may be kept in the regular organization, or it may be spun outside the current division or company—a *spinout venture*. The name *skunkworks* derives from a project initiated years ago by Lockheed (whose Advanced Development Program is still called internally as the Skunk Works). In this structure, a group of researchers are pulled out of their familiar departments and routine activities to concentrate on specific innovation targets.[7] Several recent examples are presented in Figure 12.2.

The project structure provides several advantages. Technical personnel develop more diverse knowledge through work on many projects; technical and other personnel gain familiarity with the overall project and each other's contributions; the cross-functional nature of the team leads to greater speed to market; and the powerful project leader provides direction and assumes responsibility for the team. In sum, if a

[5]Eduardo Armando and Eduardo Vasconcellos, op. cit., and Karl T. Ulrich and Steven D. Eppinger, *Product Design and Development*, 2nd ed., McGraw-Hill, 2000, pp. 28–29.

[6]S. Wheelwright and K. Clark, *Revolutionizing Product Development* (New York: The Free Press, 1992). See also discussion in Barczak, op. cit.

[7]Marianne Jelinek, "Organizing for Innovation," in V. K. Narayanan and Gina C. O'Connor (eds.), *Encyclopedia of Technology & Innovation Management* (Chichester, UK: John Wiley, 2010), Chapter 29.

FIGURE 12.2 How Big Companies Use Skunkworks

From the first skunkworks (at Lockheed Martin in 1943), this structure has allowed employees to work on high-level and sometimes secret projects. The skunkworks provides separation between the innovators and the rest of the company, which is considered critical to speed and privacy. The examples show that skunkworks can be organized in several creative ways.

Oracle: Hired engineers to work on custom cloud apps, big data analytics, cybersecurity, and the Internet of Things. The two Solution Engineering Centers are located in Reston, VA, and Denver, far from Oracle's Silicon Valley headquarters. The skunkworks is organized as a separate unit within Oracle and will work only on products for internal use at Oracle.

Walmart: Launched an incubator in Silicon Valley in 2017, named Store No. 8, designed to explore the future of retailing. The startup is focused on the development of a mobile app for retail shopping and is located in Silicon Valley and New York City.

Google X (now renamed X): Has housed several secret "moon shot" research projects designed to "improve the human condition." One well-known outcome was Google's self-driving car, but X has also worked on space elevators, robotics projects, and others. X is now considered a separate company under the Alphabet corporate umbrella.

Symantec: Launched its Symantec Ventures in March 2017, with the intention of giving startups in the cyberspace industry access to its ecosystem (data and market insights). By providing startups with access, it expects they will be able to speed up time to market. It is also considering the possibility of acquiring some of the startups in the future.

Dupont: Created the Delaware Innovation Space, in collaboration with the University of Delaware and the state government of Delaware. This is a 100,000-square-foot physical space set up to house scientifically focused startups and managed by a board comprised of representatives from all three of the institutions. Dupont is also considering the startups as possible future acquisitions.

Source: Valentina Zarya, "5 Corporate Skunkworks You Should Know About," *fortune.com*, June 15, 2017; and Marziah Karch, "Google X: The Secret Google Lab," *lifewire.com*, November 24, 2018.

project requires serious integration of several functional areas, a project structure is a good organizational choice.[8]

The relative advantages of high versus low projectization are summarized in Figure 12.3. As the figure shows, low projectization is associated with greater R&D specialization and communication within the R&D effort, while high projectization allows for more R&D diversification and improved communication between R&D and other functional areas.

In some cases, an intermediate structure is required, for example on projects that require both speed to market and technical superiority. To achieve a balance between the technical strengths of the functional structure and the integrative strengths of the project structure, a firm may choose a **matrix structure**. As shown in Figure 12.1, several matrix options exist. The **functional matrix** structure is the most lightweight of the options. Here, a team exists, with people from the various departments (such as manufacturing, R&D, and marketing), but the project is still close to the current business. Team members think like functional specialists, and functional area managers still hold most of the power. In the **balanced matrix** structure, both functional and project views are critical—neither ongoing business nor the new product should be the driver. The most heavyweight structure of the three is the **project matrix**, which recognizes the occasional need for stronger project push. This structure is characterized by high

[8]Eduardo Armando and Eduardo Vasconcellos, op. cit.

FIGURE 12.3
Advantages of
Low and High
Projectization

Low Projectization	High Projectization
Greater specialization of R&D personnel	Greater diversification of R&D personnel
Improved communication among R&D personnel	Improved communication between R&D and other functional areas
Less duplication of R&D effort	Better project integration
Focus on technical quality	Focus on faster project completion
R&D personnel like working with people of similar specialties and backgrounds	R&D personnel like working with and learning from people from diverse functional areas
Clear functional leader who manages all specialized R&D personnel	Clear project leader who is responsible for the entire project

Source: Adapted from Eduardo Armando and Eduardo Vasconcellos, "Organization for Innovation," in Praveen Gupta and Brett E. Trusko (editors), *Global Innovation Science Handbook*, New York: McGraw-Hill, 2014, p. 663.

projectization and strong project managers. Team members are project people first and functional people second.

The discussion indicates that ventures should be particularly suited for new-to-the-world products, and the examples given in Figure 12.2 suggest that some firms have found them quite useful for developing their most radical and forward-thinking new products. Some firms, however, have found highly projectized teams to be difficult to establish and/or to manage and have moved back toward a more lightweight approach. Matrix structures also have drawbacks, as they can be difficult to manage, and can become unreasonably complicated and incur high overheads. There are inevitably role-conflict issues in any matrix structure: Should team members put first priority on the project or on the function they represent? In extremely complex cases, a matrix structure can be detrimental to innovation. Operational difficulties ascribed to a rigorous organizational structure have been blamed for Hewlett-Packard's lack of innovative performance over several years.[9] These firms find that encouraging cooperation among team members is perhaps more important than the details of the organizational structure of the team; one cannot just throw people together and call them a team.[10]

Other organizational issues arise as well. Should a radical innovation be "incubated" within the venture team, only to be integrated within the firm if it gains some acceptance in the marketplace? Research on twelve large firms and their ongoing innovative efforts suggests that the best procedure is to manage the relationship between the venture's management and that of the present firm, including all issues of leadership and transition of management. Three competencies tied to radical innovation were identified:

- *Discovery.* Creating, recognizing, and articulating radical innovation opportunities.
- *Incubation.* Transitioning the radical opportunity into a business proposal.

[9]See Jelinek, op. cit.
[10]Barbara Dyer, Ashok K. Gupta, and David Wilemon, "What First-to-Market Companies Do Differently," *Research-Technology Management*, March–April 1999, pp. 15–21.

- *Acceleration.* Ramping up the business so that it is comparable to other businesses within the parent organization.[11]

Another Look at Projectization

Despite the difficulties in implementation, firms do need to consider projectization as a way to get the team members working together effectively. Any time two or more people from different departments or functions of a firm gather to work on a project, conflicts arise. When a sales manager, for example, goes to a new products *committee* meeting, there is little doubt about priorities because committee members are engineers or marketers first and committee members second. The sales manager is "functionalized," not projectized. Committee members want the company to make a profit; they are not disloyal. But they have independent opinions about how any particular new product may contribute to profit. The sales manager may see a new package size as meeting customer demands and adding sales; the engineer may believe production costs will go up more than the sales volume; accounting objects to another line item that may just split customers' current purchases and add to cost; R&D says work on the new package size will pull a key person off a far more important project needed next year.

These are legitimate issues, not idle concerns. Increasing projectization can help to handle them. If a project is important and faces lots of opposition of the types just mentioned, then we increase the projectization. If the opposition is very high, an empowered venture team may be called for. On the other hand, if the product development will entail only minor variations to a standard product or platform, it is possible that lower projectization will be the preferred option.

Different firms manage these issues in different ways. Toyota, for example, has been successful with integrated product innovation while retaining a functionally based organization. It accomplishes this in several ways:

- Written communication between employees of different functional areas is stressed. Emphasis is placed on concise (one- or two-page) reports to minimize paperwork overload.
- There is close supervision between supervisors and new hires within each functional area, resembling a student-mentor relationship.
- "Chief engineers" are the lead designers on a new car project. Their role is to design the overall approach and to manage the large team of engineers that will actually fill in the details.
- In-house training of engineers is stressed. Engineers are rotated widely throughout the company to avoid setting up functional chimneys.
- Relatively simple, standardized work processes are used to keep everyone on track.
- A set of design standards is maintained to promote predictability in the new product process.[12]

[11]Gina Colarelli O'Connor and Richard DeMartino, "Organizing for Radical Innovation: An Exploratory Study of the Structural Aspects of RI Management Systems in Large, Established Firms," *Journal of Product Innovation Management*, 23(6), 2006, pp. 475–497.

[12]Durward K. Sobek II, Jeffrey K. Liker, and Allen C. Ward, "Another Look at How Toyota Integrates Product Development," *Harvard Business Review*, July–August 1998, pp. 36–49.

Building a Team

Most managers and almost all researchers have concluded that new products teams must be created to fit their situations. There is no right method or paradigm, just as there is no right method of concept testing or spelling out a product innovation charter. Neither are there right people; most team members and team leaders tell of their own personal growth during such assignments. Sales managers and scientists alike must become something else, something appropriate to a group task.

Establishing a Culture of Collaboration

Few people disagree with the importance of culture in business. For product improvements and near line extensions, the new products people must take the culture of the ongoing organization. At Kraft Heinz, for example, the Big Red brand team (managing Heinz tomato ketchup and related products) will dominate new products activity. But as the task becomes tougher, firms will need to foster a culture of **collaboration** that will help them harness creativity, share information among departments, encourage growth of intellectual capital, and get more efficient in new product development.[13]

There are several elements critical to driving a culture that fosters innovation.[14] First of these is to encourage *continuous learning*. It is important for the team to work closely with customers, using the concept testing techniques we stressed earlier, to learn iteratively and to keep on track with customer needs. Postmortems on failed products, as well as "postvivems" on successes, should be done to understand what worked and can be replicated and what did not. Conversations across business units should be encouraged, to share best practices as well as knowledge gained from the failures. We have also previously mentioned that many companies allow their employees a certain percentage of their company time on innovative new ideas; this company policy also encourages a culture of learning and innovation.

A second key element is *acceptance of risk*. An innovative culture encourages risk taking. Team members should not feel their job or career is on the line should their product fail. Top management should recognize that calculated risk-taking, some trial and error, and some failure are required for long-term success and dissuade personnel of any fear of failure. To mitigate the chance of failure, the team can let their idea incubate longer as they ensure the product comes to market in the right form. This minimizes lengthy and costly iteration in the future.

Accountability is also an important element and needs to be established for the project team. Team members should be incented for dedication to innovation and commitment to revenue growth from innovation. Therefore, accountability metrics should include process as well as outcome measures. That is, pipeline sufficiency metrics

---

[13]For a perspective on the importance of sharing information across functional areas, see Michael Song, Jinhong Zie, and C. Anthony Di Benedetto, "Message and Source Factors, Market Uncertainty, and Extrafunctional Information Processing: Hypotheses and Empirical Evidence," *IEEE Transactions on Engineering Management*, 48(2), 2001, pp. 223–238.

[14]This section is drawn from Andria Long, "Journey to Innovation Excellence," in Praveen Gupta and Brett E. Trusko (eds.), *Global Innovation Science Handbook*, New York: McGraw-Hill, 2014, pp. 681–696.

(such as number of ideas currently being worked on) as well as pipeline performance metrics (sales revenues achieved by launched products over a three-year horizon) should be used. We discuss the issue of how best to compensate team members for their activities later in this chapter.

Finally, the role of top management and the *product champion* cannot be ignored. Senior management can communicate the importance of innovation to the company's mission and encourage long-term thinking about investment in innovation. They should empower team members to make the routine decisions on their projects while also supporting any major go/no-go decisions. They can ensure that a proper focus is maintained on innovation, which means resisting the temptation to divert long-term resource commitment of innovation (people and money) to short-term brush fires. High-performance projects usually require a product champion who takes ownership of the project and is fully committed to its success. We will explore the role of the champion later in this chapter.

Selecting the Team Leader

Given the overall strategy and the decision on just how much team the firm needs for the job at hand, it is time to select a leader. Sometimes this is automatic—for example, when the firm uses a product manager system and the new product concerns an addition to a particular person's product line, or when, as in the case of 3M's Post-It notes, the project originates from a particular person's technology.

Leaders must be *general managers*. They must be able to spot the need for change and convince others of this need. They also need to get potential team members to accept the idea of being on a team, ensure their commitment, encourage information sharing, increase interaction, and generally feel comfortable working with people from other functional areas.[15] They lead without direct authority and so must win personal support. Team leaders must have strong self-confidence (based on knowledge and experience, not just ego), have empathy (be able to look at things from another person's point of view), have a good self-awareness of how others see them, and be experts in personal communication. But the irony is that even all this is probably not enough. It has been said that a new products project really needs two leaders: a creative, inspiring type for early on and a tough disciplinarian for the later phases. Rare is the person who can be both.

Sometimes people wonder whether the leader should be chosen first or selected by the team members themselves. The latter is an attractive idea and is used occasionally. But senior management usually prefers to pick the leader and then let that leader identify the team players. This increases the likelihood of good team chemistry and commitment but also ensures that a capable leader is leading. Senior management can also help increase the leader's chance of success by providing appropriate resources and empowering the leader to make key decisions. In addition, the team leader should view his or her position as a full-time commitment![16] Many companies recognize the difficulties in locating talented leaders and highly prize those that they do find. Toyota

---

[15]Avan R. Jassawalla and Hemant C. Sashittal, "Strategies of Effective New Product Leaders," *California Management Review*, 42(2), Winter 2000, pp. 34–51.

[16]Jassawalla and Sashittal, op. cit.

and Honda, for example, have them stay on as managers of their cars after launch and then assign them to the start of another new car project (rather than to the track to the top executive positions).

Selecting the Team Members

When selecting the members of a new product team, it is important to remember that each one of them is on the team as the representative of a group of others "back home" in their department. The R&D team member can't do all the technical work, and may do none, but does stimulate, direct, and encourage others in R&D to do it. This is usually in the face of competition from other R&D representatives on other teams, who are also trying to win time for *their* projects. The same goes for team members from the other functions. Chrysler wants team members to be change agents. Bausch & Lomb (B&L) wants members to have real functional influence and a broad-business view. B&L believes so strongly in teams that a conference speaker from the firm brought along (and introduced) five core members of his team.

How many members should a team have? First, let's distinguish the core team, ad hoc team, and extended team. The *core team* includes those people who are involved in *managing* functional clusters. Thus, one marketing person may represent, speak for, and guide 10 to 12 others in the sales and marketing areas. The core team members are active throughout and are supported by *ad hoc team* members. Ad hoc members are those from important departments (such as packaging, legal, and logistics) whose importance is brief in time and thus not needed on the core team.

Extended team members may come from another division of the firm, corporate staff, or another firm. Though extended team members can come from just about anywhere, firms are increasingly seeing the value of including key suppliers on the team. Sharing of information on product and technical plans between manufacturing firms and their suppliers can reduce problems associated with technological uncertainty and help both participants reach their long-term goals.[17] The firm's purchasing department may be a core or ad hoc team member and serve as the liaison with the supplier firm. Additionally, greater coordination with external partner firms may also facilitate internal cooperation between functional areas.[18]

To illustrate the benefits of supplier interaction, Dell Computers has close ties with the external suppliers of its processors, peripherals, and software, and as a result can quickly and easily customize products in response to customer needs. DAF, a small European truck manufacturer, depends on the knowledge provided by its injection systems supplier, Bosch. These firms, in fact, view themselves as partners, despite the size difference between them. Bosch supplies injection systems to DAF, which in turn

---

[17]Kenneth J. Petersen, Robert B. Handfield, and Gary L. Ragatz, "A Model of Supplier Integration into New Product Development," *Journal of Product Innovation Management*, 20(4), 2003, pp. 284–299; and C. Anthony Di Benedetto, Roger J. Calantone, Erik VanAllen, and Mitzi M. Montoya-Weiss, "Purchasing Joins the NPD Team," *Research-Technology Management*, 46(4), July–August 2003, pp. 45–51.

[18]Bas Hillebrand and Wim G. Biemans, "Links Between Internal and External Cooperation in Product Development: An Exploratory Development Study," *Journal of Product Innovation Management*, 21(2), March 2004, pp. 110–122.

supplies quick, reliable information to Bosch. The partnership allows Bosch to better anticipate the needs of its other customers.[19]

The Role of the Project Champion

Any project needs support. We have already discussed the importance of top management support in establishing an innovative culture. But individual projects need constant support and nurturing. Without this support, a high-potential project may never come to fruition just because senior people lose interest, a required technical breakthrough is slow in coming, a political conflict diverts attention to other projects, and so on. An individual who commits to a product, promotes it, and does whatever is required to push it forward in the firm is known as the **product champion** (sometimes called the *project champion* or simply *champion*). Another term you may encounter is the *promotor*, which means the person who "pushes the idea forward." The champion within the firm plays a role similar to that of the entrepreneur starting up a new business. The champion's challenge is to push past the **roadblocks** and bypass corporate hierarchy and persuade other people in the firm (including from several functional areas) to support the innovation.[20] Champions will not win every time, but their task is to see that no project dies without a fight. Champions also play a key role in bringing information to the new product team through both their contacts within the organization and their external network.[21]

In many cases, the project manager may act as the product champion. In other cases, the champion is self-appointed, such as a technical person who was involved in the discovery leading to the project. It can be a senior level executive. But whoever champions a new product project, there are several roles that may be filled by the champion, the importance of which may depend on the type of innovation.[22] The *power promotor* is the champion who has power and resources within the firm. He or she may be able to use that power to get senior management to favor this project and to commit the required human and financial resources for development. The *expert promotor* provides technical knowledge and support, gathers information, and builds expertise so that the team can quickly gain the required technical competence. The *process promotor* knows

---

[19]For the Dell example: G. Tomas M. Hult and K. Scott Swan, "Special Issue on New Product Development and Supply Chain Management: From the Special Issue Guest Editors," *Journal of Product Innovation Management*, 20(5), 2003, pp. 333–336; for the DAF example, Finn Wynstra, Mathieu Weggeman, and Arjan van Weele, "Exploring Purchasing Integration in Product Development," *Industrial Marketing Management*, 32(1), 2003, pp. 69–83.

[20]Stephen K. Markham and Lynda Aiman-Smith, "Product Champions: Truths, Myths, and Management," *Research-Technology Management*, 44(3), May–June 2001, pp. 44–50; and Stephen K. Markham, "Moving Technologies from Lab to Market," *Research-Technology Management*, 45(6), November–December 2002, pp. 31–42.

[21]Jane M. Howell and Christine M. Shea, "Individual Differences, Environmental Scanning, Innovation Framing, and Champion Behavior: Key Predictors of Project Performance," *Journal of Product Innovation Management*, 18(1), January 2001, pp. 15–27.

[22]This section is drawn from Søren Salomo and Hans Georg Gemünden, "Promotors and Champions of Innovation: Barriers to Innovation and Innovator Roles," in V. K. Narayanan and Gina Colarelli O'Connor, *Encyclopedia of Technology & Innovation Management*, West Sussex, UK: Wiley, 2010, pp. 263–268; see also A. Griffin, R. L. Price, M. M. Maloney, B. A. Vojak, and E. W. Sim, "Voices from the Field: How Exceptional Electronic Industrial Innovators Innovate," *Journal of Product Innovation Management*, 26, 2009, pp. 222–240.

the firm's organization and politics intimately, and diplomatically establishes connections among the required participants. The *relationship promotor* has ties outside the organization and may be critical in finding an open innovation partner who will cooperate on a promising project. Finally, the *technological gatekeeper* works with R&D to establish a communication exchange network, collecting technical information and sharing it with team members and others in the organization.

Network Building

So far, our people focus has been on the team leader and the team members. But sometimes there is no team. As seen in Chapter 1, many new products are simply improvements or close line extensions, and often these are developed in the functional mode, within the ongoing organization, and without a special team. In addition, the extended team includes people well outside the core and ad hoc team. In all of these cases, the participants who actually do the new product work comprise a network.

A **network** consists of nodes, links, and operating relationships. *Nodes* are people important to the project in some way. *Links* are how they are reached and what important ties they have to others in the network. *Operating relationships* are how these people are contacted and motivated to cooperate in the project. Who are the nodes? There is no simple answer here. In fact, any given project may enlist the support of hundreds (or even thousands) of people. Only judgment can decide how many of them should be put into a formal network and managed.

Network makers admit it is easier to draw nodes and linkage lines in a diagram than to implement a network in an organization. But there is no choice, and networks are an aid, even if quite informal or just mental pictures. Perhaps their greatest danger is that they can easily become bureaucracies. One manager, when asked during a training program, refused to draw up the network for a project he was then managing. He said he did not want to see it all on one sheet and risk being overpowered by its complexity. And he did not want his team to see it and thus get a better idea of the massive indirect costs involved in the activity.

Training the Teams

An appointed team is not yet ready to operate. There must be **top management support** (discussed later) and, hopefully, a good image around the firm. Other managers sometimes come to doubt or fear a team, and they can isolate or ostracize it.

But the real need at this time is training. It would be nice to say we have a large cadre of experienced new product team members and leaders, but usually we do not. Generally, firms start a team off with an intensive two- or three-day training session for the team members. At many firms, this pretraining is so critical that teams may spend a month on it. But training sessions cannot bring team members up to the needed skill levels unless there is considerable skill to begin with.

Managing the Team

Managing a team of the type being developed for more important projects in the new products field is extremely difficult. A couple of studies found that most firms reported having well-defined new products processes but were often less successful in

FIGURE 12.4
Guiding
Principles in
New Product
Process
Implementation

Clarity of Goals and Objectives. Spell out what needs to be done, by whom, and when, at all phases of the new products process. Provide materials, training, and clearly specified metrics for measurement of new product impact. Make sure there is a shared vision, common focus and direction, and excellent communication across all team members.

Ownership. Commitment (a desire to do whatever is needed to make the project succeed) is important, but so is ownership, which goes beyond commitment. Ownership means that team members feel they can make a difference and want to do so. Their very identity is tied up in the project's outcome. Provide the kinds of rewards and recognition that encourage all team members to share the new products process and to put forth that extra effort. Build mutual confidence across team members.

Leadership at both senior and team levels. Senior management must visibly support new products and lead by example. Responsibility ultimately resides at the top, though decision making can be assigned appropriately to different managerial levels. At the team level, leadership can take the form of support, facilitation, and encouragement.

Integration with business processes. This means all upstream activities affected by the new products process. Their inputs and outputs need to be linked to new product development; a centralized business process organization may facilitate this.

Flexibility. Adjust the new products process as the environment and objectives change. The goal is to remain a world-class product developing organization; this requires the firm to allow each project or each team the required amount of flexibility in, for example, the number of projects currently underway or the length of time devoted to each stage.

Source: Based on Jeffrey M. Davidson, Allen Clamen and Robin A. Karol, "Learning from the Best New Product Developers," *Research-Technology Management*, July–August 1999, pp. 12–18; and Edward F. McDonough III, "Investigation of Factors Contributing to the Success of Cross-Functional Teams," *Journal of Product Innovation Management* 17, no. 3, May 2000, pp. 221–235.

implementation. Firms with the most success in new products tended to have several common principles guiding implementation, including clarity of roles and responsibilities, a sense of commitment and ownership, cooperation, strong team leadership, and flexibility. Figure 12.4 provides more detail.[23] A term that is now emerging to describe high-performance teams is **charged behavior**: In addition to commitment and

[23]Jeffrey M. Davidson, Allen Clamen, and Robin A. Karol, "Learning from the Best New Product Developers," *Research-Technology Management*, 42(4), July–August 1999, pp. 12–18; and Edward F. McDonough III, "Investigation of Factors Contributing to the Success of Cross-Functional Teams," *Journal of Product Innovation Management*, 17(3), May 2000, pp. 221–235.

cooperation, team members derive enjoyment from working together. Encouragement to take risks, quality focus, interdepartmental linkages, exposure to customer input, and the nature of competition, among other factors, are positively related to charged behavior.[24]

A few special thoughts on management and implementation follow.[25]

Cross-Functional Interface Management

As we have seen, product innovation involves people from many different functional areas and backgrounds: sales and marketing, R&D, design, engineering, manufacturing, operations, and so on. Part of the challenge of new products is managing the **interfaces** across the functional areas, as the key functions *must* cooperate often and effectively to improve product development performance.[26] Most new products people can identify with stereotypical complaints such as "Those marketers can't get through the day without a two-hour lunch at the most expensive restaurant in town." And this one: "Ever try to get a scientist to say clearly yes or no?" Or, "Why don't manufacturing people ever admit they goofed up?" These are wildly unfair generalizations. In fact, cross-functional problems are often much less combative than they are sometimes depicted, and people on these interfaces often get along very well.[27] But they do differ on their general time frame, for one thing, and on their measure of success for another. And frictions between functional areas can exist, threatening the project. All participants, including top management, must recognize these frictions and deal with them to minimize any possible negative effects.

Most interface management is straightforward, and experienced managers often know just what to do. Much research has focused on managing the friction between functional areas. The highlights of the research findings can be summed in three statements:

- Top managers get the interfaces they deserve because they can eliminate most of the problems any time they choose to do so.
- Interface management primarily takes time, not skills. One new product manager said he solved his team's problems by giving at least 40 percent of his

---

[24]Rajesh Sethi and Carolyn Y. Nicholson, "Structural and Contextual Correlates of Charged Behavior in Product Development Teams," *Journal of Product Innovation Management*, 18(3), May 2001, pp. 154–168.

[25]For a discussion of the performance appraisal, pay, promotion, organizational culture, team leader, member selection, empowerment, and related topics, see Patricia J. Holahan and Stephen K. Markham, "Factors Affecting Multifunctional Team Effectiveness," in M. Rosenau, A. Griffin, G. Castellion, and N. Anscheutz, *The PDMA Handbook of New Product Development* (New York: John Wiley, 1996).

[26]See Kenneth B. Kahn, "Market Orientation, Interdepartmental Integration, and Product Development Performance," *Journal of Product Innovation Management*, 18(5), September 2001, pp. 314–323.

[27]For evidence that there is general agreement across functional areas, see Roger J. Calantone, C. Anthony Di Benedetto, and Ted Haggblom, "Principles of New Product Management: Exploring the Beliefs of Product Practitioners," *Journal of Product Innovation Management*, 12(3), June 1995, pp. 235–247; and X. Michael Song, Mitzi M. Montoya-Weiss, and Jeffrey B. Schmidt, "Antecedents and Consequences of Cross-Functional Cooperation: A Comparison of R&D, Manufacturing, and Marketing Perspectives," *Journal of Product Innovation Management*, 14(1), January 1997, pp. 35–47.

time to seeing that all key players spent a lot of time with each other, on and off the job.

- Participants who continue to be a problem should be taken out of new product team situations; they get some perverse satisfaction out of reactions to their behavior.

At the most innovative firms, one sees real relationships across functions, and not just structured work assignments. 3M, for example, encourages early, informal communication among marketing, technical, and manufacturing staff (3M employees refer to this as the three-legged stool). Team members bounce ideas off one another and provide resources and information informally to each other. Design of employees' working environment can be used to stimulate cross-functional integration. Many new facilities (such as Hoffman-LaRoche's New Jersey research and marketing facility and Glaxo-Wellcome's lab in the United Kingdom) are designed with coffee bars on every floor to encourage cross-functional shop talk, and workstations can be designed such that they are easy to move (thus facilitating the process of reorganizing into teams). Sony and other Japanese companies rotate their managers through marketing, product development, manufacturing, and finance, thus developing well-rounded managers.[28]

Keep in mind, however, that even with these new approaches to teams, conflicts can still arise. In fact, a little conflict is a good thing. Healthy disagreements between functional areas can lead to more critical analysis and, ultimately, bring vitality to new product development. How conflict is managed, however, is of critical importance. Integrative conflict management styles such as confrontation (collaborative problem solving to reach a mutually agreeable solution) and give-and-take (reaching an acceptable compromise solution) are better at fostering a positive environment for innovation than dysfunctional styles such as withdrawal (avoiding the issue), smoothing (seeking a superficial solution), or forcing a solution (see Figure 12.5).[29] Also, no one functional area should dominate the process.

If marketing, manufacturing, or R&D are viewed as the *de facto* leader, good cross-functional collaboration and better new product performance are unlikely to be facilitated. Equal status seems to work best.[30]

[28]See Eric M. Olson, Rachel Cooper, and Stanley F. Slater, "Design Strategy and Competitive Advantage," *Business Horizons*, 41(2), March–April 1998, pp. 55–61; S. W. F. (Onno) Omta and Jo M. L. van Engelen, "Preparing for the 21st Century," *Research-Technology Management*, 41(1), January–February 1998, pp. 31–35; and Karen Anne Zien and Sheldon A. Buckler, "From Experience: Dreams to Market: Crafting a Culture of Innovation," *Journal of Product Innovation Management*, 14(4), July 1997, pp. 274–287.

[29]David H. Gobeli, Harold F. Koenig, and Iris Bechinger, "Managing Conflict in Software Development Teams: A Multi-Level Analysis," *Journal of Product Innovation Management*, 15(5), September 1998, pp. 423–435; and Barbara Dyer and X. Michael Song, "Innovation Strategy and Sanctioned Conflict: A New Edge in Innovation?" *Journal of Product Innovation Management*, 15(6), November 1998, pp. 505–519.

[30]Kenneth B. Kahn, "Department Status: An Exploratory Investigation of Direct and Indirect Effects on Product Development Performance," *Journal of Product Innovation Management*, 22(6), November 2005, pp. 515–526.

FIGURE 12.5   Five Conflict Management Styles

Conflict Management Style	Definition	Example
Confrontation	Collaboratively solve the problem to reach a solution the parties are committed to.	Debate the issue, conduct customer interviews, generate possible solutions, find the one most supported by customers.
Give and Take	Reach a compromise solution that the parties find acceptable.	Negotiate a set of features to build into the product to keep the project moving ahead.
Withdrawal	Avoid the issue or the disagreeable party.	Team members with unpopular positions don't think it's worth the trouble and back out of the decision.
Smoothing	Minimize the differences and find a superficial solution.	Accommodate to the team members that are strongly committed to certain product features, for the sake of group harmony.
Forcing	Impose a solution.	Project manager steps in and makes the decisions.

Source: Adapted from David H. Gobeli, Harold F. Koenig, and Iris Bechinger, "Managing Conflict in Software Development Teams: A Multi-Level Analysis," *Journal of Product Innovation Management* 14, no. 5, September 1998, pp. 423–435.

Overcoming Barriers to Market Orientation

We still see signs of compartmentalized thinking in many new product developing firms; that is, functional areas tend to focus on their own goals. Information either does not flow across departments efficiently or it is interpreted differently by different departments. This problem should be surmountable by establishing empowered cross-functional teams (discussed in this chapter) and implementing a house of quality procedure for translating customer input to product specifications (as seen in Chapter 10). A related problem that still surfaces is inertia: Market information is not used if it does not conform to specifications. As we have seen in this chapter, it is critical for management to create an environment of mutual trust among employees of all functional areas; higher levels of trust mean that managers will be more open to suggestions that might cause change in "the way things are done." Clearly, while we have seen great improvements in recent years on these issues, the problems remain, and more improvement still needs to be made.[31]

Ongoing Management of the Team

A pressing problem on new product teams is keeping the group enthusiastic. As work goes on, as creative needs are not met, as efforts fail, and as people get tensed up, it is imperative to give what one manager calls pep talks. Burnout is a genuine and not uncommon problem, and the innovation-derailing patterns of behavior that new

[31]Marjorie E. Adams, George S. Day, and Deborah Dougherty, "Enhancing New Product Development Performance: An Organizational Learning Perspective," *Journal of Product Innovation Management*, 15(5), September 1998, pp. 403–423.

products face are almost unbelievable. Some team leaders set up defenses against the well-intentioned suggestions they know will come up—a product variation, a technology that just appeared, or a new advertising approach. Such suggestions are terribly distracting if not kept away from the team.

Another aspect of the team management problem may appear trivial—the ability to run *effective meetings*. New product people seem to be in meetings continuously. Some product innovators have caught on to this need and are now studying their own team meetings for ways to speed them up and improve the decisions.

Changes in team membership over the duration of the project can also cause problems. Losing key people from the team might cause important information to get lost. There is also a *job security* issue. In many firms, climbing the corporate ladder within one's functional area (from junior to senior marketer or researcher, for example) is seen as a more secure road to promotion than is team membership. A clear career path for scientists seems to be especially important. One study showed that among the most innovative firms, there was a "dual ladder" system: Scientists could be promoted into management or choose to stay in the laboratory without financial penalty. At the more poorly performing firms, the common feeling is that "you have to get out of research to get ahead in this company."[32]

Team Compensation and Motivation

A delicate issue in team management is the matter of compensation. Team leaders and team members are usually paid a straight salary or salary plus bonus. Bonuses are equally split among company performance, individual performance, and project accomplishment. It is rare to have compensation ride on the new product's performance.[33] The reasons for this are strong: Employees should be treated equally (fairly), team members do not have the financial risks of an entrepreneur, and it is easier to transfer managers into and out of teams if compensation plans are equal. Still, all agree that finding good people willing to risk career-bypass by serving on a new products team and motivating them to give the necessary high level of effort and stress is a legitimate problem.[34] Firms that use equity awards, such as stock shares and product profit-sharing, tend to be smaller ones located in Silicon Valley.

Many firms use a combination of monetary and nonmonetary rewards (such as prizes, formal recognition, or even permission to work on pet projects on company time) to motivate their teams. According to the CPAS study, the most commonly used rewards are project completion celebrations, the opportunity to work on a bigger and more meaningful project, getting written up in a special newsletter, plaques and pins, and award dinners.[35]

[32]S. W. F. (Onno) Omta and Jo M. L. van Engelen, op. cit.

[33]See Albert Page, op. cit., p. 278.

[34]Hollister B. Sykes, "Incentive Compensation for Corporate Venture Personnel," *Journal of Business Venturing*, 7, 1992, pp. 253–265.

[35]Gloria Barczak, Abbie Griffin, and Kenneth B. Kahn, "Perspective: Trends and Drivers of Success in NPD Practices: Results of the 2003 PDMA Best Practices Study," *Journal of Product Innovation Management*, 26(1), January 2009, pp. 3–23.

Using only monetary rewards can lead to problems. Some may feel that the satisfaction of being on a successful team is reward enough, and the money isn't necessary. Others may complain that all team members get rewarded (even the lazy ones!)—a problem that is compounded if the same dollar figure is awarded to everyone on the team. Some may be resentful if their multimillion-dollar idea was rewarded with only a $1,000 bonus![36]

It has been suggested that firms align their reward structures to characteristics of the project. If the project is relatively long or less complex, rewards tied to the project's profit outcome tend to enhance performance; for risky projects, it is preferable to reward the team's processes during product development (procedures, behaviors, completion of phases in the new products process, and so on). Outcome-based rewards in this latter case may be viewed as too risky or difficult and may be rejected by the project team. Firms can also consider rewarding the team at frequent milestones (much like mountain climbers celebrate getting to the first base, then celebrate again at the summit), as this can help boost team spirit and positively affect organizational culture.[37]

TRW's Cleveland automotive group has instituted Project ELITE (Earnings Leadership in Tomorrow's Environment) to motivate and compensate its teams. In this endeavor, specific goals are set for each team project and also for each individual, and 10 to 25 percent of pay is tied to the accomplishment of these individual and team goals. DuPont uses a "360-degree" review process in which team members are evaluated by peers, subordinates, and supervisors. Motorola is one of many firms that rewards team behavior rather than team results. Motorola recognizes that teams often need to take risks to make progress, and rewarding only results might make them risk-averse. It also makes sense to have one person in charge of the nonmonetary recognition programs, modifying them occasionally to make sure the rewards are always worthwhile.[38]

Closing the Team Down

Strong differences of opinion arise regarding when a new product team should be closed down and the product turned over to the regular organization. Some firms *close out early*, well before the item is marketed; they bring in operating people a little at a time.[39] A second practice lets the team prepare for the marketing (for example, write the plan or train the people), but, at the last minute, the *regular people launch it.*

[36]Perry Pascarella, "Compensating Teams," *Across the Board*, February 1997, pp. 16–22. See also Shikhar Sarin and Vijay Mahajan, "The Effect of Reward Structures on the Performance of Cross-Functional Product Development Teams," *Journal of Marketing*, 65(2), April 2001, pp. 35–53.

[37]Shikhar Sarin and Vijay Mahajan, op. cit., and Erika B. Seamon, "Achieving Growth through an Innovative Culture," in P. Belliveau, A. Griffin, and S. M. Somermeyer, *The PDMA Toolbook 2 for New Product Development* (New York: John Wiley, 2004).

[38]These examples and suggestions are from Pascarella, op. cit., and J. Gregory Kunkel, "Rewarding Product Development Success," *Research-Technology Management*, 40(5), September–October 1997, pp. 29–31.

[39]Charles Heckscher, "The Failure of Participatory Management," *Across the Board*, 54(6), November–December 1995, pp. 16–21. Heckscher notes that permanent or "semi-permanent" teams tend to build walls around themselves, and recommends that teams be abandoned as soon as possible.

When this is done, the key team people are usually kept close to the action to help solve problems. A third, and rarer, practice lets the team actually *market the item* and either become the nucleus of its standing management as a new division or turn it over to the regular organization after it has been successfully established. Honda keeps team leaders as ongoing managers of its new products for two or three major design upgrades (six to nine years) and then reassigns them to a new development program.

No matter when the ongoing staff takes over, they should be brought into the action in a way that lets them link into the new product organization. As one manager put it, "Treat this as a whirling gear being meshed with an idle gear; send a few people into the ongoing organization early, to get the idle gear up to a speed where it can accept the rest of the new operation."

Virtual Teams[40]

Many firms now take advantage of available technology to assemble virtual teams that meet and share information electronically in place of traditional or colocated teams. Virtual teams are a way for firms to take advantage of local expertise and incorporate it into their global new products processes, and also to develop products that could be sold globally. By definition, a **virtual team** is one whose members are linked electronically (via the Internet) to each other and also to partners such as customers, contractors, and the like. The obvious benefit of virtual teams is the ability to communicate despite geographic dispersion. In addition, virtual teams can meet in *synchronous* mode (everyone is on the computer or the phone and communicating at the same time) or in *asynchronous* mode (participants enter the site individually and can come and go as they please). Synchronous methods of communication include video or audioconferencing, instant messaging, live application sharing; e-mail and shared document repositories are examples of asynchronous methods. Both are commonly used; however, asynchronous meetings avoid time zone problems and working around holidays.

A virtual team can be defined in terms of its geographic dispersion, namely, how far apart the members are. But one should also consider configurational dispersion: do all members exist in isolation, connected only virtually? Or is there, say, a central new car development team in Detroit and several other virtual participants who work alone? What about a team in Detroit, a team in Tokyo, and a team in Munich? All of the above are different configurations that suggest different work styles. There is also temporal configuration: what time zones the team members are in, whether their work schedules overlap, and so on. Team leaders should try to work around time zone problems:

---

[40]Much of this section is drawn from Hans J. Thamhain, "Managing Product Development Project Teams," in Kenneth B. Kahn, George Castellion and Abbie Griffin (eds.), *The PDMA Handbook of New Product Development* (New York: John Wiley & Sons, 2005), pp. 127–143; and Mitzi M. Montoya, Anne P. Massey, Yu-Ting Caisy Hung, and C. Brad Crisp, "Can You Hear Me Now? Communication in Virtual Product Development Teams," *Journal of Product Innovation Management*, 26(2), March 2009, pp. 139–155.

for example, the Australian team members should not feel that *every* team meeting is at 2 a.m. local time![41]

Virtual team participants will note that these teams pose their own sets of challenges. Team members must be familiar and comfortable with the technology. Performance measurement and managerial control may be more difficult, and dealing with power conflicts may be more challenging than in a face-to-face format. Further, the whole idea of virtual teams may not fit too well with the values or cultures within many firms, or may not be universally adopted by all team members. Firms with a very hierarchical chain of command or poor teamwork skills in general tend to have difficulties with implementing virtual teams. Because of problems like this, firms often complement virtual teams with at least some traditional team meetings. In fact, research in both the United States and the Netherlands finds that traditional and virtual communication channels complement and strengthen each other, and that firms should explore both colocation and information technology that supports virtual teams, depending on the nature of the knowledge that needs to be shared among members.[42] Nevertheless, experienced virtual team participants admit that the latest communication technologies have put virtual teams on a par with traditional team structures, as long as commitment and trust are maintained.[43]

Although virtual teams can be used whenever there are geographic distances between team members, they really become important in the case of global teams. Given the available technology, team leaders will see virtual teams as a wonderful opportunity to bring in firm expertise residing in research facilities located throughout the world. But the challenge posed by global virtual teams is greater, as they must overcome cultural as well as communication barriers. More on global teams continues in the next section.

Managing Globally Dispersed Teams

More firms than ever are taking a global perspective on new product development and building teams composed of individuals based in different countries. In a survey of product managers, more than half of the responding firms reported using globally dispersed teams (GDTs) for at least some of their new product efforts, and they said that the use of GDTs is expected to continue increasing.[44]

[41]N. S. Lockwood, M. M. Montoya, and A. P. Massey, "Virtual Teams in New Product Development: Characteristics and Challenges," in K. B. Kahn, S. E. Kay, R. J. Slotegraaf, and S. Uban (eds.), *The PDMA Handbook of New Product Development* (Hoboken, NJ: John Wiley, 2013), Ch. 12, p. 196.

[42]Michael Song, Hans Berends, Hans van der Bij, and Mathieu Weggeman, "The Effect of IT and Co-location on Knowledge Dissemination," *Journal of Product Innovation Management*, 24(1), January 2007, pp. 52–68.

[43]See Robert Jones, Robert Oyung, and Lisa Pace, *Working Virtually: Challenges of Virtual Teams* (Hershey, PA: Cybertech Publishing, 2005).

[44]Edward F. McDonough III, Kenneth B. Kahn, and Gloria Barczak, "An Investigation of the Use of Global, Virtual, and Colocated New Product Development Teams," *Journal of Product Innovation Management*, 18(2), March 2001, pp. 110–120. For a good reference on coordinating global R&D efforts, see Yves Doz, Jose Santos, and Peter Williamson, *From Global to Metanational: How Companies Win in the Knowledge Economy* (Boston, MA: Harvard Business School Press, 2001).

It is easy to see why GDTs have increased in prominence. Increasing product complexity and accelerated product life cycles put pressure on new product teams to gather expertise wherever it resides. If Braun, for example, developed a new battery-powered shaver suitable for use in the shower, it would need to gain expertise in materials and components, mechanics, and shaving emulsion that normally would be out of its purview. Additionally, changes to the battery or other components may also be required. Since we now have the capacity to coordinate team activities using computer-driven communication technology, it would be possible for Braun to tap into expertise on these issues even if it resides on other continents![45]

Global new product teams pose special challenges to managers due to communication challenges and cultural differences. Global business meetings are often carried out in English, and while all team members may speak English, their levels of ability may vary considerably. A multicultural, heterogeneous team should, on paper, include people with many diverse perspectives and ways of thinking, which should therefore lead to greater creativity and better problem solving. The downside is that communications breakdowns are likely to be more common, and cultural misunderstandings can occur, so it is up to top management and team leadership to get the desired cross-cultural synergy.[46] One must also consider that global team meetings are usually conducted electronically due to physical distances between team members. Since in-person meetings may be rare, even more communications problems or possibilities for misunderstandings can ensue. Nevertheless, despite these challenges, some research has found that globally dispersed teams may be better than colocated teams in terms of effectiveness and efficiency, so long as they are good at teamwork issues such as good communication, good cohesion, strong effort, and mutual support.[47]

GDTs also have a more difficult task in completing design reviews, as regular meetings in a central location obviously are nearly impossible. GDTs use videoconferencing, audioconferencing, e-mail, and phone to discuss design changes and can also use 3D printing to communicate their ideas three-dimensionally. Many firms operating globally have turned to Visual Issues Management software that allows all participants to visualize the designs in three dimensions, do mark-ups, flag problems, and track changes. Designers, engineers, and other experts can be brought into the new products process at the very earliest phases and easily identify potential problems before

[45]The shaving example is from Roger Leenders, Jan Kratzer, and Jo van Engelen, "Building Creative Virtual New Product Development Teams," in P. Belliveau, A. Griffin, and S. M. Somermeyer (eds.), *The PDMA Toolbook 2 for New Product Development* (New York: John Wiley, 2004), Chapter 5.

[46]Michael Song and Mark E. Parry, "Teamwork Barriers in Japanese High-Technology Firms: The Sociocultural Differences between R&D and Marketing Managers," *Journal of Product Innovation Management*, 14(5), September 1997, pp. 356–367; B. M. Wren, W. E. Souder, and D. Berkowitz, "Market Orientation and New Product Development in Global Industrial Firms," *Industrial Marketing Management*, 29(6), November 2000, pp. 601–611; Preston G. Smith and Emily L. Blanck, "From Experience: Leading Dispersed Teams," *Journal of Product Innovation Management*, 19(4), July 2002, pp. 294–304; and K. Sivakumar and Cheryl Nakata, "Designing New Global Product Teams: Optimizing the Effects of National Culture on New Product Development," *International Marketing Review*, 20(4), 2003, pp. 397–445.

[47]M. Hoegl, H. Ernst, and L. Proserpio, "How Teamwork Matters More as Team Member Dispersion Increases," *Journal of Product Innovation Management*, 24(2), 2007, pp. 156–165.

they become costly to fix. Overall, engineering and reengineering costs are reduced and speed to market is increased using such tools.[48]

There are many examples of virtual GDTs that have successfully overcome these communications difficulties. Boeing used Web-based new product systems to integrate its rocket engine designers and its partner firms scattered across several geographic locations, resulting in enormous reductions in design time, development costs, and the number of component parts. As another example, Xerox uses the Web to integrate the efforts of its product designers in Rochester, New York, its engineers in Shanghai, and its manufacturing plants in Hong Kong.[49] Ford coordinates its worldwide car development efforts through its Global Product Development System and Global Vehicle programs. It employs global platforms in which one group will do exhaust system engineering for all cars worldwide, another for steering column engineering, and so forth, claiming significant engineering cost reductions and more successful new launches, such as the Fusion.[50] Certainly, multinational firms that encourage glob-ally dispersed research and development activities accumulate and use knowledge more effectively, resulting in greater innovative capability. In sum, the most important drivers of successful international new product teams are having an innovative, global culture, committing sufficient resources to R&D, and obtaining the support of top management.[51]

Digital Equipment Corporation had great success with its GDT (which it named the Columbus Team), composed of members from five U.S. locations as well as Switzerland, France, and Japan. It had to put several measures into effect to over-come GDT-related hurdles, however. A major problem was team motivation: The typical team member felt more allegiance to his or her own local network and not to the Columbus Team, and getting agreement on team goals proved difficult. To overcome this problem, Digital allowed team members some say as to the tasks they should perform, so that they would contribute to the team project while at the same time "look good" to others in their local network. To overcome communications barriers, Digital found that team members liked audioconferencing at the start of the project (since casual comments could be made). Computer conferencing and e-mail worked better in later phases when team members were working more at

---

[48]Steve Bashada, "Visual Issues Management: Improving Product Development," *Time Compression*, September–October 2009, pp. 24–25.

[49]Rajesh Sethi, Somendra Pant, and Anju Sethi, "Web-Based Product Development Systems Integra-tion and New Product Outcomes: A Conceptual Framework," *Journal of Product Innovation Man-agement*, 20(1), January 2003, pp. 37–56; and Muammar Ozer, "Using the Internet in New Product Development," *Research-Technology Management*, 46(1), January–February 2003, pp. 10–17.

[50]The Ford example and quote are from Gary S. Vasilash, "Developing More Faster at Ford," *Time Compression*, September–October 2009, pp. 34–35.

[51]See Ajax Persaud, "Enhancing Synergistic Innovative Capability in Multinational Corporations: An Empirical Investigation," *Journal of Product Innovation Management*, 22(5), September 2005, pp. 412–429; and Ulrike de Brentani and Elko J. Kleinschmidt, "Corporate Culture and Commit-ment: Impact on Performance of International New Product Development Programs," *Journal of Product Innovation Management*, 21(5), September 2004, pp. 309–333.

their own pace, and it became increasingly important to retain transcripts of conversations.[52]

Many firms such as Philips, AT&T, and IBM have programs in place that actively support team diversity. Philips uses job rotation in which employees ("expatriates") are sent to foreign locations, often to serve in a different functional area within the company, for an average of five to seven years. The drug company Schering shuttles its technical people between its Berlin and Richmond, Virginia, research centers. Other firms use "visiting researchers," foreign technical specialists who visit R&D headquarters to pick up firm knowledge. Recognizing that hair care varies across countries, the Japanese chemical company Kao uses reciprocal visiting researchers—from Japan to Germany and from Germany to Japan—to develop hair care products. Predevelopment takes place in Tokyo, while development activities are centered in Darmstadt, Germany.[53]

For many firms, GDTs are here to stay since they offer a practical and cost-efficient alternative to relocating employees and research facilities to a central location. GDT members in foreign markets can also provide local expertise for developing new products for their particular markets. So far, GDTs have, in general, not performed as well as domestic teams. This may be partially due to the fact that GDTs are such a new concept for many firms. There is also some new evidence suggesting that GDTs have their own drawbacks: For example, it may be more difficult to discuss or interpret very complex problems using e-mail or a company intranet than by meeting in person. Some researchers are finding that "in-between" teams that offer flexibility in physical proximity and mode of communication are more creative than either in-person teams or totally virtual teams. With greater experience in global team management, however, GDT performance will likely increase.[54]

Summary

This chapter covered issues surrounding the subject of the team: what a team is, the various organization options, setting up a team and managing it through to completion—selecting the leader, selecting the team members, training them, and so forth.

As a closing thought, there are two new types of new product teams emerging on the scene. One is a higher-level, multifunctional group (often heads of the key functions) whose task is to *manage the project teams*. As teams proliferate, they need a reporting home of some type. The other emerging team is a group of experienced new products people whose task is to *assist project teams in developing appropriate processes to follow*. The latter may just be a person with the title *New Products Process Manager*. Process is critical, and a firm needs some place to house the **organization learning** constantly taking place.

[52]Edward F. McDonough III, "Meeting the Challenge of Global Team Management," *Research-Technology Management*, 43(4), July–August 2000, pp. 12–17.

[53]Oliver Gassmann, "Multicultural Teams: Increasing Creativity and Innovation by Diversity," *Creativity and Innovation Management*, 10(2), June 2001, pp. 88–95. A good step-by-step resource for managing dispersed teams is Parviz F. Rad and Ginger Levin, *Achieving Project Management Success Using Virtual Teams* (Ft. Lauderdale, FL: Ross Publishing, 2003).

[54]See Leenders, Kratzer, and van Engelen, op. cit., and McDonough, Kahn, and Barczak, op. cit.

Case: Provo Craft[55]

Provo Craft, located in South Jordan, Utah, has been manufacturing and distributing products and tools for crafters and hobbyists worldwide. Over its history, Provo Craft has been a successful producer of sticker, paper, and stamp products and takes pride in its customer education and customer service efforts designed to inspire creativity. Recently, however, it had shown little corporate growth.

In 2006, a new management team led by CEO Jim Thornton decided to move Provo Craft away from traditional craft products in order to seek opportunity with craft products that incorporated new technology. Thornton knew, however, that at least three major changes would need to take place: a new corporate culture was needed, new talent had to be hired, and a new creative process would have to be instituted.

A cultural shift within the organization proved to be a challenge. For many years, Provo Craft depended on technology developed by outside contractors, and this would have to change. Provo Craft began soliciting customer feedback, scanning changes in the market and in technology, and then designing specific products internally. That is, for the first time, Provo Craft was going to go through the full new products process in-house, from idea generation to design specification, marketing planning, and launch. This required hiring the right people. Typical of the new hires was Jim Colby, senior VP of product development, formerly of Hewlett-Packard. His first mission was to identify the employees most adaptable to the new in-house development program and to complement these with new hires that would share the company's vision and culture. New employees would possess engineering and technology skills, but also understand project management and be passionate about their work.

In addition to a new culture and new people, Provo Craft instituted a new creative process. Colby said that at in-house brainstorming sessions, "we gather great minds together in a room with a whiteboard, plenty of pizza, and a lot of sticky notes. We invite employees from multiple disciples such as marketing, finance, legal, HR, and sales. . . . We spend hours batting around ideas, discussing market needs and competitive positioning." At these meetings, the "mantra is, we never say we can't do it . . . all things are possible; no idea is a bad idea." In addition, employees are motivated by a financial bonus if they develop a product that is ultimately marketed.

Brainstorming sessions are followed by formal market research, which investigates (1) what customers are passionate about, (2) what the best value proposition to offer is, and (3) how the product can be developed so that it is affordable to customers and profitable for the company. Focus groups are used at this stage, following Bill Gates's adage that "your most unhappy customers are your greatest source of learning." Noncustomers as well as customers are included at this stage. This information is complemented by customer blogs and comments gathered on Provo Craft's own Twitter and Facebook pages. As Colby noted, "Social media open a whole new avenue for gathering data directly from your target customer." Provo Craft also meticulously follows protocols to protect intellectual property. Due to legal considerations, Provo Craft does

[55]This case is adapted from Jim Colby, "Provo Craft Develops a True NPD Culture—How A Small Company Succeeded at Innovation," *Visions*, 34(3), 2010, pp. 26–28; and https://home.cricut.com.

not solicit ideas directly from customers. Once promising product concepts are identified, they are placed into a product roadmap that projects five years into the future, and the development phase begins.

In sum, Colby says, developing a new product in-house can be considerably expensive, and for those responsible, it can be a "make-or-break career decision. . . . However, you can certainly eliminate risk by following the right processes and building the right team." He also notes that product innovation is a "continual learning process . . . any time you become complacent in your role, in your people, or in your process, it's probably time for a change."

How successful was Provo Craft? At the time of corporate change, the company's big seller was the Cricut, an electronic cutter with a very loyal fan base. Soon after adopting the new corporate culture, Provo Craft successfully launched several award-winning, innovative new products such as the Gypsy for Cricut (which stores Cricut cartridges, allowing users to take their entire library with them to scrapbooking parties), the Yudu screen-printing machine, the Cricut Cake (a personal electronic cutter that is used to decorate cakes and baked goods using Cricut cartridges), and many others.

Discuss the role of corporate culture at Provo Craft. What were the key changes made in corporate culture that led to the remarkable turnaround in product development? Can you make any recommendations to Mr. Colby to further improve the organizational climate for new products within Provo Craft, based on the material presented in this chapter?

Case: Ford Fusion[56]

By the mid-1980s, Ford and other carmakers were noticing that car requirements in different parts of the world were converging. For example, North American drivers accustomed to larger cars were demanding smaller ones, while many Europeans were looking for somewhat bigger and more comfortable cars with more powerful engines. This trend suggested to Ford the possibility of developing a new car for the global market, using the skills and specializations of its U.S. and European R&D centers. Out of this effort, the Mondeo (known as the Contour in the North American market) was created.

Ford Europe took project leadership for the Mondeo, as the car was more similar to European than to North American Ford models. Ford selected its assembly plant in Gand, Belgium, as the coordination site for the project. Several global working groups addressed specific technical issues. A Program Control Group was assembled consisting of the leaders of the working groups, as well as a Product Committee chaired by Ford Europe's president. A Coordination Group was established to keep the activities of all other groups coordinated. Coordination among groups was facilitated through the Web, videoconferencing, and other means of telecommunication. Suppliers were also global: 47 were European and another 20 were North American–based. The Mondeo

[56]This case is derived from Vittorio Chiesa, "Global R&D Project Management and Organization: A Taxonomy," *Journal of Product Innovation Management*, 17(5), September 2000, pp. 341–359; https://media.ford.com; www.netcarshow.com/ford/2013-fusion; and interviews with Alan Mulally available on YouTube at www.youtube.com/watch?v=oTUjg4b3_zg.

was introduced at the Geneva car exhibition of 1993 and launched in the United States a little over a year later. It was also sold in Japan through a Ford-Mazda joint venture.

Since the Mondeo, their first global car, Ford has continued to refine and upgrade its global car development programs. In fact, Ford attributes much of its recent success to increased efficiencies stemming from its Global Product Development System and Global Vehicle programs. As with car companies worldwide, Ford makes use of global platforms to support multiple brands. But, according to Derrick M. Kuzak, a senior manager of Global Product Development at Ford, the global platform approach is even more all-encompassing. He says, "Think about a product development that allows you to be faster in time to market, depending on the complexity of the vehicle, by 25 to 40 percent. . . .Think about one group doing the engineering on a system for every vehicle globally." Where in the past, each new products project would have its own, say, exhaust engineer, now one group would handle the exhaust system for all cars sold globally on the same platform. This uniformity contributes to what Ford calls "Vehicle DNA." Since steering wheel design and engineering are done by one team and applied across all cars, steering wheels on all Fords will have a distinctive, familiar grip or "feel," regardless of where they were made or sold. This familiarity runs through all components of the car, even down to the same "sound signature" emanating from a Ford I-4 engine. Ford claims to have slashed new car engineering costs by 60 percent between 2005 and 2008, thanks to their global product development efforts, while launching successful new products (including the Ford Fusion) and breathing new life into older models (the F-150 truck).

According to Ford CEO Alan Mulally, Ford management recognized that global wants exist in the car market. Customers from different parts of the world have similar wants with respect to quality, handling, fuel economy, safety, and design, with only a few regional differences; the existence of these similarities potentially provides Ford with competitive advantage. The goal in the development of the Fusion, therefore, was to design a car that would lead in all the important attributes: excellent fuel economy (up to 100 miles per gallon for the plug-in hybrid) while also fun to drive.

The Fusion incorporates several new technologies that improve safety, such as a system that keeps drivers in the correct lane, assists in parallel parking, and senses traffic in the driver's "blind spot." In addition, the SYNC® communications and entertainment system allows a voice-activated link to the car's audio features, and MyFord Touch® permits the driver to interact with various vehicle systems through voice or a touch screen. These features minimize driver distraction and also improve safety. External design focused on a distinctive sleek profile (different from most other similarly sized sedans) communicates simplicity and nimbleness. The Fusion's appearance was felt to be the next step in the evolution of a "global design language" for future development of smaller cars in the global product line. The Fusion's chief engineer, Adrian Whittle, noted that the design objective was to show customers "that Fusion not only delivers a superior visual experience but also feels like quality to the customer."

One interesting challenge in developing the Fusion for the world market was the design of the front-end architecture. The Fusion would need to meet standards that differ by market and sometimes are in conflict. The final design met head-on and offset barrier standards required by North American law while at the same time confirming to European pedestrian protection standards. Extensive computer modeling, as well as

180 crash tests, were conducted to ensure all global standards were met. Overall, Ford engineers targeted top ratings on all safety benchmarks set by all markets in which the Fusion would be sold.

The Fusion is produced at manufacturing facilities in Hermosillo, Mexico, and Flat Rock, Michigan. There are a total of 234 suppliers from 32 countries on five continents. Ford claims to have achieved 80 percent global parts commonality.

CEO Mulally refers to Ford's global collaboration efforts as the "One Ford Culture": building great cars, improving efficiency, while maintaining a customer focus. According to Mulally, this means starting with a commitment to world-class cars and taking advantage of product engineering and management capabilities located around the world. It also means continuous improvement in all aspects of car design that global customers prioritize: fuel efficiency, safety, design, and handling.

Assess Ford's efforts at managing the efforts of its various global teams, and how global car development matured from the days of the Mondeo to the development of the Fusion. What are the strengths and, importantly, the weaknesses of the procedure used in the development of the Fusion? What would you recommend for Ford to do differently, if anything? Could they have used global development teams as described in this chapter to any greater extent? If so, how?

CHAPTER THIRTEEN

Product Use Testing

Setting

The first output of technical development is a prototype, which is checked against the protocol statement that guided its development and perhaps sent it to the marketplace for a confirmatory prototype concept test. The methodology for that is essentially the same as the original concept test, except now we have a more tangible expression of the idea. Usually the end user is not satisfied that the prototype will work, so more development work is done. The cycle continues until the firm has a good approximation of what the eventual product will be—a prototype that stakeholders like.

At this time, most firms like to make up a quantity of prototypes, whether on the bench (i.e., a single working unit of a new remote control, made by designers) or in some small-scale pilot production setup. And for the first time, they can give the end user a product concept that is in a *form for extended use*—no more guessing about whether it *would* or *might* satisfy the needs, based on internal laboratory, or bench, testing. Our task is to devise a method for testing the end-users' experience with the new item, and we call the activity **product use testing** or *field testing*, or *user testing*. Sometimes it is called **market acceptance testing**, though this term may also mean *market* testing, as in Chapter 16. Product use testing is the topic of this chapter.

We begin the chapter with a statement on the role of marketing through Phase IV, development. Though the actual designing of the prototypes may be out of the marketer's hands, marketing makes important contributions throughout this phase, and its contributions accelerate rapidly as we near the end of Phase IV and approach Phase V, launch. With this in mind, we then explore the process of product use testing in detail.

The importance of product use testing is clear, as it shows up in several of the key concepts driving the whole new product process—the *unique superior product*, the *repeat buying percentage* in the A-T-A-R paradigm, and the *requirements in the protocol*. A product that does not meet end-user needs fails on one of the three key causes of failure.

One other reminder: This chapter applies equally to services and to goods. On the www.baddesigns.com Web site are many examples of poor signage marking roads, highways, parking lots, and the like. It is almost a certainty that these poor signs had not been tested for clarity.

The Role of Marketing During Development

Marketing Is Involved from the Beginning of the Process

The role of the marketing personnel changes and accelerates as the product nears the end of the development phase and moves closer to launch. Years ago, when firms were still predominantly practicing the "selling concept" (i.e., "we sell what we make"), the role of marketing was simple: to sell the products that the firm makes. Marketing didn't really need to get involved in product development until technical personnel had basically done their job. With all this discussion of teams and speed to market, it is clear most firms aren't following this concept any more—or can't, if they want to stay competitive. Marketing people are now involved from the very beginning of the new products process. Throughout the process, they advise the new products team about how the product development under way fits in with the firm's marketing capabilities (such as sales and sales training, service availability, distribution strengths, etc.) and the market's needs. By early involvement, they can help the product succeed, as they represent the issues and concerns having to do with the marketing of the product.

It is too easy to say that marketing's role is to gather information from the marketplace. Too often, that means that marketing plays a gatekeeper role, funneling information from the marketplace to the new product team that it thinks is important and possibly missing out on other, more critical information in doing so. The whole team needs to focus on the marketplace, not just marketing. All team members, be they technical personnel, design engineers, or marketing, can gather information. Indeed, the whole idea behind lead user analysis (see Chapter 4) is that key customers are part of the team itself and provide information directly. A really market-oriented firm thinks of marketing's task not as information *gathering*, but as information *coordination*—deciding what information the various sources have (customers, lead users, distributors, etc.) and what information the members of the new products team need.

A good illustration is provided by DuPont's development in the 1960s of an unusual ethylene polymer named Surlyn.[1] It was originally a totally technology-driven product with apparently interesting properties: It was strong, resilient, clear, and bouncy. It was envisioned, among other things, as a coating for golf balls—and, after much initial resistance from the golf ball manufacturers, was eventually adopted as the replacement for rubber-based ballata golf ball covers. Marketing eventually found out that there was a bigger market out there that was very interested in Surlyn—but not for the attributes originally thought to be most important. Surlyn, as it turned out, has exceptional oil- and grease-resistance properties that made it an excellent sealer for the meat packing industry. Further applications were found over the years: as an adhesive for juice boxes and an extrusion coating for paper. As more market information was gathered, the scientists were able to modify the process and develop related polymers for other applications, such as bowling pins and ski boots. Clearly, the original technology-push innovation had done an about-face, and market needs were now driving further technical development.

[1] Parry M. Norling and Robert J. Statz, "How Discontinuous Innovation Really Happens," *Research-Technology Management*, 41(3), May–June 1998, pp. 41–44.

Manufacturing's role has similarly evolved over the years. They also are involved in the new products process from the beginning, advising the team on the manufacturability of the product under consideration. Like marketing, manufacturing understands the need to be involved early and resents being left out of the early phases of the process. The Hewlett-Packard (HP) DeskJet printer, for example, represented a new direction for HP: new products, markets, and customers, and a new product development process. Manufacturing got involved in the process at the very beginning. In fact, manufacturing engineers were moved to the R&D site and used as a resource by the design engineers throughout. The process went so well, designers lobbied to get even more manufacturing engineers! As a result of this project, manufacturing engineers increased in status within HP.[2]

Marketing Ramp-Up, or the "I Think We've Got It" Phase

While they make contributions to the process throughout, the roles of both marketing and manufacturing change as the process moves along. Often, an important turning point occurs when the early prototypes are made and are passing performance tests. A new pharmaceutical to combat hypertension, for example, may be showing promising results in early animal testing. We might call this point the "I think we've got it" phase, and it is here that the team's whole attitude toward the project changes. Up to this point, the technical people on the team played the predominant role, with marketing and manufacturing acting more in an advisory capacity. Now, however, marketing's role increases, as marketing people have to crank up their operations. They have to begin planning field sales and service availability for the product, investigating packaging and branding options, bringing in the advertising agency representatives, and so on. In short, the "I think we've got it" phase is where marketing's work for launch begins.[3]

It's also where manufacturing's responsibilities pick up. In new product development, we often hear of "manufacturing ramp-up"—the point at which manufacturing personnel plan the full-scale production of the product (which up until now has just been manufactured in small quantities, sufficient for prototype evaluation). Just like manufacturing ramps up from prototypes to full production, marketing can be said to ramp up for product launch—and marketing ramp-up begins here.

Why Do Product Use Testing?

Once the prototype is ready, marketing begins an important part of the ramp-up process: assessing the physical prototype among real customers. Note: As we saw previously in Chapter 3, a prototype could be in a crude, early form or could be a finished

---

[2]Dorothy Leonard-Barton, H. Kent Bowen, Kim B. Clark, Charles A. Holloway, and Steven C. Wheelwright, "How to Integrate Work and Deepen Expertise," *Harvard Business Review*, September–October 1994, pp. 121–130.

[3]See discussion of the relative workloads of the marketing and technical personnel as the product moves from development to launch in Behnam Tabrizi and Rick Walleigh, "Defining Next-Generation Products: An Inside Look," *Harvard Business Review*, November–December 1997, pp. 116–124.

or nearly finished product. **Use testing** means testing the prototype under normal operating conditions. Consumers put a tire on a car and drive it; technicians put notebook computers in the hands of warehouse personnel; a bank installs a new check cashing service at three branch points, and so on. Makers of a building-block set for children will put kids in a focus group room and watch how they play with the set (Do they like it? Do they follow the instructions or use their imagination? Do they get tired of it quickly?), while at the same time the parents are surveyed regarding price points (Would you pay $70 for a set with 100 pieces, or $50 for a set with 75 pieces?). The product will probably not be perfect at this time, for more reasons than poor design. An example of *manufacturing* difficulties came from Weyerhaeuser. Their Ultra Softs disposable diapers worked very well, and sold at a discount price. But the pilot plant was a poor predictor of full-scale production. There were production line fires and other breakdowns, and suppliers refused to sign long-term contracts on the key diaper liner.[4] Testing should continue until the team is satisfied that the new product does indeed solve the problem or fill the need that was expressed in the original protocol.

Is Product Use Testing Really Necessary?

Here is a composite statement of what we commonly hear at product use testing time:

> "We've been working on this thing for months (or years), and we've spent a ton of money on it. Experts were called as needed. Market research showed that end users would want a product like this. Why dally around any longer? Top management is leaning on us for the revenues we promised, and we continue to hear that a key competitor is working on something similar. Look, we're now in an up mode; stopping to test suggests to management that we don't have faith in what we've been doing. Besides, customers can't just take the new item and try it fairly; they have to learn how to use it, then work it into their system, listen to our ads (or reps) advising them what to do and how good the results are. Worst of all, a competitor can get his hands on our creation and beat us to the market! No, it's just not worth the time and money to do extended use testing."

Now, sometimes that statement is a fact, not an argument. For example, the first picture telephone probably could not be use-tested by end users—there was no network of others with whom to use the phone. (Of course, virtual picture phones are available to everyone now through Skype, FaceTime, and so on.) Same for the first color TV, when there were no programs being broadcast in color. How could the Internet have been use-tested, or Facebook? Hopefully, it won't be as bad a situation as that in a well-known cartoon, where one lab scientist holds up a flask and says to another scientist, "It may well bring about immortality, but it will take forever to test it."

Are These Arguments Correct?

These arguments are persuasive, especially when put forth by the person on the top floor who has funded the work to date. But, except for very rare cases such as with the

---

[4]Alecia Swasy, "Diaper's Failure Shows How Poor Plans, Unexpected Woes Can Kill New Products," *The Wall Street Journal*, October 9, 1990, p. B1.

FIGURE 13.1
Variable Gains and Losses from Program of Product Use Testing

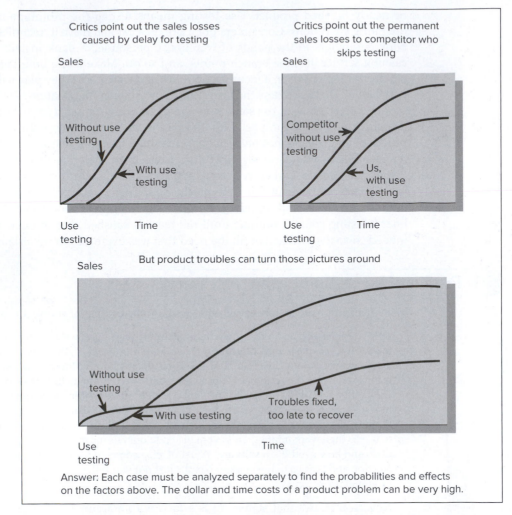

Critics point out the sales losses caused by delay for testing

Sales

Without use testing

With use testing

Use testing   Time

Critics point out the permanent sales losses to competitor who skips testing

Sales

Competitor without use testing

Us, with use testing

Use testing   Time

But product troubles can turn those pictures around

Sales

Without use testing

With use testing

Troubles fixed, too late to recover

Use testing   Time

Answer: Each case must be analyzed separately to find the probabilities and effects on the factors above. The dollar and time costs of a product problem can be very high.

picture phone, they are incorrect. What we have is an unknown, with much still to be learned. The user whose problem started the project still hasn't told us that our product *solves* that problem.

Even more, the risks and costs of use testing are usually small compared to the loss of the earnings flow from a successful product (see Figure 13.1). About the only argument that really carries weight is the competitive one, and then only when our new product can be copied and marketed, fast. Many food products are like this, as are other items where there is no technical accomplishment involved. If use testing clearly makes us second (or even third) into the market, most firms will opt for immediate marketing—without use testing. And, of course, they expect to fail often. Food products suffer an 80–90 percent failure rate, based on the minor improvements they offer, the small retail availability such products can get, and the fickleness of consumers who apparently cannot predict their behavior in a concept test.

But, even in consumer packaged-goods industries, there should be more serious consideration of the counter arguments *for* use testing. They include the following.

Assessing Competitive Reaction

A firm developing new items is well advised to build its innovation on a technology base where it has some insulation from competitive copying (see the strategy discussions in Chapter 3). Second, competitors today are finding that copying someone else has small gains—others will copy *them*, price competition will take the profits away, the imitator usually copies the innovator's mistakes too, and the competitors we must worry about most are themselves involved in technology-based developments that cannot be thrown over on short notice.

The Complexity of Customer Needs

In almost every industry, there is no one, simple, end-user need. Any new item foists onto the end user a learning curve. There are trade-offs, and there is "baggage"—things that came with the new item that often surprise even the developer. For example, imagine you were working for GTE Airfone, the technology that permits phone calls to go from ground to seated individuals on airborne planes. Though at first it seems that airlines would be interested in this product, adoption was extremely slow. It turns out that many fliers just don't want to be disturbed during their rare quiet times. And nearby passengers don't think much of the idea either. End use is indeed complex, and there is no way it can be simulated in laboratories, where use is isolated from user mistakes, competitive trashing of the concept, and objections by those in the user firm or family whose work or life is disrupted by the change. In addition, for new-to-the-world products, several product use tests may be needed for a company to get it right— what is important is that the company learns from its errors.

Customers' Communication of Their Needs

End users also often have trouble communicating their wants and their satisfactions, short of having the finished item or at least a realistic prototype. Research on smartphone users may indicate they are looking for a thinner phone with a bigger screen. When presented with a prototype of a new, ultrathin, six-inch-wide phone, however, they will likely say this is not what they really wanted! The phone is too wide to put in one's pocket, and so thin that it bends or cracks easily. Plus, the ultrathin design might have required other trade-offs (such as use of a different battery pack that requires recharging every two hours) that would be unacceptable to the user. A product use test would help identify what the customer really needs and avoid R&D work on the wrong attributes.

iRobot, manufacturer of the Roomba robotic vacuum, conducted product use testing in early 2017 prior to launch of their Roomba Series 900. The Series 900 marked a significant improvement over the basic Roomba in that it could draw a map of the targeted floor and thereby could clean more effectively. The beta version of the new model was introduced with limited availability, and purchasers had to apply to participate in the beta test. The beta test allowed iRobot to determine whether the mapping feature or other advanced features were interesting to potential consumers and to focus R&D efforts and make adjustments where necessary, before bringing the new series to market.[5]

Assurance of Delivery of a Quality Product

Recall the idea of the augmented product—where there is a core benefit, then a formal product, and then the many augmentations of service, warranty, image, financing, and so on. The new products process tends to focus on the core benefit and the formal product, and even that may have implementation problems. But firms often just *assume* they will be able to deliver the outer ring of augmented product quality—the sales force will be able to explain the new item well; early product breakdowns will not chase other potential buyers away; the finance division will approve generous financing arrangements; the advertising effectively answers competitors' claims; and warehouse personnel won't make a simple mistake and destroy half the product. These things do happen.

To bypass product use testing is a gamble that should be considered only when there is just cause. The burden of proof is on whoever argues for skipping this important step. If, in fact, thorough product use testing cannot be done, try at least to work some product use testing into the early marketing of the product (e.g., in the rollout method discussed in Chapter 16) and try to have some alternatives ready to switch to as a hedge against negative outcomes.

Knowledge Gained from Product Use Testing

As can be seen from the preceding examples, there is ample opportunity for the firm to learn from product use testing and to use the knowledge gained to make the product more suitable to the desired market. Figure 13.2 shows the key pieces of knowledge that use tests provide.

Pre-Use Sense Reactions

Almost every product gives the user a chance to react to immediate sensations of color, speed, durability, mechanical suitability, and so on. Initial reactions are important, especially on service products. For example, car manufacturers know that the most important single reaction of a potential new car buyer is the impression upon first entering a dealership. In the marketing of a new car, for example, the dealership may be designed deliberately to create a good impression; follow-up research can determined if the desired positive impression was attained.

Early Use Experiences

This is "does it work" knowledge. Key specifics are such things as ease of use, surface variables, can they manage it, are there still bugs, and is there any evidence of what the item will eventually do.

---

[5]Evan Ackerman, "iRobot Launches Beta Program to Test Smarter Home Features for Roombas," *IEEE Spectrum*, January 3, 2018.

FIGURE 13.2
Set of New
Knowledge
from Product
Use Tests

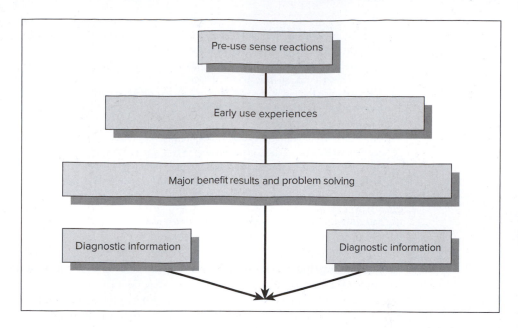

Alpha and Beta Tests

This latter point is a special problem. Computer hardware and software firms, for example, are under great competitive pressure and prefer to run **beta tests**. These are short-term use tests, at selected external customer sites, sometimes preceded by internal **alpha tests** with employees. These are designed to tell the manufacturers one thing: Does this product work, free of bugs? In fact, some have their people competing to see who can find the most bugs in a new item—better now than later.[6] Beta tests are not designed to tell them about meeting customer needs and solving problems—such testing takes longer than the few weeks usually allowed on computer products.

The term *beta testing*, originally used in the software industry, is now frequently heard in all sorts of other settings, though computer firms still seem to be the leaders at beta testing. Beta testing provides several important benefits to developers (of software, or products in general). Most obviously, any bugs would be quickly identified by users and fixed to their satisfaction. In addition, good beta testing ensures that only a high-quality product will reach stores. Beta testing can also assess the usability and performance of the product. For example, a new software application may work properly on Apple phones but not on Samsung phones. Despite extensive internal development, only extensive beta testing with real users will identify this kind of problem. Beta testing can also identify features that the beta testers thought were missing or could be improved, so be sure to ask for feature requests and feature improvements.

---

[6]Douglas W. Clark, "Bugs Are Good: A Problem-Oriented Approach to the Management of Design Engineering," *Research-Technology Management*, 43(3), May–June 1990, pp. 23–27.

FIGURE 13.3
Common Pitfalls of Beta Testing

- Beta test site firm has no internal capacity to test the performance of the product at the required level and lacks the funding to hire an outside firm to do the test.
- Developer puts in a wishy-washy performance requirement like "user-friendly," which is meaningless unless a measurable specification is defined.
- Testing is done too late in the new product process, which almost ensures that development time will be extended and production delays will occur. Doing testing in increments throughout the process is a way to avoid this pitfall.
- Developers attempt to bypass beta testing, relying only on alpha testing of their own products. By definition they are too close to the product to critically test it and find problems.
- Developers ignore early negative results, hoping that the product will improve by itself during the new product process. All beta test results, whether positive or negative, need to be honestly evaluated.

Source: From Robert Stoy, "Assembled Product Development," in M. D. Rosenau, A. Griffin, G. Castellion, and N. Anscheutz, eds., *The PDMA Handbook of New Product Development*, John Wiley & Sons, Inc., 1996, pp. 271–286.

Finally, beta testing can help build brand awareness and, if successful, generate anticipation for the finalized product.[7]

There are other concerns regarding beta test implementation. If done too late in the new products process, design may already be essentially fixed—or, if design changes are required, they may delay the launch. But if a beta version of a new computer program is released before major bugs are worked out, the lukewarm results may get picked up in the popular computer press, damaging the product's reputation. Further, the firm testing the new product may need to obtain information from the beta test site customer (such as economic value), which might strain the supplier-customer relationship. Figure 13.3 summarizes the more common pitfalls of beta testing.[8]

Gamma Testing

Beta testing may not meet all of the developer's needs. In a beta test, users may not have had time to judge whether the new product met their needs or was cost-effective for them. A new phone may work beautifully in field testing, but once it has been launched it may become clear that the batteries are faulty and drain too quickly under normal use conditions. As a result, a third term is becoming popular, **gamma testing** (gamma being the third Greek letter after alpha and beta). It designates the ideal product use test, where the item is put through its paces and thoroughly evaluated by the end user. To pass this test, the new item must solve whatever problem the customer had, no matter how long it takes. Gamma testing is so critical on new medicines and medical equipment that the United States demands it; such testing can take up to 10 years.

Even though gamma testing is the ideal test (and is urged here), firms anxious to save time and money or to leapfrog competitors nevertheless opt to go with beta

[7]Anonymous, "6 Key Steps to Follow for Beta Testing Your Products," https://hackernoon.com/6-key-steps-to-follow-for-beta-testing-your-products-cba0e71fc497, Nov. 26, 2017.

[8]Beta testing is a complex subject. One very helpful study is Robert J. Dolan and John M. Matthews, "Maximizing the Utility of Consumer Product Testing: Beta Test Design and Management," *Journal of Product Innovation Management*, 10(4), September 1993, pp. 318–330. For a full discussion of the benefits and risks of beta testing, see Robert Dolan, *Managing the New Product Development Process* (Reading, MA: Addison-Wesley, 1993), pp. 221–232.

testing. Some virtually have to—carmakers, for example. New car models are typically beta-tested by market users who drive them on a prepared track, dealers who drive them on the carmaker's proving grounds, and automotive magazine writers and test drivers. But testing is generally not conducted over a time period long enough to really judge whether the new car actually meets family needs.

Diagnostic Information

New products managers are looking for how items are used and what mistakes are made. Use tests often suggest ways to improve performance or to reduce cost. General Foods carried to the very last test the issue of the relative proportions of instant coffee and roasted grains for Mello Roast; it needed the best trade-off between the lower cost of the grains and the effect on flavor. New product developers also seek specific pieces of information needed to back up their claims. Marketers want confirmation of target markets and product positionings. Product integrity is also on trial during a use test since only the users' perceptions tell us whether the parts tie together into a meaningful whole and whether the product fits the application. Lastly, developers are watching for any other red flag, a signal that users had some problems understanding the new item or were slow to accept the results they got, and so on.

Apple and other software manufacturers may use *case-based research* as a very comprehensive form of product use testing that runs parallel to the software's development process, from early concept to finished product. The first stage is *investigation*: The developer interviews users to learn their expectations and how they will likely use the product. In the *development* stage, users are encouraged to try early prototypes of the new software and explore its menus and features. As an interesting twist, they speak out loud during product use, describing any problems they encounter. This stage is followed by a preliminary beta test with end users in a real work environment. Product use problems are identified at this stage, and solutions to all of these will be provided in the software instruction manual. This is all followed by a standard beta test.[9]

Decisions in Product Use Testing

Any product use test, whether one of several or alone, whether industrial or consumer, whether for the domestic or global marketplace, should be crafted carefully, and several key decisions must be made. First and foremost, managers should decide what it is they *need to learn* from the product use test. Though what we need to learn is totally situation specific, the objectives should still be clear and should include the requirements spelled out in the protocol. (See Chapter 10.) Some managers like to do what is often called a *potential problem analysis* at this point. The remainder of this section examines other key questions faced in product use testing.

Who Should Be in the User Group?

Some use testing is done with *lab personnel* at the plants where the products are first produced. Alexander Graham Bell became the first telephone user when he called his assistant.

[9]Matthew Holloway, "A Better Way to Test Interface Design," *Innovation*, Summer 1994, pp. 25–27.

Experts are the second testing group (e.g., the cooking staff in a test kitchen). Car companies have styling professionals; wine and coffee companies have tasters. Experts will give more careful consideration than will typical users and probably will express more accurate reactions. They will not be interested in the same things that interest customers, however.

The third test group option, *employees*, is widely utilized though often criticized. Company loyalties and pressures and employees' lifestyles and customs may distort opinions and attitudes. Obvious problems of possible bias can be overcome to some extent by concealing product identities and by carefully training and motivating the employee panel.

Stakeholders are the next choice, and the set includes customers and noncustomers, users and nonusers, resellers, end-user advisers (such as architects), users of competitive products, repair organizations, and technical support specialists whose reactions to new products have been sought.

Market researchers doing the use testing are very careful to pick the right number of stakeholders. Sample size may vary from 3 to 6 on experts, 30 or more for employees, and from 20 to several thousand for end users. As one might expect, sample size is primarily a function of what is being tested. Any sample should be representative of the entire population for which the product is targeted and the results should be accurate (have *validity*) and reproducible (have *reliability*). A hair products firm marketed a new hair tonic for men after use testing, and it flopped, primarily because it was tested in humid areas of the country. In drier areas, the product evaporated too quickly to do the user any good.

No matter who you choose as your beta testers, be sure they sign nondisclosure agreements. Secrecy is an important part of a beta test, and it is important to choose testers who can be trusted not to reveal competitive information (and also to carry out the beta test responsibilities on time).[10]

How Should We Reach the User Group?

There are several options here. First, we must decide on mode of contact: *Mail* and *personal* are the most common. The mail method is more limited than personal contact in type of product and depth of questioning, but it is more flexible, faster, and cheaper. Burlington Industries used the telephone to ask people to serve on special one-time mail panels that evaluated new fabrics. Business-to-business firms often insist on personal contact, since they need a closeness far beyond that on most consumer products.

Second, there is a choice between *individual* contact and *group* contact. Most firms prefer individual contact, especially at this critical point in the development cycle, but it may be cheaper to deal with groups.

Third, the individual mode of contact brings up the question of *location*. Should the test be conducted at the *point of use* (home, office, or factory), or should it be conducted at a *central location* (test kitchen, shopping center, theater, or van)? The point-of-use location is more realistic and permits more variables to operate. But it offers poor experimental control and permits easy misuse. In contrast, the central location offers very complete facilities (such as kitchens, two-way mirrors, eating areas, pseudo stores), good experimental control, speed, and lower cost. The central location

---

[10]Anonymous, "6 Key Steps to Follow for Beta Testing Your Products," op. cit.

approach is winning, but industrial firms will almost certainly stay with on-site studies. Sometimes one can be creative—TV networks sometimes test new pilot programs in Las Vegas, not at all representative, but oddly, a place where a wide range of people have the time and desire to look at pilots between time spent at the slot machines and blackjack tables. Other possible central locations for product use testing include marketing research firm facilities, trade shows, highway rest stops (same principle as Las Vegas: one can meet a wide variety of people), and even factory tours, such as at Ben & Jerry's Vermont headquarters.

Should We Disclose Our Identity?

A key issue, **identity disclosure**, concerns how much the user should be told about the brand or maker identity of the product. Some testers prefer open disclosure, while others (the majority) prefer to keep it secret. It may be that the brand cannot be hidden—as with many cars, some shoes, and many business products. People have perceptions about various firms and brands. Knowing a new item's brand introduces halo-image effects, maybe distorting user reactions. It helps to think about what is being tested. Developers may need a competitive comparison (only **blind tests** can determine this). Or they may want to know if users *perceive* the new item to be better (honest perception requires brands). A good compromise is to do both, first a blind test, followed by a branded test. This covers most of the issues. Service products can rarely be tested blind.

How Much Explanation Should We Provide?

Some people conduct use tests with virtually *no comment* other than the obvious "Try this." But such tests run the risk of missing some of the specific testing needs. A second degree of explanation, called *commercial*, includes just the information the customer will get when actually buying the product later. The third level is *full explanation*. It may be necessary to include a great deal of information just to ensure the product is used properly; a drug company may give its salespeople weeks of training in the use test for a new treatment. Some people do one round of testing with full explanation, followed by a brief round at the commercial level.

How Much Control over Product Use Should There Be?

Most new medicines can be tested legally only under the control of physicians. This *total control* is essential when accurate data are required and when patient safety is a concern. Many industrial products also require total control to avoid dangerous misuse.

But most testers want users to experiment, to be free to make some mistakes, and to engage in behavior representative of what will happen later when the product is marketed. For example, a new blend of coffee may be tested under conditions of perfect water, perfect measuring, and perfect perking, but it should also be tested in the kitchen the way the average person will do it—right or wrong.[11] By providing this kind

[11]It has been said that one of the best ways to mislead product planners is to establish exacting controls in product use tests that won't be duplicated in the real world. See Robert J. Lavidge, "Nine Tested Ways to Mislead Product Planners," *Journal of Product Innovation Management*, 1(2), 1984, pp. 101–105.

FIGURE 13.4   Types of Product Use Tests, as Applied to a New Toothbrush

Type	Products	Instructions
Monadic	The new product alone.	Try this new toothbrush, and tell me how you like it.
Sequential monadic	Back-to-back monadic tests.	Same as on monadic
Paired comparison*	The new product and another toothbrush (1)—the market leader or (2) one known to be the best or (3) the leader in the segment selected for the new product or (4) the one currently used by the testee.	Try these, and tell me how you like them, which you prefer, etc.
Triangular comparison*	The new product and two of the others. A variation is to use two variants of the new product and one of the others.	Same as on paired comparison.

*These multiple-product techniques can employ either of two product use approaches:
Side-by-side: Please brush your teeth with this toothbrush, and then brush again with the other one. Then give me your reactions.
Staggered (often called a sequential monadic): Please use this toothbrush for a week, and then switch to the other for a week. Then give me your reactions.

of freedom, the company can see how the product is likely to be misused. If Heublein had extensively product-use-tested its 1970s-era Wine & Dine meals (pasta, sauce mix, and a bottle of cooking wine containing salt and spices, all in a box), they would have identified a problem that hit them in the marketplace instead: Many customers just drank the salted wine, gagged, and vowed never to buy the product again![12]

So two modes of looser control—*supervised* and *unsupervised*—have developed. If a conveyor belt manufacturer wants to test a new type of belting material, the manufacturer's technical and sales personnel (maybe even their vendor's people) will be at the user's plant when the material is installed (supervised mode). After early runs indicate there are no mistakes, the belting people go back home, and the material is left to run in an unsupervised mode for the full testing period (though developer personnel are never "very far away").

Services are almost always under some supervision because they cannot be "taken home" to use. Often, restaurants test new menus in a few locations (supervised mode) and then roll them out if everything works well.

How Should the Test Be Conducted?

The product may be tested in many combinations, but four ways are standard (see Figure 13.4):

- In a **monadic** test, where the respondent tests a single product for a period of time. Services usually must be monadic, though there are exceptions.
- In a **sequential monadic** test, where there are back-to-back monadic tests with the same respondent. It is sometimes called a *staggered paired comparison*.

---

[12]Robert M. McMath and Thom Forbes, *What Were They Thinking?* (New York: Times Business, 1996).

- In a **paired comparison,** where use of the test product is interspersed with that of a competitive product.
- In a **triangular comparison**, similar to paired comparison but with two competitive products versus one test product (or two test products versus one competitor).

More sophisticated experimental designs exist, but they are only used in special situations.[13] The monadic test is the simplest; it represents normal usage of products. It is probably also the most *valid* of these tests (that is, it most closely represents normal product usage). But it is less *sensitive* in results (that is, changes in price or other attributes affect customer preferences markedly). The usual *side-by-side* or simultaneous form of paired comparison is the most unrealistic test, but it is by far the most sensitive. A *sequential monadic* is probably the ideal combination, though it takes longer. In the staggered format, a user may try out a toothbrush for one week, then change to another for the second week, then go back to the first one.

Even monadic tests usually involve a silent competitor—the product being used before the new one appeared. When an established category (such as photocopiers) is involved, then it is almost a must to test a new product against the category leader. But in the absence of an established category, as was the case with the first fax machine or the first PDA, what does the developer do? The first cell phone should have been tested against traditional landline phones, for example. If there is no direct predecessor, product developers usually just run a monadic test and then ask the user to compare the new product with whatever procedure was being followed before.

Over What Time Period Should the Test Be Conducted?

Some use tests require a *single* product experience (this may be all that is needed for a taste test); some require use over *short periods* of up to a week; and some require use over *extended periods* of up to six months. The longer period is needed if substantial learning is required (a shift in a paradigm), if initial bias must be overcome, or if the product entails an acquired taste. A longer period is also needed if the product faces a full range of variations in use (for example, a new smartphone may find application by final consumers, small business owners, multinationals, and hospitals or other institutions). Again, researchers opt more often to use several modes. The initial, quick test predicts the early reactions of those people we call innovators. Failure here, even if perceptions are unjustified, often dooms a good product. On the other hand, favorable initial impressions must be sustained well past the novelty stage. Many products have flared briefly before sputtering to an early death.

Tests over a month long are rare on consumer products and difficult to defend to management. But if a new piece of business equipment will be positioned on its cost-cutting advantage, the use test had better run long enough for the user to see a significant cost reduction. Incidentally, those long tests of paint panels in the fields along highways are lab tests, not use tests. There is no testing of user carelessness in application, thick versus thin paint coatings, and the many other variations one gets in a true

---

[13]For added information on such matters as experimental designs, sequencing of stimuli, and sample design, see Howard R. Moscowitz, *Product Testing and Sensory Evaluation of Foods* (Westport, CT: Food and Nutrition Press, 1983).

home use test. Apple gets closer when they test a new device with common indignities such as spilled soda and simulated bouncing in a car trunk. But again, this is not true use testing, where customers can think of far more creative ways to destroy a product (such as in the anecdote about the computer user who was using the pop-out CD drive as a coffee cup holder).

What Should Be the Source of the Product Being Tested?

Generally speaking, three different sources of the product are employed in a use test—*batch, pilot plant,* and *final production*. If the firm will employ just one type of use testing, then the final production material is far and away the best. Batch product should be used alone only if the production process is prohibitively expensive.

As with many other phases of product development, the decision on source of product is a trade-off between the cost and the value of information. Being penny-wise at this point has proven over and over to be pound-foolish.

Often overlooked is the product left in the hands of users at the end of the test. In most cases, the product should be collected and examined for clues about user problems and actions during the test. If a patent application will follow soon, it is very important to pick up *all* of the product; otherwise, developers risk losing the originality requirement of the patenting process.

What Should Be the Form of the Product Being Tested?

One view favors testing the *best single product* the organization has developed, as identified by concept tests or market analyses. The opposing view favors building *variants* into the test situation—colors, speeds, sizes, and so on. The latter approach is more educational but also much more costly. Services are almost always tested in multiple variations, given that it is usually easy to make the changes. The decision rests on several factors—the first being how likely the lead variant is to fail. No one wants to elaborately test one form of the product and then have that form fail.

Further, what effect will added variants have on users' understanding of the test? The more they test, the more they understand, and the more they can tell us. For example, a maker of aseptic packaging for fruit juices realized the juice and the package were both new to consumers, so the firm tested orange juice in the new package first and subsequently tested the new apple and cranberry juices. (Incidentally, the firm shipped the orange juice to its European factory for packaging so that it would spend the same time in the box as did the apple and cranberry juices.[14])

How Should We Record Respondents' Reactions?

Essentially, three options are available, as demonstrated by Figure 13.5. First, a five- or seven-point verbal rating scale is generally used to record basic *like/dislike* data. Second, the respondent is usually asked to compare the new product with another product, say, the leader or the one currently being used, or both; this is a *preference score.*

---

[14]Regardless of what the form is, the test product should be representative of the product that will actually be launched—not of significantly higher or lower quality (yes, this happens!). This is another of Lavidge's ways to mislead product planners. See Robert Lavidge, op. cit.

FIGURE 13.5
Data Formats for Product Use Tests

Like/Dislike

Product A:

	1	2	3	4	5
	Dislike strongly	Dislike some	Neutral	Like some	Like very much

Test product:

Which of these words best describes your overall satisfaction with the test product? (circle one)

    Happy   Contented   So-so   Unhappy   Angry

Preference

What was your preference between the two products?
- ☐ Much prefer C
- ☐ Somewhat prefer C
- ☐ Don't care either way
- ☐ Somewhat prefer M
- ☐ Much prefer M

Descriptive/Diagnostic

For each attribute below, please check your feelings about the test product:

Tastes great |——|——|——|——|——|——| Tastes awful

On which of the following applications would you want to use the new material?

- ☐ Floors
- ☐ Ceilings
- ☐ Walls
- ☐ Roofs
- ☐ Inside cabinets
- ☐ Other—please specify: _____

What changes would you like to see made in the test product?

_____

This can be obtained several ways; for example, a respondent may be asked to allocate 11 points between the new and comparison products. A 10–1 allocation would show strong preferences while a 6–5 allocation would reveal that the respondent is almost indifferent between the two. Third, for diagnostic reasons, testers usually want *descriptive information* about the product that covers any and all important attributes. Examples include taste, color, disposability, and speed. A semantic differential scale is the most common here. This is where we gather all of the other information called for in the objectives.

The researchers of a new sausage product presumed from early concept testing that the ideal sausage would have low levels of greasiness and saltiness, and several test products were developed accordingly. Needless to say, use testing proved just the opposite—the two top sausages in the test ranked first and second in saltiness, and they were among the greasiest. Some of the least greasy test products had some of the lowest overall scores. We have come to expect the unexpected and plan for it.

Marketing research has spawned a large group of exotic research methodologies found to be useful occasionally in new product testing. For example, brain wave measurements help disclose users' inner thoughts, especially if they have a strong emotional reaction to the product being tested. Voice pitch analysis (that is, testing for stress in the respondent's voice patterns much like in lie-detector tests) has been used to overcome product testers' efforts to be helpful and avoid hurting the tester's feelings.

Testers can also be asked to keep journals of their daily experiences with the product (noting, for example, what they liked or found hard to use about the product). Another way of gathering data is to have testers participate in discussion boards. If one user mentioned a particularly desirable new feature or a really troublesome weakness, several others on the board might join in and one could get a sense of how widespread these opinions are.[15]

One additional piece of information is very important at this point—intent to purchase. Recall that near the end of the concept test, we asked respondents how likely they thought they would be to try the product if it became available on the market (the top-two-boxes question). We have now asked them how well they liked the product and whether it was preferred to their currently used product. So again, we ask the buying intention question, this time as a measure of use test results, still not a predictor of actual trial rates.

In many *business* product use tests, the market research flavor of this section is missing. They want all relevant information and get it by close personal investigations and observations. Users may find applications the developers didn't even think of. There are few formal questionnaires in evidence.[16]

How Should We Interpret the Figures We Get?

Testers have long realized that they want *comparative* figures, not just *absolutes*. That is, if 65 percent of the users liked a product, how does that percentage compare with previous tests of somewhat similar items? If previous winners all scored over 70 percent on the "like" question, then our 65 percent isn't very impressive.

The 70 percent figure is a *norm*. Where we get norms and how we use them is often a serious question. The major source is obvious: the library of past experiences, thoroughly studied and averaged. The files of marketing research supplier firms are also helpful, but norms pulled from the air at committee meetings are virtually worthless.

[15]Anonymous, "6 Key Steps to Follow for Beta Testing Your Products," op. cit.

[16]A review of some practice along these lines is Aimee L. Stern, "Testing Goes Industrial," *Sales and Marketing Management*, March 1991, pp. 30–38.

Should We Compensate the Testers?

Especially in the case of a lengthy and involved product use test, it may make sense to reward the testers. They deserve something for the time and effort they devoted to helping you test your product. They can be offered discounts, promotional codes, or other financial incentives. But here one has to be careful. Too large a reward, and the participants may skip key details or overlook bugs; too small a reward and they will not be motivated to even do the test. For this reason, a good strategy might be to not announce the reward until the test is complete. Remember that if the reward is perceived to be fair, that tester might be willing to do another test for you in the future. Of course, be sure to reward only those testers who actually completed the test in a satisfactory manner.[17]

Summary

Chapter 13 has dealt with the issues of whether a product solves customer problems, how it compares to other products in this regard, and what else can be learned about it at this point. Getting this type of information would seem critical, but strong pressures are exerted to skip product use testing. We talked about the arguments for skipping and showed why they should be followed only when they are overpowering.

That paved the way for discussion of the many dimensions of product use tests, ranging from "What we want to learn from the test" to "Who should conduct it?" Each dimension has several options, and selecting from among them usually follows an analysis of the situation.

At the end of the testing, the product may have to be routed back into technical work to resolve problems, or it may be dropped. Otherwise, we now proceed to commercialization and the preparation of finished product, which, of course, is just a later version of the concept going into the greatest use test of all: marketing. Marketing is the topic of Chapters 14 and 15.

Case: Chipotle[18]

The restaurant chain Chipotle had undergone a food safety crisis in 2015, resulting in financial woes and some restaurant closings. Since that time, the company has attempted to recover from the crisis and draw customers back who may have lost

---

[17]Anonymous, "6 Key Steps to Follow for Beta Testing Your Products," op. cit.

[18]This case is based on several sources including: Timothy B. Leetim, "Chipotle's Food Safety Crisis, Explained," *vox.com*, December 21, 2015; Hollis Johnson and Kate Taylor, "Chipotle Just Opened a Test Kitchen That Serves Margaritas and Queso – Here's What It's Like to Visit," *businessinsider.com*, July 15, 2017; Kate Taylor, "People Are Slamming Chipotle's Queso – But the Cheesy Dip Is Actually Good Now If You Order It Correctly," *businessinsider.com*, December 3, 2017; Kate Taylor and Hollis Johnson, "Chipotle Hinted It Might Add a New Menu Item That Has Long Been on the Secret Menu – Here's the Verdict," *businessinsider.com*, February 6, 2018; Rachel Abrams, "Chipotle Will Test a Quesadilla, and a New Strategy," *nytimes.com*, June 21, 2018; Brittany Shoot, "Chipotle Will Roll Out New Non-Burrito Menu Items Including a Milkshake," *fortune.com*, June 21, 2018; and Serena Maria Daniels, "Chipotle Testing Bacon, Nachos and Late-Night Deals in Select Cities," *forbes.com*, August 12, 2018.

confidence, partially through development and launch of new additions to the menu. In particular, Chipotle has been focusing on new snack products that might encourage customer traffic during nonpeak hours.

Chipotle's original value proposition since its founding was "food with integrity"—healthy options to fast-food offerings, at a slightly higher price point. The menu has been relatively limited, consisting mainly of bowls and burritos in different combinations of ingredients. One high-potential new product is nachos, which have already progressed through the early stages of product testing. Nachos are, in fact, on Chipotle's "secret menu" (not listed on the regular menu, but if a customer asked for them, a worker can make them). Nachos are made using Chipotle's tortilla chips, with queso cheese and any available toppings desired by the customer. In February 2018, Chipotle's CEO at the time, Steve Ells, announced to investors that the company was thinking of testing nachos, as well as possibly some other new menu items. An early review of Chipotle's queso noted that the queso was tasty when served in a bowl or burrito but not well suited to nachos due to its texture.

After internal development, Chipotle added nachos to the menu of its NEXT test kitchen in Manhattan in June 2018. The NEXT test kitchen looks like a regular Chipotle restaurant, but inside this one location alone, test products are available on the menu. After success in the test kitchen, the nachos were test marketed in two cities (Minneapolis-St. Paul and Denver). The test markets allowed Chipotle to monitor sales of the nachos, as well as whether sales of other, more expensive items were adversely affected. There was concern among industry analysts and investors that the nachos would cannibalize sales of existing menu items. (Nachos are priced at about $5.00, while the average bowl or burrito is sold for about $7.50.)

During 2018, Chipotle tried several other products in the NEXT test kitchen, including quesadillas, salads, avocado tostadas, and milkshakes. In addition, Chipotle introduced applewood-smoked bacon in a limited test market (eight restaurants in Orange County, California). While many of these may seem to be obvious additions to the Chipotle menu, it must be kept in mind that the restaurant has been profitable keeping to its limited bowls-and-burritos menu. Making quesadillas and other items will require purchase of new grills and rethinking of the production assembly line. The current grills can heat tortillas in a few seconds but would require two and a half minutes to prepare a quesadilla, which can be problematic for a quick-service restaurant. Plus, all new product launches are being launched into a fiercely competitive market; with the recent memory of the food safety crisis on the minds of customers, Chipotle cannot afford for the new items to be a failure.

For a look inside the Chipotle test kitchen, watch this video: www.youtube.com/watch?v=qTCdy36XDCg.

Comment on the testing procedure used by Chipotle, focusing on the two stages (test kitchen, followed by limited test market). Will this reduce Chipotle's margin of error? What can go wrong at the test kitchen stage? What can go wrong at the test market stage? Would you make any recommendations for other kinds of testing to complement the ones currently used by the company?

Case: Product Use Testing for New Consumer Nondurables[19]

In the competitive consumer nondurables market, new products seem to be launched all the time. Failure rates tend to be on the high side, mostly because the manufacturers often try out several products, see what "sticks," and prune out the rest. Nevertheless, with careful product use testing, one can identify potential problems with the product and seek to correct them before a costly launch mistake is made.

Here are several new products that have been launched by some of the bigger-name packaged goods manufacturers. Few could really be called "new-to-the-world" products, though all of them posed at least some risk to the manufacturer.

- *Kellogg's Special K Plus:* A Special K cereal brand extension with added calcium. The product is sold in a milk-carton-shaped box (a gable top) to reinforce the calcium idea. The package contains about the same amount of cereal as a standard cereal box and is easily reclosed using a plastic seal to keep the product fresh. About $15 million is planned for the product launch.
- *Coca-Cola Surge:* Coca-Cola's response to Mountain Dew, Pepsi's popular drink aimed at active Generation Xers. Surge has a citrus flavor and is designed to compete for the extreme-sports segment against Mountain Dew and Gatorade, as well as other established soft drinks and sports drinks. A Norwegian launch (under the name "Urge") has already proven successful, and about $50 million is slated for product commercialization.
- *Uncle Ben's Rice with Calcium:* Another familiar brand to which calcium was added, Uncle Ben's Rice with Calcium was supported by the American Dietetic Association. Extensive television and print advertising featuring Eloise the "spokes-cow" was planned.
- *Avert Virucidal Tissues:* Developed and marketed by Kimberly-Clark, this was essentially Kleenex treated with vitamin C derivatives that killed cold and flu germs if you used it when you sneezed or blew your nose.
- *Wheaties Dunk-A-Ball Cereal:* From the makers of Wheaties, General Mills. This was a sweetened corn-and-wheat cereal for kids, shaped like basketballs. Advertising noted that kids could "play with it before eating" and that it would be "available for a limited time only."

Given that these products were all launched into highly competitive markets, time was of the essence in rolling them out. For the moment, however, the issue of product use testing is at hand. What do you think would be the biggest concerns, or unknowns, about each of these products that might be unearthed using product use testing? Using the list of product use testing decisions given in this chapter, make recommendations as to how some (or all) of these could have been product use tested prior to launch.

[19]This case is based on products found in the New Product Works collection, which was bought in 2018 by the marketing research company Ipsos. The collection includes consumer products of all types, including many failures by major companies. A short article and a video providing background on the collection is found at https://spotlight.ipsos-na.com/newproductworks/. For further information, see Janet Miller, "Ann Arbor 'Product Museum' Showcases Consumer Items From Around Globe — and Drives Innovation," *Ann Arbor News,* Nov. 14, 2010; and Amy Whitesall, "New Product Works," *secondwavemedia.com,* May 28, 2008.

FIGURE V.1

Launch

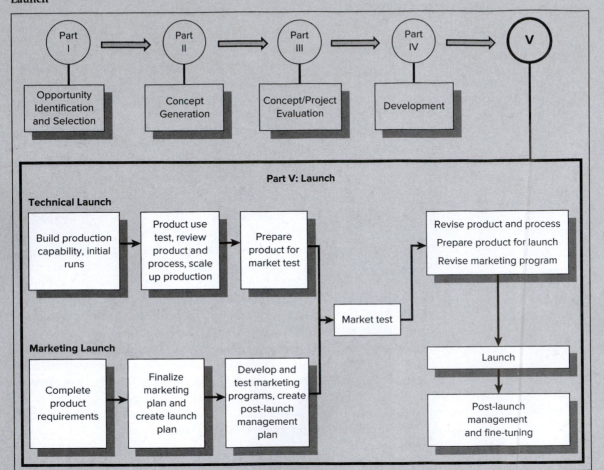

PART FIVE

Launch

We saw in Part IV that both marketing and technical activity take place throughout the development process. The intensity of activity on the marketing side may be relatively low, especially early in development, and there may be long periods of almost total inactivity as technical work gets hung up somewhere. But, as we have seen in Chapter 13, a point is reached in the development process where the balance of activity shifts more toward marketing. We depicted the parallel marketing and technical activity during the development phase in Figure IV.1. Similarly, these "twin streams" of activity carry on through the launch phase, as is shown in Figure V.1.

Somewhere in the process, management becomes convinced that the new product should be marketed. This starts what we will call the launch phase, sometimes called *commercialization*. All of the functions (engineering, production, marketing, and so on) are working before and after the launch decision. The change is often triggered by a commitment to produce the new item and to risk the high costs of building a plant.

At the end of development and throughout launch, marketing activity picks up intensity. But remember, that marketing actually begins near the start of the project. The product innovation charter calls for a market focus—usually a particular use or user. That will eventually become our target market. After concept generation, concept testing uses a concept statement that soon will turn into our product positioning statement. But marketing activities after that cool for a while, until technical can come up with a prototype that seems to show it meets the protocol statement of requirements (see Chapter 9). Of course, this brief description does not match most service products—on them, there is far less technical development work, and the whole process telescopes dramatically. And, as Figure V.1 shows, there is a lot happening on the technical side of the launch, including making the initial production runs, scaling up to full production, getting sufficient product prepared for market testing, and making last-minute revisions to product and process.

The next three chapters deal with the activities during launch. Launch planning decisions use all of the previous activity and a great deal of new thinking and testing to build eventually toward launch capability. As will be shown in upcoming chapters, launch planning can be thought of in several phases. In strategic launch planning, the strategic decisions of marketing (such as targeting and positioning) are made; in tactical launch planning, tactics are developed to implement the strategic plan. In a later phase, the strategic and tactical decisions are tested in the marketplace. All of these phases comprise Chapters 14 through 16. One could also add the phase of launch management, or managing the new product to success. Chapter 17 examines launch management because its planning is done at the same time, and it concerns the postannouncement period.

In the final launch plan, the new products team must accept some givens. That is, the firm has an established operation—one or more sales forces, a financial situation, and so on. Teams can skirt some of these limitations, but not all of them. So the first several launch plan "decisions" are not really decisions in the voluntary sense; they are called **strategic givens**. Next, the team will make a set of **strategic decisions** on matters where there are options, such as positioning, branding, packaging, and the like. These are difficult, often critical, often involve a large commitment of human and financial resources, and are usually hard to change once the decision is made.[1] Some may even be included among the strategic givens. Finally, many **tactical decisions** must be made, though in this book we will only be able to include the most important of these. As you will see, these align rather closely with traditional marketing program decisions such as promotion, pricing, and distribution. Chapter 14 deals with the strategic givens and the strategic decisions, and Chapter 15 looks at the tactics. Be warned: Terms in the new products field are flexible, and one person's tactic is another person's strategy and still another person's given.

Closing Part V is a chapter on public policy issues. These are with us throughout the process, but they come to the fore at time of launch and thereafter. One caution is appropriate: Chapters 14 and 15 cover an activity that many people do not understand. They *think* they do, and some of them are actually in marketing departments. Our problem is not that people draw a blank—blanks are easy to fill in. Instead, we suffer from the existence of many myths—conditions *people think exist but do not*. Figure V.2 lists 11 of these myths. We encourage you to keep these in mind and perhaps refer to them from time to time. As you read the next two chapters, see if you can find what makes each one of them a myth. Check your answers with those at the end of Chapter 15.

[1]M. De Bruyne, R. K. Moenaert, A. Griffin, S. Hart, E. J. Hultink, and H. Robben, "The Impact of New Product Launch Strategies on Competitive Reaction in Industrial Markets," *Journal of Product Innovation Management*, 19, 2002, p. 161.

FIGURE V.2
Some Common
Myths about
Marketing
Planning for
New Products

Here are some statements that we often hear around people who have not done much new product marketing. All are myths, as explained at different places in Chapters 14 and 15. See if you can figure out the reasons on your own, and then check your answers with those at the end of Chapter 15.

1. *Marketing people make the decisions that constitute a marketing plan.*
2. *The technical work is essentially complete when the new item hits the shipping dock. Marketing people take over.*
3. *It's important that marketing people be required to use strategy-tactics paradigms. Clear thinking helps rein in their excess exuberance and excitement.*
4. *The marketer's task is to persuade the end-user to use our new product.*
5. *The more sales potential there is in a market segment, the better that segment is as a target candidate.*
6. *The PIC guides the development stage and the marketing plan guides the launch stage.*
7. *The pioneer wins control of a new market.*
8. *A new product's goals are of two general types: sales (dollars or shares) and profits (dollars or ROIs).*
9. *People generally are pretty smart buyers—they will not be influenced by meaningless package designs.*
10. *A launch is not a game—when we say go, that's it, sink or swim, and it had better be swim.*
11. *As with Broadway shows, opening night is the culmination of everything we have been working for.*

CHAPTER FOURTEEN

Strategic Launch Planning

Setting

At this point in the new products process, the team is ready to build the actual marketing plan. The task should be easy if the new item is an improvement to items already in the line. In such cases, there is actually little to decide, as little is changed. If the product is "really new" (to the world or to the firm), the challenge facing the firm is more substantial, as it may need to rely on new communication or distribution strategies in order to sell unfamiliar products, often to unfamiliar markets.[2] Firms often do not place enough emphasis on up-front strategic planning for product commercialization (such as defining strategic purpose or competitive positioning), especially in the case of new-to-the-world products.[3] Weak strategic planning then shows up when the product reaches the market, and tactical errors (such as insufficient resource allocation) can compound the problem.

No matter how new-to-the-world the product is, the firm should think of product commercialization in two sets of decisions. **Strategic launch decisions** include both *strategic platform* decisions that set overall tones and directions and *strategic action* decisions that define to whom we are going to sell and how. **Tactical launch decisions** are marketing mix decisions such as communication and promotion, distribution, and pricing that are typically made after the strategic launch decisions and define how the strategic decisions will be implemented. For example, one platform decision that often gets overlooked is the level of aggressiveness. If it is decided to be very aggressive (a platform decision), the target market (an action decision) must be rather broad, and the introductory advertising plan (a tactical decision) will probably call for mass media and a strong attention-getting campaign.

Aside from those mentioned above, strategic launch decisions include the desired innovativeness of the product, the time to market, the competitive stance or positioning,

[2]Yikuan Lee and Gina Colarelli O'Connor, "The Impact of Communication Strategy on Launching New Products: The Moderating Role of Product Innovativeness," *Journal of Product Innovation Management*, 20(1), 2003, pp. 4–21.

[3]Michael Song and Mitzi M. Montoya-Weiss, "Critical Development Activities for Really New versus Incremental Products," *Journal of Product Innovation Management*, 15(2), March 1998, pp. 124–135.

the driver of new product development (market, technology, or both), and many others. Many of these decisions will have been made earlier in the new products process, at product innovation charter (PIC) or product protocol specification, and may be very difficult or expensive to change at this point, hence the term **strategic givens**. They are frequently difficult or costly to change once made. They do, however, determine the strategic context for the marketing plan and thus influence the tactical decisions made later. The tactical decisions are more easily modified. The strategic launch decisions are covered here in Chapter 14; the tactical launch decisions come in Chapter 15.

Product commercialization often turns out to be the most expensive and risky part of the new products process due to the financial commitments to both production and marketing made once the go-ahead is given. It is also often the most poorly managed.[4] As an example, a new Gillette blade can incur total production and marketing costs in the range of $1 billion. Despite the financial risks, proficiency in carrying out the launch process is critical to success. Researchers that study launch tend to find that most of the factors contributing to new product success are controllable—that is, rather than taking a "hope for the best" attitude, managers can achieve better success rates by improving product launch practice.[5]

To improve practice at the launch phase, it is important to have heavy marketing input, primarily because marketing will guide the implementation of the plan. The market launch plan itself may be called a business plan or marketing plan. Robert Cooper noted five requirements for an effective market launch plan:[6]

- The market launch plan is treated as a key part of the new products process, as central to this process as the development phase.
- Planning for the market launch begins early in the new products process (we touched on this when discussing the marketing ramp-up).
- The market launch plan is based on good-quality market intelligence that has been gathered throughout the new products process.
- Sufficient human and financial resources are devoted to the market launch.
- Salespeople, technical support people, and other customer service people who are engaged in the product launch should be part of the new product team.

The Strategic Givens

We begin by assessing the strategic givens, seen first in the introduction to Part V. These are decisions that are already made for us, so to speak; they come with the territory when a project is undertaken. Often we tend to forget them and their

[4]Roger Calantone and Mitzi M. Montoya-Weiss, "Product Launch and Follow-On," in William E. Souder and J. D. Sherman (eds.), *Managing New Technology Development* (New York: McGraw-Hill, 1994), pp. 217–248.

[5]Mitzi M. Montoya-Weiss and Roger Calantone, "Determinants of New Product Performance: A Review and Meta-Analysis," *Journal of Product Innovation Management*, 11(5), November 1994, pp. 397–417.

[6]These are suggested by Robert G. Cooper, "New Products: What Separates the Winners from the Losers and What Drives Success," in K. B. Kahn, S. E. Kay, R. J. Slotegraaf, and S. Uban (eds.), *The PDMA Handbook of New Product Development* (Hoboken, NJ: John Wiley, 2013), Ch. 1, p. 16.

importance. They cover the full range of the organization's operations and are often set in concrete without our knowing it. They comprise that awful resistance to change that new products people frequently lament. In fact, they are such a problem that top managements often set up skunkworks in order to try to be immune from whatever restrictions are common within the firm.

If these restrictions are really important and recognized in advance, they are put into the PIC guidelines. But some items here called givens are far more subtle, perhaps being held for reasons that new products people don't even know about. Many are pure and simple habit, convenient and comfortable routines. The point is, they need to be identified and studied. The launch team needs to be aware of such restrictions and to consider whether it wants to challenge them.

Revisiting the Strategic Goals

Early in the new products process, when the PIC was being developed, a basic set of strategic goals was outlined, and these goals have led the new products team up to this point. That original set may still be complete. Usually, though, much has been learned in the new products process, competitive conditions may have changed, and customer or management needs may have changed. Therefore, at this early point in the launch planning process, the goals should be revisited and updated.

Unfortunately, business firms use a complex set of measures as goals, and there is no one universally accepted set.[7] The most used set of measures for individual products is as follows (from lists numbering in the hundreds):

Customer Acceptance Measures	**Product Level Performance**
Customer acceptance (use)	Product cost
Customer satisfaction	Time to launch
Revenue (dollar sales)	Product performance
Market share	Quality guidelines
Unit volume	
Financial Performance	**Other**
Cash-to-cash (time to break even)	Nonfinancial measures peculiar to the new product
Margins	being launched
Profitability (internal rate of return,	Example: competitive effect, image change,
return on investment)	morale change

The **cash-to-cash** metric in the list, sometimes called the **time-to-break-even metric**, is simply the time between the initial cash investment and the time of

[7]Abbie Griffin and Albert L. Page, "An Interim Report on Measuring Product Development Success and Failure," *Journal of Product Innovation Management*, 10(4), September 1993, pp. 291–308.

payment for the finished product, and it is becoming increasingly popular.[8] Using the cash-to-cash metric, the firm must also keep in mind that they need to be efficient and effective in getting the product to market—not just fast. The cash-to-cash metric is improved by using suppliers that efficiently achieve order fulfillment, practice effective inventory management, and successfully collect accounts receivable. Perhaps for this reason, cash-to-cash first caught on with supply chain managers, though new product teams have recognized its usefulness. As one example, Toyota uses lean manufacturing techniques in its Japanese manufacturing plants and has applied these same techniques in its U.S. plants. These techniques focus on just-in-time delivery of parts from suppliers, reducing inventory levels at parts distribution centers, increasing supplier on-time delivery, and improving inventory turnover. As a result, Toyota continuously improves its cash-to-cash metric, both in its domestic and U.S. production.[9]

Regardless of how measures are expressed, there should be absolutely no doubt in the minds of any launch planners about what the launch is to produce or achieve.

Strategic Platform Decisions

Each launch planning team will want to make up its own list of platform decisions because they vary too much from industry to industry, goods to services, and industrial to packaged goods. One place to start, however, is by considering just how new the product is to the world and to the firm (recall our discussion of "what is a new product" back in Chapter 1).

Type of Demand Sought

Different levels of product newness require different kinds of impact the launch activities must have on demand:

- For a new-to-the-world product: The firm must develop an entry strategy with the emphasis on stimulating **primary demand** for the product category. The launch plan must stimulate adoption of the new product category and lead to diffusion through the marketplace. For a product improvement or upgrade to existing product (such as the newest smartphone or laptop with the latest features): The launch is expected to achieve **customer migration** (that is, existing customers should be encouraged to migrate to the new product), with switch-in from competitors' customers where possible. The goal here is to stimulate **replacement demand**.

- For a new entry or line addition in an established market (such as a new soft drink by Pepsi or a new cereal by Kellogg): The emphasis is on stimulation of

[8]For resources on the cash-to-cash metric, see R. Bowman, "From Cash to Cash: The Ultimate Supply-Chain Measurement Tool," *Supply Chain Brain*, June 2001; and M. Farris and P. Hutchinson, "Cash to Cash: The New Supply Chain Metric," *International Journal of Physical Distribution and Logistics Management*, 32(4), 2002, pp. 288–298.

[9]For more information on Toyota's cash-to-cash initiatives, see T. Feare, "Optimizing a Supply Chain," *Modern Materials Handling*, 55(13), 2000, p. 61; and J. Liker and Y. Wu, "Japanese Automakers, U.S. Suppliers and Supply-Chain Superiority," *Sloan Management Review*, Fall 2000, pp. 81–94.

selective demand (drawing market share away from competition). The launch plan must stimulate trial purchase, which is a precursor to adoption. Pepsi's objective is to get loyal Coca-Cola drinkers to break their habit at least once to try the newcomer brand.[10]

In addition to type of demand sought, several other strategic platform decisions may need to be made.

Permanence

On *permanence*, there are three options. The first is the usual one—we are *in to stay*, and no thought is given to getting out. The second is *in to stay if we meet our goals*. This cautions against alliances that would make escape difficult; it is especially useful when a firm is using the new product to enter another sphere of activity. Such a market development project can be tentative—probe an area, try hard to make it a winner, but pull out if competitive capability is inadequate.

The third option is *temporary*. Some new brands are planned to be only temporarily on the market. Coca-Cola, for example, might launch a lemon- or lime-flavored cola to temporarily gain more shelf space, to lure loyal Pepsi drinkers away with an unexpected flavor, or to bring in curious shoppers who value variety. Many new toys and games, frozen yogurt flavors, diet products, and exercise programs seem to appear every year. Customers like variety and are more willing than ever to try something new, especially if it seems fashionable, youthful, or modern.[11] Baskin-Robbins has a basic range of ice cream flavors but runs others in and out to give variety. A food company may have a short-term product designed as a tie-in to a popular movie or TV program (Kellogg's, for example, regularly features fruit-flavored snacks tied in to cartoons or movies, changing them on a frequent basis). Occasionally, a temporary product will catch on and become permanent. Many tactical decisions change if the plan is temporary—using contract manufacturing rather than building a new plant and borrowing a sales force from agents or other manufacturers.

Aggressiveness

Aggressiveness refers to an attitude as much as to dollars. An *aggressive entry* seeks lots of attention early on, so most of the promotional dollars are spent early, and most of the resources go to getting early trial. In contrast, some firms will slink into the market with a *cautious entry*. They are uncertain about something important—maybe product performance, maybe competitive reaction, maybe sales force capability to deal with a new type of market. This is not a negative posture, just one where being aggressive has a risk the firm wants to avoid. For example, some firms like to enter a new market cautiously so as not to alarm the leaders in that market.

---

[10]Joseph P. Guiltinan, "Launch Strategy, Launch Tactics, and Demand Outcomes," *Journal of Product Innovation Management*, 16(6), November 1999, pp. 509–529.

[11]Dan Herman, "Introducing Short-Term Brands: A New Branding Tool for a New Consumer Reality," *Journal of Brand Management*, 7(5), May 2000, pp. 330–340.

FIGURE 14.1
Product Line Replacement Strategies

Butt-on product replacement	The existing product is simply dropped when the replacement is announced. Example: Gillette's marketing of Fusion and dropping of Mach 3.
Low-season switch	Same as butt-on, but arranging the switch at a low point between seasons. Tour companies use this switch when they develop their new catalogs.
High-season switch	Same as butt-on, but arranging the new item at the top of a season. Example: Video game manufacturers use this strategy often, putting new replacement items out during the holiday buying season.
Roll-in, roll-out	Another version of butt-on, but arranged by a sequence of market segments. Fiat launched the new 500 in Italy first, then rest of Europe, then North America.
Downgrading	Keeping the earlier product alongside the new, but with decreased support. Example: Older computer chips are marketed alongside newer ones but with less channel support.
Splitting channels	Putting the new item in a different channel or diverting the existing product into another channel. Example: Old electronic products often and up in discounter channels.

Needless to say, there are variations on these. Samsung has so many flat-screen TVs that it is continuously renewing older ones, shifting the emphasis as it goes along. The important point is: Have *some* strategy decision and a plan. And have it early enough in launch planning that the total market offer (including augmentation such as service, warranty, and brand image) can be built to suit the strategy.

Source: Adapted from John Saunders and David Jobber, "Product Replacement: Strategies for Simultaneous Product Deletion and Launch," *Journal of Product Innovation Management* 11(5), 1994, pp. 433–450.

Third, the aggressiveness can be *balanced*. This simply means the firm is not trying to be pugnacious or slinking. The average of all new product introductions in a given industry would be balanced, but this does not mean normal; for some firms, aggressive is normal.

Product Line Replacement

Most new products relate to existing products in the company's **product line**; they do not enter markets new to the firm. Naturally, the issue arises: How should we manage the replacement of the existing by the new? The firm has several clearly different strategic options, as shown in Figure 14.1.[12]

The technologically strongest firms cannibalize their own products (and production processes) with newer, higher-performance versions (Gillette has done this for years—about one new blade technology every eight or nine years). Probably any one industry will have no more than a few innovators that can build their new product strategy around cannibalism. Other firms, the imitators, succeed by following the leader firms and making incremental improvements to their products. In other words, imitators move up the performance curve (with, say, improved printers) while the

[12] John Saunders and David Jobber, "Product Replacement: Strategies for Simultaneous Product Deletion and Launch," *Journal of Product Innovation Management*, 11(5), November 1994, pp. 433–450.

innovators create whole new curves with higher performance limits (such as next-generation printers, scanners, and software).[13]

The decision on when to launch the next generation of product is a tricky one but is likely to depend on at least three important forces: the competitive environment, customer expectations, and profit margins.

Image

The issue here is: Will the new product need *an entirely new image, a major change in an existing image, a tweaking of an existing image*, or *no image change*? For example, the button strategy of market replacement can destroy the prior brand if necessary to properly position the new. But the side-by-side strategy needs a continuing positive image in the item being upgraded. Images can be quite resilient and long-lasting, so changing them should not be undertaken lightly. Yet an image can also be distorted by an almost trivial mistake in an ad or a label, and establishing a new image can be expensive.

Once these higher-order decisions are made, we can turn our attention to what you may think of as the *real* marketing planning decisions: target market, product positioning statement, and creating unique value for the chosen target.

The Target Market Decision

Competition today forces the overwhelming majority of companies to market new items to specific target groups. Markets are so complex that one product cannot come close to meeting all needs and desires.

Alternative Ways to Segment a Market

There may be thousands of ways that new product marketers use to target a specific market segment. Yet each of these can be classified into one of several categories.

End-Use

Athletic shoes are specific for various types of athletic activity (running shoes, basketball shoes, baseball cleats, cross-trainers, etc.). Plastics are sold for hundreds of different applications. Watch buyers have different end uses: an expensive gift, a fashionable watch, or a cheap timepiece. Many types of clothing have an end-use orientation, or at least did at some time in history (denim jeans were originally for workers, golf and polo shirts for athletes, etc.). Clothing manufacturers design for use, though not only for use.

Geographic, Demographic, and Psychographic Segmentation

Convertibles are not marketed aggressively in Norway, and snowmobiles are not popular in the southern United States. Bran cereals are often targeted to the mature segment. Jitterbug phones, with large buttons and readouts, were designed for the elderly. Oreos are made from milk chocolate in South American countries and use a less-sweet

---

[13]Michael C. Neff and William L. Shanklin, "Creative Destruction as a Market Strategy," *Research-Technology Management*, May–June 1997, pp. 33–40.

FIGURE 14.2
Joint Space Map
Showing Ideal
Points (from
Figure 7.9)

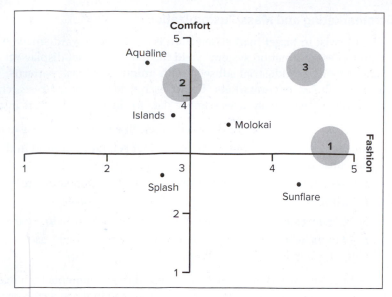

Numbers along the axes represent factor scores.

formulation in China, since taste preferences are different in those markets.[14] In addition to geodemographic segmentation, markets can be segmented according to psychographics: values, activities, and lifestyles. SRI Consulting follows trends in these variables, as well as in key demographics, using its well-known VALS (Values, Activities, and Lifestyles) questionnaire.[15] Car companies use psychographics extensively in developing new models. The Honda Element was designed for the active, youthful market who wanted stylish transportation with plenty of room to carry bicycles, camping gear, and the like for a weekend getaway.[16]

Benefit Segmentation

As we saw in Chapter 7, benefit segments are of great interest in new product development. Through surveys of customers and potential customers, we can identify segments based on benefits sought and develop products to satisfy the needs of one or more of these segments. Recall that in the joint space mapping example of Chapter 7, we identified three benefit segments in our maps of the swimsuit market (see Figure 14.2). Of course, benefit segment information in combination with brand perceptions can be very helpful in developing a positioning strategy, a topic to which we return later in this chapter.

[14]A very informative video on Oreo product adaptations around the world is available at: www.youtube.com/watch?v=75NpeAN-z4k&t=21s.

[15]Try the online version of the VALS questionnaire at www.sric-bi.com.

[16]Marc H. Meyer, "Perspective: How Honda Innovates," *Journal of Product Innovation Management*, 25(3), May 2008, pp. 261–271.

Micromarketing and Mass Customization

A current twist in target market selection is the trend toward smallness. Retail scanners and sales information systems yield the databases that display very small targets (neighborhoods or industrial subsets) with unique purchase patterns. These clusters have been labeled **micromarkets**. David Olson, new product researcher at the Leo Burnett advertising agency, uses scanner data to cluster food buyers into six groups:

Loyalists, who buy one brand at all times, like it, and don't use deals.

Rotators, who have a two- or three-product set, move around in that set, and don't use deals.

Deal-selectives, rotators whose movement is determined by presence of deals.

Price-driven, who buy all major brands, always on deals.

Store brand buyers, who, as their name implies, are loyal to a particular retailer.

Light users, who buy too little for a pattern to show. Light users comprise the biggest group in most categories.

Direct marketers and online marketers use tighter segments than mass media marketers, using *database marketing* techniques. Amazon looks at a customer's online purchase (for example, a popular book), scans its database for products that tend to be bought by other people who ordered that same book, and makes suggestions for multiple purchases. The more one purchases from Amazon, the richer the database, and the better the recommendations become. As one of countless other examples, Fingerhut (a catalog company) has a database of over 30 million households, with about 1,400 pieces of information per household (demographics, hobbies, interests, birthdays). They use their database marketing skills to support online shopping and also to tailor their direct mail offers depending on what customers are likely to buy. Mars, the candy manufacturer, is also a leader in pet food and has a database of practically every household in Germany that owns a cat, gathered from veterinarians and customer questionnaires. Mars periodically sends out samples or coupons, as well as cat birthday cards, much to the delight of the cat owners.[17]

The ultimate smallness, and the ultimate building customer value, is mass customization, which we have seen earlier in Chapter 4. Previous examples have shown the use of product configurators and user toolkits, and firms can actually practice mass customization in a variety of other ways, as seen in Figure 14.3. As shown in the figure, Planter's may sell the same peanuts to the final customer but customize packaging depending on the size of the distributor. Another extension of mass customization is **virtual product testing**. Customers build the desired product, get an assessment of the resulting price, and then state their likelihood of making a purchase. Researchers can track the way customers make the trade-offs between product features and price and thus better understand what features are and are not important in the purchase decision.[18]

[17]See Philip Kotler, *Marketing Management*, 11th ed. (Upper Saddle River, NJ: Prentice-Hall, 2003), pp. 53–55.

[18]Bill MacElroy, "Computer Configuration Figures to Change MR," *Marketing News*, April 4, 2002, p. 23.

FIGURE 14.3
Types of Mass Customization

- *Collaborative customizers* work with the customer in arriving at the optimal product. Japanese eyewear retailer Paris Miki inputs customer frame style preferences with facial features into a design system that makes frame and lens recommendations, which are further refined by customer and optician working together.

- *Adaptive customizers* let the customers do the customizing themselves according to their performance needs. Lutron Electronics markets a lighting system that allows customers to adjust lighting in several rooms simultaneously to obtain a desired ambience.

- *Cosmetic customizers* sell the same basic product to different segments, but adapt the product's presentation (such as its promotion or packaging) depending on segment needs. For example, Walmart likes larger sizes of Planter's Nuts than does 7-Eleven. Planter's now offers a wide range of package sizes and adjusts its production order-by-order according to the wishes of the retailers.

- *Transparent customizers* do not inform their customers that they are customizing the product for them. ChemStation formulates industrial soap specifically to its customers' needs but packages everything it sells in the same kind of tanks. In this case, the customer cares about whether the product works and is delivered on time, not necessarily whether it is customized.

Obviously, any of these strategies has pitfalls that need to be avoided. It would be cost-inefficient for Planter's, for example, to offer too wide a range of package sizes.

Source: *Harvard Business Review*. Exhibit from "The Four Faces of Mass Customization," by James H. Gilmore and B. Joseph Pine II, January–February 1997.

A large Japanese bicycle manufacturer, NBIC, pursues both mass customization and mass production simultaneously. The larger mass production plant uses robotics and automated assembly and is designed for high efficiency. The smaller plant is set up to produce bicycles in direct response to customer online orders. The online system allows customers to choose from literally millions of variations, and the bicycle is produced and shipped within about two weeks, at a slight price premium. What makes the two-plant system work is that product trends and changing preferences among online customers are tracked, and this customer information is forwarded to the mass-production plant. The online customers essentially act as lead users! Among other reported benefits, the craftsmen from the mass customization plant rotate to the other plant to train their mass-production colleagues, and robots designed for painting in the mass-customization plant eventually find their way into the mass-production factory.[19]

As we approach the marketing date, intense pressure builds up in the organization to add just a few more buyer types, a few more store types, and a few more uses or applications because, "The product is good for them too, isn't it?" The answer is, "not necessarily," since what makes it appealing for one segment may mean nothing to other segments; we call this the *broaden the market* fallacy. Also, targeting to diverse groups can cause dissonance in the promotion. Does a fourth grader want a peanut butter sandwich like the one shown being eaten by a senior citizen? Further, changing

[19]Suresh Kotha, "Mass-Customization: A Strategy for Knowledge Creation and Organizational Learning," *International Journal of Technology Management*, 11(7/8), 1996, pp. 846–858.

the target can be a disaster if promotional and trade-show materials and dates are all prepared; packaging, pricing, and branding are fixed; and the concept and product use tests were conducted only with the original target group.

Lastly, keep in mind that whatever we do, the end users may disagree. A few years ago, sports utility vehicles were widely adopted for regular driving use. Customers were tired of minivans, and it didn't matter what the car companies *told* us these vehicles were for (or that the government said they were trucks). Some firms capitalize on this end-user penchant by just launching the product and following up to see who the buyers are, and then focusing their promotions accordingly. This is strictly a wildcat operation—no charter, no concept testing, no use testing.

Targeting May Also Use Diffusion of Innovation

New products are innovations, and we call the spreading of their usage the *diffusion of innovation*. The original adoption and diffusion of the microwave oven was very slow, whereas it has been quite rapid for smartphones. For a cancer cure, it would be almost instantaneous.

When we used the Bass diffusion model in sales forecasting (Chapter 9), our forecasts rested on two key values: the rates of innovation and imitation. Taken together, these values define the speed of an innovation's adoption. Let's look closer now at the factors that affect this speed of the **product adoption process**: the characteristics of the innovative product and the extent to which early users encourage others to follow.

Product Characteristics

According to the classic diffusion theory of Everett Rogers, there are five factors that measure how soon a new product will diffuse into the marketplace:[20]

1. The *relative advantage* of the new product. How superior is the innovation to the product or other problem-solving methods it was designed to compete against? Google spread rapidly through the Internet community as the preferred search Web site, as it was seen to offer better search capability than other available alternatives.

2. *Compatibility.* Does it fit with current product usage and end-user activity? A *continuous* innovation requires little change or learning by customers, as compatibility with prior experiences and values is high; the more *discontinuous* the innovation, the more learning is required. Microwave ovens were slow to be adopted initially, due to the perceived differences in cooking compared to conventional methods. When first launched, digital cameras looked and operated exactly like regular film cameras people were familiar with.

3. *Complexity.* Will frustration or confusion arise in understanding the innovation's basic idea? As was seen in our discussion of value curve creation (Chapter 5), early tax preparation software was too complicated for the needs of the average person and also too expensive; Intuit's Quicken tax software better suited the

---

[20]The classic source on this subject is Everett M. Rogers, *Diffusion of Innovations* (New York: The Free Press, 1962).

needs of the typical taxpayer and at an affordable price. New devices by Apple or Samsung are usually adopted rapidly for many reasons, one of which is certainly ease of use.

4. *Divisibility* (also called *trialability*). How easily can trial portions of the product be purchased and used? Foods and beverages are quite divisible, but new homes and word processing systems are much less so. GPS devices were very expensive when they first were launched, and they were often placed in rental cars for people to try out. And most readers are familiar with the "first six months, half price" type of cable TV subscription offers.[21]

5. *Communicability* (also called *observability*). How easy is it for the user to see the benefits of using the product? The benefits of a new cologne with a nice scent are immediately noticed by the user; the benefits of using a new decay-preventing toothpaste are more difficult for the user to discern.

An innovation can be scored on these five factors, using primarily personal judgment plus the findings from market testing during earlier phases of the development. Launch plans can then be laid accordingly.

Next is the degree to which early users actively or passively encourage others to adopt a new product; if they do, its spread will be rapid. So interest has focused on the **innovators** (the first 5 to 10 percent of those who adopt the product) and on the **early adopters** (the next 10 to 15 percent of adopters). The theory of innovation diffusion states that, if we could just market our new product to those innovators and early adopters, they would spread the good news about our product to the rest of the market through word of mouth. Other categories of adopters include the **early majority** (perhaps the next 30 percent), the **late majority** (perhaps another 30 percent), and the **laggards** (the remaining 20 percent).[22]

The obvious question is, "Who will be the innovators and early adopters?" Can we identify them in advance so as to focus our early marketing on them? Not always, but they often share several traits: venturesomeness (willingness to go against social norms and try the new and different), for example, and social integration (many social or work contacts they could possibly influence); these traits apply to businesses as well as to individual consumers.[23]

Early users do come typically from the innovator group, but it is difficult to predict which ones. In the industrial setting, early *business* adopters are often (not always) the

---

[21]"Diffusion of Innovation," in V. K. Narayanan and Gina C. O'Connor (eds.), *Encyclopedia of Technology & Innovation Management* (Chichester, UK: John Wiley, 2010), Chapter 16.

[22]These are percentages of those who end up *adopting* the item. They are not percentages of the target market. Late majorities and laggards would seem to be slow, but if a product fails they may simply be the last of those daring to try the item! The last group of users who wait 90 days to try a cancer cure are quite a different group from the last of the microwave oven adopters who waited for five years. For insights on the effects of word of mouth on marketing, see Andrew M. Baker and Naveen Donthu, "Word-of-Mouth Processes In Marketing New Products: Recent Research and Future Opportunities," in Peter N. Golder and Debanjan Mitra (eds.), *Handbook of Research on New Product Development* (Cheltenham, UK: Edward Elgar, 2018), pp. 313–335.

[23]Stephane Gauvin and Rajiv K. Sinha, "Innovativeness in Industrial Organizations: A Two-Stage Model of Adoption," *Journal of Research in Marketing*, Vol. 10, June 1993, pp. 165–183.

largest firms in the industry, those who stand to make the greatest profit from the innovation, and those firms who have presidents who are younger and better educated.[24]

Geoffrey Moore's **crossing the chasm** model provides an extension to the Rogers model. Briefly, Moore suggests thinking of the innovators and early adopters as the *visionaries* and later categories as the *pragmatists*. These two new groups of adopters will differ in their expectations of the new product, and the pragmatists may not use the visionaries as their opinion leaders. That is, in Rogers's model, a neat flow of information through word of mouth, from one category to the next, is predicted to occur; Moore says that this is not necessarily so, as what the two groups are looking for in the new product can be very different. For example, visionaries may snap up the latest cell phone or music player, almost regardless of price, because it's the newest thing, they like the performance features, or they simply think it's cool. Pragmatists may be unimpressed by the newness factor and possibly couldn't care less about the new device's coolness; they may just be looking for something that works pretty well and is not so expensive. They may care more about the reviews in the mainstream publications or online sources (probably not where the visionaries get their information). Thus, the word of mouth may not effectively pass from the visionaries to the rest of the market. This is the chasm that Moore is referring to: A firm that offers a value proposition that attracts all the visionaries may never "jump over the chasm" and successfully sell into the (much larger) pragmatist market. Moore's model suggests that the firm should consider developing a value proposition that will work for pragmatists and develop a launch strategy designed to reach pragmatists.[25]

However it comes about, the target market decision essentially measures (1) how much *potential* is in each target market option, (2) how well our new product *meets the needs* of people in each of those markets, and (3) how prepared we are to compete in each—that is, our *capacity to compete* there.

Product Positioning

A **product positioning statement** is created by filling in the blank at the end of this sentence: Buyers in the target market should buy our product rather than others being offered and used because: _____. Positioning originated as a concept in advertising but is now seen as an ingredient of *total* strategy, not just an advertising strategy. Product, brand, price, promotion, and distribution must all be consistent with the product positioning statement.

Positioning alternatives fall into two broad categories. The first is to position to an **attribute** (a feature, a function, or a benefit). Attributes are the traditional positioning devices and are most popular. Thus, a tire manufacturer may position a new snow tire using a **feature**: it has the deepest treads of all comparable tires. **Function** is less frequently used, but the tire manufacturer could position the same tire in terms of higher ability to grip the road in snowy or rainy conditions. (You are not directly told how this

[24]Ralph L. Day and Paul A. Herbig, "How the Diffusion of Industrial Innovations Is Different from New Retail Products," *Industrial Marketing Management*, August 1990, pp. 261–266.

[25]The main reference is Geoffrey Moore, *Crossing the Chasm* (New York: Harper Business Essentials, 1991).

FIGURE 14.4 **Surrogate Positioning: Alternatives and Examples**

Listed below are the types of surrogates currently being used. No doubt there are many others awaiting discovery. For each, the definition is given, followed by one or more examples. The surrogates are listed in order of popularity in use. The claim in each case would be that "Our product is better than, or different than, the others because. . . ."

Nonpareil: . . . because the product has no equal; it is the best (Jaguar cars and Perrier water are sold this way).

Parentage: . . . because of where it comes from, who makes it, who sells it, who performs it, and so on. This would include a new suit or piece of furniture designed by Ralph Lauren, a new movie produced by Disney, or a new book written by Dan Brown.

Manufacture: . . . because of how the product was made. This includes *process* (Budweiser beer is beechwood-aged), *ingredients* (Fruit of the Loom underwear of pure cotton), and *design* (Audi's engineering).

Target: . . . because the product was made especially for people or firms like you. For example: an airline service specially designed for the business traveler, or Vector Tires described as being the best on wet roads.

Rank: . . . because it is the best-selling product (such as Hertz and Blue Cross/Blue Shield); not very useful on a new item unless also positioned under parent brand.

Endorsement: . . . because people you respect say it is good. May be *expert* (the many doctors who prescribed a new prescription-only pharmaceutical) or a person to be *emulated* (take your pick from the sports or entertainment celebrities that serve as spokespersons for famous brands).

Experience: . . . because its long or frequent use attests to its desirable attributes. Nuprin users, for example, claim many years of satisfactory use.

Competitor: . . . because it is just (or almost) like another product that you know and like (U.S. Postal Service Express Mail, just like the leading competitor except cheaper).

Predecessor: . . . because it is comparable (in some way) to an earlier product you liked (you liked Hershey's Kisses, so you will also like Hugs).

is done or what the specific benefit is—the emphasis is on the road-gripping function.) The tire could be probably most effectively positioned in terms of its **benefit** to the end user, namely, its ability to keep you and your family safe when driving in adverse conditions. Miller's tag line for years has been a simple statement of two benefits: "Tastes great, less filling." Similarly, Gillette sold its Fusion Proglide blade using a combination of feature, function, and benefit: the extra-thin blade (feature) causes less "tug and pull" (function), so the user can more comfortably shave against the grain (benefit).[26] Years before, a new Drano product was advertised as "thicker, stronger, faster." Once again, we see a three-way positioning statement: feature, function, and benefit (in that order).

The second alternative in positioning is to use **surrogates** (or metaphors). For example, "Use our dietary product *because it was created by a leading health expert.*" This says the product differs because of its designer. Specific reasons *why* the product is better are not given; the listener or viewer has to provide those. If the surrogate is good, the listener will bring favorable attributes to the product. See Figure 14.4 for the various surrogate positioning alternatives, their definitions, and examples of each.

[26]For a Gillette TV ad that uses this positioning, watch: www.youtube.com/watch?v=mVcg8U-S2AQ.

The perceptual mapping techniques we first encountered during concept generation and evaluation, in Chapters 6 and 7, can be profitably put to use in positioning strategy development. Consider the joint space map of Figure 14.2 again. It indicates not only the positions of the ideal brands of each benefit segment, but also the perceptions of the existing brands. We can use this map to hunt for worthwhile market gaps. We can, for example, select a position for our new brand such that it is near an ideal brand that is not served very well by existing brands. Segment 2 may be relatively large, but if there is heavy brand loyalty to the Aqualine and Islands brands, it may be difficult to get many sales there, and Segment 3 may be a better option. As a simple example, the Taylor Wine Company once identified a small group of heavy wine users and asked them what brands of wine they preferred. Surprisingly, none of the wines the heavy users bought was being positioned on its great taste. Taylor positioned a wine of theirs on taste, and succeeded immediately.

If there is no longer an open feature-function-benefit positioning that users want, developers can try to *build* preference for some unique attribute their product has. For example, most soaps are deodorizing or moisturizing soaps. Lava (a Procter & Gamble product) is not particularly strong on these two attributes. It is, however, a brand favored by car mechanics and others who get their hands very greasy. Lava's positioning essentially tells customers that they should consider a third attribute—grease-cutting ability—and Lava is the leading brand on that attribute. In some cases, a *potentially determinant attribute* may be discovered. This is an attribute that is important to many customers, but the brands are assumed to be all about the same on that attribute. Michelin, for example, positions its tires as the safest brand. While safety is clearly important to all customers, Michelin aimed to position itself as the best in safety, distancing itself from competitors.

In the remainder of this section, we will focus our attention on two of the ways in which we can increase unique value to the targeted customer—**branding** and **packaging**.

Branding and Brand Management

Trademarks and Registration[27]

Every new product must be identified, and the accurate term for what identifies products is **trademark**. Under U.S. federal law, a trademark is usually a word or a symbol. That symbol may be a sequence of letters and/or numbers (such as the Z-class Roadster), a logo (for example, Apple Inc.'s familiar apple), or a design (for example, the stylized lettering in GE, or the golden arches of McDonald's). A *word string* such as "just do it" can be a trademark, as can a *sound signature* such as the three-note NBC TV network chimes or the "Intel Inside" sound.[28] The law doesn't care how unusual the

---

[27]There are many sources for information on this topic, but the best thing a new product manager can do is make contact with the employer's in-house (or local area) trademark attorney. Most such departments have brochures for employees to study, but experts we should not try to be!

[28]Rob Osler, "On the Mark," *Marketing Management*, January–February 2007, pp. 31–36.

trademark is and just requires it to identify and differentiate the item using it. The law also requires that the firm uses, or intends to use, the trademark—this requirement is called *bona fide intent*.[29]

Most businesspeople and their customers use the term *brand* instead of *trademark*. This book uses *brand* when talking about marketing strategy and *trademark* when talking about the legal aspects. Technically speaking, services have *service marks*, not trademarks, and businesses have **trade names**. Another consideration is **registration**. Historically, and still today in most countries, the *first user* of a trademark had exclusive rights. But in the United States, you can ask that your trademark be registered. If you can get it registered, you can keep that trademark forever, even if another firm later displays proof of prior use.

The Patent and Trademark Office has certain conditions it considers when allowing a trademark to be registered. The trademark should not be immoral or misleading. The trademark should also not be too descriptive of a product type; for example, a judge once ruled that Light was too descriptive a name to be used as a cigarette brand, since the name would have identified any low-tar cigarette, not just the one firm's brand. Another condition is that the trademark should not be confusingly similar to trademarks belonging to other products. Quality Inns once tried to name a cheaper line of hotels McSleep—until McDonald's lawyers objected. The argument is that the "Mc" *formative* would lead people to believe that the hotel chain was part of McDonald's and could pose problems to McDonald's at the time the latter was building a chain of truckstop operations called McStop. Quality changed the name of the hotels to Sleep Inns. Apple Corps (the Beatles' recording company) once sued Apple Computers (now Apple Inc.) when the latter entered the music business through iTunes. In that case, however, it was ruled that the two uses were not *confusingly similar*, and both companies were permitted to keep the Apple trademark.[30]

Different types of brand names offer different amounts of protection under trademark laws. See Figure 14.5 for a description.

What happens if, shortly after launch, other manufacturers begin encroaching on our mark? We move aggressively to stop them. Aladdin began putting on its labels "Aladdin thermos bottle." Aladdin was sued by the firm that owned the thermos mark, and won; the original owner did not protect it. *Thermos* became a generic: it no longer describes one maker's brand of vacuum bottles, and any company can use it. The same thing happened to aspirin, cellophane, dry ice, shredded wheat, trampoline, yo-yo, linoleum, corn flakes, raisin bran, lanolin, nylon, and scores more; billions of dollars in value were lost. Therefore, companies aggressively protect their brand names. Coca-Cola protects both "Coca-Cola" and "Coke" to ensure that these words do not become generic terms for cola or soft drinks in general. Some Xerox Corp. advertising reminds customers that the word "Xerox" is a trademark and therefore a proper adjective. It should always be followed by a descriptive noun (as in "Xerox copier"), and never used as a verb (as in "xerox this for me").[31]

---

[29]Rob Osler, op. cit.

[30]May Wong, "Apple, Cisco, Ready for an iPhone Trace?" *businessweek.com*, February 1, 2007.

[31]Maxine S. Lans, "On Your Mark: Get Set or It May Go," *Marketing News*, September 26, 1994, p. 12.

FIGURE 14.5 Categories of Brand Names and Trademark Protection

Famous Names. Certain well-known trademarks (such as Coca-Cola and Disney) are protected by the Federal Trademark Dilution Act, which prevents other companies from using similar names, even on unrelated items. A prominent 1998 case involved the famous Victoria's Secret store, and an adult-oriented store, Victor's Secret (later Victor's Little Secret). Interestingly, the U.S. Supreme Court ruled in favor of the latter, arguing that Victoria's Secret's capacity to identify its goods were not lessened by the presence of the competitor.

Fanciful Names. Also known as neologisms, these are made-up names either comprised of real words or parts of words (Bluetooth, Ameriprise) or totally unique (Kodak, Exxon). These are distinctive and easy to protect via trademark laws, but the firm must create a meaning for a word that, by definition, doesn't have one.

Arbitrary Names. These are real words that appear to have been chosen as brand names without concern for the nature of the product or industry (Apple computers, Virgin airlines, and Web sites like Monster.com or Amazon.com). These enjoy trademark protection much like fanciful names.

Suggestive Names. These are defined as those that require some imagination to link them to the nature of the product (Coinstar coin machines, Quadra Tred tires). Suggestive names can communicate a product benefit to customers, but might be harder to protect via trademark laws. As an example, boatmaker AMF owned the Slickcraft trademark for recreational boats, but courts ruled that competitor Nescher could use the name Sleekcraft for its racing boats (since the product categories were ruled to be different enough).

Descriptive Names. (Lean Cuisine, HotJobs) are harder to protect since they are, by definition, not inherently descriptive. These names go onto a different trademark list at first (the Supplemental Register), but if the owners can create sufficient awareness after a five-year period, they can obtain a higher level of legal protection. This is what happened in the case of Rollerblades.

Generic Names. These names have become synonymous with the product category, and the original trademark holder loses the exclusive rights (see text for examples).

Source: *Marketing Management*, published by the American Marketing Association, Rob Osler, "On the Mark," January–February 2007, pp. 31–36.

Incidentally, don't forget to seek protection for the new brand in all countries where it might be marketed.

Companies can also seek **trade dress** protection. Trade dress refers to a wide range of product identifiers: In addition to brand name, it can include packaging (the familiar Coca-Cola bottle shape), product color (Brillo is the pink soap pad, SOS is blue), or décor (the distinctive red and yellow of McDonald's, for example). The extent of protection a company has is not always clear-cut, but if a firm has data that show customers identify a given trade dress with a particular brand, protection is often allowed by the courts, using the concept of *secondary meaning*. That is, the color, décor, or packaging takes on a secondary meaning, which is the name of the brand. Private brands often use trade dress to establish themselves as competitors of well-known brands—the drugstore brand of acetaminophen may be in a package that resembles the Tylenol package. Typically, courts deny the private brand absolute rights to copy the well-known brand's trade dress.[32]

[32]Paul F. Kilmer, "Trade Dress Protection 1995: A U.S. Perspective," *Journal of Brand Management*, October 1995, pp. 95–103.

What Is a Good Brand Name?

Getting a good brand is not easy, because most good combinations of letters have already been taken. But, if Billy Fuddpucker's and Orville Redenbacher can be successful brand names, then there is hope for all. Experts have given us several rules-of-thumb to follow and pitfalls to avoid (see Figure 14.6).

As Figure 14.6 shows, sometimes choosing a meaningless or even provocative brand name can have its benefits. Google was once a nonsense word, and now it is commonly used as a verb to look something up online! But this can be risky and may not always work out. Be sure the budget is sufficient for adequately creating customer awareness and understanding. If you don't have the funds to put meaning into a meaningless combination of letters, avoid that type of brand.

Given an overall marketing strategy and the role that brand will play, it is useful to have some discussions with intended users (to learn how they talk about things in this area of use)—and also with phonetic experts, who know a great deal about such things as word structures. Then brainstorm or use computers to generate large numbers of possible combinations. Computer software (such as NamePro at www.namestormers. com) is available to assist in brand name selection and development.[33]

Conduct interviews with users to screen the list down. Ask what the brands on your list mean—including in global markets (see Figure 14.7 for classic misfires). There is much support available for branding decisions at this point. A check at **www.register.com** should identify any similar brand names that might cause negative connotations or even a legal challenge. One can also turn to the Patent and Trademark Office site (**www.uspto.gov**) and search under Trademarks, as well as any trademark databases in targeted foreign countries. The site www.trademark.com can also help access trademark databases. A quick check of possible offensive or unintended meanings in foreign languages can be easily made using one of the familiar translation Web sites. Needless to say, make sure to have a good trademark attorney on your side.[34] An effective brand naming checklist is provided in Figure 14.8.

Managing Brand Equity

There is more to brand management, of course, than brand name selection. The best brand names—Coca-Cola, Levi's, Campbell, AT&T, and so on—are important assets that provide value to both the firm and its customers, as they communicate quality, build positive brand images, and encourage customer loyalty. This value is known as **brand equity**, and the firms that benefit the most from brand equity have invested in protecting this equity to maintain the value of their brand names.[35]

---

[33]The Namestormers site has links to a NamePro software demonstration as well as to a naming guide providing useful guidance on good brand name selection (including domain name selection for your firm's Web site).

[34]Useful guides in brand name development are Chiranjeev Kohli and Douglas W. LaBahn, "Creating Effective Brand Names: A Study of the Naming Process," *Journal of Advertising Research*, January–February 1997, pp. 67–75; and Lee Schaeffer and Jim Twerdahl, op. cit.

[35]The authoritative books on brand equity are David A. Aaker, *Managing Brand Equity* (New York: Free Press, 1991); and David A. Aaker and Erich Joachimsthaler, *Brand Leadership* (New York: Free Press, 2000).

FIGURE 14.6

Issues and Guidelines in Brand Name Selection

Question	Guideline
What is the brand's role or purpose?	If the brand is to aid in positioning, choose a brand name with meaning (DieHard, Holiday Inn). If purely for identification, a *neologism* (made-up word) such as Kodak or Exxon will work.
Will this product be a bridgehead to a line of products?	If so, choose carefully so as not to be a limitation in the future (Western Hotels changed name to Western International, then finally to Westin).
Do you expect a long-term position in the market?	If not, a dramatic, novelty name might be useful (such as Screaming Yellow Zonkers).
Is the name irritating or insulting to any market segment?	P&G intended to name a new detergent Dreck until it was noted that Yiddish or German definitions included garbage or body waste, and the name was changed to Dreft.

Others: Easy to understand; no hidden meanings; translates well; simple and memorable; fits corporate mission; and complements other products in the marketplace.

Brand Name Pitfalls to Avoid

Not anticipating future uses of the name. A cute name can become irrelevant; a bad name may be chosen because there was time pressure to make a decision; a regional name becomes a hindrance as the firm goes national or international. Consider US Airways, originally known as Allegheny Airlines, a name that suggests it should serve the Pittsburgh area only. An acceptable name in English or some Spanish dialects may be offensive in other Spanish dialects (the Toyota Fiera was unsuitable in Puerto Rico where the name means "ugly old woman"). Even differences between American, British, and Canadian English need to be considered. A new U.S.-made product with the brand name "EZ" (pronounced "easy") would just not sell as well in either Great Britain or Canada where most readers would pronounce the name "e-zed."

Not allocating enough time for the process. This corresponds with the idea of marketing activities being conducted throughout the product process. The brand name should not be a last-minute rush job, especially if the brand is going to be marketed across multiple countries. Consider that Procter & Gamble went to the trouble of assigning two different French brand names for Mr. Clean due to slightly different usage patterns: Monsieur Propre in French Europe, and Monsieur Net in Quebec.

Choosing the wrong comfort level. A provocative and controversial brand name such as Yahoo! may be a great strategy, certainly better than a comfortable yet uninspiring name.

Having too many individuals involved in the brand naming decision process. It works better if a team is assigned that understands brand naming and its consequences, than to let democracy or consensus rule.

Other pitfalls: Not identifying who the key decision makers are; getting "stuck" on a brand name early in the process and, knowingly or not, it is adopted without any objective feedback; not checking negative meanings in foreign markets, and, of course, not hiring the best patent attorney.

Source: Some of these points are adapted from Lee Schaeffer and Jim Twerdahl, "Giving Your Product the Right Name," in A. Griffin and S. M. Somermeyer, *The PDMA Toolbook 3 for New Product Development*, Wiley, 2007, Chapter 8.

FIGURE 14.7
Bad Brand Names

Sometimes it seems that foreign companies choose brand names that would seriously limit their sales potential in English-speaking markets.

Crapsy Fruit	French cereal
Fduhy Sesane	China Airlines snack food
Mukk	Italian yogurt
Pschitt	French lemonade
Atum Bom	Portuguese tuna
Happy End	German toilet paper
Pocari Sweat	Japanese sport drink
Zit	German lemonade
Creap	Japanese coffee creamer
I'm Dripper	Japanese instant coffee
Polio	Czech laundry detergent
Sit & Smile	Thai toilet paper
Barf	Iranian laundry detergent
Cream Pain	Japanese snack cake
Porky Pork	Japanese pork snack

Of course it works in both directions. Two famous examples are the Rolls Royce Silver Mist ("Mist" means "manure" in German), and Colgate Cue toothpaste ("Cue" is the name of a French porno magazine). Clairol also experienced problems launching its Mist Stick curling iron in Germany. The lesson is that we need to be careful when introducing brands into foreign markets.

More recently, Mon Cuisine frozen entrées were launched in the U.S., the French name undoubtedly selected to add an upscale image. Only problem was the manufacturer made a basic grammatical error (it should have used "Ma Cuisine").

Source: Anonymous, "But Will It Sell in Tulsa?" *Newsweek*, March 17, 1997, p. 8; Ross and Kathryn Petras, *The 776 Even Stupider Things Ever Said* (New York: Harper-Perennial, 1994).

FIGURE 14.8
Brand Naming Checklist

Patent attorney Mark Mondry suggests a set of guidelines for selecting brand names:

- Start with a diverse group of people. Don't let the new product team get stuck on a name they like before it is checked to see if it works strategically, or even if the firm will have the legal rights to it.
- Review the strategic goals for the product and its value proposition, as a starting point for brand name selection.
- Consider whether the names used for other products in the portfolio should be extended to avoid customer confusion.
- Consider competitors' names. Be distinctive rather than positioning your brand as the alternative to the leader. A new competitor to Apple should not call itself the Banana.
- Develop a set of good names, and narrow it down to about five or ten. Consider pronunciation, emotion, complexity, and so forth.
- Do a domain search and a trademark search. Include alternate pronunciations and spellings. No need to be surprised at the last moment by a similarly named competitor. Don't forget to check foreign markets as well.
- Choose the name, and seek domain and trademark protection. Again, do this internationally, if applicable.

Source: Mark B. Mondry, "Product Name Innovation," *Visions*, 36(2), 2012, pp. 8–9.

Innovation can be a key component of brand equity building. Under new leadership in early 2018, Taco Bell (whose parent company is YUM! Brands) launched several new additions to the menu, including Nacho Fries, and also experimented with new dining experiences, such as walk-up stands and cantinas that offer beer and alcohol. The innovative new products were supported by strategic partnerships: home delivery is now available through Grubhub in many stores nationwide (YUM! has a large financial stake in Grubhub), and other partners included Forever 21 and Cheetos. Taco Bell even arranged a tie-in with the twentieth anniversary of the movie *Demolition Man*, thus reaching the Comic-Con target audience effectively. All these activities resulted in an 8 percent system-wide increase in sales and a 5 percent same-store sales growth rate within the first year; Taco Bell was voted the top Mexican restaurant by the Harris Poll in April 2018.[36]

A brand with high equity encourages loyalty among customers, making advertising and other forms of promotion more efficient. High equity also means high brand awareness, which makes it easier for the firm to create other associations (for example, McDonald's is associated with children, clean restaurants, Ronald McDonald, etc.). Brand equity can also be associated with higher perceived quality and thus can support a premium positioning for a brand. Due to its high familiarity and positive associations, a high-equity brand can more easily be used as a bridgehead for launching **brand extensions**. In short, brand equity can provide sustainable competitive advantage—and recent work suggests that all of these brand equity advantages hold for business-to-business products as well as consumer goods.[37] One authority on branding, Kevin Lane Keller, suggested a brand report card—a list of characteristics shared by the strongest brands worldwide that can be used to assess a brand's strengths and weaknesses (see Figure 14.9).[38]

Brand extensions can be either vertical or horizontal, depending on whether the new brand is in the same product category as the parent one. Procter & Gamble extended Crest toothpaste vertically into Crest Tartar Protection, Crest Sensitivity Protection, and Crest Multicare toothpastes, and also horizontally into Crest toothbrushes and Crest Glide floss, among others. Regardless of the direction, a brand extension can boost acceptance of the new product, but problems with the new product can result in dilution of the parent brand's equity.[39]

Brand extensions must be managed carefully, as an unsuccessful extension, or too many extensions, can lead to brand equity erosion. Some companies have tried extending a well-known brand name into an inappropriate product category with disastrous results. The Frito-Lay brand has been successfully extended to many snack foods, but Frito-Lay Lemonade didn't sell. Neither did Ben-Gay aspirin, Smucker's ketchup, nor

[36]Rachel Taylor, "Taco Bell Soars on 'World-Class' Product Innovation," *qsrmagazine.com*, October 2018.

[37]Paul Mitchell, Jacqui King, and John Reast, "Brand Values Related to Industrial Products," *Industrial Marketing Management*, 30(5), July 2001, pp. 415–425.

[38]One firm that specializes in brand identity and corporate identity development is Landor Associates, www.landor.com. Their site contains a portfolio of dozens of applications, including Kellogg's, FedEx, Kodak, Seven-Up, and many others.

[39]Kuang-Jung Chen and Chu-Mei Lu, "Positive Brand Extension Trial and Choice of Parent Brand," *Journal of Product and Brand Management*, 13(1), 2004, pp. 25–36.

FIGURE 14.9
A Brand Report Card

Many different factors work together to make a strong brand. Brand managers often focus on only one or two of these factors. Here is a list of several characteristics shared by the world's strongest brands that can be used to assess the strengths of a brand and to identify points of improvement.

Characteristic	Examples
Delivers benefits desired by customers.	Starbucks offers "coffee house experience," not just coffee beans, and monitors bean selection and roasting to preserve quality.
Stays relevant.	Gillette continuously invests in major product improvements (Fusion), while using a consistent slogan: "The best a man can get."
Prices are based on value.	P&G reduced operating costs and passed on savings as "everyday low pricing," thus growing margins.
Well-positioned relative to competitors.	Lexus competes on excellent customer service, Mercedes on product superiority. Visa stresses being "everywhere you want to be."
Is consistent.	Michelob tried several different positionings and campaigns between 1970 and 1995, while watching sales slip.
The brand portfolio makes sense.	The Gap has Gap, Banana Republic, and Old Navy stores for different market segments; BMW has the 3-, 5-, and 7-series.
Marketing activities are coordinated.	Coca-Cola uses ads, promotions, catalogs, sponsorships, and interactive media.
What the brand means to customers is well understood.	Bic couldn't sell perfume in lighter-shaped bottles; Gillette uses different brand names such as Oral-B for toothbrushes to avoid this problem.
Is supported over the long run.	Coors cut back promotional support in favor of Coors Light and Zima, and lost about 50% of its sales over a four-year period.
Sources of brand equity are monitored.	Disney studies revealed that its characters were becoming "overexposed" and sometimes used inappropriately. It cut back on licensing and other promotional activity as a result.

Source: *Harvard Business Review*. Exhibit from "The Brand Report Card," by Kevin Lane Keller, February 2000.

Fruit of the Loom Laundry Detergent.[40] We have already seen how firms seeking to extend their brands globally should check for unanticipated humorous or objectionable meanings. Perhaps more subtle is the fact that humor often doesn't cross national or linguistic barriers. As a rule of thumb, humorous names tend to work best only in cases where the product will have only a limited, local market (which presumably will see the humor).[41]

Although there is no one right way to extend a brand name, there are some guidelines to follow to avoid mistakes. For instance, consider whether the brand being extended has a functional or a prestige image. Gillette could probably launch a downscale extension of the Fusion razor easily, while Mercedes risks tarnishing its reputation if it launches a low-end Mercedes car. Often, a **flagship brand** (a dominant brand in a product category, such as Hallmark Cards or Planter's Peanuts) is

[40]Robert M. McMath and Thom Forbes, *What Were They Thinking?* (New York: Times Business, 1996).
[41]Lee Schaeffer and Jim Twerdahl, "Giving Your Product the Right Name," in A. Griffin and S. M. Sodermeyer (eds.), *The PDMA Toolbook 3 for New Product Development*, New York: John Wiley, 2007, Chapter 8.

extended in this way, as its brand equity is already quite high. But flagship brands should be extended carefully, and then probably only to brands of similar or better quality to avoid risking brand name dilution and consumer confidence. There may also be international considerations. The Bayer name is best known in North America for over-the-counter pharmaceuticals, yet in Europe it is well known also as a producer of agricultural products and chemicals. Bayer pesticide might do well in Germany but probably not in the United States.[42] On the positive side, a strong parent brand, successful previous brand extensions, strong marketing support, good acceptance at the retailer level, good fit between parent brand and extension, and low perceived risk of the extension are all associated with more successful brand extensions.[43]

Brand Equity and Branding Strategies[44]

There is a variety of different branding strategies available, each with pros and cons, and there is no one-size-fits-all solution. In all cases, however, the firm must consider how the branding strategy will protect and possibly build brand equity.

Think of a spectrum of branding strategies. On one end of the spectrum are businesses that put their corporate name on every product they make. This is sometimes called an **umbrella brand** strategy. At Kellogg's, for example, every cereal carries the word "Kellogg's" as part of the brand name: Kellogg's Corn Flakes, Kellogg's Rice Krispies, and so on. The Kellogg's name is synonymous with excellence and quality in cereal, and the appearance of the company name on a new cereal or snack extends this brand equity to the new product. In similar fashion, Kraft Foods has dozens of decades-old products that include the name Kraft in the brand (Kraft Salad Dressing, Kraft Singles) or at least display the Kraft logo prominently on the package (Philadelphia Cream Cheese, Velveeta). The firm will also use corporate brands other than Kraft to roll out new products. A new nut product will carry the Planters name, a new pizza will be Di Giorno, and a new coffee is likely to be Maxwell House. Other examples are Virgin Airlines (which entered many other businesses, including publishing, soft drinks, and cell phones, all under the Virgin name), and Hard Rock Café (which extended into Hard Rock Café Resorts in Asian markets).[45]

On the other end of the spectrum are firms that seem to go out of their way not to mention the company name in the brand. None of the many detergents and cleaning products marketed by Procter & Gamble includes P&G in the brand name; the names

[42]Dennis A. Pitts and Lea Prevel Katsanis, "Understanding Brand Equity for Successful Brand Extensions," *Journal of Consumer Marketing*, 12(4), 1995, pp. 51–64; see also Sieu Meng Long, Swee Hoon Ang, and Janet Liau, "Dominance and Dilution: The Effects of Extending Master Brands," *Journal of Consumer Marketing*, 14(5), 1997, pp. 280–288.

[43]Franziska Volckner and Henrik Sattler, "Drivers of Brand Extension Success," *Journal of Marketing*, 70(2), 2006, pp. 18–34; see also Eva Martinez and Jose M. Pina, "The Negative Impact of Brand Extensions on Parent Brand Image," *Journal of Product and Brand Management*, 12(7), 2003, pp. 432–448.

[44]For dozens of examples, check out www.kelloggs.com, www.kraftfoods.com, www.thecloroxcompany.com, www.pg.com, or www.conagrabrands.com.

[45]Muammer Ozer, "A Survey of New Product Evaluation Models," *Journal of Product Innovation Management*, 16(1), January 1999, pp. 77–94.

are simply Tide, Bold, Mr. Clean, and so on. This **individual brand** strategy is consistent with P&G's historically strong brand management. The Clorox Company uses the Clorox brand on all of its bleach products. Its environmentally friendly Green Works brand also displays the Clorox brand on the packaging to communicate that the all-natural line is as effective as conventional cleaners. (More on Green Works is in the case appearing in Chapter 18.) But other products acquired by the Clorox Company over the years have never undergone a name change. The Clorox Company owns Hidden Valley Ranch salad dressing, KC Masterpiece barbecue sauce, Glad Bags, and Burt's Bees. These are high-equity brands in their own product categories, and there is nothing to be gained by using Clorox as an umbrella brand here. Interestingly, the Clorox Company does not even extend the Clorox brand to other cleaners it produces, such as 409, SOS, or Tilex (though its Handi Wipes disposable cloth towels do carry the Clorox logo on one corner of the package).

There are often possibilities for improving one's branding strategy so as to take advantage of synergies or co-branding opportunities. As a case in point, ConAgra Foods produces dozens of brands familiar throughout North America: Hunt's tomato products, Orville Redenbacher popcorn, Reddi-Wip whipped cream, Healthy Choice frozen entrees, Peter Pan peanut butter, just to name a few. None of these brands carries the ConAgra corporate name; the equity resides in the strong brands, similar to P&G or Clorox. Unlike Clorox, ConAgra's line is entirely within one category: consumer packaged food products. Consumer research showed that the ConAgra name was not well known among consumers. Executives felt that a new corporate identity would reinforce the individual brands, reinforce ConAgra's position as a top food manufacturer, and make the company more competitive. But what should they do? Adding "ConAgra" to familiar brand names like Hunt's or Peter Pan probably doesn't help them that much. ConAgra decided instead on a new slogan to be attached to every brand and advertisement ("Food You Love"), together with a new logo (a contemporary-looking smiling plate with a spoon), both unveiled in 2009. ConAgra's plan was to move on the branding spectrum closer to Kraft in terms of having a unified corporate identity while still taking advantage of its strong individual brands.

Global Branding and Positioning: Standardize or Adapt?

One consideration in global brand management is the extent to which brand names will be standardized around the world (that is, the same name is used worldwide). Gillette blades, Coca-Cola, and Kellogg's cereals are known to customers by those names everywhere they are sold. These firms use essentially the same positioning in every market as well; Gillette positions its blades as "the best a man can get" virtually everywhere.

For many other firms, achieving a standardized global presence is not an option, and quite possibly not even desirable. These firms will choose instead an adaptation strategy for its position and/or its brand names. Honda, for example, uses a high-quality position in the United States but a speed/youth positioning in Japan. BMW and Mercedes are positioned as luxury cars in the North American market, but not necessarily in their home market of Germany and neighboring countries.

A firm may also choose different names for the same product in different markets. While Tide is P&G's leading brand in North America, Ariel is their best-known name throughout Europe and Japan; similarly, Liquid Tide is Liquid Ariel in Europe. A major North American competitor of Kellogg's, General Mills, entered the European market in a joint venture with Nestlé called Cereal Partners Worldwide (General Mills provided the cereal-making expertise while Nestlé contributed experience in European distribution, sales, and advertising). Familiar North American General Mills brands such as Cheerios (as well as Europe-only brands such as Chocapic) are sold in Europe under the Nestlé name.

An interesting case is Unilever, the Anglo-Dutch conglomerate, which uses a blend of standardization and adaptation in brand name selection. Several Unilever products are sold under the same names worldwide: these include Lipton, Bertolli, Knorr, Dove, Vaseline, and many others. Cif household cleanser, originally sold in France, is known under that name there and in several other markets such as Italy, Switzerland, Turkey, and Greece, but is also known as Viss in Germany, Jif in Japan and Australia, and Vim in Canada. Perhaps the most extreme case of brand name adaptation is the fabric softener known in North America as Snuggle. Unilever sold its North American Snuggle brand in 2008, but it still sells the product in many other countries nationwide, under a wide variety of names. In Italy, the brand name is Coccolino; in France, Cajoline; in Germany and Austria, Kuschelweich; in Spain and Colombia, Mimosin; and in the Netherlands, Robijn. In all cases, the familiar teddy bear character is prominent on the package. Even though the actual product is standardized throughout the world, Unilever provides it with a local-sounding brand name in every market. (In multilingual Switzerland, the name is Comfort: simple and easy to understand in any language.) Similarly, Unilever has acquired several ice cream manufacturers around the world, including Good Humor in the United States, Langnese in Germany, Algida in Italy, and Kibon in Brazil. In each case, the familiar brand name was retained; a red heart-shaped logo is used as an identifying mark in all markets and, collectively, these are known as Heartbrand within Unilever.[46]

Global Brand Leadership[47]

The preceding section suggests that the goal is not necessarily to pursue a single global brand but rather to create a strong presence in every market through **global brand leadership**. This requires an overall global brand strategy that coordinates the brand strategies used in the individual countries and a commitment to allocate sufficient resources to brand building.

There are many ways to work toward global brand leadership. In order to achieve consistent brand management across countries, firms can develop brand manuals, set up workshops, or distribute newsletters or videos to all brand managers to serve as a guide on what the brand stands for. This goes beyond simple product attributes, as these may be copied by competitors. Intangibles (such as a quality reputation) and

---

[46]Reference: www.unilever.com.

[47]Much of this section is adapted from David A. Aaker and Erich Joachimsthaler, "The Lure of Global Branding," *Harvard Business Review*, November–December 1999, pp. 137–144.

symbols (such as the Ronald McDonald clown or the Snuggle teddy bear) should be considered as well. Mobil has set up a knowledge bank on marketing topics accessible via company intranet, and Frito-Lay runs a "market university" three times a year. Activities such as these encourage communication and sharing of successful practice among managers throughout the company. Employee empowerment is also important. P&G's Taiwanese brand team for Pantene Pro-V came up with a novel positioning: "Hair so healthy it shines." The ad campaign built around this slogan was so successful in Taiwan that it was picked up by P&G and used in 70 other countries.

Packaging

To many firms, packaging is less important, either because the goods require little packaging or because the shelf persuasiveness of packaging is not a priority. In these firms, packaging is for the most part assigned to packaging design departments. Of course, most services require no packaging. But in many other firms, packaging is of great importance, especially when the new item will be distributed through self-service environments, when the product category is already established so the new item will have to force its way in, and when many strongly entrenched competitors sit next to one another on store shelves. In such firms, packaging decisions are often made at the highest levels. In fact, more money is spent on packaging food and beverage products than on advertising them.

The Role of Packaging

Packaging can refer to *primary packaging* (the material that first envelops the product and holds it, such as a pill bottle), *secondary packaging* (the box that holds the pill bottle), or *tertiary packaging* (bulk packaging that holds secondary packages for shipment). All forms of packaging serve several roles: *containment* (hold for transporting), *protection* (from the elements and the careless), *safety* (from causing injury), *display* (to attract attention), and *information* and *persuasion*. All are important to a new products manager, sometimes enough so that there are legal problems; packaging design is a part of logo and trademark, where rights can be valuable.

But there are other roles: for example, assisting the user in some way—with instructions (pharmaceuticals or food) and with a use function (beer cans and deodorant dispensers). Other times, packages are designed to permit reusability, meet ecological demands on biodegradability, carry warnings, and meet other legal requirements. They may also aid in disposability.

The Packaging Decision

Packaging is part of the new product manager's network. The packaging decision centers on a person most often called the director of packaging. It is, however, a complex decision. Packaging decisions can involve participants from engineering, distribution, safety, legal, cost accounting, purchasing, research and development, and other departments, in addition to marketing and sales, not to mention outside interests such as vendors, distributors, shippers, advertising agencies, and the government. The packaging decision may take months; it is a key target in most accelerated development programs.

Each company tends to develop a somewhat unique approach to packaging, but there are common steps. First, a packaging person is put on a new products team. Field trips are mandatory, as is access to the various market studies that have been made. A unique packaging approach for Pfeiffer's salad dressing was found when a packaging staffer visited supermarkets and noted that salad dressings were displayed by type rather than by brand; most competitive bottles were shaped like whisk brooms with flat iron heads.

The process for package development resembles that for the product itself. Tests include dummy packages, in-store displays, color tests, visual tests, psychographic tests, physical tests, distribution tests, warehouse legibility, and even some in-store selling tests. One of the strategies sometimes used in package design is family packaging, that is, using a key design, or some other packaging element to integrate the packaging of several individual items. A package for a new Häagen-Dazs or Ben & Jerry's ice cream flavor, for example, is immediately recognizable. Coca-Cola and Pepsi are red and blue, respectively. In each case, the packages clearly belong to one set, but there are usually some individualizations, such as brand name.

Packaging can be a very powerful competitive tool. In recent years, wine and spirits have made up a larger share of the alcoholic drink market at the expense of beer. One of the ways Anheuser-Busch and competing brewers have tried to counteract this trend is through innovative packaging. See-through beer labels (technically, pressure-sensitive adhesives made from acrylate ester) that stick on the side of the bottle and look painted on are one of the newest packaging innovations. Soon after their introduction, growth in see-through labeled bottles was at over 10 percent in the United States and near 40 percent in Europe and Asia. The labels are not only attractive but can be easily designed to add special messages, such as around playoff football or Olympics time, and also allow the brewer to use the whole package—from the bottle cap to the base—for graphics and copy. Among other packaging innovations are shrink-wrap labeling and aluminum bottles for Budweiser, Bud Light, and several other Anheuser-Busch brands (including shamrock green aluminum bottles for St. Patrick's Day), and Halloween-themed aluminum bottles printed with ultraviolet ink that glow under black lights.[48]

Summary

In Chapter 14, we have extended our look at the launch planning process by going into the platform decisions and the driving decisions. Both sets have a strong effect on the strategies chosen. The chapter also looked at three of the biggest areas of decision—target market or segment, positioning of the new item for that segment, and creating unique value for that segment. We can now turn to those many things that make up the tactics portion of the marketing plan. But there is far too little space for an in-depth study in the many areas of operational marketing. We will look at those issues that give new products managers the most difficulty.

[48]"Beer Has an 'Image Crisis'; Wine and Spirits Gain," *USA Today*, January 11, 2005; Anonymous, "Labels Brewing Up Acrylate Esters Demand," *Chemical News & Intelligence*, February 27, 2006; and www.anheuser-busch.com.

Case: Tesla (B)[49]

Refer to the Tesla (A) case at the end of Chapter 10 for background information on the development of the Tesla S. This case examines the planning that led to the more affordable Model 3.

In the five years after the Model S launch, Tesla communicated with Model S buyers to determine what issues and challenges needed to be addressed in order to make a more affordable mass-produced car. Model S buyers were not only passionate high-performance car drivers, but they were also enthusiastic about electric cars in general. Furthermore, the Tesla name was getting substantial press, and sporty Model S cars driving along the highways acted as a kind of mobile billboard, building Tesla's brand image. When word came out that a mass-produced, affordable Tesla was in the works, the waiting list expanded quickly.

By July 2017, the Model 3 was launched, at a base price of $35,000 and with add-ons that could bring the sticker price up to $57,000. The problem facing Tesla at this time was sufficient production to meet the demands of the growing waiting list of customers. By April 2018, the waiting list had grown to 400,000 interested customers! Tesla produced 100,000 cars in 2017 but would need to double or even triple production in order to monetize the potential of the huge waiting list, some of whom had been waiting well over a year for the Model 3 by that point.

Comment on the launch strategy used by Tesla, for both the first launch (the Model S) and the second entry (the Model 3). What was the benefit to Tesla of entering the electric car market with the high-priced Model S? Was the decision to follow up with the lower-priced Model 3 a wise one? What were the pros and cons of this launch strategy? Reread the discussion of disruptive innovation in Chapter 2. Discuss whether Tesla is an example of either the classic or high-end disruptive innovator, and back up your position.

Case: Comparing Smartphones (C)[50]

Refer back to the Comparing Smartphones cases (A) and (B) at the end of Chapters 6 and 7. Suppose now that competitive intelligence indicates that Essential (another smartphone competitor, which runs on an Android platform) is planning a strategic relaunch of its smartphone within six months. Assume that all prices and other attributes remain about the same among the current competitors. Preannouncement buzz suggests that the new Essential phone will meet or surpass the "best" brand on light weight, screen size, resolution, and processor speed but will still lag behind in terms of battery life, internal storage, and RAM. There is no information

---

[49]This case is drawn from Jeff Dyer and David Bryce, "Tesla's High End Disruption Gamble," *Forbes*, August 20, 2015; Yonatan Levy, "The Genius of Tesla's Product Launch Strategy," *medium. com*, January 4, 2018; www.tesla.com; and other sources.

[50]See the Comparing Smartphones (A) case in Chapter 6 for further information. The Essential specifications are not based on facts and are for illustrative purposes only.

yet on the quality of the cameras. The price is rumored to be in the range of about $750–$800.

How serious is this competitive attack? What, if anything, should current competitors do now to minimize the threat posed by the new Essential phone? Or is it better to wait until the Essential relaunch occurs, and then react? (Since this is preannouncement buzz rather than real ratings, feel free to make realistic guesses at the likely levels for the Essential on each of the attributes, based on the information provided.)

CHAPTER FIFTEEN

Implementation of the Strategic Plan

Setting

Chapter 14 set up the strategic platform decisions and the strategic actions decisions. It then explored the building blocks of marketing, examining the target market and the product positioning statement. That led to actions for building value into the product for the chosen target and positioning and into the matter of brand—part of the product and part of the promotion. Now, we can move into the tactics area: how management actually sets up to communicate all of these things to the end user. The strategic implementation often calls for considerable creativity, and gets it.

The Launch Cycle

First, let's correct an impression many people have about the launch of a new product. They see the launch as a matter of announcing to the world the good news about our great new product. If it were only that simple!

What actually takes place is a **launch cycle**. The launch cycle is an expansion of the familiar introductory stage of the **product life cycle (PLC)** into substages; see Figure 15.1. It picks up the preparations during the prelaunch period, the announcement, the beachhead phase, and then the early growth stage that links the launch cycle back to the PLC.

Prelaunch and Preannouncement

The **prelaunch** stage is when we are building our capability to compete. This means the training of sales and other promotional people, building service capability, putting out *preannouncements* if they are in order, and arranging for stocking of the product at the reseller level.

The new products novice almost invariably focuses on announcement as the culmination of the entire new products process, which it clearly is not. In fact, only on very rare dramatic occasions is there one day when the announcement takes place. The car companies once keyed their announcements (with appropriate on-camera unveilings) to a date in the fall. But such drama does not play well today. In the first place, it is

FIGURE 15.1
The Launch Cycle

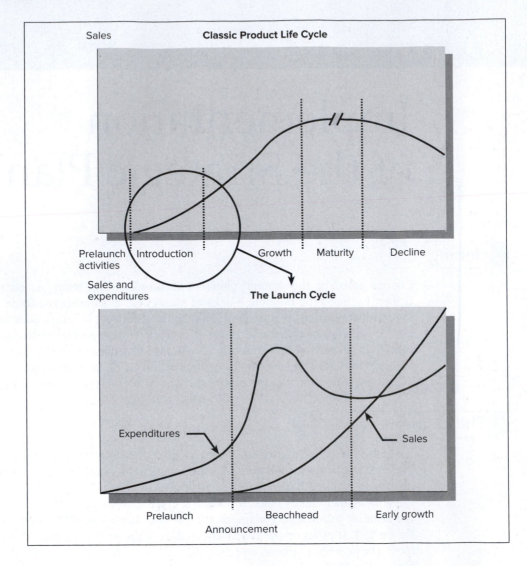

almost impossible to keep a secret, especially as the firm's formal announcement day approaches.

Instead, we see a planned sequence of announcements, often geared to keeping competitors guessing and to keeping competitors' customers from stocking up just prior to our being available. One sequence of periods goes like this: (1) nondisclosures; (2) product testing—beta testers sign confidentiality forms; (3) anticipation—position releases telling about the problem being solved; (4) influentials—press kits for editors, industry researchers, and some customers; (5) broadcast PR—full press releases, product for reviews; (6) promo pieces—the start of advertising. Stages 3 and 4 are used for preannouncements, usually subtle *signaling*, sometimes orchestrated through planned leaks by selected individuals and sometimes just allowed to happen.

Preannouncement can be used to hype interest in the upcoming product, to keep current customers from switching to a competitor, and to encourage prospective buyers to wait for the new product (rather than becoming part of the competitor's installed base of customers). Of course, in many markets, there is almost no attempt to keep secrets. The whole world knows when the next Apple watch or Galaxy phone is coming, long before the actual launch dates. This practice has occasionally received criticism, however, especially if the new product's launch is uncertain or likely to be delayed. Many of the leading high-tech firms have been criticized for not delivering software on the date promised in the preannouncement.[1]

Signaling can be done using several marketing tools. An obvious one is price. Others are advertising; trade shows; comments by salespeople; a speech by a CEO at a security analysts' luncheon in New York City, London, or Tokyo; tips from vendors of packaging or production machinery; stocking calls made on distributors or retailers; appointment of new sales representatives with certain industry experience; and so on. Some are so subtle that they are missed. But in general, they can be very effective, so much so that they constitute a field of unfair advertising law.[2]

The preannouncement decision is often tied to whether there are *network externalities*. *Indirect network externalities* exist if product sales are dependent on sales of complementary products (the more Xbox games there are, the more Xboxes Microsoft can sell). *Direct network externalities* exist if product sales are dependent on the number of people that have adopted it. The more people that have e-mail and Facebook, the more useful these products are. By contrast, videophones (as stand-alone devices) never caught on with consumers, although (as we have seen in Chapter 13) we rapidly accepted Skype, FaceTime, and other ways to make video calls using our laptops, phones, or other devices. For high-tech products with indirect network externalities, there may be two preannouncements, first to program developers and then to consumers. Indeed, Microsoft preannounced the Xbox at a game developer conference, releasing software tools enabling developers to begin designing games for use with the Xbox. When the Xbox was launched to consumers, plenty of games were already available.[3]

Preannouncement can also be used to block a competitive entry. When it became known that Ford was introducing the new Windstar minivan, Chrysler put into operation an aggressive price promotion. This brought them many buyers who otherwise might have awaited Windstar, but it also tweaked interest in Chrysler's own new minivan scheduled for the following year.[4] It is somewhat dangerous to cut the price of an item being replaced, because this can result in current buyers all deciding to await the new product; this makes it tough to clear out trade stocks of the old item. For some companies, there really is no "announcement" any more: New items are just developed and moved into the market, usually on a limited market area basis. (This will be called

[1]See discussion in T. S. Robertson, J. Eliashberg, and T. Rymon, "New Product Announcement Signals and Incumbent Reactions," *Journal of Marketing*, 59(3), July 1995, pp. 1–15.

[2]Oliver P. Heil and Arlen W. Langvardt, "The Interface between Competitive Market Signaling and Antitrust Law," *Journal of Marketing*, 58(3), July 1994, pp. 81–96.

[3]E. Le Nagard-Assayag and D. Manceau, "Modeling the Impact of Product Preannouncements in the Context of Indirect Network Externalities," *International Journal of Research in Marketing*, 18(3), September 2001, pp. 203–220.

[4]Jerry Flint, "A Van for All Seasons," *Forbes*, December 20, 1993, pp. 43–44.

a *market rollout* in Chapter 16.) There is also another risk involved in preannouncement: the product is never launched! The preannouncement might have been made simply to keep shareholders or the finance markets happy, without concern for the real danger of not being able to fulfill the signal. In the software field, this has resulted in what is called *vaporware*—signaled but not delivered until much later, if ever.

One study showed that firms with smaller shares are more likely to preannounce; large firms will avoid preannouncing if they fear government criticism of monopoly; there will be less preannouncing in industries that are very competitive; and there will be more preannouncing where switching costs are high.[5] More recent research has suggested that software firms use vaporware intentionally to gain competitive advantage, and that this seems to hold true for large as well as small firms.[6]

Announcement, Beachhead, and Early Growth

The second stage of the launch cycle—**beachhead**—gets its name from a military landing on enemy soil, a good metaphor for many launches. In a military beachhead, a standstill is followed by movement, such as a military invasion force expanding from a small strip of shoreline. In a product launch setting, beachhead refers to the heavy expenditures necessary to overcome sales inertia—Figure 15.1 illustrates this with a steeply rising expenditures curve up to the point where sales are growing at an increasing rate.

Announcement kicks off the beachhead phase, and the conditions at the time are hardly conducive to good management. Communication systems fail, unexpected problems arise, supplies become scarce, and general confusion may reign. As the months go by, a subtle change in emphasis occurs as initial announcement gives way to "reason why" and then to the rationale of trial and the reinforcement of successful experience.

The key decision in the beachhead phase is to end it—inertia has been overcome, and the product has started to move. This decision triggers a series of actions. Improvements and flankers will now be brought along as scheduled; new budgets will be approved and released; temporary marketing arrangements will be made permanent (such as a temporary sales force, an advertising agency, or a direct-mail arrangement). One new products manager said he knew this decision had been made when the firm's president stopped calling him every couple of days for the latest news.

Decisions made at launch and throughout the product life cycle need to be made in accordance with the strategic decisions made earlier. The most recent work on new product launches, interestingly, finds three common patterns for launch strategies and tactics:

- *The innovative new product.* For some products, the strategic objective is to get a foothold in the market early in the product life cycle. Common tactics accompanying this kind of launch are a broad product assortment, a new brand name and distribution channels, and a higher price.

[5]Jehoshua Eliashberg and Thomas S. Robertson, "New Product Preannouncing Behavior: A Market Signaling Study," *Journal of Marketing Research*, 25(3), August 1988, pp. 282–292.

[6]Barry L. Bayus, Sanjay Jain, and Ambar G. Rao, "Truth or Consequences: An Analysis of Vaporware and New Product Announcements," *Journal of Marketing Research*, 38(1), February 2001, pp. 3–13.

- *The offensive improvement.* The strategic objective here is different: to erect barriers to entry. Managers find it more beneficial to use existing distribution channels, high consumer promotion and advertising, and a broad product assortment.
- *The defensive addition.* For other products, the strategic objective is to increase penetration in existing markets; appropriate tactics include smaller assortments, penetration pricing, and promotions to the customer and the sales force.[7]

Lean Launch and Launch Timing[8]

A sometimes-overlooked driver of launch success is the role of the supply chain and distribution logistics. At the time of launch, manufacturing must be ramped-up to desired levels of production, the sales channel and distribution logistics should be in place, the salespeople and distributors should be sufficiently well trained on the new product, and adequate promotion to consumers and to the trade should be ready as well.

Supply chain managers try to keep the supply chain system flexible so that it can respond rapidly to sales changes. This flexibility is called a **lean launch**, and keeping the launch lean means that the firm does not commit to too much inventory during the early days of launch but can ramp up quickly should sales take off. To implement a lean launch requires coordination between sourcing, manufacturing, and delivery operations such that the length of time from raw material to consumer is minimized. Once this is in place, the firm can respond quickly to real market needs rather than stocking up on inventory that sells slower than planned (or face stockouts due to unexpectedly high sales levels). A principle that drives lean launch is **postponement**, or delaying finalization of product form and identity until late in the development process, and delaying commitment of inventory until the last possible moment. This reduces lead times, minimizing uncertainty and increasing operational flexibility until the nature of the demand is more certain.[9] Postponement actually can be manifested in two ways: *time postponement* (deploy inventory as late as possible) and *form postponement* (lock in product design as late as possible). In order to successfully implement a lean launch, firms must have good information technology systems in place so that sales can be tracked, and raw materials and inventory can be replenished effectively.

Fashion designer Burberry illustrates the benefits of lean manufacturing principles and a flexible supply chain. Lean manufacturing here is defined as producing small lot sizes to match customer demand. To do this requires excellent market research so that Burberry can identify the products and styles that are most popular, adjust quickly to changing trends, and get these to customers at lower prices. Burberry's plan is to launch

[7]E. J. Hultink, Abbie Griffin, Henry S. J. Robben, and Susan Hart, "In Search of Generic Launch Strategies for New Products," *International Journal of Research in Marketing*, 15(3), July 1998, pp. 269–286.

[8]R. J. Calantone and C. A. Di Benedetto, "Managing the Supply Chain Implications of Launch," in K. B. Kahn, S. E. Kay, R. J. Slotegraaf, and S. Uban (eds.), *The PDMA Handbook of New Product Development* (Hoboken, NJ: Wiley, 2013), Ch. 20, pp. 325–326.

[9]D. J. Bowersox, T. Stank, and P. Dougherty, "Lean Launch: Managing Product Introduction Risk Through Response-Based Logistics," *Journal of Product Innovation Management*, 16, 1999, pp. 557–568.

FIGURE 15.2 **Lean Launch: Two Examples**

Traditionally, computer vendors built and tested systems, then sent them to resellers who maintained inventory for a stocking period of about six to eight weeks. At the time of sale to the customer, the system is opened and modified to the customer's requirement. By contrast, Dell Computers pioneered the use of a lean launch method, employing flexible manufacturing techniques to build computers to order. To support this, Dell uses a lean manufacturing system. It orders parts directly from suppliers when needed for production, based on actual customer orders; in fact, Dell maintains an inventory stock of only one day's worth of component parts. By assembling to order, there is no finished inventory in the channel to manage. Since Dell revolutionized lean launch in the computer industry, others such as Compaq and Hewlett-Packard have also moved toward a build-to-order model with the intent of minimizing finished goods inventory.

The clothing manufacturer and retailer Benetton also uses lean launch to gain competitive advantage. Benetton uses electronic data interchange (EDI) technology to transmit orders from all worldwide locations to Italy on a daily basis. Thus, it can react instantly to demand by producing only the styles, colors, and sizes needed. Using computer-aided design and manufacturing (CAD/CAM) techniques, Benetton has reduced the amount of time from garment design to manufacture to less than a day: clothing designed in-house is fed into computerized garment cutting and knitting machines. Benetton also illustrates the principle of postponement in its dyeing process. Garments are knitted using un-dyed yarn, and the colors are applied only after seasonal color preferences are made available from EDI linkages. This minimizes stockouts of popular colors and also the likelihood of unsold stock of unpopular colors. Benetton also is part of a joint venture with a service company to speed up international forwarding and customs procedures, further reducing lead times to its foreign markets.

Source: D. J. Bowersox, T. Stank, and P. Dougherty (1999). "Lean Launch: Managing Product Introduction Risk Through Response-Based Logistics," *Journal of Product Innovation Management* 16, 557–568.

a new line of products monthly. By contrast, old-school fashion houses create the demands for upcoming fashion seasons themselves and design and produce their products months in advance of the anticipated demand. By being less flexible in terms of their manufacturing and supply chain, these traditional manufacturers are more likely to find themselves overstocked of some products and styles and out of stock in other items.[10]

Figure 15.2 illustrates two other firms that have successfully implemented lean launch systems.

Lean launch capability gives the firm some flexibility in timing the launch. Launch timing can be an unusually difficult thing to get right, because so many parties have a stake in it. Senior management may say that it is strategically the time for the new digital camera to be launched. But manufacturing may say that they are currently not ready to ramp up to full-scale production, which might take months. Or marketing may be delayed in getting the requisite training out to the sales force, or in setting up the distribution centers through big-box stores. But the competitor is about to launch its own version and so there can be no delay, and stockholders are holding their breath for a big, splashy, profitable launch. It can be quite difficult to find an optimal launch time, given so many conflicting opinions!

If the timing of the launch is wrong, there may be severe financial consequences even if the launch is otherwise planned well.[11] A late launch means the product does

[10]Rich Weissman, "Burberry Tightens Lead Times with Monthly Product Releases," *supplychaindive.com*, October 18, 2018; and the Burberry Web site, www.burberry.com.

[11]Fred Langerak, "Accelerated Product Development," in Jagdish N. Sheth and Naresh K. Malhotra, *Wiley International Encyclopedia of Marketing*, Volume 5, *Product Innovation and Management* (West Sussex, UK: John Wiley, 2011), p. 6.

not meet its sales potential or, in the extreme, misses the opportunity window altogether. Too early a launch, and the product may be commercialized without enough information on the marketplace, such as a clear specification of customer requirements or recent technology. The newest research on this topic suggests an interesting interplay between launch timing, lean launch, and product performance. A lean launch provides a firm with an option: since the time required to develop the new product is shorter, the firm can choose to launch earlier or later. So, manufacturing may be ready to go now, but marketing may require a few more weeks before the market is sufficiently primed; it is possible to delay the launch if necessary. (If the launch is not lean, the option to launch early is lost and management can only make a later launch.) But the firm still has to get the timing right, or the benefits derived from the lean launch will be compromised.[12]

Launch Tactics

Launch tactics planning includes selecting distribution channels, setting price and the marketing communications mix, training salespeople, and so on. For many firms, the launch phase is the single most costly and risky part of the new products process, and proficient implementation of launch tactics is related to improved new product performance.[13] We begin by reviewing the prevailing marketing mix. Consider Figure 15.3, which shows the major product launch decisions and actions pertaining to each component of the marketing mix. The product manufacturer (or service provider) can allocate its limited funds across the components of the marketing mix given in Figure 15.3—from spending to improve the product or add line extensions to it (to make the item more attractive to buyers) to having a retailer put on a big in-store promotion around the new item.

Developers have been following a mix from the very beginning—where decisions were made on research and development budgets. Pharmaceutical firms put the bulk of their money into technical research, White Consolidated (home appliances) puts it into manufacturing process development, and Avon and Mary Kay into personal selling.

The Communications Plan

Communications is the term most widely used to cover all of the information and attitude effort we put into changing how the end user sees our situation. It involves everything from technical products data to strong persuasion. The communications *requirements* are the specifics that must be communicated in our plan. They have been with us almost since the beginning of this project—for example, when we focused on skiers because we were sure our new plastics technology could deal more effectively

---

[12]Roger J. Calantone and C. Anthony Di Benedetto, "The Effects of Launch Execution and Timing on New Product Performance," *Journal of the Academy of Marketing Science*, 40(4), 2012, pp. 526–538.

[13]Fred Langerak, Erik Jan Hultink, and Henry S. J. Robben, "The Impact of Market Orientation, Product Advantage, and Launch Proficiency on New Product Performance and Organizational Performance," *Journal of Product Innovation Management*, 21(2), March 2004, pp. 79–94.

FIGURE 15.3   **Tactical Launch Decisions and Actions, Showing Influences on Demand**

Launch Tactic	Effective for
Promotion	
Advertising	Cases where awareness will stimulate trial
Coupons	Reinforcing awareness
Publicity	New and controversial technologies with high perceived usage risk
Sampling	Cases where product advantages best learned through usage
Beta Test Sites	Stimulating "sampling" and as a reference for other potential buyers
Sales and Distribution	
Shows/Demonstrations	Clarifying relative product advantages or where uncertainty exists
Technical Support	Cases of incompatibility in usage process
Distribution Structure	Cases where relative advantage strong (direct channels)
Intensity of Coverage	Cases where warranty/maintenance service needs to be offered easily
Distribution Incentives	Cases where availability needs to be stimulated
Pricing	
Introductory Pricing	High relative advantage and compatibility (skimming policy); early adoption needs to be stimulated (penetration policy)
Price Administration	Cases where economic risk needs to be reduced (i.e., through rebates or money-back guarantees)
Product	
Breadth of Assortment	Introducing new product categories with high relative advantage
Timing	
Product Deletion	High margin but strong relative advantage (fast deletion); high switching costs (slow deletion)
Preannouncing	Building hype for new products; useful if relative advantage is high

Source: Adapted from Joseph P. Guiltinan, "Launch Strategy, Launch Tactics, and Demand Outcomes," *Journal of Product Innovation Management* 16, no. 6, November 1999, p. 519.

with the need for skis to both slide and hold. A communications requirement would be to remind skiers about their problems with sticking skis, tell them we have a solution, what it is, how they can get it, and so on. This comes from the product innovation charter (PIC), from concept testing, and especially from the product protocol statement (where marketing requirements were listed alongside technical requirements). It can be quite short or long, but is a powerful tool in all that follows. It should be based on a solid understanding of the end user's attitudes and behavior.

The communications task is performed with a **communications mix**. There can be as many as four mixes: one for communications to the reseller by us, a second for communications to the end user by the reseller, a third for communications to the end user by us, and a fourth for the total communication effort by our team to the end user. Service firms and direct-selling manufacturers appreciate a simplification of this task because there is usually no reseller. Direct-selling manufacturers also benefit this way. The job here is to make the best choices—a mix from each set, imaginatively implemented. New products people, in particular, have wide freedom—a clean sheet of paper. There are some restrictions (from the "givens" in ongoing company operation), but still there is always room for creativity. For example, some firms take advantage of Internet newsgroups to boost communication among user groups and also to do follow-up customer support, though generally such impersonal communication should be coupled with human communication, if possible, to stay in touch with customers effectively.[14]

The Copy Strategy Statement

Given the requirements that communications tools are to deliver, let's look at a device designed to communicate these requirements to those who, for example, create advertising. Its name varies a lot in practice, but **copy strategy statement** is a common one. It can be used to convey to every advertising and promotion creative person the following items (among many others):

> The market segment being targeted
>
> The product positioning statement
>
> The communications mix and the pieces covered by this statement
>
> The major copy points to be communicated

The major points are usually product attributes, including features, functions, and benefits as well as uses, but they can be almost anything important to that end user making a favorable decision. For example:

> The provider of this insurance policy is the largest in the world.
>
> This brand of car floor mats is proudly made in the USA.
>
> This smartphone has no geographical limitation.
>
> Smith & Hawken indoor and outdoor furniture is now available at Target.

There is no limit. But there must be focus on any one list. Communication capabilities today are under great pressure—humans are exposed to millions of messages and thousands of firms. It's fine to list lots of points in a selling piece or an ad, but only a few of them should be on the requirements list. Only a few *must* be accomplished at this time. And the copy strategy statement should be written by the team, not by the person who will create the pieces for it.

Personal Selling

The salesperson is the workhorse of most new product introductions. Even on packaged goods, **personal selling** is clearly essential in this case, the important role of the detail salesperson in getting good retail availability and shelf position in key retail stores. The new products manager probably has to work harder than ever meeting the needs of these new professional sales operations. But, being professional, they know what will sell and are anxious to have new products if they are based on meeting customer needs. Because we are competing with other marketing managers for the limited pool of selling time with customers, getting sales support means internal marketing.

---

[14]Muammer Ozer, "Using the Internet in New Product Development," *Research-Technology Management*, 46(1), January–February 2003, pp. 10–17.

One issue that is sometimes difficult to decide is how early we should involve sales-people. An industrial firm developing new metal-grinding machinery will have down-stream customer coupling, and by the time the project is ready for marketing, the sales department has been involved for a long time; advertising people have not been. For consumer packaged goods, advertising people (including advertising agency person-nel) are involved early on, but the sales department usually is not. For services, the new product developer is apt to *be* in the sales department.

A difficult question comes up when the new product needs a new sales force—that is, one reaching markets the current one doesn't cover. Hopefully, less-disruptive adjustments can be made. Sometimes it is possible to add *some* of the uncovered cus-tomers or hire a small group of specialists to hit the major pockets of new customers.

A new product is an intrusion for the sales force. It takes time. It disrupts schedules. It involves change and risk. Salespeople often want new items to sell, but there are still negatives. Salespeople are not usually given reduced territories when asked to sell a new product. So it is important to (1) *investigate* in advance any possible reasons why salespeople might object to the new product, (2) give them all the *training and materials* they need to be effective, and (3) make sure the product is *available* in their territories when they start seeking orders. The key is to do our job such that they can do their job: have a product that customers will understand and want to try, and train the sales force to understand and communicate these things.

Over the last several years, under the prodding of very large buyers, business firms are reluctantly turning to a new mode of customer contact. Rather than have product-line-based sales forces, they are going to customer-based sales forces. Each rep sells a longer line but brings to the customer a team of company people who can address customer problems. The new approach makes customers happy (Walmart had to force the system upon its suppliers but is now Procter & Gamble's biggest single customer). A customer-based sales organization requires less of the hard-sell pushing that product-based sales forces can provide.[15]

Alliances

Technical departments have, in recent years, come to realize that they needn't have every possible technical capability required on a new product project. Instead, they form **strategic alliances** with universities, government units, private research centers, and even competitors to access what they need. Marketing people have been doing this for many years, and they still do. In fact, the trade channel itself is a strategic alliance. Independent firms sign a franchise agreement wherein each side promises to do certain things, the result of which is to accomplish a task. Manufacturers don't *have* to use retailers—consider computer makers like Dell that allow you to buy directly from the manufacturer.

Advertising is another area for alliances—long-standing agreements are signed with advertising agencies. Service organizations are often brought into a franchise situa-tion. The same can be said for warehousing companies, for competitors (to gain sales

[15]For more on this trend in sales force thinking, see Benson P. Shapiro, Adrian Slywotzky, and Stephen X. Doyle, "The High Impact Salesforce: The Investment You Can't Afford Not to Make," Harvard Business School Press, Publication No. 9-999-002, 1998.

forces that can reach markets where it is more profitable to use an established organization than to do the whole thing ourselves), and exhibit firms (for trade shows).

A-T-A-R Requirements

In Chapter 8, you met the A-T-A-R model. It displayed the four key steps that an end user must move through if there is to be satisfied adoption of a new product—Awareness, Trial, Availability, and Repeat use. It is the task of the marketing organization to accomplish these in a sufficiently large set of users to achieve financial and other goals. They make a good framework for deciding just what marketing activities will be undertaken.

Awareness

Awareness is the necessary first step toward adoption (though there are rare cases where a product can be consumed in ignorance or in a hurry, with awareness following that trial). Awareness means different things on different products and is sought aggressively by almost all new product marketers.

Measuring Awareness

Let's look at three quite different situations. First is a new candy bar. To a lover of candy bars, the mere mention of a new bar is enough to trigger interest and probably trial purchase. Second is a new bookkeeping software package being considered by the CEO of a small manufacturing firm. Mere mention is not enough; there must be considerable information because of the inconvenience of trial and the cost of the package. Third is a new method of cleaning up black water in municipal water-treatment systems, and the target is a senior civil engineer specializing in water treatment. There is so much at stake in their first trial recommendation that the senior person and his/her team may compile information over several years before making it.

All three people "heard of" their new items on a single day and in a single message. They may even have heard the positioning and understood it. But one is minutes away from trial and the others are months or years away.

Given that we want trial to follow awareness, what constitutes awareness differs greatly. There is no accepted definition, though consumer packaged goods usage tends to become standardized. For example, "Have you heard of a new chocolate-flavored nutrition bar loaded with 23 vitamins and minerals, which is low-glycemic and contains no trans fat?"[16] Some element of the positioning must be present.

Methods for Getting Awareness

People working in every industry have a good understanding of how to get awareness of a new product in their industry. The ideal probably is a mix: an announcement ad or sales call, then favorable mention by a friend, then seeing the item in use, then a reminder of some type, then getting some professional endorsement in a news account or column, then a reminder of some sort, and then an opportunity to buy it (which stimulates consideration of all the information previously gathered).

---

[16]The actual contents of a Clif Builder's Protein Bar, chocolate flavor.

Providing all these stimuli is apt to be expensive; the less the product has going for it, the more we have to spend on it. And there is never enough money to "do the job right."

Fortunately, the marketplace can help us on awareness and trial if we are following the process of this book. That's because we made sure there was a problem and then worked until we had a good *solution*. If the activity (bowling, eating, machining, surgery, or something else entirely) is important to the customer, so much the better. An interested, dissatisfied customer, for whom we have good news, needs little more than announcement to get awareness. It helps even more if the situation is newsworthy (such as sports, politics, financial markets, or health) and if the product is one that customers see in use frequently (car, television, clothing, and the like).

Stocking and Availability

Services are usually sold directly, and so are many goods. But most goods use resellers, such as distributors and retail dealers. They help us push the product down the channel, but only rarely does a new product offer them really new business without any major troubles. For example, Abbott's of New England nearly went broke trying to get its new chowder products into supermarkets. So, it persuaded some of the stores' deli counters to offer single portions of hot chowder. The products were soon in 20 percent of U.S. supermarkets.

Most resellers do a large volume of business in a rather standardized way with a small margin. Many have constraints on what they can and cannot do—franchise agreements, long-time personal relationships with sales representatives, channel leadership roles, and selling and service systems of their own. They are not at all anxious to make changes in their systems.

Therefore, their thinking should be represented in the product development process. If a distributor is large and powerful, it is a candidate for including very early in the new products process—when product attributes are still being worked on, when packaging is being designed, and so on. Otherwise, it is usually sufficient to have the resellers' views represented by experienced salespeople—sales managers and what are sometimes called *trade relations directors*.

We start with a statement of what the reseller's role will be. This role normally includes, for stocking distributors, (1) prestocking activities such as training and installation of equipment, (2) stocking of the new item, (3) preparation for promotion, including training salespeople and service people, and (4) actually doing the promotion, whether just listing the item in a catalog, adding the item to selling schedules, or working with individual buyers to determine their needs and convert interest into sales.

Somewhere along the line we have to know that resellers *can* do what we want and need, and that they *will* do it. Assuming they "can do," the "will do" is a matter of motivation, and for this we arrange a program of encouragement, based on items from the list in Figure 15.4. Without any question, proof that the new item will sell is the best motivation.[17] But channel firms can be tough if they feel mistreated.

---

[17]A 3M division tells how they choose the best channel for a new industrial product in V. Katsuri Rangan, Melvyn A. J. Menezes, and E. P. Maier, "Channel Selection for New Industrial Products: A Framework, Method, and Application," *Journal of Marketing*, 56(3), July 1992, pp. 69–82.

FIGURE 15.4 **Alternative Tools and Devices for Motivating Distributors**

A. Increase the distributor's unit volume.
1. Have an outstanding product.
2. Use pull techniques—advertising, trade and consumer shows, public relations, missionary selling.
3. Give the distributor a type of monopoly—exclusivity or selectivity.
4. Run "where available" ads.
5. Offer merchandising assistance—dollars, training, displays, points of purchase, co-op advertising, in-store demonstrations, store "events," and repair and service clinics.

B. Increase the distributor's unit margin.
1. Raise the basic percentage margin.
2. Offer special discounts—e.g., for promotion or service.
3. Offer allowances and special payments.
4. Offer to prepay allowances to save interest.

C. Reduce the distributor's costs of doing business.
1. Provide managerial training.
2. Provide dollars for training.
3. Improve the returned-goods policy.
4. Improve the service policy.
5. Drop-ship delivery to distributor's customers.
6. Preprice the merchandise.
7. Tray pack the merchandise or otherwise aid in repackaging it.

D. Change the distributor's attitude toward the line.
1. By encouragement—management negotiation, sales calls, direct mail, advertising.
2. By discouragement—threats to cut back some of the above benefits or legal action.
3. Rap sessions—talk groups, focus groups, councils.
4. Better product instruction sessions—better visuals, better instructions.

Elizabeth Arden Division of Unilever had to cancel a planned introduction of a new fragrance called Black Pearls because the firm slashed monies for department store salespeople. The stores refused to stock it, forcing Arden to plan distribution through mass merchandisers, but the whole deal was ultimately canceled, even though Black Pearls advertising had started running. The division stood to lose millions of dollars, and its president resigned by mutual consent. Moral: Don't deal carelessly with a necessary team player.

In several nonfood product categories, the practice of *stocklifting* is spreading. As an example, Midwest Quality Gloves purchased from Lowe's Home Improvement Warehouse 225,000 pairs of garden gloves made by its competitor, Wells Lamont, thus clearing the shelves to fill them with its own product. The competitor's product is then sold off to industrial customers as commodity goods or sold to firms that dispose of stocklifted goods by reselling them to close-out stores or foreign distributors.[18]

One trade channel where the players seem to have run out of creativity is that of food products. Large retailers now often "sell" their scarce space, charging

[18]Yumiko Ono, "Where Are the Gloves? They Were Stocklifted by a Rival Producer," *The Wall Street Journal*, May 15, 1998, p. A1.

manufacturers sizeable *slotting allowances*—so much per store for minimum shelf positions. Large firms can buy their way in, but smaller firms are pretty much shut out. Again, however, a really new item for which there is consumer demand will face a softer resistance.

Trial

Getting awareness is often difficult, but usually possible. The same goes for availability and some reseller promotion. Trial is another matter. This is the stumbling point for most products that fail, and it is the cause of winning products not winning a great deal more.

Trial of a new product is *limited usage*, hopefully under normal usage conditions, that will permit the customer to verify claims and learn the advantages and disadvantages of the good or service. Trial is on a scale from a taste test of a new cheese in a supermarket to a three-year experiment by a major company on a new telecommunications system. A firm can spend a fortune on free samples to generate trial. To make this investment worthwhile, there must be learning, relative to the adoption decision; thus, the cheese taste may be a full trial if taste by the tester is the only issue. But if the rest of the family has a say, or if the package may or may not keep the cheese fresh, or if the product tends to turn gray while sitting on a table or in a sandwich, then the taste test was not a trial.

Trial may be *personal, vicarious,* or *virtual.* With elevators, plant location services, and burial services, satisfactory personal trial conditions are difficult, though visiting the site of a previous buyer simulates trial. So buyers gather the trial experience of others in a vicarious experience. Virtual trial can be achieved by various electronic setups, even a pseudovirtual experience via video.

A key requirement is that a trial must have some "cost" associated with it. The more important the trial, the more the cost, or there is not enough motivation for the necessary learning to take place. The cheese taste test, just mentioned, had very little cost (a few seconds of time, possible embarrassment in the store if the taste is awful), so the customer would consider little more than the taste and perhaps color, aroma, and texture.

That is usually not enough for the next step in the process—the acceptance of the item, its adoption into a usage system, or its repeat purchase. The cheese taster probably would want to buy a small package and take it home for the *real* trial.

Barriers to Trial

Barriers to trial cause customers to delay or even permanently postpone trial. In Chapter 16, you saw several new product characteristics that influence trial rates: relative advantage, compatibility with current product usage, complexity, divisibility, and communicability. Of these, the first two, relative advantage and compatibility, probably have the greatest influence on trial and adoption. Furthermore, they can be influenced directly by launch strategies and tactics: that is, if high perceived relative advantage and/or compatibility can be achieved at the time of launch, desired levels of trial (and, ultimately, demand) will be attained.

FIGURE 15.5 **Appropriate Launch Tactics Given Relative Advantage and Compatibility**

	A. Low Relative Advantage	**B. High Relative Advantage**
1. Low Compatibility	Penetration price Slow deletion Risk-based promotion (leasing, money-back guarantees, equipment allowances) Intensive distribution	Preannounce Broad product assortments Information-based promotion (shows, demonstrations, Web sites, publicity/education) Selective distribution
2. High Compatibility	Secrecy before entry Narrow product assortments Awareness promotion (coupons, etc.) Intensive distribution	Skim price Fast deletion Usage-based promotion (samples, beta tests) to clarify benefits received Selective distribution

Source: Adapted from Joseph P. Guiltinan, "Launch Strategy, Launch Tactics, and Demand Outcomes," *Journal of Product Innovation Management* 16, no. 6, November 1999, pp. 520–521.

A framework for choosing launch tactics given levels of relative advantage and compatibility is shown in Figure 15.5. In each cell of this figure, the selected launch tactics are designed to leverage opportunities (such as a high level of compatibility) or to offset a constraint (e.g., distinguish a new product from other similar ones).

Low Relative Advantage and Low Compatibility Start with the upper left cell in Figure 15.5. Novelty products (such as Celsius "negative-calories" energy drink or Coca-Cola's Smartwater electrolyte-enhanced water) and some service products (such as a new financial service offering that bundles stocks and other investments with a credit/debit card) will fit this category: low incremental advantage and relatively incompatible with buyers' experiences. The launch plan must therefore be designed to reduce any economic or other risks associated with the product's purchase. Intensive distribution reduces search costs, while penetration price minimizes buyers' financial risk. Since the new product may not offer great advantage over products currently on the market, customer migration will be slow, and one should not delete the older product from the market quickly (and potentially annoy current customers). Promotion should also aid in risk reduction by offering money-back guarantees, warranties, or tie-ins to existing products.

High Relative Advantage and High Compatibility Now go diagonally down to the lower right cell in Figure 15.5. Here one finds products that are clearly superior on attributes that buyers consider important (such as a smartphone with more features and bigger screen size or a computer with faster operations). These are the diametric opposite of the products in the upper left cell, and recommended launch tactics consequently are the mirror images of the ones recommended above. Sampling or beta testing allows the potential user to see the product's advantages for themselves. Skimming pricing and selective distribution are recommended if the early adopters are likely to exert high search efforts in order to get the desired attributes. Because of the product's inherent benefits, customer migration will occur swiftly and deletion of the older products can be fast.

High Relative Advantage and Low Compatibility   In the upper right cell of Figure 15.5 are the new-to-the-world products that, due to their very newness, are likely to be somewhat incompatible in terms of values or use (think microwave oven or hybrid car). Launch tactics must center around directing extensive product information to prospective customers both to emphasize relative advantages and to reduce perceived incompatibility. Preannouncements may be necessary to warn prospects to prepare for the impending changes in their usage systems. Additionally, a broad assortment may be useful, especially if this helps to customize the product to different high-potential segments.

Low Relative Advantage and High Compatibility   These are the direct opposite of the products in the upper right cell of Figure 15.5: familiar products yet low relative advantage. In this cell, generating brand awareness and capitalizing on brand equity will be the most important factors in getting trial. As seen in Chapter 14, care must be taken in brand extension as a new brand with little relative performance advantage (but a cheaper price) might erode brand equity. Coors apparently was thinking of this when they launched the lower-priced Keystone brand under its own name. Intensive distribution makes sense here; additionally, distributors will be more amenable to carrying and selling a narrower assortment.

How to Overcome Those Barriers

Fortunately, development of the marketing program begins well ahead of launch because that's when most of the barrier problems should be addressed. And most of them come to developers' attention during concept testing and product use testing, as well as from experience in the industry. And most of the barriers respond to more than one solution.

Note how many of the launch tactics concern price—penetration pricing or skimming, for example. Other price tactics can include free goods, couponing, a signing bonus, deferred payment, refunding cost of competitor's stocks, price, discounts, rebates, free service, free replacement offer, cooperative advertising, direct cash payment for trying, and so on. Why is this? In most cases, the buyer is deferring trial because of anticipating loss of something—loss of time, money, or prestige, for example. The most obvious answer is to pay the buyer for such loss.

This emphasis on price has led sellers to adopt complex discount schedules (it's easier later to drop a discount than to raise the list price). Using discounts also fits with the most popular of the new product price strategies:

> *Premium*—a very high price, intended to stay that way, with clear product differentiation.
>
> *Skim*—a price clearly above the market, but appropriate to a differentiated product, nonthreatening to competition, and with room for some price manipulations.
>
> *Meet the market*—though there may be no *one* market price, this strategy says pick a price that takes price out of the play as much as possible. It is a

waste for a clearly superior product unless the marketer has no market acceptance.

Penetration—the price that is clearly low and designed to buy one's way into the market. Will be met perhaps, but in the meantime share is gained. Dangers: little room to discount, tough to raise later after share is achieved, and if met immediately, just wastes the opportunity and at a lower price.

Skim seems to achieve the benefit both ways—brings some of the product's value to our bottom line and gives marketers freedom to meet special opportunities, yet doesn't price us out of the market. Of course, if the differentiation is worth a great deal, truly making the earlier item obsolete, then premium pricing is defensible.

Repeat Purchase

If our target market buyers do a serious trial on our new item, and if we had previously been assured from the product use test that people would like it, repeat buying is virtually ensured. There are competitive actions to repel and counter. There is the continuing problem of complacency, especially in markets where our item's benefits are not crucial to anything. There is the careless new product manager who fails to keep a ready supply available for the buyer who wants to repeat.

And, as always, we need to be sure customers are satisfied with their total relationships with our firm, well beyond the product itself.

Usually, we have actions in the marketing program to encourage further usage (e.g., long-term discounts, new uses for the item, and ready availability of additional product, as well as of continued service). And we will see in Chapter 17 how a measure of repeat purchase is a key part of the postlaunch control program, in which we prepare to deal with at least some of the problems that may come up. If there is any evidence of product failure (which may be expected to happen if the product use test had to be skipped), it will be investigated promptly and corrections negotiated through the technical members of the team.

Summary

Chapter 15 was the second of a two-chapter set on the subject of marketing planning. It dealt with what some call the tactical portion of the planning task. We looked at the launch cycle, the communication program, and the requirements for success: Awareness, Trial, Availability, and Repeat purchase (A-T-A-R). Each is very difficult to attain, given the ongoing nature of life and business out there in the market and the actions of other players such as competitors. Since a marketing launch entails hundreds or even thousands of actions, we focused on those that seem most critical and the most difficult in practice.

Once the full marketing launch plan has been worked out, many firms like to devise some way to hold a dress rehearsal—just to see if there are any glitches. After all, millions of dollars may be spent in the next few months. In Chapter 16, we will look at what is called market testing. It is the third of a testing triad—with concept testing (Chapter 7) and product use testing (Chapter 13).

Case: Coca-Cola Life[19]

Founded in Atlanta, Georgia, in 1886 and still headquartered in Atlanta, the Coca-Cola Company needs no introduction. Coca-Cola products are literally found in every country in the world except Cuba and North Korea. Coca-Cola sells over 500 brands of sparkling and nonsparkling beverages worldwide and accounts for about 1.9 billion servings per day. Among its hundreds of brands are four of the global top five soft drinks: Coca-Cola, Diet Coke, Fanta, and Sprite. Other top-selling brands include Minute Maid, Honest Tea, Dasani, Powerade, and many more.

Of the hundreds of Coca-Cola brands, a great number are sold only in a few countries. Sokenbicha, for example, is a Japanese tea product sold only in Japan and in selected U.S. markets. Maaza, a calcium-enriched mango drink, is found in India, Bangladesh, the Netherlands, and Maldives. Over the years, a number of Coca-Cola products arrived on the shelves, only to disappear a few months later. These include Coke Blak (a coffee-flavored cola), Coke Vanilla, Coca-Cola with Lemon or with Lime, and many others. Some of these might have been launched for tactical reasons: to shake up consumer preferences, encourage loyal Pepsi drinkers to try a new flavor, grab shelf space, and so on. But three cola brands have, for years, been positioned as the "big three" in most countries: Coke, Diet Coke (called Coke Light in some markets), and Coke Zero Sugar. Unlike some of the smaller brands listed above, these three are considered strategic brands, globally important and managed centrally by corporate headquarters.

A quick look at international Web sites provides evidence of the strategic importance of these brands. Go to any Coca-Cola global Web page (try suffixes like .fr, .it, .de, or .in for France, Italy, Germany, and India, respectively), and the three brands are usually prominently displayed somewhere on the page.

Since 2013, there has been an attempt to add a fourth global brand, Coke Life. Originally developed by Coke researchers in Argentina and Chile, this drink uses stevia as an all-natural sweetener, uses much less sugar than regular Coke, and has no artificial sweeteners. The product was initially launched in Argentina and Chile and slowly rolled out to the global market.

A little background on this launch is required. Although Coke remains a profitable brand for the Coca-Cola company, soft drink sales have been on the decline for some time. The company has responded in several ways: investing in nonsparkling beverages such as bottled water, tea, and fruit juice and making package size changes to their soft drink lines to align better with customer preferences. But another response has been to consider the trend toward calorie counting. As far back as 1982, Coke launched Diet Coke, a sugar-free version originally sweetened with aspartame and now using NutraSweet. (In other countries, aspartame and/or

---

[19]This case is based on several sources, including Kate Taylor, "Coca-Cola's Business Shows a Bleak Future for Soda," *Business Insider*, July 27, 2016; Anonymous, "Coca-Cola Life: La Nueva Versión de la Bebida Creada in Chile y Argentina," *CNN Chile*, November 21, 2013; Justine Hofherr, "Is the New Coca-Cola 'Life' Healthier than Regular Coke? (And Will It Come to The U.S.?)," *The Boston Globe*, June 17, 2014; Harry Wallop, "Taste Test: Does Coca-Cola Life Taste Better than Regular Coke?," *The Telegraph*, August 22, 2014; and others.

other sweeteners may be used.) In 2005, Coke Zero was rolled out. This also contains artificial sweeteners but is claimed to be closer in taste to Coke (Diet Coke has a somewhat different flavor). By 2017, Coke Zero was reformulated and renamed Coca-Cola Zero Sugar. While the actual mix of sweeteners varies from one market to another, Coca-Cola Zero Sugar, like Diet Coke, is sweetened with only artificial sweeteners.

This brings us to the Coca-Cola Life launch. With three cola products on the market, Coca-Cola felt there was room for a product that delivered full taste and few calories, while still being all-natural with no artificial sweeteners. In Argentina and other South American countries, stevia (an all-natural sugar substitute derived from plants) was already popular, and Coca-Cola rolled out the new Coca-Cola Life product. This does contain some sugar as well as stevia, but it contains only about 60 percent of the calories of Coca-Cola (about 27 calories per 100 mL).

The product was first sold in Argentina in June 2013 and then Chile in November 2013, positioned as a drink for healthy lifestyles. The original Argentinian ad, showing a young couple raising a child, was an award-winning commercial and can be seen at: www.youtube.com/watch?v=xPb1t3jU3sI. Coca-Cola Life packaging was mostly green (later labels added a touch of red, the Coca-Cola company color). (Green is used very prominently in the advertisement as well.)

Coca-Cola chose to roll out Coca-Cola Life slowly into the global market. In 2014, it entered Sweden and the U.K., as well as the United States (but in relatively limited distribution). By 2015, it was in France, Australia, and several other markets. By 2018, it was in about 40 markets worldwide.

Coca-Cola Life has had mixed success in its first five years of existence. It was dropped in Australia after about two years, due to low sales, and replaced with a similar product, Coca-Cola with Stevia, which contains more stevia and less sugar than Coke Life. Similarly, in the U.K., after the 2014 launch resulted in low sales, the product was reformulated and the new version contained even less sugar. Nevertheless, due to continued slow sales coupled with an uptick in Coca-Cola Zero Sugar sales in the U.K., Coke Life was discontinued there in 2017. Interestingly, blind taste tests in the U.K. found that people preferred Life to other Coca-Cola products.

Is Coca-Cola Life a good strategic addition to Coca-Cola's product range? What are the pros and cons of adding this product to the "big three" strategic cola brands, effectively creating a "big four" in some markets?

Coca-Cola chose a very slow geographic rollout of Coca-Cola Life. What are the advantages of this strategy? Are there any disadvantages to entering slowly? Would it make sense for Coca-Cola to try another rollout strategy (for example, entering in certain distribution channels and then expanding into other channels through time)?

ANSWERS TO FIGURE V.2

1. *Teams* make these decisions, not one functional group.
2. Marketing people have been in all along. And there should be no "taking over" because technical people should stay.
3. These paradigms *aid thinking*. Exuberance and excitement we have, but they don't replace thinking.

4. Not *marketing's*—the *entire firm's*. Every part of the firm has contributed to what we offer the end user. Hopefully, the end user has a problem and will welcome the product.

5. A good target market has several dimensions, not just sales potential. A large piece of a favorable segment may be much more profitable.

6. The PIC guides *all* phases—it is a strategic plan for the entire operation through to whatever its goals call for.

7. Data don't support this. Quite often, a follower comes up with the winning design.

8. Goals may be expressed in customer satisfaction terms too, but there are usually other goals unique to the situation—for example, build a bridge to new market dominance.

9. Perhaps if really meaningless, but they should be meaningful, helpful in telling the product story.

10. The launch is *managed*—if we start to sink, let's hope there is a large bucket handy. (See Chapter 17.)

11. Opening night is the first salvo in a drive to achieve the project goals—success. A successful opening night brings little profit, but a long run brings a big one.

CHAPTER SIXTEEN

Market Testing

Setting

At this time, glance back at Figure V.1 in the introduction to Part V. It shows the basic new products process and where we are at this time. We have a physical product or the complete specifications for a new service. Early concept testing showed a need, and the use test indicated the emerging product met that need without serious drawbacks. And we have a marketing plan.

Now what do we do? Market the item quickly before competition finds out what we are up to? Or find a way to check out what we have done to see if it really looks as if we will be successful, before spending a lot of money on the launch? The option open to us is called **market testing**. This chapter gives the overall picture for market testing and introduces several methods commonly used: pseudo sale, controlled sale, and full sale.

We also discuss trends in market testing: As firms make a greater commitment to accelerated time to market, we are seeing a movement toward quicker, less-costly market testing methods that provide the required information as efficiently as possible. For example, **test marketing** (selling the product in two or more representative cities) is in fact now a relatively minor market testing technique. It's still done on some occasions, but it has lost much ground to newer, faster, and cheaper methods. (Don't confuse the terms *test marketing* and *market testing*!) Scanner-based methods are, of course, a big part of the trend in obtaining quick, reliable marketplace information. Many firms have replaced the traditional test market with a product rollout (initially limited-distribution sale, gradually expanded to the full market).

Recall that we have been stressing speed to market and the role of the new product team in accelerating time to market, starting in Chapter 1 and throughout this book. It is only fitting that we are seeing many new types of market testing grow in popularity relative to test marketing, given their advantages of cost, speed, and accuracy.

The Market Testing Decision

The full set of market testing technique options will come later. First, we need to get a feeling for the decision to test or not to test.

When Is the Decision Made?

The decision of whether and how to test can be made at many different times (see Figure 16.1). On the one hand, the longer we wait, the more we will know about our

FIGURE 16.1
Decision Matrix on When to Market Test

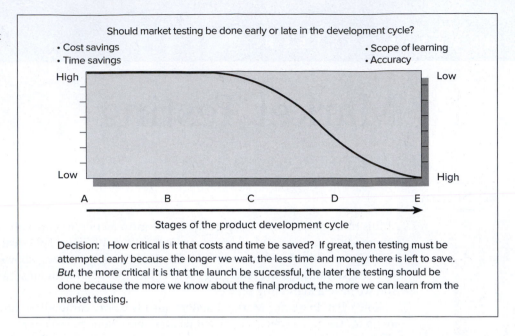

Should market testing be done early or late in the development cycle?

- Cost savings
- Time savings

- Scope of learning
- Accuracy

Stages of the product development cycle

Decision: How critical is it that costs and time be saved? If great, then testing must be attempted early because the longer we wait, the less time and money there is left to save. *But*, the more critical it is that the launch be successful, the later the testing should be done because the more we know about the final product, the more we can learn from the market testing.

product and its marketing program; that makes testing more useful and more reliable. But the longer we wait to do the test, the higher the costs, the later the entry, the more damage competitors can do, and so on. The solution is to begin the testing as soon as a technique can be found that will tell us *what we need to know*. Some consumer products market testing actually begins before the product is even firmed up—it works with a concept statement! Other market testing, such as that with an appliance manufacturer or carmaker, cannot be done until we have everything in place ready to go.

Is This an Easy Decision to Make?

Any time we make a new product, we cannot really be sure about *anything*. With a few rare exceptions, *everything* we think we know about the new product and its marketing is not a fact—it is an opinion, a guess, a judgment, a hope, possibly an order from above. The full scenario of the new item's marketing will be played out on a playing field where all too many people still have to react to something. Even they cannot be sure of their reaction, especially when we aren't completely sure what our offer will be, and we surely cannot anticipate what competition will tell buyers about it.

It takes a strong manager to say at this point, "I know we have spent a fortune, and we are running late, but I am not convinced we have made the right decisions. I want to take a couple of months (or more) to be sure." What kind of confidence does that inspire in the typical top management?

Keep in mind that asking for a market test is not a confession of failure on the team's part. This is also true in other fields. Trial performances of a new Broadway play may be staged in Detroit, Boston, or the Midwest to make minor or major revisions. In product development, as in stage productions, the decision *not* to do the test would seem to require the burden of proof.

It is true that many products underwent no market testing and were successful. But there are far too many counterexamples that show what can happen when the market test is skipped or does not test the entire marketing plan. Carter-Wallace, the makers of Nair hair removal cream, developed a version of their product for men for use on arms, legs, and back (some swimmers, cyclists, or other athletes would be interested in this product). They chose the name "Nair for Men." Would you advocate going to the market without at least testing the name? To the target audience, does "Nair" mean "the most established name in hair removal cream" or "something my sister would use"? Would they have responded better to a name like "Michael Jordan Performance Cream"? The latter, while more suggestive of athletic performance, would have lost the equity of the Nair name, namely, its quality reputation.[1]

Think about some of the new product failures introduced in the case at the end of Chapter 13: Avert Virucidal Tissues, Uncle Ben's Rice with Calcium, and so forth—or about whatever favorite new product failure comes to mind. We may never know to what extent these products were market tested. But it is a safe bet to say that these manufacturers wish they had done a better job in the market test!

Market Tests Must Have Teeth

Figure 16.2 shows how market testing relates to other testing—the three major tests covering the three major causes for new product failure—concept testing for "lack of need," product use testing for "product does not meet need," and market testing for "marketed poorly." Many times a firm is in a hurry at all three of those times, so it first skips the concept test, then it skips the field use testing, and then, if it also skips market testing, it will be flying blind. Once in a while, the firm gets it right and nothing is lost by skipping the market test. Years ago, Campbell executives were reportedly so excited about the concept of Spaghetti-Os that they bypassed test markets and went right to launch and never looked back. This is very risky, of course, and not what we recommend here; most firms would do at least some kind of market test of the type we will see in this chapter. But the market test must have teeth, meaning that managers are willing to take action based on the results. In some cases, negative market test results are ignored because the product team does not want to kill the CEO's pet project!

Regardless of the kind of market test used, planners go to the trouble of market testing to gain two important insights. First, this is the opportunity to obtain *solid forecasts of dollar and unit sales*—not the general market figures or ranges of possible shares that guided earlier planning decisions. Second, the planners need *diagnostic information* to help them revise and refine anything about the launch that seems to require it—product, packaging, communication effort, or anything else. To gather solid quantitative forecasts and the diagnostic information and then, for whatever reason, not use it is asking for trouble.

Market tests must have teeth—poor market test results should not be ignored. Remember in Chapter 7 when we noted that in early phases we could have relatively low hurdles so as not to terminate a promising concept before it was fully worked out?

---

[1] When in market testing, the Nair for Men name tested well in online surveys, and the product was successfully launched under this name.

FIGURE 16.2
How Market
Testing Relates
to the Other
Testing Steps

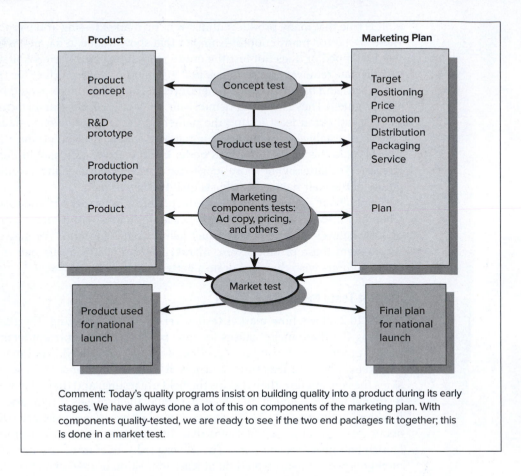

Comment: Today's quality programs insist on building quality into a product during its early stages. We have always done a lot of this on components of the marketing plan. With components quality-tested, we are ready to see if the two end packages fit together; this is done in a market test.

We needed to establish more difficult hurdles at the time of concept evaluation, because committing to development of a new concept is costly and time-consuming, and it incurs opportunity costs since other promising concepts are not developed. At this very late phase in the process, the same principle applies. For a product that passes the market test, the next phase is launch, and as the examples show, the amounts at stake escalate sharply at this point!

The Factors for Deciding Whether to Market Test

Each new product project has a unique situation, but here are the most common important factors considered in the market test decision.

Any Special Twists on the Launch

Did the original charter dictate a tight time schedule? There may be special considerations such as the need for new volume to help sell off an operation or the need to assist a new CEO to get off to a quick start. Does the charter limit the funds for the project such that it *must* be rolled out, growing to each new phase as profits come in from earlier phases? Is this launch part of a far bigger launch program, for example, where the firm is trying to gain new industry experience in one world market to permit a critical expansion into another world market?

What Information Is Needed

We look first to see if this is one of those situations where huge sums of money have been spent and careers staked, yet no one knows what will really happen out there when the item becomes available. Conditions permitting, there is a strong argument for thorough market testing. This is partly to avoid a huge loss from market rejection but also to protect against being surprised by too *much* volume. Supermarkets and food producers were not prepared for the growth in demand for organic food products and have scrambled to find new global sources of organic ingredients and increase domestic production.[2] Later launches have been supported by the rollout market testing process discussed later in this chapter.

One experienced Procter & Gamble (P&G) market researcher said he considers skipping the market test if the following conditions exist:

1. Capital investments are small and forecasts are conservative.
2. The use tests went well and consumer interest is high.
3. The company knows the business well and has been successful there.
4. Advertising is ready and successfully tested; sales promotion plan does not depend on perfect execution.[3]

Interestingly, one way P&G market tests new products is to list them, together with their retail price, on their Web site. They judge the likely interest in a new product by how many customers click on the site and order the product. P&G's Crest Whitestrips, the home tooth-whitening kit, sold at a relatively high $44 at the time of its launch and was initially offered only on whitestrips.com. E-mails to potential consumers were used to encourage visiting the Web site, in addition to TV and magazine ads. The response to the online campaign was very promising: About 12 percent of visitors to the site bought the kit, accounting for about 144,000 kits sold in the first eight months. With these results, it was relatively easy for P&G to overcome retailers' skepticism about the high price per kit and to convince them to stock the product.[4]

Another type of information need is more *operational*. It is for learning, as in learning *how* to do something that the launch requires. A launch involves all functions, each with its own needs. The manufacturing and production department needs to plan around solid volume estimates and must also at this point identify any difficulties in ramping up from smaller batch sizes to full-scale production. The service department (whether internal or contracted out) needs to know what the likely service demands will be so that it can be sufficiently prepared. The firm needs to know about any special needs or requirements from outside vendors or resellers. In addition, will product

[2]Anonymous, "Demand for Organic Food Exceeds Supply," *foxnews.com*, July 6, 2006; updated January 13, 2015.

[3]Robert E. Davis, "The Role of Market Research in the Development of New Consumer Products," *Journal of Product Innovation Management*, 10(4), September 1993, pp. 309–317.

[4]John Gaffney, "How Do You Feel about a $44 Tooth-Bleaching Kit?" *Business 2.0*, October 2001, p. 46.

acceptance by customers be as expected, or will customer adoption require a significant, unforeseen change in purchasing habits? And what is the likely effect of product cannibalization? To what extent will the new product's sales volume come at the expense of other products already on the market?

The above conditions argue *for* information, but today's managers anticipate this problem by building in customer involvement. Firms that rely on the voice of the customer from the very beginning (as we have seen back in Chapter 4, even having customers as members of their new product teams) get early answers to lots of questions. Some firms approach this level of involvement by having customers pay for the material used in product use testing. Additionally, **total quality management** programs familiar in many firms force some of the learning needed for items earlier in this list.

Costs

Market test costs include: (1) direct costs of the test—fees to market research firms, (2) costs of the launch itself—for production, selling, and so on, and (3) lost revenue that a national launch would have brought. Sometimes the costs of launch are so great that firms don't even consider market testing. For example, in the automobile industry, their big cost is getting the finished product; once they have cars, there is little inclination to market them in a limited geographical area, or so they have felt. Many Japanese automakers, nevertheless, will roll out new cars through the West Coast first as a market test.

Methods of Market Testing

Marketers have developed a seemingly endless array of market testing methods for new products. One firm uses a very large company cafeteria. Another uses small foreign divisions. In the Chipotle case in Chapter 13, you saw how this company uses one single Manhattan restaurant as a test site for new products. But the methods tend to fall into one of the following three general categories. Figure 16.3 shows where each of the methods is most useful.

Pseudo Sale

This approach asks potential buyers to do something (such as say they would buy *if* the product were actually available, or pick the item off the shelf of a *make-believe store*). The action is distinct and identifiable, and much of the marketing strategy is utilized in the presentation; but the key factor here is little pain for the buyer—no spending, no major risk. It is, as the name says, a **pseudo sale**. It can be done early.

Controlled Sale

Here the buyer must make a purchase. The sale may be quite formal or informal, but it is conducted under *controlled conditions*. The method is still research because the product has not been released for regular sale. Some key variable (often distribution) is not opened up but is contrived. **Controlled sale** is more vigorous than the pseudo sale, however, and much more revealing.

FIGURE 16.3
Methods
of Market
Testing and
Where Used

| | Product Categories Where Useful | | | | |
| | Industrial | | Consumer | | |
	Goods	Services	Packaged	Durables	Services
Pseudo sale					
Speculative sale	■	■		■	■
Simulated test marketing			■	■	■
Controlled sale					
Informal selling	■	■		■	
Direct marketing	■			■	
Minimarketing	■		■	■	
Full sale					
Test marketing	■	■	■	■	■
Rollout					
By application	■	■			
By influence	■	■			■
By geography	■	■	■	■	
By trade channel	■		■	■	

Full Sale

In a **full sale**, the firm has decided to fully market the product (this is not the case in the above methods). But it wants to do so on a limited basis first to see if everything is working right. Barring some catastrophe, the product will go to full national launch.

Pseudo Sale Methods

Product innovators use two approaches to get potential users to make some expression of commitment resembling a sale without actually laying out money. The **speculative sale** method asks them if they would buy it, and the **simulated test market (STM)** method creates a false buying situation and observes what they do.

Speculative Sale

This is a technique used primarily by firms in business-to-business markets and consumer durables. It sounds very similar to the technique used in concept and product use tests, differing as follows:

> In the *concept test*, we give the new item's positioning claim and perhaps something about its form or manufacture. Then we ask, "How likely would you be to buy a product like this, if we made it?"

> In *product use testing*, we give customers some of the product, have them use it in some normal way, and then ask the same question, "How likely would you be to buy a product like this, if we made it?"

> In the *pseudo sale method* called "*speculative*," we go to the customer, give them the full pitch on the product in a version close to ultimate marketing, answer questions, negotiate prices, and lead up to the closing question, "If we make this product available as I have described it, would you buy it?"

This testing is typically done by regular salespeople using selling materials that are developed and ready to go. They make pseudo sales calls—presenting the new product as though it were available for purchase. The difference this time is that the product is real, as are the price, delivery schedules, selling presentation, and so on. The target customer is real, and the positioning is clear. The buyer has little to do except make a decision. That decision may be just to ask for some samples to try, but that's okay. Trial is industry's way of making the first purchase and is really what we are trying to measure at this time.

Although the tool is typically used for business products, it can be used for certain consumer products. Rubbermaid is an example. Rubbermaid sells its products essentially by a push strategy, with some image advertising to consumers, but product presentation is confined to store counters. This setting can be duplicated easily, so Rubbermaid uses the speculative method in a setting that looks much like a focus group concept test (except using a finished product with information on usage, pricing, and so on). The consumer faces a situation much like that in a store and can easily speculate on whether a purchase would be made.

Situations where the speculative method fits include:

1. Where industrial firms have very close downstream relationships with key buyers.
2. Where new product work is technical, entrenched within a firm's expertise, and only little reaction is needed from the marketplace.
3. Where the adventure has very little risk, and thus a costlier method is not defendable.
4. Where the item is new (say, a new material or a completely new product type) and key diagnostics are needed. For example, what set of alternatives does the potential buyer see, or what possible applications come to mind first?

There is no advertising in a speculative sale market test, and the ways of using it are many. For example, some people reject the idea of making a presentation to a buyer and then admitting there is actually no product available to buy. In such cases, they simply tell buyers, "We are getting ready to market a new product, and I want to know if you might be interested."

Simulated Test Market

Packaged goods firms do a great deal of product development, yet the speculative sale method, described above, wouldn't work for them. They too wanted a method that was cheaper, more confidential, and faster than the controlled sale and full sale methods that follow. They found it in the A-T-A-R model discussed in Chapter 7. The method was a spinout from concept testing and comes very early in the development process. For being early, it is sometimes called *premarket testing*—testing that is done prior to getting ready to market—but *simulated test marketing* (STM) is the more common term today. Most usage is well ahead of the time other market testing can be used.[5] The name *simulated test market* came to be used because mathematical formulas are used to simulate the marketplace.

The central idea is to get estimates of *trial purchasing* and *repeat purchasing*. *Awareness* comes from the advertising agency's component testing, and the firm's managers supply the other factors of *market units, availability, prices,* and *costs* that are required to turn A-T-A-R into a sales forecast. An example of a typical simulated test market procedure is given in Figure 16.4, though keep in mind that practice varies considerably from one market research supplier to another.

These pretests usually involve 300 to 600 people, require 8 to 14 weeks, and cost a small fraction of a full test market (exact cost will depend on the number of sales waves). Among the prominent suppliers of STMs is BASES, a division of ACNielsen. BASES combines consumer response data (similar to that shown in Figure 16.4) with the firm's marketing plans to assess new product sales potential, allowing the manufacturer to tailor the allocation of marketing resources to improve the product's success potential. Another major supplier is Information Resources Incorporated (IRI). Among other services, IRI provides a product benchmarking service that scans an extensive database of new products to determine critical trial and repeat levels that can spell success or failure for the new product being tested.[6]

STM services are offered in various forms and are continuously being improved. Recently, for example, BASES began stopping people as they *entered supermarkets,* gave them the pitch, asked them questions, gave them a coupon, and then followed up with the store later to see how many shoppers actually bought the item that was then available in the store.[7]

[5]Don't confuse these STM models with other models, such as TRACKER, that are used for interpreting early results in test marketing cities. Marketing scientists have models to cover almost every step in the new product development and marketing process, but here we can cover only the usage leaders.

[6]Check out both of these sources' Web sites, www.acnielsen.com and www.iriworldwide.com (the latter is IRI's site). Other notable providers include the NPD Group at www.npd.com, Simmons Research at www.simmonsresearch.com, and TNS at www.tnsglobal.com.

[7]An excellent (though dated) evaluation of these STM models can be found in Allan D. Shocker and William G. Hall, "Pretest Market Models: A Critical Evaluation," *Journal of Product Innovation Management,* 3(3), September 1986, pp. 86–107.

FIGURE 16.4   A Sample Simulated Test Market Conducted as a Mall Intercept

1. Respondents are approached as they walk through the mall and invited to participate in a marketing study. (At least one major supplier does this step by telephone.) Respondents are qualified by observation before interviewing (estimates of age, sex, income, family status, and so on) and by questioning (such as product category usage) during a brief interview in the mall corridor. Employees of competitors will be eliminated at this step. Selected respondents are invited to step into a nearby research facility, which usually is one of the empty mall store areas.

2. In the facility, the respondents may be given a self-administered questionnaire asking for their attitudes and practices in one or more product categories. Then comes either individual or small-group exposure to broadcasting or print advertising stimuli. TV ads may or may not be couched in a television presentation (for example, a TV pilot program that is itself being tested). Print ads may be in what appears to be a magazine or on separate tear sheets. Several ads are presented so the respondent isn't sure what is being tested. One of the ads is for the new product being market tested. It gives the full story, including claims and price. (Note: Practice can vary, depending on the client and the company doing the testing.)

3. The respondent is then taken into another room, usually what appears to be a very small convenience store with shelves of products. The test manager gives the respondent cash or play money, not usually enough to make a purchase but enough to make such a purchase less painful. A respondent so inclined can walk right out without making a purchase, even with actual cash. The respondent shops and, hopefully, purchases the new product advertised in the first room—this yields the variable *Trial*. (One leading company does not use a mock-up store, but simply asks respondents standard buying intention questions as we used in Chapter 16 on product use testing, then gives the trial product to those who express buying interest.)

4. Most of the participants are then free to go. Perhaps 10 percent are taken into another room where a focus group is held. Another 10 percent may be asked to fill out another self-administered questionnaire covering postexposure attitudes, planned product usage, and the like. Those that purchased the product are contacted later, nonbuyers are questioned as to why they did not buy the product, and participants may be given trial packages of the product as a thank-you for doing the study.

5. Some time later (time varies with the product category involved), the respondent is contacted by telephone. The call may be identified with the mall experience or it may be camouflaged. Information is sought about such things as product usage, reactions, and future intentions. Many diagnostics are obtained at this time, such as who in the family used the product, how it was used, and products it was used with.

At the end of the call, the respondent may be offered a chance to buy more of the product. This is the first step in a *sales wave*. Product is delivered to the respondent's home by mail or another delivery system, and the call is later repeated, new information gathered, and another sale opportunity offered. The sales wave provides information on another critical variable— *repeat*.

Output

Consumers give their opinions on the product, they buy or ask for some, they react to it, and so on. But the key purpose is to estimate how well the product will sell, so the various services offer trial rate, repeat rate, market share estimates, and volume estimates. The latter come when they combine trial-and-repeat rates with the client's assumptions on awareness, retail availability, competitive actions, and the like.

A key aspect of the method is its mathematical simulation. If the client doesn't like the sales forecast from a study, variations are easily tested. For example, the model can be "asked" what amount of trial would be necessary to get to the desired market share. In turn, the cost of getting that trial (for example, by doubling the number of coupons currently planned for the introductory period or by lowering the price for a while) can be evaluated.

There are two variations on the above procedure, and the difference comes in how the data are analyzed. BASES Group, the current leading provider of the service, takes a fairly simple approach, relying on heuristics (rules of thumb derived from trial-and-error experience with previous, comparable situations). They gather the raw trial-and-repeat data from the test and calibrate them using their vast data set of thousands of comparable product introductions from the past to come out with adjusted trial and repeat measures. They then put these adjusted data through their version of the A-T-A-R model to project sales and market share.

Other leading suppliers use mathematical models, not heuristics, to derive their forecasts. This approach demands that more information be supplied by the client, but it is more useful in running simulations. One of the more prominent models is ASSESSOR, which is distinguished by its ability to make two forecasts (one using an A-T-A-R model and one using a preference model) and comparing the two to come up with market share predictions.[8] Consumer goods producers such as SC Johnson often test new products using the ASSESSOR simulated test market procedure.[9]

ASSESSOR's A-T-A-R model projects market share for a new product based on estimates of awareness, trial-and-repeat purchases. Customer data are gathered using a procedure much like that outlined in Figure 16.4. Based on the marketing mix variables of advertising (affecting awareness), distribution (affecting availability), and sales promotion (affecting number of samples received), estimates of long-run or steady-state trial-and-repeat are obtained. Multiplying steady-state trial-and-repeat rates gives the projected long-run market share. ASSESSOR allows the product manager to do "what-if" analysis, that is, to evaluate the effects of changes in marketing mix variables on market share and profit.

New Advances in STMs

We had discussed the use of virtual reality systems such as Oculus Rift in mass customization. Virtual-reality-based testing techniques have also been combined with traditional simulated test market procedures. Virtual reality provides consumers with an immersive experience and permits them to interact realistically with products via virtual shopping, virtual dressing rooms, and virtual product showrooms and demonstrations.[10] As an example, consumer goods producer Cadbury used an online virtual shopping from Decision Insight to complement its traditional research on use of retail shelf space. The virtual shopping experience showed that arranging brands and private labels of cough drops vertically results in more sales than arranging them in the frequently used checkerboard pattern (brands and private labels adjacent to one another). And Kimberly-Clark operates a 3D store simulation to conduct market research for new products.[11]

---

[8]The ASSESSOR model is described in A. J. Silk and G. L. Urban, "Pre-Test-Market Evaluation of New Packaged Goods: A Model and Measurement Methodology," *Journal of Marketing Research*, 15(2), May 1978, pp. 171–191; also see G. L. Urban and G. M. Katz, "Pre-Test-Market Models: Validation and Managerial Implications," *Journal of Marketing Research*, 20(3), August 1983, pp. 221–234.

[9]Gary L. Lilien, Arvind Rangaswamy, and Timothy Matanovich, "The Age of Marketing Engineering," *Marketing Management*, Spring 1998, pp. 48–50.

[10]Anonymous, "Virtual Reality: The Next Big Thing in Marketing Research," *clearseasresearch.com*, June 1, 2016.

[11]Anonymous, "Virtual Reality: Changing the Way Marketers Are Conducting Reearch," *online.rutgers. edu*, undated.

Criticism

The STM technique has its critics. All major packaged goods firms use one or more of the methods, but we don't know how often or with what confidence. Mathematical complexity is a problem, and some managers may therefore be suspicious of the techniques. Second, everything in the system is slightly false: The mall intercept creates false conditions at the start, then the stimuli are unrealistically administered, the store is obviously fake, and much attention is focused on the behavior of the consumers being tested. Third, the calculations require a set of givens from the client before the formulas can be run (on the percent of stores that will stock the item, for example, or on the advertising budget, on how good the advertising will be, and on competitive reaction). Most of these numbers are assumptions and/or may be biased.[12] Further, the method may be less applicable for products that are totally new to the market or that are sold predominantly by personal selling or point-of-purchase promotion.

The firms supplying the service simply ask, "What other method comes close at such an early date?" Besides, their sales forecasts are often accurate, although it is felt that perhaps as many as half of all such tested products that go on into some later form of market testing are unsuccessful there.[13] So, usage and controversy continue.

Controlled Sale Methods

Pseudo sale methods are laboratory experiments that can provide very useful information in early market tests. Marketers also require market testing methods that involve real purchasing under some real competitive environment but that can control one or more dimensions of the situation. Marketers have also wished for a market testing method that assumes distribution, or gets it automatically, without having to spend time and money to get it. This wishing has resulted in the **controlled sale** market testing methods.

Informal Selling

Much industrial selling is based on clearly identifiable product features. Product developers want potential buyers to see the product and hear the story, to make a trial purchase (or accept the offer of free trial supply), and to actually use the product. Repeat sales should follow unless product use testing was poorly done. Personal selling is the primary promotional tool, and there is little need to assess advertising.

So the obvious approach is to train a few salespeople, give them the product and the selling materials, and have them begin making calls. This informal selling method can even be handled at trade shows, either at the regular booths or in special facilities nearby. An example came from a 3M division that was in a crash program to market a new optical fiber splice; for market testing the item, the team manager found a trade show running just three months prior to launch date, where almost every potential buyer of the item would be present. As a footnote on this successful test, the night

---

[12]For a good list of pros and cons of STMs, see Muammer Ozer, "A Survey of New Product Evaluation Models," *Journal of Product Innovation Management*, 16(1), January 1999, pp. 77–94.

[13]Bruce D. Weinberg, *Roles for Research and Models in Improving New Product Development.* Cambridge, MA: Marketing Science Institute, 1990, p. 8.

before the show opened it was necessary for the team to find why some fibers were slipping out of the splices; for this, they used a toy microscope purchased at a nearby mall.[14] New product marketers have to be quick on their feet.

The presentations in the informal selling method are for real, and cash sales take place. Often, enough time remains between the order and the expected date of shipment that production can be arranged after sufficient orders are obtained.

Informal selling differs from the speculative sale method discussed earlier. There, we asked people if they *would* buy; here we ask them *to* buy. And, just as Rubbermaid was mentioned as a consumer products firm using speculative selling, we find consumer firms using informal selling. All products sold primarily by salespeople directly to end users can use it (most controlled sale methods avoid the retailer/distributor stocking problem). So can services of most types.

Direct Marketing

Another simple method of controlled sale is by **direct marketing**. Though usage of the term *direct marketing* varies, here it includes the sale of a (primarily) consumer product by the maker directly to the consuming unit, usually via online catalog or print catalog. As examples, L.L.Bean and Lands' End are large direct marketers. They can easily test a new service of some type, or a new product or product line, simply by listing it in *some* of their catalogs and counting the orders. The advantages are several: secrecy, quick feedback, low cost, database support, and ease of testing multiple variations (by using multiple catalogs).

Minimarkets

Whereas the informal selling and direct marketing methods essentially avoid distributors and retailers/dealers, a third method involves outlets on a very limited basis. The new products manager first selects one or several outlets where sale of the new product would be desirable. In no way a representative sample, these are more likely to be bigger outlets where cooperation can be obtained. Instead of using whole cities (as in test marketing), we use each store as a mini-city or **mini-market**, thus the name.

Black & Decker, for example, could contact Walmart or Home Depot and make arrangements to display and sell a new version of its Snake Lite. It could not use local TV advertising because the item is available in only one or two outlets, but the stores could list the item in *their* advertising, there could be shelf display and product demon-strations, and sales clerks could offer typical service. Some methods (such as offering a rebate or a mail-in premium) could get the names of purchasers for follow-up contact by market research people.

The mini-market situation is more realistic, actual buying situations are created, great flexibility is allowed in changing price and other variables, somewhat more confi-dentiality is possible than with test marketing, and it is cheaper. Nevertheless, it is still somewhat contrived in that the ability to get distribution is not tested—mini-market testing is a still controlled sale. Store personnel may over-attend the product, that is, pay too much attention to it and give it assistance that the item will not get when fully marketed. And, of course, sales cannot be projected to any national figure.

[14]Steve Blount, "It's Just a Matter of Time," *Sales & Marketing Management*, March 1992, pp. 32–43.

Several market research firms offer this service to manufacturers, using stores with which they have previously set up relationships and also using their fleet of vans to rapidly get the product out to more than just a few stores. At least one of the firms has special new product racks in supermarkets, where the new items are displayed. Note that this method is not very scientific; it is used to catch the first flavor of actual sale and/or to work on special problems the developers are having (such as brand confusion, price, package instructions, product misuse, or different positionings). It tells us the trial and gives some feeling about repeat.

One variation on mini-markets, **controlled-distribution scanner markets (CDSMs)**, is based on scanner technology and has received much attention in the consumer packaged goods field. Information Resources Inc. (IRI) and ACNielsen offer CDSM service to packaged goods manufacturers. IRI's BehaviorScan CDSM uses eight cities of around 100,000 people, for example, Marion, Indiana, and Visalia, California. In each city, it contacts all of the retail outlets for grocery store products and asks them to install scanner systems if they don't already have them, at IRI's expense. In return, the retailers agree to share the scanner data with IRI and to cooperate in a few other activities. Next, IRI sets up two panels of 1,000 families in each city. Participants agree to (1) have electronic technology installed on cable-based television sets, (2) report their exposure to print media, (3) make all of their purchases of grocery store products in the BehaviorScan stores, and (4) use a special card (much like a credit card) identifying their family. The families get various incentives (such as lottery participation) to get their initial and sustained cooperation. The key parts of this system are (1) cable TV interrupt privileges, (2) a full record of what other media (such as magazines) go into each household, (3) family-by-family purchasing, and (4) a complete record of 95 percent of all store sales of tested items from the checkout scanners. Immediate stocking and distribution in almost every store is ensured by the research firm (this too is a controlled sale method). IRI knows almost every stimulus that hits each individual family, and it knows almost every change that takes place in each family's purchase habits.

For example, assume Kraft wants to market test a new version of cheddar cheese called Cajun. It contracts with IRI to buy the cheese category in one or more of the eight cities. It then places Cajun in a city and starts local promotion. Another of the cities can be used temporarily as a control. Kraft gets the right to put its commercials (via cable interrupt) into whichever of the homes (for example, younger families) it chooses. Kraft knows whether the families watched TV at the times of the commercials, whether they bought any of the Cajun, whether they bought it again, and so on. The two panels in each city allow Kraft to use two different positionings in its TV advertising, one positioning for each of the panels. The variations and controls stretch the imagination. Kraft can find out how many of the upscale homes that watched the initial commercial bought some of the product within the next two days and what they bought on their prior purchase, what they paid, what else they bought at the time, and the like.

ACNielsen offers a similar CDSM, its Consumer Panel Service. Nielsen's panel includes well over 120,000 households nationwide. It differs from BehaviorScan in a couple of major ways. Instead of the special card used by IRI families, Nielsen families have a scanner-like wand with which they record their purchases at home; this information is transmitted daily to Nielsen. This means that the Nielsen panel can track purchases from all retailers, not just participating stores, but has the drawback that panel members must actively scan all their purchases at home. Nielsen is also equipped to send test TV ads over the air, rather than only to cable households.[15]

Scanner Market Testing

There are many variations on mini-market testing, all designed to meet special situations and needs. One of them, **scanner market testing**, also came out of IRI's BehaviorScan system.

Once BehaviorScan was established, clients began asking the firm for more scanner data (fast and detailed in contrast to traditional market audit data that were slow and with less detail). They wanted to keep the BehaviorScan laboratories, but they also wanted data on large areas, preferably the entire country. So IRI developed what became known as InfoScan, a system of auditing sales out of outlets selling grocery store products. These audits were done in stores with scanner systems, and the data were reported for major metropolitan markets—first a few, and now over a hundred. In fact, the coverage is so complete that the InfoScan total market service is bought now as a national system, or it can be bought for single markets.

IRI has such good contacts with the stores it uses that, for a price, they can ensure stocking of a new product. Without this assurance, the sell-in is left to whatever the firm can do. So InfoScan data can be used in a *mini-market test*—for example, buying market stocking in Indianapolis and Denver and measuring sales of the new item there. Most mini-market test methods (see above) are in a small subset of stores and thus do not allow advertising in the areas' leading media—all local media are available in an InfoScan market. Or InfoScan data can be used in a *test market* where they introduce the new item by *natural sell-in*, regular calls on retailers and wholesalers in, say, Nashville and Albuquerque. If they want to, they can buy store data for two other cities, say, Rochester and Kansas City, where they do *not* sell the new product, for comparison with the two where it is being sold. The city pairs are not as carefully selected and matched as they are in traditional test marketing. Or, third, InfoScan data can be used where a firm starts selling a new product in major markets of the west, moves it out to nearby markets in the mountain states, and so on across the country. In a moment, we will see that this is a *rollout* market test.

InfoScan thus is a *method of market test design and data gathering*. By itself, it is not a method of market testing, but it supports most of them. To help in this, IRI has also developed household panels in all of their markets so that clients can follow individual family purchases, taking on some aspects of their own BehaviorScan laboratory system. Some consumer firms' managers call InfoScan a *live* test market to distinguish it from the simulated test marketing models, and others call it an *in-market* test to distinguish it from the smaller city laboratories of the BehaviorScan electronic testing service.[16] Since the manufacturer can obtain so much information from one provider

---

[15]For more information, check out the IRI and Nielsen Web sites: www.iriworldwide.com and www.acnielsen.com.

[16]IRI goes much further in designing variations on the basic service. For example, besides the controlled *market* testing just described, they also offer controlled *store* testing where activities in one chain are studied.

(purchases, household demographics and media behavior, and response to promotions and prices), InfoScan and its competitors are known as **single-source systems**. The excitement of single-source systems is the flexibility to do many different things in many different markets, with coordinated services, in rich detail, and (best of all) in a matter of days.

Again, ACNielsen is a direct competitor with a similar offering, SCANTRACK Services, which gathers data weekly from over 4,800 food and food/drug stores in 50 major markets. Data are also available from drug stores, mass merchandisers, and convenience stores, and for product categories in which nonscanner sales are more common, such as tobacco or candy, the scanner data are augmented with store audit data. Nielsen also provides Nielsen Food Index (NFI) reports. Managers can then obtain SCANTRACK and NFI reports online from Nielsen. Retailers also use their own scanner data to test alternative price points and shelf placements.

To meet the ever-increasing demands of consumer packaged goods marketers, both Nielsen and IRI offer expert system services that cut through the enormous amount of scanner data to provide useful reports to managers. IRI offers Sales Partner, which cuts through retail scanner data to identify key selling arguments and write reports that manufacturer sales reps can use when calling on retailers. Another IRI product, CoverStory, writes a brief market research report (including visuals and graphs) for product managers highlighting notable trends and events regarding their products. Nielsen offers Sales Advisor, which develops summaries of sales data and effective presentations of marketing information, again for the manufacturer's sales force to use on sales calls.[17]

Full Sale Methods

In full sale market testing, *all* variables are *go*, including competition and the trade. They test the realities of national introduction. First will come test marketing, and then the fastest growing method of all, rollout.

Test Marketing

Test marketing refers to that type of market testing in which a representative piece of the total market (usually, one or more metropolitan markets in and around cities) is chosen for a dress rehearsal. When we hear that a new product is being tested in Evansville, Boise, or Dubuque, it is probably in the form of a test market. What typically happens is that a firm first picks, say, two cities in which to sell the new product and two cities very similar to the first where the product is not sold. All four are watched closely; stocking of the new product is audited; sales are audited—either by the InfoScan system or some other method of collecting store purchase data and store inventories from which sales can be calculated. What they had, plus what they bought, less what they have left over on the auditor's next call equals what they must have sold (ignoring what walked out).

[17]Check the two firms' Web sites for the most up-to-date information.

The *purpose* of most test marketing today has changed. Whereas the early purpose was to predict profits and thus help decide *whether* to go national, firms today use it more to fine-tune their plans and learn *how best* to do so. Test marketing is too expensive to be used as a final exam.

An illustrative example of how a firm fine-tuned a marketing plan is given by Searle in their development of NutraSweet (aspartame) artificial sweetener. When NutraSweet was first developed, Searle originally thought the natural target market would be artificial sweetener users who disliked saccharin's aftertaste. In regional test markets, they found that the real target market was quite different and actually much larger and more lucrative: dissatisfied sugar users. It turned out that many saccharin users actually preferred saccharin's taste.[18] Similarly, when P&G was preparing to launch Febreze fabric refresher designed to lift odors from fabrics (a new product category), an extensive two-year test market was conducted in Phoenix, Tucson, Salt Lake City, and Boise. While Febreze was originally targeted to a niche market (smokers looking to remove cigarette odor from clothes), the test market showed that the potential market was much wider: Families with young children or pets were found to be heavy users.[19]

Pros and Cons

In contrast to other test methods, test marketing is intended to offer typical market conditions, thereby allowing the best sales forecast and the best evaluation of alternative marketing strategies. It reduces the risk of a total or major flop.

The test market offers the most abundant *supply of information* (such as sales, usage, prices, reseller reactions and support, publicity, and competitive reactions) and many less important but occasionally valuable by-products. For example, a smaller firm can use successful test market results to help *convince national distributors* to chance stocking the item.

The test market also permits *verifying production*: any manufacturing problem (such as ineffective or unsafe packaging) can be identified during the test market rather than later during national launch. Other firms have been surprised by the effects of *humidity* or *temperature, abuse* by distribution personnel, *ingenious undesirable uses* of the product, and *general misunderstanding* by company or distributive personnel.

Of course, the method is *expensive*: Direct costs per city are substantial; many indirect costs (for preparing product, special training, and so on) must be considered as well. These costs are often acceptable if the data are accurate, thus allowing the test markets to be projected to a national sales figure. But *test market results are not really projectable*. We cannot control all *environmental factors*; company people tend to *overwork* a test program; dealers may *overattend or underattend*; and the constant temptation exists to *sweeten the trade package* unrealistically in fear that inadequate distribution will kill the entire test.

---

[18]Gary S. Lynn, Mario Mazzuca, Joseph G. Morone, and Albert S. Paulson, "Learning Is the Critical Success Factor in Developing Truly New Products," *Research-Technology Management*, May–June 1998, pp. 45–51.

[19]Anonymous, "Odor Removal Spray Introduced," *Supermarket News*, July 13, 1998, p. 44; and Jack Neff, "P&G Shifts Ad Focus for Rollout of Febreze," *Advertising Age*, April 6, 1998, p. 16.

FIGURE 16.5   **A Risk of Test Marketing: Showing Your Hand to the Competitor**

- Kellogg tracked the sale of General Foods' Toast-Ems while they were in test market. Noting they were becoming popular, they went national quickly with Pop-Tarts before the General Foods' test market was over.
- After having invented freeze-dried coffee, General Foods was test-marketing its own Maxim brand when Nestlé bypassed them with Taster's Choice, which went on to be the leading brand.
- While Procter & Gamble were busy test-marketing their soft chocolate chip cookies, both Nabisco and Keebler rolled out similar cookies nationwide.
- The same thing happened with P&G's Brigade toilet-bowl cleaner. It was in test marketing for three years, during which time both Vanish and Ty-D-Bol became established in the market.
- While Campbell was test-marketing Prego spaghetti sauce, Ragú increased advertising and promotion (to skew the results of the Prego test), and also developed and rolled out new Ragú Homestyle sauce.
- General Foods' test market results for a new frozen baby food were very encouraging, until it was learned that most of the purchases were being made by competitors Gerber, Libby, and Heinz.

Sources: J. P. Guiltinan and G. W. Paul, *Marketing Management: Strategies and Programs*, 4th ed. (New York: McGraw-Hill, 1991); G. L. Urban and S. H. Star, *Advanced Marketing Strategy* (Englewood Cliffs, NJ: Prentice-Hall, 1991); E. E. Scheuing, *New Product Management* (Columbus, OH: Bell & Howell, 1989); Robert M. McMath and Thom Forbes, *What Were They Thinking?* (New York: Times Business, 1998); G. A. Churchill, *Basic Marketing Research* (Fort Worth, TX, Dryden, 1998); and others.

In addition, there is the question of *time*. A good test may take a year or more, which gives competition a full view of the test firm's strategy, time to prepare a reaction, and even the chance to leapfrog directly to national marketing on a similar item (see examples in Figure 16.5). At one time, P&G would test market most new products extensively. Now, it goes directly from a successful STM to national launch with many products, though in some cases, where higher risks or uncertainties were present (such as Febreze, as noted earlier), a full-scale test market of as long as three years may still be employed. Similarly, Starbucks conducted traditional test markets in selected cities when launching Via, its instant coffee product, before rolling it out into the North American market and then worldwide. Though seemingly a simple product launch, management correctly recognized the risks, which justified the extensive testing. For example, Starbucks needed to determine if Via would be perceived as a high-quality product worthy of the Starbucks name, whether the features most desired by Starbucks drinkers (rich, flavorful coffee) would be deliverable in instant form, whether Starbucks drinkers would be skeptical of any instant coffee, whether the individual packet format would be accepted or desired, and so on. Moreover, a major failure with Via might have tainted the overall Starbucks brand equity.[20]

Also, *competitors can mess up a test market city* with a flood of coupons and other devices to falsely decrease the test product's sales. A product manager in the cereal industry once said that his firm used to issue valuable coupons for its own product when it noticed a competitor was conducting a test market. When asked why his company didn't try anything more involved or exciting, he simply replied, "It works!"

[20]Julie Jargon, "Starbucks Takes New Road with Instant Coffee: Company Launches Marketing Campaign and Taste Challenge to Tout Its Portable, Less Expensive Product Via," *The Wall Street Journal*, September 29, 2009, p. A29.

As another tactic, competitive salespeople might even be tempted to make bulk new product purchases, falsely increasing the test product's sales reports.[21]

The Test Parameters

A large body of test market literature is available, and most of the leading market research consulting firms stand ready to design tests appropriate to any situation, so no depth of detail is needed here. The most common questions are "Where should we test?" and "How long should the test run?"

Picking Test Markets   Each experienced test marketer has an ideal structure of cities or areas. Ad agencies keep lists. Picking two or three to use is not simple, but usually the demographics and level of competition should be representative, the distribution channel should not be too difficult to get in, and there are no regional peculiarities in product consumption. One interesting consideration is media coverage: To avoid wasted exposures, the selected market usually has print and broadcast media that cover just that market, not a huge surrounding area.

Duration of Test   There is no one answer to the question of how long a test market should last, as made clear by one marketing vice president who said he needed 24 to 36 months for a new plant care item but only 6 to 9 months for a candy snack. See Figure 16.6 for some data on purchase cycles; the wide variations are just one factor in the duration decision.

The Rollout

Test marketing is not dead, but marketers now prefer a market testing method called **rollout**, sometimes called *limited marketing*. It gives the dress rehearsal value of a test market but avoids many of its problems. Indeed, many firms will say they do not do market tests but do frequently use rollouts.

Many rollouts take the form of *geographic rollouts*, where a new product is introduced in a single city or market, information is gathered, the company learns from the limited-market experience, and the product is eventually released to a broader market. For example, in August 2018, Ben & Jerry's Ice Cream started rolling out a non–ice cream product, Cookie Dough Chunks, in chocolate chip and peanut butter–chocolate chip flavors. The idea for this unconventional product came from the observation that some consumers enjoyed picking out and eating the cookie dough that Ben & Jerry's added to some of their ice cream flavors; this observation meant that there might be a market for cookie dough chunks sold separately. The decision was to initiate the rollout in Ben & Jerry's Scoop Shops in their home state of Vermont, allowing them to monitor interest and excitement about the new product and predict likely acceptance if rolled out nationally. The company also promoted the new product through Instagram, hoping to generate interest and enthusiasm through social media word of mouth.[22]

---

[21]This technique is still being used, this time in the book industry, where some authors have made purchases in those stores whose sales are being audited for inclusion in national bestseller lists. Most firms have urged salespeople to recruit neighbors to make purchases and spur stocking by stores.

[22]Olivia Harrison, "Ben & Jerry's Created the Best Edible Cookie Dough Ever, but You Can Only Get It in One Place," *refinery29.com*, August 24, 2018; and Sarah Weinberg, "The Fate of Ben & Jerry's Snackable Cookie Dough Is in Vermonters' Hands," *delish.com*, August 21, 2018.

FIGURE 16.6   Purchase Cycles on Selected Product Categories

	Average Purchase Frequency (weeks)	Average Four-Week Penetration (percent)		Average Purchase Frequency (weeks)	Average Four-Week Penetration (percent)
Air fresheners	6	12.3%	Fruit drinks	4	27.8%
Baking supplies:			Presweetened		
Brown sugar	17	13.6	powdered		
Cake mixes	10	29.6	drinks	8	13.2
Chewable			Laundry care:		
vitamins	26	0.8	Heavy-duty		
Cleaners:			detergents	5	50.4
All-purpose			Soil and stain		
cleaners	35	3.4	removers	25	4.7
Window			Liquid bleach	6	18.3
cleaners	27	7.1	Margarine	3	71.7
Rug cleaners	52	2.4	Milk additives	9	11.8
Bathroom			Mouthwash	13	9.7
cleaners	25	4.2	Pet food:		
Coffee	3	53.1	Cat (total)	2	14.1
Frozen foods:			Dog (dry)	4	23.2
Frozen entrees	6	19.5	Dog (total)	2	41.8
Frozen pizza	8	21.1	Raisins	18	8.3
Furniture polish	27	7.0	Salad dressings	6	32.9
Hair care:			Salad toppings	8	1.2
Hair color	12	4.7	Snacks	3	17.7
Shampoo	8	23.4	Steak sauce	23	5.4
Juices/drinks:			Toothpaste	9	33.1
Fruit juices	3	33.6			

Note: The first column is the average time between purchases of the category cited, by the households in the ADTEL panel. The second column is the percentage of panel households that make at least one purchase in a four-week period. Both figures contribute to the decision on test market duration.
Source: ADTEL, Inc.

Geographic rollouts are often used in global launches, where one or a few *lead countries* receive the product first; the company tracks sales and then rolls out to other parts of the world. As seen in the Chapter 15 case, Coca-Cola Life, sweetened with stevia and intended for the global market, was originated by its product developers in Argentina and Chile and was initially marketed there before being rolled out to many other markets.[23] One 3M division markets items in Argentina before rolling them out to the countries in Europe. Colgate follows a lead country strategy and, for example, marketed Palmolive Optims shampoo in the Philippines, Australia, Mexico, and Hong Kong before rolling it out into Europe, Asia, and other world markets.

[23]Anonymous, "Coca-Cola Life: La Nueva Versión de la Bebida Creada in Chile y Argentina," *CNN Chile*, November 21, 2013.

As the examples show, the starting areas are not necessarily representative areas, but more typically are areas where the company thinks it has the right people, or the right markets, to get the rollout started. Some firms, in fact, want the area to be difficult, not easy. For example, Miles Laboratories was marketing diabetes self-testing glucometers and realized that two of its sales divisions would have to cooperate; the Diagnostic salespeople knew the technology, and the Consumer Healthcare salespeople knew the retail druggists. They picked New York City, saying, "Because of the complexity of the market, if we could be successful in New York City, we could roll it out to other parts of the country with reasonable assurance of success."[24]

Second, there is no doubt about the company's intentions in any of these examples. These are not market tests conducted before the launch. These are the *actual launches of the products*. It is just done in a gradual way, with the intention of eventually reaching the full intended market. See Figure 16.7 for the decision on when to roll out and how far to increase the rollout before switching to a full national launch.

FIGURE 16.7
The Patterns of Information Gained at Various Stages of a Rollout

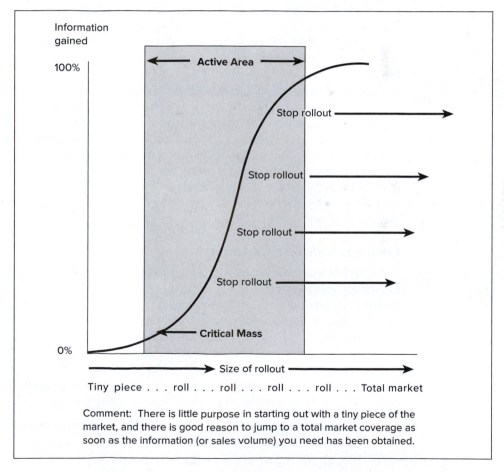

Comment: There is little purpose in starting out with a tiny piece of the market, and there is good reason to jump to a total market coverage as soon as the information (or sales volume) you need has been obtained.

[24]Leslie Brennan, "Meeting the Test," *Sales and Marketing Management*, March 1990, p. 60.

It is important to note that rollout does not have to be planned geographically. An alternative rollout is by *application* or *end-user segment*. For example, an industrial adhesives firm may develop a new adhesive that works on many applications, including fastening bricks to steel plates, fastening insulation siding to the two-by-four studs in a house, and fastening shingles onto plywood roofing sheets. It has been field-tested in all three applications and has been tested in informal selling to roofing firms in one use (shingles), where it received a good response. Should the firm offer it for all three applications at once? Arguments against this include (1) the adhesive has not been market tested in the first two applications, (2) such action would strain resources, (3) multiple uses might confuse customers, all of whom are in the construction field and will hear of all three selling efforts, and (4) the new products manager wants to have some successful experience to talk about when entering the brick and siding fields because they are highly competitive. The answer here is to roll out by *end-user segment*. Market the new adhesive in the shingles business first, gain experience, build up some cash flow, and establish credibility. Then gradually begin selling it to the siding firms and make whatever changes are indicated. Still later, roll it on into the brick field.

Another kind of rollout is by *distributor*. What if the adhesives firm developed a new product with only one major application, and the product (1) was only marginally better and (2) required lots of training for the distributors' reps. The adhesives firm could choose to begin selling the adhesive through one of its best (and friendliest) distributors, a firm willing to go along on the new item. When that went well, it could gradually roll it out to other distributors with whom it had increasingly less *influence*, using prior successes to persuade them. Toy and game companies use this kind of channel rollout as well. A new line of dolls or miniature cars might be rolled out exclusively at Walmart, since this retailer represents a large percentage of toy sales in the U.S. market. If the product sells well there, and the retailer experiences no difficulties in inventorying or restocking the toy, they move to smaller chains and independent toysellers.

Contrasts with Test Marketing

A rollout has many advantages. The biggest are that it gives management most of the knowledge learned from a test market, it has an escape clause without losing the full budget if the product flops, and yet the company is well on its way to national availability as early rollout results start coming in. This is important in the competitive battle because test marketing gives the competition time to launch their products while we are still in test market or getting geared up to go national.

Does this sound like the best of all worlds? What's the catch? In many situations, there isn't any catch, and the technique is justifiably growing rapidly. Other firms may find rollouts to be just as big a risk as full launch. Here is why:

1. Their biggest investment may be in a new production facility, and to roll out requires the full plant at the start.
2. They may be in an industry where competitors can move very fast (for example, because no patent or new facilities are required), so a slow marketing gives them as much chance to leapfrog as would test marketing.

3. Available distributors are powerful and may not be interested in playing along with a rollout of a product that can fail. (A big-name toy and game manufacturer has channel power too, and might have an easier time convincing Walmart to take on a product being rolled out.)

4. They need the free national publicity that only a full national launch can get them; rollouts tend not to be newsworthy (though the Ben & Jerry's example suggests that social media might be a way around this problem in an inexpensive manner).

Wrap-Up on Market Testing Methodologies

Each of the 10 methods in the three categories of Figure 16.3 can be used alone, and many firms use the one they think is best in terms of cost and what they can learn. But some firms want a system of two or more techniques.

Such firms usually begin with a pseudo sale method—the speculative format if they are industrial or in a business where personal selling is the major marketing thrust, or a form of STM if they are in consumer packaged goods. Pseudo sale is cheap and quick. Learning is limited, but it is a good leg up on the problem. It often doesn't hold up the process.

The firm then turns to one of the controlled sale methods, especially informal selling for industrial firms or mini-markets for consumer firms. If the second test will be the last, firms tend to slide directly into a full-sale method. Thus, an industrial firm might use a speculative sale followed by an applications rollout. A packaged goods firm might start with an STM followed by a geographical rollout, or an STM followed by a mini-market and then full launch. Advances in information technology ensure that firms will have quicker and better data available at the individual household and business firm level far out into the future.

Summary

This chapter has presented market testing: the evaluation of the product together with its marketing plan. The techniques of market testing vary from the simplistic (and quite unreliable) one, of making a sales presentation about the new product to potential buyers and then asking them if they would buy it if available, to a rollout.

The appropriate market testing methodology for any particular new product cannot be stipulated here. Some new product innovation is of such low risk that no market testing can be defended. The toughest issue of all is probably that of technology-based firms that develop what they feel the customer needs and *will* want; but customers don't *know* they want these new items until they have had a long chance to see them and think about them. Examples are many, ranging from the bathtub to the microwave oven. As a result, technical innovators sometimes distrust any kind of intermediate testing.

At the time of entering any market test (including rollout) and at the time of national launch, many firms have adopted some of the thinking of space launches: using a launch control system to prepare them for unexpected, but possible, traumatic events. This is the topic of Chapter 17.

Case: Chick-fil-A[25]

Consumers have long sought simplicity and convenience when shopping. But the arrival of Blue Apron in 2012 and competitors such as Plated and HelloFresh suggested that, for many, convenience could be provided in the form of a meal kit—a box ordered online containing every ingredient one would need to make dinner at home, perfectly measured, nothing more or less. The idea simplifies the shopping experience while still allowing the consumer to prepare dinner expertly at home. The success of these delivery startups has not gone unnoticed, as Amazon and Walmart have entered the market with their own meal kit offerings, ordered online. Grocery chains such as Whole Foods and Wegman's have also introduced their own versions of meal kits.

In 2018, the restaurant chain Chick-fil-A decided to explore the possibilities in the meal kit business, with their Mealtime Kits. Much like its online and in-store competitors, Mealtime Kits provide pre-portioned ingredients for full recipes, all centered around Chick-fil-A's famous chicken. Dinner preparation at home takes about 30 minutes. Each kit serves two people and costs $15.89. Five different Mealtime Kit recipes are available: Chicken Parmesan, Chicken Enchiladas, Dijon Chicken, Pan Roasted Chicken, and Chicken Flatbread. Regular Chick-fil-A customers might find these recipes interesting or even surprising, since none of these is on the regular menu at the restaurant.

To test the viability of Mealtime Kits, Chick-fil-A planned a limited rollout in its hometown of Atlanta. From August to November 2018, Mealtime Kits were available at 150 Chick-fil-A restaurants in the Atlanta area. Customers were able to order the kit inside the restaurant at the counter, at the drive-thru window, or online through the Chick-fil-A One mobile app. In addition, Chick-fil-A provided a form on its Web site so that customers nationwide could express their enthusiasm for the meal kit coming to a nearby restaurant. The regional rollout and online form provided Chick-fil-A with valuable insights to determine if the meal kit should be rolled out to the nationwide market.

A consumer study of meal kits conducted in 2018 by investors.com revealed some interesting facts. When customers make meal kits at home, they tend to say that the food tastes and smells better than if they had made the same recipe without the help of a meal kit. According to Packaged Facts, meal kit sales revenues in 2017 reached $5 billion, estimated to increase to $10 billion by 2020. Although the largest share of current meal kit sales are online, Chick-fil-A believes that it can get a share of this business by getting customers to come in and pick up the kits.

Make a recommendation to Chick-fil-A for market testing this product. What would be the key information you would need to gain from the limited rollout? From the online forms? Would you recommend any other kind of market testing? And how would you ensure that the results you obtained were valid?

[25]This case is based on Anonymous, "Chick-fil-A's Hometown Customers Get First Opportunity to Try New Meal Kits Concept," https://thechickenwire.chick-fil-a.com; other sources on the corporate Web site, www.chick-fil-a.com; Alex Conrad, "Blue Apron's Got Big Plans for Dinner—But So Do Its Hungry Rivals," *forbes.com*, October 14, 2014; and Russ Britt, "Will Investors Eat Up the Fresh New Industry of Meal Kits?," *investors.com*, June 25, 2018.

CHAPTER SEVENTEEN

Launch Management

Setting

Once the new product is ready to market, the long trek through the development process may appear to be ended. The people involved in the program are happy, satisfied, and anxious for a well-earned rest.

But the group was charged with launching a *winning* product. Just as managerial control over the *development process* was needed (checking actual progress against the plan and making adjustments where it appeared there would be trouble meeting the schedule), control over the *marketing of the new product* is needed. Launch management lasts until the new product has finished its assault on given objectives, which may take as long as six months to a year for industrial goods and commercial services or as little as a few weeks for some consumer packaged goods.

What We Mean by Launch Management

Comparing a NASA space capsule to a youngster's slingshot will explain the subject of this chapter. After firing a rock at a crow in the upper branches of a tree, the youngster quickly panics and runs if the rock sails well over the crow and heads directly for the kitchen window in the neighbor's house. That's when the youngster would rather be in the NASA control headquarters in Houston, Texas, because NASA scientists launch *guided* space capsules, not *unguided* slingshot rocks. NASA would have anticipated that an in-flight directional problem *might* occur and thus would simply make an in-flight correction, allowing the space capsule to continue its *controlled* flight. Not having in-flight corrective powers, the youngster simply runs. That is, good tracking systems make successful launching of new products more likely.[1]

Whether it is a NASA rocket launch or a new product launch, the post-launch assessment has the same basic purpose: to learn from the experience, and to correct mistakes. To adapt the NASA analogy to the product launch situation, one can use a

---

[1]People marketing new products are not the only ones using NASA-type systems today. Manufacturing quality control managers have the same difficulties in anticipating problems that might endanger product quality, watching to see if these problems are coming up, and being ready to do something if they do.

gap analysis matrix. There are five major areas in the gap analysis matrix that can be measured and compared to the expected plan:

- Market window accuracy.
- Executive support.
- The business case.
- Sales preparedness.
- Cross-functional alignment.[2]

First, *market window accuracy* should be measured. If a product's market window of profitability is shorter than expected, this may indicate a turning point in the life cycle and may require strategic thinking for the next product put into development. Second is *executive support*. Senior management vision and a hard-working, knowledgeable product champion are essential to good launch supervision and coordination. Any weaknesses in the level of support provided to the new product should be identified and corrected. Next, the *business case* should be validated. A solid business case, showing desirable financial projections, is critical in making the go decision. If the product fails to live up to financial performance expectations, it may signal that certain market or competitive details had been overlooked. *Sales preparedness* is also checked. This means getting commitments from sales managers, hiring and motivating the sales force, and providing sufficient training and materials to help them do their job. Again, weaknesses here can be found and fixed for the next launch. Finally, the extent of *cross-functional alignment* should be considered. Good communication must exist throughout the organization in order to develop products that really address customer needs in a satisfactory way. Audits can be used to identify and correct any communication flaws in the firm.

Post-launch is also a good time to make sure the product portfolio is in alignment, and that all products are consistent with the firm's PIC. If any portfolio imbalances are found, they can be corrected through careful selection of future products for development.

The following section provides details on how a launch management system can realistically be applied.

The Launch Management System

A launch management system contains the following steps.

1. *Spot potential problems.* The first step in getting ready to play NASA on a new product launch is to identify all potential weak spots or potential troubles. These problems occur either in the firm's actions (such as poor advertising or poor manufacturing) or in the outside environment (such as competitive retaliation). As one manager said, "I look for things that will really hurt us if they happen, or don't happen."

[2]The gap analysis matrix is from Steven Haines, "Post-Launch Product Management," in K. B. Kahn, S. E. Kay, R. J. Slotegraaf, and S. Uban (eds.), *The PDMA Handbook of New Product Development* (Hoboken, NJ: John Wiley, 2013), Ch. 21, pp. 344–345.

2. *Select those to control.* Each potential problem is analyzed to determine its expected impact. Expected impact means we multiply the damage the event would cause by the likelihood of the event happening. The impact is used to rank the problems and to select those that will be "controlled" and those that won't.

3. *Develop contingency plans for the control problems.* Contingency plans are what, if anything, will be done if the difficulties actually occur. The degree of completeness in this planning varies, but the best contingency plans are ready for *immediate* action. For example, "We will boost commission on the new item from 7 percent to 10 percent, by fax to all sales reps" is a contingency plan. It's ready to be put to work immediately. "We will undertake the development of a new sales compensation plan" is no contingency plan.

4. *Design the tracking system.* As with NASA, the *tracking system* must send back usable data fast. We must have some experience so we can evaluate the data (Is our slowdown in technical service typical on big electronic devices like ours, or do we have a problem building?). There should be *trigger points* (for example, trial by 15 percent of our customers called on, by the end of the first month). These points (if not met) trigger the contingency plan. Without them, we just end up arguing. Remember, money to execute a contingency plan has to come from somewhere (someone else's budget), and thus every plan faces opposition from people who want to delay implementing it.

If a problem cannot be tracked, no matter how important its impact may be, then we don't have it under control. For example, a competitor's decision to cut price by 35 percent is an act; it cannot be tracked like dealer stocking percentages can be. But we *can* have a contingency plan ready if it happens. This situation is not ideal because managerial control tries to anticipate a problem before it gets here; then we implement the remedial action in time to soften the negative effects. (See Figure 17.1.)

On the following pages, we will look in depth at each of these four steps in planning and executing a launch management system.

Step One: Spot Potential Problems

Four techniques are used to develop the list of potential problems. First is the *situation analysis* made for the marketing planning step. For example, government lawyers may recently have criticized an ingredient used in the product. Or buyers may have indicated a high level of satisfaction with present products on the market, suggesting trouble in getting them to try our new one. The *problems* section in the marketing plan will have summarized most of the potential troubles from the situation analysis.

A second technique is to *role-play what competitors will do* after they have heard of the new product. Vigorous devil's advocate sessions can turn up scary options that competitors may exercise—they usually have more options than we think of at first glance.

Third, we *look back over all the data* accumulated in the new product's file. Start with the original concept test reports, then the screening forms, the early lab testing, the rest of the use tests (especially the longer-term ones with potential customers), and records of all internal discussions. These sources contain lots of potential troubles, some of which we had to ignore in our efforts to move the item along.

FIGURE 17.1
Graphic
Application of
the General
Tracking
Concept (with
Remedial
Action)

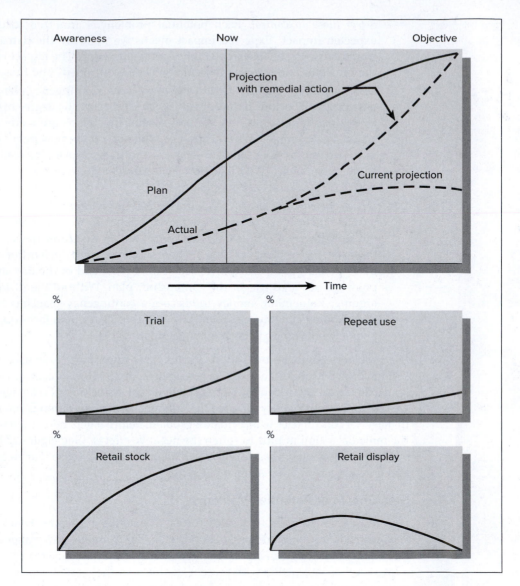

For example, a food product had done well in all studies to date, except when the project leader ran a simulated test market (see Chapter 16). The sales forecast from the research firm came out very low. Study of the data indicated that consumers interviewed by the research firm had given a trial forecast of 5 percent, whereas the agency and the developer had been anticipating a trial of 15 percent. The difference was highly significant because success depended on which estimate was right. The developers believed *they* were right, so they stopped the STM tests and introduced the product. But they made trial the top-priority item on the problem list. Shortly after introduction, surveys showed that 15 percent was the better estimate, and the

FIGURE 17.2
A-T-A-R
Launch Control
Patterns
(Actual) for
Three Pharma-
ceutical/
Nutritional
Products

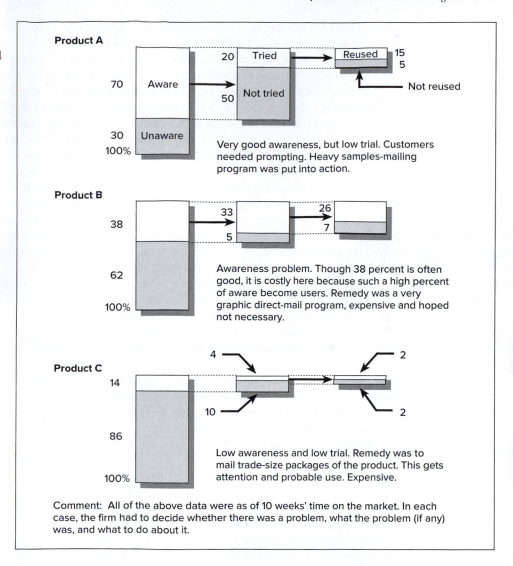

Product A

70 Aware

20 Tried

Reused 15

5

50 Not tried

Not reused

30 Unaware

100%

Very good awareness, but low trial. Customers needed prompting. Heavy samples-mailing program was put into action.

Product B

38

33

26

5

7

62

100%

Awareness problem. Though 38 percent is often good, it is costly here because such a high percent of aware become users. Remedy was a very graphic direct-mail program, expensive and hoped not necessary.

Product C

14

4

2

10

2

86

100%

Low awareness and low trial. Remedy was to mail trade-size packages of the product. This gets attention and probable use. Expensive.

Comment: All of the above data were as of 10 weeks' time on the market. In each case, the firm had to decide whether there was a problem, what the problem (if any) was, and what to do about it.

contingency plan was happily discarded. But they were ready if action had been warranted.[3]

Fourth, it is helpful to start with a satisfied customer or industrial user and work back from that satisfaction to determine the *hierarchy of effects* necessary to produce it. On consumer packaged goods, this hierarchy is the same one used earlier in the A-T-A-R model. Figure 17.2 shows that model when applied to the marketing of three ethical pharmaceutical and nutritional specialty items. Note that each product

[3]From the files of David W. Olson, vice president of New Product Research at Chicago advertising agency Leo Burnett.

had a different problem and required different remedial action (contingency plan). All three items were marketed by one firm in one year.

But the hierarchy of effects will vary in other situations. Thus, for example, the satisfaction point for an industrial drill may be "known, provable, substantially lower output cost." But reaching that point requires the customer to measure actual costs. It also requires the customer to have data on what the drills cost previously. These are like rungs on a ladder—the customer cannot get to the top (satisfaction) without having stepped on the rungs of "know previous costs" and "know actual costs of the new drill." Both are potential problems, given that most firms do not have such sophisticated cost systems.

Later in this chapter (in Figure 17.7) you will see a sample launch management plan for a new industrial multimeter. There the five key potential problems were: salespeople will fail to call as requested, salespeople will fail to understand the product, potential customers do not order a trial instrument, buyers do not place quantity orders after the trial, and a competitor markets a similar item. All were potential "killers," and one of them did strike.

Another example concerned a consumer durable product—this time a combination of the sturdy mountain bike and the thin-framed nimbler racing bike. But Huffy, the manufacturer, failed to anticipate one potential problem that became a $5 million mistake. Huffy chose to distribute the new bike through their regular channels (mass merchandisers and big-box discounters). Unfortunately, the special hybrid bikes needed individual sales attention at the point of sale; such knowledgeable salespeople only work at bike specialty shops. A launch management system might have discovered this soon enough to permit necessary changes.[4]

All of this is not to say the companies were wrong—all new products are a gamble, and we never have enough time and money to do the job "right." But the problems represent what we are looking for when we do our launch management—knowing what bad event might happen, we can at least be on the lookout for it and hopefully have something in place ready to go if it does happen.

Interestingly, one problem usually overlooked is the possibility of being too successful. It sounds like a nice kind of problem to have, but it can be expensive and should be anticipated if there is any particular reason to think it might happen.

Before leaving the matter of potential killer problems, don't forget that the firm has yet to prove it can do what it proposes to do—that is, produce and distribute a product that does what we claim it will. So launch management plans also contain problem items such as:

- Vendors fail to deliver the new parts in the volume promised.
- The new conveyor lines will be stretched to their limit. The stress limits provided by suppliers may be in error, and/or our manufacturing workforce may misuse the technology.
- Samples of the new product are critical in this introduction, yet we have not proven our ability to package the small units needed.

---

[4]"Flops," *BusinessWeek*, August 16, 1993, pp. 76–82.

These too are potential problems. Any one of them can cause the new item to fail, so we must manage our way through them too. Incidentally, this reinforces a key issue in new products management today: The development does not end when the item arrives at the shipping dock. It ends when enough good-quality product has performed satisfactorily in the hands of the end user. The full team manages the launch management operation.

Last, note that one item has not been mentioned—actual sales. We do not "control" sales and do not have tracking lines and contingency plans for low sales. It might seem we should, and most launch management plans put together by novices include sales. But stop to think. If the sales line is falling short of the forecast, what contingency plan should be ordered into action? Unless you know what is *causing* poor sales, you don't know what solution to use.

Instead, we use the above efforts to list the main reasons why sales may be low and then track *those reasons*. If we have anticipated properly, tracked properly, and instituted remedies properly, then sales will follow. Otherwise, when sales lag, we have to stop, undertake research to find out what is happening, plan a remedial action, prepare for it, and then implement it. By then, it's far too late. Contingency planning is a hedge bet; it is a gamble, like insurance. Most contingency planning is a waste, and we hope it all will be.

Step Two: Select the Control Events

No one can managerially control the scores of potential problems that come from the analysis in step one. So the planner's judgment must cut the list down to a number the firm can handle. (See Figure 17.3 for a graphic representation of what follows.) Some

FIGURE 17.3
Decision Model for Building Launch Control Plan

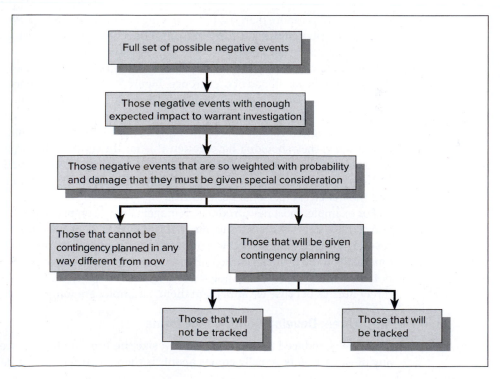

FIGURE 17.4
Expected
Effects Matrix
for Selection of
Control Events

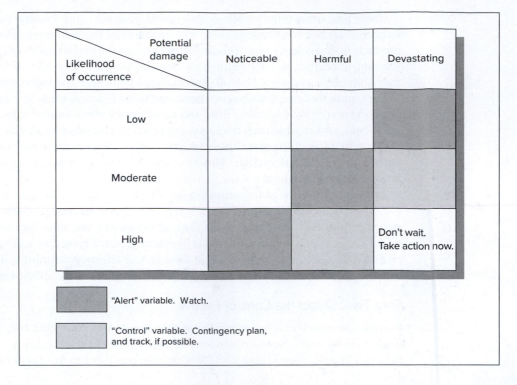

people say never more than six, but a shaving system by Gillette heavily advertised and globally distributed would surely warrant more contingency planning than the launch of a new line of jigsaw blades.

The judgment used to reduce the list of problems is usually based on the potential damage and the likelihood of occurrence. Figure 17.4 shows an **expected effects matrix**, indicating how the two factors combine to produce nine different categories of four types. Those with little harm and little probability can safely be ignored. Others farther down the diagram cannot be. At the bottom/right are problems that should be taken care of now; they shouldn't have gotten this far. In between are problems handled as suggested by the patterns on the boxes. How they are handled is situational, depending on time pressure, money for contingencies, the firm's maturity in launch management, and the managers' personal preferences.

For example, most new products managers have been burned on previous launches and so have developed biases toward certain events. They may have been criticized so severely for forgetting something on a previous launch that they never forget it again. One new products manager recommended that the problems be sorted into two piles—potholes and sinkholes. Potholes are harmful, but sinkholes are disaster. Potholes rarely hurt us because we anticipate them; sinkholes are tough to anticipate.

Step Three: Develop Contingency Plans

Once we've reduced the problem list to a size the firm can handle, we have to ask: "If any of those events actually comes about, is there anything we can do?" For example, although competitive price cuts and competitive product imitation are on many lists, there is usually little the firm can do. The competitor is going to try to hold most of its share, and the developer is usually better off to ignore those actions and sell on the uniqueness of the new item.

For the other events, our planned reaction depends on the event. Let's take two different types: a company failure and a negative buyer action (consumer failure). The most common company failure is inadequate distribution, particularly at the retail or dealer level. Correcting the problem usually just depends on how high a price the company is willing to pay.

Retailers sell the one thing they have—shelf space exposure to store traffic. Shelf space goes to the highest bidder, so if a new product comes up short, the remedy is to raise the bid—special promotions, more pull advertising, a better margin, and so on (see Chapter 15). These were rejected options when the marketing program was put together, so contingency planners usually have lots of alternatives from which to choose.

A consumer failure is handled the same way. To get awareness, the marketers' program called for particular actions (sales calls, advertising, and so on). If it turns out that awareness is low, we usually do more of the same action—increase sales calls, or whatever. If people are not actually trying the new item, we have ways of encouraging trial (such as mailing samples or trade packages as in Figure 17.2 or giving out coupons).

Many product developers have marveled at how easy good contingency thinking is while preparing to launch, compared to doing it under the panic conditions of a beach-head disaster.

Step Four: Design the Tracking System

We now have a set of negative outcomes, for most of which we have standby contingency plans ready to go. The next step is developing a system that will tell us when to implement any of those contingency plans. The answer lies in the concept of tracking.

Tracking

The tracking concept in new product launch shares many similarities with tracking projectiles launched into space. There is a blast-off, a breakout of the projectile into an orbit or trajectory of its own, possible modification on that trajectory during flight, and so on. The launch controller is responsible for tracking the projectile against its planned trajectory and for making whatever corrections are necessary to ensure that it goes where it is supposed to go.

Applying this tracking concept to new products was as natural as could be. Earlier, Figure 17.1 showed the graphic application of the basic concept to a new product.

Three essentials are involved: First is the ability to lay the *planned trajectory*. What is the expected path? What is reasonable, given the competitive situation, the product's features, and the planned marketing efforts? An experienced firm with hundreds of successfully launched products may be able to set a realistic trajectory path for a new product based on past experience with similar products.

Firms that lack this kind of extensive experience can sometimes acquire the data it needs from such outside sources as advertising agencies, marketing research firms, trade media, or industry pools. Such ready-made options are important in these days of global marketing; fortunately, there is an increase of market research data and service organizations with international operations.

Second, there must be an *inflow of actual data* indicating progress against the plan. This means quick and continuing marketing research geared to measure the variables being tracked. As an illustrative example, a short list of the kinds of questions used by Leo Burnett Company when tracking a new product is provided in Figure 17.5.

Third, we have to *project the probable outcome* against the plan. Unless the outcome can be forecast, we have little basis for triggering remedial action until the outcome is at hand. The key is speed—learning fast that a problem is coming about, early enough to do something that prevents it or solves it.

Selecting the Actual Tracking Variables

Now we hit perhaps the toughest part of launch management. How will we actually measure whether one of our key problems is coming about?

If the problem is some specific step of action or mind, like awareness, then the answer is clear—find out how many people are aware of the new item. Trial is easy; repeat purchase is easy. What about trade support? Many new product marketers fear

FIGURE 17.5   **Questions from a New Product Tracking Study**

Category Usage Questions

In the past six months, how many times have you bought (product category)?
What brands of (product category) have you ever heard of?
Have you ever heard of (brand)? (Ask for four to six brands)
Have you ever bought (brand)? (Ask for four to six brands)
About how many times have you bought (brand) in the past six months?

Advertising Awareness Questions

Do you recall seeing any advertising for (brand)? (Ask all brands respondent is aware of.)
Describe the advertising for (brand).
Where did you see the advertising for (brand)?

Purchase Questions

Have you ever bought (brand)?

If "Yes":	**If "No":**
How many times have you bought (brand)?	Did you look for (brand) in the store?
How likely are you to buy (brand) again?	Why didn't you try (brand)?
What did you like/dislike about (brand)?	How likely are you to try (brand) in the future?
What do you think of the price of (brand)?	

Each response is interpreted by Leo Burnett Company according to standard guidelines or norms. For example, the repurchase likelihood is measured on a five-point scale, and a modified "top-two-boxes" score is used: 100% of the "Definitely's" +50% of the "Probably's." For the price question, the norm is no more than 30% should say "fair" or "poor" value.
Source: Adapted from David W. Olson, "Postlaunch Evaluation for Consumer Goods," in M. Rosenau, A. Griffin, G. Castellion, and N. Anscheutz (eds), *The PDMA Handbook of New Product Development*, John Wiley & Sons, Inc., 1996, pp. 395–411.

they will not get the push they need. But does trade support mean stocking the product? Displaying the product? Advertising the product locally? Giving presale service? Gearing up to give postsale service? The launch planner has to decide.

We need relevant, measurable, and predictable tracking variables. A variable is *relevant* if it identifies the problem, *measurable* if we can get a statistic showing it is or isn't, and *predictable* if we know the path that the statistic should follow across the page.

Look back to Figure 17.1. The top graph displays awareness: "Have you heard of . . . ?" It is a percentage of all people in the target market. The track line, labeled *plan,* shows what we *expect* to happen. The broken line shows what we find *is* happening and what we fear *will* happen if we do nothing. The tracking variable is relevant, measurable, predictable.

But let's look at dealer support. At the bottom of Figure 17.1 is a track of retail stocking, the percentage of target dealers who have stocked the item so far. This too is relevant, measurable, and predictable (based on our past experience). But what about shelf space? The height of the stocking, the number of facings, and the department in which it occurs are all aspects of shelf space. They differ in relevance; they are all tough to measure without actually calling on stores and looking at the shelves; and we are apt to lack the experience we need to predict them. Figure 17.1 also shows retail display, but such a track is mainly a guess.

Selecting the Trigger Points

Given that we have found useful variables for warning that a problem is coming about, the last step is deciding in advance how bad it has to be before turning the contingency plan loose. Say, for example, we have a low budget situation and are worried that customers may not hear of our new item—low awareness. If our objective for three months out is 40 percent of customers aware, and tracking shows we actually have only 35 percent, should we release the standby e-mail promotion program?

This is not an easy decision to make under beachhead conditions, for political reasons as well as for time constraints. Doubling the emphasis on social media promotion may be seen as a signal that the original broadcast advertising has failed. This admission is not popular, and arguments will be made that the advertising is working as planned and the awareness will soon increase.

To avoid these no-win situations, agree in advance what level will be the trigger and put the triggering decision in the hands of a person with no vested interest. With this, the tracking plan is complete. With diligent implementation, the launch will probably be "controlled to success."

Nontrackable Problems

What do we do when we have a problem that worries us but cannot be tracked because we can't find a variable for it, or because we don't have a track that the variable should follow, or because there is nothing we can do if the problem is found to be coming about? The answer is, very little.

Typically, management watches sales, and, if they are falling below the forecast, someone is asked to find out why. This means interviewing salespeople, customers, distributors, and so on. It's a difficult inquiry because things are changing so fast and because most participants have vested interests—they may not reveal the true problem even if they know it.

When the cause is found, a remedy is devised. If it's not a fast-moving market, time may be available to get the new product back into a good sales pattern. If it's too late, the new item is dumped or milked for a while. The loss may be very little if the costs of launch were low, as they often are for small firms, for line extensions, and for products that were never expected to amount to much.

Effective Innovation Metrics[5]

Deciding on the right metrics to use to evaluate a firm's new products process is clearly difficult. Yet effective metrics are needed for success with current projects, as well as for continued improvement. Marketing experts David Reibstein and Venkatesh Shankar advocate the use of an **innovation dashboard** that establishes performance metrics for innovation inputs, process effectiveness, and performance outcomes.[6] Figure 17.6 presents some of the most typically used measures for each of these three categories. Input metrics include R&D spending, number of employees devoted to innovation, and number of new ideas in the pipeline. Process effectiveness metrics include number of new products introduced, time to market, number of patents filed, and budgeted versus actual time and cost incurred. Finally, performance metrics include percentage of sales derived from new products, number of successful new products, return on investment in innovation, time to break even, and improvement in customer satisfaction.

Much can be learned about metrics by examining the practices of some of the best-performing firms. For example, Boeing uses cost, quality, and reliability metrics in the

FIGURE 17.6
Metrics for
Innovation

Input Metrics	Process Metrics	Performance Metrics
R&D spending	Number of new products introduced	Percent of sales from new products
Number of employees devoted to innovation	Average time to market	Number of new products
Number of new ideas in pipeline	Number of patents filed and commercialized	Return on investment in innovation
Number of projects in development	Budgeted versus actual time and cost incurred	Breakeven time
Percent of ideas sourced from outside the firm	Percent of projects that result in a launch	Improvement in customer satisfaction

Source: Adapted from David Reibstein and Venkatesh Shankar, "Innovation Metrics," in Jagdish N. Sheth and Naresh K. Malhotra, *Wiley International Encyclopedia of Marketing*, Volume 5, *Product Innovation and Management* (West Sussex, UK: John Wiley, 2011), p. 93.

[5]The examples in this section are taken from Mark J. Deck, "An Up-Close Look at Using Metrics Effectively Across the Life Cycle: Examples from Boeing, ChevronTexaco, Air Products, and Sprint," *Visions*, 24(1), January 2005, pp. 14–16.

[6]David Reibstein and Venkatesh Shankar, "Innovation Metrics," in Jagdish N. Sheth and Naresh K. Malhotra, *Wiley International Encyclopedia of Marketing*, Volume 5, *Product Innovation and Management* (West Sussex, UK: John Wiley, 2011), pp. 91–96.

development of new airplanes. But Boeing VP Chris Chadwick says that *soft metrics* are also very useful. One used at Boeing is "help needed." Product team leaders are encouraged to ask for help when they run into a development problem; no requests for "help needed" is a signal that a project might be running into trouble. Boeing also uses forward-looking metrics to predict possible problems ahead of time. A metric such as weight maturity, for example, alerts Boeing to whether they are on track to meet eventual target weight constraints.

Another useful idea is to get external validation for metrics. ChevronTexaco has metrics for its capital programs, which it benchmarks using an external firm that specializes in this kind of analysis. This allows ChevronTexaco to assess its own cost and performance, not just with respect to internal goals, but also in comparison to competitive firms. ChevronTexaco also makes metrics meaningful for decision makers. Too often, managers don't pay attention to metrics, since their impact is never really communicated to them. At ChevronTexaco, managers are trained and certified in the use of metrics in decision making. In addition, Boeing, ChevronTexaco, and many other firms tie individual incentives to performance on important metrics.

If there are too many or overly complex metrics, they will become a problem unto themselves. To avoid "paralysis by analysis," for example, Air Products (a gas and chemical company) uses only a handful of metrics at the highest level, such as financial return relative to objectives. At the middle level of management, a few additional metrics are added, such as product cost indexes and marketing efficiency; lower levels within the firm are concerned with more tactical metrics. Sprint, the communications services provider, does much the same thing. According to Assistant Vice President Mike Coffey, Sprint senior management uses a scorecard with eight or fewer metrics for each product they offer. Sprint also prioritizes metrics, recognizing that in their line of work, customer satisfaction and operational performance are the most important. Coffey says, "When customers are happy, that's a leading indicator of their intention to keep using the service."

An additional advantage of having fewer metrics is that metrics can be in conflict. Accelerated time to market is a good thing, but not if it means sacrificing quality. Air Products focuses on product reuse, which improves total cost of capital (one important metric), but lower cost of capital also has the effect of worsening an engineering efficiency metric, engineering cost divided by total capital. According to Naser Chowdhury, director of Global Product Management, this sort of metric conflict does occur, but needs to be avoided.

Finally, metrics need to be adjusted and fine-tuned through time, so that they are aligned with business goals—and firms need to learn from their metrics. At Boeing, a review known as Program Independent Assessment is designed to help identify new metrics and drop older ones, and also to assess how well current metrics are being used on each product project.

As a final thought, we are observing an increased use of social media metrics in launch management.[7] We have previously seen the use of social media early in the new

---

[7]Amy Kenley, "Social Media and New Product Development," in K. B. Kahn, S. E. Kay, R. J. Slotegraaf, and S. Uban (eds.), *The PDMA Handbook of New Product Development* (Hoboken, NJ: John Wiley, 2013), Ch. 17, pp. 283–291.

products process, notably in open innovation efforts such as P&G's Connect and Develop, in which new ideas can be solicited and commented on by the online community. In fact, social media can be profitably used for launch management as well. During product launch, customer feedback can be gained via online sources, measured and compared to products already on the market. Sentiment analysis tools can be used to categorize the overall positive or negative sentiment about the product as expressed online, as well as to identify opportunities for improvement. Insights about after-sale service can be obtained from online sources and shared among service providers so as to improve customer support.

A Sample Launch Management Plan

Figure 17.7 shows a sample launch management plan. In it are samples of real-life problems, specific variables that were selected to track them, trigger points, and the standby contingency plans ready to go into effect. Note particularly that this was not a large firm, it had no market research department, and it was not then sophisticated in how to launch new products. Still, the plan covers the main bases, permits launch management to be in the hands of available managers, and provides effective action if any of the possible problems come about.

Larger firms with big budgets will have more sophisticated plans, but in principle they will be exactly the same—problem, tracking variable, trigger point, and remedial plan ready to go. Very small firms may have the energy to deal with only a few problems; the manager may use what we call *eyeball control* to move around the market and find if they are coming about, and then have in mind what will be done if they are.

But, whether in the mind, in the format of Figure 17.7, or in a sophisticated formal plan, the essentials are the same.

Launch Management and Knowledge Creation[8]

Of course, we are learning throughout the new products process. During product development, we may discover activities or processes that we would like to duplicate in other product projects or standardize throughout the firm, or may identify technologies that could be reused elsewhere to minimize risks and costs and shorten development time. But in particular, much important knowledge can be created at the postlaunch phase by conducting an after-action review (AAR), and AAR practitioners include some of the most successful innovating firms today, with Harley-Davidson, Sprint, and Ford among them.

An AAR is designed to capture the events leading up to the product launch and to try to understand the thinking behind the actions taken. The goal is to identify what went right (so it can be duplicated) and what went wrong (to identify weak areas in the firm's processes that need to be fixed). A good AAR includes statements of planned objectives

---

[8]Much of this section is taken from Ken Bruss, "Gaining Competitive Advantage by Leveraging Lessons Learned," in A. Griffin and S. M. Somermeyer, *The PDMA Toolbook 3 for New Product Development* (New York: John Wiley, 2007), Chapter 15.

FIGURE 17.7   Sample Launch Management Plan

Setting: This launch control plan is for a small or medium-sized industrial firm that is marketing a unique electrical measuring instrument. The device must be sold to the general-purpose (i.e., factory) market, whereas past company products have been sold primarily to the scientific R&D market. The firm has about 60 salespeople, but its resources are not large. No syndicated (e.g., audit firm) services are available in this market.

Only a few parts of the marketing plan are presented here, but the control plan does contain the total set of control problems, a plan to measure those that could be measured, and what the firm planned to do if each problem actually occurred.

Potential Problem	Tracking	Contingency Plan
1. Salespeople fail to contact general-purpose market at prescribed rate.	Track weekly call reports. The plan calls for at least 10 general purpose calls per week per rep.	If activity falls below this level for three weeks running, a remedial program of one-day district sales meetings will be held.
2. Salespeople may fail to understand how the new feature of the product relates to product usage in the general-purpose market.	Tracking will be done by having sales manager call one rep each day. Entire sales force will be covered in two months.	Clarification will be given to individual reps on the spot, but if first 10 calls suggest a widespread problem, special teleconference calls will be arranged to repeat the story to the whole sales force.
3. Potential customers are not making trial purchases of the product.	Tracking by instituting a series of 10 follow-up telephone calls a week to prospects who have received sales presentations. There must be 25 percent agreement on product's main feature and trial orders from 30 percent of those prospects who agree on the feature.	Remedial plan provides for special follow-up telephone sales calls to all prospects by reps, offering a 50 percent discount on all first-time purchases.
4. Buyers make trial purchase but do not place quantity reorders.	Track another series of telephone survey calls, this time to those who placed an initial order. Sales forecast based on 50 percent of trial buyers reordering at least 10 more units within six months.	No remedial plan for now. If customer does not rebuy, there is some problem in product use. Since product is clearly better, we must know the nature of the misuse. Field calls on key accounts will be used to determine that problem, and appropriate action will follow.
5. Chief competitor may have the same new feature (for which we have no patent) ready to go and markets it.	This situation is essentially untrackable. Inquiry among our suppliers and media will help us learn quicker.	Remedial plan is to pull out all stops on promotion for 60 days. A make-or-break program. Full field selling on new item only, plus a 50 percent first-order discount and two special mailings. The other trackings listed above will be monitored even more closely.

FIGURE 17.8
A Sample
After-Action
Review

Objectives:

1. Send the customer sample by end December
2. Send the revised samples by end February
3. Reduce test time in half (from one minute to 30 seconds)

Results:

Objective 1 missed by a week, objectives 2 and 3 achieved

Reasons for Variances?

New product did not achieve performance requirements spelled out in the product spec.
Too much time (six weeks) was lost in redesign and remanufacturing as a result.
Not enough time was allocated for hardware or software changes.
But:
Team was able to reduce test time due to newly developed efficient testing.

Lessons Learned:
We probably relied too much on generic, off-the-shelf processes and packages, not all of which were appropriate in this setting.
Internally, we had been calling this product a "derivative" of existing products, but indeed the testing procedure was much more complex than for existing products, which should have been accounted for in the plan.

Source: Adapted from Ken Bruss, "Gaining Competitive Advantage by Leveraging Lessons Learned," in A. Griffin and S. M. Somermeyer, *The PDMA Toolbook 3 for New Product Development*, John Wiley & Sons, Inc., 2007, Ch. 15.

and actual results, an attempt to rationalize the observed variances, a statement of what has been learned, and an outline for the next steps. An illustrative example is provided in Figure 17.8. The AAR need not be terribly formal—in some cases, a couple of individuals meeting briefly after a customer visit might suffice—but nevertheless it must be done. Some firms delay the AAR until a year after release, in order to assess how well the new product did, or whether it achieved its planned targets. Participants in the AAR should include the new product team leader and possibly just about anyone else who has some direct experience with the project. If this results in an unworkably large number of individuals, break them up into meaningful subgroups, run several AARs in parallel, then bring the subgroups together to discuss what had been learned. As is often the case in group discussion settings, having a good, trained facilitator can make all the difference.

Some products unintentionally live short lives. Occasionally, however, products are marketed that the managers know from the start will be on the market only a short time. Such products include fad products, temporary fillers of a hole in a product line, products keyed to a market participant's special needs, and *occasional* products. One producer of occasional products is Baskin-Robbins, which has a standing set of flavors always available and another stable of flavors that move into and out of the line.

Temporary products have much less need for launch management, mainly because there is nothing that can be done—everything is committed. Advertising and personal selling monies are needed to load up distributor/retailers (no out-of-stocks can be allowed because they represent permanently lost sales) and to build immediate sales. Sales promotion works only on awareness and trial. There are no follow-on products scheduled, production is contracted out if possible, inventories are moved out, and production runs are matched to the reorder rate. No long-term service facilities are built, prices are held steady (or at the most, reduced), and most effort after announcement is put into market intelligence needed to know when sales are leveling and heading down. By the time any launch problems are identified, the time to solve them is past.

Product Failure

Despite everyone's best efforts, products do sometimes fail or appear to be failing. When the product appears to be in decline, the firm first thinks of how additional money can best be spent, and strategy is reviewed. Of course, time permitting, the product can be changed or standby add-ons can be sent to market while longer-term changes are being made. If the market situation is particularly difficult and solutions lie only in longer-time product changes, it may be necessary to pull the product temporarily, or, at best, stop all promotion and hold the market in a freeze until the problem solution has been found. If things in the development area don't move along successfully fast, it is usually necessary to abandon the product; that is, to abandon the market opportunity. Most firms have many new product options and like to get their losers out of sight and out of mind. The politics are bad, people are scurrying to escape the sinking ship, critics are reminding everyone how they predicted this trouble, and so on. Of course, if new plants were built, if major promotional programs were undertaken, or in any other way major financial commitments were made, then there will be efforts to hold on—at least until there has been time to put through a relaunch.

The product deletion decision is obviously a complex one with a potentially strong ripple effect. One team of researchers has suggested a stepwise process for the product deletion decision (see Figure 17.9). In this process, the firm must first decide whether the product's performance merits consideration for deletion. It then explores ways by which the viability of the product might be restored through quality or price adjustments or perhaps targeting new markets. Before making the deletion decision, the firm must systematically evaluate the full effect of the deletion on overheads, expenses, and capacity utilization and also determine whether the deletion would leave a major hole in the firm's product line. Finally, if deletion is necessary or inevitable, its speed must be determined (i.e., get rid of the product immediately, milk it for several quarters or even years, sell it off, etc.).[9]

Some evidence exists that new-to-the-world product projects may be harder to shut down. In these cases, managers tend to be more optimistic about the chances of success, be more emotionally committed to the project, and be more likely to want to continue the project right through to launch. Sometimes, the evaluation steps in the new products process identify strong signals indicating potential problems, but are ignored. In other cases, the evaluation is not done thoroughly, and clear Go/No Go decisions are not

---

[9]George J. Avlonitis, Susan J. Hart, and Nikolaos X. Tzokas, "An Analysis of Product Deletion Scenarios," *Journal of Product Innovation Management*, 17(1), January 2000, pp. 41–56.

FIGURE 17.9
A Stepwise Product Deletion Process

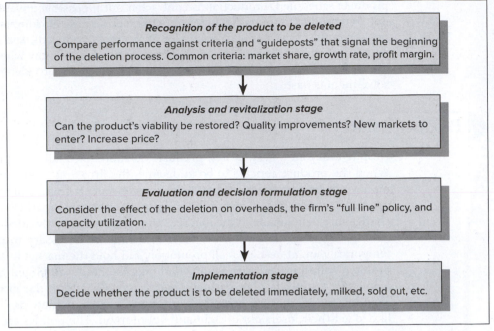

Source: Adapted from George J. Avlonitis, Susan J. Hart, and Nikolaos X. Tzokas, "An Analysis of Product Deletion Scenarios," *Journal of Product Innovation Management* 17, no. 1, January 2000, pp. 41–56.

made. Some products that do get eliminated may even come back, possibly under another name. In our rush to speed products to market quicker, we must not lose sight of the need to halt poor products sooner![10]

If a product or product line is discontinued, it may still hold revenue opportunities. It can be sold to another firm outright. Alternatively, the firm can sell the rights to the product or its brand name, its formulation or blueprints, its manufacturing process, its distribution channel, its technology or core subassemblies, or the whole business unit.[11] Another possibility is for the firm to consolidate its position—to become the big fish in an admittedly shrinking pond (see some examples in Figure 17.10). Actually, there is an advantage to this strategy: There is low threat of new competition entering the market. Any of these opportunities should be explored if feasible.

If **abandonment** is necessary, the manager's job is not finished. A lot of people need to be notified (including customers, governments, distributors, and trade groups). If

---

[10]Jeffrey B. Schmidt and Roger J. Calantone, "Are Really New Product Development Projects Harder to Shut Down?" *Journal of Product Innovation Management,* 15(2), March 1998, pp. 111–123; and Jeffrey B. Schmidt and Roger J. Calantone, "Escalation of Commitment during New Product Development," *Journal of the Academy of Marketing Science,* 30(2), 2002, pp. 103–118.

[11]Patricia A. Katzfey, "Product Discontinuation," in M. Rosenau, A. Griffin, G. Castellion, and N. Anscheutz (eds.), *The PDMA Handbook of New Product Development* (New York: John Wiley, 1996), pp. 413–425.

FIGURE 17.10

Consolidation Strategies at Work

About a hundred years ago, detachable, disposable paper collars were part of a waiter's uniform. As these fell out of style, there remained only one firm still making the collar. When this firm was acquired by another company, it sent out letters to its customers that the price of its paper collars would double. The new owner recognized that there was a small yet captive demand for this kind of collar.

A kitchen cabinet manufacturer bought a large wagon-wheel manufacturing plant, with the intention of turning it into a location for cabinet manufacture. It soon found that it had just taken over one of the last wagon-wheel plants in the United States, and continued to sell wagon wheels profitably for some time thereafter (including many to gardeners or landscapers, who use them as planters).

Push lawnmowers declined in popularity as gasoline-powered mowers of all shapes and sizes, and riding mowers, took over the suburban lawn care market. One firm, American Lawnmower, had about a 95 percent share of the market for push mowers. In recent years, many homeowners have switched back to push mowers for their simplicity, environmental friendliness, and nostalgia, and sales have rebounded.

After transistors had completely replaced vacuum tubes in televisions, radios, and other devices, RCA and GE abandoned vacuum tube manufacture. One company located in Illinois realized that there would be demand for vacuum tubes in special applications, aggressively bought out small competitors, and achieved a profitable position in the market.

The advantage here is that there is little threat of new competition entering the market. (Would GE really want to reinvest in vacuum tubes at this point, or Ford in wagon wheels?)

Source: Examples are from Laurence P. Feldman, "From Paper Collars to Vacuum Tubes: Life at the End of the Product Life Cycle," *Visions,* October 1997, p. 10.

persons or firms have become dependent on the product, it may be necessary to have a gradual stock-reduction program, a stockpiling of parts, and a period of repair service. The cost and required time duration of this after-the-fact support needs to be estimated.

Summary

This chapter brings us to the point where we introduce the product. We have the product, we have the marketing program for it, and we are prepared to control its way to success.

The requirements of launch management are a plan, measurement of progress in the market, analysis of events to determine if prearranged contingency actions should be put into play, and continuing study to ensure that any problem becomes known as soon as possible so action can be taken to avert or at least ameliorate it.

Launch management and tracking are especially tough because most of the activity is out in the marketplace, variables will change, and measurements are difficult and expensive (not like walking through the factory in the eyeball control method). But the methodology is available, and when the situation warrants this effort, a new products manager can certainly gain from it.

We can now turn our attention to a topic ever-present in new products work: Are there public policy issues involved in the new product's manufacture, distribution, use, or disposal? Are there ethical issues involved? What the developer thinks is, of course, not the point. What does the public think? What do government people think? This issue is the subject of Chapter 18.

Case: Gillette[12]

For decades, the Gillette Company (a division of Procter & Gamble) has followed a simple strategy for success: replace excellent blade technology with an even better one. Over the years, Gillette has brought us the Blue Blade, the Platinum Plus, the Trac II, the Atra, the Sensor, then the SensorExcel.

In April 1998, Gillette launched the Mach3, a three-bladed pivoting cartridge system. A key element of the Mach3's design was the positioning of the three blades: each blade was a little closer to the face than the previous one. This patented design reduced the irritation caused by the third blade. In 2003, Wilkinson Sword (a division of Edgewell Personal Care), one of Gillette's key competitors, launched a four-blade system, the Schick Quattro, which soon started drawing market share away from the Mach3. The success of the Quattro suggested that customers were willing to accept shaving systems with more than three blades and encouraged Gillette to plan a multi-blade system.

Gillette never launched a four-blade system. In 2006, Gillette leaped over the competition and launched the Fusion, a five-blade system with lubricating strips on both sides and one extra trimming blade on the back. In addition to having more blades, the Fusion also placed the blades closer together in the cartridge for a close, comfortable shave, and also came in a battery-powered model (the Fusion Power) that vibrates, adding to shaving comfort.

Fusion was an immediate success. Despite a price point about a dollar higher per cartridge than Mach3, 4 million razors were sold in the first two months. An important part of the marketing support for the Fusion was an extensive, worldwide television advertising campaign featuring globally recognized athletes such as Tiger Woods, Thierry Henry, and Roger Federer.

Nevertheless, Gillette received some criticism and skepticism at the time of the Fusion launch. A story in *Consumer Reports* found no additional performance benefits beyond what the Mach3 offered, and critics wondered why as many as five blades were needed for a good shave. Customers were skeptical at first of the five-blade system, especially after so many years of Gillette promotion promising that the Mach3 was "the best a man can get." Some even recalled satirical TV ads on comedy programs such as *MadTV* for 17-blade systems and wondered if Gillette was going in that direction. It was also troubling to Gillette executives that, while the razors were selling well, sales of the cartridge refills were lagging. This was a real cause for concern, for two reasons. Low sales of refills would suggest that customers viewed the Fusion as a novelty product and were not building loyalty; also, in the razor business, refills are much more profitable

---

[12]This case is based on Mark Maremont, "How Gillette Brought Its Mach3 to Market," *The Wall Street Journal*, April 15, 1998, p. B-1; www.gillette.com; Amy Tsao, "Schick vs. Gillette" Hardly a Close Match," *bloomberg.com*, November 10, 2003; Leanne Davis, "Gillette: Product and Marketing Innovation," mkstrat.files.wordpress.com/2013/01/gillette-case.pdf; Sue Byrne, "Which Shave Club Has the Best Razor?," *consumerreports.org*, April 25, 2016; Lauren Thomas, "Gillette One Ups Dollar Shave Club with On-Demand Razor Ordering Service Where You Text to Order," *cnbc.com*, May 9, 2017; Sarah Brookbank, "P&G, Gillette Launch Heated Razor, Test Waters with Indiegogo Campaign," *cincinnati.com*, Sept. 18, 2018; Anonymous, "The Heated Razor By GilletteLabs: Sold Out," *indiegogo.com*, Anonymous, "Gillette's Heated Razor Creates the Comfort of a Hot Towel with Every Stroke," *designboom.com*.

than the cheaply priced handles. Despite the initial skepticism, the Gillette Fusion has been a top-seller and major generator of revenue for Gillette.

So it may (or may not) have been a surprise when the next competitive move was not a six- or seven-blade system. Instead, low-cost competitors such as Dollar Shave Club and Harry's have emerged, offering a good honest shave at a low price. Rather than stressing high-tech blades, these competitors offered convenience, in the form of mail delivery. Of these, Dollar Shave Club is an intriguing example. Founded in 2011, it was immediately successful as a low-cost blade-by-mail club. The original Dollar Shave Club advertising, humorously promoting the benefits of joining the club and poking fun at the high-tech blades sold by competitors, can be seen here: www.youtube.com/watch?v=ZUG9qYTJMsI.

By 2016, Dollar Shave Club was acquired by Unilever, propelling this multinational into one of the leading blade competitors worldwide. By 2017, Gillette's sales in its grooming segment had declined by 6 percent, with the entry of the low-cost competitors considered to be a major reason. Though the initial Dollar Shave Club blades were promoted as low-tech, by 2018 the company was offering only a four- and a six-blade cartridge, as well as many other grooming products, all still sold through mail delivery.

Gillette responded to the mail-order blade business by launching the Gillette Shave Club (later renamed Gillette On Demand), a mail-order service promising three-day delivery and flexible price points. Nevertheless, Gillette wanted to maintain its high-quality image and was hesitant to lower its prices. Rather than competing on low price alone, Gillette has turned again to technological innovation; however, the days of simply adding more blades to the cartridge may be over. Customers seem to have reached the point where the additional blade will not improve the shave quality enough to justify the higher blade cost. The most recent innovation from Gillette's research unit (GilletteLabs) is the Heated Razor, which promises a blade with the "comfort of a hot towel with every stroke." Flex disc technology enables the blade to fit smoothly on the face, while also maximizing heat flow. The razor is waterproof and comes with an electric charger. A short video describing the technology can be viewed here: www.designboom.com/technology/gilette-heated-razor-gilettelabs-10-08-2018.

Gillette made the Heated Razor available in a market test through the crowdfunding service Indiegogo. The test was judged to be a major success, as the test batch sold out quickly, and customers were curious about this new-generation razor.

Based on what you see in this case, what was the effect of the mail-order competitors on the blade market? What accounts for their success at this time, given the dominance of Gillette and Schick/Wilkinson Sword for decades in the world blade market? What are the risks involved in Gillette's decision to roll out high-tech "really new" products such as the Heated Razor, especially now that the mail-order competitors are drawing substantial market share and changing the face of competition in this market? What strategic role does design play at Gillette? Also, comment on the aggressive marketing and rollout plans used by Gillette to support their product launches. What are the pros and cons?

Public Policy Issues

Setting

Along the way through the past 17 chapters, we have been dealing with the various problems of developing and launching a new product. But, to simplify things, we have deferred until now some major questions of public policy. They concern the relationship between the firm (the people, as well as the products and services) and the citizenry. In every country on earth, there are ways in which the new product function is limited or directed, and usually for very good reason. So managers need to know the rules, and they need to understand the edges of the law where issues may be unclear.

Chapter 18 gives the life cycle of a public concern, discusses the attitudes of business regarding product innovation and public policy, and deals with the most critical of the concerns—product liability. It then goes into the other concerns, such as sustainability and the environment, and some related managerial issues.

Bigger Picture: A Cycle of Concerns

The environment has been on the public consciousness more than ever before, and many companies have decided to seek solutions in their own ways. Walmart has looked into building low-energy stores, while General Electric is building ultra-high-efficiency products. Why so much attention in recent years? Certainly, media coverage of environmental concerns has been high, and the U.S. Environmental Protection Agency has established a comprehensive climate policy. These factors have led to greater awareness at the grassroots level. Chief executive officers sometimes explain their sudden environmental concerns as a "personal awakening" to climate threats. But there is more to it: Big investors know that limits on carbon dioxide outputs are coming, so they exert pressure on firms to find a solution. Car companies have successfully launched hybrid and electric vehicles to minimize the air pollutants from combustion engines, and they have worked on other alternative power sources for cars of the future. But what if several years of research efforts produce a gas combustion engine that is 1,000 times more efficient than the ones used today in cars? That might be more efficient than hydrogen cell power and should not be ruled out as one of the targets for cars 20 years in the future. Managers will sometimes turn to **technology roadmaps** to play out alternative

FIGURE 18.1
Life Cycle of a
Public Concern

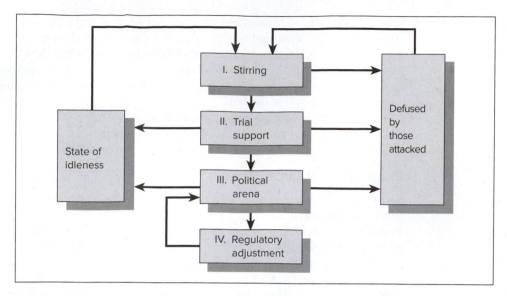

scenarios into the future and develop plans.[1] No matter what the industry, the environment is squarely in the mainstream, and if they hadn't been doing so already, firms have to develop policy on what to do next.[2] Through time, firms in other industries (tobacco, chemicals, pharmaceuticals, fast foods, and so on) have received their share of public scrutiny, for environmental reasons, health reasons, or others.

All public pressure situations go through a life cycle of the following phases (see Figure 18.1). See if you can identify each of these phases in the emergence of, for example, concerns about global warming or fast-food nutrition.

Phase I: Stirring

Individuals begin to sound off long before enough people have been injured or irritated to cause a general reaction. Letters to company presidents, complaints in the media, e-mail campaigns to political representatives, and tentative expressions of concern by knowledgeable authorities are typical of phase I. Most people ignore these periods, but they are easy to identify, looking back. Consequently, the stirring phase may last a long time—decades, in fact. The problem for new products managers is that they don't know if the issue will flare up or will die away.

Phase II: Trial Support

As the stirrings over an issue increase, a champion may decide to take it on as a cause. Such champions used to be individuals and were often unknown, as Ralph Nader was when he tackled auto safety in the 1960s. Today, cause support tends to come from

[1]Richard E. Albright and Beebe Nelson, "Product and Technology Mapping Tools for Planning and Portfolio Decision Making," in P. Belliveau, A. Griffin, and S. M. Somermeyer (Eds.), *The PDMA Toolbook 2 for New Product Development*, 2004, Hoboken, New Jersey: John Wiley & Sons.

[2]Michelle Conlin (Ed.), "The Best Ideas." *BusinessWeek*, December 18, 2006, pp. 97–107; and the U.S. Environmental Protection Agency Web site, www.epa.gov.

organizations whose leaders are attempting to marry the basic unrest in a situation with a desire for contribution and publicity. The key question to these organizations often is, "How widespread is the unpublicized unrest?" Or, "How dramatic can the headlines be made?" This may sound crass, but remember, there are scores of budding issues at any time, and an organization may lose its power if it squanders its scarce resources on issues that die out.

In any event, phase II is a period when the would-be leader and the muted cause are on the stump, seeking a political base. If achieved, the action moves to phase III, unless the industry being attacked can defuse the situation or the cause fails to capture broad support.

Phase III: The Political Arena

By the time an issue has acquired a political base among the voting public, the opportunity for defusing has usually passed. Now, companies must gird up for political battle in state and/or federal legislatures or in the various regulatory arenas. The issue is the content of new laws or regulations, and companies usually recognize the widespread consumer demands and are only trying to achieve the least costly and least restrictive mode of meeting them. Occasionally, companies fight vigorously against settlement. Nevertheless, the political base is usually all the cause a leader needs to force some modification in a practice, one severe enough to require legislation or a court ruling.

Phase IV: Regulatory Adjustment

New regulatory legislation is rarely precise, and this imprecision leads to a period of jockeying by the adversaries over its interpretation. The Consumer Product Safety Act, for example, directed the **Consumer Product Safety Commission** to order the seizure of any "imminently hazardous consumer products," four terms that are each impossible to define. Imprecision may well be a necessary or even wise approach in regulation. The phase often lasts for years, and sometimes general shifts in a country's political thinking cause various issues to move into or out of the idle state.

Business Attitudes toward Product Issues

Business firms deal with public policy issues on a much broader base than just new products, so they have reached a structure of beliefs on this matter of interface between business and society. Most of those beliefs support product innovation, and society agrees. Granted, there are some issues that we haven't yet figured out. For example, how do we pay the costs of product misuse where the consumer was unable to read and understand labels? What is the responsibility of a food company whose customers want great taste but whose government wants quality nutrition? In general, most of the headlines today are for problems that came up years ago, and our concerns are "at the margin"—that is, dealing in areas of temporary uncertainty and change.

The new product that causes unexpected concern on the public policy front is probably the result of careless management. Note, *unexpected*. A lot of our problems we expect and in most cases have methods to avoid them, or hedge bets, or prepare to deal with them. Of course, no manager can walk through the minefield of federal and regional legislators, regulators, trial lawyers, aggrieved customers, and leaders of popular causes without occasionally tripping up.

Current Problem Areas

New products managers face many specific problem areas as they attempt to deal with social and legal pressures—product liability is the most complex, and at the moment the most frustrating, partly because of the seriousness of the potential suits and the costs of error.

These issues are worldwide, though our discussion will mainly use North American examples. Members of the European Union are still wrestling with the product liability question because of their 1985 commitment to strict liability. Although going slower than it was supposed to, the directive will apparently be implemented. Germany and the Scandinavian countries are world leaders in environmental issues. China more recently instituted a product liability law; many other nations in the world have yet even to face this issue.

Product Liability

The scenario here is simple: You buy a product and are injured. The injury may have come when you carried the product home, when you opened it, when you stored it, when you used it, when you tried to repair it, or when you disposed of it. If you were injured and if you think the maker or the reseller of the product did (or didn't do) something that caused the injury, then you have a product liability claim. If guilty, the accused party is liable for the cost and the pain of the injury, plus punitive damages as well.

Historically, **product liability** applied to goods, not services, and there have been many lost attempts to extend the law to cover services. Yet services are products (both in fact and as we use the terms in this book); they are sold and bought in good faith, injuries do occur, and some redress should be possible. For example, an engineering consulting firm gave an opinion that a building was in good shape; the buyer later found this untrue when an injury took place. Negligence on services can produce a product liability case.

How important is product liability? Most suits are settled out of court, so we don't have good dollar data. Undoubtedly, the costs can be enormous for the company involved.

Typology of Injury Sources

Here is a list of the ways we get into trouble, and most of them are double trouble for *new* products.

1. Many products have *inherent risks*. For example, blood transfusion carries the risk of hepatitis infection, and dynamite will explode. Because the risk cannot be avoided, we get more understanding in the courts.

2. *Design defects* can cause the manufacture of an unsafe product in three different ways. First, the design may create a *dangerous condition*, say a steam vaporizer whose center of gravity is so high that the unit is likely to spill. Second, an essential *safety device* may be absent. For example, a hair dryer may lack an overheat cutoff

switch. Third, the design may call for *inadequate materials*, which perform their function at first but may eventually deteriorate and become dangerous.

3. *Defects in manufacture* have perhaps always been a new products problem. Inadequate quality techniques may result in defective units even if the product is well designed. Poorly welded ladders are an example.

4. The manufacturer may produce an acceptable product but *fail to provide adequate instructions for use or warnings against particular uses*. If used improperly, the lawnmower is a potentially dangerous device. The instructions should tell the user how to use it *and* how not to use it. But courts are much more interested in how strong the warnings are against misuse, even of the unforeseeable kind. With the high risk of lawsuits, firms often go to what seem to be absurd lengths to ensure they have adequate warning labels (thus, a lawnmower may sport a label reading, "do not pick up the mower to trim hedges"; see Figure 18.2). What constitutes adequate warning will never be known for sure, but here is what courts have used in recent years. The warning should be placed conspicuously on the product; it should be where the user most likely can be expected to see it; it should communicate the level of danger; it should instruct the user in how to avoid the potential hazard; sellers should not engage in marketing activities that vitiate an otherwise adequate warning; and it should not be accompanied by statements that the product is safe. The user should be told what may happen if the warning is ignored. Makers must also be prepared to prove that the user *got* the warning, not just that the maker *posted* it.

5. Finally, dangers sometimes appear *after use*, and the manufacturer's liability may continue into this period. For example, manufacturers of spray cans have to urge that the discarded cans not be burned in fireplaces.

FIGURE 18.2
Which Are the Real Product Warning Labels?

1. On a disposable razor: "Do not use this product during an earthquake."
2. On a rock garden: "Eating rocks may lead to broken teeth."
3. On a roll of Life Savers: "Not for use as a flotation device."
4. On a hair dryer: "Do not use while sleeping."
5. On a piano: "Harmful or fatal if swallowed."
6. On a cardboard windshield sun shade: "Warning: Do not drive with sun shield in place."
7. On shin guards: "Shin guards cannot protect any part of the body they do not cover."
8. On syrup of ipecac: "Caution: may induce vomiting."
9. On an iron: "Do not iron clothes while being worn."
10. On a plastic sled: "Not to be eaten or burned."
11. On work gloves: "For best results, do not leave at crime scene."
12. On a cell phone: "Don't try to dry your phone in a microwave oven."
13. On a carpenter's router: "This product not intended for use as a dentist's drill."
14. On a blender: "Not for use as an aquarium."
15. On a stroller: "Always remove child from stroller before folding."
16. On a washing machine: "Do not put any person in this washer."
17. On a fireplace log: "Caution: risk of fire."
18. On a laser printer cartridge: "Do not eat toner."
Solutions appear at the end of the Chapter 18 case.

Sources: '20/20' report, ABC Television, October 28, 1998, Michigan Lawsuit Abuse Watch Web site (www.mlaw.org), and other sources.

FIGURE 18.3   Forms and Sources of Product Liability

A manufacturer or reseller may be found guilty of product liability via these four routes:

	Negligence	Warranty	Strict Liability	Misrepresentation
Source	Common law, 1800s; Once required privity, but dropped in 1960.	Uniform Commercial Code; Enhanced by Magnuson Moss Act.	Court decisions, 1960s.	Common law.
Conditions	Defective product by design or manufacture, and with failure to warn.	Defective product: Implied warranty of merchantability or of fitness for particular purpose. Express warranty; Untrue claim.	Defective product: No requirement for negligence or privity, and no disclaimer is allowed. Reasonably foreseeable.	Untrue claim or misrepresentation that led to injury. User relied on it. No need for defective product.
Defense	Not negligence; product not defective	Not implied by common usage. Not actually stated. Normal puffery.	Buyer knew, so assumed risk. Unforeseeable misuse. Product not defective.	Was truthful. Normal puffery. Buyer should have known better.

Note: We must approach the product liability matter cautiously because of the tendency of the press to distort problems. For example, it was widely publicized recently that an overweight physician with a heart condition had bought a lawnmower, suffered a heart attack while starting the mower, and was awarded $1.8 million. In fact, court records showed that the mower mechanism *was defective* and required an *abnormally large number of pulls*. The doctor, incidentally, *did not have a heart condition*. Casual readers of the press rarely have enough information to reach a good judgment, though they do form opinions.

The Four Legal Bases for Product Liability

The four main routes to liability for a product manufacturer are shown in Figure 18.3. All cases require a basis for the claim, and the manufacturer has to have done something—at the very minimum, make, sell, or lease the product to someone.[3]

Negligence

In the 1880s, under common law, injury claimants had to prove that (1) the manufacturer was *negligent* in operations, let the product become defective and thus injurious, and (2) there was direct sale from the manufacturer to the injured user (*privity*). Perhaps a wagon maker was careless and failed to attach a wheel securely to the axle.

[3]A good general source on the following issues is George D. Cameron, *Business Law: Legal Environment, Transactions, and Regulation* (Plano, Texas: Business Publications, 1989).

The wheel came off, the driver was injured, and **negligence** was easy to establish. The wagon maker failed to exercise ordinary care (the care that a reasonable person would use). The mistake could be made by salespeople, advertising, labeling, retailers, and wholesalers because one aspect of negligence is *failure to warn*.

In 1916, a court ruled that a defectively manufactured product was "inherently dangerous"; it didn't have to be sold direct. By 1966, every state had accepted this line of reasoning, and lack of privity as a defense against negligence was useless.

Warranty

It was still difficult to prove negligence. Thus warranty, a development of the first half of the 20th century, is relevant. **Warranty** is a promise, and if a promise can be proved and is not fulfilled, the seller can be charged with breach of warranty, whether negligent or not. A careful manufacturer of a new product may still be found guilty of causing injury.

Warranty is express or implied. An *express warranty* is any statement of fact made by the manufacturer about a product, whether made by salespeople, retailers, or others. The major issue with express warranty is the degree of puffing a court will allow. *Implied warranty* arises when a maker offers a product for a given use. An implied *warranty of fitness for a particular purpose* is part of the sales contract and means the product is of average quality and can be used for the purposes for which such products are customarily used. The buyer is justified to depend on the seller being right—an expert who knows how people customarily use the item.

But there was constant court bickering over who said what to whom and whether the distributor could have known as much as the maker. Our society is too complex for law that confuses more than clarifies, so we next experienced the development of the strict liability concept.

Strict Liability

Under the concept of **strict liability**, the seller of an item has the responsibility for *not putting a defective product on the market*. If the product is defective, the manufacturer can be sued by any injured party even if that party was only a bystander. *There need be no negligence; there need be no direct sale; no statement by the seller will relieve the liability.*

However, the manufacturer may be able to use three key defenses. The first is *assumption of risk*. If the user of the product learns of the defect and continues to use it regardless of the danger, a suit may not be sustained. Second, the manufacturer has the defense of *unforeseeable misuse*, meaning the injury occurred because the user misused the product in a way that the seller could not reasonably have anticipated. Managers of new products may lack the expected experience, yet courts expect them to be completely marketwise. Third, the defense may be that the product, though causing injury, is not defective. For example, a man hit his eye on the pointed top of a small ventilation window on the side of his car. Though he leaned over and accidentally bumped the window, the jury held that this injury did not mean the window was defective. Presumably, the plaintiff should have been more careful.

Misrepresentation

Actually, a product itself doesn't have to be defective (as it does in the three other preceding situations) so long as an injury took place when the product was used on

misrepresentation (intentional or not) by the seller. These cases are rare, but an example was the helmet manufacturer who made a helmet for motorcyclists and showed a motorcyclist wearing one in a picture on the carton. An experienced police officer bought one for use while riding on duty, but the helmet was not made to be used as a safety helmet. The court ruled there had been misrepresentation.

Other Legislation

Many industries have had unique problems leading to specialized legislation. The Food and Drug Administration, for example, was created in 1906. There are restrictions on alcoholic beverages, automobiles, scientific instruments, metals, and scores more. Attention frequently goes to the Consumer Product Safety Act and its Consumer Product Safety Commission (CPSC). Although the commission's direct impact has been much less than anticipated, the indirect impact has been substantial. It has the power to set standards for products, order the recall of products (see next section), issue public warnings about possible problem products, stop the marketing of new products, ban present or proposed products, and levy substantial civil and criminal penalties. Manufacturers have made many changes to avoid trouble with the law.

Planning for the Product Recall[4]

Any firm may one day face a product recall. To ensure that the recall will be handled properly and successfully, there are crisis management steps that can be taken prior to, during, and after the recall.

Prior to the recall, have a crisis management plan in place. Designate a single individual as the recall program coordinator. He or she will be the spokesperson to the media and to regulatory bodies. Make sure this individual is well informed in dealing with the media and will not buckle under the intense media questioning that might occur. Make sure there are effective channels for communicating with consumers as well as intermediaries such as retailers.

At the time of the crisis, assess the safety risk and take corrective action. When a single blood sugar level meter was found to be defective, LifeScan (a Johnson & Johnson subsidiary) recalled all 600,000 meters on the market at that time. Make sure final customers as well as intermediaries are informed of the risks. Toymakers can easily recall all defective toys sitting on retailers' shelves, but getting the word out to individual consumers is more challenging. A broad media publicity campaign (including on social media) may be required. This is where the crisis management preparation comes in handy. The moment the crisis hits is not the ideal time to start writing press releases and finding contact information for media personnel!

Finally, after the recall, the goal is to restore the company's reputation and to monitor recall effectiveness, ultimately to ensure that sales and market share rebound.

One of the most famous recall cases was the Tylenol cyanide tampering case in the early 1980s. The manufacturer, Johnson & Johnson (J&J), handled all aspects of the recall.

[4]This section (including many of the examples) derives from Barry Berman, "Planning for the Inevitable Product Recall," *Business Horizons*, March–April 1999, pp. 69–77.

A single, high-ranking spokesperson (the CEO) made all statements to the media, while the company immediately removed all product from store shelves, ran a successful publicity campaign to consumers, and scrambled to find the source of the cyanide. When the source was identified as package tampering, J&J developed tamper-resistant packaging as well as new, tamper-proof product forms such as gelcaps and geltabs. The new, safer product and packaging was relaunched several months later, and the media praised J&J's efforts. Tylenol sales were soon higher than they had been before the crisis.

Sustainability and the Environment

Sustainable design refers to either new product design or delivery that reduces negative impacts on the environment. There is no question that sustainability has become a critical consideration in product development. In 2011, the Sustainability and Innovation Global Executive Study found that about 24 percent of companies were "embracers" of sustainability, which meant:

- They have a business case for sustainability;
- They consider sustainability to be necessary to be competitive;
- Sustainability is considered a permanent part of their management agenda.[5]

Further, embracers are more likely to recognize that sustainability strategies will help draw new customers, build market shares, and grow profit margins in current markets. Similarly, about one-third of the companies in the 2012 CPAS study[6] felt that sustainability was a contributing factor to their new product profits. Most firms do consider sustainability as part of their business strategy, even if they do not agree with the embracers on all three of the preceding points. It may be difficult to quantify the financial benefit of investment in sustainability, which might dampen the enthusiasm of some firms to make a commitment. Yet this does not dissuade those companies that have truly embraced sustainability as part of their business strategy.

Sustainability, and other corporate social responsibility programs, has a triple-bottom-line objective: the company should be profitable, customers should get a satisfactory product, and society should benefit in some way. This can be called a "win-win-win" outcome. It is easy for a company to jump on the sustainability bandwagon and make overblown claims about its products or services (this practice is known as **greenwashing**). But embracers actually make adjustments in their business strategy to actively incorporate sustainability; it is not empty words from the marketing department. Corporate strategy scholar Michael Porter has written that the firms that are most successful at corporate social responsibility do not view investment in these activities as inconsistent with their corporate mission: on the contrary, they are essential to achieving the corporate mission.[7] Now, a growing number of firms have a

[5]K. Hannaes et al., *Sustainability: The "Embracers" Seize Advantage*, MIT Sloan Management Review Research Report, Winter 2011.

[6]S. K. Markham and H. Lee, "Product Development and Management Association's 2012 Comparative Performance Assessment Study," *Journal of Product Innovation Management*, 30(3), 2013, pp. 409–429.

[7]M. E. Porter and M. R. Kramer, "The Competitive Advantage of Corporate Philanthropy," *Harvard Business Review*, 80, 2002, pp. 5–16.

FIGURE 18.4   **Integrating Sustainability into the Business Mission**

The Body Shop's environmental agenda is well known. Unlike competitors in the cosmetics industry that focus on glamor and emotion, The Body Shop stresses all-natural ingredients and a natural lifestyle.

Ben & Jerry's Ice Cream supports sustainable practices in farming, as well as non-genetically modified ingredients, humane and cage-free farms, and several other social causes.

Patagonia is a leader among clothing manufacturers in its mission of eco-friendliness, fair labor, and corporate responsibility throughout the supply chain.

Mars Drinks (a division of Mars Inc.) studied the environmental impact of coffee packaging throughout the product process, from raw material to distribution and post-use, eventually producing single-serve coffee packaging for the business-to-business market that significantly reduces the carbon footprint.

Kickstarter has supported several environmental new product initiatives by startups: Genusee makes frames for eyeglasses from water bottles; Huskee Cup makes reusable coffee mugs from coffee husk waste; and Luke's Toy Factory makes a line of eco-friendly toy trucks made from a durable wood-hybrid material including sawdust from furniture manufacture.

Sources: W. C. Kim and R. Mauborgne, "Creating New Market Space," *Harvard Business Review*, 77, January–February 1999, pp. 83–93; J. L. Hardcastle, "Six Sustainable Packaging Trends to Watch in 2016," from www.environmentalleader.com, January 22, 2016; C. A. Di Benedetto, "Corporate Social Responsibility as an Emerging Business Model in Fashion Marketing," *Journal of Global Fashion Marketing*, 8(4), 2017, pp. 251–265; and company Web sites. Kickstarter examples from Heather Clancy, "How Kickstarter is Encouraging Designers to Consider Circularity and Other Environmental Factors," *greenbiz.com*, November 30, 2018.

sustainability manager or environmental specialist as an integral part of the new product development team.[8]

One company that seems to have embraced sustainability and taken advantage of the emerging demand for sustainable products is Clorox. In recent years, Clorox has repositioned Brita water filters and pitchers as an alternative to water in plastic bottles, acquired Burt's Bees and expanded it into an all-natural line of personal care products, and developed the Green Works line of all-natural cleaning products.[9] (Clorox will be revisited in the Clorox Green Works case at the end of this chapter.) In the clothing industry, a leader is Patagonia. From its earliest days designing outdoor wear, Patagonia has aimed to make products that are sustainable as well as durable. In addition, the company makes donations to environmental initiatives throughout the world and also minimizes waste in clothing manufacturing—something that is a real concern in the textile industry. Patagonia fosters strong relationships with its worldwide suppliers, monitors their human rights practices, and provides employees with desirable work environments.[10]

Several other examples of large and small companies appear in Figure 18.4. As shown in the figure, some of the smaller firms turned to Kickstarter to help build their businesses; Kickstarter in fact, encourages entrepreneurs to consider environmental issues such as sustainable sourcing at the earliest stages of product development.

In some cases, the sustainability effort is industry-wide. VinylPlus is a European-wide voluntary commitment to sustainable product development in the polyvinyl chloride (PVC) industry. It offers a sustainability label to companies in the building

[8]E. Genç and C. A. Di Benedetto, "Cross-Functional Integration in the Sustainable New Product Development Process: The Role of the Environmental Specialist," *Industrial Marketing Management*, 50, October 2015, pp. 150–161.

[9]Hannaes et al., 2011.

[10]Patagonia Web sites, www.patagonia.com/company-info.html and www.patagonia.com/corporate-responsibility.html.

and construction industries that identifies the PVC products they use as high performance in terms of sustainability (responsible sourcing, recycling, energy policies, and supply chain management requirements, among others). Several European PVC manufacturers have already been awarded this label after an auditing process carried out by VinylPlus.[11] A similar industry initiative, SPICE, was cofounded by L'Oréal and now includes many other cosmetics companies such as Avon, LVMH, and Shiseido; this initiative focuses on sustainability and eco-friendliness of product packaging.[12]

All too often, unfortunately, there is a gap between good intentions and execution.[13] Managers want to do the right thing environmentally, but are under pressure to make profits, especially when the economy is weak. Therefore, strong support for environmental concerns from top management is critical. The best success in sustainable design occurs when the firm aligns its business objectives with its environmental initiatives. If this occurs, product teams will feel supported in pursuing projects that have longer-term environmental benefits and not feel obliged to pick the low-hanging fruit (make only incremental green improvements to their products). Firms that take a leadership position in sustainable design may discover that this becomes their sustainable competitive advantage. Government mandates on fuel emission, waste management, and other environmental issues are becoming more stringent; managers can effectively incorporate these mandates into their long-term business objectives. It is now up to us to focus on environmental consequences of our products throughout the new products process: to understand customer needs, to design products to solve environmental problems creatively, and to learn the effects of our creations by testing.

Green marketing expert Jacquelyn Ottman notes that firms need to think beyond the obvious when designing products with environmental benefits. She suggests five realistic, actionable strategies for firms to promote sustainable design:

- *Innovate at the system level.* Consider the resources used in manufacture of the product, as well as what happens to the product during and after use. Then think about how the product relates to this entire system. Soladey, a Japanese manufacturer, developed a toothbrush with a photocatalytic titanium dioxide rod in the handle. When used in a bright room, the brush initiates a chemical reaction that breaks down plaque, eliminating the need for toothpaste. The makers of the gDiaper developed a new washable diaper with a disposable lining that can be flushed down the toilet. This keeps disposable diapers out of the landfill.

- *Use new materials, rather than just cutting down on current materials.* Coca-Cola uses a recyclable "plant bottle" that uses up to 30 percent plant-based materials such as sugar cane and sugar production by-products. The plant bottle reduces carbon emissions by as much as 25 percent. Ingeo, a bioplastic manufactured by Natureworks, is made entirely from polylactic acid derived from corn fermentation. Earlier, you read about the Adidas Parley running shoes made from fibers reclaimed from recycled plastic bottles.

[11]Leanne Taylor, "VinylPlus Launches Game Changing Sustainability Mark for PVC Building and Construction Products," *britishplastics.uk*, November 15, 2018.

[12]Lucy Whitehouse, "Schwan Cosmetics Joins Sustainable Packaging Initiative for Cosmetics," *cosmeticsdesign-europe.com*, November 14, 2018.

[13]For a good discussion of these issues, see Jim Todhunter, "Going Green Without Seeing Red," *Visions*, 33(3), October 2009, pp. 6–7.

FIGURE 18.5
Public Policy Problems and the New Products Process

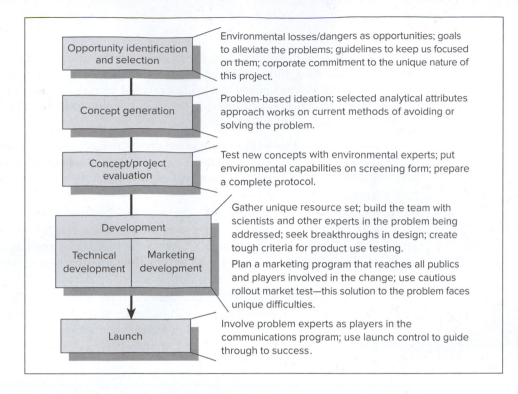

* *Develop new technologies to solve environmental challenges.* Many new advances have been made in the lightbulb industry, including light-emitting diodes that are more efficient than compact fluorescent lamp lighting and last twice as long. Capturing and using solar energy is another possibility. A new hand-held charger by Solio can power cell phones, digital cameras, and other devices for as much as 56 hours using sunlight.
* *Develop new business models.* Zipcar and other similar car-share services allow someone who needs a car for a few hours to rent at low hourly rates; gas is included in the fee, and the individual does not incur car-owner worries like insurance, maintenance, or parking.
* *Restore the environment.* The ultimate way to think of eco-friendly innovation is to try to reduce environmental damage through new technologies and business models. Procter & Gamble provides PUR, a powder that removes pollutants and other impurities from water, to third-world nations. BASF has developed an ozone catalyst for car radiators that converts up to 80 percent of ground-level ozone into oxygen. This is already standard equipment on Volvos and many other cars worldwide.[14]

See Figure 18.5 for how the overall new product system contributes to public policy problems just as it does to other problems.

[14]This discussion and all examples are derived from Jacquelyn Ottman, "Five Ways to Eco-Innovate," *Visions*, 36(3), 2012, pp. 6–7.

Product Piracy[15]

In some industries (video/audio products, computer software, pharmaceuticals, and brand-name clothing and fragrances), **product piracy** is a major problem, especially in foreign markets. Product piracy is actually a catchall term that includes several categories of illegal activities, which threaten the brand equity and intellectual property of firms in these and other industries:

1. *Counterfeiting.* This is the unauthorized production of goods that are protected by trademark, copyright, or patent. Counterfeit goods range from low price and quality to excellent quality; often a giveaway is that the product lacks the manufacturer's original warranty.

2. *Brand Piracy.* This is defined as the unauthorized use of copyrighted or patented goods or brands. Again, product quality can range from very low (the "$20 Rolex") to extremely high. Cartier and other watch and fragrance companies have initiated thousands of legal actions to attempt to stamp out brand piracy.

3. *Near Brand Usage.* Here, the pirate manufacturer uses slightly different brand names such as Channel fragrances, Panasanic camcorders, Kuma running shoes with a pouncing bear logo instead of a puma (*kuma* being Japanese for "bear"), Sunbucks coffee, or Tonny Hilfiger clothes (all real examples!). Moral: Buyer beware, and check the package carefully.

4. *Intellectual Property Copying.* Some of the most highly publicized cases in recent years have involved the unauthorized copying of intellectual property, especially CDs and DVDs containing computer software or entertainment. One estimate figures that 75 million CDs are illegally copied in China alone. Other industries such as pharmaceuticals and car or plane parts are also affected.

In many foreign markets, especially developing economies such as China, the laws governing intellectual property protection and product piracy are very lax. In fact, in many lesser-developed countries (LDCs), intellectual property is seen as a public good, and easy access to it boosts economic development, ultimately closing the gap between the LDC and developed economies.[16] Figure 18.6 shows several ways that firms from developed economies can protect themselves from product piracy, or at least reduce its effects to some degree. In addition to seeking legal recourse or government protection, simply communicating with the market and educating them about the risks of buying pirated products can be an effective action to take.

---

[15]Much of this section draws from Laurence Jacobs, A. Coksun Samli, and Tom Jedlik, "The Nightmare of International Product Piracy," *Industrial Marketing Management*, 30, 2001, pp. 499–509.

[16]Subhash C. Jain, "Problems in International Protection of Intellectual Property Rights," *Journal of International Marketing*, 4(1), 1996, pp. 9–32.

FIGURE 18.6 **Protection against Product Piracy**

1. Communication: Announce that your product has been pirated and that only the real thing offers top value and should be sought out. It was good enough to have been pirated, suggesting that it is of good quality! Especially works if there is a safety or health risk involved. Brazilian consumers were concerned about pirated contraceptives and anticancer drugs.
2. Legal recourse: A NAFTA agreement requires trading partners to enforce intellectual property rights. GATT allows a nation to restrain imports from countries where piracy is a problem. A firm can begin the process of getting legal protection by registering with the U.S. Customs Service.
3. Government: The U.S. Trade Representation lists the countries with the biggest piracy problem—currently China and Taiwan. A country can get a nation with a poor track record denied most-favored-nation status, but this is a severe penalty and rarely imposed. A problem is that there are not enough "policemen" to enforce all the international agreements.
4. Direct Contact: Get the counterfeit goods off the store shelves. Sometimes the counterfeiting is ignored, because of the costs of litigation and enforcement, risk of bad publicity, and the fact that top government officials may be in on the deal! Another possibility is for the injured company to try to buy the pirate firm.
5. Labeling: Put holograms or "DNA security markers" (that encode product manufacturing information) on the genuine goods' labels. Holograms can be copied but do increase the counterfeiter's costs. The security markers are generally too costly for most counterfeiters.
6. Strong Proactive Marketing: Cut prices, spend aggressively on advertising, encourage customers to buy the genuine article. Get distributors' support in cutting down on the counterfeit products. Keep changing the product or its packaging.
7. Piracy as Promotion: Wide availability of pirated Word software could have the effect of spreading the adoption of Word as the world's word processing standard. Microsoft could then add features available only to genuine product owners via valid registration numbers or could offer product support only to genuine owners.

Source: *Industrial Marketing Management*, Vol. 30, Laurence Jacobs, A. Coksun Samli and Tom Jedlik, "The Nightmare of International Product Piracy," pp. 499–509.

Designing Products for Emerging Markets[17]

Another concern facing product developers is the unlocked potential in developing markets such as China and India, or in third-world countries. Many companies would love to increase their presence in these emerging markets, but one must keep in mind that salaries and standards of living may be very different, as well as the attributes or performance levels expected of products. Therefore, when considering these markets, one must keep in mind that the right product, be it a new mode of transportation, a new farming implement, or a medical device, may significantly improve people's lives, and it is ethically correct to pursue these markets. One should also remember that the "right" product here is not necessarily last year's model or a dumbed-down version of this year's model. It may be that a whole new product is developed from the ground up for developing markets, due to their particular needs and constraints. Figure 18.7 shows several important considerations in developing new products for emerging markets. Global R&D expert Gunjan Bagla suggests that product managers from developed nations need to consider several basic questions when entering emerging markets:

- Should I, and can I, develop new products or new technology in the emerging market?

[17]Gunjan Bagla, "Product Development in Emerging Markets," *Visions*, 35(3), 2011, pp. 44–45.

FIGURE 18.7 Success Factors for Entering Emerging Markets

1. *Adapt the Innovation Strategy.* Adapt organizational structure and culture so that development of lower-cost, lower-tech products receive attention, not just products aimed at the "top of the pyramid." Siemens has a strategic initiative known as SMART ("simple, maintenance-friendly, affordable, reliable, and timely-to-market") to develop products for previously-missed markets.

2. *Meet the New Customers.* Learn about them. Listen to the voice of these customers. Go to meet them in their own cultural environment. Nokia engineers have done ethnographic research in India and Nepal to determine specific customer needs (such as screens that can be read in bright sunlight or address books using icons that can be used by the illiterate).

3. *Offer a New Price-Performance Ratio.* To do this, it might be better to design a product from scratch than to try to strip features out of an existing product. The Dacia Logan, designed by Renault and built in Romania, is low-cost ($6500 purchase price), carries five people, is half as expensive to service as a regular Renault, and can be easily serviced by basic mechanics (it does not need to go to a Renault dealership for service).

4. *Apply "Ghandian" Engineering.* The mindset of headquarters employees needs to change, toward an attitude of willing product simplification. The answer is not always to find the newest technology. Automotive supplier Bosch made adjustments to simple technologies to provide parts for the inexpensive Tata Nano, designed for sale in India. For example, the injection technology used in the Nano was adapted from two-wheeler technology.

5. *Localize R&D Activities.* New products for emerging markets are often best developed in those very markets. This keeps development costs low and taps the knowhow of local engineers who may come up with cheap, unconventional solutions. GE's R&D facility in Bangalore developed an inexpensive, portable electrocardiogram (ECG) that suited the needs of local doctors. The engineers also adapted an Indian portable-ticket printer for use as the ECG printer.

6. *Adapt Marketing and Sales.* Learn how marketing is different in the target country, and adapt. Nokia has had success selling through a network of 90,000 points of sale in India by adapting to local methods. In rural neighborhoods, customers prefer talking to salespeople in person, so sales vans pass by occasionally, and salespeople teach people about cell phones and provide after-sale service.

7. *Introduce New Business Models.* Nokia-Siemens developed a new business model using smart technology (Village Connection) that reduces capital expenditure for phone companies, allowing them to enter low-end market segments profitably despite very low monthly spending per capita on phone services.

8. *Find a Local Partner.* Use the partner's expertise to learn quickly about local market conditions. Having a local partner helps overcome any appearance of foreignness. GE brings professors from top Indian universities to spend their sabbatical at the Bangalore facility, and cooperates with the Indian Institute of Technology on research projects.

Source: Anna Dubiel and Holger Ernst, "Success Factors of New Product Development for Emerging Markets," in K. N. Kahn, S. E. Kay, R. J. Slotegraaf and S. Uban (Eds.), *The PDMA Handbook of New Product Development* (Hoboken, NJ: John Wiley), 2013, Ch. 6, pp. 100–114.

- Should I just take my current product and de-feature it, or should I build a totally new product for the emerging market?
- Should the product be designed in the developing market? Who would be responsible, an in-house team or contract designers?
- If I develop a product for an emerging market, do I risk having it reimported to my home market where it might cannibalize sales?
- Can I trust that technical talent recruited in the emerging market will be helpful?
- Are there any intellectual property risks if I do development or engineering in an emerging market?

Obviously, there is no one right answer to these questions, but they must not be ignored. In some cases, a very clever and inexpensive new product can be built from

FIGURE 18.8 Frugal Innovation

Nokia developed a cell phone charger for the Indian market that works on bike power. A "dynamo" transmits current generated by the revolution of the front wheel to a bracket located on the handlebars. This is a practical cell phone charger for a market where millions of people use bicycles as their primary means of transportation and where electrical power is unreliable and often unavailable through the night.

German manufacturer Siemens has a corporate technology center in Goa, India, where a very low-cost medical scanner was developed (it costs about $500 per unit to produce, about a quarter of the cost of a typical scanner of this type). Rather than redesigning and dumbing-down a Western model, the entire scanner was redesigned in such a way as to meet the needs of doctors in developing countries while minimizing costs. The key to the redesign was embedding the camera in the "heart" of the scanner.

Source: Gunjan Bagla, "Product Development in Emerging Markets," *Visions*, 35(3), 2011, pp. 44–45.

FIGURE 18.9 Grassroots Frugal Innovation for Emerging Markets

A potter living in a rural part of Gujarat, India, developed a refrigerator made of clay that requires no electricity and costs about $50. Water evaporating through the clay creates a cool environment inside the refrigerator, which can keep food cool for up to five days.

The Indian company Frugal Digital has launched two innovative products: a low-cost schoolroom projector with a USB port that connects to a phone for navigation, and a health monitor (temperature, pulse, blood pressure, and so on) made from an old alarm clock and inexpensive Indian-made parts.

Other entrepreneurs have developed an inexpensive windmill made of bamboo; a biomass gasifier that converts farm waste into fuel, which generates power in regions lacking electricity; a highly efficient motorcycle tractor; and prosthetic limbs for amputees that cost $45.

Source: Eden Yin and Jaideep C. Prabhu, "Innovation in China and India," in Peter N. Golder and Debanjan Mitra (editors), *Handbook of Research on New Product Development*, Cheltenham, UK: Edward Elgar, 2018, pp. 146–170.

the ground up for the emerging market, which would suit the needs there better than "dumbing-down" an existing product. Illinois company Sun Ovens, for example, sells solar-powered cooking devices in 130 countries worldwide. Indian manufacturer Godrej launched a low-cost refrigerator with no compressor, relying on using conversion of electrical energy instead to maintain low temperature; though it uses a less efficient method of cooling, the refrigerator also has no moving parts, which makes it ideal in third-world markets where repair shops are scarce.[18] Figure 18.8 describes Nokia's bicycle-powered cell phone charger and Siemens' medical scanner, both developed for the Indian market. These all illustrate **frugal engineering**—designing and manufacturing new products with minimal resources.

Small entrepreneurial startups are sometimes behind groundbreaking examples of frugal innovation, born perhaps out of necessity in some cases. As Figure 18.9 shows, people can be quite ingenious when coming up with simple, workable solutions that suit the needs of emerging markets.

[18]The oven example is from Kelly Weidner, "Subsistance Marketplaces: From Impactful Research to Practical Innovation," *Visions*, 35(2), 2011, pp. 16–19; the refrigerator example is from Bagla, *Visions*, op. cit.

The Underlying Issues

A few really tough issues thread their way through the preceding confusions. They are such that we will never be free of problems working in the public policy area. One of them is, *What are reasonable goals for action here?* A risk-free existence is totally unreasonable. Zero-defect quality control is a goal in many firms. But, with the complexity in most of today's consumer products, nothing short of government decree would stop consumers from making errors—and then only because they would not be making any decisions at all. Besides, even if we could hope to reach a 99.99 percent level of risk reduction, that would still leave about 30,000 people on the wrong side of the statistic in the United States alone. Worldwide, the number would certainly be much higher.

Another one is the *trade-off problem*. Even when a particular situation seems to have a clear-cut guiding principle, we often find a contrary principle of equal merit. Which of two worthy options should be accepted?

A third is, *Where should the costs fall?* In many of the controversies that affect new products, the argument is not so much *what should be done as who should pay for it*. Assuming (1) no production system can ever make products perfectly and (2) no consumer group will ever use products with perfect wisdom, there will always be injuries and waste. Who should pay? Governments are already under pressure for tax reduction. Insurance companies know the negative reactions to inflated rates. So the no-fault approach is becoming popular—or, as the manufacturer says, the *total*-fault approach. The manufacturer assumes all responsibility and is expected to pass along the costs somehow.

Summary

This concludes our trip through a troublesome dimension of the new products process. The pressures are very real, and the difficulties are at times almost overwhelming. Some unresolved issues have no answers, and new variations in the general problem areas will continue to unfold.

New products managers, however, are finding they can manage under these circumstances if they do their homework well. Avoiding needless troubles requires that they understand the process, stay close to their legal departments, get management's support at critical times, and follow up marketing with more aggressive launch management than ever before used in American industry. All temptations are to do just the opposite because time can be the Achilles' heel of new products management, as we have seen more than once.

Although we have covered the major areas of product policy concerns in the new products field, you should know that there are far more problems and issues buried in the labs, plants, and offices of today's new products manager. Every industry has scores of them.

The point here is this: Thousands of people deal with these troublesome issues every day—they know the problems and they have worked out a balance between need to know and need to move ahead. They manage, risks and all.

Case: Clorox Green Works[19]

In the last 15 or so years, concerned consumers have demanded "environmentally friendly" or "green" versions of their favorite products. Manufacturers soon learned that meeting this emerging demand posed particular challenges. For one thing, consumers are skeptical of green claims, possibly because some products with questionable credentials were marketed aggressively, and misleadingly, as environmentally friendly. Customer skepticism is likely to keep getting stronger. Consumers are becoming more educated about green issues and concerns, and the days of slapping a green flag on the label and calling your product environmentally friendly are over. Another issue is that many consumers have come to expect that the green version of items such as household cleaners may be twice as expensive as the conventional brand and may also be less effective. Even labeling becomes an issue. What do you write on the label that properly conveys the intended message and doesn't unintentionally put off customers? Green? Natural? Good for the environment? Organic? Ecologically friendly? Small wonder that green products have not experienced expected levels of market penetration.

The Clorox Company set out to approach the green consumer market with a new line of household cleaning products. The Green Works line was launched in 2008 and was in fact the first family of natural cleaning products ever launched by a major consumer-goods manufacturer. The line, which includes an all-purpose cleaner, a toilet bowl cleaner, and other cleaning products, was an immediate success and had captured a large share of the natural cleaning products market only a few months after launch. What accounts for the success of this line? Industry experts suggest that Clorox did two things very well with this launch: (1) They identified a new, underserved market segment and learned everything they could about them, and (2) they designed and launched a product that met all of that segment's key needs, not just a couple of important ones.

For years, Clorox was interested in the issues of health and wellness and had accumulated a large bank of consumer data. This came in handy, as the Clorox product team was able to identify an emerging segment relatively early. Although many consumers had a general objective of "doing something good for the environment," this particular segment had something more in mind: their health and well-being and that of their family. They liked the performance of standard cleaning products but thought they contained too many potentially dangerous chemicals. Members of this market segment saw themselves playing a key role in their family: keeping the home safe. The product team named this segment the "Chemical-Avoiding Naturalist." Clorox market research found that this target consumer was very likely to be the primary shopper for the family, and 85 percent of the segment membership was female.

For women in this market segment, not just any "green" product would do. This consumer's belief (that she was first and foremost the protector of the family) would imply that she might not be fanatical about buying green products in any case; rather,

[19]This case draws largely from Sumi N. Cate, David Pilosof, Richard Tait, and Robin Karol, "The Story of Clorox Green Works™—In Designing a Winning Green Product Experience Clorox Cracks the Code," *Visions*, 33(1), March 2009, pp. 10–14.

this customer has a strong emotional commitment to the family. Nevertheless, a line of products with the cleaning power of conventional cleaners, but with no harsh chemicals, would be attractive to this customer.

Development of the new product line began with the positioning statement. Clorox first had to choose what terminology should figure in the value proposition that would best appeal to their targeted segment. Their demographic research found that terms like "green," "sustainable," or "carbon-neutral" would not be clear enough or could be interpreted multiple ways. "Organic" was considered, but its use is government-regulated and might be troublesome for Clorox. The product team settled on "natural," mostly because it worked with the target customer and also team members felt it played to Clorox's core competencies (it could be easily communicated and advertised, and it was a reasonable and reachable objective for the firm).

With a combination of personal interviews and in-home ethnographic "fly-on-the-wall" research, the product team gained an understanding of the Chemical-Avoiding Naturalist. This research suggested that this segment had several must-have expectations of the product, all of which would have to be met. It would have to support the emotional commitment of protecting her family and the environment (by drastically reducing the amount of harsh chemicals) but without compromising performance, convenience, or ease of use. It would need to be priced at an acceptable level and widely available, and the information about the product's benefits would need to be credible and trustworthy. The product team realized that focusing exclusively on one or two of these expectations would not be good enough. This consumer will not switch over to an all-natural product if performance was sacrificed or if the price premium was too high.

The ethnographic research found that customers knew that natural ingredients like vinegar could be used as cleaners, and some even made their own cleaners at home. Many expressed familiarity with plant-based cleaning ingredients and wondered why cleaners had to have harsh chemicals in them at all. These and related research findings led the Clorox team to develop its own definition of natural: 99 percent free of petrochemicals, derived from plants or minerals, biodegradable and nontoxic, and not chemically processed or tested on animals. (The ideal, 100 percent free of petrochemicals, was not considered feasible, because components such as fragrances, colors, and preservatives are not always available in natural form; 99 percent was close enough for Clorox to make a "virtually" all-natural claim.)

Care was taken such that the product line would have all of the must-have expectations. Conventional cleaning products sold in the $2.00 to $3.00 range, while many natural competitors sold for over $7.00 per bottle. The targeted retail price for the new line was set at $3.00 to $4.00 per bottle, which was felt to be acceptable to this segment. Since conventional products were sold almost everywhere (grocery stores, convenience stores, pharmacies, and so on), it was felt that intensive distribution was critical for the new line as well. The credibility angle was covered by having full disclosure on the label as well as providing extensive information on the product Web site. Clorox also received a rare endorsement from the Sierra Club and was recognized by the Environmental Protection Agency's "Design for the Environment" Formulator Program. The aesthetic appearance was also not forgotten: The product itself as well as its packaging would have to convey cleanliness and simplicity, as well as performance.

For example, while a colorless and odorless product might have conveyed an all-natural image, customers might wonder if it would be any more effective than plain water! Finally, a clever brand name (Clorox Green Works) was chosen. "Green Works" effectively summarizes the dual benefits of the product line: environmentally conscious, but also powerful ("it works"). The inclusion of "Clorox" in the name was not accidental, as the team wanted to leverage the Clorox effectiveness and trust brand equity. Finally, the word "natural" appears prominently on every label.

Of course, the products really had to deliver, but new advances in surfactant (cleaning agent) and solvent chemistry were making plant-based ingredients more effective. Clorox was able to rely on natural ingredients such as coconut oil (surfactant), natural polysaccharides (thickeners), and corn-based ethanol (solvent) to deliver acceptable levels of cleaning power that might not have been possible several years earlier. In fact, once launched, Green Works products performed as well or better than conventional products.

The product launch was a success. Clorox was able to get Green Works products into all major retailers and encouraged them to display them prominently in their stores. The launch of a highly effective new green product also received a fair amount of publicity in the press at the time.

What can be learned from the development of Clorox Green Works? What accounted for the remarkable success of the line? (Think of at least three clear reasons.) What were the major difficulties or hurdles faced by the product team? How could a firm in a different product category, or a service provider, apply some of the best practices described in this case?

Case: Sustainability and the Fashion Industry[20]

Many firms include corporate social responsibility (CSR) as a central part of their business model. CSR implies a commitment to a "win-win-win" or "triple-bottom-line" objective: the firm makes satisfactory sales and profits, customers are happy with the products they receive, and there is some meaningful benefit to society. CSR is often an explicit part of the firm's corporate mission.

For many firms, sustainability is an important element of their CSR commitment. As an example, in response to consumer concerns for sustainable and organic food, health food stores started appearing in the 1960s. This small initiative has developed over the years into a major industry, with leading grocery chains such as Whole Foods

---

[20]This case is based on the following: E. Ritch, M. Schröder, C. Brennan, and M. Pretious (2011), "Sustainable Consumption and the Retailer: Will Fashion Ethics Follow Food?" in C. D'Souza, M. Taghian, and M. Polonsky, *Readings and Cases in Sustainable Marketing: A Strategic Approach to Social Responsibility*, Prahran, Australia: Tilde University Press, 176–198; M. Polonsky (2011), "Green Marketing: What Does the Future Hold?" in C. D'Souza, M. Taghian, and M. Polonsky, *Readings and Cases in Sustainable Marketing: A Strategic Approach to Social Responsibility*, Prahran, Australia: Tilde University Press, 245–256; C. A. Di Benedetto, "Corporate Social Responsibility as an Emerging Business Model in Fashion Marketing," *Journal of Global Fashion Marketing*, 8(4), 2017, pp. 251–265; and www.gcufairfashioncenter.org. The Bolt Threads example is from Anonymous, "Emeryville's Creative Culture Helps Foster Artistic Endeavors and Scientific Information," *bizjournals. com*, November 16, 2018.

committed to offering organic produce, sustainable sources for meat and fish, and so on. Nevertheless, the fashion industry has been generally slower to move in this direction. A consumer who might choose organic over conventionally grown vegetables at Trader Joe's may not give any thought as to whether a new shirt they are buying at a department store is made from organic cotton.

There is much evidence that the textile industry is one of the environmentally "dirtiest" ones, from the use of pesticides and toxic dyes, to wasteful use of land and water, to manufacturing and post-consumer waste. According to GCNYC The Fair Fashion Center, textiles are the second largest industry in terms of water use and production of pollutants. They are responsible for 10 percent of global carbon emissions, and 85 percent of textiles eventually go into landfills. The relatively slower progress by the fashion industry in this regard, however, suggests there is much potential for improvement, in particular as more competitors view sustainability initiatives as a key part of their CSR commitment.

There are already many successful sustainability and socially responsible initiatives by both small and large fashion firms. Patagonia and L.L.Bean are two major clothing producers that stress long-lasting clothing and timeless fashions; Ray-Ban has done much the same with eyewear. Some big fashion merchandisers also have an environmentally friendly corporate mission: Kering (owner of Stella McCartney's environmentally concerned fashion company) focuses on sustainability in their supply chain. In addition, many small startups have been at the forefront of sustainable fashion. Bolt Threads applies bioengineering processes to turn silk proteins grown in yeast and cells grown in corn stalks into materials such as Microsilk, which is used in the production of ties and hats. A later Bolt creation, which received support from a Kickstarter campaign, is Melo, a material produced from mushrooms that is similar in appearance to leather. Other smaller companies are working on no-wash jeans (which cuts down on the use of water as well as detergent chemicals), cotton textile waste recycled into renewable fiber, and seaweed-based ink for screen printing on clothing.

Nevertheless, the fashion industry has lagged behind others in terms of commitment to sustainability and the environment. Sustainable marketing researcher Elaine Ritch and her colleagues identified four obstacles slowing down the uptake of "slow fashion" by consumers:

- *Insufficient consumer product information.* Unlike the food industry, where product labels such as "organic" or "fair trade" are commonplace, fashion retailers tend not to use much consumer labeling concerning sourcing, sustainability, or fair trade. Consumer information tends to be somewhat uneven. They may know the benefits of "buying local" (to cut down on emissions caused by transportation) or avoid products thought to be produced in sweatshops. But other issues, such as the use of energy in textile production or the health of cotton farmers, receive less attention, and consumers are consequently less knowledgeable.

- *Accessibility.* Retailers have not made organic or fair-trade clothing available in big enough numbers for the mass market, and/or have not promoted them sufficiently. Even those consumers who are committed to sustainability and the environment may conclude there are not too many sustainable choices with respect to clothing.

- *Unfashionable perception.* Despite the actions of many leading fashion designers and clothing manufacturers, as discussed, many consumers believe that sustainable equals unfashionable. Fashionability implies changing styles and preferences, which runs counter to the principles of sustainability.
- *High prices.* Sustainable or organic clothing is often more expensive, as is the case with household cleaners or other consumer goods. Customers may actually buy sustainable clothing in place of conventional alternatives, even if there is a price premium, but side-by-side comparisons in stores are not common. By contrast, grocery stores will place organic and conventional produce together, making it easy for customers to choose.

Play the role of a consultant to the fashion industry. Recommend positive steps that participants in the fashion industry can take to overcome each of the four obstacles. What would you recommend to a large manufacturer or fashion design firm? A small startup founded on a sustainable mission (such as Bolt Threads)? What about the role of fashion retailers (bricks-and-mortar stores, or online retailers)?

Case: CSR at Starbucks[21]

Advertising expert Charles R. ("Ray") Taylor has noted a great increase in CSR activities in recent years. Using Super Bowl ads as a metric for CSR activity, about 6.4 percent of Super Bowl ads from 2008 to 2017 had CSR content; this percentage increased to 25 percent in Super Bowl 2018. Companies as varied as Anheuser-Busch, Verizon, and Hyundai, among others, tied their advertising content to appeals supporting, respectively, hurricane relief, first responders, and pediatric cancer research. Professor Taylor notes that this trend is related to the preferences of millennials, who have a positive attitude toward brands that are tied to social responsibility. Millennials are not only a large, brand-loyal, and price-sensitive target, but they are a growing target as well, and companies increasingly are seeing the value in incorporating and promoting a relevant CSR initiative.

As competition on the CSR battlefield intensifies, firms will need to do more to ensure that their CSR appeals will stand out. Professor Taylor suggests three guidelines: choose an uncontroversial CSR appeal (hurricane relief and the other examples cited would certainly fit); avoid messages that sound political and that might alienate some of the loyal customer base; and keep in mind that customers know that companies are in business to make a profit and therefore might be skeptical of CSR claims.

Professor Taylor's recommendations are consistent with those of a recent survey by Clutch, a research organization. Clutch researchers found that consumers are expecting companies to make a commitment to CSR. But for this commitment to be most

[21]This case is based on the following: Leia Klingel, "Starbucks Pledges Millions to Help Struggling Coffee Farmers," *foxbusiness.com*, September 26, 2018; Charles Taylor, "What Gillette Could Learn from CSR Ads in the Super Bowl," *forbes.com*, January 17, 2019; Toby Cox, "How Businesses Can Approach Corporate Social Responsibility and Public Relations," *clutch.com*, February 6, 2019; Anonymous, "Starbucks C.A.F.E. Practices," *scsglobalservices.com*; and the Starbucks Web site, www.starbucks.com.

effective, the businesses should consider consumers' values, the unique purpose of their brand(s), and how it can make the most impact with its CSR initiatives. The Clutch study found that companies in the food and grocery industries, technology companies, fashion companies, and those in health and beauty services as well as restaurants, among others, should make firm commitments to CSR efforts.

One firm that has established a reputation for effective CSR is Starbucks. The principle of CSR can be expressed in terms of the "triple-bottom-line." Using Starbucks as an example, the triple-bottom-line refers to (1) customers getting a satisfying product, (2) Starbucks achieves profit objectives, and (3) Starbucks gives back in some meaningful way to society. One of their best-known CSR initiatives is their support for local coffee farmers who provide their supply. Starbucks is committed to and invests in programs that strengthen farmer communities and also protect the environment. For example, Starbucks works collaboratively with nongovernmental organizations that assist farming communities. The company provides bridge loans to farmers to help them get through the growing season until they can make income at harvest time, and also provides farmer support centers. In conjunction with Conservation International, Starbucks has developed C.A.F.E. (Coffee and Farmer Equity) Practices standards to ensure that their coffee is grown and processed in a sustainable fashion. These and other actions not only benefit the farmers but also ensure a supply of high-quality coffee and other products for years to come.

As of 2018, Starbucks had invested over $70 million in farmer programs. In September 2018, they committed an additional $20 million to small farmers who were hurt financially by falling coffee prices (in some cases, coffee production costs were actually above sales price). The farmers most affected by rising production costs are those working in difficult-to-harvest areas (for example, mountainous regions in Colombia), where it is not possible to use machines to automate coffee bean picking, and farmers must pay workers to pick them by hand.

Discuss the CSR initiatives of Starbucks. Check online to see if you can add more initiatives in addition to the ones listed in this case. How well does Starbucks rate in terms of the criteria for effective CSR, as presented by Professor Taylor and/or by the Clutch survey findings? In your opinion, is Starbucks CSR effective, and why or why not? Can you recommend other suitable CSR initiatives? What can Starbucks (or any other large company) do to ensure that consumers see their CSR actions as sincere, and not just a way to get good public relations?

ANSWERS TO FIGURE 18.2

Almost all of the warning labels in the figure are real! The real ones are: 2 (rock garden), 4 (hair dryer), 6 (windshield sun shade), 7 (shin guards), 9 (iron), 10 (sled), 12 (cell phone), 13 (router), 15 (stroller), 16 (washing machine), 17 (fireplace log), 18 (printer cartridge). In fact, several of these have won "worst of" awards. The best source for details on odd warning labels is the list of Wacky Warning Labels published by Michigan Lawsuit Abuse Watch, http://mlaw.org/wwl/pastwinners.html.

Sources of Ideas Already Generated

New product ideas come from many places, some of which are peculiar to particular firms or industries. Here are the more broadly used sources, in addition to the ones discussed in Chapter 4.

Employees

Many types of employees can be sources of new product concepts. Salespeople are an obvious group, but so are technical groups, manufacturing, customer service, and packaging employees, and, in the case of general consumer products, any employee who uses the products. Manufacturing and engineering personnel are frequently part-time inventors who should be encouraged to submit their ideas. These people need to know that their ideas are wanted, and special mechanisms (and even cultures) must usually be constructed to gather those ideas.

Employee suggestion systems are not always dependable but sometimes yield useful results. The most helpful suggestions come from employees whose work brings them in contact with customer problems. For example, a drill manufacturer's service department found that many drills were burning out because customers were using them as electric screwdrivers. Adding a clutch mechanism to the drill created a new product. Complaint-handling departments also become familiar with consumers' use of products. Salespeople know when a large order is lost because the firm's product is not quite what the customer wanted.

Customers

The greatest source of new product ideas is the customer or user of the firm's products or services, although their ideas are usually only for product improvement or nearby line extensions. Some people believe the majority of all new products in certain industries originate with users. Because some specialized user groups are personally involved with devices, new products people occasionally delegate new product concept development to them. Similarly, auto parts and components manufacturers look to their giant original equipment manufacturers buyers for new product initiatives. Many customer suggestions are too incremental in nature, however, and not always useful to product teams looking for the next radical idea. Chapter 10 discusses how one can obtain the voice of the customer to get more high-potential ideas from customers.

Resellers

Brokers, manufacturers' reps, industrial distributors, large jobbers, and large retail firms may be quite worthwhile sources. In fact, some mass merchandisers have their own new products departments and invite manufacturers to bid on specifications. Many industrial representatives are skilled enough to be special advisers to their clients, and selling agents in the toy industry not only advise but actually take on the new products function if the manufacturer wishes.

One chemical distributor suggested using a low-cost polyethylene bag to line steel drums to prevent corrosion; and a millwork producer learned about a new competitive entry from a dealer and then suggested how the new item could be improved. Both suggestions were successfully implemented.

Suppliers/Vendors

Most manufacturers of plastic housewares are small and thus look to the large plastics firms for advice. Virtually all producers of steel, aluminum, chemicals, metals, paper, and glass have technical customer service departments. One of their functions is to suggest new products made of the firm's basic material.

Competitors

New product idea generators are interested in competitors' activities, and competitors' new products may be an indirect source for a leapfrog or add-on new product; but competitors are rarely sources of new product ideas except in industries where benchmarking has been accepted as a strategy. The first firms bringing a new product to a particular market segment (such as the smaller city banks) do use their innovative competitors as sources, but this is effective only when market segments are insulated. Car and truck makers, forklift truck manufacturers, and other similar manufacturing companies will routinely buy competitive products and conduct *teardown analysis*, sometimes known as *backwards engineering*. They will disassemble the competitive product into thousands of component parts, catalog them, and mount them on panels so others can examine them. Teardown analysis can provide insights on competitive component costs and may suggest potential improvements.

The Invention Industry

Every industrialized country has an "industry" consisting of a nucleus of inventors surrounded by firms and organizations that help them capitalize on their inventions. Though tending to lose out to corporate research centers, individual inventors still submit almost a fourth of all patent applications. The auxiliary or supportive group includes:

Venture capital firms	Banks
Inventors' schools	Inventors' councils
Attorneys	Small Business Administration
Trademark and patent offices	Technology expositions
Consultants on new business	Patent shows
Patent brokers and others	Inventor newsletters
Inventor assistance firms	State entrepreneurial aid programs
Individual investors	University innovation centers

Other new organizations are merging the financial, legal, and managerial consulting assistance that inventors usually require, either as venture firms that actually take over and develop the idea or as facilitator firms that reach out to established manufacturers. In the meantime, some firms have what they call "inventors' farm systems" to get both quantity and variety of invention input. Outstanding Corporate Award winner Nordic-Track makes inventors their primary source of new products and cultivates that group with almost as much marketing effort as used on their customers.

Miscellaneous

Among the many other sources of outside new product ideas are the following:

1. **Consultants.** Most management consulting firms do new products work, and some specialize in it—for example, McKinsey, Arthur D. Little, Mercer, and PRTM. Some consulting firms are devoted exclusively to new products work and include idea generation as one of their services. Unfortunately, the stigma of being "outsiders" is strong in the new products field, as exemplified by the not-invented-here syndrome.

2. **Advertising agencies.** This source of new product ideas is badly underrated. Most agencies have the creative talent and the product/market experience to generate new product concepts. Some agencies have full-blown new products departments, and some take their concepts all the way to market, including premarket tests and rollouts. Consumer product agencies do more new products work than industrial agencies do, although the West Coast agencies specializing in the computer industry render a wide range of services because their clients are often small.

3. **Marketing research firms.** Normally, marketing research firms get involved in the idea-generating process by assisting a client with need assessment. They rarely stumble across an opportunity that they pass along to a client. Some of the

bigger marketing research firms such as AC Nielsen also serve as management consultants.

4. **Retired product specialists.** Industrial new products people, particularly those with technical strength, often retire from their firms and become part-time consultants to other firms. One company actually tracks the retirements of all qualified specialists in its industry. Conflict-of-interest problems may arise, and divulging competitive secrets is ethically questionable, but most arrangements work around these problems easily.

5. **Industrial designers.** Industrial design firms sometimes function as part of a team implementing a new product decision that has already been made. However, many industrial designers are extremely creative. Industrial design firms and individual industrial designers are increasingly capitalizing on their own new product strengths. As noted in Chapter 11, industrial designers are increasingly part of the core new products team, due to their knowledge of ergonomics, materials, and sustainability, in addition to their aesthetic know-how. Industrial design departments of universities are sometimes assigned by government and other service organizations to do original new products work.

6. **Other manufacturers.** Most firms have potentially worthwhile new product ideas that they do not want because these ideas conflict with the firm's strategy. These ideas are sometimes allowed to remain idle. But, as discussed in Chapter 4, firms are turning to outward open innovation to monetize these ideas, through licensing, partnership, outright sale, or some other mechanism.

7. **Universities.** Professors and students occasionally offer new product ideas, especially in schools of engineering, the sciences, and business. Dentists, physicians, and pharmacists are scientific groups that play a major role in new products work, and firms will sometimes set up their R&D labs near leading research universities to encourage partnership and dialogue.

8. **Research laboratories.** Most of the world's leading countries now have at least one major research laboratory that will do new products work on contract from manufacturers and that occasionally comes up with interesting new product ideas. Notable research laboratories include the Battelle Memorial Institute (Columbus, Ohio), Illinois Institute of Technology, and Stanford Research Institute International.

9. **Governments.** The Patent Office of the U.S. government offers several services designed to help manufacturers find worthwhile new product ideas. The *Official Gazette* provides a weekly listing of (1) all new patents issued, (2) condensed descriptions of the patented items, and (3) which patents are for sale or license. Patent Office reports and services also make known what government patents and foreign patents are available.

The military services have a want list of products that they would like to buy; the Department of Agriculture will help manufacturers with new products; and state governments have programs to aid industries.

One by-product of today's regulation of business is increased assistance from regulators for solving such problems as unsafe products and unsafe working conditions. For example, the Occupational Safety and Health Act stimulated several companies to develop first-aid kits.

10. **The media.** The hundreds of technical and scientific journals, trade journals, online newsletters, and monographs are occasionally sources of ideas for new products. Most of the ideas indirectly result from accounts of new products activity.

11. **International.** Minnetonka executives got the idea for pump toothpaste while browsing in a German supermarket. Powdered Tide was developed by scientists in Cincinnati, but Liquid Tide used a formula for surfactants from Japan and a mineral salts antagonist from Belgium. Unfortunately, few firms have systematic programs to find ideas from other countries. Some establish foreign offices to monitor various technologies, others ask their advertising agencies' foreign offices to gather ideas, and still others subscribe to one or more reporting services.

Managing These Idea Sources

These sources of ideas do not function without special effort. For example, salespeople must be trained how to find users with good ideas and how to coax the ideas from them. International markets must be covered on the spot by trained people. Studying the competition must be systematic to catch every change in competitors' products. Each special source is also a potential source for the competition, and the firm that uses these sources most appropriately will acquire the best ideas.

Other Techniques of Concept Generation

Chapters 4, 5, and 6 presented the leading ideation techniques with the best track records and the greatest chance of producing valuable new product concepts. Perhaps hundreds of other techniques are available, some of which are proprietary (confidential to the consulting firm that originated each), and some of which are techniques given here but with different names.

Here below you will find many effective techniques that are used in new concept ideation. Try one, or more, of these and see what you can come up with!

Techniques to Aid Problem Analysis

Composite Listing of Needs Fulfilled

By simply listing the many needs met by currently available products, there is a good chance some otherwise overlooked need will come to mind. This mechanical process is successful only if the listing is pushed to one's mental limits.

Market Segmentation Analysis

By using one segmentation dimension on top of another, an analyst can develop a hierarchy of smaller and smaller market segments. For example, liquid soap segmentation could use sex, age, body part cleaned, ethnic groups, and geographic location. All possible combinations of these would yield thousands of groups—for example, elderly women using liquid soap to wash their faces in New York City, or mechanics working in car repair facilities thoroughly washing grease off their hands. Each combination is potentially a group whose needs are peculiar and currently unmet. (Psychographic and behavioral segments are especially useful.)

Dreams

This approach analyzes the dreams of people who are currently studying the problem(s). Dreams offer a greater range of insights, equitably involve other persons in the problem situation, and offer paranormal aspects of the dream itself. Various famous people, including novelist Robert Louis Stevenson, have attributed part of their creativity to dreams. Chapter 4 mentioned the scientist August Kekulé who envisioned the circular shape of the benzene molecule in a dream about a snake biting its own tail.

Techniques to Aid Scenario Analysis

There are many techniques for finding meaningful seed trends (trends that could be extended). Some are discussed in Chapter 5, and here are six more.

Trend People

Many believe certain people have a predictive sense and should be watched. *Women's Wear Daily* is one publication that uses this method, and the people it watches are well known to regular readers. This method helps the publication fulfill its promise to bring "breaking news about fashion" to its readership.

Trend Areas

Many major changes in American life and practice traditionally begin on the West Coast and gradually make their way east. Although television and other mass media have reduced the time lag, some firms station personnel in California just to be closer to the changes going on there.

Hot Products

The automobile, television, the computer, and the Internet have had a dramatic effect on lifestyles. Netflix and similar streaming services forever changed how people obtain home entertainment. One way to gather meaningful seed trends is to study such products and their effects. But watch out, because it is possible some trends could turn out to be short-lived fads.

Technological Roadmapping

This approach predicts when one technology will substitute for another and seeks the implications of the substitution for all products and systems involving either the new or the old. Doing this involves time series analysis, graphic analysis, and forecasts by technical people. We have recently seen this in the car industry, as experts predicted the replacement of combustion engines over time with hybrid and then electric cars, and the need for auto services to keep up (electric car repair, battery replacement, charging stations, and so on).

Technical Innovation Follow-On

This procedure analyzes the implications for technical breakthroughs across a broad spectrum of technology, not just the immediate technology in which the breakthrough came. For example, a breakthrough in solar heating could be analyzed for effects in plumbing, clothing, furniture, or even entertainment.

Cross-Impact Analysis

First, list all possible changes that may occur over the next 20 years in a given area of activity (say, transportation). Then, apply these changes to other areas of activity, much as is done in technical innovation follow-on. The difference is that this method is not restricted to forecastable breakthroughs.

Techniques to Enhance Group Creativity

Phillips 66 Groups

To increase participation, Dr. J. Donald Phillips broke Osborn's 12-person groups into subgroups of six members each, sending the subgroups to break-off rooms for six minutes each, rearranging the subgroups, sending the new subgroups off for another six minutes, and so on. Rearrangement was Phillips's key to eliminating the problem of dominant or conflicting personalities. The Phillips 66 groups are sometimes called *buzz groups, free association groups*, and *discussion 66 groups*.

Brainstorming Circle

This approach forces the conversational sequence around a circle, and each person expands or modifies the idea expressed by the prior person in the circle. The brainstorming circle is more orderly and forces all persons to participate equally.

Reverse Brainstorming

This approach concentrates on a product's weaknesses or problems rather than on solutions or improvements. The discussion attempts to ferret out every criticism of, say, a vacuum cleaner. Later, attempts are made to eliminate the weaknesses or solve the problems.

Tear-Down

The rule of suspended judgment is reversed in this approach. Instead of avoiding criticism, tear-down requires it, and participants must find something wrong with the previous idea to get a talking turn.

And Also

In this approach, each speaking participant enlarges or extends the previous idea. No lateral moves are permitted unless the chain runs dry. The approach has been called *idea building and modification*.

Gordon Method

Prior to developing synectics, W. J. J. Gordon used groups that were not told what the problem was. In this method, if a discussion is to develop new ideas for recording musical performances, the group is encouraged to discuss opera. Eventually the leader turns the discussion toward the problem but still without divulging it.

Delphi

Although occasionally touted for ideation, Delphi is really a method of organizing a forecasting survey. Panels of experts are compiled; they are sent a questionnaire calling for forecasts within a given area of activity (e.g., hospitals or data processing); the questionnaires are tabulated and summarized; the results are returned to the panel for their reaction and alteration; new summaries are prepared; the results are sent out again, and so on. The iterations continue until conformity is reached or until impasse is obvious. In certain situations, the Delphi method has been deemed effective, and it can be used quite easily. It is especially desirable where the industry itself is new and there are no historical data to aid forecasters.

Think Tanks

This too is more a matter of organizing people than a mechanism of stimulating creativity. Think tanks are centers of intensive scientific research. The key to success here is the environment, which is thought to be stimulating to creativity. If the people in a think tank are charged with converting their outlandish ideation into useful products for marketing, the term *skunkworks* is often applied; we learn more about skunkworks in Chapter 12.

Techniques of the Analytical Attribute Approach

Benefit Analysis

All of the benefits that customers or users receive from the product under study are listed in the hope of discovering an unrealized benefit or unexpectedly absent benefit.

Use Analysis

Listing the many ways buyers make use of a given product is also sometimes revealing. Some firms spend large sums of money asking consumers to tell them of new uses. Johnson Wax got into the car-polishing business when it found that its floor wax was being used on cars. One must contact users, however—not just list the uses already known to the company.

Function Analysis

In between feature and use is an activity called *function*. Thus, for shampoos, we know the chemicals and product features present, and we may know the full reasons for using shampoos. But it is also creative to list all possible ways that shampoos function— scraping, dissolving, depositing, evaporating, and so on. One could also list all the possible consumer uses of shampoo: cleaning, conditioning, making hair manageable, fighting split ends or grease, and so on.

Attribute Extension

Also called *parameter analysis*, this technique begins with any attribute that has changed recently and then extends that change. Thus, for example, bicycle seats have gotten smaller and smaller. Extending that idea, one might imagine a bicycle with no seat at all; what would such a bicycle look like, and what would it be used for?

Relative Brand Profile

Every brand name is flexible or elastic, meaning it can be stretched to cover different product types. People can understand a Minute Maid jelly or Minute Maid soup. But they will find it harder to accept other "stretchings"—such as Minute Maid meats. Various market research techniques can be used to make these measurements, and any stretch that makes sense to the buyer is a potential new product. Incidentally, this thinking applies to goods and services, industrial as well as consumer.

Pseudo Product Test

By using what psychologists call a *projective technique*, one can ask consumers to evaluate what is presented to them as a proposed product but is actually an unidentified product currently on the market. They will typically find unique characteristics matching the needs they have. These attributes can then be the base for a new product.

Hierarchical Design

Here an organization chart design is formed, with product usage at the top and material types fanning out below. One such design began with deodorants, followed at the second level by roll-on, stick, and aerosol. The brands were listed under roll-ons. Under each brand could be package size or target market segment. Another design had light construction at the top, followed by wood, steel, and concrete. Wood was broken into metal roof, tar or shingle roof, and so on. The technique is mainly a way of forcing one to see all aspects of a situation, which is the essence of the analytical attribute approach.

Weaknesses

All weaknesses of a product or product line (the company's own and those of the competition) are identified. This primarily defensive technique identifies line extensions and flanker products, and possibly even new-and-improved products. Every resolvable weakness offers a new product concept.

Achilles' Heel

Some analysts prefer to prune the list of weaknesses to one or two that are so serious, a competitor might capitalize on them.

Techniques to Enhance Lateral Search

One school of thought holds that all "nearby" creativity produces only insignificant line extensions and modifications. These people have only disdain for matrixes, analogy, and attribute analysis. They insist the mind must be pushed beyond where it wants to go in a lateral search. Marketers too often think "vertically" when coming up with new ideas. Does introducing yet another soft drink flavor or shampoo name create any new customers or profitability? Some of the techniques mentioned in Chapter 5, such as TRIZ or the value curve approach, aid in lateral search of this type.

Here are some additional recommended techniques to stimulate lateral search.

Free Association

This approach begins when the ideator writes down one aspect of the product situation being studied—a product attribute, a use, or a user. The trick then is to let the mind roam wildly while jotting down every idea that comes out. The process is repeated for other aspects of the product situation. The associations are usually quite direct in the early stages when creativity is being stimulated; but with time, they become much less related and much more valuable as insights.

Stereotype Activity

Here one asks, "How would _____ do it?" The blank is filled in with a stereotype. Particular individuals can also be used, and the question can be reversed to ask what the stereotype would not do. Thus, a bicycle manufacturer might ask, "What type of bicycle would a senator ride? Has a loudspeaker on it? It pedals both ways? It backpedals?"

Cross-Field Compilation

As scientific disciplines have become increasingly blurred, a creative technique has been developed to bridge the between-field barriers. If a firm works primarily in the chemical area, its product developers may systematically scan developments in, say, physics or biology. Scientists in those fields may not know that some of their ideas have applications in chemistry.

Key-Word Monitoring/Tracking

This approach involves monitoring media sources and tallying the number of times key words appear. One firm used this approach to spot increasing use of the zodiac, and it promptly marketed a series of successful products featuring the zodiac symbols. This method is closely allied to the Big Winner approach discussed later.

Use of the Ridiculous

Just to show that anything can be done, some ideators deliberately try to force themselves to use ridiculous approaches. In one session, participants were asked to write out the most preposterous methods of joining two wires together. One answer was, "Hold them with your teeth," and another was, "Use chewing gum." Those present were astounded to realize they had just reinvented alligator clips, and they promptly gave serious consideration to the chewing gum. It turns out that some ingredients in chewing gum may sometime be marketed for use in wiring!

Study of Other People's Failures

Any product that has failed offers a chance for the next trier to spot its problem. The New Product Works collection (see the Product Use Testing case in Chapter 13) displays thousands of product failures, including some of those included in the Chapter 13 case. The failures apparently stimulate creativity.

Lateral Thinking—Avoidance

Some people have stressed the use of avoidance techniques to keep an idea from dominating thinking as it has in the past.

Keep asking, "Is there another way of looking at this?"

Keep asking, "Why?"

Deliberately rotate attention to a phase or aspect of the problem other than the logical one.

Find an entry point into the problem other than the one habitually used.

List all possible alternatives to every aspect of the analysis.

Deliberately seek nonstandard concepts other than those inherent to the problem. Try "unconcepting" or "disconcepting," or try dropping a concept.

Fractionalize concepts and other aspects of the problem.

Bridge two or more concepts to form still other concepts.

Other people call the approach *disparate thinking, zigzag,* and *divergent thinking.* This method was claimed to have partially solved a long-standing problem of light bulb theft in the Boston subway—light bulbs were made to screw in counterclockwise.

Creative Stimuli

The idea subject is specified first—the problem, the product, and so on. Then the tangible goal is stipulated—the desired result or what the specified idea should accomplish. Last, a long list of words, names, and phrases is studied for ideas that accomplish the tangible goal. These are proven stimulants (why, we don't know). Some of them are:

Guest stars	Charity	Family	Photography
Alphabet	Education	Timeliness	Interview
Truth	His and hers	Video	Testimonials
Outer space	Style	World	Decorate
Chart	Nation	Birth	Showmanship
Gauge scale	Weather	Ethnic	Floor, wall
Zipper	Habit, fad	Push button	Participation
Fantasy	Transportation	Snob appeal	Music
Folklore	Symbolism	Romance	Direct mail
Subconscious	Calendar	Parody	Seasons
Hobbies	Rhinestones	Graphics	Strawberry
Holidays	Curiosity	Sketch	Telephone

Big Winner

Many successful firms, teams, or individuals in sports, politics, television, and so on are uniquely in tune with the thinking of society. Studying these big winners may lead to principles that can be generalized to new products. Consider the biggest new electronic gadget, the hottest celebrity, the most recent championship winner, or the most popular app as a starting point.

Competitive Analysis

Many firms claim that by studying the strategic plans and actions of competitors, they can detect new product approaches, especially defensive ones. For this purpose they watch competitive announcements, surveys, financial reports, trade show exhibits, detailed analyses of their products, and other such techniques. Life-cycle models help a firm estimate when competitors will take over any of its markets and thus stimulate new products to defensively cannibalize sales.

Technological Mapping

This is a form of relevance-tree forecasting in which the competitive capability of each competitor is predicted. It lays the groundwork for decisions to push or play down certain technologies in the home firm. Strategic analysis permits direct forecasting of probable future changes in competitors' technological commitments by studying mergers, acquisitions, sell-offs, patent applications, patent sales, and so on. A keen analyst can predict major market swings and thus suggest new product opportunities (or lack of opportunities) for the firm.

A

Aaker, David A., 363n, 370n
AAR (After Action Review), 432, 434
Abandonment, 436
Abraham, Don, 64n, 65n
Absolute screens, imposing, 174
Accelerated product development (APD), 38
Accelerated time to market, 248
Acceleration competency, 301
Acceptance risk strategy, 172
Accumulated data, examining prior to launch, 421
Achilles' Heel technique, 472
ACNielsen, 403, 410
Acquisition, acquiring market strengths, 71
Activity category, for exploration, 124
Ad hoc team members, 304
Adams, Dan, 267n
Adams, Marjorie E., 7n, 19n, 310n
Adaptive conjoint analysis, 151
Adaptive customizers, 355
Adaptive product, developing, 74
Adequate warning, 444
Adidas Ultraboost X Parley shoes case, 82–83
Adopter categories, 221
Advertising agencies, 465
Affinity groupings, 254
After Action Review (AAR), 432, 434
After use dangers, 444
Aggressive entry, 350
Agile product development, 37–38
Agile-Stage-Gate, 37
Åhlström, Pär, 41
Aid to management, protocol as, 265
Aiman-Smith, Lynda, 305n
Air Multiplier (fan), 124
Air Products, 431
Airblade (hand dryer), 123–124
Ajamian, Greg A., 32n
Albaum, Gerald S., 202n
Albright, Richard E., 441n

Ali, Abdul, 41n
All commodity volume (ACV), 179
Allegiance to functional areas, 96
Alliances, 384–385
Allyn, Welch, 72
Alpha tests, 329–330
Altshuller, G. S., 157
Amazon, 12, 46, 49, 60, 112, 157, 194–195, 354, 418
Ambidextrous firms, 53
Analogy, 154–155
Analysis, managerial side of, 214
Analytic Hierarchy Process (AHP), 208–210
Analytical attribute techniques, 141, 143, 471–472
And also technique, 470
Andersen, Scot, 117n, 118
Ang, B. W., 199n
Ang, Swee Hoon, 368n
Anheuser-Busch, 372, 461
Announcements, 375, 377
Anscheutz, Ned F., 16n, 184n, 187n, 283n, 308n, 330n, 428n, 436n
Antil, John H., 176n
Apple Computer, 11, 41, 106, 112
Appleyard, Melissa M., 109n
Applications engineering, 74
Aquafresh White Trays case, 117–118
Arbitrary names, protection of, 362
Archer, Trevor, 108n
Arm & Hammer, 14
Art and entertainment, testing concepts, 181
Assumption of risk defense, 446
Asynchronous mode, meeting in, 313
A-T-A-R concept (awareness-trial-availability-repeat), 175
A-T-A-R model, 176–180
  forecasting sales using, 219–220
  launch control patterns, 423
  requirements, 385–391
  sales forecast, 224, 403
Attribute analysis techniques, 143
Attribute Dependency Template, 154

Attribute extension, 471–472
Attribute(s)
  positioning to, 358
  types of, 141–142
Augmentation dimensions in a protocol, 253
Augmented product concept, 246
Auto industry, new product process, 52
Automobile project screening, 209
Availability, 179, 386–388
Avert Virucidal Tissues, 341
Avlonitis, George J., 435n, 436n
Avoidance strategy, 172
Avoidance techniques, 474
Awareness, 178, 385–386, 429

B

B&L (Bausch & Lomb), 69, 138
Baba, Yasunori, 293n
baddesigns.com Web site, 322
Bagla, Gunjan, 453, 453n, 455n
Bai, F., 199n
Baker, Kenneth G., 202n
Baking soda, use of, 14
Balanced entry, 351
Balanced matrix option, 298
Bangle, C., 287n
Bannon, Lisa, 71n
Barbera, Brad, 255n, 277n
Barczak, Gloria, 7n, 19n, 67n, 167n, 290n, 297n, 311n, 314n
Barrier problems, overcoming, 390–391
Barriers
  bridging between-field, 473
  to creativity, 96
  overcoming to market orientation, 310
  to trial, 388–389
Bart, Christopher K., 67n, 70n
BASES group, data banks of, 182
BASES II, 224
BASF, 451

Bashada, Steve, 316n
Baskin-Robbins, occasional
    products, 434
Bass, Frank M., 221n, 223n
Bass diffusion model, 221–223
Batch concept, 36
Batch product in use testing, 336
Battelle Memorial Institute, 466
Bausch & Lomb (B&L), 69, 138,
    160, 304
Bay City Electronics case, 235–239
Bayer, 368
Bayuk, Linda M., 43n
Bayus, Barry L., 106n, 378n
Bazooka effect, 134–135
Beachhead stage of the launch
    cycle, 378–379
Beale, Claire-Juliette, 136n, 137n
Beam, Henry H., 279n
Bechinger, Iris, 309n, 310n
Beckley, Fred R., 291n
BehaviorScan CDSM, 408
Bell, Alexander Graham, 92, 331
Belliveau, P., 6n, 32n, 48n, 66n,
        72n, 77n, 103n, 105n, 108n,
        121n, 123n, 126n, 141n, 172n,
        254n, 281n, 312n, 315n, 441n
Benefit(s)
    of a product, 142
    putting first, 97
    used in positioning, 359
Benefit analysis, 471
Benefit segmentation, 189, 190, 353
Benefit segments, identifying,
    189–192
Benetton, using lean launch, 380
Berends, Hans, 290n, 314n
Berkowitz, D., 315n
Berman, Barry, 447n
Berman, Dennis, 73n
Bertels, Heidi, 52n
Beta testing, common pitfalls of, 330
Beta tests, 329–330
"better sameness," avoiding, 255
Between-field barriers, bridging, 473
Biemans, Wim G., 304n
Big business, new products
    management as, 6
Big winners, studying, 475
Bionicle (electronic toy), 26

Black & Decker, 61, 285, 289, 407
Blanck, Emily L., 315n
Blau, Gary E., 23n, 78n
Blind tests, 333
Blount, Steve, 407n
BMW, 113, 149, 281, 282, 287,
    292, 369
Boeing, 42, 114, 292, 316, 430–431
Boggs, R. W., 43n
Bohr, Neils, 92
Boike, Doug, 7n
Bona fide intent, 361
Bond, Edward U., III, 33n, 232n
Bosch, 111, 304–305, 454
Bothersomeness technique, 125
Bottom-up approach to strategy
    development, 232
Bottom-up platform procedure, 61
Bowen, H. Kent, 324n
Bower, Joseph L., 48n
Bowersox, D. J., 379n, 380n
Bowman, R., 349n
Boyce, Scott, 32n
Boyer, Ray, 94n
Boyle, Dan, 130
Brainsketching, 135
Brainstorming, 134–135, 318, 470
Brand, 361
Brand equity, 62, 363–368
Brand extensions, 366, 368
Brand names, 361, 362, 363, 365
Brand piracy, 452
Brand platforms, 62
Brand report card, 367
Branded tests, 333
Branding and brand management,
    360–371
Branding strategies, 368–369
Brandon, Dave, 195
Bread and Butter projects, 80, 81
Breakthrough innovation, system
    for, 47
Breakthrough products, 21
Brennan, Leslie, 415n
Brentani, Ulrike de, 9n, 10n, 60n,
    61n, 316n
Briggs, Robert O., 135n
Broaden the market fallacy, 355
Brodie, Roderick J., 187n
Brown, Peter, 54n

Bruss, Ken, 432n, 434n
Bryce, David, 49n
Buckler, Sheldon A., 95n, 309n
Build-test-feedback-revise
    process, 51
Bunch, Paul R., 23n, 78n
Burhenne, Wim, 149n
Burnout, on new product teams, 310
Business analysis, comprehensive,
    33–34
Business attitudes, toward product
    issues, 442
Business case, validating in a gap
    analysis matrix, 420
Business model innovation, 49
Business processes, integration
    with, 307
Business-to-business (B2B) product
    development, 268
Butt-on product replacement, 351
Buying intention questions, 182
Buying unit, 178
Buzz groups, 470

C

CAD (computer-aided design),
    291, 292
CAE (computer-aided
    engineering), 291
Calantone, Roger J., 10n, 18n, 41n,
        48n, 70n, 109n, 110n, 113n,
        209n, 304n, 308n, 347n, 379n,
        381n, 436n
Calder, Josh, 64n, 65n
CAM (computer-aided
    manufacturing), 291
Cameron, Allan, 55
Cameron, George D., 445n
Campbell Soup Company, 95, 174,
    228, 268, 363, 397
Candy wrapper, silent, 129
Cankurtaran, Pinar, 40n
Capacity to compete, 358
Car crashworthiness, 292
Car design, 283
Car industry
    ergonomic trade-offs in, 149
    platform planning, 59
Carbon monoxide monitor, 122

Careers, in new product development, 17–18

Carlson, Maureen, 198n

CAs (Customer attributes), in HOQ, 259, 261

Case-based research, 331

Cash-to-cash metric, 43, 348–349

Castellion, George, 16n, 21n, 43n, 69n, 126n, 184n, 187n, 283n, 308n, 313n, 330n, 428n, 436n

Cate, Sumi N., 457n

Category platform, 63

Cattin, Philippe, 149n

Cautious entry, 350

Cavusgil, S. T., 10n, 18n

CDSMs (Controlled-distribution scanner markets), 408

Cemex, as on-time supplier, 123

Central location approach, 332

Cereality (cereal franchise), 104

Chadwick, Chris, 431

Champions, 211
  product, 303, 305

"change or die" situation, at LEGO, 26

Channel rollout, 416

Channels, splitting, 351

Charged behavior, 307

Checklists, 152–154

Chemical-Avoiding Naturalist, 457, 458

Chen, Kuang-Jung, 366n

Chesbrough, Henry, 109, 109n

ChevronTexaco, 431

Chick-fil-A case, 418

Chiesa, Vittorio, 319n

China, electronics, 9

Chipotle case, 339–340

Choice-based conjoint analysis, 151

Choperena, Alfredo M., 39n

Chowdhury, Naser, 431

Christensen, Clayton M., 48n

Christiansen, Ole Kirk, 25

Chunks, 283, 284–285

Churchill, Gilbert A., 412n

Clamen, Allen, 32n, 307n

Clark, Barney, 55

Clark, Douglas W., 329n

Clark, Kim B., 39n, 298n, 324n

Clausing, Don, 258n, 261n, 262n

Clorox Company, brand strategy, 369

Clorox Green Works case, 449, 457–459

Closed innovation model, 111

Clouse, S. F., 223n

Coast (soap), development of, 134

Coca-Cola, 104, 181, 450

Coca-Cola life case, 392–394

Coca-Cola Surge, 341

Co-creation, 64, 65

Coffey, Mike, 431

Colby, Jim, 318, 318n, 319

Collaboration, culture of, 302–303

Collaborative customizers, 355

Colocation in the design process, 290

Comer, Donald, 45n

Comments about a new concept, 189

Commercialization, 34, 343

Commercialized concept statements, 186–187

Commonality, level of, 62

Communicability of new products, 357

Communications, 381–383

Communications mix, 382

Company failure, correcting, 427

Company within a company, 59

Comparative figures, versus absolutes, 338

Comparative Performance Assessment Study (CPAS), 7, 67, 167

Compatibility, of new products, 356

Compensation, as a team management issue, 311–312

Competencies, tied to radical innovation, 300

Competitive analysis, 475

Competitive comparisons, putting into a protocol, 253

Competitive information in the concept statement, 187

Competitive products, benchmarking, 252

Competitive reaction, assessing, 327

Competitors
  messing up a test market, 412
  showing your hand to, 412
  as sources of product ideas, 464
  surrogate positioning, 359

Complexity, 93, 356–357

Component Control Template, 154

Components, of a product, 283

Comprehensive prototype, 286–287

Computer programs, for brainstorming, 136

Computer-aided design and manufacturing (CAD/CAM) techniques, 380

Computer-aided design (CAD), 291, 292

Computer-aided engineering (CAE), 291

ConAgra Foods, brand strategy, 369

Concept(s), 181–182
  defined, 100
  identifying poor, 182
  of a new product, 98
  translation of, 98–99

Concept development, 174

Concept evaluation at Amazon case, 194–195

Concept evaluation, product line considerations in, 169–170

Concept generation
  as a creative task, 142
  phase, 30, 31–32, 35
  techniques, 138, 468–475

Concept Lab, at LEGO, 26

Concept selection, challenges of, 198

Concept statements
  commercialized, 186–187
  development of, 119
  preparing, 183–187

Concept testing, 32, 174, 180, 397
  conjoint analysis in, 192
  prototypes in, 151–152
  purposes of, 182–183
  research, 183–189
  as treacherous, 193

Concept testing and development, 180–183

Concept/project evaluation phase, 30, 32, 36

Concurrent system, 244

Conflict management styles, 309, 310

Confrontation, as a management style, 310

Conjoint analysis, 147–152
  in concept testing, 192

Conjoint results, 150
Conlin, Michelle, 441n
Consolidation strategies, 437
Constantineau, Larry A., 203n
Consultants, as sources of product
    ideas, 465
Consumer buying unit, 178
Consumer failure, contingency
    plans for, 427
Consumer Product Safety
    Commission (CPSC), 442, 447
Consumers
    designing products and
        services, 104
    sensing, 64, 65
Contingency plans
    for control problems, 421
    developing, 426–427
    system for implementing, 427–430
Continuous innovation, 356
Contour (car), 319
Control, over product during use
    testing, 333–334
Control events, selection of, 425–426
Controlled problems, selecting
    during launch, 421
Controlled sale, 400
Controlled sale methods, 406–410
Controlled-distribution scanner
    markets (CDSMs), 408
Cooper, Alan, 294n
Cooper, Bob, 78
Cooper, Jacquelin, 31n, 111n,
    112n, 169n
Cooper, Rachel, 278n, 309n
Cooper, Robert G., 7n, 14n, 16n,
    18, 19n, 20n, 21n, 22n, 23,
    23n, 37n, 38, 38n, 41n, 51n,
    59, 59n, 60n, 61n, 67n, 69n,
    70, 77n, 78n, 79n, 81n, 95n,
    113n, 114n, 124n, 128n, 186n,
    200n, 203n, 214n, 232n, 233,
    233n, 234n, 347, 347n
Coover, Harry W., 91, 91n
Coproducer, customer as, 72
Copy strategy statement, 383
Core benefits, of protocol, 247
Core competencies, 70
Core team, 304
Cornish, Edward, 215n

Corporate identity, design to build
    or support, 280–281
Corporate planning, ongoing, 29–30
Corporate strategy, 250, 253
Cosmetic customizers, 355
Cost reductions, new products as, 14
Costs
    of abandoning projects, 240
    of market testing, 400
    of test marketing, 411
Counterfeiting, 452
Crawford, C. Merle, 41n, 42n
Creation process, inputs required
    by, 97
Creative abrasion, 96
Creative customer problem solving
    case, 139–140
Creative firms, 94
Creative people, 94
Creative personnel, transferring, 94
Creative stimuli, 140, 474
Creativity, 12, 91–95
Creativity Templates, 153, 154
Creativity-stimulating
    techniques, 138
Crest Whitestrips, 117, 399
Creusen, Mariëlle E. H., 286n
Cricut electronic cutter, 319
Crisp, C. Brad, 313n
Cristiano, John J., 263n
Cross-cultural synergy, 315
Cross-field compilation, 473
Cross-functional alignment, 420
Cross-functional
    communication, 200
Cross-functional diversity, 96
Cross-functional interface
    management, 308–309
Cross-functional teams, 20, 38,
    263, 296
Cross-impact analysis, 470
Crossing the chasm model, 358
Crowdsourcing, 106–108
Crown Equipment Corporation, 280
Cruise, Tom, 160
Crunch time periods, 39
CSR at Starbucks case, 461–462
Culling factors, 206
Cultural differences, GTDs
    and, 315

Culture of collaboration,
    establishing, 302–303
Cumulative expenditures curve,
    170–172
Curtis, Carey C., 224n, 264n
Customer(s)
    communication of needs, 327–328
    "going deep" with, 268
    meeting new, 454
    as sources of product ideas,
        463–464
Customer and market analysis, 217
Customer attributes (CAs), in
    HOQ, 259, 261
Customer desires, converting into
    blueprint, 257–258
Customer franchise, 71
Customer group market sources, 72
Customer knowledge, poor, 93
Customer migration, achieving, 349
Customer needs
    complexity of, 327
    design to meet, 279–280
Customer site visits, 128
Customer surveys, 121
Customer-based sales forces, 384
Cutherell, David, 283n
Cycle of concerns, 440–442
Cycle time, 38, 248
    acceleration, 42
    metric, 39
    reduction program, 40
Cyclone Grinder, 278

D

Da Vinci, Leonardo, 92
Dacia Logan (car), 454
Dahan, Ely, 152n
Dahl, D. W., 155n
Dangerous condition from a design
    defect, 443
Danneels, Erwin, 47n, 53n
Darroch, Jenny, 13n
Database marketing, 354
Davenport, Thomas H., 92n
Davidson, Jeffrey M., 307n
Davis, John, 206n
Davis, Robert E., 399n
Day, George S., 310n

Day, Ralph L., 358n
Day in the life research, 128
de Bont, Cees J. P. M., 150n
de Brentani, Ulrike, 9n, 10n, 60n, 61n, 316n
De Bruyne, M., 344n
de Mozota, Brigitte Borja, 280n
De Vreede, Gert-Jan, 135n
Dealer support, 429
Deal-selective food buyers, 354
Decay curves, 172
Decision matrix, on when to market test, 396
Decision points, 19
Deck, Mark J., 112n, 430n
Decking, 292
Defects in manufacture, 444
Defensive addition launch pattern, 379
Dehoff, Kevin, 9n
Del Monte Foods, 137
Deliverables, 245
Dell Computers, pioneered lean launch methods, 380
Delphi probe forecasting technique, 216
Demand, type sought, 349–350
DeMartino, Richard, 301n
Demographic market segmentation, 352–353
den Ouden, Elke, 113n
Derivative products, 285
DeRose, Rodger L., 206n
Descriptive information, gathering, 337
Descriptive names, protection of, 362
Design, 17
    continuous improvement in, 293–294
    described, 276–277
    factors for, 285–286
    role of, 278–283
    sustainable, 448
Design defects, 443–444
Design dimensions, 282
Design engineers, 289
Design for assembly (DFA), 292
Design for disassembly, 282
Design for manufacturability (DFM), 291–292

Design parameters, 252
Design-driven innovation, 277
Designer decaf example, 99–100
"Destination therapy," 56
Detailed specifications, 252–253
Determinant attributes, 144, 147, 183
Determinant gap maps, 143–145
DeTore, Arthur, 61n
Development, 271–274, 323–324
Development phase, 30, 33–34, 36
Development process, managing, 248
Development stage in case-based research, 331
DFA (Design for assembly), 292
DFM (Design for manufacturability), 291
Di Benedetto, C. Anthony, 41n, 209n, 223n, 277n, 302n, 304n, 308n, 358n, 379n, 381n, 449n, 459n
Diagnostic information, 331, 397
Diagrams, as a concept statement, 185
Dial-A-Pharmacist service, 45
Dickinson, John R., 150n
Differentiation, 279
Diffusion of innovation, 176, 221, 356–358
Digital colocation, 290
Digital Designer, launched by LEGO, 26
Digital Equipment Corporation, GDT, 316
Digital preassembly, 293
Dimensional analysis, 152
Direct interviewing, 188
Direct marketing, 407
Direct network externalities, 377
Disagreements, between functional areas, 309
Disciplines panel, 137–138
Discontinuities, 46
Discontinuous innovation, 356
Discount schedules, complex, 390
Discovery competency, 300
Discovery-driven planning, 47
Discussion 62
    groups, 470
Disparate thinking, 474

Displacement Template, 154
Disruptive innovations, 48–49
Disruptive projects, resources to, 80
Distributors, 73, 387
Divergent thinking, 474
Divisibility of new products, 357
DNA security markers, 453
Dolan, Robert J., 151n, 330n
Dominiquini, Jennifer, 112n
Domino's Pizza, 123, 129
Domino's Pizza case, 195–197
Dougherty, Deborah, 310n
Dougherty, P., 379n, 380n
Dove soap bars, 14, 15
Downgrading, 351
Doyle, J. Patrick, 195, 196
Doyle, Stephen X., 384n
Doz, Yves, 314n
Drawings, as a concept statement, 183
Dreams, aiding problem analysis, 468–469
Dröge, Cornelia, 48n, 110n
Drucker, Peter F., 296, 296n
Dual Cyclone bagless vacuum cleaner, 5, 123
Dual-drive combinations, 73
Dual-drive strategy, 71
Dubiel, Anna, 454n
DuPont, 323
DuPont case, 267–268
Durgee, Jeffrey F., 129n
Dyer, Barbara, 300n, 309n
Dyer, Jeffrey H., 49n, 194n, 212n, 291n, 373n
Dynamic leap scenario, relevance tree form of, 131
Dynamic leap studies, 131
Dysfunctional styles, 309
Dyson, James, 5, 123–124, 275

E

Early adopters, 357
Early expenditures curve, 170
Early launch, 381
Early majority, 357
Early use experiences, 328
Easterday, Thomas, 282
Echambadi, Raj, 149

Econometric analysis forecasting technique, 216
Edgar, Dan, 267n
Edgett, Scott J., 19n, 20n, 41n, 77n, 78n, 79n, 80, 81n, 95n, 124n, 203n, 232n, 233n, 234n
Edison, Thomas, 92
Ee, Darren, 113n
Effective innovation metrics, learning, 430–432
Eisenbach, Jorg M., 53n
Electronic brainstorming, 135–136
Electronic data interchange (EDI) technology, 380
Elgar, Edward, 102n
Eliashberg, Jehoshua, 377n, 378n
Elizabeth Arden Division, of Unilever, 387
Ellis, Lynn W., 224n, 264n
Ells, Steve, 340
Emerging markets, designing products for, 453–455
Emerging trends, studying, 64
Emotional appeal in design, 285, 286
Empathy, lack of, 93
Employees, 332, 463
Emulation, as a level of innovativeness, 75
Endorsement surrogate positioning, 359
End-use
    focusing on, 72
    market segmentation, 352
    market sources, 72
End-user experience, 71
End-user segment, roll out by, 416
Engineering characteristics (ECs), in HOQ, 259, 262, 263
Engineers, sources of talented, 9
Englund, Randall L., 79n, 80n, 232n
Enkel, E., 109n
"Enoughness," search of, 64, 65
Environment, 448–451
    design for, 282–283
    on the public consciousness, 440
Eppinger, Steven D., 157, 157n, 276n, 281n, 283n, 285n, 286n, 298n
Equity awards for team members, 311

Ergonomics, design with attention to, 282
Ernst, Holger, 315n, 454n
Estimates, reliance on, 224–225
Ethnographic market research, 127
Ettlie, John E., 53n
Evaluation system
    for basic new products process, 167–169
    design, 177
    for new products, 166–167
    planning for new product concept, 172–175
Evaluation tasks, 19, 21, 34–37
Evaluation techniques, 168
Evamy, Michael, 276n, 289n
Evink, Janis R., 279n
Evolution, from concept to new product, 36
Evolving product, 35
Executive support, measuring in a gap analysis matrix, 420
Expected effects matrix, 426
Expected impact, of potential problems, 421
Experience surrogate positioning, 359
Expert Choice software, 208, 209
Experts
    going to, 125
    as a testing group, 332
Explanation in product use testing, 333
Express warranty, 446
Extend study, 131
Extended team members, 304
Extent of process change, 79
Extent of product change, 79
External mandates, 31
Exxon Chemical, 79
ExxonMobil, 53
Eyeball control, 432

F

Factor analysis, 145
Factors
    for industrial designers, 285–286
    in scoring models, 201
Failure to warn, 446

Failure(s), study of other people's, 473
Famous names, protection of, 362
Fanciful names, protection of, 362
Farley, John U., 222n
Farris, M., 349n
Feare, T., 349n
Feasibility, 200
Feature-function-benefit triad, 360
Features, 141–142, 358
Febreze fabric refresher, 411
FedEx, service development, 45
Feldman, Laurence P., 275n, 437n
Feynman, Richard, 91
Field testing, 322
Final production product in use testing, 336
Financial analysis
    challenges in, 215
    different methods on new products, 231
    life cycle concept of, 226–227
    of new products, 235
    timing of, 173
Financial forecasting methods, 231
Financials in a protocol, 253
Fingerhut (catalog company), database, 354
Firms, with global innovation culture, 10
First to mindshare, 39
First-to-market, as a risky strategy, 74
Firth, D. R., 223n
Fisher, Eden, 32n
Flagship brands, extending, 368
Flashlight, dimensional attributes of, 153
Fleming, Alexander, 13, 92
Flexibility, 307
Flint, Jerry, 377n
Fluke Corporation, 128
Fly on the wall research, 128
Flynn, Craig, 246n
Focus groups, 126–127, 255
Focused prototypes, 51, 286–287
Foley, Kevin, 117n
Food and Drug Administration, 447
Food buyers, clustering, 354
Food products, trade channel, 387
"Food with integrity," 340

Forbes, Thom, 334n, 367n, 412n
Forcing, as a management style, 310
Ford Fusion case, 319–321
Ford Motor Company, 128, 316, 319–320
Forecasting
    long-term, 215
    models, 223–224
    reducing dependence on, 227–231
    survey, 471
    techniques, 216
    what you know, 227
Forecasting sales, using traditional methods, 216–217
Form
    of product being tested, 336
    required by creation process, 97
Form postponement, 379
Formats, for concept testing, 183–186
Fountoulakis, Stavros, 32n
Franke, Nikolaus, 104, 104n, 105n, 107n, 109, 109n
Free association, 470, 473
Front-end architecture, of the Ford Fusion, 320
Front-loading design problems, 292
Frugal engineering, 455n
Fujimoto, Takahiro, 39n, 292n
Full profile conjoint analysis, alternatives to, 151
Full sale, 401, 410–417
Full screen, 32, 165, 199–201
Full-profile conjoint analysis, 151
Fully screened concept, 36
Function(s)
    positioning to, 358
    of a product, 141–142
Function activity, 471
Function analysis, 471
Functional elements, of a product, 283
Functional matrix structure, 299
Functional representative, on a new products team, 17
Functional structure option, for teams, 297
Future, professional forecaster's view of, 133
Fuzzy gates, 21

G

Gaffney, John, 399n
Galidor (electronic toy), 26
Galileo, 92
Gamma testing, 330–331
Gap analysis, 143–147
Gap analysis matrix, 419–420
Gap maps, 143–145
Garcia, Rosanna, 46n, 48n
Gartenberg, Chaim, 54n
Gaskin, Steve, 150n
Gassmann, Oliver, 109n, 317n
Gates, Bill, 318
Gault, Stanley C., 161
Gauvin, Stéphane, 357n
gDiaper, 450
Genç, E., 449n
General Electric (GE), 46, 52, 92, 116, 440
    R&D facilities in Bangalore, 454
General managers, leaders as, 303
General Motors, 72
Generation Y males, targeting, 83
Generic names, protection of, 362
Geniuses, thinking strategies, 92
Geographic market segmentation, 352–353
Geometric layout, creating for a product, 284–285
Ghandian engineering, 454
Gibson, Richard, 73n
Gilbert, James Patrick, 290n
Gillette case, 438–439
Gillette Co., 15, 31, 438
Gilmore, James H., 355n
Githens, Gregory D., 172n, 195n
Give and take, as a management style, 310
GlaxoSmithKline (GSK), 110, 117–118
Global brand leadership, 370–371
Global branding and positioning, 369–370
Global business meetings, 315
Global innovation culture, 10
Global new product teams, 10, 11, 315
Global operations, managing, 10

Global platform approach, 320
Global teams, 290
Globalization, increasing, 9–11
Globally dispersed teams (GDTs), managing, 314–317
"glocal" product, 61
Goals, 73–74
Gobeli, David H., 297n, 309n, 310n
Godrej (manufacturer), 455
Goffin, Keith, 292n
Goh, Nicky, 113n
Goldenberg, Jacob, 91n, 134n, 154n
Golder, Peter N., 23n, 91n, 102n, 106n, 109n, 156n, 223n, 256n, 357n, 455n
Go/No Go decision, 20, 21, 173, 232, 303, 435
Go/No Go point, 33
Google, 102
Google Glass case, 115–116
Gordon, W. J. J., 470
Gordon method, 470
Gorilla research, 128
Gorski, Christine, 121n
Governments, as sources of product ideas, 466–467
Graham, Ben, 102n
Graham, Robert J., 79n, 80n, 232n
Green design, 282
Green marketing, 450
Green Works line, 449, 457
"Greenfield Markets," identifying, 63
Greenwashing, 448
Gretzky, Wayne, 130
Griffin, Abbie, 6n, 7n, 16n, 21n, 32n, 40n, 43n, 48n, 50n, 51, 51n, 66n, 67n, 69n, 70n, 72n, 74n, 77n, 103n, 105n, 108n, 121n, 123n, 126n, 141n, 167n, 172n, 184n, 187n, 191n, 192n, 216n, 254, 254n, 258n, 261n, 263n, 264n, 281n, 283n, 305n, 308n, 311n, 312n, 313n, 315n, 330n, 344n, 348n, 364n, 367n, 379n, 428n, 432n, 434n, 436n, 441n
Griffith, David A., 10n
Grossman, Jeffrey C., 135n
Group contact with the user group, 332

Group creativity, 134, 470–471
Group rewards, 95
Group support systems (GSS) software, 135–136, 188
Group think, 93
Growth, goals and objectives, 73
GSK (GlaxoSmithKline), 110, 117–118
GTE Airfone, 327
Guided launch, concept of, 419–420
Guidelines in a PIC, 74–75
Guiltinan, Joseph P., 350n, 382n, 389n, 412n
Guinness Breweries, idea bank, 94
Gupta, Ashok K., 300n
Gupta, Praveen, 107n
Gustafsson, Anders, 108n

H

Haas, Al, 129n
Haggblom, Ted, 308n
Haggerty, Matthew K., 289n
Hainer, Herbert, 83
Haines, Steven, 420n
Hall, William G., 403n
Hamel, Gary, 6n
Handfield, Robert B., 304n
Hannaes, K., 448n
Hargadon, Andrew, 95n
Hart, Susan J., 344n, 379n, 435n, 436n
Hartley, Janet L., 39n
Hauser, John R., 254n, 254, 258n, 261n, 262n
Haworth Inc., 279
Heart pump industry, 55–57
Heart pumps, 56, 181
Heavy product, identifying, 124
Heavyweight teams, 297
Heckscher, Charles, 312n
Heil, Oliver P., 377n
Heinekamp, Eric J., 121n
Hentschel, Uwe, 145n
Herbig, Paul A., 358n
Herman, Dan, 350n
Hertenstein, Julie H., 276n
Heuristics (rules of thumb), 12, 224, 405
Hey, Jonathan, 135n

Hierarchical decision tree in AHP, 209
Hierarchical design, 472
Hierarchy of effects, 423
High-season switch, 351
Hillebrand, Bas, 304n
Hines, Andy, 64n, 65n
Hippel, Eric von, 108n
Hoechst-U.S.'s scoring model, 233
Hoegl, M., 315n
Holahan, Patricia J., 308n
Hollmann, Thomas, 43n
Holloway, Charles A., 324n
Holloway, Matthew, 331n
Hollow-gate problem, 21
Holograms on products, 453
Honda, 61, 75, 83–86, 95, 128, 290, 304, 313, 369
Honda Element case, 83–86
Hoover Company, 72
Horovitz, Bruce, 74n
Hot products, aiding scenario analysis, 469
House of quality (HOQ), 257–262
Houston, Mark B., 33n, 232n
Howell, Jane M., 305n
HTC U11, 159
Huberty, Tim, 127n
Huffy, hybrid bikes, 424
Hulland, John S., 231n
Hult, G. Tomas M., 305n
Hultink, Erik Jan, 344n, 379n, 381n
Hung, Yu-Ting Caisy, 313n
Hurdle rates, 231, 241
Huston, Larry, 110n
Hutchinson, P., 349n
Hyland, Joanne, 6n, 48n

I

I Love My Dog initiative, 137
Iansiti, Marco, 41n, 292n
IBM, 60, 61, 95, 113, 279, 317
IDEA awards case, 294–295
Idea bank at creative firms, 94
Idea building and modification, 470
Idea concept, 35
Idea generation, obstacles to, 93
Idea sources, 467
Ideal brands, rating, 190

Ideation, as constant, 89
Ideation Group, 279
Identity disclosure in product use testing, 333
IFF (International Flavors and Fragrances), 104, 105
Ikea, 11
Illinois Institute of Technology, 466
Image for a product, 352
Imitation, as a level of innovativeness, 74–75
Immediate action, contingency plans ready for, 421
Implied warranty, 446
Importance map, 189
Importance ratings, 189
Inadequate materials, in a design, 444
Income-statement-based net present value (NPV), 224
Incremental new products, 22
Incubation competency, 300
Incubation period, 47
India, automotive engineering, 9
Indiegogo case, 116–117
Indirect network externalities, 377
Individual brand strategy, 369
Individual contact with the user group, 332
Industrial designers, 285–286, 287, 466
Industrial product innovation, 149
Industrial Research Institute, scoring model, 203
Inflow of actual data during tracking, 428
Influencers, reaching full set of, 188
Informal selling method, 406–407
Information coordination, marketing's task in, 323
Information needs, for new product launch, 399
Information Resources Incorporated (IRI), 403
InfoScan system, 409
Inherent risks of products, 443
Initial diffusion rate, 221
Injury sources, typology of, 443–445
In-market test, 409

InnoHub, as a form of open innovation, 113
Innovation, 17, 91–92
    diffusion of, 356–358
    disruptive, 48–49
    metrics for, 430–432
Innovation dashboard, 430
Innovation engine, guidance system needed for, 27
Innovation strategy, adapting, 454
Innovative new product launch pattern, 378
Innovative products, growth potential of, 221
Innovativeness
    degree of, 66, 74–75
    relation to success, 16
Innovators, 93–94, 357. *See also* Creative people
Input metrics, 430
Institute for the Study of Business Markets (ISBM), 268
Instructions, for use, 444
Intel, 15
Intellectual property (IP), 110, 113–114, 452
Intent to purchase information, 338
Interaction design, 294
Interface management, 308
Interfaces
    in the design process, 287–291
    managing across functional areas, 308
Internal concept generation, 119–120
Internal mandates, 31
Internal marketing, 274
Internal rate of return (IRR), 215, 224
Internal records, 121
International Flavors and Fragrances (IFF), 104, 105
International sources of product ideas, 467
Interviewing
    customers, 126, 254
    preparing for concept evaluation, 188–189
Interviews, taping, 254–255
Intuition, 12
Invention, 17
Invention industry, 464–465

Investigation stage in case-based research, 331
Investment, outflows, 239
IP (Intellectual property)
    copying, 452
    in open innovation, 110, 113
iPhone X, 159
iPod, development of, 11
iPod Touch, marketing, 255
IRI (Information Resources Incorporated), 403, 408
IRR (Internal rate of return), 215, 224
Itemized response to ideas, 96

J

Jacobs, Laurence, 452n, 453n
Jain, Sanjay, 378n
Jain, Subhash C., 452n
Jana, Reena, 55n, 106n
Jargon, Julie, 412n
Jaruzelski, Barry, 9n
Jassawalla, Avan R., 303n
Jedlik, Tom, 452n, 453n
Jelinek, Mariann, 113n, 114n, 298n
Jennings, Kyle E., 135n
JetBlue, excellent service development, 444
Joachimsthaler, Erich, 363n, 370n
Job security, 311
Jobber, David, 351n
Jobs, Steve, 31, 255, 255n, 277n
Johnson, Albert, 32n
Johnson, Hollis, 339n
Johnson & Johnson, 21, 95, 112, 136, 447
Johnson Wax, use analysis, 471
Johnston, Zachary T., 43n
Joint space maps, 190, 191, 353
Jones, Dow, 13n
Jones, Robert, 314n
Journal of Product Innovation Management, 23
Joyce, Caneel K., 135n
Judges for a scoring model, 206–207
Jury of executive opinion forecasting technique, 216
Just-in-time delivery of parts, 349
Just-in-time life, 64

K

Kahn, Kenneth B., 7n, 19n, 20n, 21n, 37n, 43n, 46n, 51n, 67n, 69n, 77n, 81n, 104n, 167n, 187n, 216n, 217, 217n, 218n, 220n, 224n, 290n, 308n, 309n, 311n, 313n, 314n, 317n, 347n, 379n, 420n, 431n
Kalil, Thomas, 135n
Kalwani, Manohar U., 46n
Karlsson, Christer, 41n
Karol, Robin A., 307n, 457n
Katsanis, Lea Prevel, 62n, 368n
Katz, Gerald M., 254n, 257, 259n, 261n, 263n, 264n, 405n
Katzfey, Patricia A., 436n
Kawasaki, Jet Skis, 256
Kawasaki, Guy, 255, 255n
Kay, Mary, 381
Kay, S. E., 20n, 43n, 46n, 51n, 77n, 81n, 104n, 187n, 217n, 314n, 347n, 379n, 420n, 431n, 454n
Keko, Elio, 102n, 106n, 107n
Kekulé, August, 92, 469
Keller, Kevin Lane, 366n, 367n
Kelley, Thomas, 134, 134n
Kellogg Company, 62, 341, 368, 369, 370
Kenley, Amy, 431n
Key-word monitoring, 473
Khanwilkar, Pratap, 56
Kieffer, Don, 246n
Kilmer, Paul F., 362n
Kim, Cheol, 157n
Kim, W. C., 155, 155n, 157n, 449n
Kimberly-Clark (K-C), 71, 114, 341, 405
Kindle, 46
King, Jacqui, 366n
Kingon, Angus I., 72n
Kinko's, FedEx acquisition of, 45
Kleinschmidt, Elko J., 9n, 10n, 16n, 19n, 20n, 60n, 61n, 67n, 77n, 78n, 79n, 81n, 95n, 124n, 203n, 232n, 233n, 234n, 316n
Koen, Peter A., 32n, 53n, 59, 59n, 68
Koenig, Harold F., 309n, 310n
Kohli, Chiranjeev, 363n

Kotha, Suresh, 355n
Kotler, Philip, 354n
Kramer, M. R., 448n
Krapfel, Robert, Jr., 41n
Kratzer, Jan, 315n
Kristensson, Per, 108n
Kroemer, Karl H. E., 282n
Krohe, James, Jr., 96n
Krubasik, E. G., 42n
Kuczmarski, Thomas D., 15n, 43n, 46n, 203n
Kunkel, J. Gregory, 312n
Kuzak, Derrick M., 320

L

LaBahn, Douglas W., 41n, 363n
Laboratories, technological strengths in, 71
Labrich, Kenneth, 13n
Lafley, A. G., 111
Lager, Thomas, 261n
Laggards, 221, 357
Laitner, Diana, 67n
Lambert, Denis, 39n
Lambert, Fred, 241n
Langerak, Fred, 40n, 380n, 381n
Langvardt, Arlen W., 377n
Lans, Maxine S., 361n
Larson, Eric W., 297n
Late launch, 380
Late majority, 221, 357
Lateral search, techniques enhancing, 472–475
Launch, 34, 398–399
    control plan, 425
    cycle, 375–379
    management, 34, 419–420
    management plan, 432, 433
    management system, 420–430
    phase, 30, 34, 36–37, 45, 341
    planning, 344
    tactics, 381–384, 389
Launch timing, 379–381
LaunchPoint Technologies, 56
Lavidge, Robert J., 333n, 336n
Lawrence, C., 223n
LDCs (Lesser-developed countries), intellectual property as a public good, 452

Le Nagard-Assayag, E., 377n
Lead user analysis, 48
Lead users, 108
    characteristics of, 108
    interviewing, 126
    new product ideas from, 108–109
Leader, selecting for a team, 303–304
Leadership, 227, 307
Lean launch, 379–381
Leap method, 131
Leap studies, 131
Lee, Hyunjung, 7n, 8n, 9n, 52n, 75n, 167n, 448n
Lee, Yikuan, 346n
Leenders, Roger, 315n
Lees, Gavin, 184n, 186n
Legislation, affecting liability, 447
LEGO Group
    open innovation system, 112
    new products, 25–29
LEGOLAND parks, 26
Lehmann, Donald R., 222n
Lehnerd, Alvin, 61n
Lehr, L. W., 94n
Leonard-Barton, Dorothy, 127n, 324n
Lesser-developed countries (LDCs), intellectual property as a public good, 452
Levacor Heart Pump case, 55–57
Leverage capabilities, 71
Leveraged creativity, 74
Levin, Ginger, 317n
Liau, Janet, 368n
Licensing, 71
lickety-stick process, 52, 135
Lieberman, M. B., 75n
Liefer, Richard, 6n, 46n
Life cycle, of a public concern, 440–442
Life cycle analysis, 217
Life Savers Company, using props, 138
Lifecycle concept, of financial analysis, 226–227
LifeScan, recall of all meters, 447
Light users, food buyers as, 354
Lightweight teams, 297
Liker, Jeffrey K., 263n, 301n, 349n
Lilien, Gary L., 108n, 136n, 149n, 208n, 405n

Limited marketing, 413
Limited usage, trial as, 388
Links, in a network, 306
Live test market, 409
Living thing, project as, 226
Local partner, finding, 454
Lockwood, N. S., 314n
Logo, as a trademark, 360
Long, Sieu Meng, 368n
Long-run market share, expressing, 219
Lopez, Al, 53
Loser, avoiding the big or sure, 167
Low-cost development and marketing, strategy of, 228
Low-season switch, 351
Loyalists, food buyers as, 354
Lu, Chu-Mei, 366n
Lucas, George, 71
Luckey, Palmer, 54
Lynn, Gary S., 47n, 52n, 411n

M

MacCormack, Alan, 292n
MacElroy, Bill, 354n
MacMillan, Ian C., 47n
Magnetic levitation technology, 56
Magrath, Allen J., 63n
Mahajan, Vijay, 221n, 222n, 223n, 312n
Maier, E. P., 386n
Mail method, of user group contact, 332
Makridakis, Spyros, 216n
Malhotra, Naresh K., 9n, 31n, 186n, 380n, 430n
Management. *See* Senior management; Top management
Managerial side of analysis, 214
Managers, handling problems, 225–231
Manceau, D., 377n
Mandolia, Rishu, 46n, 94n
Mangalindan, J. P., 12n
Manufacturability, design for, 282–283
Manufacture, design for ease of, 279
Manufacture surrogate positioning, 359

Manufactured goods, compared to services, 43
Manufacturers role of, 324
  as sources of product ideas, 466
Manufacturing ramp-up, 324
Map of snacks, 143–145
Marcus, Burton H., 125n
Maremont, Mark, 438n
Marion, Tucker J., 60n
Market acceptance testing, 322
Market drivers, 72–73
Market opportunities, 76
Market orientation, overcoming barriers to, 310
Market rollout, 377–378
Market satisfaction gap (MSG), 268
Market segmentation analysis, 468
Market share
  converting into long-run sales, 220
  as a goal, 73
  sense of, 182
Market status, goals and objectives, 73
Market testing, 34, 395
  asking for, 396–397
  conditions for skipping, 399
  decision, 395–400
  factors for deciding whether to, 398–400
  having teeth, 397–398
  methods of, 400–401
  relating to other testing, 397, 398
  rollouts, 228
Market window accuracy, 420
Marketed concept, 36
Marketing, 6
  role during development, 323–324
  role in development, 273–274
Marketing date, as tentative, 173
Marketing decisions, interlacing with technical, 33
Marketing department, direct inputs from, 121–122
Marketing mix, reviewing, 381
Marketing plan, 29, 33
Marketing ramp-up, 22, 324
Marketing research firms, 465–466
Marketing tasks in development, 30

Marketplace, effects on market testing, 400
Markets, segmenting, 352–353
Markham, Stephen K., 7n, 8n, 9n, 19n, 43n, 52n, 72n, 75n, 167n, 203n, 305n, 308n, 448n
Mars (candy manufacturer), database of cat owners, 354
Marsh, Sarah J., 94n
Marshall, Jeneanne, 278n
Martin, Justin, 181n
Martinez, Eva, 368n
Mass customization, 72, 104, 354–356
Mass production, 355
Massey, Anne P., 313n, 314n
Matanovich, Timothy, 149n, 405n
Matrix hell, 263
Matrix structures, 299–300
Matthews, John M., 330n
Mattimore, Bryan, 138n
Mauborgne, Renée, 155, 155n, 449n
Mazursky, David, 154n
Mazzuca, Mario, 52n, 411n
McBride, Sarah, 215n
McCamey, David A., 43n
McDonald, Rory, 48n
McDonald's, 361
McDonough, Edward F., III, 290n, 307n, 314n, 317n
McGahan, Anita M., 48n
McGrath, M. E., 59n
McGrath, Rita Gunther, 47n, 59n
McMath, Robert M., 334n, 367n, 412n
Meadows, Lee, 108n
Media sources of product ideas, 467
Medquest, 56
Meet the market price, 390
Meetings, running effective, 311
Menezes, Melvyn A. J., 386n
Mercedes Benz case, 241–243
Merck, 23, 102
Methé, David T., 71n
Metrics, external validation for, 431
Meyer, Marc H., 61n, 83n, 353n
Michalko, Michael, 92n
Michelin, 102
Micromarkets, targeting, 354
Microsoft, 102
Microwave oven, 13, 181
Miles, Morgan P., 13n

Miles Laboratories, 415
Miller, Charles, 141n
Miller, William, 186n
Min, Sungwook, 46n
Mindstorms (electronic toy), 26
Minimarket test, 409
Minimarkets, controlled sales in, 407–409
Misrepresentation, 445, 446–447
Mission statements, 59
Mitchell, Paul, 366n
Mitigation risk strategy, 172
Mitra, Debanjan, 102n, 106n, 109n, 156n
Miyabe, Junichiro, 71n
Models, as a concept statement, 185
Modular products, 60
Modularization, 60
Moenaert, R. K., 344n
Molitor, Graham T. T., 133, 133n
Monadic test, 334, 335
Monaghan, Tom, 195
Mondeo (car), 319
Mondry, Mark, 365, 365n
Monetary and nonmonetary rewards, 311
Montgomery, D. B., 75n
Montoya, Mitzi M., 304n, 308n, 313n, 314n, 346n, 347n
Moore, Geoffrey, 358, 358n
Moran, John J., 260n, 261n
Moreau, P., 155n
Morone, Joseph G., 52n, 411n
Morrison, P. D., 108n
Morton, Peter D., 108n
Moscowitz, Howard R., 335n
Moss, Roberta, 19n
Motivation, of teams, 311–312
Motorola, 290, 312
Moulson, Tom, 283n
Mozart, 92
Mudambi, Ram, 10n
Mudambi, Susan, 10n
Mueller, James L., 281n
Mulally, Alan, 319n, 320
Muller, Eitan, 221n, 223n
Multifunctional group, managing project teams, 317
Multifunctional product development, 20
Multifunctional team, 245

Multiple coverage strategy, 131
Multiple regression forecasting technique, 216
Multiple-objective strategic portfolio model, 80
Munsch, Ken, 277
Musk, Elon, 212
Myths, about marketing planning, 344–345

N

Nabisco, 412
Nader, Ralph, 441
"Nair for Men," 397
Nakata, Cheryl, 315n
Narayanan, V. K., 13n, 46n, 113n, 114n, 223n, 229n, 230n, 297n, 298n, 305n, 357n
Narrative format for a concept test, 184
Natural sell-in, 409
Nature, imitating, 138
Natureworks, 450
Nauyalis, Carrie T., 198n
Navarra, Pietro, 10n
NBIC, mass customization, 355
Near brand usage, 452
Need/benefit, as a creation process input, 97
Needs fulfilled, composite listing of, 468
Neeleman, David, 44
Neff, Jack, 411n
Neff, Michael C., 352n
Negligence, 445–446
Nelling, Edward, 229n, 230n
Nelson, Beebe, 441n
Neologism, as a brand name, 362, 364
Net loss on cannibalized sales, 240
Net present value (NPV), 202, 215, 229
Netflix, 46, 49, 107, 469
Network, 306
Network building, 306
Network externalities, 377
New product(s), 14, 46
    all not planned, 13
    approaches, 102
    causing unexpected concern, 442

differentiating, 60
financial analysis, 235
as key, 59
sales forecasting for, 215–216
New Product Blueprinting, 268
New product concepts, 98, 102–103, 181–182
New product evaluation system, 167
New product line category, 15
New product lines, 14
New product story, 25–29
New product strategy, 22
New product tracking study, questions from, 428
New products, importance of, 6–9
New products management, 6
New products process, 18–22, 25, 28
    difficulty of, 6–7
    evaluations in, 166–170
    goal of, 20
    implementation guiding principles, 307
    improving, 225–226
    phases in, 29–34
New products process manager, 17, 317
New products strategy, 59–66
New products team, 11
New resource, 31
New service development process, 43
New technology, concepts embodying, 181
New Zealand Wool Testing Authority, 187
Newell Brands, 161
New-to-the-firm products, 14
New-to-the-world products, 14, 15, 46–48, 349, 435
Nguyen, Hang T., 109n
Nicholson, Carolyn Y., 308n
Nielsen. See ACNielsen
Nielsen Food Index (NFI) reports, 410
Nike, 63, 104, 112
Nissan, focus groups, 127
Nobeoka, Kentaro, 293n
Nodes of a network, 306
No-fault approach, 456
Nokia, 454, 455
Nokia-Siemens, 454

Non-laboratory technology, 71
Nonpareil surrogate positioning, 359
Nontrackable problems, 429–430
NordicTrack, 465
Norling, Parry M., 323n
Norms, from product use testing, 338
Not-invented-here syndrome, 465
nPower PEG (Personal Energy Generator), 64
NPV (Net present value), 202, 215, 229
Nussbaum, Bruce, 122n, 127n, 135n, 279n, 280n
NutraSweet, 13, 392, 411

O

Objectives, in a PIC, 73–74
Observability of new products, 357
Observing, consumers, 125
Occasional products, 434
Oce, idea bank, 94–95
O'Connor, Gina Colarelli, 6n, 13n, 46n, 47, 48n, 113n, 114n, 129n, 223n, 229n, 230n, 297n, 298n, 301n, 305n, 346n, 357n
Oculus rift case, 54–55
Offensive improvement launch pattern, 379
Official Gazette, 466
Olay Regenerist, 111
Olson, David W., 354, 423n, 428n
Olson, Eric M., 278n, 309n
Olympic figure-skating method, 205
Omniscient proximity, 125
Omta, S. W. F. (Onno), 309n, 311n
"On decision" option, 21
One-on-one interviewing, 126
Ongoing strategies, covering product innovation, 31
Online communities, 136–137
Ono, Yumiko, 387n
Oobeya Room, 245, 246
Open innovation, 109–114
Operating relationships of a network, 306
Operations, 12, 13
Opportunities, evaluating and ranking, 76
Opportunity (real start), 35
Opportunity analysis, special, 30

Opportunity concept, 35
Opportunity cost, 171
Opportunity identification, 29–31,
    35, 63–64, 76
Opportunity Identification and
    Selection, 2, 3–4, 29–31
Options-pricing theory, 228
Oratech LLC, 117–118
Organization learning, housing, 317
Organizational structure options, 297
Ortt, Roland J., 150n
Osborn, Alex, 134
Osler, Rob, 360n, 361n, 362n
Ottman, Jacquelyn A., 282n,
    450, 451n
Ottum, Brian, 187n, 191n, 192n
Outcomes, projecting probable, 428
Outsourcing, 110
Outstanding Corporate Innovator
    award, 23, 45
Overbeeke, Kees, 291n
Overheads, applicable, 240
Overlapping phases, 38
"Over-the-wall" product
    development, 38
Oysters, 80, 81
Oyung, Robert, 314n
Ozer, Muammer, 316n, 368n,
    383n, 406n

P

P&G. See Procter & Gamble (P&G)
Pace, Lisa, 314n
Packaging, 371–372
Page, Albert L., 67n, 74n, 311n, 348n
Paired comparison, 335
Pant, Somendra, 316n
Paper collars, disposable, 437
Parallel processing, 38
Paralysis by analysis, 228, 431
Parameter analysis, 471
Parentage surrogate positioning, 359
Park, C. Whan, 96n
Parry, Mark E., 315n
Pascarella, Perry, 312n
Patent and Trademark Office,
    361, 363
Patent Office of the U.S.
    government, 466

Paul, G. W., 412n
Paul, Ronald L., 184n
Paulson, Albert S., 46n, 52n, 411n
PDMA (Product Development &
    Management Association), 7,
    17, 23, 67
Pearls, 80
Pekny, Joseph F., 23n, 78n
Penetration price, 391
Penicillin, discovery of, 13
Penn Racquet Sports, 73
People dimension of product
    development, 174–175
Perception, of a customer
    problem, 122
Perceptual gap analysis, 143
Perceptual gap maps, 143, 145–146
Perceptual mapping techniques, 360
Perceptual maps, 145
Pereira, Joseph, 71n
Performance metrics, 430
Performance parameters, 252
Performance specs, 252
Permanence options, of
    products, 350
Perry, Tekla S., 95n
Persaud, Ajax, 316n
Personal accolades for creatives, 95
Personal computer, introduction
    of, 46
Personal contact, concept testing
    through, 188
Personal selling, 383–384
Personal sense, prime benefit as, 180
Personal trial conditions, 388
Peters, Lois S., 46n
Petersen, Kenneth J., 304n
Petras, Ross and Kathryn, 365n
Pfizer, 13, 233
Phased new products process, 18–19
Philips Electronics, 113, 317
Phillips, J. Donald, 470
Phillips 66 groups, 470
Phone interviews, 126
PIC. See Product innovation
    charter (PIC)
Piller, F., 104n
Pillsbury, 102
Pilosof, David, 457n
Pilot concept, 36

Pilot plant product, in use testing, 336
Pina, Jose M., 368n
Pine, B. Joseph, II, 355n
Pisano, Gary P., 49n, 106n
Pitts, Dennis A., 62n, 368n
Platt, Marjorie B., 276n
PLC (Product life cycle), 375
PMT (Portfolio Management
    Team), 45
Poetz, Marion K., 107n
Poh, K. L., 199n
Point-of-use location, 332
Political arena phase for a public
    issue, 442
Portfolio, role in, 241
Portfolio management approach, 38
Portfolio Management Team
    (PMT), 45
Porter, M. E., 448n
Positioning, 251
Postannouncement speed, 39
Postponement
    principle of, 41
    of product form and identity, 379
Postshipping technical speed, 39
Potential problem analysis, 331
Potholes, 173–174, 253, 426
Power Train Group, at Honda, 85
Pragmatists, 358
Prahalad, C. K., 108n
Pratt, Anthony Lee, 290n
Prayer groups, avoiding, 127
Preannouncements, 375–378
Predecessor surrogate
    positioning, 359
Preference score, 336
Prelaunch stage of the launch
    cycle, 375
Premarket speed, 39
Premarket testing, 200, 403
Premium price, 390
Prescreening process, 182–183
Pressure, intense, 12
Pretechnical evaluation, 32
Prevo, Gert Jan, 102n, 106n, 107n
Price, in the concept statement, 187
Price, Raymond L., 50n
Price strategies for new products,
    390–391
Price tactics, for launch, 390

Price-driven food buyers, 354
Pricing, 239
Primary criteria in AHP, 209
Primary demand, stimulating, 349
Primary packaging, 371
Private online communities, 136
Privity, 445
Probe-and-learn process, 52
Problem(s)
　gathering, 120–132
　solving, 133–138
　sorting and ranking, 125
　spotting potential during launch,
　　420, 421–425
Problem analysis, 122–130
Problem areas, current, 443
Problem find-solve approach, 32
Problem-based approach, 119
Problem-based ideation, 119–120
Process concept, 36
Process innovation, 13
Process metrics, 430
Procter & Gamble (P&G)
　Coast (soap), 134
　common set of ingredients, 61
　Crest Whitestrips, 399
　cutting development time, 42
　Febreze and Dryel, 171–172
　Febreze fabric refresher, 411
　PUR, 451
　research centers, 11
Proctor, Tony, 136n
Produceability engineer, 291
Product(s)
　as groups of attributes, 141–142
　improvements and revisions to
　　existing, 14
　launching next generation of, 352
　speeding to market, 38–43
Product adoption process, 356
Product architecture, 283–285
Product attributes, 141–142, 251–253
Product category, for exploration, 124
Product champions, 50, 51, 305
Product characteristics, 356–358
Product commercialization, 346
Product concept statement, 100–102
Product concepts, 31, 96–102,
　181–182
　evaluation preceding, 167–169

Product configurators, 104
Product definition, 32, 245
Product deletion decision, 435–436
Product deliverables, 248
Product description, 32
Product design, 287, 288, 289
　Dieter Rams's principles, 276
　impact of 3D printing on, 293
Product development, 18, 23
　strategic elements of, 5–23
Product Development &
　Management Association
　(PDMA), 7, 17, 23, 67
Product diffusion, 221–223
Product engineering, 288
Product enhancements, 156–157
Product experience, 71
Product failure, 435–437
Product families, 61
Product function analysis, 129
Product goals, 278–283
Product ideas, sources of new,
　463–467
Product innovation, 13. See also
　Innovation
Product innovation charter (PIC),
　18, 22, 31, 38, 59, 66–70,
　90–91, 226
　arena section, 70–73
　background section of, 70
　of LEGO, 27
　development of, 58
　eliminating new product
　　ideas, 180
　goals and objectives section of,
　　73–74
　preparing, 75–76
　reconsidering, 232–234
　sections of, 70–75
　special guidelines section of,
　　74–75
Product innovation gap, 31
Product innovation management,
　5–6
Product integrity
　as a guideline, 75
　testing, 331
Product issues, business attitudes
　toward, 442
Product liability, 443–447

Product life, 239
Product life cycle (PLC), 375
Product line analysis, 217
Product lines
　additions to existing, 14, 16
　considerations in concept
　　evaluation, 169–170
　replacement, 351–352
Product piracy, 452–453
Product planning, 6
Product platforms, 59
　establishing, 285
　strategy, 60
Product portfolio
　analysis, 76–81
　establishing, 28
　management, 18
Product positioning, 251, 358–360
Product protocol, 32. See also
　Protocol(s)
Product protocol for entrepreneurs
　case, 265–267
Product recall, planning, 447–448
Product schematic, 284
Product Use Testing for New
　Consumer Nondurables
　case, 341
Product use testing (PUT), 322, 397
　arguments against and for,
　　325–328
　conducting, 334–335
　data formats, 337
　decisions in, 331–339
　knowledge gained from,
　　328–331
　necessity for, 325–328
　reasons for, 324–325
　risks and costs of, 326
Production, verifying within a test
　market, 411
Production requirements in a
　protocol, 250, 253
Profile sheet, 207–208
Profit flow (real finish), 35
Profit forecast, 178
Profits, goals and objectives,
　73–74
Program Evaluation Review
　Technique (PERT) chart, 272
Progress reports, 34

Project ELITE (Earnings Leadership in Tomorrow's Environment), at TRW, 312
Project evaluation, 32, 170
Project manager, 17
Project matrix option, 299
Projective technique, 472
Projectization, 297, 298, 301
Proprietary online panels (POPs), 136
Proprinter dot-matrix printer, 279
Props, using, 138
Proserpio, L., 315n
Protocol(s), 245
  components of, 253
  concept, 36
  contents of, 249–253
  for a home trash disposal/recycling system, 250
  integrating and focusing role of, 247
  in new products process, 257
  preparation, 245
  process, difficulty of, 264–265
  purposes of, 247–248
  spelling out, 212
Prototypes, in concept testing, 151–152
Prototype(s), 33
  concept, 36
  as concept statements, 185
  concept testing, 181
  developing, 286–287
  evaluating, 33
  testing, 44, 322
Provo Craft case, 318–319
Prügl, Reinhard, 109n
Prusak, Laurence, 92n
Pseudo product test, 472
Pseudo sale, 400, 401–406
Psychographic market segmentation, 352–353
Public concerns, life cycle of, 440–442
Published sources, for problem analysis, 125–126
Pujari, Ashish, 67n, 70n
Purcell, Rick W., 264n
Purchase intentions, forecasting sales, 218

Push mowers, 437
PUT. *See* Product use testing (PUT)

Q

Qualitative research technique, 126, 152–158
Quality, focusing on, 38
Quality Function Deployment (QFD), 32, 257–264
Quality product, assurance of delivery of, 328
Quantitative approaches, 158
Quantitative innovation diffusion models, 221

R

R&D (research & development), 6, 9, 454
Rad, Parviz F., 317n
Rae, Jeneanne Marshall, 278n, 289n
Rafii, Farshad, 290n
Ragatz, Gary L., 304n
Ramaswamy, Venkat, 108n
Rangan, V. Katsuri, 386n
Rangaswamy, Arvind, 136n, 149n, 208n, 405n
Rank surrogate positioning, 359
Rao, Ambar G., 378n
Ray-Ban case, 160–161
Raynor, Michael, 48n
Rayport, Jeffrey F., 127n
RC (Rider Counterbalance) lift truck, 280
Ready-made new product ideas, 102–114
Really-new products, 14
Real-options analysis, 228–229
Reast, John, 366n
Recall program coordinator, designating, 447
Registration, 361
Regulatory adjustment phase for a public issue, 442
Regulatory requirements in a protocol, 253
Reibstein, David, 430, 430n
Reilly, Richard R., 47n, 52n
Reimann, Bernard C., 239n
Reinertsen, Donald G., 20n, 170n

Relative advantage, of new products, 356
Relative brand profile, 472
Relevance Tree form of dynamic leap scenarios, 132
Relevance-tree forecasting, 475
Reliability of a sample, 332
Repeat, A-T-A-R definition, 178, 179
Repeat buying percentage, 322
Repeat purchase rate, 219–220, 391
Replacement demand, stimulating, 349
Replacement Template, 154
Repositionings, 14
Required rate of return, 228, 229, 240
Requirements, in the protocol, 322
Research & development (R&D), 6, 9, 454
Research laboratories, as sources of product ideas, 466
Research results, analyzing, 189–192
Resellers, 386, 464
Resource preparation, 33
Respondent group, defining, 187–188
Respondents, 188–189, 336–338
Response situation, selecting, 188
Retired product specialists, 466
Reverse brainstorming, 124, 470
Reverse income statement, 47
Rewards
  monetary and nonmonetary, 312
  special for creative achievement, 95
Rice, Mark P., 6n, 48n
Rigby, Darrell, 114n
Risk, managing, 228
Risk curve, 240
Risk strategies, for new products, 172
Risk/payoff matrix, 170–172
Roadblocks
  pushing past, 305
  removal of, 95–96
Robben, Henry S. J., 31n, 344n, 379n, 381n
Robertson, David, 25n, 27, 62n
Robertson, Thomas S., 377n, 378n
Robinson, William T., 46n
Rogers, Everett M., 356, 356n
Role playing, 129, 138, 421

Roll-in, roll-out, 351
Rolling evaluation, 173
Rolling evolution, 272
Rollout market test, 409
Rollout method, 413–417
Rosenau, Milton D., Jr., 16n, 184n, 187n, 252n, 260n, 261n, 283n, 308n, 330n, 428n, 436n
Rotators, food buyers as, 354
Rubbermaid case, 161–162
Rubbermaid Inc., push strategy, 402
Rydholm, Joseph, 127n
Rymon, T., 377n

S

Saaty, Thomas L., 208n
Safe Keep Monitors, from Coleman, 122
Safety device, absent, 443
Safety measures, differentiating JetBlue, 44
Sakkab, Nabil, 110n
Sales
  contingency plans ready for, 425
  forecasts of dollar and unit, 397
Sales analysis, conducting, 217
Sales forecasting
  for new products, 215–216
  problems with, 224–225
  using A-T-A-R model, 219–220
  using purchase intentions, 218
Sales peak, time and magnitude of, 223
Sales preparedness, 420
Salesperson, 383
Salomo, Sören, 9n, 10n, 60n, 61n, 305n
Samli, A. Coksun, 452n, 453n
Sample size for a product use test, 332
Samsung Galaxy S9, 159
Sanderson, R. Hedley, 187n
Santori, Mike, 52
Santos, Jose, 314n
Sarin, Shikhar, 312n
Sashittal, Hemant C., 303n
Satellite radio, forecasting sales of, 215
Sattler, Henrik, 368n

Saunders, John, 351n
SC Johnson Company, 121, 405
Scanner market testing, 409–410
Scenario analysis, 130–132, 217
  compared to problem analysis, 161
  guidelines for conducting, 131–132
  techniques aiding, 469–470
Scenario writing forecasting technique, 216
Scenarios, forms of, 131
Schaeffer, Lee, 363n, 364n, 367n
Schematic elements, clustering, 284
Schematics. *See* Product schematic
Scheuing, E. E., 412n
Schirr, Gary R., 104n, 107n
Schmidt, Jeffrey B., 10n, 18n, 41n, 186n, 209n, 308n, 436n
Schnaars, Steven, 75n, 131n
Schoormans, Jan P. L., 150n, 286n
Schreier, Martin, 104n, 105n, 107n, 109n
Schwarzenegger, Arnold, 140
Scope creep, 69
Scorers for a scoring model, 206–207
Scoring, 205
Scoring models, 199, 201–208
  aspects of, 211–212
  combined financial and strategic, 233
  for full screen of new product concepts, 204
  misusing, 211
ScotchGard fabric protector, 13
Screening, 32
Screening procedure in a scoring model, 202–207
Scriven, Eric, 206n
Scrubbing Bubbles Automatic Shower Cleaner, 121
Seamon, Erika B., 66n, 123n, 234, 234n, 312n
Searle, NutraSweet, 411
Searls, K., 108n
Sebell, Mark Henry, 130n
Second but best strategy, 74
Secondary meaning, 362
Secondary packaging, 371
Seibert, Rebecca, 32n
Selective demand, stimulation of, 349–350

Seller, misrepresentation by, 446–447
Senior management, role in radical new products, 53
Sense reactions, pre-use, 328, 329
Sensing consumers, 64, 65
Sensitivity testing, 207, 240
Sequential monadic test, 334, 335
Serendipitous planning, 13
Serial innovators, role of, 50–51
Service delivery personnel, 44–45
Service development process, 43
Service industries, platforms in, 62
Service marks, 361
Services, 43–46, 443
Sethi, Anju, 316n
Sethi, Rajesh, 96n, 308n, 316n
Shalit, Gene, 129
Shankar, Venkatesh, 430, 430n
Shanklin, William L., 352n
Shapiro, Benson P., 384n
Sharma, Subhash, 222n
Shea, Christine M., 305n
Shelf space, selling, 429
Sheth, Jagdish N., 9n, 31n, 186n, 380n, 430n
Shin, G. C., 10n, 18n
Shirouzu, Norihiko, 127n, 128n, 129n
Shop talk, encouraging cross-functional, 309
Shorter, Lee, 117n
Shugan, Steven A., 156n
Siau, Keng L., 136n
Siemens, 111, 454, 455
Sierra Club, 458
Signaling, 376–377
Signed agreement, protocol as, 245
Signode Corporation, 73
Silent competitor, 335
Simple regression forecasting technique, 216
Simple time series forecasting technique, 216
Simulated test market (STM) method, 401, 403–406
Simulation analyses, 293
Sinclair, Steven A., 144n
Single-source systems, 410
Sinha, Rajiv K., 357n

Sinkholes, 426

Situation analysis, 421

Situations, approving instead of numbers, 227–228

Sivakumar, K., 9n, 315n

Sketches, as a concept statement, 184–185

Skim price, 389

Skunkworks, 59, 298, 348

Slater, Stanley F., 39n, 278n, 309n

Slotegraaf, R. J., 20n, 43n, 46n, 51n, 77n, 81n, 104n, 187n, 217n, 314n, 347n, 379n, 420n, 431n, 454n

Slotting allowances, 388

Slywotzky, Adrian, 384n

SMART (simple, maintenance-friendly, affordable, reliable, and timely-to-market), 454

Smartphones, 43, 123, 158–160

Smets, Gerda, 291n

Smith, Daniel C., 96n

Smith, Preston G., 20n, 40, 315n

Smithers, Rebecca, 124n

Smoothing, as a management style, 310

Sobek, Durward K., II, 301n

Social cohesion, 96

Social media metrics, in launch management, 431

Sodermeyer, S. M., 281n, 367n

Soft metrics, 431

Soladey (manufacturer), 450

Solano, Brandon, 195, 196

Solio, hand-held charger, 451

Somermeyer, S. M., 6n, 32n, 48n, 66n, 72n, 77n, 103n, 105n, 108n, 121n, 123n, 126n, 141n, 172n, 191n, 192n, 216n, 254n, 261n, 263n, 264n, 312n, 315n, 364n, 432n, 434n, 441n

Sommer, Anita F., 38n

Song, Michael, 290n, 302n, 308n, 309n, 314n, 315n, 346n

Sonnack, M., 108n

Sony Xperia XZ2, 159

Souder, W. E., 315n, 347n

Sound signature, as a trademark, 360

Spaghetti-Os, concept of, 397

Speculative sale method, 402–403

Speed to market, design for, 278–279

Speeding to market, risks and guidelines in, 41–43

Speedstorming, 135

Spielberg, Steven, 26

Spinout venture, 298

Spiral development, 51–52

Splitting channels, 351

Sports teams, 296–297

Sprint, 431

Sproles, George, 283n

Srinivasan, V., 152n

Staggered paired comparison, 334

Stakeholder contacts, 126–128

Stakeholders, 187
    needs and problems of, 120, 122
    as a test group, 332

Stalling, Edward C., 144n

Stanford Research Institute International, 466

Stank, T., 379n, 380n

Stanko, Michael A., 110n

Star, S. H., 412n

Starbucks, test markets launching Via, 412

Stated concept, 35

State-of-the art breakthrough, 74

Static leaps, 131

Statt, Nick, 54n

Statz, Robert J., 323n

Steelcase, 186, 225, 279

Stepwise product deletion process, 436

Stereotype activity, 139, 140, 473

Stern, Aimee L., 338n

Stevens, Laura, 194n

Stevenson, Robert Louis, 469

Stimuli words and phrases, 474

Stirring phase for a public issue, 441

STM (Simulated test market) method, 401, 403–406

Stock, Gregory N., 94n

Stocking distributors, 386–388

stock-keeping units (SKUs), at LEGO, 26

Stocklifting, 387

Store brand buyers, 354

Story, Molly Follette, 281n

Stoy, Robert, 330n

Strategic alliances, 41, 384

Strategic categories, examples of, 79

Strategic Decision Group (SDG), portfolio evaluation model, 79, 81

Strategic decisions, set of, 344

Strategic elements, 18, 22–23

Strategic focus, identifying, 27

Strategic givens, 344, 347–348

Strategic goals, revisiting, 348–349

Strategic launch decisions, 346

Strategic launch planning, 344

Strategic plan, implementation of, 375–391

Strategic planning, 29, 161

Strategic platform decisions, 349–352

Strategy statements, 67

Strauss, Levi, 129

Stremersch, Stefan, 102n, 106n, 107n

Strict liability, 445, 446

Subaru, 282

Success, reason for, 16

Success/failure analysis, 231

Successful concept, 37

Suggestive names, protection of, 362

Sultan, Fareena, 222n

Sun Ovens, 455

Sundgren, Niklas, 61n

Sunk costs, 241

Supervised control in product use testing, 334

Supplier interaction, benefits of, 304

Suppliers/Vendors, as sources of product ideas, 464

Supply chain, 379

Surlyn, DuPont's development of, 323

"Surprise" products, 89

Surrogates, 175
    positioning using, 359

Sustainability and the fashion industry case, 459–461

Sustainable design, 448–451

Sutton, Robert L., 95n

Swaddling, David C., 141n

Swan, K. Scott, 305n

Swasy, Alecia, 325n

Swatch watches, 279

Switching model, 219–220

Sykes, Hollister B., 311n

Synchronous mode, meeting in, 313

T

Tabrizi, Behnam, 324n
Taco Bell, 366
Tactical decisions, 344, 346–347
Tactical launch decisions, 346, 382
Tactical launch planning, 344
Tait, Richard, 457n
Tanaka, Takashi, 246n
Target market(s), 249–251
Target market decision, 352–358
Target surrogate positioning, 359
Targeting error, 93
Tata Nano, 454
Tauber, Edward M., 125n
Taylor, Kate, 155n
Team(s)
    building, 302–306
    changes in membership, 311
    closing down, 312–313
    kinds of, 296–297
    managing, 306–313
    rewarding team behavior, 312
    structuring, 297–301
    supporting diversity, 317
    training, 306
    virtual, 313–314
Team guidance, 69
Team leaders, 17
Team members, selecting, 304–305
Team selection, guidelines for
    QFD, 263
Teamwork, 11
Tear-down technique, 470
Technical and marketing
    departments, 121–122
Technical innovation follow-on
    procedure, 469
Technical tasks in development, 30
Technological mapping, 475
Technological roadmapping
    approach, 469
Technological strengths, in
    laboratories, 71
Technology, 71
    drivers, 71–72
    opportunities, 76
    required by creation process, 97
Teflon, 13, 267
Templates for creativity, 154

Temporary products, 350, 434
Tertiary packaging, 371
Tesla case, 212–213, 373
Test market, InfoScan data
    used in, 409
Test marketing, 395, 410–413
    contrasted with rollouts,
        416–417
    risk of showing your hand, 412
Tested concept, 35
Testing, sources of product for, 336
Thamhain, Hans J., 21n, 313n
Think tanks, 471
Third-generation new products
    process, 22
Thomas, Jerry W., 93n
Thomas, Robert J., 180n
Thomke, Stefan, 292n, 293n
Thompson, James D., 47n
Thoratec (company), 55
Thornton, Jim, 318
Threadless, 107
3-D CAD, benefits of, 293
3M Company, 94, 104
3M Telecom Enclosure Division, 105
"360-degree" review process, at
    DuPont, 312
Time period for product use testing,
    335–336
Time postponement, 379
Time series and regression
    forecasts, 217
Time to market, 20, 39
Time-to-break-even metric, 348
Timing, 253
Todhunter, Jim, 450n
Toilet brushes, 98
Top management
    speeding products to market, 41
    support for teams, 306
Top-down platform procedure, 61
Top-down strategic approach, 232
Top-two-boxes score, 182, 185,
    189, 218
Toro, 73
Total quality management
    programs, 400
Total-fault approach, 456
Tottie, Magnus, 261n
Toyama, Ryoko, 71n

Toyota Motor Co.
    integrated product integration, 301
    sport-utility vehicles, 129
T-P-M linkage, 72
Tracking concept, in marketing,
    427–428
Tracking system, designing, 421,
    427–430
Tracking variables, 428–429
Trade dress protection, 362
Trade names, 361
Trade relations directors, 386
Trademarks, 360, 361
Trade-off analysis, 147–152
Trade-off problem, 456
Training, teams, 306
Transfer risk strategy, 172
Transition management team, 48
Transparent customizers, 355
Transparent self, 64, 65
Tremont Electric, 64
Trend areas, observing, 469
Trend people, observing, 469
Trial, of new products, 178, 388–391
Trial Support phase, 441–442
Trialability of new products, 357
Triangular comparison, 335
Trigger points, 421, 429
Tritle, Gary, 206n
TRIZ, 157–158
Trusko, Brett E., 107n
Trust, environment of mutual, 310
Twerdahl, Jim, 363n, 364n, 367n
Two-Bottle Tote, 252
Tzokas, Nikolaos X., 435n, 436n

U

Uban, S.,20n, 43n, 46n, 51n, 77n,
    81n,104n, 187n, 217n, 314n,
    347n, 379n, 420n, 431n, 454n
Ulrich, Karl T., 62n, 157, 157n, 276n,
    281n, 283n, 285n, 286n, 298n
Ultra Softs disposable diapers,
    production problems, 325
Ulwick, Anthony W., 256n
Umbrella brand strategy, 368
Umbria, 137
UMI (University Microfilms
    International), 73

Uncle Ben's Rice with Calcium, 341, 397
Underutilized resource, 31
Unforeseeable misuse defense, 446
Unilever, 370, 387, 439
Unique superior product, 16, 322
Universal design, 280
Universities, as sources of product ideas, 466
University Microfilms International (UMI), 73
Unstable product specifications, 69
Unsupervised control in product use testing, 334
Urban, Glen L., 219n, 231n, 405n, 412n
Use analysis, 471
Use of the ridiculous, 140, 473
Use testing, 324–325
User groups, 331–333
User testing, 322
User toolkits, 102, 103–106
User-oriented design, 280

V

Vacuum tube manufacture, 437
Validity of a sample, 332
Value, of an established brand, 62
Value added, offering, 16
Value curve creation, 155–156
van den Bulte, C., 223n
van der Bij, Hans, 290n, 314n
Van Der Legt, Remko, 135n
van Engelen, Jo M. L., 309n, 311n, 315n
van Putten, Alexander B., 47n
van Weele, Arjan, 305n
VanAllen, Erik, 304n
Vaporware, 378
Variants in product use testing, 336
Varma, Vishal A., 23n, 78n
"Vehicle DNA," 320
Vence, Deborah L., 14n, 15n
Vendors, 291, 464
Verbal rating scale, recording like/ dislike data, 336
Verganti, Roberto, 106n, 277, 277n

Veryzer, Robert W., 129n, 276n, 280n
Viagra, 13
Vicarious experience, 388
Vicarious trial, 388
Vickery, S. K., 70n
Virtual communities, 136
Virtual made real, 64, 65
Virtual product testing, 354
Virtual reality (VR), 54, 106, 152, 186
Virtual teams, 313–314
Visionaries, 358
Visions newsletter, 23
"Visiting researchers," 317
Visual equity across products, 280
Visual Issues Management software, 315
Vogel, Brian L., 289n
Voice of the customer (VOC), 48, 126, 254–257
Voice pitch analysis, 338
Vojak, Bruce A., 50n, 305n
Volckner, Franziska, 368n
Volpetti, Stefano, 160
von Hippel, Eric, 103n, 105n, 108n, 109n
Vriens, Marco, 149n

W

Wagon-wheel manufacturing plant, 437
Walgreen's, 45
Walleigh, Rick, 324n
Walter, James, 62n
Ward, Allen C., 301n
Warning, adequate, 444
Warranty, 446
Watson, Thomas, 95
Weaknesses technique, 472
Weggeman, Mathieu, 290n, 305n, 314n
Weighted average cost of capital, 240
Weightings, for scoring models, 207
Weinberg, Bruce D., 231n, 406n
Weiner, Russell, 195, 196
Wessel, Maxwell, 48n
What-if analysis, 217, 220, 405

Wheaties Dunk-A-Ball Cereal, 341
Wheelwright, Steven C., 216n, 298n, 324n
Whirlpool, Trash Smasher compactor, 138
White, Chelsea C., III, 263n
White Elephants, 80
Whitney, Daniel E., 289n
Whittle, Adrian, 320
Wilby, Carolyn P., 150n
Wildcatting, 249
Wilemon, David, 300n
Williamson, Peter, 314n
Wilson, H. James, 92n
Wilson, Peter, 134n
Withdrawal, as a management style, 310
Wittink, Dick R., 149n
Wojtas, Mary G., 282n
Wong, May, 361n
Woodside, Arch G., 187n
Word string, as a trademark, 360
Working capital, 239
World Car platform, of Honda, 61
Wren, B. M., 315n
Wright, Malcolm, 184n, 186n
Wu, Y., 349n
Wynett, Craig, 91
Wynstra, Finn, 305n

X

Xerox, 316

Y

YouTube, 60, 115, 196

Z

Zarya, Valentina, 107n
Zero-defect quality control, 456
Ziamou, Paschalina (Lilia), 131n
Zien, Karen Anne, 95n, 309n
Zigzag, 474
Zipcar, 451
Zirger, B. J., 39n
Zook, Chris, 114n
Zuckerberg, Mark, 160
Zuo, L., 155n